Stanley Gibbons

Great Britain CONCISE Stamp Catalogue

2006 edition

STANLEY GIBBONS LTD

By Appointment to
Her Majesty The Queen
Stanley Gibbons Ltd., London
Philatelists

Published by *Stanley Gibbons Publications*
Editorial, Sales Offices and Distribution Centre: Parkside,
Christchurch Road, Ringwood,
Hants BH24 3SH

First Edition — May 1986
Second Edition — May 1987
Third Edition — May 1988
Fourth Edition — May 1989
Fifth Edition — May 1990
Sixth Edition — May 1991
Seventh Edition — May 1992
Eighth Edition — April 1993
Ninth Edition — April 1994
Tenth Edition — April 1995
Eleventh Edition — April 1996
Twelfth Edition — April 1997
Thirteenth Edition — April 1998
Fourteenth Edition — April 1999
Fifteenth Edition — May 2000
Sixteenth Edition — April 2001
Seventeenth Edition — April 2002
Eighteenth Edition — April 2003
Nineteenth Edition — April 2004
Twentieth Edition — May 2005
Twenty-first Edition—April 2006

ISBN: 0-85259-621-9

Item No. 2887 (06)
Printed and bound by Polestar Wheatons Ltd, Exeter.

Stanley Gibbons Holdings Plc.
Stanley Gibbons Ltd,
Stanley Gibbons Auctions
399 Strand, London WC2R 0LX

Auction Room and Specialist Departments.
Open Monday–Friday, 9.30 a.m. to 5.00 p.m.
Shop: Open Monday–Friday 9 a.m. to 5.30 p.m.
and Saturday 9.30 a.m. to 5.30 p.m.
Telephone: 020 7836 8444, Fax: 020 7836 7342,
E-mail: *enquiries@stanleygibbons.co.uk* and
Internet: *www.stanleygibbons.com* for all departments.

Stanley Gibbons Publications
Gibbons Stamp Monthly
Parkside, Christchuch Road, Ringwood, Hants BH24 3SH
Telephone: 01425 472363 (24 hour answerphone service),
Fax: 01425 470247 and E-mail: *info@stanleygibbons.co.uk*
Publications Mail Order, Freephone 0800 611622.
Monday–Friday 8.30 a.m. to 5.00 p.m.

Fraser's
399 Strand, London WC2R 0LX
Open Monday–Friday 9.00 a.m. to 5.30 p.m.
and Saturday 10.00 a.m. to 4.00 p.m.
Telephone: 020 7836 8444,
Fax: 020 7836 7342,
E-mail: *info@frasersautographs.co.uk*
and Internet: *www.frasersautographs.com*

Great Britain Philatelic Societies
The Great Britain Philatelic Society.
Hon. Membership Secretary: Peter Tanner, "High Standings",
13 Hubeerts Close, Gerrards Cross, Bucks SL9 7EN.

The Modern British Philatelic Circle.
Hon. Membership Secretary: A. J. Wilkins, 3 Buttermere
Close, Brierley Hill, West Midlands, DY5 3SD.

The Great Britain Collectors' Club.
Secretary: Mr. Parker A. Bailey, 17 Greenwood Road,
Merrimack, NH03054, U.S.A.

The Great Britain Concise Catalogue
2006 Edition

The Concise Catalogue, now in its 21st year of publication, has established itself as an essential guide for the "one-country" collector of Great Britain.

The popularity of Great Britain stamps continues to grow — the Concise Catalogue supplies the information to enhance your collection.

- ✦ All issues from the Penny Black of 1840 to 21 March 2006 including Regional, Postage Due, Official and Postal Fiscal stamps.
- ✦ All different stamp designs are illustrated.
- ✦ Every basic stamp listed, including those with different watermarks or perforations and those showing graphite lines or phosphor bands.
- ✦ Unmounted mint and mounted mint prices quoted for 1887 "Jubilee" series and all King Edward VII and King George V issues.
- ✦ Missing colours, missing embossing, watermark errors, imperforate errors and phosphor omitted varieties from those stamps normally issued with phosphor bands.
- ✦ Gutter Pairs and "Traffic light" Gutter Pairs listed in mint sets.
- ✦ First Day Covers for Special Issues from 1924 and for King Edward VIII and King George VI definitives. For the present reign the coverage also extends to Sponsored Booklet panes and Regionals. All British Post Office special First Day of Issue postmarks are illustrated and priced on cover.
- ✦ Post Office Picture Cards (PHQ cards) are priced as sets, both mint and used with First Day of Issue postmarks.
- ✦ Presentation, Collector and Gift Packs, including the scarce versions with foreign inscriptions.
- ✦ Quick-reference diagrams for listed Machin decimal booklet panes.
- ✦ Design Index for Commemorative and Special Stamps after the Philatelic Information Section.
- ✦ Machin and commemorative underprints given separate catalogue numbers.
- ✦ Post Office Yearbooks.
- ✦ Royal Mail Postage Labels priced in mint or used sets and on British Post Office First Day Covers.
- ✦ Notes on Postage Due bisects based on research by Mr. P. Frost.
- ✦ Wartime issues for the Channel Islands.
- ✦ Separate section for Post Office Stamp Booklets with dated editions of King George VI listed separately.
- ✦ Post Office Label Sheets, popularly known as 'Generic Smilers'.
- ✦ Helpful introductory section providing definitions and guidance for the collector and including all watermark illustrations shown together to assist identification.
- ✦ Specimen overprints are now listed up to 1952.
- ✦ Addresses for specialist philatelic societies covering Great Britain stamps.
- ✦ Recently discovered errors and varieties listed. See Nos. 236awi, 418c, 630b, 712a, 716g, 755b, 757d, 783b, 828d, 881a, 887e, 889d, 895f, 895f, 895g, 896d, 904b, 914d, 943ab, 1221a, 1329a, 1423b, 1578Ec, 1617a, 1662a, 1845a, 2115a, 2115a, 2125a, 2126a, 2170a, 2212a, 2265b, 2277a, S1pb, S1pc and O9ca.

We would like to thank all those who have assisted in the compilation of this catalogue. Special thanks for amendments to this edition are due to Messrs P. Hobden, A. Musry, M. Richardson, D. Smythe, J. Townend and J. Tremayne.

HUGH JEFFERIES
LESLEY BRINE

STANLEY GIBBONS PUBLICATIONS
OVERSEAS REPRESENTATION

Stanley Gibbons Publications are represented overseas by the following sole distributors (*), distributors (**) or licensees (***)

Australia *Lighthouse Philatelic (Aust.) Pty Ltd** Locked Bag 5900 Botany DC New South Wales 2019 Australia

*Stanley Gibbons (Australia) Pty Ltd**** Level 6 36 Clarence Street Sydney New South Wales 2000 Australia

Belgium and Luxembourg** *Davo* c/o Philac Rue du Midi 48 Bruxelles 1000 Belgium

Canada* *Lighthouse Publications (Canada) Ltd* 255 Duke Street Montreal Quebec Canada H3C 2M2

Denmark** *Samlerforum/Davo* Ostergade 3 DK7470 Karup Denmark

Finland** *Davo* c/o Kapylan Merkkiky Pohjolankatu 1 00610 Helsinki Finland

France* *Davo France* (Casteilla) 10 Rue Leon Foucault 78184 St. Quentin Yvelines Cesex France

Hong Kong** *Po-on Stamp Service* GPO Box 2498 Hong Kong

Israel** *Capital Stamps* PO Box 3769 Jerusalem 91036 Israel

Italy* *Ernesto Marini Srl* Via Struppa 300 I-16165 Genova GE Italy

Japan** *Japan Philatelic Co Ltd* PO Box 2 Suginami-Minami Tokyo Japan

Netherlands* *Davo Publications* PO Box 411 7400 AK Deventer Netherlands

New Zealand*** *Mowbray Collectables* PO Box 80 Wellington New Zealand

Norway** *Davo Norge* A/S PO Box 738 Sentrum N-01 05 Oslo Norway

Singapore** *Stamp Inc Collectibles Pte Ltd* 10 Ubi Crescent # 01-43 Ubi Tech Park Singapore 408564

Sweden* *Chr Winther Sorensen* AB Box 43 S-310 Knaered Sweden

Contents

Prices

> The prices quoted in this catalogue are the estimated selling prices of Stanley Gibbons Ltd at the time of publication. They are, *unless it is specifically stated otherwise*, for examples in fine condition for the issue concerned. Superb examples are worth more; those of a lower quality considerably less.

All prices are subject to change without prior notice and Stanley Gibbons Ltd may from time to time offer stamps below catalogue price. Individual low value stamps sold at 399, Strand are liable to an additional handling charge. Purchasers of new issues are asked to note that the prices charged for them contain an element for the service rendered and so may exceed the prices shown when the stamps are subsequently catalogued.

No guarantee is given to supply all stamps priced, since it is not possible to keep every catalogued item in stock.

Quotation of prices.
The prices in the left-hand column are for unused stamps and those in the right-hand column are for used.

A dagger (†) denotes that the item listed does not exist in that condition and a blank, or dash, that it exists, or may exist, but no market price is known.

Prices are expressed in pounds and pence sterling. One pound comprises 100 pence (£1 = 100p).

The method of notation is as follows: pence in numerals (e.g. 5 denotes five pence); pounds and pence up to £100, in numerals (e.g. 4·25 denotes four pounds and twenty-five pence); prices above £100 expressed in whole pounds with the "£" sign shown.

Unused and Used stamps.
The prices for unused stamps of Queen Victoria issued before 1887 are for lightly hinged examples. Unused stamps of the 1887 "Jubilee" issue and from the reigns of King Edward VII and King George V are priced in both unmounted and mounted condition. Unused prices for King Edward VIII to Queen Elizabeth II issues are for unmounted mint (though when not available, mounted mint stamps are often supplied at a lower price). Prices for used stamps are for postally used examples.

Prices quoted for bisects on cover or on large piece are for those dated during the period officially authorised.

Minimum price.
The minimum price quoted is 10 pence. For individual stamps prices between 10 pence and 95 pence are provided as a guide for catalogue users. The lowest price *charged* for individual stamps or sets purchased from Stanley Gibbons Ltd is £1.

Set prices.
Set prices are generally for one of each value, excluding shades and varieties, but including major colour changes. Where there are alternative shades, etc., the cheapest is usually included. The number of stamps in the set is always stated for clarity.

The mint prices for sets containing *se-tenant* pieces are based on the prices quoted for such combinations, and not on those for individual stamps. The used set price is for single stamps.

Used sets containing *se-tenant* combinations are usually worth the same as the prices quoted for the cheapest First Day Cover.

Gutter Pairs.
These, and traffic light gutter pairs, are priced as complete sets.

Used on Cover prices.
To assist collectors, cover prices are quoted in a third column for postage and Official stamps issued in the reign of Queen Victoria and in boxed notes for the 1887 "Jubilee" issue and for King Edward VII and King George V stamps.

The cover should be of non-philatelic origin, bearing the correct postal rate for the period and distance involved and cancelled with the markings normal to the offices concerned. Purely philatelic items have a cover value only slightly greater than the catalogue value for the corresponding used stamps. This applies generally to those high-value stamps used philatelically rather than in the normal course of commerce.

Oversized covers, difficult to accommodate on an album page, should be reckoned as worth little more than the corresponding value of the used stamps. The condition of a cover affects its value. Except for "wreck covers", serious damage or soiling reduce the value where the postal markings and stamps are ordinary ones. Conversely, visual appeal adds to the value and this can include freshness of appearance, important addresses, old-fashioned but legible handwriting, historic town-names, etc. The prices quoted are a base on which further value would be added to take account of the cover's postal historical importance in demonstrating such things as unusual, scarce or emergency cancels, interesting routes, significant postal markings, combination usage, the development of postal rates, and so on.

First Day Cover prices.
Prices are quoted for commemorative first day covers from 1924 British Empire Exhibition pair onwards. These prices are for special covers (from 1937) franked with complete sets and cancelled by ordinary operational postmarks to the end of 1962 or the various standard "First Day of Issue" markings from 1963.

Prices are provided for King Edward VIII and King George VI definitives on plain covers with operational postmarks of the first day of issue. For some values special covers also exist and these are worth more than the prices quoted.

The Philatelic Bureau and other special "First Day of Issue" postmarks provided by the Post Office since 1963 are listed under each issue. Prices quoted are for these postmarks used on illustrated covers (from 1964 those produced by the Post Office), franked with complete sets.

The British Post Office did not introduce special First Day of Issue postmarks for definitive issues until the first instalment of the Machin £sd series, issued 5 June 1967, although "First Day" treatment had been provided for some Regional stamps from 8 June 1964 onwards. Prices for the First Day Covers from 1952 to 1966, showing definitive stamps are for the stamps indicated, used on illustrated envelopes and postmarked with operational cancellations.

From 1967 onwards the prices quoted are for stamps as indicated, used on illustrated envelopes and postmarked with special First Day of Issue handstamps. Other definitives issued during this period were not accepted for "First Day" treatment by the British Post Office.

Guarantee
All stamps are guaranteed genuine originals in the following terms:

If not as described, and returned by the purchaser, we undertake to refund the price paid to us in the original transaction. If any stamp is certified as genuine by the Expert Committee of the Royal Philatelic Society, London, or by B.P.A. Expertising Ltd, the purchaser shall not be entitled to make any claim against us for any error, omission or mistake in such certificate.

Consumers' statutory rights are not affected by the above guarantee.

The recognised Expert Committees in this country are those of the Royal Philatelic Society, 41 Devonshire Place, London W1G 6JY, and B.P.A. Expertising Ltd, P.O. Box 137, Leatherhead, Surrey KT22 0RG. They do not undertake valuations under any circumstances and fees are payable for their services.

Contacting the Catalogue Editor

The Editor is always interested in hearing from people who have new information which will improve or correct the Catalogue. As a general rule he must see and examine the actual stamps before they can be considered for listing; photographs or photocopies are insufficent evidence.

Submissions should be made in writing to the Catalogue Editor, Stanley Gibbons Publications. The cost of return postage for items submitted is appreciated, and this should include the registration fee if required.

Where information is solicited purely for the benefit of the enquirer, the editor cannot undertake to reply if the answer is already contained in these published notes or if return postage is omitted. Written communications are greatly preferred to enquiries by telephone and the editor regrets that he or his staff cannot see personal callers without a prior appointment being made. Correspondence may be subject to delay during the production period of each new edition.

Please note that the following classes of material are outside the scope of this Catalogue:

(a) Non-postal revenue or fiscal stamps.
(b) Postage stamps used fiscally.
(c) Local carriage labels and private local issues.
(d) Punctured postage stamps (perfins).
(e) Telegraph stamps.
(f) Bogus or phantom stamps.
(g) Railway or airline letter fee stamps, bus or road transport company labels.
(h) Postal stationery cut-outs.
(i) All types of non-postal labels and souvenirs.
(j) Documentary labels for the postal service, e.g. registration, recorded delivery, airmail etiquettes, etc.
(k) Privately applied embellishments to official issues and privately commissioned items generally.
(l) Stamps for training postal staff.

We regret we do not give opinions as to the genuineness of stamps, nor do we identify stamps or number them by our Catalogue.

General Abbreviations

Alph	Alphabet
Anniv	Anniversary
Brt	Bright (colour)
C,c	Chalky paper
C.	Overprinted in carmine
Des	Designer; designed
Dp	Deep (colour)
Eng	Engraver; engraved
Horiz	Horizontal; horizontally
Imp, Imperf	Imperforate
Inscr	Inscribed
L	Left
Litho	Lithographed
Lt	Light (colour)
mm	Millimetres
MS	Miniature sheet
O,o	Ordinary paper
Opt(d)	Overprint(ed)
P, Perf	Perforated
Photo	Photogravure
Pl	Plate
Pr	Pair
Ptd	Printed
Ptg	Printing
PVA	Polyvinyl alcohol (gum)
R	Right
R.	Row
Recess	Recess-printed
T	Type
Typo	Typographed
Un	Unused
Us	Used
Vert	Vertical; vertically
W or wmk	Watermark
Wmk s	Watermark sideways

(†) = Does not exist.

(—) (or blank price column) = Exists, or may exist, but no market price is known.

/ between colours means "on" and the colour following is that of the paper on which the stamp is printed.

Printers

B.W.	Bradbury Wilkinson & Co, Ltd.
D.L.R.	De La Rue & Co, Ltd, London, and (from 1961) Bogota, Colombia. De La Rue Security Print (*formerly Harrison & Sons Ltd*) from 8 September 1997.
Enschedé	Joh. Enschedé en Zonen, Haarlem, Netherlands.
Harrison	Harrison & Sons, Ltd, High Wycombe.
J.W.	John Waddington Security Print, Ltd, Leeds.
P.B.	Perkins Bacon Ltd, London.
Questa	Questa Colour Security Printers, Ltd.
Waterlow	Waterlow & Sons, Ltd, London.
Walsall	Walsall Security Printers, Ltd.

Philatelic information

Catalogue Numbers

The catalogue number appears in the extreme left column. The boldface Type numbers in the next column are merely cross-reference to illustrations. Catalogue numbers in the *Gibbons Stamp Monthly* Supplements are provisional only and may need to be altered when the lists are consolidated.

Our Catalogue numbers are universally recognised in specifying stamps and as a hallmark of status.

Inverted and other watermark varieties incorporate "Wi", etc., within the number. Other items which appear in this Catalogue but not *Part 1 (British Commonwealth) Catalogue,* incorporate "Ea", etc.

Catalogue Illustrations

Stamps and first day postmarks are illustrated at three-quarters linear size. Stamps not illustrated are the same size and format as the value shown, unless otherwise indicated. Overprints, surcharges and watermarks are normally actual size. Illustrations of varieties are often enlarged to show the detail. Illustrations of miniature sheets are half linear size and their dimensions, in millimetres, are stated with the width given first.

Designers

Designers' names are quoted where known, though space precludes naming every individual concerned in the production of a set. In particular, photographers supplying material are usually named only when they also make an active contribution in the design stage; posed photographs of reigning monarchs are, however, an exception to this rule.

Printing Errors

Errors in printing are of major interest to this Catalogue. Authenticated items meriting consideration would include: background, centre or frame inverted or omitted; centre or subject transposed; error of colour; error or omission of value; double prints and impressions; printed both sides; and so on. Designs *tête-bêche*, whether intentionally or by accident, are listable. Colours only partially omitted are not listed. However, stamps with embossing, phosphor or both omitted and stamps printed on the gummed side are included.

Printing technology has radically improved over the years, during which time photogravure and lithography have become predominant. Varieties nowadays are more in the nature of flaws which are almost always outside the scope of this book.

In no catalogue, however, do we list such items as: dry prints, kiss prints, doctor-blade flaws, colour shifts or registration flaws (unless they lead to the complete omission of a colour from an individual stamp), lithographic ring flaws, and so on. Neither do we recognise fortuitous happenings like paper creases or confetti flaws.

Paper Types

All stamps listed are deemed to be on "ordinary" paper of the wove type and white in colour; only departures from this are normally mentioned.

A coloured paper is one that is coloured right through (front and back of the stamp). In the Catalogue the colour of the paper is given in *italics*, thus:

purple/*yellow* = purple design on yellow paper.

Papers have been made specially white in recent years by, for example, a very heavy coating of chalk. We do not classify shades of whiteness of paper as distinct varieties. The availability of many postage stamps for revenue purposes made necessary some safeguard against the illegitimate re-use of stamps with removable cancellations. This was at first secured by using fugitive inks and later by printing on chalky (chalk-surfaced) paper, both of which made it difficult to remove any form of obliteration without also damaging the stamp design. We have indicated the existence of the papers by the letters "**O**" (ordinary) and "**C**" (chalky) after the description of all stamps where the chalky paper may be found. Where no indication is given the paper is "ordinary".

Our chalky paper is specifically one which shows a black mark when touched with a silver wire. Stamps on chalk-surfaced paper can easily lose this coating through immersion in water.

Perforation Measurement

The gauge of a perforation is the number of holes in a length of 2 cm.

The Gibbons *Instanta* gauge is the standard for measuring perforations. The stamp is viewed against a dark background with the transparent gauge put on top of it. Though the gauge measures to decimal accuracy, perforations read from it are generally quoted in the Catalogue to the nearest half. For example:

Just over perf 12¾ to just under 13¼ = perf 13
Perf 13¼ exactly, rounded up = perf 13½
Just over perf 13¼ to just under 13¾ = perf 13½
Perf 13¾ exactly, rounded up = perf 14

However, where classification depends on it, actual quarter-perforations are quoted. Perforations are usually abbreviated (and spoken) as follows, though sometimes they may be spelt out for clarity.

P 14: perforated alike on all sides (read: "perf 14").

P 14 x 15: the first figure refers to top and bottom, the second to left and right sides (read: "perf 14 by 15"). This is a compound perforation.

Such headings as "P 13 x 14 (vert) and P 14 x 13 (horiz)" indicate which perforations apply to which stamp format— vertical or horizontal.

From 1992 onwards most definitive and greetings stamps from both sheets and booklets occur with a large elliptical (oval) hole inserted in each line of vertical perforations as a security measure. The £10 definitive, No. 1658, is unique in having two such holes in the horizontal perforations.

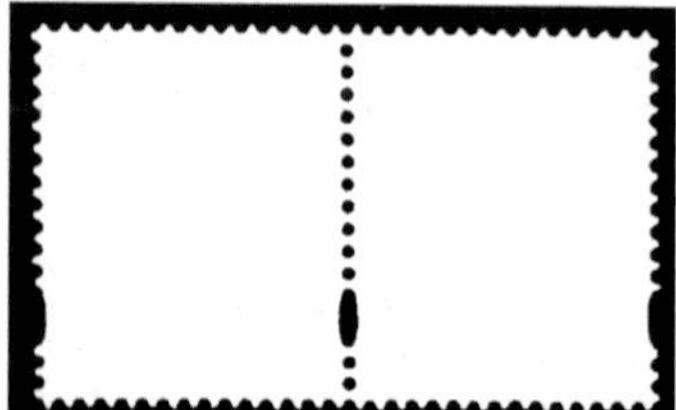

Elliptical Perforations

Perforation Errors

Authenticated errors, where a stamp normally perforated is accidentally issued imperforate, are listed provided no traces of perforations (blind holes or indentations) remain. They must be provided as pairs, both stamps wholly imperforate, and are only priced in that form.

Numerous part-perforated stamps have arisen from the introduction of the Jumelle Press. This has a rotary perforator with rows of pins on one drum engaging with holes on another. Engagement is only gradual when the perforating unit is started up or stopped, giving rise to perforations "fading out", a variety mentioned above as not listed.

Stamps from the Jumelle printings sometimes occur imperforate between stamp and sheet margin. Such errors are not listed in this catalogue, but are covered by the volumes of the *Great Britain Specialised Catalogue*.

Pairs described as "imperforate between" have the line of perforations between the two stamps omitted.

Imperf between (horiz pair): a horizontal pair of stamps with perfs all around the edges but none between the stamps.

Imperf between (vert pair): a vertical pair of stamps with perfs all around the edges but none between the stamps.

Imperf between (vertical pair)

Imperf horizontally (vertical pair)

Where several of the rows have escaped perforation the resulting varieties are listable. Thus:

Imperf vert (horiz pair): a horizontal pair of stamps perforated at top and bottom; all three vertical directions are imperf—the two outer edges and between the stamps.

Imperf horiz (vert pair): a vertical pair perforated at left and right edges; all three horizontal directions are imperf—the top, bottom and between the stamps.

Varieties of double, misplaced or partial perforation caused by error or machine malfunction are not listable, neither are freaks, such as perforations placed diagonally from paper folds, nor missing holes caused by broken pins.

Phosphor Issues

Machines which sort mail electronically have been introduced progressively and the British Post Office issued the first stamps specially marked for electronic sorting in 1957. This first issue had easily visible graphite lines printed on the back beneath the gum (see Nos. 561/6). They were issued in the Southampton area where the experiment was carried out.

The graphite lines were replaced by phosphor bands, activated by ultra-violet light. The bands are printed on the front of the stamps and show as a matt surface against the usual smooth or shiny appearance of the untreated surface of the paper. The bands show clearly in the top or bottom horizontal margins of the sheet.

The first phosphor issues appeared in 1959 (see Nos. 599/609) and these stamps also had graphite lines on the back. Further details will be found in the listings above No. 599 and 619. From 1962 onwards most commemoratives were issued in versions with or without bands. From 1967 all commemorative stamps had phosphor bands, but from 1972 they were replaced by "all-over" phosphor covering the entire area of the stamp.

After a considerable period of development a special paper was produced in which the phosphor had been incorporated into the coating. From 15 August 1979 to April 1996 phosphorised paper was accepted for use generally, replacing phosphor bands on most issues for all values except the second class letter rate. Phosphorised paper can only be identified by ultra-violet light. The Stanley Gibbons Uvitec Micro ultra-violet lamp is firmly recommended for use in identifying the phosphor stamps listed in this Catalogue. *Warning*. Never stare at the lighted lamp but follow the manufacturer's instructions. Phosphor bands were reintroduced for all issues from April 1996.

During the years 1967 to 1972, when all issues, except the high values, should have shown phosphor bands, a number of stamps appeared with them omitted in error. These varieties are listed in this Catalogue. Stamps with "all-over" phosphor omitted can only be detected by the use of an ultra-violet lamp and these varieties are listed in the Stanley Gibbons *Great Britain Specialised Catalogue*. Note that prices are for unmounted mint examples only. Varieties such as double bands, misplaced or printed on the back are not listed in this Catalogue.

Gum Description

All stamps listed are assumed to have gum of some kind and original gum (o.g.) means that which was present on the stamp as issued to the public. Deleterious climates and the presence of certain chemicals can cause gum to crack and, with early stamps, even make the paper deteriorate. Unscrupulous fakers are adept in removing it and regumming the stamp to meet the unreasoning demand often made for "full o.g." in cases where such a thing is virtually impossible.

The gum normally used on stamps has been gum arabic until the late 1960's when synthetic adhesives were introduced. Harrison and Sons Ltd for instance use *polyvinyl alcohol*, known to philatelists as PVA (see note above SG723).

Colour Identification

The 200 colours most used for stamp identification are given in the Stanley Gibbons Stamp Colour Key. The Catalogue has used the Colour Key as a standard for describing new issues for some years. The names are also introduced as lists are rewritten, though exceptions are made for those early issues where traditional names have become universally established.

In compound colour names the second is the predominant one, thus:

orange-red = a red tending towards orange.

red-orange = an orange containing more red than usual.

When comparing actual stamps with colour samples in the Colour Key, view in a good north daylight (or its best substitute: fluorescent "colour-matching" light). Sunshine is not recommended. Choose a solid portion of the stamp design; if available, marginal markings such as solid bars of colour or colour check dots are helpful. Shading lines in the design can be misleading as they appear lighter than solid colour. Furthermore, the listings refer to colours as issued: they may deteriorate into something different through the passage of time.

Shades are particularly significant when they can be linked to

Multi-value Coil Strip

specific printings. In general, shades need to be quite marked to fall within the scope of this Catalogue.

Modern colour printing by lithography is prone to marked differences of shade, even within a single run, and variations can occur within the same sheet. Such shades are not listed.

Errors of Colour

Major colour errors in stamps or overprints which qualify for listing are: wrong colours; albinos (colourless impressions), where these have Expert Committee certificates; colours completely omitted, but only on unused stamps (if found on used stamps the information is usually footnoted) and with good credentials, missing colours being frequently faked.

Colours only partially omitted are not recognised. Colour shifts, however spectacular, are not listed.

Booklet Stamps

Single stamps from booklets are listed if they are distinguishable in some way (such as watermark or phosphor bands) from similar sheet stamps.

Booklet panes are listed where they contain stamps of different denominations se-tenant, where stamp-size printed labels are included, or where such panes are otherwise identifiable. Booklet panes are placed in the listing under the lowest denomination present.

In the listing of complete booklets the numbers and prefix letters are the same as used in the Stanley Gibbons *Great Britain Specialised Catalogue.*

Coil Stamps

Stamps only issued in coil form are given full listing. If stamps are issued in both sheets and coils, the coil stamps are listed separately only where there is some feature (e.g. watermark sideways or gum change) by which single stamps can be distinguished. Coil strips containing different values *se-tenant* are also listed.

Coil join pairs are generally too random and easily faked to permit listing; similarly ignored are coil stamps which have accidentally suffered an extra row of perforations from the claw mechanism in a malfunctioning vending machine.

Gutter Pairs

In 1988 the recess-printed Castle high value definitives were issued in sheets containing four panes separated by a gutter margin. All modern Great Britain commemoratives and special stamps are produced in sheets containing two panes separated by a blank horizontal or vertical margin known as a gutter. This feature first made its appearance on some supplies of the 1972 Royal Silver Wedding 3p and marked the introduction of Harrison & Sons' new "Jumelle" stamp-printing press. There are advantages for both the printer and the Post Office in such a layout which has been used for most commemorative issues since 1974.

The term "gutter pair" is used for a pair of stamps separated by part of the blank gutter margin as illustrated below. Most printers include some form of colour check device on the sheet margins, in addition to the cylinder or plate numbers. Harrison & Sons use round "dabs", or spots of colour, resembling traffic lights. For the

Booklet Pane with Printed Labels

Se-tenant Pane of Four

Gutter pair

Traffic Light Gutter Pair

period from the 1972 Royal Silver Wedding until the end of 1979 these colour dabs appeared in the gutter margin. There was always one example to every double pane sheet of stamps. They can also be found in the high value Machin issue printed in photogravure. Gutter pairs showing these "traffic lights" are worth considerably more than the normal version.

From the 2004 Entente Cordiale set, Walsall reintroduced traffic lights in the gutters of certain sets. Where these extend over more than one section of gutter margin on any value, they are priced in blocks rather than pairs.

Miniature Sheets

A miniature sheet contains a single stamp or set with wide inscribed or decorated margins. The stamps often also exist in normal sheet format. This Catalogue lists, with **MS** prefix, complete miniature sheets which have been issued by the Post Office and which are valid for postal purposes.

Stamps from miniature sheets, not also available in normal sheet format, are not individually listed or priced in this catalogue.

Se-tenant Combinations

Se-tenant means "joined together". Some sets include stamps of different design arranged *se-tenant* as blocks or strips and, in mint condition, these are usually collected unsevered as issued. Such *se-tenant* combinations are supplied in used condition at a premium over the used prices of the individual stamps. See also the note on Set Prices.

Presentation and Souvenir Packs

Special Packs comprising slip-in cards with printed commemorative inscriptions and notes on the back and with protective covering, were introduced in 1964 for the Shakespeare issue. Definitive issues first appeared in Presentation Packs in 1960. Notes will be found in the listings to describe souvenir books issued on special occasions.

Issues of 1968–1969 (British Paintings to the Prince of Wales Investiture) were also issued in packs with text in German for sale through the Post Office's German Agency and these are also included.

Collectors packs, first called gift packs, containing commemoratives issued in the preceding twelve months, first appeared in 1967. These are listed and priced.

Yearbooks

Special Post Office Yearbooks were first available in 1984. They contain all of the commemorative issues for one year in a hardbound book, illustrated in colour complete with slip case. These are listed and priced.

Commemorative First Day Covers

Until 1963 the Post Office did not provide any special first day of issue postmark facilities for collectors. Several philatelic organisations and stamp dealers did produce pictorial covers for the various commemorative issues and collectors serviced these to receive ordinary operational postmarks. Occasionally a special

Miniature Sheet containing a set of stamps

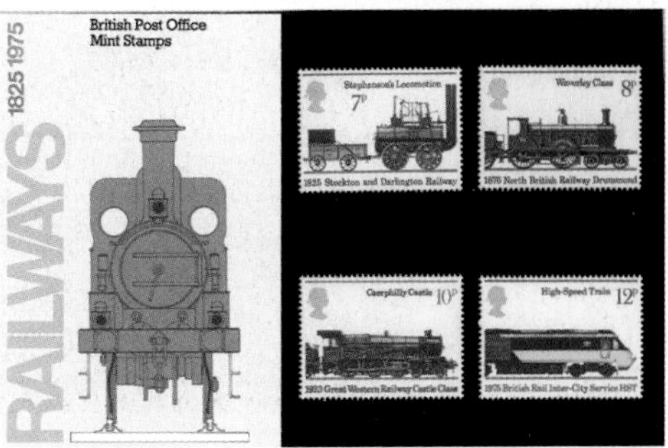

13 August 1975 Public Railways Presentation Pack

Type A. First day of Issue Slogan

Type B. Large Handstamp

Type C. Small Handstamp

Type D. Maltese Cross

Type E

Type F. £ Sign

Type G. Three Lions

Type H. Four Castles

Type I. Windsor Keep

Type J. Millennium (2000 issues are inscr "Beyond 2000")

Type K. Arms of Post Office

Illustrations shown sixty six per cent.

handstamp was produced which coincided with a new stamp issue, or relevant slogan postmarks, like the 1953 "Long Live the Queen" type, were in general use at the time.

On 21 March 1963 the Post Office installed special posting boxes at eleven main post offices so that collectors could obtain "uniformly high standard" impressions, from normal operational postmarks, for their first day covers. From 7 May 1963 special "First Day of Issue" slogans (Type A) were aplied to mail posted in these special boxes, whose number had, by then, risen to thirty. The Philatelic Bureau accepted orders by post for such covers from the issue of 16 May 1963 onwards.

The slogan type was replaced on 23 April 1964 by "First Day of Issue" handstamps (Type B). These were, initially, of considerable size, but were later replaced by smaller versions (Type C) which remained in use at nearly 200 principal offices until the Christmas issue of 2 November 1998. From 1970 the Bureau postmarks as Type C were inscribed "British Philatelic Bureau".

Since 1972 the Post Office has provided for virtually all issues an additional "alternative" pictorial "First Day of Issue" cancellation, at a location connected with the issue. Being available from the Bureau, these cancellations are illustrated and listed in this catalogue.

From 12 January 1999 (Millennium Inventors' Tale issue) the "alternative" pictorial postmark has been applied to all covers posted in special first day boxes throughout the country, replacing the local, non-pictorial, cancels. A bilingual version is used when the "alternative" office is in Wales. For collectors who prefer plain postmarks a non-pictorial version of the "alternative" postmark is available from Royal Mail Special Handstamp Centres.

"First Day of Issue" postmarks of standard or pictorial type have occasionally been provided on a "one-off" basis for places linked to particular stamp issues, eg Weymouth for the 1975 Sailing set. Such postmarks, which are not available from the Bureau, are footnoted only.

Royal Mail established Special Handstamp Centres in 1990 where all sponsored special handstamps and many "First Day of Issue" postmarks are now applied.

Pictorial local "First Day of Issue" postmarks were in use between 1988 and 1998 applied to covers posted in first day boxes and sent to main offices or Special Handstamp Centres. These included Birmingham (1993–98), Durham (1988–98), City of London (1989–98), London (1993–98), Newcastle upon Tyne (1992–94), and St Albans (1995–98). Different designs were used at the Glasgow Handstamp Centre for various places, 1993–98. As these postmarks were not available from the Bureau they are not included in this catalogue.

Post Office Label Sheets

This catalogue lists complete "Generic Smilers" sheets in a section following the booklet listings. "Personalised" and "Corporate" sheets are not listed, neither are identifiable single stamps from label sheets.

No Value Indicated Stamps

From 22 August 1989 various definitive and special stamps appeared inscribed "2nd", "1st" or "E" instead of a face value. These were sold at the current minimum rates for these services which were as follows:

Inland Postage Rate	*2nd Class*	*1st Class*
5 September 1988	14p.	19p.
2 October 1989	15p.	20p.
17 September 1990	17p.	22p.
16 September 1991	18p.	24p.
1 November 1993	19p.	25p.

Inland Postage Rate	*2nd Class*	*1st Class*
8 July 1996	20p.	26p.
26 April 1999	19p.	26p.
17 April 2000	19p.	27p.
8 May 2003	20p..	28p
1 April 2004	21p..	28p
7 April 2005	21p.	30p.
3 April 2006	23p	32p

European Airmail Rate	
26 April 1999	30p.
25 October 1999	34p.
27 April 2000	36p.
2 July 2001	37p.
27 March 2003	38p.
1 April 2004	40p.
7 April 2005	42p.
3 April 2006	44p

PHQ Card cancelled on First Day of Issue

PHQ Cards

From 1973 the Post Office produced sets of picture cards to accompany commemorative issues which can be sent through the post as postcards. Each card shows an enlarged colour reproduction of one stamp, initially of a single value from one set and subsequently of all values. The Post Office gives each card a "PHQ" serial number, hence the term. The cards are usually on sale shortly before the date of issue of the stamps, but there is no officially designated "first day".

Cards are priced in fine mint condition for complete sets as issued. Used prices are for cards franked with the stamp affixed, on the obverse, as illustrated above, or reverse; the stamp being cancelled with an official postmark for first day of issue.

Watermark Types

Stamps are on unwatermarked paper except where the heading to the set states otherwise.

Watermarks are detected for Catalogue description by one of four methods: (1) holding stamps to the light; (2) laying stamps face down on a dark background; (3) by use of the Morley-Bright Detector, which works by revealing the thinning of the paper at the watermark; or (4) by the more complex electric watermark detectors such as the Signoscope.

The diagram below shows how watermark position is described in the Catalogue. Watermarks are usually impressed so that they read normally when looked through from the printed side. However, since philatelists customarily detect watermarks by looking at the back of the stamp, the watermark diagram also makes clear what is actually seen. Note that "G v R" is only an example and illustrations of the different watermarks employed are shown in the listings. The illustrations are actual size and shown in normal positions (from the front of the stamps).

AS DESCRIBED (Read through front of stamp)		AS SEEN DURING WATERMARK DETECTION (Stamp face down and back examined))
GvR	Normal	GvR
GvR	Inverted	GvR
GvR	Reversed	GvR
GvR	Reversed and inverted	GvR
GvR	Sideways	GvR
GvR	Sideways inverted	GvR

Watermark Errors and Varieties

Watermark errors are recognised as of major importance. They comprise stamps showing the wrong watermark devices or stamps printed on paper with the wrong watermark. Stamps printed on paper showing broken or deformed bits on the dandy roll, are not listable.

Underprints

From 1982 various values appeared with underprints, printed on the reverse, in blue, over the gum. These were usually from special stamp booklets, sold at a discount by the Post Office, but in 1985 surplus stocks of such underprinted paper were used for other purposes.

2 Small Crown
4 Large Crown
9 (Extends over three stamps)
13 V R
15 Small Garter
16 Medium Garter
17 Large Garter
20 Emblems
33 Spray of Rose
39 Maltese Cross
40 Large Anchor
47 Small Anchor
48 Orb
49 Imperial Crown
100 Simple Cypher
15 Multiple Cypher
110 Single Cypher
111 Block Cypher
117 PUC £1
125 E 8 R
127
133
153 Tudor Crown
165 St. Edward's Crown
179 Multiple Crowns
F5 Double-lined Anchor
F6 Single-lined Anchor
POSTAL FISCALS

General Types of watermark as seen through the front side of the stamp

In this Catalogue stamps showing underprints are priced mint only. Used examples can be obtained, but care has to be taken in floating the stamps since the ink employed to print the device is solvent in water.

Underprint Types

1 Star with central dot

2 Double-lined Star

3 Double-lined "D"

4 Multiple double lined stars

5 Multiple double-lined "D"

(Types **4**/**5** are shown ¾ actual size)

Note: Types 4/5 are arranged in a random pattern so that the stamps from the same sheet or booklet pane will show the underprint in a slightly different position to the above. Stamps, when inspected, should be placed the correct way up, face down, when comparing with the illustrations.

Specimen Stamps

From 1847 stamps have been overprinted "SPECIMEN" for a variety of purposes, including the provision of samples to postmasters, as a security overprint on printers' or official reference copies and, from 1859, on examples of current British stamps sent to the International Bureau of the Univeral Postal Union for distribution to member nations.

Numerous styles were employed for these "Specimen" overprints, which are now listed in this catalogue up to the end of the reign of King George VI. The different types are illustrated here. Note that for ease of reference type numbers are the same as those given in the *Stanley Gibbons Great Britain Specialised Catalogue* and "missing" type numbers may have been used on stamps outside the scope of this catalogue or may refer to "Cancelled" overprints, which are, likewise, not listed here.

SPECIMEN 1	SPECIMEN 2
SPECIMEN 4	SPECIMEN 5
SPECIMEN 6	SPECIMEN 7
SPECIMEN 8	SPECIMEN 9
SPECIMEN 10	SPECIMEN 11
SPECIMEN 12	SPECIMEN 13
SPECIMEN 15	SPECIMEN 16
SPECIMEN 17	SPECIMEN 22
SPECIMEN 23	SPECIMEN 26
SPECIMEN 29	SPECIMEN 30
SPECIMEN 31	SPECIMEN 32

"Specimen" stamps are listed at the end of each reign and following the Departmental Official, Postage Due and Postal Fiscal sections with the Stanley Gibbons number of the unoverprinted stamps shown in brackets after the colour, followed by the plate number (where shown on the stamp) and the types of "Specimen" overprints found. The different types are not listed here and where more than one type was used the price given is for the cheapest version. Imperforate "Specimen" overprints are also not listed, unless the stamp was normally issued in that form.

More detailed listings will be found in Volumes 1 and 2 of the *Great Britain Specialised Catalogue*.

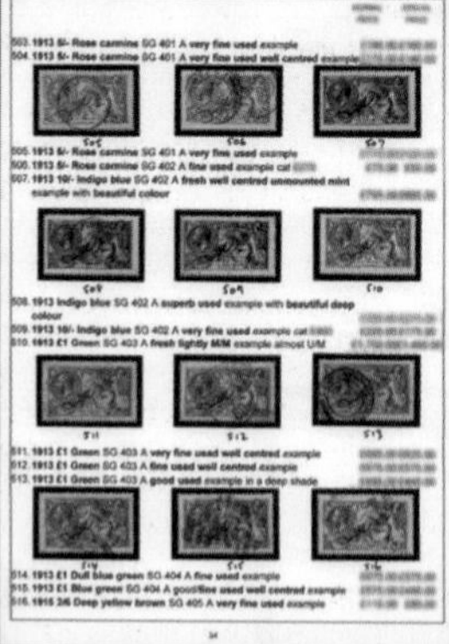

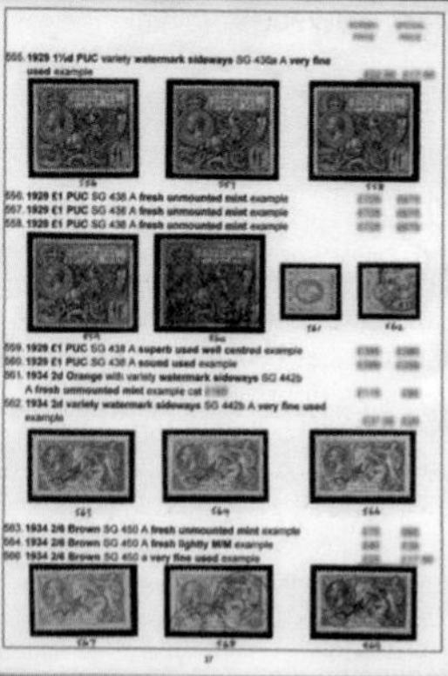

Commemorative Design Index

This index gives an easy reference to the inscriptions and designs of the Special Stamps 1953 to April 2000. Where a complete set shares an inscription or type of design, then only the catalogue number of the first stamp is given in addition to separate entries for stamps depicting popular thematic subjects. Paintings, inventions, etc., are indexed under the name of the artist or inventor, where this is shown on the stamp.

1. £.s.d. ISSUES 1953–70

2. DECIMAL CURRENCY 1971-2004

UNITED KINGDOM OF GREAT BRITAIN AND IRELAND

QUEEN VICTORIA

20 June 1837–22 January 1901

MULREADY ENVELOPES AND LETTER SHEETS, so called from the name of the designer, William Mulready, were issued concurrently with the first British adhesive stamps.

1d. black	Envelopes:	£250 unused;	£350 used.
	Letter Sheets:	£225 unused;	£325 used.
2d. blue	Envelopes:	£325 unused;	£1200 used.
	Letter Sheets:	£300 unused;	£1400 used.

LINE-ENGRAVED ISSUES

GENERAL NOTES

Brief notes on some aspects of the line-engraved stamps follow, but for further information and a full specialist treatment of these issues collectors are recommended to consult Volume 1 of the Stanley Gibbons *Great Britain Specialised Catalogue*.

Alphabet I

Alphabet II

Alphabet III

Alphabet IV

Typical Corner Letters of the four Alphabets

Alphabets. Four different styles were used for the corner letters on stamps prior to the issue with letters in all four corners, these being known to collectors as:

Alphabet I. Used for all plates made from 1840 to the end of 1851. Letters small.

Alphabet II. Plates from 1852 to mid-1855. Letters larger, heavier and broader.

Alphabet III. Plates from mid-1855 to end of period. Letters tall and more slender.

Alphabet IV. 1861. 1d. Die II, Plates 50 and 51 only. Letters were hand-engraved instead of being punched on the plate. They are therefore inconsistent in shape and size but generally larger and outstanding.

While the general descriptions and the illustrations of typical letters given above may be of some assistance, only long experience and published aids can enable every stamp to be allocated to its particular Alphabet without hesitation, as certain letters in each are similar to those in one of the others.

Blued Paper. The blueing of the paper of the earlier issues is believed to be due to the presence of prussiate of potash in the printing ink, or in the paper, which, under certain conditions, tended to colour the paper when the sheets were damped for printing. An alternative term is bleuté paper.

Corner Letters. The corner letters on the early British stamps were intended as a safeguard against forgery, each stamp in the sheet having a different combination of letters. Taking the first 1d. stamp, printed in 20 horizontal rows of 12, as an example, the lettering is as follows:

Row 1. A A, A B, A C, etc. to A L.

Row 2. B A, B B, B C, etc. to B L.

and so on to

Row 20 T A, T B, T C, etc. to T L.

On the stamps with four corner letters, those in the upper corners are in the reverse positions to those in the lower corners.

Thus in a sheet of 240 (12 × 20) the sequence is:

	AA	BA	CA		LA
Row 1.				etc. to	
	AA	AB	AC		AL
	AB	BB	CB		LB
Row 2.				etc. to	
	BA	BB	BC		BL
	and so on to				
	AT	BT	CT		LT
Row 20.				etc. to	
	TA	TB	TC		TL

Placing letters in all four corners was not only an added precaution against forgery but was meant to deter unmarked parts of used stamps being pieced together and passed off as an unused whole.

Dies. The first die of the 1d. was used for making the original die of the 2d., both the No Lines and White Lines issues. In 1855 the 1d. Die I was amended by retouching the head and deepening the lines on a transferred impression of the original. This later version, known to collectors as Die II, was used for making the dies for the 1d. and 2d. with letters in all four corners and also for the 1½d.

The two dies are illustrated above No. 17 in the catalogue.

Double letter

Guide line in corner

Guide line through value

Double Corner Letters. These are due to the workman placing his letter-punch in the wrong position at the first attempt, when lettering the plate, and then correcting the mistake; or to a slight shifting of the punch when struck. If a wrong letter was struck in the first instance, traces of a wrong letter may appear in a corner in addition to the correct one. A typical example is illustrated.

Guide Lines and Dots. When laying down the impressions of the design on the early plates, fine vertical and horizontal guide lines were marked on the plates to assist the operative. These were usually removed from the gutter margins, but could not be removed from the stamp impression without damage to the plate, so that in such cases they appear on the printed stamps, sometimes in the corners, sometimes through "POSTAGE" or the value. Typical examples are illustrated.

Guide dots or cuts were similarly made to indicate the spacing of the guide lines. These too sometimes appear on the stamps.

Ivory Head

"Ivory Head". The so-called "ivory head" variety is one in which the Queen's Head shows white on the back of the stamp. It arises from the comparative absence of ink in the head portion of the design, with consequent absence of blueing. (See "Blued Paper", on page 1).

Line-engraving. In this context "line-engraved" is synonymous with recess-printing, in which the engraver cuts recesses in a plate and printing (the coloured areas) is from these recesses. "Line-engraved" is the traditional philatelic description for these stamps; other equivalent terms found are "engraving in *taille-douce*" (French) or "in *intaglio*" (Italian).

Plates. Until the introduction of the stamps with letters in all four corners, the number of the plate was not indicated in the design of the stamp, but was printed on the sheet margin. By long study of identifiable blocks and the minor variation in the design, coupled with the position of the corner letters, philatelists are now able to allot many of these stamps to their respective plates. Specialist collectors often endeavour to obtain examples of a given stamp printed from its different plates and our catalogue accordingly reflects this depth of detail.

Maltese Cross

Type of Town postmark

Cheltenham
Penny Post

Type of Penny Post cancellation

Example of 1844 type postmark

Postmarks. The so-called "Maltese Cross" design was the first employed for obliterating British postage stamps and was in use from 1840 to 1844. Being hand-cut, the obliterating stamps varied greatly in detail and some distinctive types can be allotted to particular towns or offices. Local types, such as those used at Manchester, Norwich, Leeds, etc., are keenly sought. A red ink was first employed, but was superseded by black, after some earlier experiments, in February 1841. Maltese Cross obliterations in other colours are rare.

Obliterations of this type, numbered 1 to 12 in the centre, were used at the London Chief Office in 1843 and 1844.

Some straight-line cancellations were in use in 1840 at the Penny Post receiving offices, normally applied on the envelope, the adhesives then being obliterated at the Head Office. They are nevertheless known, with or without Maltese Cross, on the early postage stamps.

In 1842 some offices in S.W. England used dated postmarks in place of the Maltese Cross, usually on the back of the letter since they were not originally intended as obliterators. These town postmarks have likewise been found on adhesives.

In 1844 the Maltese Cross design was superseded by numbered obliterators of varied type, one of which is illustrated. They are naturally comparatively scarce on the first 1d. and 2d. stamps.

Like the Maltese Cross they are found in various colours, some of which are rare.

Re-entry

"Union Jack" re-entry

Re-entries. Re-entries on the plate show as a doubling of part of the design of the stamp generally at top or bottom. Many re-entries are very slight while others are most marked. A typical one is illustrated.

The "*Union Jack*" re-entry, so-called owing to the effect of the re-entry on the appearance of the corner stars (see illustration) occurs on stamp L K of Plate 75 of the 1d. red, Die I.

T A (T L)

M A (M L)

Varieties of Large Crown Watermark

I

II

Two states of Large Crown Watermark

Watermarks. Two watermark varieties, as illustrated, consisting of crowns of entirely different shape, are found in sheets of the Large Crown paper and fall on stamps lettered M A and T A (or M L and T L when the paper is printed on the wrong side). Both varieties are found on the 1d. rose-red of 1857, while the M A (M L) variety comes also on some plates of the 1d. of 1864 (Nos. 43, 44) up to about Plate 96. On the 2d. the T A (T L) variety is known on plates 8 and 9, and the M A (M L) on later prints of plate 9. These varieties may exist inverted, or inverted reversed on stamps lettered A A and A L and H A and H L, and some are known.

In 1861 a minor alteration was made in the Large Crown watermark by the removal of the two vertical strokes, representing fleurs-de-lis, which projected upwards from the uppermost of the three horizontal curves at the base of the Crown. Hence two states are distinguishable, as illustrated.

CONDITION–IMPERFORATE LINE-ENGRAVED ISSUES

The prices quoted for the 1840 and 1841 imperforate Line engraved issues are for "fine" examples. As condition is most important in assessing the value of a stamp, the following definitions will assist collectors in the evaluation of individual examples.
Four main factors are relevant when considering quality.

(a) Impression. This should be clean and the surface free of any rubbing or unnatural blurring which would detract from the appearance.
(b) Margins. This is perhaps the most difficult factor to evaluate. Stamps

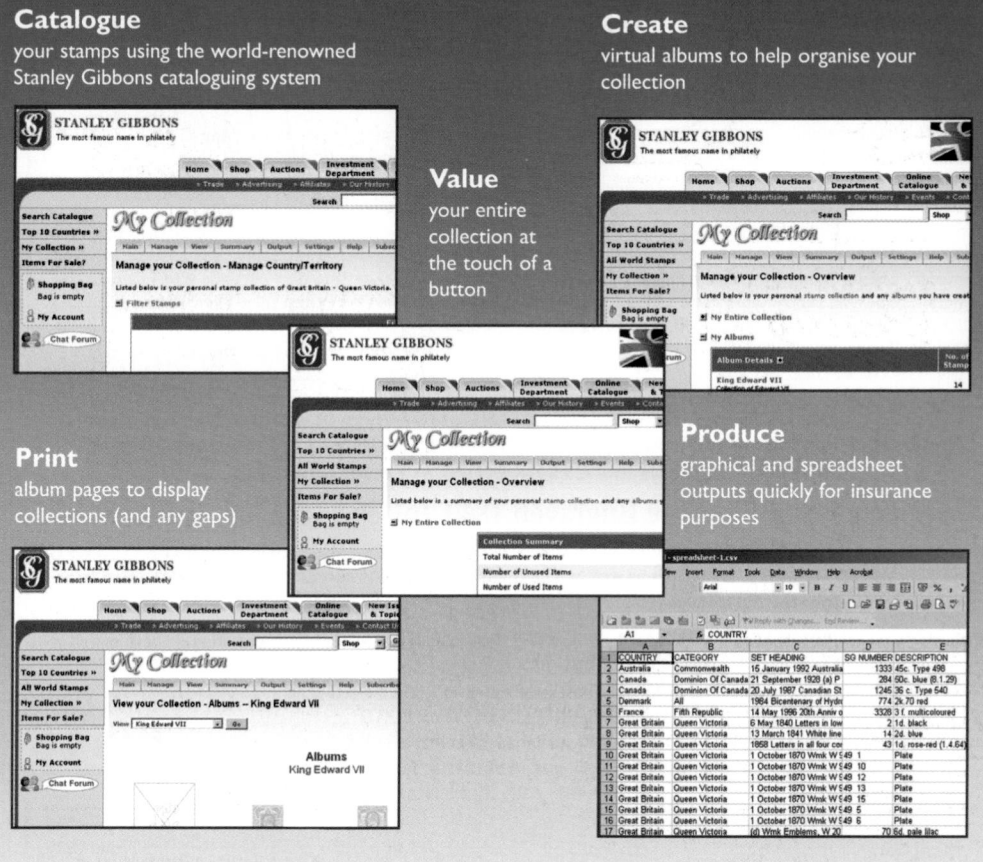

described as "fine", the standard adopted in this catalogue for pricing purposes, should have margins of the recognised width, defined as approximately one half of the distance between two adjoining unsevered stamps. Stamps described as "very fine" or "superb" should have margins which are proportionately larger than those of a "fine" stamp. Examples with close margins should not, generally, be classified as "fine".

(c) Cancellation. On a "fine" stamp this should be reasonably clear and not noticeably smudged. A stamp described as "superb" should have a neat cancellation, preferably centrally placed or to the right.

(d) Appearance. Stamps, at the prices quoted, should always be without any tears, creases, bends or thins and should not be toned on either the front or back. Stamps with such defects are worth only a proportion of the catalogue price.

Good

Fine

Very Fine

Superb

The actual size illustrations of 1840 1d. blacks show the various grades of quality. When comparing these illustrations it should be assumed that they are all from the same plate and that they are free of any hidden defects.

PRINTERS. Nos. 1/53a were recess-printed by Perkins, Bacon & Petch, known from 1852 as Perkins, Bacon & Co.

STAMPS ON COVER. Prices are quoted, for those Victorian and Edwardian issues usually found used on cover. In general these prices refer to the cheapest versions of each basic stamp with other shades, plates or varieties, together with unusual frankings and postmarks, being worth more.

1

1a

2 Small Crown

(Eng Charles and Frederick Heath)

1840 (6 May). *Letters in lower corners. Wmk Small Crown,* W **2**. *Imperf.*

			Un	*Used*	*Used on cover*
1	**1**	1d. intense black	£7500	£350	
2		1d. black	£6000	£275	£475
		Wi. Watermark inverted	£15000	£1400	
3		1d. grey-black (worn plate	£7000	£350	
4	**1a**	2d. dp full blue.	£20000	£825	
5		2d. blue	£15000	£650	£1700
		Wi. Watermark inverted	£35000	£3000	
6		2d. pale blue	£20000	£700	

The 1d. stamp in black was printed from Plates 1 to 11. Plate 1 exists in two states (known to collectors as 1a and 1b), the latter being the result of extensive repairs.

Repairs were also made to plates 2, 5, 6, 8, 9, 10 and 11, and certain impressions exist in two or more states.

The so-called "Royal reprint" of the 1d. black was made in 1864, from Plate 66, Die II, on paper with Large Crown watermark, inverted. A printing was also made in carmine, on paper with the same watermark, normal.

For 1d. black with "VR" in upper corners see No. V1 under Official Stamps.

The 2d. stamps were printed from Plates 1 and 2.

Plates of 1d. black

	Un	*Used*	*Used on cover*
1*a*	£8000	£300	£550
1*b*	£6000	£275	£475
2	£6000	£275	£475
3	£8750	£325	£575
4	£6000	£300	£500
5	£6000	£275	£500
6	£6500	£275	£500
7	£6750	£300	£600
8	£8500	£350	£675
9	£9000	£420	£800
10	£12000	£600	£1600
11	£11000	£3800	£8500

Varieties of 1d. black

		Un	*Used*
a.	On *bleuté* paper (Plates 1 to 8) *from*	—	£500
b.	Double letter in corner *from*	£6250	£300
bb.	Re-entry *from*	£6500	£325
bc.	"PB" re-entry (Plate 5, 3rd state)	—	£5500
c.	Guide line in corner	£6250	£300
cc.	Large letters in each corner (E J, I L, J C and P A) (Plate 1b) *from*	£6250	£425
d.	Guide line through value	£6250	£325
g.	Obliterated by Maltese Cross		
	In red	—	£300
	In black	—	£275
	In blue	—	£5000
	In magenta	—	£2000
	In yellow	—	—
h.	Obliterated by Maltese Cross with number in centre *from*	—	£6000
	No. 1	—	£6000
	No. 2	—	£6000
	No. 3	—	£6000
	No. 4	—	£6000
	No. 5	—	£6000
	No. 6	—	£6000
	No. 7	—	£6000
	No. 8	—	£6000
	No. 9	—	£6000
	No. 10	—	£6000
	No. 11	—	£6000
	No. 12	—	£6000
i.	Obliterated "Penny Post" in black (without Maltese Cross) *from*	—	£2500
j.	Obliterated by town postmark (without Maltese Cross)		
	In black *from*	—	£4000
	In yellow *from*	—	£22000
	In red *from*	—	£4000
k	Obliterated by 1844 type postmark in black *from*	—	£950

Plates of 2d. blue

Plate		*Un*	*Used*	*Used on cover*
1	*Shades from*	£15000	£650	£1700
2	*Shades from*	£20000	£700	£2000

Varieties of 2d. blue

		Un	Used
a.	Double letter in corner	—	£700
aa.	Re-entry	—	£750
b.	Guide line in corner	—	£675
c.	Guide line through value	—	£675
e.	Obliterated by Maltese Cross		
	In red	—	£700
	In black	—	£650
	In blue	—	£7500
	In magenta	—	£6500
f.	Obliterated by Maltese Cross with number in centre from		
	No. 1	—	£6000
	No. 2	—	£6000
	No. 3	—	£6000
	No. 4	—	£6000
	No. 5	—	£6000
	No. 6	—	£6000
	No. 7	—	£6000
	No. 8	—	£6000
	No. 9	—	£6000
	No. 10	—	£6000
	No. 11	—	£6000
	No. 12	—	£5500
g.	Obliterated "Penny Post" in black (without Maltese Cross) *from*	—	£4500
h.	Obliterated by town postmark (without Maltese Cross) in black *from*	—	£3500
i.	Obliterated by 1844 type postmark		
	In black *from*	—	£1500
	In blue *from*	—	£9000

1841 (10 Feb). *Printed from "black" plates. Wmk* W **2**. *Paper more or less blued. Imperf.*

			Un	Used	Used on cover
7	1	1d. red-brown (*shades*)	£1250	75·00	£175
		a. "PB" re-entry (Plate 5, 3rd state)	—	£1500	
		Wi. Watermark inverted (Plates 1b, 8 and 10) *from*	—	£1250	

The first printings of the 1d. in red-brown were made from Plates 1b, 2, 5 and 8 to 11 used for the 1d. black.

1d. red-brown from "black" plates

Plate	Un	Used	Used on cover
1*b*	£8000	£275	£475
2	£5500	£225	£325
5	£2000	£125	£275
8	£2000	£110	£225
9	£2000	£110	£225
10	£1500	£110	£225
11	£1500	90·00	£225

1841 (late Feb). *Plate 12 onwards. Wmk* W **2**. *Paper more or less blued. Imperf.*

			Un	Used	Used on cover
8	1	1d. red-brown	£400	15·00	25·00
		Wi. Watermark inverted	£2000	£250	
8*a*		1d. red-brown on very blue paper	£450	15·00	
9		1d. pale red-brown (worn plates)	£500	25·00	
10		1d. deep red-brown	£600	30·00	
11		1d. lake-red	£3500	£600	
12		1d. orange-brown	£1200	£150	

Error. No letter "A" in right lower corner (Stamp B (A), *Plate* 77)

12*a*	**1**	1d. red-brown	—	£8500

The error "No letter A in right corner" was due to the omission to insert this letter on stamp B A of Plate 77. The error was discovered some months after the plate was registered and was then corrected.

There are innumerable variations in the colour shade of the 1d. "red" and those given in the above list represent colour groups each covering a wide range.

Varieties of 1d. red-brown, etc.

		Un	Used
b.	Re-entry from	—	60·00
c.	Double letter in corner from	—	25·00
d.	Double Star (Plate 75) "Union Jack" re-entry	£15000	£2200
e.	Guide line in corner	—	18·00
f.	Guide line through value	—	22·00
g.	Thick outer frame to stamp	—	22·00
h.	Ivory head	£400	22·00
j.	Left corner letter "S" inverted (Plates 78, 105, 107) *from*	—	£120
k.	P converted to R (Plates 30/1, 33, 83, 86) *from*	—	60·00
l.	Obliterated by Maltese Cross		
	In red	—	£3500
	In black	—	45·00
	In blue	—	£500
m.	Obliterated by Maltese Cross with number in centre		
	No. 1	—	£135
	No. 2	—	£135
	No. 3	—	£160
	No. 4	—	£400
	No. 5	—	£135
	No. 6	—	£110
	No. 7	—	£110
	No. 8	—	£110
	No. 9	—	£135
	No. 10	—	£225
	No. 11	—	£225
	No. 12	—	£225
n.	Obliterated "Penny Post" in black (without Maltese Cross)	—	£550
o.	Obliterated by town postmark (without Maltese Cross)		
	In black *from*	—	£500
	In blue *from*	—	£1200
	In green *from*	—	£2200
	In yellow *from*	—	—
	In red *from*	—	£6500
p.	Obliterated by 1844 type postmark		
	In blue *from*	—	£175
	In red *from*	—	£5000
	In green *from*	—	£1750
	In violet *from*	—	£2500
	In black *from*	—	15·00

Stamps with thick outer frame to the design are from plates on which the frame-lines have been straightened or recut, particularly Plates 76 and 90.

For "Union Jack" re-entry see General Notes to Line-engraved Issues.

In "P converted to R" the corner letter "R" is formed from the "P", the distinctive long tail having been hand-cut.

KEY TO LINE-ENGRAVED ISSUES

S.G Nos.	*Description*	*Date*	*Wmk*	*Perf*	*Die*	*Alphabet*
	THE IMPERFORATE ISSUES					
1/3	1d. black	6.5.40	SC	Imp	I	I
4/6	2d. no lines	8.5.40	SC	Imp	I	I
	PAPER MORE OR LESS BLUED					
7	1d. red-brown	Feb 1841	SC	Imp	I	I
8/12	1d. red-brown	Feb 1841	SC	Imp	I	I
8/12	1d. red-brown	6.2.52	SC	Imp	I	II
13/15	2d. white lines	13.3.41	SC	Imp	I	I
	THE PERFORATED ISSUES					
	ONE PENNY VALUE					
16*a*	1d. red-brown	1848	SC	Roul	I	I
16*b*	1d. red-brown	1850	SC	16	I	I
16*c*	1d. red-brown	1853	SC	16	I	II
17/18	1d. red-brown	Feb 1854	SC	16	I	II
22	1d. red-brown	Jan 1855	SC	14	I	II
24/5	1d. red-brown	28.2.55	SC	14	II	II
21	1d. red-brown	1.3.55	SC	16	II	II
26	1d. red-brown	15.5.55	LC	16	II	II
29/33	1d. red-brown	Aug 1855	LC	14	II	III
	NEW COLOURS ON WHITE PAPER					
37/41	1d. rose-red	Nov 1856	LC	14	II	III
36	1d. rose-red	26.12.57	LC	16	II	III
42	1d. rose-red	1861	LC	14	II	IV
	TWO PENCE VALUE					
19, 20	2d. blue	1.3.54	SC	16	I	I

S.G Nos.	Description	Date	Wmk	Perf	Die	Alphabet
23	2d. blue	22.2.55	SC	14	I	I
23*a*	2d. blue	5.7.55	SC	14	I	II
20*a*	2d. blue	18.8.55	SC	16	I	II
27	2d. blue	20.7.55	LC	16	I	II
34	2d. blue	20.7.55	LC	14	I	II
35	2d. blue	2.7.57	LC	14	I	III
36*a*	2d. blue	1.2.58	LC	16	I	III
	LETTERS IN ALL FOUR CORNERS					
48/9	½d. rose-red	1.10.70	W9	14	—	
43/4	1d. rose-red	1.4.64	LC	14	II	
53*a*	1½d. rosy mauve	1860	LC	14	II	
51/3	1½d. rose-red	1.10.70	LC	14	II	
45	2d. blue	July 1858	LC	14	II	
46/7	2d. thinner lines	7.7.69	LC	14	II	

Watermarks: SC = Small Crown, T 2. LC = Large Crown, T 4.
Dies: See notes above No. 17 in the catalogue.
Alphabets: See General Notes to this section.

3 White lines added

1841 (13 Mar)–51. *White lines added. Wmk* W **2**. *Paper more or less blued. Imperf.*

				Un	Used	Used on cover
13	3	2d.	pale blue	£3500	85·00	
14		2d.	blue	£3000	75·00	£250
		Wi.	Watermark inverted	£7000	£550	
15		2d.	dp full blue	£4000	85·00	
15*aa*		2d.	violet-blue (1851)	£14000	£1000	

The 2d. stamp with white lines was printed from Plates 3 and 4.

No. 15aa came from Plate 4 and the quoted price is for examples on thicker, lavender tinted paper.

Plates of 2d. blue

Plate	Un	Used
3 shades.....*from*	£3000	85·00
4 shades.....*from*	£3500	75·00

Varieties of 2d. blue

		Un	Used
a.	Guide line in corner	—	90·00
b.	Guide line through value	£3250	90·00
bb.	Double letter in corner	—	90·00
be.	Re-entry	£4250	£140
c.	Ivory head	£3250	85·00
e.	Obliterated by Maltese Cross		
	In red	—	£15000
	In black	—	£200
	In blue	—	£3000
f.	Obliterated by Maltese Cross with number in centre		
	No. 1	—	£450
	No. 2	—	£450
	No. 3	—	£450
	No. 4	—	£425
	No. 5	—	£550
	No. 6	—	£425
	No. 7	—	£750
	No. 8	—	£600
	No. 9	—	£750
	No. 10	—	£875
	No. 11	—	£550
	No. 12	—	£350
g.	Obliterated by town postmark (without Maltese Cross)		
	In black *from*	—	£1250
	In blue *from*	—	£2000
h.	Obliterated by 1844 type postmark		
	In black *from*	—	75·00
	In blue *from*	—	£650
	In red *from*	—	£12000
	In green *from*	—	£2500

1841 (Apr). *Trial printing (unissued) on Dickinson silk-thread paper. No wmk. Imperf.*

16 **1** 1d. red-brown (Plate 11) £4000

Eight sheets were printed on this paper, six being gummed, two ungummed, but we have only seen examples without gum.

1848. *Wmk* W **2**. *Rouletted approx* 111/2 *by Henry Archer.*

16*a* **1** 1d. red-brown (Plates 70, 71) £8500

1850. *Wmk* W **2**. P 16 *by Henry Archer.*

			Un	Used	Used on cover
16*b*	1	1d. red-brown (Alph 1) (from Plates 90–101) *from*	£1500	£475	£1000
		*b*Wi. Watermark inverted	—	£1500	

1853. *Wmk* W **2**. *Government Trial Perforation.*

16c **1** 1d. red-brown (p 16) (Alph II) (*on cover*) .... † £12000

SEPARATION TRIALS. Although the various trials of machines for rouletting and perforating were unofficial, Archer had the consent of the authorities in making his experiments, and sheets so experimented upon were afterwards used by the Post Office.

As Archer ended his experiments in 1850 and plates with corner letters of Alphabet II did not come into issue until 1852, perforated stamps with corner letters of Alphabet I may safely be assumed to be Archer productions, if genuine.

The Government trial perforation is believed to have been done on Archer's machines after they had been purchased in 1853. As Alphabet II was by that time in use, the trials can be distinguished from the perforated stamps listed below by being dated prior to 24 February 1854, the date when the perforated stamps were officially issued.

Die I, Alphabet I, stamps from plates 74 and 113 perforated 14 have been recorded for many years, but it is now generally recognised that the type of comb machine used, producing one extension hole in the side margins, cannot be contemporary with other trials of this period.

Die I

Die II

4 Large Crown

Die I: The features of the portrait are lightly shaded and consequently lack emphasis.

Die II (Die I retouched): The lines of the features have been deepened and appear stronger.

The eye is deeply shaded and made more lifelike. The nostril and lips are more clearly defined, the latter appearing much thicker. A strong downward stroke of colour marks the corner of the mouth. There is a deep indentation of colour between lower lip and chin. The band running from the back of the ear to the chignon has a bolder horizontal line below it than in Die I.

1854–57. Paper more or less blued.

(a) *Wmk Small Crown*, W **2**. P 16.

			Un	Used	Used on cover
17	1	1d. red-brown (Die I) (24.2.54) ..	£275	20·00	40·00
		a. Imperf three sides (horiz pair)	†	—	
		Wi. Watermark inverted	—	£150	
18		1d. yellow-brown (Die I)	£325	40·00	
19	3	2d. dp blue (Plate 4) (12.3.54)	£2750	85·00	£130
		a. Imperf three sides (horiz pair) .	†	—	
		Wi. Watermark inverted	—	£210	
20		2d. pale blue (Plate 4)	£2750	90·00	
20*a*		2d. blue (Plate 5) (18.8.55)	£5000	£275	£425
		*a*Wi. *Watermark inverted*	—	£600	

21	1	1d. red-brown (Die II) (22.2.55) .	£300	50·00	90·00
		a. Imperf (Plates 2, 14)			
		Wi. Watermark inverted................	£650	£175	

(b) Wmk Small Crown, W **2**. P 14.

22	1	1d. red-brown (Die I) (1.55)	£500	70·00	£125
		Wi. Watermark inverted	—	£225	
23	3	2d. blue (Plate 4) (22.2.55)	£5000	£200	£300
		Wi. Watermark inverted................	—	£450	
23*a*		2d. blue (Plate 5) (4.7.55)	£6000	£275	£400
		b. Imperf (Plate 5)			
		*a*Wi. Watermark inverted	—	£500	
24	1	1d. red-brown (Die II) (27.2.55)..	£450	45·00	75·00
		Wi. Watermark inverted	£1250	£175	
24*a*		1d. dp red-brown (very blue paper) (Die II)	£525	70·00	
25		1d. orange-brown (Die II)	£1400	£140	

(c) Wmk Large Crown, W **4**. P 16.

26	1	1d. red-brown (Die II) (15.5.55) .	£800	80·00	£180
		a. Imperf (Plate 7)			
		Wi. Watermark inverted	—	£225	
27	3	2d. blue (Plate 5) (20.7.55)..........	£6500	£350	£450
		a. Imperf	—	£5500	
		Wi. Watermark inverted	—	£600	

(d) Wmk Large Crown, W **4**. P 14.

29	1	1d. red-brown (Die II) (6.55)	£200	15·00	30·00
		a. Imperf (*shades*) (Plates 22, 24, 25, 32, 43)	£2250	£2200	
		Wi. Watermark inverted	£750	£100	
30		1d. brick-red (Die II)	£275	35·00	
31		1d. plum (Die II) (2.56)	£1800	£500	
32		1d. brown-rose (Die II)...............	£275	35·00	
33		1d. orange-brown (Die II) (3.57)	£425	40·00	
34	3	2d. blue (Plate 5) (20.7.55)..........	£1900	50·00	£130
		Wi. Watermark inverted	—	£225	
35		2d. blue (Plate 6) (2.7.57)	£2200	50·00	£130
		a. Imperf	—	£5500	
		b. Imperf horiz (vert pair)	†	—	
		Wi. Watermark inverted	—	£225	

*17/35a **For well-centred, lightly used +125%**

1856–58. *Wmk Large Crown,* W **4**. *Paper no longer blued.*

(a) P 16.

36	1	1d. rose-red (Die II) (26.12.57)	£1500	60·00	£130
		Wi. Watermark inverted	—	£250	
36*a*	3	2d. blue (Plate 6) (1.2.58)	£6750	£325	£450
		*a*Wi. Watermark inverted	—	£575	

(b) Die II. P 14.

37	1	1d. red-brown (11.56)	£800	£225	£500
38		1d. pale red (9.4.57)	75·00	15·00	
		a. Imperf	£1800	£1500	
39		1d. pale rose (3.57)	75·00	25·00	
40		1d. rose-red (9.57)	40·00	9·00	20·00
		a. Imperf	£1800	£1500	
		b. Imperf vert (horiz pair)	†	—	
		Wi. Watermark inverted................	£120	60·00	
41		1d. dp rose-red (7.57)	90·00	12·00	

1861. *Letters engraved on plate instead of punched (Alphabet IV).*

42	1	1d. rose-red (Die II) (Plates 50 & 51)	£200	30·00	50·00
		a.Imperf	—	£3250	
		Wi.Watermark inverted	£350	70·00	

*36/42a **For well-centred, lightly used +125%**

The original die (Die I) was used to provide roller dies for the laying down of all the line-engraved stamps from 1840 to 1855. In that year a new master die was laid down (by means of a Die I roller die) and the impression was retouched by hand engraving by William Humphrys. This retouched die, always known to philatelists as Die II, was from that time used for preparing all new roller dies.

One Penny. The numbering of the 1d. plates recommenced at 1 on the introduction of Die II. Plates 1 to 21 were Alphabet II from which a scarce plum shade exists. Corner letters of Alphabet III appear on Plate 22 and onwards. As an experiment, the corner letters were engraved by hand on Plates 50 and 51 in 1856, instead of being punched (Alphabet IV), but punching was again resorted to from Plate 52 onwards. Plates 50 and 51 were not put into use until 1861.

Two Pence. Unlike the 1d. the old sequence of plate numbers continued. Plates 3 and 4 of the 2d. had corner letters of Alphabet I, Plate 5 Alphabet II and Plate 6 Alphabet III. In Plate 6 the white lines are thinner than before.

In both values, varieties may be found as described in the preceding issues—ivory heads, inverted watermarks, re-entries, and double letters in corners.

The change of perforation from 16 to 14 was decided upon late in 1854 since the closer holes of the former gauge tended to cause the sheets of stamps to break up when handled, but for a time both gauges were in concurrent use. Owing to faulty alignment of the impressions on the plates and to shrinkage of the paper when dampened, badly perforated stamps are plentiful in the line-engraved issues.

5

6

Showing position of the plate number on the 1d. and 2d. values. (Plate 170 shown)

1858–79. *Letters in all four corners. Wmk Large Crown,* W **4**. *Die II* (1d. and 2d.). P 14.

					Used on cover
			Un	*Used**	
43	5	1d.rose-red (1.4.64)......................	15·00	2·00	6·00
44		1d.lake-red	15·00	2·00	
		a.Imperf............................. *from*	£5000	£2500	
		Wi.Watermark inverted......... *from*	75·00	25·00	

*43/4a **For well-centred, lightly used +125%**

Plate	*Un*	*Used*	*Plate*	*Un*	*Used*
71..................	35·00	3·00	118................	50·00	2·00
72..................	40·00	4·00	119................	45·00	2·00
73..................	40·00	3·00	120................	15·00	2·00
74..................	40·00	2·00	121................	40·00	9.50
76..................	35·00	2·00	122................	15·00	2·00
77..................	—	£120000	123................	40·00	2·00
78..................	90·00	2·00	124................	28·00	2·00
79..................	30·00	2·00	125................	40·00	2·00
80..................	45·00	2·00	127................	55·00	2·25
81..................	45·00	2·20	129................	40·00	8·00
82..................	90·00	4·00	130................	55·00	2·25
83..................	£110	7·00	131................	65·00	16·00
84..................	60·00	2·25	132................	£130	22·00
85..................	40·00	2·25	133................	£110	9·00
86..................	50·00	4·00	134................	15·00	2·00
87..................	30·00	2·00	135................	95·00	26·00
88..................	£130	8·00	136................	90·00	20·00
89..................	40·00	2·00	137................	28·00	2·25
90..................	40·00	2·00	138................	18·00	2·00
91..................	55·00	6·00	139................	60·00	16·00
92..................	35·00	2·00	140................	18·00	2·00
93..................	50·00	2·00	141................	£110	9·00
94..................	45·00	5·00	142................	70·00	24·00
95..................	40·00	2·00	143................	60·00	15·00
96..................	45·00	2·00	144................	95·00	20·00
97..................	40·00	3·50	145................	30·00	2·25
98..................	50·00	6·00	146................	40·00	6·00
99..................	55·00	5·00	147................	50·00	3·00
100................	60·00	2·25	148................	40·00	3·00
101................	60·00	9·00	149................	40·00	6·00
102................	45·00	2·00	150................	15·00	2·00
103................	50·00	3.50	151................	60·00	9·00
104................	75·00	5·00	152................	60·00	5.50
105................	90·00	7·00	153................	£100	9·00
106................	55·00	2·00	154................	50·00	2·00
107................	60·00	7·00	155................	50·00	2·25
108................	80·00	2·25	156................	45·00	2·00
109................	85·00	3.50	157................	50·00	2·00
110................	60·00	9·00	158................	30·00	2·00
111................	50·00	2·25	159................	30·00	2·00
112................	70·00	2·25	160................	30·00	2·00
113................	50·00	12·00	161................	60·00	7·00
114................	£250	12·00	162................	50·00	7·00
115................	90·00	2·25	163................	50·00	3·00
116................	75·00	9·00	164................	50·00	3·00
117................	45·00	2·00	165................	45·00	2·00

No Rip Off!

…ll the stamp collection but I couldn't decide …uld be the best person to go to. Mrs Jones …ext door said "why don't you try that nice …m Coventry, he did very well for me" so …ot" I gave him a ring and he was very …e and friendly on the telephone and … to give me advice on what would be best for me

No Pressure - Selling a stamp collection is often a difficult personal decision. We understand that when the time comes, you will not just be looking for a fair price, but also that the transaction is handled in a friendly and sensitive manner. We are long standing members of the Philatelic Traders Society, with a good reputation for our honest and reliable dealings, both buying and selling. We intend to be around for many more years by continuing this policy.

The Very Best Price Ever? - Of course we can't guarantee that in every instance, but we can assure you, that as well as being entirely without obligation, any offer made will be highly competitive. We also believe that by giving potential vendors two options, we can offer a more flexible and comprehensive service than most.

Two Ways To Sell Your Stamps

1 We Buy

Collections, Accumulations, Stocks.

We have never yet had to turn down a lot because it is too valuable, and can usually provide immediate payment,for collections up to £100,000. The bulk of our purchases however comprise lots of £200-£10,000 in value, so if yours is a more modest collection, don't be shy!

2 Auction

Our wide ranging and loyal clientele means that we have a strong demand for anything in stamps, postal history, postcards and cigarette cards. Our commission charges to vendors are among the lowest.

We Will Travel To Value Suitable Lots

There is no charge for this service. For less valuable properties, we can arrange collection at our expense. Alternatively, you can forward material by registered post for our written valuation by return

For a friendly and personal service telephone 01926 634809 or fax 01926 634819 and ask to speak to myself of my colleague Robin Taylor

Tony Lester Auctions

The Sidings, Birdingbury Road, Marton, Nr. Rugby CV23 9RX
Website: www.tonylester.co.uk
Email:stamps@ukonline.co.uk

Plate	Un	Used	Plate	Un	Used
166	45·00	6·00	196	50·00	5·00
167	45·00	2·00	197	55·00	9·00
168	50·00	8·00	198	40·00	6·00
169	60·00	7·00	199	55·00	6·00
170	35·00	2·00	200	60·00	2·00
171	15·00	2·00	201	30·00	5·00
172	30·00	2·00	202	60·00	8·00
173	70·00	9·00	203	30·00	16·00
174	30·00	2·00	204	55·00	2·25
175	60·00	3.50	205	55·00	3·00
176	60·00	2·25	206	55·00	9·00
177	40·00	2·00	207	60·00	9·00
178	60·00	3·50	208	55·00	16·00
179	50·00	2·25	209	50·00	9·00
180	60·00	5·00	210	65·00	12·00
181	45·00	2·00	211	70·00	20·00
182	90·00	5·00	212	60·00	11·00
183	55·00	3·00	213	60·00	11·00
184	30·00	2·25	214	65·00	18·00
185	50·00	3·00	215	65·00	18·00
186	65·00	2·25	216	70·00	18·00
187	50·00	2·00	217	70·00	7·00
188	70·00	10·00	218	65·00	8·00
189	70·00	7·00	219	90·00	70·00
190	50·00	6·00	220	40·00	7·00
191	30·00	7·00	221	70·00	16·00
192	50·00	2·00	222	80·00	40·00
193	30·00	2·00	223	90·00	60·00
194	50·00	8·00	224	£125	50·00
195	50·00	8·00	225	£2200	£650

The following plate numbers are known imperf (No. 44a); 72, 79, 80, 81, 82, 83, 84, 85, 86, 87, 88, 90, 91, 92, 93, 96, 97, 98, 100, 101, 102, 103, 104, 105, 107, 108, 109, 112, 113, 114, 116, 117, 120, 121, 122, 136, 137, 142, 146, 148, 158, 162, 164, 166, 171, 174, 191 and 202.

The numbering of this series of 1d. red plates follows after that of the previous 1d. stamp, last printed from Plate 68.

Plates 69, 70, 75, 126 and 128 were prepared for this issue but rejected owing to defects, and stamps from these plates do not exist, so that specimens which appear to be from these plates (like many of those which optimistic collectors believe to be from Plate 77) bear other plate numbers. Owing to faulty engraving or printing it is not always easy to identify the plate number. Plate 77 was also rejected but some stamps printed from it were used. One specimen is in the Tapling Collection and six or seven others are known. Plates 226 to 228 were made but not used.

Specimens from most of the plates are known with inverted watermark. The variety of watermark described in the General Notes to this section occurs on stamp M A (or M L) on plates up to about 96 (Prices from £110 used).

Re-entries in this issue are few, the best being on stamps M K and T K of Plate 71 and on S L and T L, Plate 83.

			Un	Used*	Used on cover
45	6	2d. blue (thick lines) (7.58)	£300	10·00	35·00
		a. Imperf (Plate 9)		—	£5000
		Wi. Watermark inverted	£800	£160	
		Plate			
		7	£1200	45·00	
		8	£1100	32·00	
		9	£300	10·00	
		12	£1800	£120	
46		2d. blue (thin lines) (1.7.69)	£325	20·00	50·00
		Wi. Watermark inverted	£1250	£160	
47		2d. dp blue (thin lines)	£325	20·00	
		a. Imperf (Plate 13)	£6000		
		Plate			
		13	£325	20·00	
		14	£425	25·00	
		15	£400	25·00	

*45/7 **For well-centred, lightly used +125%**

Plates 10 and 11 of the 2d. were prepared but rejected. Plates 13 to 15 were laid down from a new roller impression on which the white lines were thinner.

There are some marked re-entries and repairs, particularly on Plates 7, 8, 9 and 12.

Stamps with inverted watermark may be found and also the T A (T L) and M A (M L) watermark varieties (see General Notes to this section).

Though the paper is normally white, some printings showed blueing and stamps showing the "ivory head" may therefore be found.

7

Showing the plate number (9)

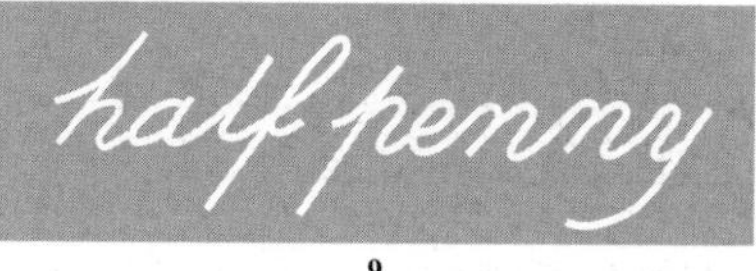

9

1870 (1 Oct). *Wmk W* **9**, *extending over three stamps*. P 14.

			Un	Used*	Used on cover
48	7	½d. rose-red	90·00	15·00	55·00
49		½d. rose	90·00	15·00	
		a. Imperf (Plates 1, 4, 5, 6, 8, 14) *from*	£2750	£1800	
		Wi. Watermark inverted	—	£100	
		Wj. Watermark reversed	—	£100	
		Wk. Watermark inverted & reversed	£225	75·00	
		Plate			
		1	£225	70·00	
		3	£150	35·00	
		4	£130	25·00	
		5	90·00	15·00	
		6	£100	15·00	
		8	£300	95·00	
		9	£4500	£700	
		10	£110	15·00	
		11	£100	15·00	
		12	£100	15·00	
		13	£100	15·00	
		14	£100	15·00	
		15	£150	35·00	
		19	£175	50·00	
		20	£250	70·00	

*48/9a **For well-centred, lightly used +200%**

The ½d. was printed in sheets of 480 (24 × 20) so that the check letters run from

AA XT
to
AA TX

Plates 2, 7, 16, 17 and 18 were not completed while Plates 21 and 22, though made, were not used.

Owing to the method of perforating, the outer side of stamps in either the A or X row (ie the left or right side of the sheet) is imperf.

Stamps may be found with watermark inverted or reversed, or without watermark, the latter due to misplacement of the paper when printing.

8

Position of plate number

1870 (1 Oct). *Wmk* W **4**. P 14.

			Un	Used*	Used on cover
51	8	1½d. rose-red	£375	50·00	£200
52		1½d. lake-red	£375	50·00	
		a. Imperf (Plates 1 & 3) *from*	£4000	†	
		Wi. Watermark inverted	—	£300	
		Plate			
		(1)	£550	70·00	
		3	£375	50·00	

Error of lettering. OP–PC for CP–PC (Plate 1)

53	**8**	1½d. rose-red	£12000	£1200

Prepared for use in 1860, *but not issued; blued paper.*

53a	**8**	1½d. rosy mauve (Plate 1)	£5000	
		b. Error of lettering, OP–PC for CP–PC	—	†

*51/3 **For well-centred, lightly used +125%**

Owing to a proposed change in the postal rates, 1½d. stamps were first printed in 1860, in rosy mauve, No. 53a, but the change was not approved and the greater part of the stock was destroyed, although three or four postally used examples have been recorded.

In 1870 a 1½d. stamp was required and was issued in rose-red. Plate 1 did not have the plate number in the design of the stamps, but on stamps from Plate 3 the number will be found in the frame as shown above. Plate 2 was defective and was not used.

The error of lettering OP–PC on Plate 1 was apparently not noticed by the printer, and therefore not corrected.

EMBOSSED ISSUES

Volume 1 of the Stanley Gibbons Great Britain Specialised Catalogue gives further detailed information on the embossed issues.

PRICES. The prices quoted are for cut-square stamps with average to fine embossing. Stamps with exceptionally clear embossing are worth more.

10 11 12

13 Position of die number

(Primary die engraved at the Royal Mint by William Wyon. Stamps printed at Somerset House)

1847–54. *Imperf (For paper and wmk see footnote).*

			Un	*Used*	*Used on cover*
54	**10**	1s. pale green (11.9.47)	£8250	£750	£1000
55		1s. green	£8250	£800	
56		1s. dp green	£9000	£800	
		Die 1 (1847)	£8250	£750	
		Die 2 (1854)	£9000	£825	
57	**11**	10d. brown (6.11.48)	£5500	£1000	£1900
		Die 1 (1848)	£6000	£1000	
		Die 2 (1850)	£5500	£1000	
		Die 3 (1853)	£5500	£1000	
		Die 4 (1854)	£6000	£1000	
		Die 5			
58	**12**	6d. mauve (1.3.54)	£6500	£800	
59		6d. dull lilac	£6500	£800	£1250
60		6d. purple	£6500	£800	
		Wi. Watermark upright	—	£800	
		Wj. Watermark inverted	—	£800	
		Wk. Watermark inverted & reversed	£6500	£800	
61		6d. violet	£9000	£2200	

The 1s. and 10d. are on "Dickinson" paper with "silk" threads. The 6d. is on paper watermarked V R in single-lined letters, W 13, which may be found in four ways—upright, inverted, upright reversed, and inverted reversed.

The die numbers are indicated on the base of the bust. Only Die 1 (1 W W) of the 6d. was used for the adhesive stamps. The 10d. is from Die 1 (W.W.1 on stamps), and Dies 2 to 5 (2W.W., 3W.W., 4W.W. and 5W.W.) but the number and letters on stamps from Die 1 are seldom clear and many specimens are known without any trace of them. Because of this the stamp we previously listed as "No die number" has been deleted. That they are from Die 1 is proved by the existence of blocks showing stamps with and without the die number. The 1s. is from Dies 1 and 2 (W.W.1, W.W·2).

The normal arrangement of the "silk" threads in the paper was in pairs running down each vertical row of the sheets, the space between the threads of each pair being approximately 5 mm and between pairs of threads 20 mm. Varieties due to misplacement of the paper in printing show a single thread on the first stamp from the sheet margin and two threads 20 mm apart on the other stamps of the row. Faulty manufacture is the cause of stamps with a single thread in the middle.

Through bad spacing of the impressions, which were handstruck, all values may be found with two impressions more or less overlapping. Owing to the small margin allowed for variation of spacing, specimens with good margins on all sides are not common.

Double impressions are known of all values.

Later printings of the 6d. had the gum tinted green to enable the printer to distinguish the gummed side of the paper.

SURFACE-PRINTED ISSUES

GENERAL NOTES

Volume 1 of the Stanley Gibbons Great Britain Specialised Catalogue gives further detailed information on the surface-printed issues.

"Abnormals". The majority of the great rarities in the surface printed group of issues are the so-called "abnormals", whose existence is due to the practice of printing six sheets from every plate as soon as made, one of which was kept for record purposes at Somerset House, while the others were perforated and usually issued. If such plates were not used for general production or if, before they came into full use, a change of watermark or colour took place, the six sheets originally printed would differ from the main issue in plate, colour or watermark and, if issued would be extremely rare.

The abnormal stamps of this class listed in this Catalogue and distinguished, where not priced, by an asterisk (*) are:

No.	
78	3d. Plate 3 (with white dots)
152	4d. vermilion, Plate 16
153	4d. sage-green, Plate 17
109	6d. mauve, Plate 10
124/*a*	6d. pale chestnut & 6d. chestnut, Plate 12
145	6d. pale buff, Plate 13
88	9d. Plate 3 (hair lines)
98	9d. Plate 5 (see footnote to No. 98)
113	10d. Plate 2
91	1s. Plate 3 ("Plate 2")
148/50	1s. green, Plate 14
120	2s. blue, Plate 3

Those which may have been issued, but of which no specimens are known, are 2½d. wmk Anchor, Plates 4 and 5; 3d. wmk Emblems, Plate 5; 3d. wmk Spray, Plate 21, 6d. grey, wmk Spray, Plate 18; 8d. orange, Plate 2; 1s. wmk Emblems, Plate 5; 5s. wmk Maltese Cross, Plate 4.

The 10d. Plate 1, wmk Emblems (No. 99), is sometimes reckoned among the abnormals, but was an error, due to the use of the wrong paper.

Corner Letters. With the exception of the 4d., 6d. and 1s. of 1855–57, the ½d., 1½d., 2d. and 5d. of 1880, the 1d. lilac of 1881 and the £5 (which had letters in lower corners only, and in the reverse order to the normal), all the surface-printed stamps issued prior to 1887 had letters in all four corners, as in the later line-engraved stamps. The arrangement is the same, the letters running in sequence right across and down the sheets, whether these were divided into panes or not. The corner letters existing naturally depend on the number of stamps in the sheet and their arrangement.

Imprimaturs and Imperforate Stamps. The Post Office retained in their records (now in the National Postal Museum) one imperforate sheet from each plate, known as the Imprimatur (or officially approved) sheet. Some stamps were removed from time to time for presentation purposes and have come on to the market, but these imperforates are not listed as they were not issued. Full details can be found in Volume 1 of the Great Britain Specialised Catalogue.

However, other imperforate stamps are known to have been issued and these are listed where it has been possible to prove that they do not come from the Imprimatur sheets. It is therefore advisable to purchase these only when accompanied by an Expert Committee certificate of genuineness.

Plate Numbers. All stamps from No. 75 to No. 163 bear in their designs either the plate number or, in one or two earlier instances, some other indication by which one plate can be distinguished from another. With the aid of these and of the corner letters it is thus possible to "reconstruct" a sheet of stamps from any plate of any issue or denomination.

Surface-printing. In this context the traditional designation "surface-printing" is synonymous with typo(graphy)—a philatelic term—or letterpress—the printers' term—as meaning printing from (the surface of) raised type. It is also called relief printing, as the image is in relief (in French, *en épargne*), unwanted parts of the design having been cut away. Duplicate impressions can be electrotyped or stereotyped from an original die, the resulting *clichés* being locked together to form the printing plate.

Wing Margins. As the vertical gutters (spaces) between the panes, into which sheets of stamps of most values were divided until the introduction of the Imperial Crown watermark, were perforated through the centre with a single row of holes, instead of each vertical row of stamps on the inner side of the panes having its own line of perforation as is now usual, a proportion of the stamps in each sheet have what is called a "wing margin" about 5 mm wide on one or other side.

The stamps with "wing margins" are the watermark Emblems and Spray of Rose series (3d., 6d., 9d., 10d., 1s. and 2s.) with letters D, E, H or I in S.E. corner, and the watermark Garter series (4d. and 8d.) with letters F or G in S.E. corner. Knowledge of this lettering will enable collectors to guard against stamps with wing margin cut down and re-perforated, but note that wing margin stamps of Nos. 62 to 73 are also to be found re-perforated.

PRINTERS. The issues of Queen Victoria, Nos. 62/214, were typo by Thomas De La Rue & Co.

PERFORATIONS. All the surface-printed issues of Queen Victoria are perf 14, with the exception of Nos. 126/9.

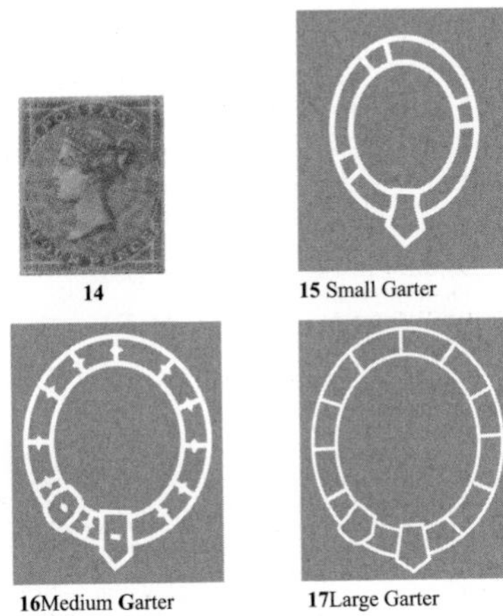

14 **15** Small Garter

16Medium **G**arter **17**Large Garter

1855–57. *No corner letters.*

(a) Wmk Small Garter, W **15**. *Highly glazed, deeply blued paper* (31 *July* 1855)

			Un	Used*	Used on cover
62	**14**	4d. carmine (*shades*)	£5000	£375	£650
		a. Paper slightly blued	£5250	£375	
		b. White paper	—	£750	
		Wi. Watermark inverted	—	£900	

(b) *Wmk Medium Garter*, W **16**.

(i) *Thick, blued highly glazed paper* (25 February 1856).

			Un	Used*	Used on cover
63	**14**	4d. carmine (*shades*)	£5750	£425	£650
		a. White paper	£4750		
		Wi. Watermark inverted	—	£900	

(ii) *Ordinary thin white paper* (September 1856).

			Un	Used*	Used on cover
64	**14**	4d. pale carmine .	£4500	£350	£550
		a. Stamp printed double	†	—	
		Wi. Watermark inverted	—	£750	

(iii) *Ordinary white paper, specially prepared ink* (1 November 1856).

			Un	Used*	Used on cover
65	**14**	4d. rose or dp rose	£4250	£350	£500

(c) *Wmk Large Garter,* W **17**. *Ordinary white paper* (January 1857).

			Un	Used*	Used on cover
66	**14**	4d. rose-carmine .	£1400	£100	£175
		a. Rose .	£1100	£100	
		aWi. Watermark inverted	—	£280	
		aWj. Watermark inverted & reversed			
		b. Thick glazed paper	£3000	£275	
		bWi. Watermark inverted			

*62/6b **For well-centred, lightly used** +125%

18

19

20 Emblems wmk (normal)

20a Watermark error, three roses and shamrock

20b Watermark error, three roses and thistle

(d) *Wmk Emblems,* W **20**.

			Un	Used*	Used on cover
69	**18**	6d. deep lilac (21.10.56)	£1100	£120	
70		6d. pale lilac	£900	95·00	£175
		a. Azure paper	£4500	£700	
		b. Thick paper	£2200	£275	
		c. Error. Watermark W **20a**			
		Wi. Watermark inverted	—	£250	
		Wj. Watermark reversed			
		Wk. Watermark inverted & reversed			
71	**19**	1s. deep green (1.11.56)	£2200	£375	
72		1s. green	£1250	£260	£350
73		1s. pale green	£1250	£260	
		a. Azure paper	—	£1500	
		b. Thick paper	—	£300	
		c. Imperf		†	—
		Wi. Watermark inverted	—	£425	
		Wj. Watermark reversed	—	£1000	
		Wk. Watermark inverted and reversed			

*69/73b **For well-centred, lightly used** +125%

KEY TO SURFACE-PRINTED ISSUES 1855–83

S.G. Nos.	*Description*	*Watermark*	*Date of Issue*
	NO CORNER LETTERS		
62	4d. carmine	Small Garter	31.7.55
63/5	4d. carmine	Medium Garter	25.2.56
66/a	4d. carmine	Large Garter	Jan 1857
69/70	6d. lilac	Emblems	21.10.56
71/3	1s. green	Emblems	1.11.56
	SMALL WHITE CORNER LETTERS		
75/7	3d. carmine	Emblems	1.5.62
78	3d. carmine (dots)	Emblems	Aug 1862
79/82	4d. red	Large Garter	15.1.62
83/5	6d. lilac	Emblems	1.12.62
86/8	9d. bistre	Emblems	15.1.62
89/91	1s. green	Emblems	1.12.62
	LARGE WHITE CORNER LETTERS		
92	3d. rose	Emblems	1.3.65
102/3	3d. rose	Spray	July 1867
93/4	4d. vermilion	Large Garter	4.7.65
96/7	6d. lilac	Emblems	7.3.65
104/7	6d. lilac	Spray	21.6.67
108/9	6d. lilac	Spray	8.3.69
122/4	6d. chestnut	Spray	12.4.72
125	6d. grey	Spray	24.4.73

S.G. Nos.	*Description*	*Watermark*	*Date of Issue*
98	9d. straw	Emblems	30.10.65
110/11	9d. straw	Spray	3.10.67
99	10d. brown	Emblems	11.11.67
112/14	10d. brown	Spray	1.7.67
101	1s. green	Emblems	19.1.65
115/17	1s. green	Spray	13.7.67
118/20*b*	2s. blue	Spray	1.7.67
121	2s. brown	Spray	27·2.80
126/7	5s. rose	Cross	1.7.67
128	10s. grey	Cross	26.9.78
129	£1 brown-lilac	Cross	26.9.78
130, 134	5s. rose	Anchor	25.11.82
131, 135	10s. grey-green	Anchor	Feb 1883
132, 136	£1 brown-lilac	Anchor	Dec 1882
133, 137	£5 orange	Anchor	21.3.82

LARGE COLOURED CORNER LETTERS

S.G. Nos.	*Description*	*Watermark*	*Date of Issue*
138/9	2½d. rosy mauve	Anchor	1.7.75
141	2½d. rosy mauve	Orb	1.5.76
142	2½d. blue	Orb	5·2.80
157	2½d. blue	Crown	23.3.81
143/4	3d. rose	Spray	5.7.73
158	3d. rose	Crown	Jan 1881
159	3d. on 3d. lilac	Crown	1.1.83
152	4d. vermilion	Large Garter	1.3.76
153	4d. sage-green	Large Garter	12.3.77
154	4d. brown	Large Garter	15.8.80
160	4d. brown	Crown	9.12.80
145	6d. buff	Spray	15.3.73
146/7	6d. grey	Spray	20.3.74
161	6d. grey	Crown	1.1.81
162	6d. on 6d. lilac	Crown	1.1.83
156a	8d. purple-brown	Large Garter	July 1876
156	8d. orange	Large Garter	11.9.76
148/50	1s. green	Spray	1.9.73
151	1s. brown	Spray	14.10.80
163	1s. brown	Crown	24.5.81

Watermarks:		
	Anchor	**W 40, 47**
	Cross	**W 39**
	Crown	**W 49**
	Emblems	**W 20**
	Large Garter	**W 17**
	Medium Garter	**W 16**
	Orb	**W 48**
	Small Garter	**W 15**
	Spray	**W 33**

21

22

23

24

25 Plate 2

A. White dots added

B. Hair lines

1862–64. *A small uncoloured letter in each corner, the* 4d. *wmk Large Garter,* W **17**, *the others Emblems,* W **20**.

			Un	*Used**	*Used on cover*
75	**21**	3d. dp carmine-rose (Plate 2) (1.5.62)	£3250	£400	
76		3d. brt carmine-rose	£1500	£250	£450
		Wi. Watermark inverted	—	£450	
77		3d. pale carmine-rose	£1500	£250	
		b. Thick paper	—	£350	
		Wj. Watermark reversed			
78		3d. rose (with white dots, Type A, Plate 3) (8.62)	£20000	£8000	
		a. Imperf (Plate 3)	£4000		
79	**22**	4d. brt red (Plate 3) (15.1.62)	£1350	£110	
80		4d. pale red	£1100	90·00	£200
		Wi. Watermark inverted	—	£225	
81		4d. brt red (Hair lines, Type B, Plate 4) (16.10.63)	£1500	£110	
82		4d. pale red (Hair lines, Type B, Plate 4)	£1350	90·00	£200
		a. Imperf (Plate 4)	£3000		
		Wi. Watermark inverted	—	£250	
83	**23**	6d. dp lilac (Plate 3) (1.12.62)	£1450	£110	
84		6d. lilac	£1400	90·00	£170
		a. Azure paper	—	£900	
		b. Thick paper	—	£225	
		c. Error. Shamrock missing from wmk (stamp TF)			
		d. Error. Watermark W **20b** (stamp TF)	—	£6000	
		Wi. Watermark inverted	—	£280	
		Wj. Watermark reversed			
		Wk. Watermark inverted and reversed			
85		6d. lilac (Hair lines, Plate 4) (20.4.64)	£1800	£180	£275
		a. Imperf (watermark inverted)	£3000		
		Eb. Imperf and watermark upright			
		c. Thick paper	£2200	£225	
		d. Error. Watermark W **20b** (stamp TF)			
		Wi. Watermark inverted	—	£350	
		Wj. Watermark reversed			
		Wk. Watermark inverted and reversed			
86	**24**	9d. bistre (Plate 2) (15.1.62)	£3250	£400	£575
		Wi. Watermark inverted	—	£525	
		Wj. Watermark reversed	—	£600	
		Wk. Watermark inverted and reversed			
87		9d. straw	£2750	£350	
		a. On azure paper			
		b. Thick paper	£3500	£425	
		c. Error. Watermark W **20b** (stamp TF)	†	—	
88		9d. bistre (Hair lines, Plate 3) (5.62)	£13500	£7500	
89	**25**	1s. dp green (Plate No. 1 Plate 2) (1.12.62)	£2500	£350	
90		1s. green (Plate No. 1 Plate 2)	£1700	£175	£275
		a. "K" in lower left corner in white circle (stamp KD)	£5500	£950	
		aa. "K" normal (stamp KD)	—	£1250	
		b. On azure paper			
		c. Error. Watermark W **20b** (stamp TF)			
		d. Thick paper	—	£275	
		da. Thick paper, "K" in circle as No. 90a	—	£2100	
		Wi. Watermark inverted	—	£275	
		Wj. Watermark reversed			
		Wk. Watermark inverted and reversed	—	£275	
91		1s. dp green (Plate No. 2 = Plate 3)	£20000		
		a. Imperf	£3800		
		aWi. Watermark inverted	£2800		

*75/91 **For well-centred, lightly used +125%**

The 3d. as Type **21**, but with network background in the spandrels which is found overprinted SPECIMEN, was never issued.

The plates of this issue may be distinguished as follows:

3d.	Plate 2	No white dots.
	Plate 3	White dots as Illustration A.
4d.	Plate 3	No hair lines. Roman I next to lower corner letters.
	Plate 4	Hair lines in corners. (Illustration B.). Roman II.
6d.	Plate 3	No hair lines.
	Plate 4	Hair lines in corners.
9d.	Plate 2	No hair lines.
	Plate 3	Hair lines in corners. Beware of faked lines.
1s.	Plate 2	Numbered 1 on stamps.
	Plate 3	Numbered 2 on stamps & with hair lines.

The 9d. on azure paper (No. 87a) is very rare, only one confirmed example being known.

The variety "K" in circle, No. 90a, is believed to be due to a damaged letter having been cut out and replaced. It is probable that the punch was driven in too deeply, causing the flange to penetrate the surface, producing an indentation showing as an uncoloured circle.

The watermark variety "three roses and a shamrock" illustrated in W **20a** was evidently due to the substitution of an extra rose for the thistle in a faulty watermark bit. It is found on stamp TA of Plate 4 of the 3d., Plates 1 (No. 70c), 3, 5 and 6 of the 6d., Plate 4 of the 9d. and Plate 4 of the 1s.

Similar problems occurred on stamp TF of the 6d. and 9d. Here the shamrock emblem became detached and a used example of the 6d. (No. 84) is known showing it omitted. It was replaced by a third rose (**W 20b**) and this variety exists on the 6d. (Nos. 84/5 and 97) and 9d. (Nos. 87 and 98).

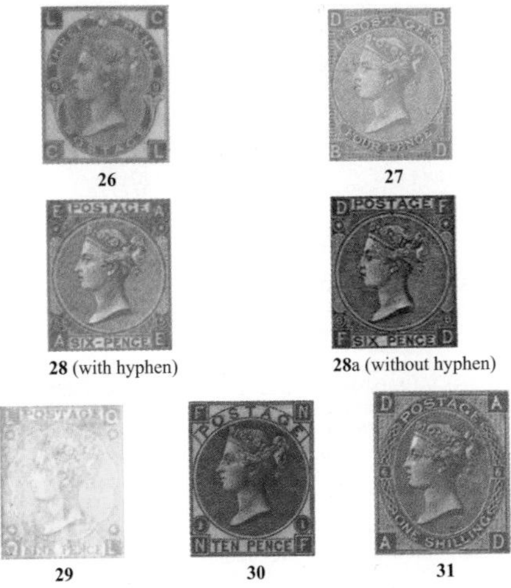

26 **27**

28 (with hyphen) **28a** (without hyphen)

29 **30** **31**

1865–67. *Large uncoloured corner letters. Wmk Large Garter* (4d.); *others Emblems.*

			Un	Used*	Used on cover
92	**26**	3d. rose (Plate 4) (1.3.65)	£1350	£180	£275
		a. Error. Watermark W **20a**	£2750	£900	
		b. Thick paper	£1350	£200	
		Wi. Watermark inverted	—	£350	
		Wj. Watermark reversed			
		Wk. Watermark inverted and reversed			
93	**27**	4d. dull vermilion (4.7.65)	£525	85·00	
94		4d. vermilion	£450	55·00	£125
		a. Imperf (Plates 11, 12)	£1750		
		Wi. Watermark inverted	£475	55·00	
		Plate			
		7 (1865)	£550	£100	
		8 (1866)	£500	60·00	
		9 (1867)	£500	60·00	
		10 (1868)	£550	£110	
		11 (1869)	£500	60·00	
		12 (1870)	£475	55·00	
		13 (1872)	£500	55·00	
		14 (1873)	£550	85·00	
96	**28**	6d. dp lilac (with hyphen)(7.3.65)	£1100	£130	
97		6d. lilac (with hyphen)	£725	80·00	£120
		a. Thick paper	£825	£110	
		b. Stamp doubly printed (Plate 6)	—	£12000	
		c. Error. Watermark W **20a** (Pl 5, 6) *from*	—	£750	
		d. Error. Watermark W **20b** (Plate 5)			
		Wi. Watermark inverted	—	£175	
		Wj. Watermark reversed			
		Wk. Watermark inverted and reversed	†	—	
		Plate			
		5 (1865)	£725	80·00	
		6 (1867)	£2200	£150	
98	**29**	9d. straw (Plate 4) (30.10.65)	£2200	£500	£800
		a. Thick paper	£2500	£625	
		b. Error. Watermark W **20a**	—	£1200	
		c. Error. Watermark W **20b** (stamp TF)			
		Wi. Watermark inverted	—	£700	
99	**30**	10d. red-brown (Plate 1) (11.11.67)	*	£25000	
101	**31**	1s. green (Plate 4) (19.1.65)	£1450	£170	£250
		a. Error. Watermark W 20a	—	£1100	
		b. Thick paper	£1600	£250	
		c. Imperf between (vert pair)	—	£9000	
		Wi. Watermark inverted	—	£380	
		Wj. Imperf watermark inverted			

*92/101c **For well-centred, lightly used** +**100%**

From mid-1866 to about the end of 1871 4d. stamps of this issue appeared generally with watermark inverted.

Unused examples of No. 98 from Plate 5 exist, but this was never put to press and all evidence points to such stamps originating from a portion of the Imprimatur sheet which was perforated by De La Rue in 1887 for insertion in albums to be presented to members of the Stamp Committee (*Price* £15000 *un*).

The 10d. stamps, No. 99, were printed in error on paper watermarked "Emblems" instead of on "Spray of Rose".

32

33 Spray of Rose

34

1867–80. *Wmk Spray of Rose.* W **33**.

			Un	Used*	Used on cover
102	**26**	3d. dp rose (12.7.67)	£800	85·00	
103		3d. rose	£450	55·00	90·00
		a. Imperf (Plates 5, 6, 8) *from*	£2750		
		Wi. Watermark inverted	£750	£175	
		Plate			
		4 (1867)	£825	£190	
		5 (1868)	£450	55·00	
		6 (1870)	£475	55·00	
		7 (1871)	£550	60·00	
		8 (1872)	£525	55·00	
		9 (1872)	£525	60·00	
		10 (1873)	£650	£110	
104	**28**	6d. lilac (with hyphen) (Plate 6) (21.6.67)	£1100	80·00	£160
		a. Imperf			
		Wi. Watermark inverted	—	£225	
105		6d. dp lilac (with hyphen) (Plate 6)	£1100	80·00	
106		6d. purple (with hyphen) (Plate 6)	£1100	£110	
107		6d. brt violet (with hyphen) (Plate 6) (22.7.68)	£950	90·00	
108	**28a**	6d. dull violet (without hyphen) (Plate 8) (8.3.69)	£550	80·00	
		Wi. Watermark inverted	—	£225	
109		6d. mauve (without hyphen)	£500	80·00	£120
		a. Imperf (Plate Nos. 8 & 9)	£4750	£3250	
		Wi. Watermark inverted	—	£200	
		Plate			
		8 (1869, mauve)	£500	£110	

		9 (1870, mauve)	£500	80·00	
		10 (1869, mauve)	*	£22000	
110	**29**	9d. straw (Plate No. 4)(3.10.67)	£1700	£275	£425
		Wi. Watermark inverted	—	£475	
111		9d. pale straw (Plate No. 4)	£1600	£250	
		a. Imperf (Plate 4)	£5000		
112	**30**	10d. red-brown (1.7.67)	£2300	£300	£700
		Wi. Watermark inverted	—	£650	
113		10d. pale red-brown	£2300	£325	
114		10d. deep red-brown	£3250	£475	
		a. Imperf (Plate 1)	£5000		
		Plate			
		1 (1867)	£2300	£300	
		2 (1867)	£22000	£8500	
115	**31**	1s. deep green (13.7.67)	£725	38·00	
117		1s. green	£650	35·00	55·00
		a. Imperf between (horiz pair) (Pl 7)			
		b. Imperf (Plate 4)	£3250	£1800	
		Wi. Watermark inverted	£1500	£150	
		Plate			
		4 (1867)	£825	50·00	
		5 (1871)	£650	35·00	
		6 (1871)	£1000	35·00	
		7 (1873)	£1000	60·00	
118	**32**	2s. dull blue (1.7.67)	£2200	£175	£675
		Wi. Watermark inverted	—	£450	
119		2s. dp blue	£2750	£175	
		a. Imperf (Plate 1)	£7000		
120		2s. pale blue	£2750	£200	
		aa. Imperf (Plate 1)	£7000		
120*a*		2s. cobalt	£11000	£2200	
120*b*		2s. milky blue	£9250	£1400	
		Plate			
		1 (1867)	£2200	£175	
		3 (1868)	*	£7000	
121		2s. brown (Plate No. 1) (27.2.80)	£15000	£2800	
		a. Imperf	£15000		
		b. No watermark	†	—	
		Wi. Watermark inverted	—	£3800	

*102/21 **For well-centred, lightly used +75%**

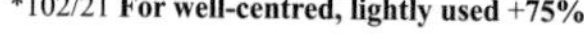

Examples of the 1s. from Plates 5 and 6 without watermark are postal forgeries used at the Stock Exchange Post Office in the early 1870s.

1872–73. *Uncoloured letters in corners. Wmk Spray,* W **33**.

			Un	*Used**	*Used on cover*
122	34	6d. dp chestnut (Plate 11)(12.4.72)	£875	90·00	
122*a*		6d. chestnut (Plate 11) (22.5.72)	£650	50·00	90·00
		Wi. Watermark inverted	—	£200	
122*b*		6d. pale chestnut (Plate 11) (1872)	£550	50·00	
123		6d. pale buff (19.10.72)	£600	85·00	£200
		Wi. Watermark inverted	—	£200	
		Plate			
		11 (1872, pale buff)	£600	85·00	
		12 (1872, pale buff)	£2000	£250	
124		6d. chestnut (Plate 12) (1872)	*	£2750	
124*a*		6d. pale chestnut (Plate 12) (1872)	*	£2750	
125		6d. grey (Plate No. 12) (24.4.73)	£1400	£200	£250
		a. Imperf	£3800		
		Wi. Watermark inverted	£3000	£400	

*122/5 **For well-centred, lightly used +50%**

35

36

37

38

39 Maltese Cross

40 Large Anchor

1867–83. Uncoloured letters in corners.

(a) Wmk Maltese Cross, W **39**. P 15½ × 15.

			Un	*Used**
126	**35**	5s. rose (1.7.67)	£5000	£600
127		5s. pale rose	£5000	£600
		a. Imperf (Plate 1)	£10000	
		Plate		
		1 (1867)	£5000	£600
		2 (1874)	£7500	£950
128	**36**	10s. greenish grey (Plate 1) (26.9.78)	£38000	£2500
129	**37**	£1 brown-lilac (Plate 1) (26.9.78)	£50000	£3750
		(b) Wmk Anchor, W **40**. P 14. *(i) Blued paper*		
130	**35**	5s. rose (Plate 4) (25.11.82)	£18000	£3750
		Wi. Watermark inverted	—	£7000
131	**36**	10s. grey-green (Plate 1) (2.83)	£60000	£4500
132	**37**	£1 brown-lilac (Plate 1) (12.82)	£80000	£8000
133	**38**	£5 orange (Plate 1) (21.3.82)	£40000	£11000
		(ii) White paper.		
134	**35**	5s. rose (Plate 4)	£14000	£2700
135	**36**	10s. greenish grey (Plate 1)	£60000	£3500
136	**37**	£1 brown-lilac (Plate 1)	£85000	£7000
137	**38**	£5 orange (Plate 1)	£9000	£4000

*126/37 **For well-centred, lightly used +75%**

41

42

43

44

45

46

47 Small Anchor

48 Orb

1873–80. *Large coloured letters in the corners.*

(a) Wmk Anchor, W **47**.

			Un	Used*	Used on cover
138	**41**	2½d.rosy mauve (*blued paper*) (1.7.75)	£700	£120	
		a.Imperf			
		Wi.Watermark inverted	£1250	£250	
		Plate			
		1 (*blued paper*) (1875)	£700	£120	
		2 (*blued paper*) (1875)	£5500	£1250	
		3 (*blued paper*) (1875)	—	£4250	
139		2½d. rosy mauve (*white paper*)	£500	80·00	£140
		Wi.Watermark inverted	£850	£180	
		Plate			
		1 (*white paper*) (1875)	£500	80·00	
		2 (*white paper*) (1875)	£500	80·00	
		3 (*white paper*) (1875)	£775	£120	

Error of Lettering L H—F L *for* L H—H L (*Plate* 2).

140	**41**	2½d.rosy mauve	£14000	£1900	

(b) Wmk Orb, W **48**.

141	**41**	2½d.rosy mauve (1.5.76)	£425	50·00	80·00
		Wi.Watermark inverted	£650	£100	
		Plate			
		3 (1876)	£925	£100	
		4 (1876)	£425	50.00	
		5 (1876)	£425	50.00	
		6 (1876)	£425	50.00	
		7 (1877)	£425	50.00	
		8 (1877)	£425	50.00	
		9 (1877)	£425	50.00	
		10 (1878)	£475	65·00	
		11 (1878)	£425	50·00	
		12 (1878)	£425	50·00	
		13 (1878)	£425	50·00	
		14 (1879)	£425	50·00	
		15 (1879)	£425	50·00	
		16 (1879)	£425	50·00	
		17 (1880)	£1250	£240	
142	**41**	2½d.blue (5.2.80)	£375	40·00	75·00
		Wi.Watermark inverted	£850	£175	
		Plate			
		17 (1880)	£375	55·00	
		18 (1880)	£400	40·00	
		19 (1880)	£375	40·00	
		20 (1880)	£375	40·00	

(c) Wmk Spray, W **33**.

143	**42**	3d. rose (5.7.73)	£350	45·00	60·00
		Wi.Watermark inverted	£850	£225	
144		3d.pale rose	£400	45·00	
		Plate			
		11 (1873)	£350	45·00	
		12 (1873)	£400	45·00	
		14 (1874)	£425	45·00	
		15 (1874)	£350	45·00	
		16 (1875)	£350	45·00	
		17 (1875)	£400	45·00	
		18 (1875)	£400	45·00	
		19 (1876)	£350	45·00	
		20 (1879)	£480	85·00	
145	43	6d.pale buff (Plate 13) (15.3.73)	*	£15000	
146		6d. dp grey (20.3.74)	£400	60·00	£100
147		6d.grey	£400	60·00	
		Wi. Watermark inverted	£850	£225	
		Plate			
		13 (1874)	£400	60·00	
		14 (1875)	£400	60·00	
		15 (1876)	£400	60·00	
		16 (1878)	£400	60·00	
		17 (1880)	£675	£140	
148	**44**	1s. dp green (1.9.73)	£650	£120	
150		1s. green	£500	£100	£170
		Wi. Watermark inverted	£1000	£225	
		Plate			
		8 (1873)	£575	£120	
		9 (1874)	£575	£120	
		10 (1874)	£575	£140	
		11 (1875)	£575	£120	
		12 (1875)	£500	£100	
		13 (1876)	£500	£100	
		14 (—)*	*	£22000	
151		1s. orange-brown (Plate 13) (14.10.80)	£3250	£575	£1100
		Wi. Watermark inverted	£6000	£900	

(d) Wmk Large Garter, W **17**.

152	**45**	4d. vermilion (1.3.76)	£1750	£425	£850
		Wi. Watermark inverted	—	£700	
		Plate			
		15 (1876)	£1750	£425	
		16 (1877)	*	£22000	
153		4d. sage-green (12.3.77)	£900	£250	£450
		Wi. Watermark inverted	—	£500	
		Plate			
		15 (1877)	£1000	£275	
		16 (1877)	£900	£250	
		17 (1877)	*	£15000	
154		4d. grey-brown (Plate 17)(15.8.80)	£1500	£450	£1100
		a. Imperf	£7000		
		Wi. Watermark inverted	—	£900	
156	**46**	8d. orange (Plate 1) (11.9.76)	£1100	£300	£450
		Wi. Watermark inverted	—	£650	

*138/56 **For well-centred, lightly used +100%**

1876 (July). *Prepared for use but not issued.*

156*a*	**46**	8d. purple-brown (Plate 1)	£6500		

49 Imperial Crown

3d

(50)

1880–83. *Wmk Imperial Crown,* W **49**.

			Un	Used*	Used on cover
157	**41**	2½d. blue (23.3.81)	£350	28·00	45·00
		Wi. Watermark inverted	—	£325	
		Plate			
		21 (1881)	£350	35·00	
		22 (1881)	£350	35·00	
		23 (1881)	£350	28·00	
158	**42**	3d. rose (3.81)	£400	80·00	£140
		Wi. Watermark inverted	—	£380	
		Plate			
		20 (1881)	£550	£130	
		21 (1881)	£400	80·00	
159	**50**	3d. on 3d. lilac (C.) (Plate 21) (1.1.83)	£450	£130	£350
		Wi. Watermark inverted			
160	**45**	4d. grey-brown (8.12.80)	£350	60·00	£140
		Wi. Watermark inverted	—	£550	
		Plate			
		17 (1880)	£350	60·00	
		18 (1882)	£350	60·00	
161	**43**	6d. grey (1.1.81)	£350	65·00	£120
		Wi. Watermark inverted	—	£550	
		Plate			
		17 (1881)	£400	65·00	
		18 (1882)	£350	65·00	

162	**50**	6d. on 6d. lilac (C.) (Plate 18) (1.1.83)	£500	£130	£350
		a. Slanting dots (various) *from*	£950	£350	
		b. Opt double	—	£9000	
		Wi. Watermark inverted	£1400	£550	
163	**44**	1s. orange-brown (24.5.81)	£500	£140	£450
		Wi. Watermark inverted	£1400	£600	
		Plate			
		13 (1881)	£625	£140	
		14 (1881)	£500	£140	

*157/63 **For well-centred, lightly used +75%**

The 1s. plate 14 (line perf 14) exists in purple but was not issued in this shade (*Price* £7500 *unused*). Examples were included in a few of the Souvenir Albums prepared for members of the "Stamp Committee of 1884".

52

53

54 55

56

1880–81. Wmk Imperial Crown, W **49**.

164	**52**	½d. dp green (14.10.80)	45·00	10·00	20·00
		a. Imperf	£1800		
		b. No watermark	£5500		
		Wi. Watermark inverted	—	£325	
165		½d. pale green	45·00	15·00	
166	**53**	1d. Venetian red (1.1.80)	22·00	10·00	18·00
		a. Imperf	£1800		
		Wi. Watermark inverted	—	£250	
167	**54**	1½d. Venetian red (14.10.80)	£175	45·00	£130
		Wi. Watermark inverted	†	—	
168	**55**	2d. pale rose (8.12.80)	£225	90·00	£225
		Wi. Watermark inverted	£1100	£500	
168*a*		2d. dp rose	£250	90·00	
169	**56**	5d. indigo (15.3.81)	£625	£110	£225
		a. Imperf	£3250	£2750	
		Wi. Watermark inverted	—	£3250	

*164/9 **For well-centred, lightly used +75%**

Two used examples of the 1d. value have been reported on the Orb (fiscal) watermark.

57

Die I

Die II

1881. Wmk Imperial Crown, W **49**.

(a) 14 dots in each corner, Die I (12 July).

170	**57**	1d. lilac	£200	30·00	50·00
		Wi. Watermark inverted	—	£500	
171		1d. pale lilac	£200	30·00	

(b) 16 dots in each corner, Die II (13 December).

172	**57**	1d. lilac	2·50	2·00	3·00
		Wi. Watermark inverted	40·00	25·00	
172*a*		1d. bluish lilac	£375	£125	
173		1d. deep purple	2·50	2·00	
		a. Printed both sides	£750	†	
		b. Frame broken at bottom	£800	£300	
		c. Printed on gummed side	£700	†	
		d. Imperf three sides (pair)	£5000	†	
		e. Printed both sides but impression on back inverted	£800	†	
		f. No watermark	£3250	†	
		g. Blued paper	£4000		
174		1d. mauve	2·50	1·50	
		a. Imperf (pair)	£2750		

*170/4 **For well-centred, lightly used +50%**

1d. stamps with the words "PEARS SOAP" printed on the back in orange, blue or mauve price from £500, unused.

The variety "frame broken at bottom" (No. 173b) shows a white space just inside the bottom frame-line from between the "N" and "E" of "ONE" to below the first "N" of "PENNY", breaking the pearls and cutting into the lower part of the oval below "PEN".

KEY TO SURFACE-PRINTED ISSUES

1880–1900

S.G. Nos.	*Description*	*Date of Issue*
164/5	½d. green	14.10.80
187	½d. slate-blue	1.4.84
197/*e*	½d. vermilion	1.1.87
213	½d. blue-green	17.4.1900
166	1d. Venetian red	1.1.80
170/1	1d. lilac, Die I	12.7.81
172/4	1d. lilac, Die II	12.12.81
167	1½d. Venetian red	14.10.80
188	1½d. lilac	1.4.84
198	1½d. purple & green	1.1.87
168/*a*	2d. rose	8.12.80
189	2d. lilac	1.4.84
199/200	2d. green & red	1.1.87
190	2½d. lilac	1.4.84
201	2½d. purple on blue paper	1.1.87
191	3d. lilac	1.4.84
202/4	3d. purple on yellow paper	1.1.87
192	4d. dull green	1.4.84
205/*a*	4d. green & brown	1.1.87
206	4½d. green and carmine	15.9.92
169	5d. indigo	15.3.81
193	5d. dull green	1.4.84
207	5d. purple & blue, Die I	1.1.87
207*a*	5d. purple & blue, Die II	1888
194	6d. dull green	1.4.84
208/*a*	6d. purple on rose-red paper	1.1.87
195	9d. dull green	1.8.83
209	9d. purple & blue	1.1.87
210/*b*	10d. purple & carmine	24.2.90
196	1s. dull green	1.4.84
211	1s. green	1.1.87
214	1s. green & carmine	11.7.1900
175	2s.6d.lilac on blued paper	2.7.83
178/9	2s.6d. lilac	1884
176	5s. rose on blued paper	1.4.84
180/1	5s. rose	1884
177/*a*	10s. ultramarine on blued paper	1.4.84
182/3*a*	10s. ultramarine	1884
185	£1 brown-lilac, wmk Crowns	1.4.84
186	£1 brown-lilac, wmk Orbs	6.1.88
212	£1 green	28.1.91

Note that the £5 value used with the above series is listed as Nos. 133 and 137.

58

59

60

1883–84. *Coloured letters in the corners.* Wmk Anchor, W **40**.

(a) Blued paper.

			Un	*Used**
175	**58**	2s.6d. lilac (2.7.83)	£4000	£1200
176	**59**	5s. rose (1.4.84)	£10000	£3500
177	**60**	10s. ultramarine (1.4.84)	£32000	£7500
177*a*		10s. cobalt (5.84)	£38000	£11000

(b) White paper.

178	**58**	2s.6d. lilac	£450	£140
179		2s.6d. deep lilac	£550	£175
		a. On blued paper	£6000	£2500
		Wi. Watermark inverted	—	£5500
180	**59**	5s. rose	£875	£200
		Wi. Watermark inverted	†	£7000
181		5s. crimson	£775	£200
182	**60**	10s. cobalt	£25000	£6500
183		10s. ultramarine	£1700	£475
183*a*		10s. pale ultramarine	£1900	£475

*175/83a **For well-centred, lightly used +50%**

For No. 180 perf 12 see second note below No. 196.

61

Broken frames, Plate 2

1884 (1 Apr). Wmk Three Imperial Crowns, W **49**.

185	**61**	£1 brown-lilac	£22000	£2200
		a. Frame broken	£35000	£3800
		Wi. Watermark inverted	—	£10000

1888 (Feb). Watermark Three Orbs, W **48**.

186	**61**	£1 brown-lilac	£50000	£3500
		a. Frame broken	£60000	£6000

*185/6a **For well-centred, lightly used +50%**

The broken-frame varieties, Nos. 185a and 186a, are on Plate 2 stamps JC and TA, as illustrated. See also No. 212a.

62

63

64

65

66

1883 (1 Aug). (9d.) or **1884** (1 Apr) (others). Wmk Imperial Crown, W **49** (sideways on horiz designs).

187	**52**	½d. slate-blue	20·00	7·00	12·00
		a. Imperf	£2000		
		Wi. Watermark inverted	—	£250	
188	**62**	1½d. lilac	95·00	38·00	£100
		a. Imperf	£2000		
		Wi. Watermark inverted	—	£200	
189	**63**	2d. lilac	£175	70·00	£110
		a. Imperf	£2200		
		Wi. Watermark sideways inverted			
190	**64**	2½d. lilac	75·00	12·00	25·00
		a. Imperf	£2200		
		Wi. Watermark sideways inverted	£400		
191	**65**	3d. lilac	£190	85·00	£125
		a. Imperf	£2200		
		Wi. Watermark inverted	†	£800	
192	**66**	4d. dull green	£425	£175	£250
		a. Imperf	£2500		
193	**62**	5d. dull green	£425	£175	£250
		a. Imperf	£2700		
194	**63**	6d. dull green	£450	£200	£275
		a. Imperf	£2700		
		Wi. Watermark sideways inverted	£700		
195	**64**	9d. dull green (1.8.83)	£875	£375	£1800
		Wi. Watermark sideways inverted	£1400	£600	
196	**65**	1s. dull green	£950	£200	£475
		a. Imperf	£4250		
		Wi. Watermark-inverted			

*187/96 **For well-centred, lightly used** +100%

The above prices are for stamps in the true dull green colour. Stamps which have been soaked, causing the colour to run, are virtually worthless.

Stamps of the above set and No. 180 are also found perf 12; these are official perforations, but were never issued. A second variety of the 5d. is known with a line instead of a stop under the "d" in the value; this was never issued and is therefore only known unused (*Price* £14000).

71 72 73

74 75 76

77 78 79

80

81

82

Die I

Die II

Die I: Square dots to right of "d".
Die II: Thin vertical lines to right of "d".

1887 (1 Jan)–**92**. *"Jubilee" issue. New types. The bicoloured stamps have the value tablets, or the frames including the value tablets, in the second colour.* Wmk Imperial Crown, W **49** (Three Crowns on £1).

			Unmtd Mint	*Mtd Mint*	*Used**
197	**71**	½d. vermilion	2·25	1·50	1·00
		a. Printed on gummed side	£2250	£1400	
		b. Printed both sides			
		c. Doubly printed	—	£12000	
		d. Imperf	—	£2200	
		Wi. Watermark inverted	40·00	30·00	25·00
197*e*		½d. orange-vermilion	2·25	1·50	1·00
198	**72**	1½d. dull purple & pale green	22·00	15·00	7·00
		a. Purple part of design double	—	—	£6500
		Wi. Watermark inverted	£850	£550	£350
199	**73**	2d. green & scarlet	£450	£350	£225
200		2d. grey-green & carmine	40·00	8·00	12·00
		Wi. Watermark inverted	£850	£575	£375
201	**74**	2½d. purple/*blue*	35·00	22·00	3·00
		a. Printed on gummed side	£5500	£4500	
		b. Imperf three sides	—	£3500	
		c. Imperf	—	£4000	
		Ed. Missing "d" in value	†	†	£5500
		Wi. Watermark inverted	£1400	£900	£700
202	**75**	3d. purple/*yellow*	35·00	22·00	3·25
		a. Imperf (wmk inverted)	—	£5500	
		Wi. Watermark inverted	—	—	£550
203		3d. deep purple/*yellow*	35·00	22·00	3·25
204		3d. purple/*orange* (1890)	£900	£500	
205	**76**	4d. green & purple-brown	50·00	30·00	13·00
		aa. Imperf	—	£6000	
		Wi. Watermark inverted	£800	£550	£350
205*a*		4d. green & dp brown	50·00	30·00	13·00
206	**77**	4½d. green & carmine (15.9.92)	15·00	10·00	40·00
		Wi. Watermark inverted			
206*a*		4½d. green & dp brt carmine	£750	£500	£400
207	**78**	5d. dull purple & blue (Die I)	£700	£500	85·00
207*a*		5d. dull purple and blue (Die II) (1888)	50·00	35·00	11·00
		Wi. Watermark inverted	—	—	£600
208	**79**	6d. purple/*rose-red*	50·00	30·00	10·00
		Wi. Watermark inverted	£2200	£1500	£750
208*a*		6d. deep purple/*rose-red*	50·00	30·00	11·00
209	**80**	9d. dull purple & blue	90·00	60·00	40·00
		Wi. Watermark inverted	£3000	£2000	£750
210	**81**	10d. dull purple and carmine (*shades*) (24.2.90)	70·00	45·00	38·00
		aa. Imperf	—	£6000	
		Wi. Watermark inverted	£3500	£2500	£750
210*a*		10d. dull purple and deep dull carmine	£600	£400	£200
210*b*		10d. dull purple & scarlet	£110	60·00	45·00
211	**82**	1s. dull green	£300	£200	60·00
		Wi. Watermark inverted	£900	£575	£375
212	**61**	£1 green (28.1.91)	£5000	£3000	£650
		a. Frame broken	£10000	£6000	£1750
		Wi. Watermark inverted	—	£60000	£6000

*197/212a **For well-centred, lightly used +50%**

The broken-frame varieties, No. 212a, are on Plate 2 stamps JC or TA, as illustrated above No. 185.

½d. stamps with "PEARS SOAP" printed on the back in orange, blue or mauve, price from £500 each.

No used price is quoted for No. 204 as it is not possible to authenticate the paper colour on stamps in used condition.

1900. *Colours changed.* Wmk Imperial Crown, W **49**.

213	**71**	½d. blue-green (17.4)	2·25	1·75	2·00
		a. Printed on gummed side	—	—	—
		b. Imperf	—	£4000	
		Wi. Watermark inverted	40·00	30·00	30·00
214	**82**	1s. green & carmine (11.7)	80·00	50·00	£125
		Wi. Watermark inverted	£1500	£850	£750
Set of 14			£775	£500	£325

*213/14 **For well-centred, lightly used +50%**

The ½d. No. 213, in bright blue, is a colour changeling caused by a constituent of the ink used for some months in 1900.#

USED ON COVER PRICES

No. 197	£6	No. 205	£35	No. 209	£200
No. 198	£22	No. 206	£75	No. 210	£225
No. 200	£24	No. 207	£150	No. 211	£125
No. 201	£6	No. 207*a*	£40	No. 213	£6
No. 202	£30	No. 208	£75	No. 214	£850

SPECIMEN OVERPRINTS (Queen Victoria)

1841–70. *Line-engraved issues.*

S1	1d. red-brown (No. 8) (1)	£2200
S2	2d. blue (No. 13) (1)	£3500
S3	2d. deep blue (No. 19) (2)	£1100
S4	2d. blue (No. 23) (2)	£1100
S5	1d. red-brown (No. 29) (2)	£450
S6	1d. rose-red (No. 38) (6, 7, 10)	£175
S7	1d. rose-red (No. 43) (various plates) (1, 6, 8, 9)	£150
S8	2d. blue (No. 45) (1, 7)	£400
S9	2d. blue (No. 46) (pl 14, 15) (6, 8, 9, 10)	£200
S10	½d. rose-red (No. 48) (various plates) (2, 8, 9, 10)	£175
S11	1½d. rosy-mauve (No. 53a) (2, 6)	£1250
S12	1½d. rose-red (No. 51) (pl 1) (2, 6)	£350
	a. Plate 3 (8, 9, 10)	£225

1847–54. *Embossed issues.*

S13	1s. pale green (No. 54) (red opt)	£1750
	a. Black opt (1, 2)	£1750
S14	10d. brown (No. 57) (1, 2)	£1750
S15	6d. mauve (No. 58) (1, 2)	£2000

1855–57. *Surface-printed issues. No corner letters.*

S16	4d. carmine/*blued* (No. 62) (23)	£650
S17	4d. carmine/*blued* (No. 63) (2)	£600
S18	4d. carmine (No. 64) (2)	£600
S19	4d. rose (No. 65) (4)	—
S20	4d. rose (No. 66) (2, 7)	£325
S21	6d. deep. lilac (No. 69) (2, 4, 7, 8)	£350
S22	6d. lilac (No. 84) (2, 5, 8)	£350
S23	6d. lilac (No. 85) (2)	£350
S24	1s. deep green (No. 71) (2, 4, 7)	£550

1862–64. *Surface-printed issues small uncoloured corner letters.*

S25	3d. rose, shaded spandrels (–) (2, 6)	£700
S26	3d. deep carmine-rose (No. 75) (2, 5, 6, 8)	£275
S27	3d. rose (No. 78) (2)	£1000
S28	4d. bright red (No. 79) (2, 5, 6, 8)	£250
S29	4d. bright red (No. 81) (2)	£300
S30	6d. deep lilac (No. 83) (2, 5, 8)	£350
S31	6d. lilac (No. 85) (2)	£350
S32	9d. bistre (No. 86) (2, 6)	£400
S33	1s. deep green (No. 89) (pl 1) (2, 5, 8)	£300
S34	1s. deep green (No. 91) (pl 2) (2)	£2400

1865–73. *Surface-printed issues, large uncoloured corner letters.*

S35	3d. rose (No. 92) (pl 4) (2)	£2250
S36	3d. rose (No. 102) (pl 5) (8)	£200
	a. Plate 6 (2, 8)	£200
	b. Plate 7 (2, 6)	£200

	c. Plate 8 (8)	£200
	d. Plate 10 (2, 8, 9)	£200
S37	4d. vermilion (No. 93) (pl 14) (8)	£250
S38	6d. deep lilac (No. 96) (pl 5) (2)	£3500
S39	6d. dull violet (No. 108) (pl 8) (1, 8)	£300
S40	6d. mauve (No. 109) (pl 9) (6, 8)	£300
S41	6d. chestnut (No. 122) (pl 11) (2, 6, 8)	£250
S42	6d. grey (No. 125) (pl 12) (6, 8, 9)	£300
S43	9d. straw (No. 98) (pl 4) (20)	£600
S44	9d. straw (No. 110) (pl 4) (2, 8, 9, 10, 11)	£300
S45	10d. red-brown (No. 112) (pl 1) (2, 5, 6, 8, 9, 10, 11)	£375
S46	1s. green (No. 101) (pl 4) (2)	£400
S47	1s. green (No. 115) (pl 4) (1, 8, 9)	£275
	a. Plate 5 (2, 6, 8, 9)	£275
	b. Plate 6 (8, 9)	£275
	c. Plate 7 (9)	£275
S48	2s. dull blue (No. 118) (Pl 1) (2, 5, 8, 9, 10, 11)	£400
S49	2s. brown (No. 121) (Pl 1) (9)	£2000

1867–83. *Wmk Maltese Cross or Anchor.*

S50	5s. rose (No. 126) (pl 1) (2, 6)	£750
S51	5s. pale rose (No. 127) (pl 2) (8, 9)	£800
S52	5s. rose (No. 130) (pl 4) (9)	£2500
S53	10s. greenish grey (No. 128) (pl 1) (8, 9)	£2500
S54	10s. grey-green (No. 131) (pl 1) (9)	£550
S55	£1 brown-lilac (No. 129) (pl 1) (9)	£4500
S56	£1 brown-lilac (No. 132) (pl 1) (9)	£7500
S57	£1 brown-lilac (No. 136) (pl 1) (6, 9)	£7000
S58	£5 orange (No. 133) (pl 1) (9, 11)	£2400
S59	£5 orange (No. 137) (pl 1) (9, 11, 16)	£2800

1873–80. *Large Coloured Corner Letters.*

S60	2½d. rosy mauve (No. 138) (pl 1) (8)	£200
S61	2½d. rosy mauve (No. 141) (pl 3) (10)	—
	a. Plate 5 (9)	£180
	b. Plate 6 (8, 9)	£180
	c. Plate 7 (9)	£180
	d. Plate 10 (9)	£180
	e. Plate 16 (9)	£180
S62	2½d. blue (No. 142) (pl 17) (9)	£120
S63	2½d. blue (No. 157) (pl 23) (9)	£140
S64	3d. rose (No. 143) (pl 14) (2)	£210
	a. Plate 17 (8, 9)	£200
	b. Plate 18 (8, 9, 10)	£200
	c. Plate 19 (9, 10)	£200
S65	3d. rose (No. 158) (pl 21) (9)	£200
S66	4d. vermilion (No. 152) (pl 15) (9)	£325
S67	4d. sage-green (No. 153) (pl 15) (9)	£275
	a. Plate 16 (9)	£275
S68	4d. grey-brown (No. 154) (pl 17) (9)	£250
S69	4d. grey-brown (No. 160) (pl 17) (9)	£210
	a. Plate 8 (9)	£225
S70	6d. deep grey (No. 146) (pl 14) (8, 10)	£225
	a. Plate 15 (8, 9)	£225
	b. Plate 16 (9)	£225
S71	6d. grey (No. 161) (pl 18) (9)	£225
S72	8d. purple-brown (No. 156a) (pl 1) (8, 9)	£2000
S73	8d. orange (No. 156) (pl 1) (8, 9)	£225
S74	1s. green (No. 150) (pl 11) (8)	£225
	a. Plate 12 (8, 9, 10)	£225
	b. Plate 13 (9)	£225
S75	1s. orange-brown (No. 151) (pl 13) (9)	£325
S76	1s. orange-brown (No. 163) (pl 13) (9)	£225
	a. Plate 14 (9)	£225

1880–83. *Wmk Imperial Crown.*

S77	½d. deep green (No. 164) (9)	50·00
S78	1d. Venetian red (No. 166) (9)	90·00
S79	1d. lilac (14 dots) (No. 170) (9)	50·00
S80	1d. lilac (16 dots) (No. 172) (9, 12)	50·00
S81	1½d. Venetian red (No. 167) (9)	60·00
S82	2d. pale rose (No. 168) (9)	85·00
S83	3d. on 3d. lilac (No. 159) (9)	£200
S84	5d. indigo (No. 169) (9, 12, 13)	£120
S85	6d. on 6d. lilac (No. 162) (9)	£200

1883–84. *Wmk Anchor or Three Imperial Crowns (£1).*

S86	2s.6d. lilac (No. 175) (9, 11, 12, 13)	£400
S87	5s. rose (No. 176) (9, 11)	£1000
S88	5s. crimson (No. 181) (9, 11, 12, 13)	£375
S89	10s. ultramarine (No. 177) (9)	£1300
S90	10s. cobalt (No. 177a) (9)	£2500
S91	10s. cobalt (No. 182) (9)	£1500
S92	10s. ultramarine (No. 183) (9, 11, 13)	£400
S93	£1 brown-lilac (No. 185) (9, 11, 12)	£1600
S94	£1 brown-lilac (No. 186) (11)	£4000

1883–84. *Wmk Imperial Crown.*

S95	½d. slate-blue (No. 187) (9)	40·00
S96	1½d. lilac (No. 188) (9)	70·00
S97	2d. lilac (No. 189) (9)	70·00
S98	2½d. lilac (No. 190) (9)	70·00
S99	3d. lilac (No. 191) (9)	70·00
S100	4d. dull green (No. 192) (9)	£150
S101	5d. dull green (No. 193) (9)	£150
S102	6d. dull green (No. 194) (9)	£180
S103	9d. dull green (No. 195) (9)	£300
S104	1s. dull green (No. 196) (9)	£250

1887. *"Jubilee" issue. Wmk Imperial Crown.*

S105	½d. vermilion (No. 197) (9, 10, 12)	32·00
S106	1½d. dull purple & pale green (No. 198) (6, 9, 12)	45·00
S107	2d. green and scarlet (No. 199) (9, 10, 12)	50·00
S108	2½d. purple/*blue* (No. 201) (6, 9, 12, 13)	60·00
S109	3d. purple/*lemon* (No. 202) (6, 9, 12)	45·00
S110	4d. green and purple-brown (No. 205) (6, 9, 10, 12)	45·00
S111	4½d. green and carmine (No. 20b) (9, 13)	£300
S112	5d. dull purple and blue (No. 207) (9, 12)	90·00
S113	5d. dull purple and blue (No. 207a) (9, 12)	50·00
S114	6d. purple/*rose-red* (No. 208) (9, 10, 12)	50·00
S115	9d. dull purple and blue (No. 209) (6, 9, 12)	55·00
S116	10d. dull purple and carmine (No. 210) (9, 13, 15)	80·00
S117	1s. dull green (No. 211) (9, 10, 12)	55·00
S118	£1 green (No. 212) (9, 11, 13, 15, 16)	£700

1900. *Colours changed. Wmk Imperial Crown.*

S119	½d. blue-green (No. 213) (11, 15)	£200
S120	1s. green & carmine (No. 214) (15)	£400

KING EDWARD VII

22 January 1901 – 6 May 1910

PRINTINGS. Distinguishing De La Rue printings from the provisional printings of the same values made by Harrison & Sons Ltd. or at Somerset House may prove difficult in some cases. For very full guidance Volume 2 of the Stanley Gibbons *Great Britain Specialised Catalogue* should prove helpful.

Note that stamps perforated 15×14 must be Harrison; the 2½d., 3d. and 4d. in this perforation are useful reference material, their shades and appearance in most cases matching the Harrison perf 14 printings.

Except for the 6d. value, all stamps on chalk-surfaced paper were printed by De La Rue.

Of the stamps on ordinary paper, the De La Rue impressions are usually clearer and of a higher finish than those of the other printers. The shades are markedly different except in some printings of the 4d., 6d. and 7d. and in the 5s., 10s. and £1.

Used stamps in good, clean, unrubbed condition and with dated postmarks can form the basis of a useful reference collection, the dates often assisting in the assignment to the printers.

PRICES. For Nos. 215/456a prices are quoted for unmounted mint, mounted mint and used stamps.

USED STAMPS. For well-centred, lightly used examples of King Edward VII stamps, add the following percentages to the used prices quoted below:

De La Rue printings (Nos. 215/66)—3d. values + 35%, 4d. orange + 100%, 6d. + 75%, 7d. & 1s. + 25%, all other values + 50%.

Harrison printings (Nos 267/86)—all values and perforations + 75%.

Somerset House printings (Nos. 287/320)—1s. values + 25%, all other values + 50%.

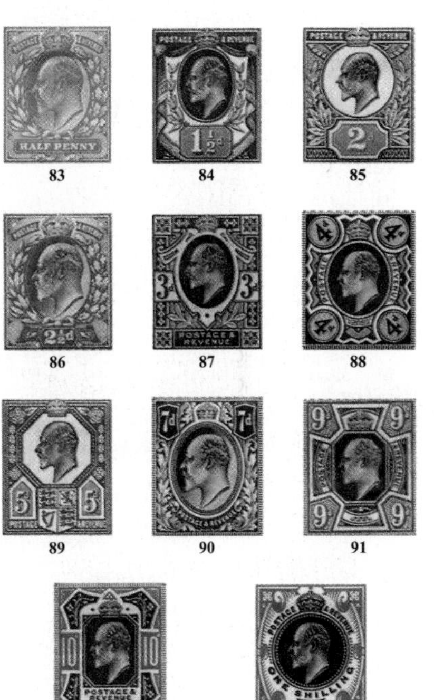

83 84 85 86 87 88 89 90 91 92 93

94 95 96

97

(Des E. Fuchs)

1902 (1 Jan)–**10**. *Printed by De La Rue & Co.* Wmk Imperial Crown W **49** (½d. to 1s. Three Crowns on £1); Anchor, W **40** (2s.6d. to 10s.). Ordinary paper. P 14.

			Unmtd mint	Mtd mint	Used
215	83	½d. dull blue-green (1.1.02)	2·50	2·00	1·50
		Wi. Watermark inverted	£2750	£2000	£1000
216		½d. blue-green	2·50	2·00	1·50
217		½d. pale yellowish green (26.11.04)	2·50	2·00	1·50
218		½d. yellowish green	2·50	2·00	1·50
		a. Booklet pane. Five stamps plus St. Andrew's Cross label (6.06)	£500	£350	
		b. Doubly printed (bottom row on one pane) (Control H9)	£30000	£20000	
		Wi. Watermark inverted	20·00	12·00	9·00
219		1d. scarlet (1.1.02)	2·50	2·00	1·50
220		1d. brt scarlet	2·50	2·00	1·50
		a. Imperf (pair)	—	£20000	
		Wi. Watermark inverted	7·00	4·00	3·00
221	84	1½d. dull purple and green (21.3.02)	70·00	35·00	18·00
222		1½d. slate-purple & green	85·00	38·00	18·00
		Wi. Watermark inverted	—	—	£600
223		1½d. pale dull purple and green (*chalk-surfaced paper*) (8.05)	65·00	40·00	18·00
224		1½d. slate-purple & bluish green (*chalk-surfaced paper*)	65·00	40·00	15·00
225	85	2d. yellowish green and carmine-red (25.3.02)	70·00	45·00	18·00
		Wi. Watermark inverted	£22000		
226		2d. grey-green and carmine-red (1904)	90·00	50·00	24·00
227		2d. pale grey-green and carmine-red (*chalk-surfaced paper*) (4.06)	70·00	40·00	24·00
		Wi. Watermark inverted			
228		2d. pale grey-green and scarlet (*chalk-surfaced paper*) (1909)	70·00	40·00	24·00
229		2d. dull blue-green and carmine (*chalk-surfaced paper*) (1907)	£150	70·00	45·00
230	86	2½d. ultramarine (1.1.02)	30·00	20·00	10·00
231		2½d. pale ultramarine	30·00	20·00	10·00
		Wi. Watermark inverted	—	—	£2500
232	87	3d. dull purple/*orange-yellow* (20.3.02)	70·00	40·00	12·00
		Wi. Watermark inverted			
		a. Chalk-surfaced paper (3.06)	£300	£150	70·00
232*b*		3d. dp purple/*orange-yellow*	70·00	40·00	12·00
232*c*		3d. pale reddish purple/*orange-yellow* (*chalk-surfaced paper*) (3.06)	£300	£150	60·00

233		3d. dull reddish purple/*yellow* (*lemon back*) (*chalk-surfaced paper*)	£300	£150	75·00
233*b*		3d. pale purple/*lemon* (*chalk-surfaced paper*)	75·00	35·00	15·00
234		3d. purple/lemon (*chalk-surfaced paper*)	75·00	35·00	15·00
235	**88**	4d. green & grey-brown (27.3.02)	£110	50·00	30·00
		Wi. Watermark inverted			
236		4d. green & chocolate-brown	£110	50·00	30·00
		a. Chalk-surfaced paper (1.06)	65·00	40·00	18·00
		Wi. watermark inverted			£6500
238		4d. deep green and chocolate-brown (*chalk-surfaced paper*) (1.06)	65·00	40·00	18·00
239		4d. brown-orange (1.11.09)	£275	£150	£130
240		4d. pale orange (12.09)	40·00	20·00	15·00
241		4d. orange-red (12.09)	40·00	20·00	15·00
242	**89**	5d. dull purple and ultramarine (14.5.02)	£125	55·00	20·00
		a. Chalk-surfaced paper (5.06)	£100	50·00	20·00
244		5d. slate-purple and ultramarine (*chalk-surfaced paper*) (5.06)	£100	50·00	20·00
		Wi. Watermark inverted	£5500	£3250	
245	**83**	6d. pale dull purple (1.1.02)	70·00	35·00	18·00
		a. Chalk-surfaced paper (1.06)	70·00	35·00	18·00
246		6d. slate-purple	70·00	35·00	18·00
248		6d. dull purple (*chalk-surfaced paper*) (1.06)	70·00	35·00	18·00
		Wi. Watermark inverted	—	—	£2500
249	**90**	7d. grey-black (4.5.10)	20·00	10·00	18·00
249*a*		7d. dp grey-black	£150	£110	£100
250	**91**	9d. dull purple and ultramarine (7.4.02)	£175	80·00	60·00
		a. Chalk-surfaced paper (6.05)	£200	80·00	60·00
		aWi. Watermark inverted	—	—	£2000
251		9d. slate-purple & ultramarine	£175	80·00	60·00
		a. Chalk-surfaced paper (6.05)	£175	80·00	60·00
254	**92**	10d. dull purple and carmine (3.7.02)	£190	80·00	60·00
		a. No cross on crown	£500	£300	£200
		b. Chalk-surfaced paper (9.06)	£190	80·00	60·00
255		10d. slate-purple and carmine (*chalk-surfaced paper*) (9.06)	£190	80·00	60·00
		a. No cross on crown	£550	£300	£200
256		10d. dull purple and scarlet (*chalk-surfaced paper*) (9.10)	£200	80·00	60·00
		a. No cross on crown	£550	£300	£200
257	**93**	1s. dull green and carmine (24.3.02)	£175	80·00	35·00
		a. Chalk-surfaced paper (9.05)	£175	80·00	35·00
259		1s. dull green & scarlet (*chalk-surfaced paper*) (9.10)	£175	80·00	50·00
260	**94**	2s.6d. lilac (5.4.02)	£475	£220	£140
		Wi. Watermark inverted	£4000	£3000	£2000
261		2s.6d. pale dull purple (*chalk-surfaced paper*) (7.10.05)	£500	£2250	£150
		Wi. Watermark inverted	£5000	£4000	£2500
262		2s.6d. dull purple (*chalk-surfaced paper*)	£500	£225	£150
263	**95**	5s. brt carmine (5.4.02)	£675	£350	£200
		Wi. Watermark inverted	—	—	£3500
264		5s. dp brt carmine	£675	£350	£200

USED ON COVER PRICES

No. 215	£2.50	No. 217	£2.50	No. 219	£2.50
No. 222	£30	No. 225	£32	No. 230	£22
No. 232	£30	No. 236a	£40	No. 240	£35
No. 242	£50	No. 245	£50	No. 249	£195
No. 250	£200	No. 254	£225	No. 257	£150
No. 260	£700	No. 263	£950		

265	**96**	10s. ultramarine (5.4.02)	£1500	£650	£450
266	**97**	£1 dull blue-green (16.6.02)	£2500	£1600	£650
		Wi. Watermark inverted	—	£30000	£15000

97a

1910 (May). *Prepared for use, by De La Rue but not issued.* Wmk Imperial Crown, W **49**. P 14.

266*a*	**97**	2d. Tyrian plum		—	£60000

One example of this stamp is known used, but it was never issued to the public.

1911. *Printed by Harrison & Sons. Ordinary paper.* Wmk Imperial Crown W **49**.

(a) P 14.

267	**83**	½d. dull yellow-green (3.5.11)	3·50	2·75	1·50
		Wi. Watermark inverted	30·00	15·00	15·00
268		½d. dull green	4·00	3·00	1·50
269		½d. dp dull green	15·00	11·00	6·00
270		½d. pale bluish green	70·00	40·00	40·00
		a. Booklet pane. Five stamps plus St. Andrew's Cross label	£750	£500	
		b. Watermark sideways	†	†	£22000
		c. Imperf (pair)	—	£22000	†
271		½d. brt green (fine impression) (6.11)	£375	£250	£150
272		1d. rose-red (3.5.11)	12·00	8·00	12·00
		Wi. Watermark inverted	30·00	15·00	12·00
		a. No wmk (brick-red)	55·00	40·00	45·00
273		1d. dp rose-red	12·00	8·00	12·00
274		1d. rose-carmine	80·00	55·00	30·00
275		1d. aniline pink (5.11)	£900	£550	£300
275*a*		1d. aniline rose	£275	£180	£140
276	**86**	2½d. brt blue (10.7.11)	£120	55·00	30·00
		Wi. Watermark inverted	£1100	£800	
277	**87**	3d. purple/*lemon* (12.9.11)	£160	65·00	£180
277*a*		3d. grey/*lemon*	£5500	£3000	
278	**88**	4d. brt orange (12.7.11)	£175	65·00	50·00

(b) P 15×14.

279	**83**	½d. dull green (30.10.11)	65·00	40·00	45·00
279*a*		½d. dp dull green	75·00	40·00	45·00
280		1d. rose-red (4.10.11)	65·00	38·00	25·00
281		1d. rose-carmine	35·00	15·00	15·00
282		1d. pale rose-carmine	40·00	22·00	15·00
283	**86**	2½d. brt blue (14.10.11)	50·00	22·00	15·00
284		2½d. dull blue	50·00	22·00	15·00
		Wi. Watermark inverted	—	—	£500
285	**87**	3d. purple/*lemon* (22.9.11)	70·00	45·00	15·00
285*a*		3d. grey/*lemon*	£3250	£2250	
286	**88**	4d. brt orange (11.11.11)	60·00	30·00	15·00
Set of 5			£250	£130	90·00

USED ON COVER PRICES

No. 267	£4	No. 272	£18	No. 276	£50
No. 277	£550	No. 278	£175	No. 279	£100
No. 281	£30	No. 283	£35	No. 285	£40
No. 286	£65				

1911–13. *Printed at Somerset House. Ordinary paper.* Wmk as 1902–10. P 14.

287	**84**	1½d. reddish purple and bright green (13.7.11)	85·00	40·00	35·00
288		1½d. dull purple & green	50·00	25·00	28·00
289		1½d. slate-purple and green (9.12)	55·00	28·00	28·00
290	**85**	2d. dp dull green & red (8.8.11)	50·00	25·00	20·00
291		2d. dp dull green & carmine	50·00	25·00	20·00

292		2d. grey-green and bright carmine (carmine shows clearly on back) (11.3.12)..	50·00	25·00	25·00
293	**89**	5d. dull reddish purple and bright blue (7.8.11)............	55·00	30·00	20·00
294		5d. deep dull reddish purple and bright blue	50·00	30·00	20·00
295	**83**	6d. royal purple (31.10.11).......	90·00	50·00	85·00
296		6d. bright magenta (*chalk-surfaced paper*) (31.10.11).	£12500	£7500	
297		6d. dull purple	50·00	30·00	20·00
298		6d. reddish purple (11.11)	50·00	30·00	25·00
		a. No cross on crown (various shades)...............................	£950	£600	
299		6d. very deep reddish purple (11.11)	90·00	40·00	
300		6d. dark purple (3.12)..............	50·00	30·00	
301		6d. dull purple "Dickinson" coated paper* (3.13)...........	£300	£170	
303		6d. deep plum (*chalk-surfaced paper*) (7.13)	50·00	28·00	70·00
		a. No cross on crown	£1250	£800	
305	**90**	7d. slate-grey (1.8.12)	25·00	15·00	22·00
306	**91**	9d. reddish purple and light blue (24.7.11)	£175	80·00	75·00
306*a*		9d. dp dull reddish purple and dp brt blue (9.11)...............	£175	80·00	75·00
307		9d. dull reddish purple and blue (10.11)	£110	60·00	60·00
307*a*		9d. dp plum & blue (7.13)........	£110	60·00	60·00
308		9d. slate-purple and cobalt-blue (3.12)	£175	95·00	£100
309	**92**	10d. dull purple and scarlet (9.10.11)	£150	80·00	75·00
310		10d. dull reddish purple and aniline pink.......................	£450	£275	£225
311		10d. dull reddish purple and carmine (5.12)	£120	70·00	60·00
		a. No cross on crown	£2000	£1250	
312	**93**	1s. dark green and scarlet (13.7.11)	£190	£100	60·00
313		1s. deep green and scarlet (9.10.11)	£140	70·00	35·00
		Wi. Wmk inverted....................	£200	£110	†
314		1s. green & carmine (15.4.12).	£125	55·00	35·00
315	**94**	2s.6d. dull greyish purple (15.9.11)	£900	£600	£350
316		2s.6d. dull reddish purple	£500	£220	£150
		Wi. Watermark inverted...........	†	†	—
317		2s.6d. dark purple	£500	£220	£150
318	**95**	5s. carmine (29.2.12)..............	£675	£350	£180
319	**96**	10s. blue (14.1.12)....................	£1500	£700	£500
320	**97**	£1 dp green (3.9.11)	£2500	£1600	£700

*No. 301 was on an experimental coated paper which does not respond to the silver test.

USED ON COVER PRICES					
No. 288	£50	No. 290	£50	No. 293	£65
No. 297	£85	No. 305	£195	No. 307	£190
No. 311	£225	No. 314	£160	No. 316	£950
No. 318	£950				

SPECIMEN OVERPRINTS (King Edward VII)

1902–10. *Printed by De La Rue & Co. Ordinary paper.*

S121	½d. dull blue-green (No. 215) (15)................	£200
S122	½d. yellowish green (No. 218) (17, 22)..........	£200
S123	1d. scarlet (No. 219) (15, 16, 17, 22)............	£150
S124	1½d. dull purple and green (No. 221) (15)	£200
	a. chalk-surfaced paper (No. 223) (17)........	£500
S125	2d. yellowish green and carmine-red (No. 225) (16)...	£350
	a. chalk-surfaced paper (No. 227) (17)........	£500
S126	2d. Tyrian plum (No. 266a) (17)....................	£35000
S127	2½d. ultramarine (No. 230) (15, 17)................	90·00
S128	3d. dull purple/*orange-yellow* (No. 232) (15)	£250
	a. chalk-surfaced paper (No. 223a) (17)......	£500
S129	4d. green and grey-brown (No. 235) (16)......	£300
S130	4d. brown-orange (No. 239) (17)..................	£500
S131	5d. dull purple and ultramarine (No. 242) (16)...	£200
	a. chalk-surfaced paper (No. 242a) (17)......	£500
S132	6d. pale dull purple (No. 245) (15)	£250
	a. chalk-surfaced paper (No. 245a) (17)......	£500
S133	7d. grey-black (No. 249) (17)	£500
S134	9d. dull purple and ultramarine (No. 250) (16)...	£225
	a. chalk-surfaced paper (No. 250a) (17)......	£500
S135	10d. dull purple and carmine (No. 254) (16)...	£350
	a. chalk-surfaced paper (No. 254b) (17)......	£500
S136	1s. dull green and carmine (No. 257) (16).....	£250
	a. chalk-surfaced paper (No. 257a) (17)......	£500
S137	2s.6d. lilac (No. 260) (15, 16)	£250
	a. chalk-surfaced paper (No. 261) (17)........	—
S138	5s. bright carmine (No. 263) (16, 17)...........	£280
S139	10s. ultramarine (No. 265) (16, 17)................	£350
S140	£1 dull blue-green (No. 266) (16, 17)..........	£850

1911. *Printed by Harrison & Sons.* P 14.

S141	½d. dull yellow-green (No. 267) (22)............	£200
S142	1d. rose-red (No. 272) (22)	£200
S143	3d. purple/*lemon* (No. 277) (22)	£175
S144	4d. bright orange (No. 278) (22)..................	£175

1911. *Printed by Harrison & Sons.* P 15×14.

S145	2½d. bright blue (No. 283) (22).......................	—

1911–13. *Printed by Somerset House.* P 14.

S146	2d. deep dull green and red (No. 290) (22)....	£180
S147	5d. dull reddish purple and bright blue (No. 293) (22)..	—
S148	6d. dull purple (No. 297) (22).......................	£250
S149	7d. slate-grey (No. 305) (26).........................	£250
S150	9d. reddish purple and light blue (No. 306) (22)...	£275
S151	10d. dull purple & scarlet (No. 309) (22)	£250
S152	1s. dark green and scarlet (No. 312) (22, 23, 26)	£250
S153	2s.6d. dull greyish purple (No. 315) (22)..........	£250
S154	5s. carmine (No. 318) (26)	—
S155	£1 deep green (No. 320) (22).......................	£1250

KING GEORGE V

6 May 1910 – 20 January 1936

Further detailed information on the issues of King George V will be found in Volume 2 of the Stanley Gibbons *Great Britain Specialised Catalogue*.

PRINTERS. Types **98** to **102** were typographed by Harrison & Sons Ltd, with the exception of certain preliminary printings made at Somerset House and distinguishable by the controls "A.11", "B.11" or "B.12" (the Harrison printings do not have a full stop after the letter). The booklet stamps, Nos. 334/7, and 344/5 were printed by Harrison only.

WATERMARK VARIETIES. Many British stamps to 1967 exist without watermark owing to misplacement of the paper, and with either inverted, reversed, or inverted and reversed watermarks. A proportion of the low-value stamps issued in booklets have the watermark inverted in the normal course of printing.

Low values with *watermark sideways* are normally from stamp rolls used on machines with sideways delivery or, from June 1940, certain booklets.

STAMPS WITHOUT WATERMARK. Stamps found without watermark, due to misplacement of the sheet in relation to the dandy roll, are not listed here but will be found in the *Great Britain Specialised Catalogue*.

The 1½d. and 5d. 1912–22, and ½d., 2d. and 2½d., 1924–26, listed here, are from whole sheets completely without watermark.

98

99

Simple Cypher

For type difference with T **101/2** see notes below the latter.

Die A

Die B

Dies of Halfpenny

Die A. The three upper scales on the body of the right hand dolphin form a triangle; the centre jewel of the cross inside the crown is suggested by a comma.

Die B. The three upper scales are incomplete; the centre jewel is suggested by a crescent.

Die A

Die B

Dies of One Penny

Die A. The second line of shading on the ribbon to the right of the crown extends right across the wreath; the line nearest to the crown on the right hand ribbon shows as a short line at the bottom of the ribbon. Die B. The second line of shading is broken in the middle; the first line is little more than a dot.

(Des Bertram Mackennal and G. W. Eve. Head from photograph by W. and D. Downey. Die eng J. A. C. Harrison)

1911–12. Wmk Imperial Crown, W **49**. P 15×14.

321	**98**	½d. pale green (Die A) (22.6.11)	10·00	5·00	4·00
322		½d. green (Die A) (22.6.11)	8·00	4·00	4·00
		a. Error. Perf 14 (8.11)	—	£14000	£700
		Wi. Watermark inverted	£16000	—	£1250
323		½d. bluish green (Die A)	£400	£300	£180
324		½d. yellow-green (Die B)	18·00	12·00	1·50
325		½d. bright green (Die B)	13·00	8·00	1·50
		a. Watermark sideways	—	—	£3500
		Wi. Watermark inverted	20·00	10·00	4·50
326		½d. bluish green (Die B)	£250	£160	£100
327	**99**	1d. carmine-red (Die A) (22.6.11)	10·00	4·50	2·50
		c. Watermark sideways	†	†	—
		Wi. Watermark inverted	£1500	£900	£800
328		1d. pale carmine (Die A) (22.6.11)	25·00	14·00	3·00
		a. No cross on crown	£700	£425	£275
329		1d. carmine (Die B)	15·00	7·00	3·00
		Wi. Watermark inverted	22·00	12·00	4·00
330		1d. pale carmine (Die B)	15·00	10·00	4·00
		a. No cross on crown	£900	£550	£350
331		1d. rose-pink (Die B)	£200	£110	40·00
332		1d. scarlet (Die B) (6.12)	65·00	45·00	18·00
		Wi. Watermark inverted	65·00	45·00	18·00
333		1d. aniline scarlet (Die B)	£300	£200	£110

For note on the aniline scarlet No. 333 see below No. 343.

1912 (Aug). *Booklet stamps.* Wmk Royal Cypher ("Simple"), W **100**. P 15×14.

334	**98**	½d. pale green (Die B)	75·00	40·00	40·00
335		½d. green (Die B)	75·00	40·00	40·00
		Wi. Watermark inverted	75·00	40·00	40·00
		Wj. Watermark reversed	£800	£600	£350
		Wk. Watermark inverted and reversed	£800	£600	£350
336	**99**	1d. scarlet (Die B)	40·00	30·00	30·00
		Wi. Watermark inverted	40·00	30·00	30·00
		Wj. Watermark reversed	£1000	£750	
		Wk. Watermark inverted and reversed	—	—	£200
337		1d. bright scarlet (Die B)	40·00	30·00	30·00

101

102

Multiple Cypher

Type differences

½d. In T **98** the ornament above "P" of "HALFPENNY" has two thin lines of colour and the beard is undefined. In T **101** the ornament has one thick line and the beard is well defined.

1d. In T **99** the body of the lion is unshaded and in T **102** it is shaded.

1912 (1 Jan). Wmk Imperial Crown, W **49**. P 15×14.

338	**101**	½d. deep green	28·00	15·00	8·00
339		½d. green	15·00	8·00	4·00
340		½d. yellow-green	15·00	8·00	4·00
		a. No cross on crown	£170	£100	50·00
		Wi. Watermark inverted	£1000	£750	£400
341	**102**	1d. bright scarlet	10·00	5·00	2·00
		a. No cross on crown	£140	80·00	50·00
		b. Printed double, one albino	£275	£180	
		Wi. Watermark inverted	£450	£300	£225
342		1d. scarlet	10·00	5·00	2·00
343		1d. aniline scarlet*	£250	£175	£100
		a. No cross on crown	£1500	£1000	

*Our prices for the aniline scarlet 1d. stamps, Nos. 333 and 343, are for the specimens in which the colour is suffused on the surface of the stamp and shows through clearly on the back. Specimens without these characteristics but which show "aniline" reactions under the quartz lamp are relatively common.

1912 (Aug). Wmk Royal Cypher ("Simple"), W **100**. P 15×14.

344	**101**	½d. green	14·00	7·00	3·00
		a. No cross on crown	£180	£100	50·00
		Wi. Watermark inverted	£225	£140	60·00
		Wj. Watermark reversed	£180	£100	50·00
		Wk. Watermark inverted and reversed	15·00	8·00	4·50
345	**102**	1d. scarlet	15·00	8·00	4·50
		a. No cross on crown	£160	£100	3·00
		Wi. Watermark inverted	20·00	13·00	50·00
		Wj. Watermark reversed	30·00	20·00	13·00
		Wk. Watermark inverted and reversed	16·00	9·00	9·00

1912 (Sept). Wmk Royal Cypher ("Multiple"), W **103**. P 15×14.

346	**101**	½d. green (Oct)	20·00	12·00	8·00
		a. No cross on crown	£160	£100	60·00
		b. Imperf	£200	£130	
		c. Watermark sideways	†	†	£2750
		d. Printed on gummed side	—	—	†
		Wi. Watermark inverted	20·00	12·00	15·00
		Wj. Watermark reversed	20·00	12·00	9·00
		Wk. Watermark inverted and reversed	30·00	20·00	
347		½d. yellow-green	20·00	15·00	8·00
348		½d. pale green	25·00	15·00	8·00
349	**102**	1d. bright scarlet	25·00	18·00	10·00
350		1d. scarlet	25·00	18·00	10·00
		a. No cross on crown	£200	£120	50·00
		b. Imperf	£200	£130	
		c. Watermark sideways	£225	£130	£150

		d. Watermark sideways. No cross on crown	£1100	£750	
		Wi. Watermark inverted	25·00	15·00	15·00
		Wj. Watermark reversed	25·00	15·00	15·00
		Wk. Watermark inverted and reversed	£1200	£800	£450

104 105 106

107 108

No. 357ab

No. 357ac

No. 357a

Die I

108b Die II

Two Dies of the 2d.

Die I.—Inner frame-line at top and sides close to solid of background. Four complete lines of shading between top of head and oval frame-line. These four lines do not extend to the oval itself. White line round "TWOPENCE" thin.

Die II.—Inner frame-line further from solid of background. Three lines between top of head and extending to the oval. White line round "TWOPENCE" thicker.

(Des Bertram Mackennal (heads) and G. W. Eve (frames). Coinage head (½, 1½, 2, 3 and 4d.); large medal head (1d., 2½d.); intermediate medal head (5d. to 1s.); small medal head used for fiscal stamps. Dies eng J. A. C. Harrison) (Typo by Harrison & Sons Ltd., except the 6d. printed by the Stamping Department of the Board of Inland Revenue, Somerset House. The latter also made printings of the following which can only be distinguished by the controls: ½d. B.13; 1½d. A.12; 2d. C.13; 2½d. A.12; 3d. A12, B.13, C.13; 4d. B.13; 5d. B.13; 7d. C.13; 8d. C.13; 9d. agate B.13; 10d. C.13; 1s. C.13)

1912–24. Wmk Royal Cypher, W **100**. Chalk-surfaced paper (6d.). P 15×14.

351	**105**	½d. green (16.1.13)	3·00	1·00	1·00
		a. Partial double print (half of bottom row) (Control G15)	—	£16000	
		b. Gummed both sides			
		Wi. Watermark inverted	4·00	3·00	1·50
		Wj. Watermark reversed	25·00	15·00	7·00
		Wk. Watermark inverted and reversed	6·00	4·00	3·00
352		½d. bright green	3·00	1·00	1·00
353		½d. deep green	10·00	5·00	2·00
354		½d. yellow-green	10·00	6·00	3·00
355		½d. very yellow (Cyprus) green (1914)	£7500	£5000	†
356		½d. blue-green	60·00	40·00	25·00
357	**104**	1d. bright scarlet (8.10.12)	3·00	1·00	1·00
		a. "Q" for "O" (R. 1/4) (Control E14)	£200	£150	£140
		ab. "Q" for "O" (R. 4/11) (Control T22)	£400	£350	£175
		ac. Reversed "Q" for "O" (R. 15/9) (Control T22)	£375	£300	£225
		ad. Inverted "Q" for "O" (R. 20/3)	£450	£375	£225
		b. *Tête-bêche* (pair)	—	£55000	†
		Wi. Watermark inverted	4·00	2·00	1·00
		Wj. Watermark reversed	30·00	17·00	8·00
		Wk. Watermark inverted and reversed	6·00	3·00	2·50
358		1d. vermilion	9·00	5·00	2·50
359		1d. pale rose-red	22·00	15·00	2·50
360		1d. carmine-red	20·00	11·00	5·00
361		1d. scarlet-vermilion	£175	£125	50·00
		a. Printed on back	£375	£275	†
362	**105**	1½d. red-brown (15.10.12)	6·00	4·00	1·50
		a. "PENCF" (R. 15/12)	£275	£200	£150
		b. Booklet pane. Four stamps plus two printed labels (2.24)	£550	£450	
		Wi. Watermark inverted	9·00	5·00	2·00
		Wj. Watermark reversed	55·00	40·00	10·00
		Wk. Watermark inverted and reversed	15·00	8·00	6·00
363		1½d. chocolate-brown	20·00	11·00	2·00
		a. No watermark	£275	£180	£110
364		1½d. chestnut	9·00	5·00	1·00
		a. "PENCF" (R. 15/12)	£140	£100	80·00
365		1½d. yellow-brown	30·00	20·00	16·00
366	**106**	2d. orange-yellow (Die I) (20.8.12)	14·00	8·00	3·00
367		2d. reddish orange (Die I) (11.13)	10·00	6·00	3·00
368		2d. orange (Die I)	8·00	4·00	3·00
		Wi. Watermark inverted	20·00	12·00	10·00
		Wj. Watermark reversed	20·00	12·00	10·00
		Wk. Watermark inverted and reversed	15·00	8·00	8·00
369		2d. brt orange (Die I)	8·00	5·00	3·00
370		2d. orange (Die II) (9.21)	8·00	5·00	3·50
		Wi. Watermark inverted	30·00	20·00	20·00
		Wk. Watermark inverted and reversed	£100	70·00	60·00
371	**104**	2½d. cobalt-blue (18.10.12)	22·00	12·00	4·00
371*a*		2½d. bright blue (1914)	22·00	12·00	4·00
372		2½d. blue	22·00	12·00	4·00
		Wi. Watermark inverted	90·00	60·00	60·00
		Wj. Watermark reversed	35·00	20·00	20·00
		Wk. Watermark inverted and reversed	35·00	20·00	20·00
373		2½d. indigo-blue* (1920)	£3000	£2000	£1200
373*a*		2½d. dull Prussian blue* (1921)	£1200	£700	£600
374	**106**	3d. dull reddish violet (9.10.12)	22·00	12·00	3·00
375		3d. violet	10·00	5·00	3·00
		Wi. Watermark inverted	£125	75·00	75·00
		Wj. Watermark reversed	£200	£125	£125
		Wk. Watermark inverted and reversed	30·00	20·00	20·00
376		3d. bluish violet (11.13)	15·00	9·00	3·00
377		3d. pale violet	17·00	10·00	3·00
378		4d. dp grey-green (15.1.13)	55·00	35·00	10·00
379		4d. grey-green	25·00	15·00	2·00
		Wi. Watermark inverted	40·00	25·00	25·00
		Wj. Watermark reversed	95·00	50·00	50·00
		Wk. Watermark inverted and reversed	60·00	35·00	35·00

380		4d. pale grey-green	40·00	25·00	5·00
381	107	5d. brown (30.6.13)	25·00	15·00	5·00
		Wi. Watermark inverted	£600	£375	£375
		Wj. Watermark reversed	†	†	—
		Wk. Watermark inverted and reversed	£350	£225	£225
382		5d. yellow-brown	25·00	15·00	5·00
		a. No watermark	£950	£700	
383		5d. bistre-brown	£200	£110	60·00
384		6d. dull purple (1.8.13)	45·00	25·00	10·00
385		6d. reddish purple (8.13)	30·00	15·00	7·00
		a. Perf 14 (9.20)	£145	90·00	£110
		Wi. Watermark inverted	60·00	40·00	40·00
		Wj. Watermark reversed	£1500	£1000	
		Wk. Watermark inverted and reversed	40·00	20·00	20·00
386		6d. deep reddish purple	45·00	27·00	5·00
387		7d. olive (1.8.13)	35·00	20·00	10·00
		Wi. Watermark inverted	70·00	40·00	40·00
		Wj. Watermark reversed	†	†	—
		Wk. Watermark inverted and reversed	£2250	£1600	
388		7d. bronze-green (1915)	90·00	60·00	25·00
389		7d. sage-green (1917)	£110	70·00	18·00
390		8d. black/*yellow* (1.8.13)	55·00	32·00	11·00
		Wi. Watermark inverted	£160	£100	£100
		Wj. Watermark reversed	£240	£160	£160
		Wk. Watermark inverted and reversed	£2750	£2000	
391		8d. black/yellow-buff (granite) (5.17)	60·00	40·00	15·00
392	108	9d. agate (30.6.13)	30·00	15·00	6·00
		a. Printed double, one albino			
		Wi. Watermark inverted	£150	90·00	90·00
		Wk. Watermark inverted and reversed	90·00	60·00	60·00
393		9d. deep agate	45·00	25·00	6·00
393*a*		9d. olive-green (9.22)	£225	£110	30·00
		aWi. Watermark inverted	£900	£650	£600
		aWk. Watermark inverted and reversed	£800	£550	£500
393*b*		9d. pale olive-green	£250	£120	40·00
394		10d. turquoise-blue (1.8.13)	40·00	22·00	20·00
		Wi. Watermark inverted	£2750	£1800	£1100
		Wk. Watermark inverted and reversed	£350	£225	£200
394*a*		10d. deep turquoise-blue	£150	90·00	30·00
395		1s. bistre (1.8.13)	35·00	20·00	4·00
		Wi. Watermark inverted	£250	£180	£140
		Wk. Watermark inverted and reversed	85·00	50·00	50·00
396		1s. bistre-brown	55·00	35·00	12·00
Set of 15			£475	£250	95·00

Imperf stamps of this issue exist but may be war-time colour trials.

†The impression of No. 361a is set sideways and is very pale. Nos. 362a and 364a occur on Plates 12 and 29 and are known from Controls L18, M18, M19, O19 and Q21. The flaws were corrected by 1921.

*No. 373 comes from Control O20 and also exists on toned paper.

No. 373*a* comes from Control R21 and also exists on toned paper, but both are unlike the rare Prussian blue shade of the 1935 2½d. Jubilee issue.

Examples of the 2d., T **106** which were in the hands of philatelists, are known bisected in Guernsey from 27 December 1940 to February 1941.

See also Nos. 418/29.

1913 (Aug). *Wmk Royal Cypher ("Multiple"), W* **103**. P 15×14.

397	105	½d. brt green	£250	£150	£180
		a. Watermark sideways	†	†	£18000
		Wi. Watermark inverted	£600	£450	
398	104	1d. dull scarlet	£350	£225	£225
		Wi. Watermark inverted	£750	£550	

Both these stamps were originally issued in rolls only. Subsequently sheets were found, so that horizontal pairs and blocks are known but are of considerable rarity.

109

A

110 Single Cypher

Major Re-entries on 2s.6d.

Nos. 400a and 406a

No. 415b

(Des Bertram Mackennal. Dies eng J. A. C. Harrison. Recess)

High values, so-called "Sea Horses" design: T **109**. *Background around portrait consists of horizontal lines, Type* A. *Wmk Single Cypher, W* **110**. P 11×12.

1913 (30 June). *Printed by Waterlow Bros & Layton.*

399	109	2s.6d. deep sepia-brown	£700	£250	£160
400		2s.6d. sepia-brown	£550	£225	£140
		a. Re-entry (R. 2/1)	£2250	£1200	£600
401		5s. rose-carmine	£1000	£400	£275
402		10s. indigo-blue (1 Aug)	£1800	£700	£425
403		£1 green (1 Aug)	£4500	£2200	£1200
404		£1 dull blue-green (1 Aug)	£4500	£2200	£1400

*399/404 **For well-centred, lightly used+35%**

1915 (Oct–Dec). *Printed by De la Rue & Co.*

405	109	2s.6d. deep yellow-brown	£600	£250	£200
		Wi. Watermark inverted	£1600	£950	
406		2s.6d. yellow-brown	£450	£225	£190
		a. Re-entry (R. 2/1)	£2200	£1250	£600
		Wi. Watermark inverted	£1250	£650	
		Wj. Watermark reversed	£1200	£650	
		Wk. Watermark inverted and reversed	£2750	£1500	
407		2s.6d. pale brown	£450	£225	£190
		a. Re-entry (R. 2/1)	£2200	£1250	£600
		Wi. Watermark inverted	£1250	£650	
		Wj. Watermark reversed	£1250	£700	
408		2s.6d. sepia (seal-brown)	£450	£225	£190
		Wi. Watermark inverted	£1250	£650	
		Wj. Watermark reversed	£1200	£650	
409		5s. brt carmine	£850	£375	£300
		Wi. Watermark inverted	£3500	£2000	
		Wj. Watermark reversed	£3500	£2000	
		Wk. Watermark inverted and reversed	—	£6000	
410		5s. pale carmine	£900	£450	£280
411		10s. deep blue (Dec)	£4000	£2250	£875
412		10s. blue	£2800	£1800	£700

		Wi. Watermark inverted and reversed	—	—	†
413		10s. pale blue	£3000	£2000	£700

*405/13 **For well-centred, lightly used +45%**

No. 406/7 were produced from the original Waterlow plates as were all De La Rue 5s and 10s printings. Examples of No. 406/7, 410 and 411 occur showing degrees of plate wear.

1918 (Dec)–**19**. *Printed by Bradbury, Wilkinson & Co, Ltd.*

413*a*	**109**	2s.6d. olive-brown	£225	£100	65·00
414		2s.6d. chocolate-brown	£280	£125	70·00
415		2s.6d. reddish brown	£280	£125	70·00
415*a*		2s.6d. pale brown	£250	£110	65·00
		b. Major re-entry (R. 1/2)	£1200	£650	£400
416		5s. rose-red (1.19)	£450	£250	£110
417		10s. dull grey-blue (1.19)	£800	£375	£160
Set of 4 (inc. no. 403)			£5500	£2500	£1400

*413a/17 **For well-centred, lightly used +35%**

DISTINGUISHING PRINTINGS. Note that the £1 value was only printed by Waterlow.

Waterlow and De La Rue stamps measure exactly 22 mm vertically. In the De La Rue printings the gum is usually patchy and yellowish, and the colour of the stamp, particularly in the 5s., tends to show through the back. The holes of the perforation are smaller than those of the other two printers, but there is a thick perforation tooth at the top of each vertical side.

In the Bradbury Wilkinson printings the height of the stamp is 223/4 or 23 mm due to the use of curved plates. On most of the 223/4 mm high stamps a minute coloured guide dot appears in the margin just above the middle of the upper frame-line.

For (1934) re-engraved Waterlow printings see Nos. 450/2.

UNITED KINGDOM OF GREAT BRITAIN AND NORTHERN IRELAND

111 Block Cypher

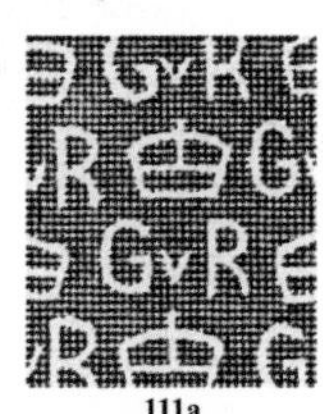

111a

The watermark Type **111a**, as compared with Type **111**, differs as follows: Closer spacing of horizontal rows (12½ mm instead of 14½ mm). Letters shorter and rounder. Watermark thicker. The dandy roll to produce watermark Type **111a** was provided by Somerset House in connection with experiments in paper composition undertaken during 1924–25. These resulted in a change from rag only paper to that made from a mixture including esparto and sulphite.

(Typo by Waterlow & Sons, Ltd (all values except 6d.) and later, 1934–35, by Harrison & Sons, Ltd (all values). Until 1934 the 6d. was printed at Somerset House where a printing of the 1½d. was also made in 1926 (identifiable only by control E.26). Printings by Harrisons in 1934–35 can be identified, when in mint condition, by the fact that the gum shows a streaky appearance vertically, the Waterlow gum being uniformly applied, but Harrisons also used up the balance of the Waterlow "smooth gum" paper)

1924 (Feb)–**26**. *Wmk Block Cypher, W* **111**. P 15×14.

418	**105**	½d. green	2·00	1·00	1·00
		a. Watermark sideways (5.24)	18·00	9·00	3·25
		aWi. Watermark sideways inverted	£450	£350	
		b. Doubly printed	£11000	£8000	†
		c. No watermark	£3000	—	—
		Wi. Watermark inverted	7·00	3·50	1·00
419	**104**	1d. scarlet	2·00	1·00	1·00
		a. Watermark sideways	35·00	20·00	15·00
		b. Experimental paper, W **111a** (10.24)	40·00	22·00	
		c. Partial double print, one inverted	—	£7500	
		d. Inverted "Q" for "O" (R. 20/3)	£600	£375	
		Wi. Watermark inverted	7·00	4·00	1·50
420	**105**	1½d. red-brown	2·00	1·00	1·00
		a. *Tête-bêche* (pair)	£700	£500	£800
		b. Watermark sideways (8.24)	20·00	19·00	3·50
		bWi. Watermark sideways inverted	—	£600	
		c. Printed on the gummed side	£650	£400	
		d. Booklet pane. Four stamps plus two printed labels (3.24)	£200	£150	
		e. Ditto. Watermark sideways	£7000	£6000	
		f. Experimental paper, W **111a** (10.24)	90·00	60·00	70·00
		g. Double impression	—	£14000	†
		Wi. Watermark inverted	3·50	2·00	1·00
421	**106**	2d. orange (Die II) (7.24)	4·00	2·50	2·50
		a. No watermark	£1500	£800	
		b. Watermark sideways (7.26)	£175	£100	£100
		c. Partial double print	—	£18000	†
		Wi. Watermark inverted	45·00	30·00	20·00
422	**104**	2½d. blue (10.10.24)	10·00	5·00	3·00
		a. No watermark	£2250	£1600	
		b. Watermark sideways	†	†	£6000
		Wi. Watermark inverted	70·00	40·00	30·00
423	**106**	3d. violet (10.10.24)	20·00	10·00	2·50
		Wi. Watermark inverted	70·00	40·00	30·00
424		4d. grey-green (10.10.24)	28·00	12·00	2·50
		a. Printed on the gummed side	£3000	£2000	†
		Wi. Watermark inverted	£170	90·00	65·00
425	**107**	5d. brown (17.10.24)	40·00	20·00	3·00
		Wi. Watermark inverted	£110	70·00	50·00
426		6d. reddish purple (*chalk-surfaced paper*) (9.24)	20·00	12·00	2·50
		Wi. Watermark inverted	75·00	60·00	35·00
		Wk. Watermark inverted and reversed	£425	£275	£175
426*a*		6d. purple (6.26)	6·00	3·00	1·50
		aWi. Watermark inverted	75·00	50·00	30·00
427	**108**	9d. olive-green (11.11.24)	40·00	12·00	3·50
		Wi. Watermark inverted	£110	75·00	60·00
428		10d. turquoise-blue (28.11.24)	85·00	40·00	40·00
		Wi. Watermark inverted	£2750	£1750	£1200
429		1s. bistre-brown (10.24)	50·00	22·00	3·00
		Wi. Watermark inverted	£575	£350	£325
Set of 12			£250	£110	60·00

There are numerous shades in this issue.

The 6d. on chalk-surfaced and ordinary papers was printed by both Somerset House and Harrisons. The Harrison printings have streaky gum, differ slightly in shade, and that on chalk-surfaced paper is printed in a highly fugitive ink. The prices quoted are for the commonest (Harrison) printing in each case.

112

(Des H. Nelson. Eng J. A. C. Harrison. Recess Waterlow)

1924–25. *British Empire Exhibition. W* **111**. P 14.

(a) Dated "1924" (23.4.24).

430	**112**	1d. scarlet	12·00	10·00	11·00
431		1½d. brown	20·00	15·00	15·00
Set of 2			30·00	25·00	26·00
First Day Cover					£400

(b) Dated "1925" (9.5.25).

432	**112**	1d. scarlet	25·00	15·00	30·00
433		1½d. brown	60·00	40·00	70·00
Set of 2			80·00	55·00	£100
First Day Cover					£1500

113

114

115

St. George and the Dragon

117

(Des J. Farleigh (T **113** and **115**), E. Linzell (T **114**) and H. Nelson (T **116**). Eng C. G. Lewis (T **113**), T. E. Storey (T **115**), both at the Royal Mint; J. A. C. Harrison, of Waterlow (T **114** & **116**). Typo by Waterlow from plates made at the Royal Mint, except T **116**, recess by Bradbury, Wilkinson from die and plate of their own manufacture)

1929 (10 May). *Ninth U.P.U. Congress, London.*

(a) W **111**. P 15×14.

434	**113**	½d. green	3·00	2·25	2·25
		a. Watermark sideways	70·00	35·00	35·00
		Wi. Watermark inverted	30·00	12·00	10·00
435	**114**	1d. scarlet	3·00	2·25	2·25
		a. Watermark sideways	£130	60·00	60·00
		Wi. Watermark inverted	30·00	12·00	10·00
436		1½d. purple-brown	3·00	2·25	1·75
		a. Watermark sideways	70·00	35·00	35·00
		b. Booklet pane. Four stamps plus two printed labels	£275	£225	
		Wi. Watermark inverted	15·00	5·00	6·00
437	**115**	2½d. blue	18·00	10·00	10·00
		Wi. Watermark inverted	£2750	£1800	£900

(b) W **117**. P 12.

438	**116**	£1 black	£1000	£750	£550
Set of 4 (to 2½d.)			24·00	15·00	14·50
First Day Cover (4 vals.)					£550
First Day Cover (5 vals.)					£7500

PRINTERS. All subsequent issues were printed in photogravure by Harrison & Sons Ltd *except where otherwise stated.*

118

119

120

121

122

1934–36. *W* **111**. P 15×14.

439	**118**	½d. green (17.11.34)	1·00	50	50
		a. Watermark sideways	15·00	8·00	3·50
		aWi. Watermark sideways inverted	£375	£275	75·00
		b. Imperf three sides	£3750	£2500	
		Wi. Watermark inverted	20·00	9·00	1·25
440	**119**	1d. scarlet (24.9.34)	1·00	50	50
		a. Imperf (pair)	£2800	£2000	
		b. Printed on gummed side	£725	£550	
		c. Watermark sideways (30.4.35)	30·00	15·00	6·00
		cWi. Watermark sideways inverted	£125	75·00	
		d. Double impression	†	†	£17000
		e. Imperf between (pair)	£5000	£3000	
		f. Imperf (three sides) (pair)	£3000	£2000	
		Wi. Watermark inverted	20·00	9·00	3·00
441	**118**	1½d. red-brown (20.8.34)	1·00	50	50
		a. Imperf (pair)	£950	£600	
		b. Imperf (three sides) (lower stamp in vert pair)	£1900	£1200	
		c. Imperf between (horiz pair)			
		d. Watermark sideways	13·00	8·00	4·00
		dWi. Watermark sideways inverted			
		e. Booklet pane. Four stamps plus two printed labels (1.35)	£150	£100	
		Wi. Watermark inverted	8·00	4·00	1·00
442	**120**	2d. orange (19.1.35)	1·50	75	75
		a. Imperf (pair)	£4750	£4000	
		b. Watermark sideways (30.4.35)	£200	£110	75·00
443	**119**	2½d. ultramarine (18.3.35)	2·50	1·50	1·25
444	**120**	3d. violet (18.3.35)	3·00	1·50	1·25
		Wi. Watermark inverted	—	—	£850
445		4d. dp grey-green (2.12.35)	4·00	2·00	1·25
		Wi. Watermark inverted	†	†	£800
446	**121**	5d. yellow-brown (17.2.36)	13·00	6·50	2·75
447	**122**	9d. dp olive-green (2.12.35)	20·00	12·00	2·25
448		10d. turquoise-blue (24.2.36)	30·00	15·00	10·00
449		1s. bistre-brown (24.2.36)	40·00	15·00	1·25
		a. Double impression	—	—	†
Set of 11			95·00	50·00	20·00

Owing to the need for wider space for the perforations the size of the designs of the ½d. and 2d. were once, and the 1d. and 1½d. twice reduced from that of the first printings.

The format description, size in millimetres and S.G. catalogue number are given but further details will be found in the *Great Britain Specialised Catalogue*, Volume 2.

Description	*Size*	*S.G. Nos.*	*Date of Issue*
½d. intermediate format	18.4×22.2	—	19.11.34
½d. small format	17.9×21.7	439	14.2.35
1d. large format	18.7×22.5	—	24.9.34
1d. intermediate format	18.4×22.2	—	1934
1d. small format	17.9×21.7	440	8.2.35
1½d. large format	18.7×22.5	—	20.8.34
1½d. intermediate format	18.4×22.2	—	1934
1½d. small format	17.9×21.7	441	7.2.35
2d. intermediate format	18.4×22.2	—	21.1.35
2d. small format	18.15×21.7	442	1935

There are also numerous minor variations, due to the photographic element in the process.

The ½d. imperf three sides, No. 439b, is known in a block of four, from a sheet, in which the bottom pair is imperf at top and sides.

Examples of 2d., T **120**, which were in the hands of philatelists are known bisected in Guernsey from 27 December 1940 to February 1941.

B

123

(Eng. J.A.C. Harrison. Recess Waterlow)

1934 (16 Oct). *T* **109** *(re-engraved). Background around portrait consists of horizontal and diagonal lines, Type* B. *W* **110**. P 11×12.

450	**109** 2s.6d. chocolate-brown	£150	70·00	40·00
451	5s. bright rose-red	£400	£160	85·00
452	10s. indigo	£500	£340	80·00
Set of 3		£1000	£525	£190

There are numerous other minor differences in the design of this issue.

(Des B. Freedman)

1935 (7 May). *Silver Jubilee. W* **111**. P 15×14.

453	**123** ½d. green	1·00	1·00	1·00
	Wi. Watermark inverted	14·00	7·00	3·00
454	1d. scarlet	2·00	1·50	2·00
	Wi. Watermark inverted	14·00	7·00	4·00
455	1½d. red-brown	1·25	1·00	1·00
	Wi. Watermark inverted	5·00	3·00	1·50
456	2½d. blue	6·50	5·00	6·00
456*a*	2½d. Prussian blue	£9000	£7000	£8000
Set of 4		10·00	8·00	9·25
First Day Cover				£600

The 1d., 1½d. and 2½d. values differ from T **123** in the emblem in the panel at right.

Four sheets of No. 456a, printed in the wrong shade, were issued in error by the Post Office Stores Department on 25 June 1935. It is known that three from the sheets were sold from the sub-office at 134 Fore Street, Upper Edmonton, London, between that date and 4 July.

SPECIMEN STAMPS (King George V)

1911–12. *Wmk Imperial Crown.* P 15×14.

S156	½d. green Die 1A (No. 322) (22)	£700
	a. Die 1B (No. 324) (22)	£300
S157	1d. carmine-red, Die 1A (No. 327) (22)	£450
	a. Die 1B (No. 329) (22)	£450
S158	1d. scarlet, Die 1B (No. 332) (22)	£650

1912. *Wmk Royal Cypher ("Simple").* P 15×14.

S159	½d. green (No. 334) (22, 26)	£250
S160	1d. scarlet (No. 336) (22, 26)	£300

1912. *Wmk Imperial Crown.* P 15×14.

S161	½d. green (No. 339) (26)	£300

1912. *Wmk Royal Cypher ("Simple").* P 15×14.

S162	½d. green (No. 344) (26)	£500

1912–24. *Wmk Royal Cypher.* P 15×14.

S163	½d. green (No. 351) (23, 26)	£120
S164	1d. bright scarlet (No. 357) (23, 26)	£150
S165	1½d. red-brown (No. 362) (23, 26)	60·00
S166	2d. orange Die I (No. 368) (26)	£200
	a. Die II (No. 370) (15, 23)	£500
S168	2½d. blue (No. 372) (15, 23, 26)	85·00
S169	3d. violet (No. 375) (15, 23, 26)	£200
S170	4d. grey-green (No. 379) (15, 23, 26)	£100
S171	5d. brown (No. 381) (15, 23, 26)	£200
S172	6d. dull purple (No. 384) (15, 23, 26)	£150
S173	6d. olive (No. 387) (26)	£160
S174	8d. black/*yellow* (No. 390) (26)	£200
S175	9d. agate (No. 392) (26)	£300
S176	9d. olive-green (No. 393a) (15, 23)	£600
S177	10d. turquoise-blue (No. 394) (15, 23, 26)	£325
S178	1s. bistre (No. 395) (15, 23, 26, 31)	£300

1913. *Printed by Waterlow Bros. & Layton.*

S179	2s.6d. deep sepia-brown (No. 399) (26, 29)	£500
S180	5s. rose-carmine (No. 401) (26)	£600
S181	10s. indigo-blue (No. 402) (23, 26, 29)	£900
S182	£1 green (No. 403) (23, 26)	£2500

1915. *Printed by De La Rue & Co.*

S183	2s.6d. yellow-brown (No. 406) (23)	£1000
S184	5s. bright carmine (No. 409) (23)	£800
S185	10s. deep blue (No. 411) (26)	£2000

1918–19. *Printed by Bradbury Wilkinson & Co. Ltd.*

S186	2s.6d. olive-brown (No. 413a) (15, 23, 26, 31, 32)	£700
S187	5s. rose-red (No. 416) (15, 23, 26, 31, 32)	£900
S188	10s. dull grey-blue (No. 417) (15, 23, 26, 31, 32)	£1000

1924–26. *Wmk Block Cypher.* P15×14.

S189	½d. green (No. 418) (15, 23, 30, 32)	60·00
S190	1d. scarlet (No. 419) (15, 23, 30, 32)	60·00
S191	1½d. red-brown (No. 420) (15, 23, 30, 32)	60·00
S192	2d. orange (No. 421) (23, 32)	70·00
S193	2½d. blue (No. 422) (23, 32)	£400
S194	3d. violet (No. 423) (23, 32)	£600
S195	4d. grey-green (No. 424) (23, 32)	£500
S196	5d. brown (No. 425) (23, 26, 32)	£110
S197	6d. purple (No. 426a) (23, 26, 32)	£300
S198	9d. olive-green (No. 427) (23, 26, 32)	£110
S199	10d. turquoise-blue (No. 428) (23, 32)	£650
S200	1s. bistre-brown (No. 429) (23, 32)	£450

1924. *British Empire Exhibition Dated* "1924".

S201	1d. scarlet (No. 430) (15, 23, 30)	£500
S202	1½d. brown (No. 431) (15, 23, 30)	£500

1925. *British Empire Exhibition. Dated* "1925".

S203	1d. scarlet (No. 432) (30)	£600
S204	1½d. brown (No. 433) (30)	£600

1929. *Postal Union Congress.*

S205	2½d. blue (No. 437) (32)	—
S206	£1 black (No. 438) (32, red opt)	£2000

1934–36. *Printed in Photogravure.*

S207	½d. green (No. 439) (23, 32)	£350
S208	1d. scarlet (No. 440) (23, 32)	£400
S209	1½d. red-brown (No. 441) (23, 32)	£400
S210	2d. orange (No. 442) (30, 32)	—
S211	2½d. ultramarine (No. 443) (23)	£500
S212	3d. violet (No. 444) (23, 30)	£500
S213	4d. grey-green (No. 445) (23, 30)	£500
S214	5d. yellow-brown (No. 446) (23)	£500
S215	9d. olive-green (No. 447) (23)	£500
S216	10d. turquoise-blue (No. 448) (23, 32)	£500
S217	1s. bistre-brown (No. 449) (23, 32)	£100

1934. *Re-engraved Die.*

S218	2s.6d. chocolate-brown (No. 450) (30)	£2500
S219	5s. bright rose-red (No. 451) (30)	£2500
S220	10s. indigo (No. 452) (30)	£2500

1935. *Silver Jubilee.*

S221	½d. green (No. 453) (23)	£800
S222	1d. scarlet (No. 454) (23)	£800
S223	1½d. red-brown (No. 455) (23)	£800
S224	2½d. blue (No. 456) (23)	£800

KING EDWARD VIII

20 January – 10 December 1936

Further detailed information on the stamps of King Edward VIII will be found in Volume 2 of the Stanley Gibbons *Great Britain Specialised Catalogue*.

PRICES. From S.G. 457 prices quoted in the first column are for stamps in unmounted mint condition.

124

125

(Des H. Brown, adapted Harrison using a photo by Hugh Cecil)

1936. *W* **125**. P 15×14.

No.	Type	Description	Mint	Used
457	**124**	½d. green (1.9.36)	30	30
		a. Double impression		
		Wi. Watermark inverted	10·00	5·00
458		1d. scarlet (14.9.36)	60	50
		Wi. Watermark inverted	9·00	5·00
459		1½d. red-brown (1.9.36)	30	30
		a. Booklet pane. Four stamps plus two printed labels (10.36)	75·00	
		Wi. Watermark inverted	1·00	1·00
460		2½d. brt blue (1.9.36)	30	85
Set of 4			1·25	1·75

First Day Covers

1.9.36	½d., 1½d., 2½d. (*457, 459/60*)	£150
14.9.36	1d. (*458*)	£170

SPECIMEN STAMPS (King Edward VIII)

1936. *King Edward VIII issue.*

S225	½d. green (No. 457) (30, 32)	£500
S226	1d. scarlet (No. 458) (30, 32)	£500
S227	1½d. red-brown (No. 459) (30, 32)	£500
S228	2½d. bright blue (No. 460) (30)	£500

KING GEORGE VI

11 December 1936 – 6 February 1952

Further detailed information on the stamps of King George VI will be found in Volume 2 of the Stanley Gibbons *Great Britain Specialised Catalogue*.

126 King George VI and Queen Elizabeth

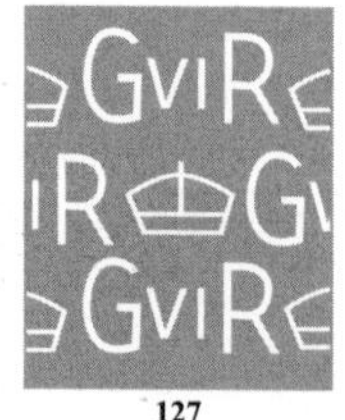

127

Colon flaw (Cyl. 7 No dot, R. 10/1, later corrected)

(Des E. Dulac)

1937 (13 May). *Coronation. W* **127**. P 15×14.

No.	Type	Description	Mint	Used
461	**126**	1½d. maroon	30	30
		a. Colon flaw	15·00	
First Day Cover				35·00

128

129

130

King George VI and National Emblems

(Des T **128/9**, E. Dulac (head) and E. Gill (frames). T **130**, E. Dulac (whole stamp))

1937–47. *W* **127**. P 15×14.

No.	Type	Description	Mint	Used
462	**128**	½d. green (10.5.37)	30	25
		a. Watermark sideways (1.38)	50	50
		ab. Booklet pane of 4 (6.40)	50·00	
		Wi. Watermark inverted	10·00	60
463		1d. scarlet (10.5.37)	30	25
		a. Watermark sideways (2.38)	20·00	9·00
		ab. Booklet pane of 4 (6.40)	£100	
		Wi. Watermark inverted	38·00	3·00
464		1½d. red-brown (30.7.37)	30	25
		a. Watermark sideways (2.38)	1·00	1·25
		b. Booklet pane. Four stamps plus two printed labels (8.37)	£100	
		c. Imperf three sides (pair)	£3500	
		Wi. Watermark inverted	15·00	1·25
465		2d. orange (31.1.38)	1·20	50
		a. Watermark sideways (2.38)	70·00	38·00
		b. Bisected (on cover)	†	40·00
		Wi. Watermark inverted	55·00	18·00
466		2½d. ultramarine (10.5.37)	40	25
		a. Watermark sideways (6.40)	70·00	32·00
		b. *Tête-bêche* (horiz pair)	£20000	
		Wi. Watermark inverted	50·00	18·00
467		3d. violet (31.1.38)	5·00	1·00
468	**129**	4d. grey-green (21.11.38)	60	75
		a. Imperf (pair)	£5000	
		b. Imperf three sides (horiz pair)	£5250	
469		5d. brown (21.11.38)	3·50	85
		a. Imperf (pair)	£6000	
		b. Imperf three sides (horiz pair)	£5250	
470		6d. purple (30.1.39)	1·50	60
471	**130**	7d. emerald-green (27.2.39)	5·00	60
		a. Imperf three sides (horiz pair)	£5000	
472		8d. brt carmine (27.2.39)	7·50	80
473		9d. dp olive-green (1.5.39)	6·50	80
474		10d. turquoise-blue (1.5.39)	7·00	80
		aa. Imperf (pair)	£6000	
474*a*		11d. plum (29.12.47)	3·00	2·75
475		1s. bistre-brown (1.5.39)	9·00	75
Set of 15			45·00	10·00

For later printings of the lower values in apparently lighter shades and different colours, see Nos. 485/90 and 503/8.

No. 465b was authorised for use in Guernsey from 27 December 1940 until February 1941.

Nos. 468b and 469b are perforated at foot only and each occurs in the same sheet as Nos. 468a and 469a.

No. 471a is also perforated at foot only, but occurs on the top row of a sheet.

First Day Covers

10.5.37	½d., 1d., 2½d. (*462/3, 466*)	45.00
30.7.37	1½d. (*464*)	45.00
31.1.38	2d., 3d. (*465, 467*)	95.00
21.11.38	4d., 5d. (*468/9*)	60.00
30.1.39	6d. (*470*)	55.00
27.2.39	7d., 8d. (*471/2*)	80.00
1.5.39	9d., 10d., 1s. (*473/4, 475*)	£450
29.12.47	11d. (*474a*)	50.00

131

132

133

(Des E. Dulac (T **131**) and Hon. G. R. Bellew (T **132**). Eng J. A. C. Harrison. Recess Waterlow)

1939–48. *W* **133**. P 14.

476	**131**	2s.6d. brown (4.9.39)	35·00	6·00
476*a*		2s.6d. yellow-green (9.3.42)	11·00	1·50
477		5s. red (21.8.39)	20·00	2·00
478	**132**	10s. dark blue (30.10.39)	£225	20·00
478*a*		10s. ultramarine (30.11.42)	20·00	5·00
478*b*		£1 brown (1.10.48)	20·00	26·00
Set of 6			£300	55·00

First Day Covers

21.8.39	5s. (*477*)	£750
4.9.39	2s.6d. brown (*476*)	£1500
30.10.39	10s. dark blue (*478*)	£2750
9.3.42	2s.6d. yellow-green (*476a*)	£1500
30.11.42	10s. ultramarine (*478a*)	£3250
1.10.48	£1 (*478b*)	£275

134 Queen Victoria and King George VI

(Des H. L. Palmer)

1940 (6 May). *Centenary of First Adhesive Postage Stamps. W* **127**. P 14½×14.

479	**134**	½d. green	30	75
480		1d. scarlet	1·00	75
481		1½d. red-brown	50	1·50
482		2d. orange	1·00	75
		a. Bisected (on cover)	†	30·00
483		2½d. ultramarine	2·25	50
484		3d. violet	3·00	3·50
Set of 6			8·75	5·25
First Day Cover				55·00

No. 482a was authorised for use on Guernsey from 27 December 1940 until February 1941.

1941–42. *Head as Nos. 462/7, but with lighter background to provide a more economic use of the printing ink. W* **127**. P 15×14.

485	**128**	½d. pale green (1.9.41)	30	30
		a. *Tête-bêche* (horiz pair)	£15000	
		b. Imperf (pair)	£5000	
		Wi. Watermark inverted	4·00	50
486		1d. pale scarlet (11.8.41)	30	30
		a. Watermark sideways (10.42)	5·00	4·50
		b. Imperf (pair)	£6000	
		c. Imperf three sides (horiz pair)	£6000	
487		1½d. pale red-brown (28.9.42)	60	80
488		2d. pale orange (6.10.41)	50	50
		a. Watermark sideways (6.42)	28·00	19·00
		b. *Tête-bêche* (horiz pair)	£15000	
		c. Imperf (pair)	£5000	
		d. Imperf pane*	£15000	
		Wi. Watermark inverted	4·00	1·00
489		2½d. light ultramarine (21.7.41)	30	30
		a. Watermark sideways (8.42)	15·00	12·00
		b. *Tête-bêche* (horiz pair)	£15000	
		c. Imperf (pair)	£4000	
		d. Imperf pane*	£10000	
		e. Imperf three sides (horiz pair)	£6000	
		Wi. Watermark inverted	1·50	1·00
490		3d. pale violet (3.11.41)	2·50	1·00
Set of 6			3·50	2·75

The *tête-bêche* varieties are from defectively made-up stamp booklets.

Nos. 486c and 489e are perforated at foot only and occur in the same sheets as Nos. 486b and 489c.

*BOOKLET ERRORS. Those listed as "imperf panes" show one row of perforations either at the top or at the bottom of the pane of 6.

First Day Covers

21.7.41	2½d. (*489*)	45·00
11.8.41	1d. (*486*)	22·00
1.9.41	½d. (*485*)	22·00
6.10.41	2d. (*488*)	60·00
3.11.41	3d. (*490*)	£110
28.9.42	1½d. (*487*)	55·00

135

136

Extra porthole aft (Cyl. 11 No dot, R. 16/1)

Extra porthole fore (Cyl. 8 Dot, R. 5/6)

Seven berries (Cyl. 4 No dot, R. 12/5)

(Des H. L. Palmer (T **135**) and R. Stone (T **136**))

1946 (11 June). *Victory. W* **127**. P 15×14.

491	**135**	2½d. ultramarine	20	20
		a. Extra porthole aft	45·00	
		b. Extra porthole fore	65·00	
492	**136**	3d. violet	20	50
		a. Seven berries	20·00	
Set of 2			40	50
First Day Cover				65·00

137

138 King George VI and Queen Elizabeth

(Des G. Knipe and Joan Hassall from photographs by Dorothy Wilding)

1948 (26 Apr). *Royal Silver Wedding. W* **127**. P 15×14 (2½d.) or 14×15 (£1).

493	**137**	2½d. ultramarine	35	20
494	**138**	£1 blue	40·00	40·00
Set of 2			40·00	40·00
First Day Cover				£425

1948 (10 May). Stamps of 1d. and 2½d. showing seaweed-gathering were on sale at eight Head Post Offices in Great Britain, but were primarily for use in the Channel Islands and are listed there (see Nos. C1/2, after Royal Mail Postage Labels).

139 Globe and Laurel Wreath

140 "Speed"

141 Olympic Symbol

142 Winged Victory

Crown flaw (Cyl. 1 No dot, R. 20/2, later retouched)

(Des P. Metcalfe (T **139**), A. Games (T **140**), S. D. Scott (T **141**) and E. Dulac (T **142**))

1948 (29 July). *Olympic Games. W* **127**. P 15×14.

495	**139**	2½d. ultramarine	35	10
496	**140**	3d. violet	35	50
		a. Crown flaw	20·00	
497	**141**	6d. bright purple	70	40
498	**142**	1s. brown	1·50	1·50
Set of 4			2·25	2·00
First Day Cover				45·00

145 Goddess Concordia, Globe and Points of Compass

146 Posthorn and Globe

Lake in Asia (Cyl. 3 Dot, R. 14/1)

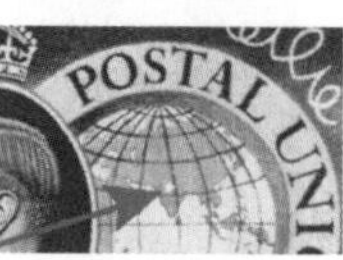
Lake in India (Cyl. 2 No dot, R. 8/2)

(Des Mary Adshead (T **143**), P. Metcalfe (T **144**), H. Fleury (T **145**) and Hon. G. R. Bellew (T **146**))

1949 (10 Oct). *75th Anniv of Universal Postal Union. W* **127**. P 15×14.

499	**143**	2½d. ultramarine	25	10
		a. Lake in Asia	30·00	
		b. Lake in India	25·00	
500	**144**	3d. violet	25	50
501	**145**	6d. bright purple	50	75
502	**146**	1s. brown	1·00	1·25
Set of 4			1·50	2·50
First Day Cover				80·00

1950–52. *4d. as No. 468 and others as Nos. 485/9, but colours changed. W* **27**. P 15×14.

503	**128**	½d. pale orange (3.5.51)	30	30
		a. Imperf (pair)	£4000	
		b. *Tête-bêche* (horiz pair)	£15000	
		c. Imperf pane*	£12000	
		Wi. Watermark inverted	50	50
504		1d. light ultramarine (3.5.51)	30	30
		a. Watermark sideways (5.51)	1·10	1·25
		b. Imperf (pair)	£4000	
		c. Imperf three sides (horiz pair)	£5000	
		d. Booklet pane. Three stamps plus three printed labels (3.52)	18·00	
		e. Ditto. Partial *tête-bêche* pane	£6000	
		Wi. Watermark inverted	4·50	2·50
505		1½d. pale green (3.5.51)	65	60
		a. Watermark sideways (9.51)	3·25	5·00
		Wi. Watermark inverted	4·50	1·00
506		2d. pale red-brown (3.5.51)	75	40
		a. Watermark sideways (5.51)	1·75	2·00
		b. *Tête-bêche* (horiz pair)	£15000	
		c. Imperf three sides (horiz pair)	£5000	
		Wi. Watermark inverted	4·25	6·50
507		2½d. pale scarlet (3.5.51)	60	40
		a. Watermark sideways (5.51)	1·75	1·75
		b. *Tête-bêche* (horiz pair)		
		Wi. Watermark inverted	1·50	1·25
508	**129**	4d. light ultramarine (2.10.50)	2·00	1·75
		a. Double impression	†	£7000
Set of 6			4·00	3·25

*BOOKLET ERRORS. Those listed as "imperf panes" show one row of perforations either at the top or at the bottom of the pane of 6.

No. 504c is perforated at foot only and occurs in the same sheet as No. 504b.

No. 506c is also perforated at foot only.

First Day Covers

2.10.50	4d. (*508*)	£120
3.5.51	½d., 1d., 1½d., 2d., 2½d. (*503/7*)	55·00

143 Two Hemispheres

144 UPU Monument, Berne

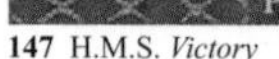
147 H.M.S. *Victory*

148 White Cliffs of Dover

149 St. George and the Dragon **150** Royal Coat of Arms

(Des Mary Adshead (T **147/8**), P. Metcalfe (T **149/50**). Recess Waterlow)

1951 (3 May). *W* **133**. P 11×12.

509	**147**	2s.6d. yellow-green	2·00	1·00
510	**148**	5s. red	40·00	1·00
511	**149**	10s. ultramarine	10·00	7·50
512	**150**	£1 brown	48·00	18·00
Set of 4			95·00	25·00
First Day Cover				£925

151 "Commerce and Prosperity" **152** Festival Symbol

(Des E. Dulac (T **151**), A. Games (T **152**))

1951 (3 May). *Festival of Britain. W* **127**. P 15×14.

513	**151**	2½d. scarlet	20	15
514	**152**	4d. ultramarine	30	35
Set of 2			40	40
First Day Cover				38·00

SPECIMEN STAMPS (King George VI)

1937. *Coronation.*

S229	1½d. maroon (No. 461) (32)	£600

1937–47. *King George VI issue.*

S230	2d. orange (No. 465) (26)	£275
S231	3d. violet (No. 467) (26)	£240
S232	4d. grey-green (No. 468) (9, 23)	£160
S233	5d. brown (No. 469) (9, 23)	£200
S234	6d. purple (No. 470) (9)	—
S235	7d. emerald-green (No. 471) (23)	£200
S236	8d. bright carmine (No. 472) (9, 23)	£200
S237	9d. deep olive-green (No. 473) (9, 23)	£200
S238	10d. turquoise-blue (No. 474) (9, 23)	£200
S239	11d. plum (No. 474a) (26)	£225
S240	1s. bistre-brown (No. 475) (9, 23)	£125

1939–48.

S241	2s.6d. brown (No. 476) (23)	£250
S242	2s.6d. yellow-green (No. 476a) (9, 23, 26, 30)	£250
S243	5s. red (No. 477) (9, 23, 26)	£250
S244	10s. dark blue (No. 478) (23)	£450
S245	10s. ultramarine (No. 478a) (9, 23)	£375
S246	£1 brown (No. 478b) (30)	—

1940. *Centenary of First Adhesive Postage Stamps.*

S247	½d. green (No. 479) (9)	—
S248	1d. scarlet (No. 480) (9)	—
S249	1½d. red-brown (No. 481) (9)	—
S250	2d. orange (No. 482) (9)	—
S251	2½d. ultramarine (No. 483) (9)	—
S252	3d. violet (No. 484) (9)	—

1941–42. *Re-engraved with lighter background.*

S253	½d. pale green (No. 485) (9)	—
S254	1d. pale scarlet (No. 486) (9)	—
S255	1½d. pale red-brown (No. 487) (9)	—
S256	2d. pale orange (No. 488) (9)	—
S257	2½d. light ultramarine (No. 489) (9)	—
S258	3d. pale violet (No. 490) (9)	—

1946. *Victory.*

S259	2½d. ultramarine (No. 491) (9)	—
S260	3d. violet (No. 492) (9)	—

1948. *Royal Silver Wedding.*

S261	2½d. ultramarine (No. 493) (30)	—
S262	£1 blue (No. 494) (30)	—

1948. *Olympic Games.*

S263	2½d. ultramarine (No. 495) (26)	—
S264	3d. violet (No. 496) (26)	—
S265	6d. bright purple (No. 497) (26)	—
S266	1s. brown (No. 498) (26)	—

1949. *75th Anniv of Universal Postal Union.*

S267	2½d. ultramarine (No. 499) (30)	—
S268	3d. violet (No. 500) (30)	—
S269	6d. bright purple (No. 501) (30)	—
S270	1s. brown (No. 502) (30)	—

QUEEN ELIZABETH II

6 February 1952

Further detailed information on the stamps of Queen Elizabeth II will be found in Volumes 3, 4 and 5 of the Stanley Gibbons *Great Britain Specialised Catalogue*.

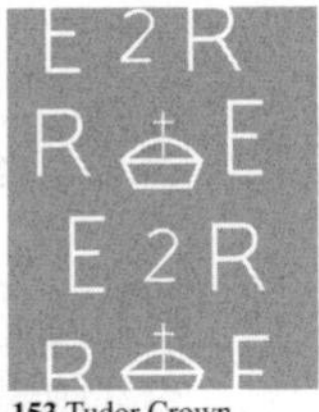

153 Tudor Crown

154

155

156

157

158

159

160

Queen Elizabeth II and National Emblems

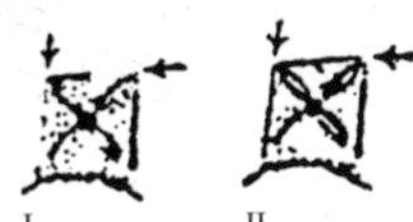

Two types of the 2½d.

Type I:— In the frontal cross of the diadem, the top line is only half the width of the cross.

Type II:— The top line extends to the full width of the cross and there are signs of strengthening in other parts of the diadem.

(Des Enid Marx (T **154**), M. Farrar-Bell (T **155/6**), G. Knipe (T **157**), Mary Adshead (T **158**), E. Dulac (T **159/60**). Portrait by Dorothy Wilding)

1952–54. *W* **153**. P 15×14.

515	**154**	½d. orange-red (31.8.53)	10	15
		Wi. Watermark inverted (3.54)	60	60
516		1d. ultramarine (31.8.53)	20	20
		a. Booklet pane. Three stamps plus three printed labels	35·00	
		Wi. Watermark inverted (3.54)	4·50	2·75
517		1½d. green (5.12.52)	10	20
		a. Watermark sideways (15.10.54)	50	70
		b. Imperf pane*		
		Wi. Watermark inverted (5.53)	60	70
518		2d. red-brown (31.8.53)	20	20
		a. Watermark sideways (8.10.54)	1·25	2·00
		Wi. Watermark inverted (3.54)	25·00	18·00
519	**155**	2½d. carmine-red (Type I) (5.12.52)	15	15
		a. Watermark sideways (15.11.54)	7·00	8·00
		b. Type II (booklets) (5.53)	1·25	1·25
		bWi. Watermark inverted (5.53)	30	75
520		3d. deep lilac (18.1.54)	1·50	90
521	**156**	4d. ultramarine (2.11.53)	3·25	1·25
522	**157**	5d. brown (6.7.53)	75	3·50
523		6d. reddish purple (18.1.54)	4·00	1·00
		a. Imperf three sides (pair)		
524		7d. bright green (18.1.54)	9·50	5·50
525	**158**	8d. magenta (6.7.53)	75	85
526		9d. bronze-green (8.2.54)	23·00	4·75
527		10d. Prussian blue (8.2.54)	18·00	4·75
528		11d. brown-purple (8.2.54)	35·00	15·00
529	**159**	1s. bistre-brown (6.7.53)	80	50
530		1s.3d. green (2.11.53)	4·50	3·25
531	**160**	1s.6d. grey-blue (2.11.53)	14·00	3·75
Set of 17			£100	40·00

See also Nos. 540/56, 561/6, 570/94 and 599/618a.

*BOOKLET ERRORS. This pane of 6 stamps is completely imperf (see No. 540a, etc).

Stamps with *sideways watermark* come from left-side delivery coils and stamps with *inverted watermark* are from booklets.

For stamps as Types **154/5** and **157/60** with face values in decimal currency see Nos. 2031/3, 2258/9 and **MS**2326.

First Day Covers

5.12.52	1½d., 2½d. (*517, 519*)	25·00
6.7.53	5d., 8d., 1s. (*522, 525, 529*)	50·00
31.8.53	½d., 1d., 2d. (*515/16, 518*)	50·00
2.11.53	4d., 1s.3d., 1s.6d. (*521, 530/1*)	£170
18.1.54	3d., 6d., 7d. (*520, 523/4*)	£110
8.2.54	9d., 10d., 11d. (*526/8*)	£225

161

162

163

164

(Des E. Fuller (2½d.), M. Goaman (4d.), E. Dulac (1s.3d.), M. Farrar-Bell (1s.6d.). Portrait (except 1s.3d.) by Dorothy Wilding)

1953 (3 June). *Coronation. W* **153**. P 15×14.

532	**161**	2½d. carmine-red	20	25
533	**162**	4d. ultramarine	1·10	1·90
534	**163**	1s.3d. deep yellow-green	5·00	3·00
535	**164**	1s.6d. deep grey-blue	10·00	4·75
Set of 4			16·00	9·00
First Day Cover				75·00

For a £1 value as Type **163** see Nos. **MS**2147 and 2380.

165 St. Edward's Crown

166 Carrickfergus Castle

167 Caernarvon Castle

168 Edinburgh Castle

169 Windsor Castle

(Des L. Lamb. Portrait by Dorothy Wilding. Recess Waterlow (until 31.12.57) and De La Rue (subsequently))

1955–58. *W* **165**. P 11×12.

No.	Type	Description	Unused	Used
536	**166**	2s.6d. black-brown (23.9.55)	9·00	2·00
		a. De La Rue printing (17.7.58)	30·00	2·50
		Wi. Watermark inverted	†	£2500
537	**167**	5s. rose-carmine (23.9.55)	35·00	4·00
		a. De La Rue printing (30.4.58)	80·00	10·00
538	**168**	10s. ultramarine (1.9.55)	85·00	14·00
		a. De La Rue printing. Dull ultramarine (25.4.58)	£225	22·00
539	**169**	£1 black (1.9.55)	£130	35·00
		a. De La Rue printing (28.4.58)	£350	65·00
Set of 4 (Nos. 536/9)			£225	50·00
Set of 4 (Nos. 536a/9a)			£575	90·00
First Day Cover (538/9)				£800
First Day Cover (536/7)				£600

See also Nos. 595/8a & 759/62.

On 1 January 1958, the contract for printing the high values, T **166** to **169**, was transferred to De La Rue & Co, Ltd. The work of the two printers is very similar, but the following notes will be helpful to those attempting to identify Waterlow and De La Rue stamps of the W **165** issue.

The De La Rue sheets are printed in pairs and have a -| or |-shaped guide-mark at the centre of one side-margin, opposite the middle row of perforations, indicating left and right-hand sheets respectively.

The Waterlow sheets have a small circle (sometimes crossed) instead of a "|-" and this is present in both side-margins opposite the 6th row of stamps, though one is sometimes trimmed off. Short dashes are also present in the perforation gutter between the marginal stamps marking the middle of the four sides and a cross is at the centre of the sheet. The four corners of the sheet have two lines forming a right-angle as trimming marks, but some are usually trimmed off. All these gutter marks and sheet trimming marks are absent in the De La Rue printings. De La Rue used the Waterlow die and no alterations were made to it, so that no difference exists in the design or its size, but the making of new plates at first resulted in slight but measurable variations in the width of the gutters between stamps, particularly the horizontal, as follows:

	Waterlow	De La Rue
Horiz gutters, mm	3.8 to 4.0	3.4 to 3.8

Later D.L.R. plates were however less distinguishable in this respect.

For a short time in 1959 the D.L.R. 2s.6d. appeared with one dot in the bottom margin below the first stamp. It is possible to sort singles with reasonable certainty by general characteristics. The individual lines of the D.L.R. impression are cleaner and devoid of the whiskers of colour of Waterlow's, and the whole impression lighter and softer.

Owing to the closer setting of the horizontal rows the strokes of the perforating comb are closer; this results in the topmost tooth on each side of De La Rue stamps being narrower than the corresponding teeth in Waterlow's which were more than normally broad.

Shades also help. The 2s.6d. D.L.R. is a warmer, more chocolate shade than the blackish brown of Waterlow; the 5s. a lighter red with less carmine than Waterlow's; the 10s. more blue and less ultramarine; the £1 less intense black.

The paper of D.L.R. printings is uniformly white, identical with that of Waterlow printings from February 1957 onwards, but earlier Waterlow printings are on paper which is creamy by comparison.

In this and later issues of T **166/9** the dates of issue given for changes of watermark or paper are those on which supplies were first sent by the Supplies Department to Postmasters.

1955–58. *W* **165**. P 15×14.

No.	Type	Description	Unused	Used
540	**154**	½d. orange-red (booklets 8.55, sheets 12.12.55)	15	15
		a. Part perf pane*	£4000	
		Wi. Watermark inverted (9.55)	20	30
541		1d. ultramarine (19.9.55)	30	15
		a. Booklet pane. Three stamps plus three printed labels	16·00	
		b. *Tête-bêche* (horiz pair)		
		Wi. Watermark inverted (9.55)	65	60
542		1½d. green (booklet 8.55, sheets 11.10.55)	25	30
		a. Watermark sideways (7.3.56)	35	70
		b. *Tête-bêche* (horiz pair)	£2500	
		Wi. Watermark inverted (8.55)	60	60
543		2d. red-brown (6.9.55)	25	35
		aa. Imperf between (vert pair)	£3500	
		a. Watermark sideways (31.7.56)	55	70
		ab. Imperf between (horiz pair)	£3500	
		Wi. Watermark inverted (9.55)	11·00	9·00
543*b*		2d. light red-brown (17.10.56)	20	20
		ba. *Tête-bêche* (horiz pair)	£1800	
		bb. Imperf pane*	£4500	
		bc. Part perf pane*	£4000	
		bWi. Watermark inverted (1.57)	9·00	7·00
		d. Watermark sideways (5.3.57)	8·00	7·00
544	**155**	2½d. carmine-red (Type I) (28.9.55)	20	25
		a. Watermark sideways (Type I) (23.3.56)	1·50	1·75
		b. Type II (booklets 9.55, sheets 1957)	45	45
		ba. *Tête-bêche* (horiz pair)	£2000	
		bb. Imperf pane*	£3500	
		bc. Part perf pane*	£3250	
		bWi. Watermark inverted (9.55)	25	70
545		3d. deep lilac (17.7.56)	25	25
		aa. *Tête-bêche* (horiz pair)	£2000	
		a. Imperf three sides (pair)	£1500	
		b. Watermark sideways (22.11.57)	18·00	17·00
		Wi. Watermark inverted (1.10.57)	1·00	1·00
546	**156**	4d. ultramarine (14.11.55)	1·25	45
547	**157**	5d. brown (21.9.55)	6·00	6·00
548		6d. reddish purple (20.12.55)	4·50	1·25
		aa. Imperf three sides (pair)	£2250	
		a. *Deep claret* (8.5.58)	4·50	1·40
		ab. Imperf three sides (pair)	£2000	
549		7d. bright green (23.4.56)	50·00	10·00
550	**158**	8d. magenta (21.12.55)	7·00	1·25
551		9d. bronze-green (15.12.55)	20·00	2·75
552		10d. Prussian blue (22.9.55)	20·00	2·75
553		11d. brown-purple (28.10.55)	50	1·10
554	**159**	1s. bistre-brown (3.11.55)	22·00	65
555		1s.3d. green (27.3.56)	30·00	1·60
556	**160**	1s.6d. grey-blue (27.3.56)	23·00	1·60
Set of 18			£160	27·00

The dates given for Nos. 540/556 are those on which they were first issued by the Supplies Dept to postmasters.

In December 1956 a completely imperforate sheet of No. 543*b* was noticed by clerks in a Kent post office, one of whom purchased it against P.O. regulations. In view of this irregularity we do not consider it properly issued.

Types of 2½d. In this issue, in 1957, Type II formerly only found in stamps from booklets, began to replace Type I on sheet stamps.

*BOOKLET ERRORS. Those listed as "imperf panes" show one row of perforations either at top or bottom of the booklet pane; those as "part perf panes" have one row of 3 stamps imperf on three sides.

For Nos. 542 and 553 in Presentation Pack, see after No. 586.

170 Scout Badge and "Rolling Hitch"

171 "Scouts coming to Britain"

172 Globe within a Compass

(Des Mary Adshead (2½d.), P. Keely (4d.), W. H. Brown (1s.3d.))

1957 (1 Aug). *World Scout Jubilee Jamboree. W* **165**. P 15×14.

557	**170**	2½d. carmine-red	50	50
558	**171**	4d. ultramarine	75	1·50
559	**172**	1s.3d. green	4·50	4·50
Set of 3			5·00	5·75
First Day Cover				25·00

173

½d. to 1½d., 2½d., 3d. 2d. Graphite-line arrangements (Stamps viewed from back)

(Adapted F. Langfield)

1957 (12 Sept). *46th Inter-Parliamentary Union Conference. W* **165**. P 15×14.

560	**173**	4d. ultramarine	1·00	1·00
First Day Cover				£140

GRAPHITE-LINED ISSUES. These were used in connection with automatic sorting machinery, first introduced experimentally at Southampton. The graphite lines were printed in black on the back, beneath the gum; two lines per stamp, except for the 2d. In November 1959 phosphor bands were introduced (see notes after No. 598).

1957 (19 Nov). *Graphite-lined issue. Two graphite lines on the back, except 2d. value, which has one line. W* **165**. P 15×14.

561	**154**	½d. orange-red	25	25
562		1d. ultramarine	40	40
563		1½d. green	1·20	1·40
		a. Both lines at left	£1200	£450
564		2d. light red-brown	1·60	2·25
		a. Line at left	£650	£225
565	**155**	2½d. carmine-red (Type II)	8·50	7·00
566		3d. deep lilac	80	50
Set of 6			12·00	10·50
First Day Cover				85·00

No. 564a results from a misplacement of the line and horizontal pairs exist showing one stamp without line. No. 563a results from a similar misplacement. See also Nos. 587/94.

176 Welsh Dragon

177 Flag and Games Emblem

178 Welsh Dragon

(Des R. Stone (3d.), W. H. Brown (6d.), P. Keely (1s.3d.))

1958 (18 July). *Sixth British Empire and Commonwealth Games, Cardiff. W* **165**. P 15×14.

567	**176**	3d. deep lilac	20	20
568	**177**	6d. reddish purple	40	45
569	**178**	1s.3d. green	2·25	2·40
Set of 3			2·50	2·75
First Day Cover				75·00

179 Multiple Crowns

1958–65. *W* **179**. P 15×14.

570	**154**	½d. orange-red (25.11.58)	10	10
		a. Watermark sideways (26.5.61)	30	40
		c. Part perf pane*	£3000	
		Wi. Watermark inverted (11.58)	40	40
		k. Chalk-surfaced paper (15.7.63)	2·50	2·75
		kWi. Watermark inverted	2·75	3·00
		l. Booklet pane. No. 570a×4	7·50	
		m. Booklet pane. No. 570k×3 *se-tenant* with 574k	9·00	
		n. Booklet pane. No. 570a×2 *se-tenant* with 574l×2 (1.7.64)	2·25	
571		1d. ultramarine (booklets 11.58, sheets 24.3.59)	10	10
		aa. Imperf (vert pair from coil)		
		a. Watermark sideways (26.5.61)	1·50	1·25
		b. Part perf pane*	£3500	
		c. Imperf pane	£4500	
		Wi. Watermark inverted (11.58)	25	20
		l. Booklet pane. No. 571a×4	10·00	
		m. Booklet pane. No. 571a×2 *se-tenant* with 575a×2 (1d. values at left) (16.8.65)	10·00	
		ma. Ditto. 1d. values at right	11·00	
572		1½d. green (booklets 12.58, sheets 30.8.60)	10	15
		a. Imperf three sides (horiz strip of 3)	£5500	
		b. Watermark sideways (26.5.61)	9·00	5·00
		Wi. Watermark inverted (12.58)	1·50	80
		l. Booklet pane. No. 572b×4	35·00	
573		2d. light red-brown (4.12.58)	10	10
		a. Watermark sideways (3.4.59)	50	1·00
		Wi. Watermark inverted (10.4.61)	£140	70·00
574	**155**	2½d. carmine-red (Type II) (booklets 11.58, sheets 15.9.59)	10	20
		a. Imperf strip of 3		
		b. *Tête-bêche* (horiz pair)	£4250	
		c. Imperf pane*	£3250	
		Wi. Watermark inverted (Type II) (11.58)	4·50	3·00
		d. Watermark sideways (Type I) (10.11.60)	25	40
		da. Imperf strip of 6		
		e. Type I (wmk upright) (4.10.61)	70	70
		k. Chalk-surfaced paper (Type II) (15.7.63)	50	80
		kWi. Do. Watermark inverted (15.7.63)	75	1·25
		l. Watermark sideways (Type II) (1.7.64)	70	1·25
575		3d. deep lilac (booklets 11.58, sheets 8.12.58)	10	20
		a. Watermark sideways (24.10.58)	25	35
		b. Imperf pane*	£3250	
		c. Part perf pane*	£3000	
		d. Phantom "R" (Cyl 41 no dot)	£350	
		Eda. Do. First retouch	20·00	

		Edb. Do. Second retouch	20·00	
		e. Phantom "R" (Cyl 37 no dot)	45·00	
		Eea.Do. Retouch	12·00	
		kWi.Do. Watermark inverted (15.7.63)	75	1·25
		Wi. Watermark inverted (11.58)	25	40
		l. Booklet pane. No. 575a×4 (26.5.61)	3·25	
576	**156**	4d. ultramarine (29.10.58)	45	35
		a. Deep ultramarine†† (28.4.65)	15	15
		ab. Watermark sideways (31.5.65)	70	55
		ac. Imperf pane*	£4000	
		ad. Part perf pane*	£3000	
		al. Booklet pane. No. 576ab×4 (16.8.65)	3·25	
		aWi. Watermark inverted (21.6.65)	60	50
577		4½d. chestnut (9.2.59)	10	25
		Ea. Phantom frame	7·50	
578	**157**	5d. brown (10.11.58)	30	40
579		6d. deep claret (23.12.58)	30	25
		a. Imperf three sides (pair)	£1250	
		b. Imperf (pair)	£1500	
580		7d. brt green (26.11.58)	50	45
581	**158**	8d. magenta (24.2.60)	60	40
582		9d. bronze-green (24.3.59)	60	40
583		10d. Prussian blue (18.11.58)	1·00	50
584	**159**	1s. bistre-brown (30.10.58)	45	30
585		1s.3d. green (17.6.59)	45	30
586	**160**	1s.6d. grey-blue (16.12.58)	4·00	40
Set of 17 (*one of each value*)			8·00	4·25
First Day Cover (577)				£250
*Presentation Pack***			£250	

*BOOKLET ERROR. See note after No. 556.

**This was issued in 1960 and comprises Nos. 542, 553, 570/1 and 573/86. It exists in two forms: (a) inscribed "10s6d" for sale in the U.K.; and (b) inscribed "$1.80" for sale in the U.S.A.

††This "shade" was brought about by making more deeply etched cylinders, resulting in apparent depth of colour in parts of the design. There is no difference in the colour of the ink.

Sideways watermark. The 2d., 2½d., 3d. and 4d. come from coils and the ½d., 1d., 1½d., 2½d., 3d. and 4d. come from booklets. In coil stamps the sideways watermark shows the top of the watermark to the left *as seen from the front of the stamp*. In the *booklet* stamps it comes equally to the left or right.

Nos. 570k and 574k only come from 2s. "Holiday Resort"experimental undated booklets issued in 1963, in which one page contained 1 × 2½d. *se-tenant* with 3×½d. (See No. 570l).

No. 574l comes from coils, and the "Holiday Resort" experimental booklets dated "1964" comprising four panes each containing two of these 2½d. stamps *se-tenant* vertically with two ½d. No. 570a. (See No. 570m).

2½d. imperf. No. 574a comes from a booklet with watermark upright. No. 574da is from a coil with sideways watermark.

No. 574e comes from sheets bearing cylinder number 42 and is also known on vertical delivery coils.

In 1964 No. 575 was printed from cylinder number 70 no dot and dot on an experimental paper which is distinguishable by an additional watermark letter "T" lying on its side, which occurs about four times in the sheet, usually in the side margins, 48,000 sheets were issued.

No. 575 is known imperforate and *tête-bêche*. These came from booklet sheets which were not issued.

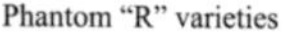
Phantom "R" varieties

179a Nos. 575d and 615a (Cyl 41 no dot) **179b** No. 575Eda

179c No. 575e (Cyl 37 no dot)

179d Phantom Frame variety Nos. 577Ea and 616Eba

3d. An incomplete marginal rule revealed an "R" on cyls 37 and 41 no dot below R. 20/12. It is more noticeable on cyl 41 because of the wider marginal rule. The "R" on cyl 41 was twice retouched, the first being as illustrated here (No. 575Eda) and traces of the "R" can still be seen in the second retouch.

No. 575d is best collected in a block of 4 or 6 with full margins in order to be sure that it is not 615a with phosphor lines removed.

The retouch on cyl 37 is not easily identified: there is no trace of the "R" but the general appearance of that part of the marginal rule is uneven.

4½d. An incomplete marginal rule revealed a right-angled shaped frame-line on cyl 8 no dot below R. 20/12. It occurs on ordinary and phosphor.

WHITER PAPER. On 18 May 1962 the Post Office announced that a whiter paper was being used for the current issue (including Nos. 595/8). This is beyond the scope of this catalogue, but the whiter papers are listed in Vol. 3 of the Stanley Gibbons *Great Britain Specialised Catalogue*.

1958 (24 Nov)–**61**. *Graphite-lined issue. Two graphite lines on the back, except 2d. value, which has one line. W* **179**. P 15×14.

587	**154**	½d. orange-red (15.6.59)	9·00	9·00
		Wi. Watermark inverted (4.8.59)	3·25	4·00
588		1d. ultramarine (18.12.58)	1·50	1·50
		a. Misplaced graphite lines (7.61)*	80	1·25
		Wi. Watermark inverted (4.8.59)	1·25	2·00
589		1½d. green (4.8.59)	90·00	80·00
		Wi. Watermark inverted (4.8.59)	60·00	48·00
590		2d. light red-brown (24.11.58)	9·00	3·50
591	**155**	2½d. carmine-red (Type II) (9.6.59)	10·00	10·00
		Wi. Watermark inverted (21.8.59)	65·00	50·00
592		3d. deep lilac (24.11.58)	50	65
		a. Misplaced graphite lines (5.61)*	£450	£380
		Wi. Watermark inverted (4.8.59)	45	75
593	**156**	4d. ultramarine (29.4.59)	5·50	5·00
		a. Misplaced graphite lines (1961)*	£1800	
594		4½d. chestnut (3.6.59)	6·50	5·00
Set of 8 (*cheapest*)			85·00	70·00

Nos. 587/9 were only issued in booklets or coils (587/8).

*No. 588a (in coils), and Nos. 592a and 593a (both in sheets) result from the use of a residual stock of graphite-lined paper. As the use of graphite lines had ceased, the register of the lines in relation to the stamps was of no importance and numerous misplacements occurred - two lines close together, one line only, etc. No. 588a refers to two lines at left or right; No. 592a refers to stamps with two lines only at left and both clear of the perforations and No. 593a to stamps with two lines at left (with left line down perforations) and traces of a third line down the opposite perforations.

(Recess D.L.R. (until 31.12.62), then B.W.)

1959–68. *W* **179**. P 11×12.

No.	Type	Description	Unused	Used
595	**166**	2s.6d. black-brown (22.7.59)	10·00	75
		Wi. Watermark inverted	£1500	
		a. B.W. printing (1.7.63)	35	40
		aWi. Watermark inverted	£1750	£175
		k. Chalk-surfaced paper (30.5.68)	50	1·50
596	**167**	5s. scarlet-vermilion (15.6.59)	55·00	2·00
		Wi. Watermark inverted	£2750	£275
		a. B.W. ptg. *Red* (*shades*) (3.9.63)	1·20	50
		ab. Printed on the gummed side	£800	
		aWi. Watermark inverted	£275	75·00
597	**168**	10s. blue (21.7.59)	55·00	5·00
		a. B.W. ptg. *Bright ultramarine* (16.10.63)	4·50	4·50
		aWi. Watermark inverted	–	£1500
598	**169**	£1 black (23.6.59)	£120	12·00
		Wi. Watermark inverted	–	£1750
		a. B.W. printing (14.11.63)	11·00	8·00
		aWi. Watermark inverted	£7000	£2500
Set of 4 (*Nos.* 595/8)			£195	17·00
Set of 4 (*Nos.* 595a/8a)			15·00	11·00
Presentation Pack (1960)*			£1100	

The B.W. printings have a marginal Plate Number. They are generally more deeply engraved than the D.L.R. showing more of the Diadem detail and heavier lines on Her Majesty's face. The vertical perf is 11.9 to 12 against D.L.R. 11.8.

*This exists in three forms: (a) inscribed "$6.50" for sale in the U.S.A.; (b) without price for sale in the U.K.; (c) inscribed "£1 18s" for sale in the U.K.

See also Nos. 759/62.

PHOSPHOR BAND ISSUES. These are printed on the front and are wider than graphite lines. They are not easy to see but show as broad vertical bands at certain angles to the light.

Values representing the rate for printed papers (and when this was abolished in 1968 for second issue class mail) have one band and others two, three or four bands as stated, according to the size and format.

In the small size stamps the bands are on each side with the single band at left (*except where otherwise stated*). In the large size commemorative stamps the single band may be at left, centre or right, varying in different designs. The bands are vertical on both horizontal and vertical designs *except where otherwise stated.*

The phosphor was originally applied typographically but later usually by photogravure and sometimes using flexography, a typographical process using rubber cylinders.

Three different types of phosphor have been used, distinguishable by the colour emitted under an ultra-violet lamp, the first being green, then blue and now violet. Different sized bands are also known. All these are fully listed in Vol. 3 of the Stanley Gibbons *Great Britain Specialised Catalogue*.

Varieties. Misplaced and missing phosphor bands are known but such varieties are beyond the scope of this Catalogue.

1959 (18 Nov). *Phosphor-Graphite issue. Two phosphor bands on front and two graphite lines on back, except 2d. value, which has one band on front and one line on back. (a) W* **165**. P 15×14.

No.	Type	Description	Unused	Used
599	**154**	½d. orange-red	4·00	3·75
600		1d. ultramarine	11·00	11·00
601		1½d. green	4·00	4·00

Examples of the 2½d., No. 606, exist showing watermark W **165** in error. It is believed that phosphor-graphite stamps of this value with this watermark were not used by the public for postal purposes.

The Presentation Pack was issued in 1960 and comprises two each of Nos. 599/609. It exists in two forms: (a) inscribed "3s 8d" for sale in the U.K. and (b) inscribed "50c" for sale in the U.S.A.

(b) W **179**.

No.	Type	Description	Unused	Used
605	**154**	2d. light red-brown (1 band)	5·00	4·25
		a. Error. W **165**	£180	£125
606	**155**	2½d. carmine-red (Type II)	22·00	18·00
607		3d. deep lilac	10·00	8·00
608	**156**	4d. ultramarine	20·00	16·00
609		4½d. chestnut	30·00	20·00
Set of 8			85·00	70·00
Presentation Pack			£300	

1960 (22 June)–**67**. *Phosphor issue. Two phosphor bands on front, except where otherwise stated. W* **179**. P 15×14.

No.	Type	Description	Unused	Used
610	**154**	½d. orange-red	10	15
		a. Watermark sideways (14.7.61)	10·00	10·00
		Wi. Watermark inverted (14.8.60)	90	90
		l. Booklet pane. No. 610a×4	40·00	
611		1d. ultramarine	10	10
		a. Watermark sideways (14.7.61)	90	90
		Wi. Watermark inverted (14.8.60)	25	30
		l. Booklet pane. No. 611a×4	9·00	
		m. Booklet pane. No. 611a×2 *se-tenant* with 615d×2† (16.8.65)	15·00	
		ma. Booklet pane. No. 611a×2 *se-tenant* with 615dEa×2 (16.8.65)	15·00	
		n. Booklet pane. No. 611a×2 *se-tenant* with 615b×2†† (11.67)	8·00	
612		1½d. green	15	15
		a. Watermark sideways (14.7.61)	10·00	10·00
		Wi. Watermark inverted (14.8.60)	12·00	9·50
		l. Booklet pane. No. 612a×4	42·00	
613		2d. light red-brown (1 band)	16·00	18·00
613*a*		2d. light red-brown (2 bands) (4.10.61).	10	15
		aa. Imperf three sides***		
		ab. Watermark sideways (6.4.67)	30	60
614	**155**	2½d. carmine-red (Type II) (2 bands)*	20	30
		Wi. Watermark inverted (14.8.60)	£170	£140
614*a*		2½d. carmine-red (Type II) (1 band) (4.10.61)	60	75
		aWi. Watermark inverted (3.62)	40·00	38·00
614*b*		2½d. carmine-red (Type I) (1 band) (4.10.61)	45·00	40·00
615		3d. deep lilac (2 bands)	60	55
		a. Phantom "R" (Cyl 41 no dot)	40·00	
		Wi. Watermark inverted (14.8.60)	50	90
		b. Watermark sideways (14.7.61)	1·75	1·75
		l. Booklet pane. No. 615b×4	20·00	
615*c*		3d. deep lilac (1 band at right) (29.4.65)	60	55
		cEa. Band at left	60	70
		cWi. Watermark inverted (band at right) (2.67)	7·00	7·00
		cWia. Watermark inverted (band at left) (2.67)	65·00	60·00
		d. Watermark sideways (band at right) (16.8.65)	5·50	5·00
		dEa. Watermark sideways (band at left)	5·50	5·00
		e. One centre band (8.12.66)	40	45
		eWi. Watermark inverted (8.67)	2·25	2·25
		ea. Wmk sideways (19.6.67)	70	50
616	**156**	4d. ultramarine	3·50	3·50
		a. Deep ultramarine (28.4.65)	25	25
		aa. Part perf pane	£4000	
		ab. Wmk sideways	35	50
		aWi. Watermark inverted (21.6.65)	40	40
		al. Booklet pane. No. 616ab×4	2·50	
616*b*		4½d. chestnut (13.9.61)	25	30
		Eba. Phantom frame	15·00	
616*c*	**157**	5d. brown (9.6.67)	25	35
617		6d. purple	30	30
617*a*		7d. bright green (15.2.67)	55	50
617*b*	**158**	8d. magenta (28.6.67)	40	45
617*c*		9d. bronze-green (29.12.66)	60	55
617*d*		10d. Prussian blue (30.12.66)	70	60
617*e*	**159**	1s. bistre-brown (28.6.67)	40	35
618		1s.3d. green	1·90	2·50
618*a*	**160**	1s.6d. grey-blue (12.12.66)	2·00	2·00
Set of 17 (*one of each value*)			7·50	8·00

The automatic facing equipment was brought into use on 6 July 1960 but the phosphor stamps may have been released a few days earlier.

The stamps with watermark sideways are from booklets except Nos. 613ab and 615ea which are from coils. No. 616ab comes from both booklets and coils.

No. 615a. See footnote after No. 586.

*No. 614 with two bands on the creamy paper was originally from cylinder 50 dot and no dot. When the change in postal rates took place in 1965 it was reissued from cylinder 57 dot and no dot on the whiter paper. Some of these latter were also released in error in districts of S.E. London in September 1964. The shade of the reissue is slightly more carmine.

***This comes from the bottom row of a sheet which is imperf at bottom and both sides.

†Booklet pane No. 611m shows the 1d. stamps at left and No. 611ma the 1d. stamps at right.

††Booklet pane No. 611n comes from 2s. booklets of January and March 1968. The two bands on the 3d. stamp were intentional because of the technical difficulties in producing one band and two band stamps *se-tenant*.

The Phosphor-Graphite stamps had the phosphor applied by typography but the Phosphor issue can be divided into those with the phosphor applied typographically and others where it was applied by photogravure. Moreover the photogravure form can be further divided into those which phosphoresce green and others which phosphoresce blue under ultra-violet light. From

1965 violet phosphorescence was introduced in place of the blue. All these are fully listed in Vol. 3 of the Stanley Gibbons *Great Britain Specialised Catalogue*.

Unlike previous one-banded phosphor stamps, No. 615c has a broad band extending over two stamps so that alternate stamps have the band at left or right (same prices either way). No. 615cWi comes from the 10s phosphor booklet of February 1967 and No. 615eWi comes from the 10s. phosphor booklets of August 1967 and February 1968.

Nos. 615a (Phantom "R") and 615Eba (Phantom frame), see illustrations following No. 586.

180 Postboy of 1660

181 Posthorn of 1660

(Des R. Stone (3d.), Faith Jaques (1s.3d.))

1960 (7 July). *Tercentenary of Establishment of General Letter Office. W* **179** *(sideways on* 1s.3d.). P 15×14 (3d.) or 14×15 (1s.3d.).

619	**180**	3d. deep lilac	50	50
620	**181**	1s.3d. green	3·75	4·25
Set of 2			3·75	4·25
First Day Cover				55·00

182 Conference Emblem

(Des R. Stone (emblem, P. Rahikainen))

1960 (19 Sept). *First Anniversary of European Postal and Telecommunications Conference. Chalk-surfaced paper. W* **179**. P 15×14.

621	**182**	6d. bronze-green and purple	1·50	50
622		1s.6d. brown and blue	8·50	5·00
Set of 2			9·75	5·50
First Day Cover				55·00

SCREENS. Up to this point all photogravure stamps were printed in a 200 screen (200 dots per linear inch), but all later commemorative stamps are a finer 250 screen. Exceptionally No. 622 has a 200 screen for the portrait and a 250 screen for the background.

184 "Growth of Savings"

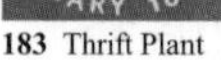

183 Thrift Plant

185 Thrift Plant

(Des P. Gauld (2½d.), M. Goaman (others))

1961 (28 Aug). *Centenary of Post Office Savings Bank. Chalk-surfaced paper. W* **179** *(sideways on* 2½d.) P 14×15 (2½d.) or 15×14 (others).

A. "Timson" Machine

623A	**183**	2½d. black and red	25	25
		a. Black omitted	£16000	
624A	**184**	3d. orange-brown and violet	20	20
		a. Orange-brown omitted	£170	
		Eb. Perf through side sheet margin	28·00	30·00
625A	**185**	1s.6d. red and blue	2·50	2·25
Set of 3			2·75	2·50
First Day Cover				65·00

B. "Thrissell" Machine

623B	**183**	2½d. black and red	2·25	2·25
624B	**184**	3d. orange-brown and violet	40	40
		a. Orange-brown omitted	£850	

2½d. TIMSON. Cyls 1E-1F. Deeply shaded portrait (brownish black).

2½d. THRISSELL. Cyls 1D-1B or 1D (dot)-1B (dot). Lighter portrait (grey-black).

3d. TIMSON. Cyls 3D-3E. Clear, well-defined portrait with deep shadows and bright highlights.

3d. THRISSELL. Cyls 3C-3B or 3C (dot)-3B (dot). Dull portrait, lacking in contrast.

Sheet marginal examples *without* single extension perf hole on the short side of the stamp are always "Timson", as are those with large punch-hole *not* coincident with printed three-sided box guide mark.

The 3d. "Timson" perforated completely through the right hand side margin comes from a relatively small part of the printing perforated on a sheet-fed machine.

Normally the "Timsons" were perforated in the reel, with three large punch-holes in both long margins and the perforations completely through both short margins. Only one punch-hole coincides with the guide-mark.

The "Thrissells" have one large punch-hole in one long margin, coinciding with guide-mark and one short margin imperf (except sometimes for encroachments).

186 C.E.P.T. Emblem

187 Doves and Emblem

188 Doves and Emblem

(Des M. Goaman (doves T. Kurpershoek))

1961 (18 Sept). *European Postal and Telecommunications (C.E.P.T.) Conference, Torquay. Chalk-surfaced paper. W* **179**. P 15×14.

626	**186**	2d. orange, pink and brown	15	20
		a. Orange omitted	£12000	
627	**187**	4d. buff, mauve and ultramarine	15	25
628	**188**	10d. turquoise, pale green and Prussian blue	15	80
		a. Pale green omitted	£9000	
		b. Turquoise omitted	£2750	
Set of 3			40	1·10
First Day Cover				6·00

189 Hammer Beam Roof, Westminster Hall

190 Palace of Westminster

(Des Faith Jaques)

1961 (25 Sept). *Seventh Commonwealth Parliamentary Conference. Chalk-surfaced paper. W* **179** *(sideways on* 1s.3d.) P 15×14 (6d.) or 14×15 (1s.3d.).

629	**189**	6d. purple and gold	25	25
		a. Gold omitted	£800	
630	**190**	1s.3d. green and blue	2·50	2·75
		a. Blue (Queen's head) omitted	£12000	
		b. Green omitted		
Set of 2			2·75	3·00
First Day Cover				30·00

191 "Units of Productivity"

192 "National Productivity"

193 "Unified Productivity"

(Des D. Gentleman)

1962 (14 Nov). *National Productivity Year. Chalk-surfaced paper. W* **179** *(inverted on* 2½d. *and* 3d.). P 15×14.

631	**191**	2½d. myrtle-green and carmine-red *(shades)*	20	20
		Ea. Blackish olive and carmine-red	25	15
		p. One phosphor band. *Blackish olive and carmine-red*	60	50
632	**192**	3d. light blue and violet *(shades)*	25	25
		a. Light blue (Queen's head) omitted	£1200	
		p. Three phosphor bands	1·50	80
633	**193**	1s.3d. carmine, light blue and deep green	1·50	2·00
		a. Light blue (Queen's head) omitted	£6500	
		p. Three phosphor bands	35·00	22·00
Set of 3 (Ordinary)			1·75	1·90
Set of 3 (Phosphor)			30·00	22·00
First Day Cover (Ordinary)				48·00
First Day Cover (Phosphor)				£150

194 Campaign Emblem and Family

195 Children of Three Races

(Des M. Goaman)

1963 (21 Mar). *Freedom from Hunger. Chalk-surfaced paper. W* **179** *(inverted)*. P 15×14.

634	**194**	2½d. crimson and pink	25	10
		p. One phosphor band	3·00	1·25
635	**195**	1s.3d. bistre-brown and yellow	1·75	1·90
		p. Three phosphor bands	30·00	23·00
Set of 2 (Ordinary)			1·75	2·00
Set of 2 (Phosphor)			30·00	24·00
First Day Cover (Ordinary)				32·00
First Day Cover (Phosphor)				52·00

196 "Paris Conference"

(Des R. Stone)

1963 (7 May). *Paris Postal Conference Centenary. Chalk-surfaced paper. W* **179** *(inverted)*. P 15×14.

636	**196**	6d. green and mauve	30	50
		a. Green omitted	£2700	
		p. Three phosphor bands	6·00	7·00
First Day Cover (Ordinary)				16·00
First Day Cover (Phosphor)				37·00

197 Posy of Flowers

198 Woodland Life

(Des S. Scott (3d.), M. Goaman (4½d.))

1963 (16 May). *National Nature Week. Chalk-surfaced paper. W* **179**. P 15×14.

637	**197**	3d. yellow, green, brown and black	15	15
		p. Three phosphor bands	55	60
638	**198**	4½d. black, blue, yellow, magenta and brown-red	25	35
		p. Three phosphor bands	2·75	3·00
Set of 2 (Ordinary)			30	50
Set of 2 (Phosphor)			3·25	3·50
First Day Cover (Ordinary)				22·00
First Day Cover (Phosphor)				40·00

Special First Day of Issue Postmark

	Ordinary	*Phosphor*
London E.C. (Type A)	24·00	30·00

This postmark was used on First Day Covers serviced by the Philatelic Bureau.

199 Rescue at Sea

200 19th-century Lifeboat

201 Lifeboatmen

(Des D. Gentleman)

1963 (31 May). *Ninth International Lifeboat Conference, Edinburgh. Chalk-surfaced paper. W* **179**. P 15×14.

639	**199**	2½d. blue, black and red	25	25
		p. One phosphor band	50	60
640	**200**	4d. red, yellow, brown, black and blue	50	50
		p. Three phosphor bands	50	60
641	**201**	1s.6d. sepia, yellow and grey-blue	3·00	3·25
		p. Three phosphor bands	48·00	28·00
Set of 3 (Ordinary)			3·25	3·50
Set of 3 (Phosphor)			48·00	28·00
First Day Cover (Ordinary)				35·00
First Day Cover (Phosphor)				55·00

Special First Day of Issue Postmark

	Ordinary	Phosphor
London	65·00	80·00

This postmark was used on First Day Covers serviced by the Philatelic Bureau.

202 Red Cross

203

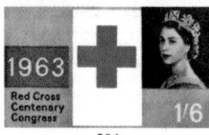

204

(Des H. Bartram)

1963 (15 Aug). *Red Cross Centenary Congress. Chalk-surfaced paper. W* **179**. P 15×14.

642	**202**	3d. red and deep lilac	25	25
		a. Red omitted	£6500	
		p. Three phosphor bands	1·10	1·00
		pa. Red omitted	£12000	
643	**203**	1s.3d. red, blue and grey	3·00	3·00
		p. Three phosphor bands	35·00	27·00
644	**204**	1s.6d. red, blue and bistre	3·00	3·00
		p. Three phosphor bands	35·00	27·00
Set of 3 (*Ordinary*)			5·00	5·75
Set of 3 (*Phosphor*)			65·00	55·00
First Day Cover (*Ordinary*)				40·00
First Day Cover (*Phosphor*)				90·00

Special First Day of Issue Postmark

	Ordinary	Phosphor
London E.C	75·00	£100

This postmark was used on First Day Covers serviced by the Philatelic Bureau.

205 Commonwealth Cable

(Des P. Gauld)

1963 (3 Dec). *Opening of COMPAC (Trans-Pacific Telephone Cable). Chalk-surfaced paper. W* **179**. P 15×14.

645	**205**	1s.6d. blue and black	2·75	2·50
		a. Black omitted	£4000	
		p. Three phosphor bands	16·00	15·50
First Day Cover (*Ordinary*)				28·00
First Day Cover (*Phosphor*)				40·00

Special First Day of Issue Postmark

	Ordinary	Phosphor
Philatelic Bureau, London E.C.1 (Type A)	45·00	50·00

PRESENTATION PACKS. Special Packs comprising slip-in cards with printed commemorative inscriptions and descriptive notes on the back and with protective covering, were introduced in 1964 with the Shakespeare issue. These are listed and priced. Issues of 1968-69 (British Paintings to the Prince of Wales Investiture) were also issued in packs with text in German for sale through the Post Office's German Agency and these are also quoted. Subsequently, however, the packs sold in Germany were identical with the normal English version with the addition of a separate printed insert card with German text. These, as also English packs with Japanese and Dutch printed cards for sale in Japan and the Netherlands respectively, are listed in Vols. 3 and 5 of the Stanley Gibbons *Great Britain Specialised Catalogue*.

206 Puck and Bottom (*A Midsummer Night's Dream*)

207 Feste (*Twelfth Night*)

208 Balcony Scene (*Romeo and Juliet*)

209 "Eve of Agincourt" (*Henry V*)

210 Hamlet contemplating Yorick's Skull (*Hamlet*) and Queen Elizabeth II

(Des D. Gentleman. Photo Harrison & Sons (3d., 6d., 1s.3d., 1s.6d.). Des C. and R. Ironside. Recess B.W. (2s.6d.))

1964 (23 Apr). *Shakespeare Festival. Chalk-surfaced paper. W* **179**. P 11×12 (2s.6d.) or 15×14 (others).

646	**206**	3d. yellow-bistre, black and deep violet-blue (*shades*)	15	15
		p. Three phosphor bands	25	30
647	**207**	6d. yellow, orange, black and yellow-olive (*shades*)	30	30
		p. Three phosphor bands	75	1·00
648	**208**	1s.3d. cerise, blue-green, black and sepia (*shades*)	75	1·00
		Wi. Watermark inverted	£600	
		p. Three phosphor bands	4·00	6·50
		pWi. Watermark inverted	£120	
649	**209**	1s.6d. violet, turquoise, black and blue (*shades*)	1·00	85
		Wi. Watermark inverted		£1300
		p. Three phosphor bands	8·00	8·00
650	**210**	2s.6d. deep slate-purple (*shades*)	2·75	2·75
		Wi. Watermark inverted	£400	
Set of 5 (*Ordinary*)			4·50	4·50
Set of 4 (*Phosphor*)			12·00	14·00
First Day Cover (*Ordinary*)				12·00
First Day Cover (*Phosphor*)				17·00
Presentation Pack (*Ordinary*)			22·00	

The 3d. is known with yellow-bistre missing in the top two-thirds of the figures of Puck and Bottom. This occurred in the top row only of a sheet.

Special First Day of Issue Postmark

	Ordinary	Phosphor
Stratford-upon-Avon, Warwicks	15·00	22·00

This postmark was used on First Day Covers serviced by the Philatelic Bureau, as well as on covers posted at Stratford P.O.

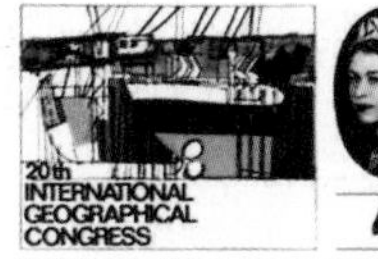

211 Flats near Richmond Park ("Urban Development")

212 Shipbuilding Yards, Belfast ("Industrial Activity")

213 Beddgelert Forest Park, Snowdonia ("Forestry")

214 Nuclear Reactor, Dounreay ("Technological Development")

(Des D. Bailey)

1964 (1 July). *20th International Geographical Congress, London. Chalk-surfaced paper. W* **179**. P 15×14.

651	**211**	2½d. black, olive-yellow, olive-grey and turquoise-blue	10	10
		p. One phosphor band	40	50
652	**212**	4d. orange-brown, red-brown, rose, black and violet	30	30
		a. Violet (face value) omitted	£180	
		c. Violet and red-brown (dock walls) omitted	£300	
		Wi. Watermark inverted	£600	
		p. Three phosphor bands	1·25	1·25
653	**213**	8d. yellow-brown, emerald, green and black	75	85
		a. Green (lawn) omitted	£9000	
		Wi. Watermark inverted	£700	
		p. Three phosphor bands	2·50	2·75
654	**214**	1s.6d. yellow-brown, pale pink, black and brown	3·50	3·50
		Wi. Watermark inverted	22·00	
		p. Three phosphor bands	28·00	22·00
Set of 4 (*Ordinary*)			4·50	4·50
Set of 4 (*Phosphor*)			30·00	24·00
First Day Cover (*Ordinary*)				22·00
First Day Cover (*Phosphor*)				40·00
Presentation Pack (*Ordinary*)			£160	

A used example of the 4d. is known with the red-brown omitted.

Special First Day of Issue Postmark

	Ordinary	Phosphor
G.P.O. Philatelic Bureau, London E.C.1 (Type B)	27·00	35·00

215 Spring Gentian

216 Dog Rose

217 Honeysuckle

218 Fringed Water Lily

(Des M. and Sylvia Goaman)

1964 (5 Aug). *Tenth International Botanical Congress, Edinburgh. Chalk-surfaced paper. W* **179**. P 15×14.

655	**215**	3d. violet, blue and sage-green	25	25
		a. Blue omitted	£5250	
		b. Sage-green omitted	£8000	
		p. Three phosphor bands	40	40
656	**216**	6d. apple-green, rose, scarlet and green	50	50
		Wi. Watermark inverted		
		p. Three phosphor bands	2·50	2·75
657	**217**	9d. lemon, green, lake and rose-red	1·75	2·25
		a. Green (leaves) omitted	£8000	
		Wi. Watermark inverted	42·00	
		p. Three phosphor bands	4·50	4·00
658	**218**	1s.3d. yellow, emerald, reddish violet and grey-green	2·50	2·50
		a. Yellow (flowers) omitted	£20000	
		Wi. Watermark inverted	£700	
		p. Three phosphor bands	25·00	20·00
Set of 4 (*Ordinary*)			4·50	4·50
Set of 4 (*Phosphor*)			30·00	24·00
First Day Cover (*Ordinary*)				24·00
First Day Cover (*Phosphor*)				40·00
Presentation Pack (*Ordinary*)			£160	

Special First Day of Issue Postmark

	Ordinary	Phosphor
G.P.O. Philatelic Bureau, London E.C.1 (Type B).	28·00	45·00

219 Forth Road Bridge

220 Forth Road and Railway Bridges

(Des A. Restall)

1964 (4 Sept). *Opening of Forth Road Bridge. Chalk-surfaced paper. W* **179**. P 15×14.

659	**219**	3d. black, blue and reddish violet	10	10
		p. Three phosphor bands	1·00	1·50
660	**220**	6d. blackish lilac, light blue and carmine-red	40	40
		a. Light blue omitted	£2700	
		Wi. Watermark inverted	2·00	
		p. Three phosphor bands	4·50	4·75
		pWi. Watermark inverted	£750	
Set of 2 (*Ordinary*)			50	50
Set of 2 (*Phosphor*)			5·00	5·75
First Day Cover (*Ordinary*)				7·00
First Day Cover (*Phosphor*)				18·00
Presentation Pack (*Ordinary*)			£400	

Special First Day of Issue Postmarks

	Ordinary	Phosphor
G.P.O. Philatelic Bureau, London E.C.1 (Type B)	20·00	28·00
North Queensferry, Fife	40·00	£130
South Queensferry, West Lothian	32·00	95·00

The Queensferry postmarks were applied to First Day Covers sent to a temporary Philatelic Bureau at Edinburgh.

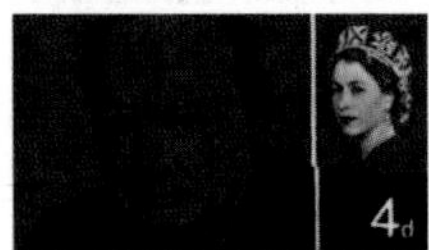

221 Sir Winston Churchill

(Des D. Gentleman and Rosalind Dease, from photograph by Karsh)

1965 (8 July). *Churchill Commemoration. Chalk-surfaced paper. W* **179**. P 15×14.

I. "REMBRANDT" Machine

661	**221**	4d. black and olive-brown	10	10
		Wi. Watermark inverted	2·25	
		p. Three phosphor bands	25	25

II. "TIMSON" Machine

661*a*	**221**	4d. black and olive-brown	35	35

III. "L. & M. 4". Machine

662*a*	–	1s.3d. black and grey	30	40
		Wi. Watermark inverted	75·00	
		p. Three phosphor bands	2·50	3·00
Set of 2 (*Ordinary*)			40	50
Set of 2 (*Phosphor*)			2·75	3·25
First Day Cover (*Ordinary*)				7·00
First Day Cover (*Phosphor*)				9·00
Presentation Pack (*Ordinary*)			65·00	

The 1s.3d. shows a closer view of Churchill's head.

Two examples of the 4d. value exist with the Queen's head omitted, one due to something adhering to the cylinder and the other due to a paper fold. The stamp also exists with Churchill's head omitted, also due to a paper fold.

4d. REMBRANDT, Cyls 1A-1B dot and no dot. Lack of shading detail on Churchill's portrait. Queen's portrait appears dull and coarse. This is a rotary machine which is sheet-fed.

4d. TIMSON. Cyls 5A-6B no dot. More detail on Churchill's portrait –furrow on forehead, his left eyebrow fully drawn and more shading on cheek. Queen's portrait lighter and sharper. This is a reel-fed two-colour 12-in. wide rotary machine and the differences in impressions are due to the greater pressure applied by this machine.

1s.3d. Cyls 1A-1B no dot. The "Linotype and Machinery No. 4" machine is an ordinary sheet-fed rotary press machine. Besides being used for printing the 1s.3d. stamps it was also employed for overprinting the phosphor bands on both values.

Special First Day of Issue Postmark

	Ordinary	Phosphor
G.P.O. Philatelic Bureau, London E.C.1 (Type B)	10·00	16·00

A First Day of Issue handstamp was provided at Bladon, Oxford, for this issue.

222 Simon de Montfort's Seal

223 Parliament Buildings (after engraving by Hollar, 1647)

(Des S. Black (6d.), R. Guyatt (2s.6d.))

1965 (19 July). *700th Anniversary of Simon de Montfort's Parliament. Chalk-surfaced paper. W* **179**. P 15×14.

663	**222**	6d. olive-green	20	20
		p. Three phosphor bands	60	1·00
664	**223**	2s.6d. black, grey and pale drab	80	1·50
		Wi. Watermark inverted	20·00	
Set of 2 (*Ordinary*)			1·00	1·25
First Day Cover (*Ordinary*)				15·00
First Day Cover (*Phosphor*)				26·00
Presentation Pack (*Ordinary*)			65·00	

Special First Day of Issue Postmark

	Ordinary
G.P.O. Philatelic Bureau, London E.C.1 (Type B)	15·00

A First Day of Issue handstamp was provided at Evesham, Worcs, for this issue.

224 Bandsmen and Banner

225 Three Salvationists

(Des M. Farrar-Bell (3d.), G. Trenaman (1s.6d.))

1965 (9 Aug). *Salvation Army Centenary. Chalk-surfaced paper. W* **179**. P 15×14.

665	**224**	3d. indigo, grey-blue, cerise, yellow and brown	25	25
		p. One phosphor band	25	40
666	**225**	1s.6d. red, blue, yellow and brown	1·00	1·50
		p. Three phosphor bands	2·50	2·75
Set of 2 (*Ordinary*)			1·00	1·50
Set of 2 (*Phosphor*)			2·50	3·00
First Day Cover (*Ordinary*)				23·00
First Day Cover (*Phosphor*)				33·00

The Philatelic Bureau did not provide First Day Cover services for Nos. 665/70.

226 Lister's Carbolic Spray

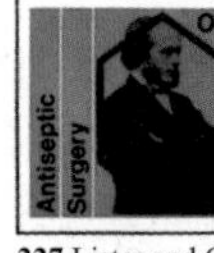

227 Lister and Chemical Symbols

(Des P. Gauld (4d.), F. Ariss (1s.))

1965 (1 Sept). *Centenary of Joseph Lister's Discovery of Antiseptic Surgery. Chalk-surfaced paper. W* **179**. P 15×14.

667	**226**	4d. indigo, brown-red and grey-black	25	15
		a. Brown-red (tube) omitted	£300	
		b. Indigo omitted	£4000	
		p. Three phosphor bands	25	25
		pa. Brown-red (tube) omitted	£2700	
668	**227**	1s. black, purple and new blue	1·00	1·10
		Wi. Watermark inverted	£325	
		p. Three phosphor bands	2·00	2·50
		pWi. Watermark inverted		
Set of 2 (*Ordinary*)			1·00	1·25
Set of 2 (*Phosphor*)			2·25	2·50
First Day Cover (*Ordinary*)				12·00
First Day Cover (*Phosphor*)				15·00

228 Trinidad Carnival Dancers

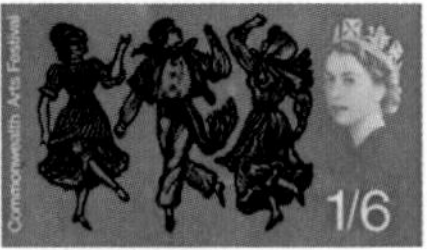

229 Canadian Folk-dancers

(Des D. Gentleman and Rosalind Dease)

1965 (1 Sept). *Commonwealth Arts Festival. Chalk-surfaced paper. W* **179**. P 15×14.

669	**228**	6d. black and orange	20	20
		p. Three phosphor bands	30	50
670	**229**	1s.6d. black and light reddish violet	80	1·10
		p. Three phosphor bands	2·50	3·50
Set of 2 (*Ordinary*)			1·00	1·25
Set of 2 (*Phosphor*)			2·75	3·50
First Day Cover (*Ordinary*)				16·50
First Day Cover (*Phosphor*)				22·00

230 Flight of Supermarine Spitfires

231 Pilot in Hawker Hurricane Mk I

232 Wing-tips of Supermarine Spitfire and Messerschmitt Bf 109

233 Supermarine Spitfires attacking Heinkel HE-111H Bomber

234 Supermarine Spitfire attacking Junkers Ju 87B "Stuka" Dive-bomber

235 Hawker Hurricanes Mk I over Wreck of Dornier Do-17Z Bomber

236 Anti-aircraft Artillery in Action

237 Air-battle over St. Paul's Cathedral

(Des D. Gentleman and Rosalind Dease (4d.×6 and 1s.3d.), A. Restall (9d.))

1965 (13 Sept). *25th Anniv of Battle of Britain. Chalk-surfaced paper. W* **179**. P 15×14.

671	**230**	4d. yellow-olive and black	1·00	1·00
		a. Block of 6. Nos. 671/6	6·00	10·00
		p. Three phosphor bands	1·25	1·50
		pa. Block of 6. Nos. 671p/6p	10·00	15·00
672	**231**	4d. yellow-olive, olive-grey and black	1·00	1·00
		p. Three phosphor bands	1·25	1·50
673	**232**	4d. red, new blue, yellow-olive, olive-grey and black	1·00	1·00
		p. Three phosphor bands	1·25	1·50
674	**233**	4d. olive-grey, yellow-olive and black	1·00	1·00
		p. Three phosphor bands	1·25	1·50
675	**234**	4d. olive-grey, yellow-olive and black	1·00	1·00
		p. Three phosphor bands	1·25	1·50
676	**235**	4d. olive-grey, yellow-olive, new blue and black	1·00	1·00
		a. New blue omitted	†	£4000
		p. Three phosphor bands	1·25	1·50
677	**236**	9d. bluish violet, orange and slate purple	1·75	2·00
		Wi. Watermark inverted	50·00	
		p. Three phosphor bands	1·75	2·50
678	**237**	1s.3d. lt grey, dp grey, black, lt blue and bright blue	1·75	2·00
		Wi. Watermark inverted	25·00	
		p. Three phosphor bands	1·75	2·50
		pWi. Watermark inverted	3·00	
Set of 8 (*Ordinary*)			8·50	8·50
Set of 8 (*Phosphor*)			10·00	12·50
First Day Cover (*Ordinary*)				25·00
First Day Cover (*Phosphor*)				28·00
Presentation Pack (*Ordinary*)			65·00	

Nos. 671/6 were issued together *se-tenant* in blocks of 6 (3×2) within the sheet. No. 676a is only known commercially used on cover from Truro.

Special First Day of Issue Postmark

	Ordinary	*Phosphor*
G.P.O. Philatelic Bureau, London E.C.1 (Type C) ...	25·00	28·00

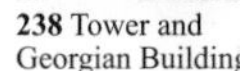

238 Tower and Georgian Buildings

239 Tower and "Nash" Terrace, Regent's Park

(Des C. Abbott)

1965 (8 Oct). *Opening of Post Office Tower. Chalk-surfaced paper. W* **179** (*sideways on* 3d.). P 14×15 (3d.) or 15×14 (1s.3d.).

679	**238**	3d. olive-yellow, new blue and bronze-green	15	15
		a. Olive-yellow (Tower) omitted	£2000	£750
		p. One phosphor band at right	15	15
		pEa. Band at left	15	15
		pEb. Horiz pair. Nos. 679p/pEa	30	50
680	**239**	1s.3d. bronze-green, yellow-green and blue	30	45
		Wi. Watermark inverted	45·00	
		p. Three phosphor bands	30	50
		pWi. Watermark inverted	50·00	
Set of 2 (*Ordinary*)			40	60
Set of 2 (*Phosphor*)			45	65
First Day Cover (*Ordinary*)				6·50
First Day Cover (*Phosphor*)				7·00
Presentation Pack (*Ordinary*)			6·00	
Presentation Pack (*Phosphor*)			6·00	

The one phosphor band on No. 679p was produced by printing broad phosphor bands across alternate vertical perforations. Individual stamps show the band at right or left.

Special First Day of Issue Postmark

	Ordinary	*Phosphor*
G.P.O. Philatelic Bureau, London E.C.1 (Type C)	10·00	12·00

The Philatelic Bureau did not provide First Day Cover services for Nos. 681/4.

240 U.N. Emblem

241 I.C.Y. Emblem

(Des J. Matthews)

1965 (25 Oct). *20th Anniv of U.N.O. and International Cooperation Year. Chalk-surfaced paper. W* **179**. P 15×14.

681	**240**	3d. black, yellow-orange and light blue	25	20
		p. One phosphor band	25	30
682	**241**	1s.6d. black, brt purple and light blue	1·00	80
		Wi. Watermark inverted	£1750	
		p. Three phosphor bands	2·75	3·00
Set of 2 (*Ordinary*)			1·00	1·00
Set of 2 (*Phosphor*)			2·50	3·25
First Day Cover (*Ordinary*)				12·00
First Day Cover (*Phosphor*)				14·00

242 Telecommunications Network

243 Radio Waves and Switchboard

(Des A. Restall)

1965 (15 Nov). *I.T.U. Centenary. Chalk-surfaced paper. W* **179**. P 15×14.

683	**242**	9d. red, ultramarine, deep slate, violet, black and pink	50	40
		Wi. Watermark inverted	14·00	
		p. Three phosphor bands	1·00	75
		pWi. Watermark inverted	70·00	
684	**243**	1s.6d. red, greenish blue, indigo, black and light pink	1·50	1·25
		a. Light pink omitted	£1500	
		Wi. Watermark inverted	55·00	
		p. Three phosphor bands	4·25	5·25
Set of 2 (*Ordinary*)			1·50	1·60
Set of 2 (*Phosphor*)			4·25	6·00
First Day Cover (*Ordinary*)				17·00
First Day Cover (*Phosphor*)				20·00

Originally scheduled for issue on 17 May 1965, supplies from the Philatelic Bureau were sent in error to reach a dealer on that date and another dealer received his supply on 27 May.

244 Robert Burns (after Skirving chalk drawing)

245 Robert Burns (after Nasmyth portrait)

(Des G. Huntly)

1966 (25 Jan). *Burns Commemoration. Chalk-surfaced paper. W* **179**. P 15×14.

685	**244**	4d. black, dp violet-blue and new blue	15	15
		p. Three phosphor bands	25	50
686	**245**	1s.3d. black, slate-blue and yellow-orange	40	70
		p. Three phosphor bands	2·25	2·25
Set of 2 (*Ordinary*)			55	85
Set of 2 (*Phosphor*)			2·50	2·25
First Day Cover (*Ordinary*)				4·00
First Day Cover (*Phosphor*)				6·00
Presentation Pack (*Ordinary*)			55·00	

Special First Day of Issue Postmarks

(35 mm diameter)

	Ordinary	*Phosphor*
Alloway, Ayrshire	12·00	12·00
Ayr	12·00	12·00
Dumfries	15·00	15·00
Edinburgh	15·00	15·00
Glasgow	15·00	15·00
Kilmarnock, Ayrshire	15·00	15·00

A special Philatelic Bureau was set up in Edinburgh to deal with First Day Covers of this issue. The Bureau serviced covers to receive the above postmarks, and other versions were applied locally. The locally applied handstamps were 38-39mm in diameter, the Bureau postmarks, applied by machine, 35mm. The Ayr, Edinburgh, Glasgow and Kilmarnock postmarks are similar in design to that for Alloway. Similar handstamps were also provided at Greenock and Mauchline, but the Bureau did not provide a service for these.

246 Westminster Abbey

247 Fan Vaulting, Henry VII Chapel

(Des Sheila Robinson. Photo Harrison (3d.). Des and eng Bradbury, Wilkinson. Recess (2s.6d.))

1966 (28 Feb). *900th Anniversary of Westminster Abbey. Chalk-surfaced paper (3d.). W* **179**. P 15×14 (3d.) or 11×12 (2s.6d.).

687	**246**	3d. black, red-brown and new blue	15	20
		p. One phosphor band	20	25
688	**247**	2s.6d. black	55	80
Set of 2			70	1·00
First Day Cover (*Ordinary*)				6·00
First Day Cover (*Phosphor*)				14·00
Presentation Pack (*Ordinary*)			45·00	

Special First Day of Issue Postmark

	Ordinary
G.P.O. Philatelic Bureau, London E.C.1 (Type B)	15·00

The Bureau did not provide a First Day Cover service for the 3d. phosphor stamp.

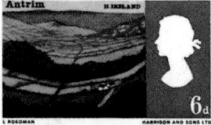

248 View near Hassocks, Sussex

249 Antrim, Northern Ireland

250 Harlech Castle, Wales

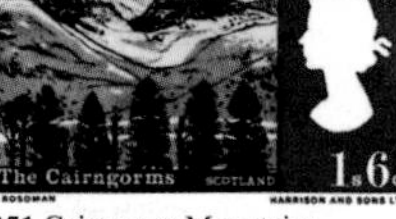

251 Cairngorm Mountains Scotland

(Des L. Rosoman. Queen's portrait, adapted by D. Gentleman from coinage)

1966 (2 May). *Landscapes. Chalk-surfaced paper. W* **179**. P 15×14.

689	**248**	4d. black, yellow-green and new blue	10	15
		p. Three phosphor bands	10	15
690	**249**	6d. black, emerald and new blue	15	20
		Wi. Watermark inverted	6·00	
		p. Three phosphor bands	15	20
		pWi. Watermark inverted	30·00	
691	**250**	1s.3d. black, greenish yellow and greenish blue	25	35
		p. Three phosphor bands	25	35
692	**251**	1s.6d. black, orange and Prussian blue	40	35

		Wi. Watermark inverted	15·00	
		p. Three phosphor bands	40	40
Set of 4 (*Ordinary*)			80	95
Set of 4 (*Phosphor*)			80	1·00
First Day Cover (*Ordinary*)				7·00
First Day Cover (*Phosphor*)				8·50

A block of four of No. 689 is known with the top right stamp showing the face value and the bottom right the Queen's head and the face value both omitted due to a paper fold.

Special First Day of Issue Postmark

	Ordinary	*Phosphor*
G.P.O. Philatelic Bureau, London E.C.1 (Type B) ...	12·00	12·00

First Day of Issue handstamps were provided at Lewes, Sussex; Coleraine, Co. Londonderry; Harlech, Merioneth and Grantown-on-Spey, Morayshire, for this issue.

252 Players with Ball

253 Goalmouth Mêlée

254 Goalkeeper saving Goal

(Des D. Gentleman (4d.), W. Kempster (6d.), D. Caplan (1s.3d.). Queen's portrait adapted by D. Gentleman from coinage)

1966 (1 June). *World Cup Football Championship. Chalk-surfaced paper. W* **179** (*sideways on* 4d.). P 14×15 (4d.) or 15×14 (others).

693	**252**	4d. red, reddish purple, bright blue, flesh and black	10	25
		p. Two phosphor bands	10	25
694	**253**	6d. black, sepia, red, apple-green and blue	15	25
		a. Black omitted	£110	
		b. Apple-green omitted	£3000	
		c. Red omitted	£5000	
		Wi. Watermark inverted	2·00	
		p. Three phosphor bands	15	25
		pa. Black omitted	£700	
695	**254**	1s.3d. black, blue, yellow, red and light yellow-olive	50	1·00
		a. Blue omitted	£200	
		Wi. Watermark inverted	£110	
		p. Three phosphor bands	50	1·00
		pWi. Watermark inverted	1·25	
Set of 3 (*Ordinary*)			70	1·00
Set of 3 (*Phosphor*)			50	1·00
First Day Cover (*Ordinary*)				20·00
First Day Cover (*Phosphor*)				22·00
Presentation Pack (*Ordinary*)			15·00	

Special First Day of Issue Postmark

	Ordinary	*Phosphor*
G.P.O. Philatelic Bureau, London E.C.1 (Type C).....	20·00	25·00

A First Day of Issue handstamp was provided at Wembley, Middx, for this issue.

255 Black-headed Gull

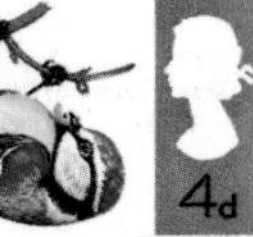

256 Blue Tit

257 European Robin

258 Blackbird

(Des J. Norris Wood)

1966 (8 Aug). *British Birds. Chalk-surfaced paper. W* **179**. P 15×14.

696	**255**	4d. grey, black, red, emerald-green, brt blue, greenish yellow and bistre	20	20
		Wi. Watermark inverted	4·00	
		a. Block of 4. Nos. 696/9	1·00	2·00
		ab. Black (value), etc. omitted* (*block of four*)	£7000	
		ac. Black only omitted*	£7500	
		aWi. Watermark inverted (block of four).	17·00	
		p. Three phosphor bands	20	20
		pWi. Watermark inverted	18·00	
		pa. Block of 4. Nos. 696p/9p	75	2·00
		paWi. Watermark inverted (*block of four*)..	75·00	
697	**256**	4d. black, greenish yellow, grey, emerald-green, brt blue and bistre ...	20	20
		Wi. Watermark inverted	4·00	
		p. Three phosphor bands	20	20
		pWi. Watermark inverted	18·00	
698	**257**	4d. red, greenish yellow, black, grey, bistre, reddish brown and emerald-green	20	20
		Wi. Watermark inverted	4·00	
		p. Three phosphor bands	20	20
		pWi. Watermark inverted	18·00	
699	**258**	4d. black, reddish brown, greenish yellow, grey and bistre**	20	20
		Wi. Watermark inverted	4·00	
		p. Three phosphor bands	20	20
		pWi. Watermark inverted	16·00	
Set of 4 (*Ordinary*)			1·00	1·00
Set of 4 (*Phosphor*)			75	1·00
First Day Cover (*Ordinary*)				8·00
First Day Cover (*Phosphor*)				8·00
Presentation Pack (*Ordinary*)			10·00	

Nos. 696/9 were issued together *se-tenant* in blocks of four within the sheet.

*In No. 696ab the blue, bistre and reddish brown are also omitted but in No. 696ac only the black is omitted.

**In No. 699 the black was printed over the bistre. Other colours omitted, and the stamps affected:

d.	Greenish yellow (Nos. 696/9) .	£575
pd.	Greenish yellow (Nos. 696p/9p)	£2500
e.	Red (Nos. 696 and 698)	£575
f.	Emerald-green (Nos. 696/8)	£110
pf.	Emerald-green (Nos. 696p/8p)	£110
g.	Bright blue (Nos. 696/7)	£400
pg.	Bright blue (Nos. 696p and 697p)	£3750
h.	Bistre (Nos. 696/9)	£100
ph.	Bistre (Nos. 696p/9p)	£2250
j.	Reddish brown (Nos. 698/9)	90·00
pj.	Reddish brown (Nos. 698p and 699p)	90·00

The prices quoted are for each stamp.

Special First Day of Issue Postmark

	Ordinary	*Phosphor*
G.P.O. Philatelic Bureau, London E.C.1 (Type C)	22·00	22·00

259 Cup Winners

1966 (18 Aug). *England's World Cup Football Victory. Chalk-surfaced paper.* W **179** (*sideways*). P 14×15.

No.	Type	Description	Unused	Used
700	**259**	4d. red, reddish purple, bright blue, flesh and black	30	30
First Day Cover				13·00

These stamps were only put on sale at post offices in England, the Channel Islands and the Isle of Man, and at the Philatelic Bureau in London and also, on 22 August, in Edinburgh on the occasion of the opening of the Edinburgh Festival as well as at Army post offices at home and abroad.

The Philatelic Bureau did not service First Day Covers for this stamp, but a First Day of Issue handstamp was provided inscribed "Harrow & Wembley" to replace the "Wembley, Middx", postmark of the initial issue.

260 Jodrell Bank Radio Telescope

261 British Motor-cars

262 "SRN 6" Hovercraft

263 Windscale Reactor

(Des D. and A. Gillespie (4d., 6d.), A. Restall (others))

1966 (19 Sept). *British Technology. Chalk-surfaced paper. W* **179**. P 15×14.

No.	Type	Description	Unused	Used
701	**260**	4d. black and lemon	15	10
		p. Three phosphor bands	10	10
702	**261**	6d. red, dp blue and orange	25	20
		a. Red (Mini-cars) omitted	£7500	
		b. Deep blue (Jaguar & inscr) omitted	£5500	
		p. Three phosphor bands	15	25
703	**262**	1s.3d. black, orange-red, slate and light greenish blue	50	40
		p. Three phosphor bands	35	40
704	**263**	1s.6d. black, yellow-green, bronze-green, lilac and deep blue	50	60
		p. Three phosphor bands	35	40
Set of 4 (*Ordinary*)			1·00	1·10
Set of 4 (*Phosphor*)			1·00	1·10
First Day Cover (*Ordinary*)				6·00
First Day Cover (*Phosphor*)				6·00
Presentation Pack (*Ordinary*)			9·00	

Special First Day of Issue Postmark

	Ordinary	*Phosphor*
G.P.O. Philatelic Bureau, Edinburgh 1 (Type C)	12·00	12·00

264

265

266

267

268

269

All the above show battle scenes and they were issued together *se-tenant* in horizontal strips of six within the sheet.

270 Norman Ship

271 Norman Horsemen attacking Harold's Troops

(All the above are scenes from the Bayeux Tapestry)

(Des D. Gentleman. Photo. Queen's head die-stamped (6d., 1s.3d.))

1966 (14 Oct). *900th Anniv of Battle of Hastings. Chalk-surfaced paper. W* **179** (*sideways on* 1s.3d.). P 15×14.

No.	Type	Description	Unused	Used
705	**264**	4d. black, olive-green, bistre, deep blue, orange, magenta, green, blue and grey	10	30
		a. Strip of 6. Nos. 705/10	1·90	6·00
		aWi. Strip of 6. Watermark inverted	45·00	
		Wi. Watermark inverted	7·00	
		p. Three phosphor bands	10	30
		pa. Strip of 6. Nos. 705p/10p	1·90	6·00
		pWi. Watermark inverted	3·00	
		paWi. Strip of 6. Watermark inverted	20·00	
706	**265**	4d. black, olive-green, bistre, deep blue, orange, magenta, green, blue and grey	10	30
		Wi. Watermark inverted	7·00	
		p. Three phosphor bands	10	30
		pWi. Watermark inverted	2·00	
707	**266**	4d. black, olive-green, bistre, deep blue, orange, magenta, green, blue and grey	10	30
		Wi. Watermark inverted	7·00	

		p. Three phosphor bands	10	30
		pWi. Watermark inverted	3·00	
708	**267**	4d. black, olive-green, bistre, deep blue, magenta, green, blue and grey	10	30
		Wi. Watermark inverted	7·00	
		p. Three phosphor bands	10	30
		pWi. Watermark inverted	3·00	
709	**268**	4d. black, olive-green, bistre, deep blue, orange, magenta, green, blue and grey	10	30
		Wi. Watermark inverted	7·00	
		p. Three phosphor bands	10	30
		pWi. Watermark inverted	3·00	
710	**269**	4d. black, olive-green, bistre, deep blue, orange, magenta, green, blue and grey	10	30
		Wi. Watermark inverted	7·00	
		p. Three phosphor bands	10	30
		pWi. Watermark inverted	3·00	
711	**270**	6d. black, olive-green, violet, blue, green and gold	10	30
		Wi. Watermark inverted	42·00	
		p. Three phosphor bands	10	30
		pWi. Watermark inverted	55·00	
712	**271**	1s.3d. black, lilac, bronze-green, rosine, bistre-brown and gold	20	75
		a. Lilac omitted	£650	
		Wi. Watermark sideways inverted (top of crown pointing to right)*	35·00	
		p. Four phosphor bands	20	75
		pa. Lilac omitted	£650	
		pWi. Watermark sideways inverted (top of crown pointing to right)*	35·00	
Set of 8 (*Ordinary*)			2·00	2·25
Set of 8 (*Phosphor*)			2·00	2·25
First Day Cover (*Ordinary*)				8·00
First Day Cover (*Phosphor*)				9·00
Presentation Pack (*Ordinary*)			9·00	

*The normal sideways watermark shows the tops of the Crowns pointing to the left, as seen from the *back of the stamp*.

Other colours omitted in the 4d. values and the stamps affected:

b.	Olive-green (Nos. 705/10)	60·00
pb.	Olive-green (Nos. 705p/10p)	60·00
c.	Bistre (Nos. 705/10)	60·00
pc.	Bistre (Nos. 705p/10p)	60·00
d.	Deep blue (Nos. 705/10)	70·00
pd.	Deep blue (Nos. 705p/10p)	70·00
e.	Orange (Nos. 705/7 and 709/10)	60·00
pe.	Orange (Nos. 705p/7p and 709p/10p)	60·00
f.	Magenta (Nos. 705/10)	60·00
pf.	Magenta (Nos. 705p/10p)	60·00
g.	Green (Nos. 705/10)	60·00
pg.	Green (Nos. 705p/10p)	60·00
h.	Blue (Nos. 705/10)	60·00
ph.	Blue (Nos. 705p/10p)	60·00
j.	Grey (Nos. 705/10)	60·00
pj.	Grey (Nos. 705p/10p)	60·00
pk.	Magenta and green (Nos. 705p/10p)	

The prices quoted are for each stamp.

Nos. 705 and 709, with grey and blue omitted, have been seen commercially used, posted from Middleton-in-Teesdale.

The 6d. phosphor is known in a yellowish gold as well as the reddish gold as used in the 1s.3d.

Three examples of No. 712 in a right-hand top corner block of 10 (2×5) are known with the Queen's head omitted as a result of a double paper fold prior to die-stamping. The perforation is normal. Of the other seven stamps, four have the Queen's head misplaced and three are normal.

MISSING GOLD HEADS. The 6d. and 1s.3d. were also issued with the die-stamped gold head omitted but as these can also be removed by chemical means we are not prepared to list them unless a way is found of distinguishing the genuine stamps from the fakes which will satisfy the Expert Committees.

The same remarks apply to Nos. 713/14.

Special First Day of Issue Postmark

	Ordinary	*Phosphor*
G.P.O. Philatelic Bureau, Edinburgh 1 (Type C)	10·00	12·00

A First Day of Issue handstamp was provided at Battle, Sussex, for this issue

272 King of the Orient

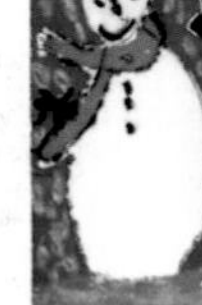

273 Snowman

(Des Tasveer Shemza (3d.), J. Berry (1s.6d.) (winners of children's design competition). Photo, Queen's head die-stamped)

1966 (1 Dec). *Christmas. Chalk-surfaced paper. W* **179** (*sideways on* 3d.). P 14×15.

713	**272**	3d. black, blue, green, yellow, red and gold	10	25
		a. Queen's head double	£550	†
		ab. Queen's head double, one albino	£550	
		b. Green omitted	£6500	
		p. One phosphor band at right	10	25
		pEa. Band at left	10	25
		pEb. Horiz pair. Nos. 713p/pEa	20	60
714	**273**	1s.6d. blue, red, pink, black and gold	30	50
		a. Pink (hat) omitted	£1300	
		Wi. Watermark inverted	15·00	
		p. Two phosphor bands	30	50
		pWi. Watermark inverted	42·00	
Set of 2 (*Ordinary*)			40	40
Set of 2 (*Phosphor*)			40	45
First Day Cover (*Ordinary*)				2·50
First Day Cover (*Phosphor*)				2·50
Presentation Pack (*Ordinary*)			12·00	

Special First Day of Issue Postmarks

	Ordinary	*Phosphor*
G.P.O. Philatelic Bureau, Edinburgh 1 (Type C)	10·00	10·00
Bethlehem, Llandeilo, Carms (Type C)	10·00	10·00

274 Sea Freight

275 Air Freight

(Des C. Abbott)

1967 (20 Feb). *European Free Trade Association (EFTA). Chalk-surfaced paper. W* **179**. P 15×14.

715	**274**	9d. deep blue, red, lilac, green, brown, new blue, yellow and black	25	20
		a. Black (Queen's head, etc.), brown, new blue and yellow omitted	£750	
		b. Lilac omitted	60·00	
		c. Green omitted	60·00	
		d. Brown (rail trucks) omitted	45·00	
		e. New blue omitted	60·00	
		f. Yellow omitted	60·00	
		Wi. Watermark inverted	45·00	
		p. Three phosphor bands	25	20
		pb. Lilac omitted	£140	
		pc. Green omitted	60·00	
		pd. Brown omitted	45·00	
		pe. New blue omitted	60·00	
		pf. Yellow omitted	£110	
		pWi. Watermark inverted	12·00	
716	**275**	1s.6d. violet, red, deep blue, brown, green, blue-grey, new blue, yellow and black	50	45
		a. Red omitted		
		b. Deep blue omitted	£375	
		c. Brown omitted	60·00	
		d. Blue-grey omitted	60·00	
		e. New blue omitted	60·00	
		f. Yellow omitted	60·00	

g. Green omitted
p. Three phosphor bands 25 40
pa. Red omitted
pb. Deep blue omitted £375
pc. Brown omitted 50·00
pd. Blue-grey omitted 60·00
pf. New blue omitted 60·00
pWi. Watermark inverted 25·00
Set of 2 (*Ordinary*) 50 65
Set of 2 (*Phosphor*) 50 60
First Day Cover (*Ordinary*) 3·00
First Day Cover (*Phosphor*) 3·00
Presentation Pack (*Ordinary*) 3·50

Special First Day of Issue Postmark

	Ordinary	*Phosphor*
G.P.O. Philatelic Bureau, Edinburgh 1 (Type C)	6·00	6·00

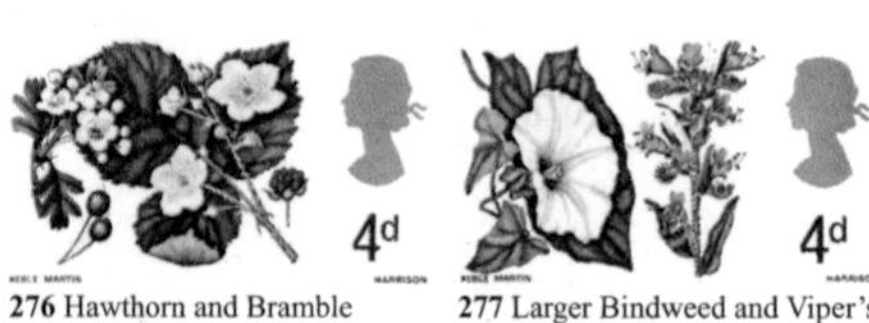

276 Hawthorn and Bramble **277** Larger Bindweed and Viper's Bugloss

278 Ox-eye Daisy, Coltsfoot and Buttercup **279** Bluebell, Red Campion and Wood Anemone

T **276/9** were issued together *se-tenant* in blocks of four within the sheet.

280 Dog Violet **281** Primroses

(Des Rev. W. Keble Martin (T **276/9**), Mary Grierson (others))

1967 (24 Apr). *British Wild Flowers. Chalk-surfaced paper. W* **179**. P 15×14.

717 **276** 4d. grey, lemon, myrtle-green, red, agate and slate-purple 20 20
a. Block of 4. Nos. 717/20 80 3·00
aWi. Block of 4. Watermark inverted 9·00
b. Grey double* £1500
c. Red omitted £2750
f. Slate-purple omitted £4500
Wi. Watermark inverted 2·00
p. Three phosphor bands 10 15
pa. Block of 4. Nos. 717p/20p 50 2·75
paWi. Block of 4. Watermark inverted 9·00
pd. Agate omitted £3000
pf. Slate-purple omitted £275
pWi. Watermark inverted 2·00

718 **277** 4d. grey, lemon, myrtle-green, red, agate and violet 20 20
b. Grey double* £1500
Wi. Watermark inverted 2·00
b. Grey double* £1500
c. Red omitted £2750
f. Slate-purple omitted £4250
Wi. Watermark inverted 2·00
p. Three phosphor bands 10 15
pd. Agate omitted £3000
pe. Violet omitted £5500
pWi. Watermark inverted 2·00

719 **278** 4d. grey, lemon, myrtle-green, red and agate 20 20
b. Grey double* £1500
Wi. Watermark inverted 2·00
p. Three phosphor bands 10 15
pd. Agate omitted £3000
f. Slate-purple omitted £4250
Wi. Watermark inverted 2·00
p. Three phosphor bands 10 15
pd. Agate omitted £3000
pWi. Watermark inverted 2·00

720 **279** 4d. grey, lemon, myrtle-green, reddish purple, agate and violet 20 20
b. Grey double* £1500
c. Reddish purple omitted £1100
d. Value omitted†
Wi. Watermark inverted 2·00
p. Three phosphor bands 10 15
Wi. Watermark inverted 2·00
pd. Agate omitted £3000
pe. Violet omitted £5500
pWi. Watermark inverted 2·00

721 **280** 9d. lavender-grey, green, reddish violet and orange-yellow 20 25
Wi. Watermark inverted 1·25
p. Three phosphor bands 15 25

722 **281** 1s.9d. lavender-grey, green, greenish yellow and orange 25 35
p. Three phosphor bands 20 30

Set of 6 (*Ordinary*) 1·00 1·25
Set of 6 (*Phosphor*) 75 1·00
First Day Cover (*Ordinary*) 5·00
First Day Cover (*Phosphor*) 6·00
Presentation Pack (*Ordinary*) 5·25
Presentation Pack (*Phosphor*) 5·25

*The double impression of the grey printing affects the Queen's head, value and inscription.

†No. 720d was caused by something obscuring the face value on R14/6 during the printing of one sheet.

Special First Day of Issue Postmark

	Ordinary	*Phosphor*
G.P.O. Philatelic Bureau, Edinburgh 1 (Type C)	10·00	12·00

PHOSPHOR BANDS. Issues from No. are normally with phosphor bands only, except for the high values but most stamps have appeared with the phosphor bands omitted in error. Such varieties are listed under "Ey" numbers and are priced unused only. See also further notes after 1971–95 Decimal Machin issue.

PHOSPHORISED PAPER. Following the adoption of phosphor bands the Post Office started a series of experiments involving the addition of the phosphor to the paper coating before the stamps were printed. No. 743c was the first of these experiments to be issued for normal postal use. See also notes after 1971–96 Decimal Machin issue.

PVA GUM. Polyvinyl alcohol was introduced by Harrisons in place of gum arabic in 1968. As it is almost invisible a small amount of pale yellowish colouring was introduced to make it possible to check that the stamps had been gummed. Although this can be distinguished from gum arabic in unused stamps there is, of course, no means of detecting it in used examples. Where the two forms of gum exist on the same stamps, the PVA type are listed under "Ev" numbers, except in the case of the 1d. and 4d. (vermilion), both one centre band, which later appeared with gum arabic and these have "Eg" numbers. "Ev" and "Eg" numbers are priced unused only. All stamps printed from No. 763 onwards were issued with PVA gum only *except where otherwise stated.*

It should be further noted that gum arabic is shiny in appearance, and that, normally, PVA gum has a matt appearance. However, depending upon the qualities of the paper ingredients and the resultant absorption of the gum, occasionally, PVA gum has a shiny appearance. In such cases, especially in stamps from booklets, it is sometimes impossible to be absolutely sure which gum has been used except by testing the stamps chemically which destroys them. Therefore, whilst all gum arabic is shiny it does not follow that all shiny gum is gum arabic.

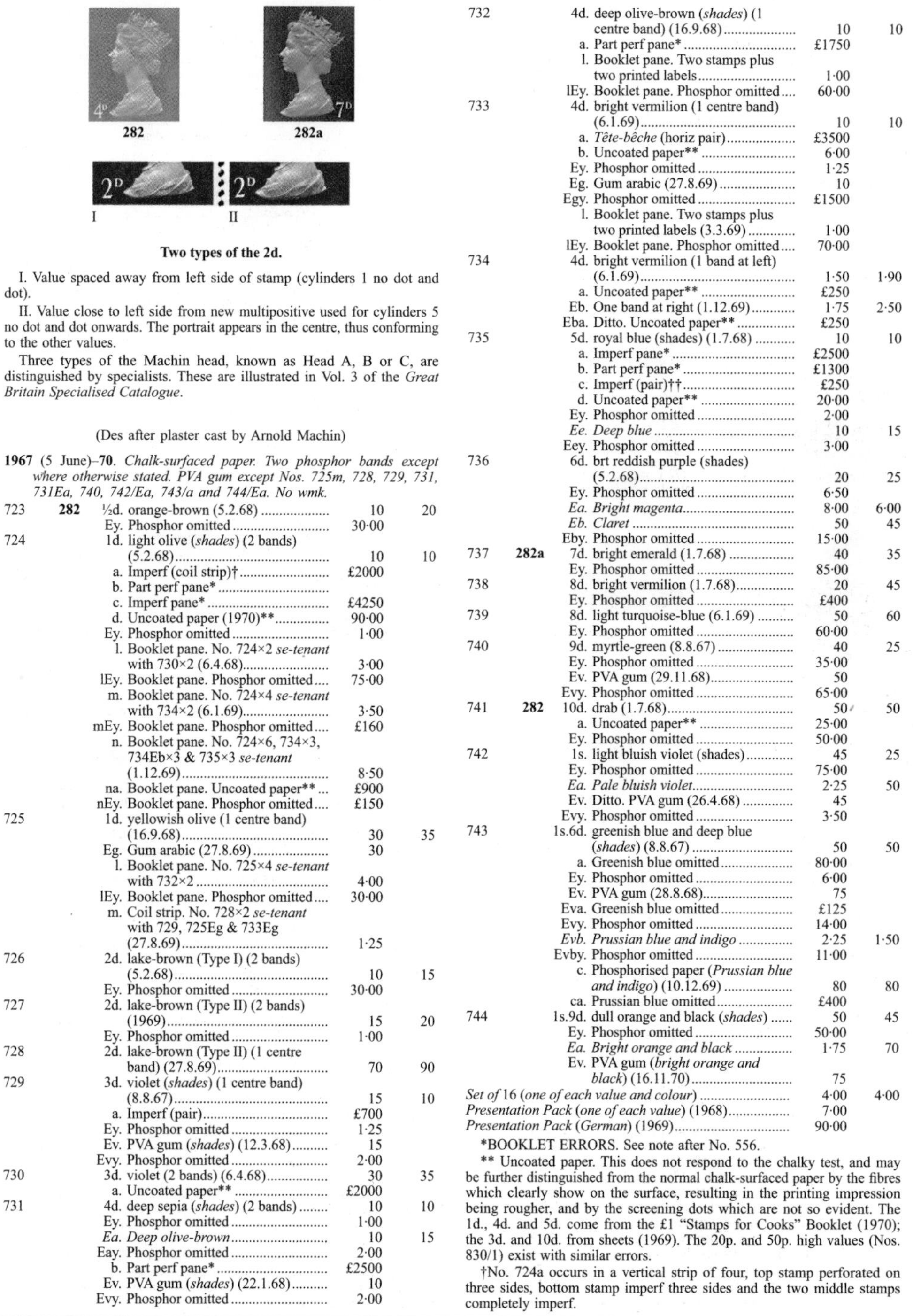

282 282a

I II

Two types of the 2d.

I. Value spaced away from left side of stamp (cylinders 1 no dot and dot).

II. Value close to left side from new multipositive used for cylinders 5 no dot and dot onwards. The portrait appears in the centre, thus conforming to the other values.

Three types of the Machin head, known as Head A, B or C, are distinguished by specialists. These are illustrated in Vol. 3 of the *Great Britain Specialised Catalogue*.

(Des after plaster cast by Arnold Machin)

1967 (5 June)–**70**. *Chalk-surfaced paper. Two phosphor bands except where otherwise stated. PVA gum except Nos. 725m, 728, 729, 731, 731Ea, 740, 742/Ea, 743/a and 744/Ea. No wmk.*

No.	Type	Description	Unused	Used
723	**282**	½d. orange-brown (5.2.68)	10	20
		Ey. Phosphor omitted	30·00	
724		1d. light olive (*shades*) (2 bands) (5.2.68)	10	10
		a. Imperf (coil strip)†	£2000	
		b. Part perf pane*		
		c. Imperf pane*	£4250	
		d. Uncoated paper (1970)**	90·00	
		Ey. Phosphor omitted	1·00	
		l. Booklet pane. No. 724×2 *se-tenant* with 730×2 (6.4.68)	3·00	
		lEy. Booklet pane. Phosphor omitted	75·00	
		m. Booklet pane. No. 724×4 *se-tenant* with 734×2 (6.1.69)	3·50	
		mEy. Booklet pane. Phosphor omitted	£160	
		n. Booklet pane. No. 724×6, 734×3, 734Eb×3 & 735×3 *se-tenant* (1.12.69)	8·50	
		na. Booklet pane. Uncoated paper**	£900	
		nEy. Booklet pane. Phosphor omitted	£150	
725		1d. yellowish olive (1 centre band) (16.9.68)	30	35
		Eg. Gum arabic (27.8.69)	30	
		l. Booklet pane. No. 725×4 *se-tenant* with 732×2	4·00	
		lEy. Booklet pane. Phosphor omitted	30·00	
		m. Coil strip. No. 728×2 *se-tenant* with 729, 725Eg & 733Eg (27.8.69)	1·25	
726		2d. lake-brown (Type I) (2 bands) (5.2.68)	10	15
		Ey. Phosphor omitted	30·00	
727		2d. lake-brown (Type II) (2 bands) (1969)	15	20
		Ey. Phosphor omitted	1·00	
728		2d. lake-brown (Type II) (1 centre band) (27.8.69)	70	90
729		3d. violet (*shades*) (1 centre band) (8.8.67)	15	10
		a. Imperf (pair)	£700	
		Ey. Phosphor omitted	1·25	
		Ev. PVA gum (*shades*) (12.3.68)	15	
		Evy. Phosphor omitted	2·00	
730		3d. violet (2 bands) (6.4.68)	30	35
		a. Uncoated paper**	£2000	
731		4d. deep sepia (*shades*) (2 bands)	10	10
		Ey. Phosphor omitted	1·00	
		Ea. Deep olive-brown	10	15
		Eay. Phosphor omitted	2·00	
		b. Part perf pane*	£2500	
		Ev. PVA gum (*shades*) (22.1.68)	10	
		Evy. Phosphor omitted	2·00	
732		4d. deep olive-brown (*shades*) (1 centre band) (16.9.68)	10	10
		a. Part perf pane*	£1750	
		l. Booklet pane. Two stamps plus two printed labels	1·00	
		lEy. Booklet pane. Phosphor omitted	60·00	
733		4d. bright vermilion (1 centre band) (6.1.69)	10	10
		a. *Tête-bêche* (horiz pair)	£3500	
		b. Uncoated paper**	6·00	
		Ey. Phosphor omitted	1·25	
		Eg. Gum arabic (27.8.69)	10	
		Egy. Phosphor omitted	£1500	
		l. Booklet pane. Two stamps plus two printed labels (3.3.69)	1·00	
		lEy. Booklet pane. Phosphor omitted	70·00	
734		4d. bright vermilion (1 band at left) (6.1.69)	1·50	1·90
		a. Uncoated paper**	£250	
		Eb. One band at right (1.12.69)	1·75	2·50
		Eba. Ditto. Uncoated paper**	£250	
735		5d. royal blue (shades) (1.7.68)	10	10
		a. Imperf pane*	£2500	
		b. Part perf pane*	£1300	
		c. Imperf (pair)††	£250	
		d. Uncoated paper**	20·00	
		Ey. Phosphor omitted	2·00	
		Ee. Deep blue	10	15
		Eey. Phosphor omitted	3·00	
736		6d. brt reddish purple (shades) (5.2.68)	20	25
		Ey. Phosphor omitted	6·50	
		Ea. Bright magenta	8·00	6·00
		Eb. Claret	50	45
		Eby. Phosphor omitted	15·00	
737	**282a**	7d. bright emerald (1.7.68)	40	35
		Ey. Phosphor omitted	85·00	
738		8d. bright vermilion (1.7.68)	20	45
		Ey. Phosphor omitted	£400	
739		8d. light turquoise-blue (6.1.69)	50	60
		Ey. Phosphor omitted	60·00	
740		9d. myrtle-green (8.8.67)	40	25
		Ey. Phosphor omitted	35·00	
		Ev. PVA gum (29.11.68)	50	
		Evy. Phosphor omitted	65·00	
741	**282**	10d. drab (1.7.68)	50	50
		a. Uncoated paper**	25·00	
		Ey. Phosphor omitted	50·00	
742		1s. light bluish violet (shades)	45	25
		Ey. Phosphor omitted	75·00	
		Ea. Pale bluish violet	2·25	50
		Ev. Ditto. PVA gum (26.4.68)	45	
		Evy. Phosphor omitted	3·50	
743		1s.6d. greenish blue and deep blue (*shades*) (8.8.67)	50	50
		a. Greenish blue omitted	80·00	
		Ey. Phosphor omitted	6·00	
		Ev. PVA gum (28.8.68)	75	
		Eva. Greenish blue omitted	£125	
		Evy. Phosphor omitted	14·00	
		Evb. Prussian blue and indigo	2·25	1·50
		Evby. Phosphor omitted	11·00	
		c. Phosphorised paper (*Prussian blue and indigo*) (10.12.69)	80	80
		ca. Prussian blue omitted	£400	
744		1s.9d. dull orange and black (*shades*)	50	45
		Ey. Phosphor omitted	50·00	
		Ea. Bright orange and black	1·75	70
		Ev. PVA gum (*bright orange and black*) (16.11.70)	75	
		Set of 16 (*one of each value and colour*)	4·00	4·00
		Presentation Pack (*one of each value*) (1968)	7·00	
		Presentation Pack (*German*) (1969)	90·00	

*BOOKLET ERRORS. See note after No. 556.

** Uncoated paper. This does not respond to the chalky test, and may be further distinguished from the normal chalk-surfaced paper by the fibres which clearly show on the surface, resulting in the printing impression being rougher, and by the screening dots which are not so evident. The 1d., 4d. and 5d. come from the £1 "Stamps for Cooks" Booklet (1970); the 3d. and 10d. from sheets (1969). The 20p. and 50p. high values (Nos. 830/1) exist with similar errors.

†No. 724a occurs in a vertical strip of four, top stamp perforated on three sides, bottom stamp imperf three sides and the two middle stamps completely imperf.

††No. 735c comes from the original state of cylinder 15 which is identifiable by the screening dots which extend through the gutters of the stamps and into the margins of the sheet. This must not be confused with imperforate stamps from cylinder 10, a large quantity of which was stolen from the printers early in 1970.

The 1d. with centre band and PVA gum (725) only came in the September 1968 10s. booklet (No. XP6). The 1d., 2d. and 4d. with centre band and gum arabic (725Eg, 728 and 733Eg respectively) only came in the coil strip (725m). The 3d. (No. 730) appeared in booklets on 6.4.68, from coils during Dec 68 and from sheets in Jan 1969. The 4d. with one side band at left (734) came from 10s. (band at left) and £1 (band at left or right) booklet se-tenant panes, and the 4d. with one side band at right (734Eb) came from the £1 booklet *se-tenant* panes only.

The 4d. (731) in shades of washed-out grey are colour changelings which we understand are caused by the concentrated solvents used in modern dry cleaning methods.

For decimal issue, see Nos. X841, etc.

First Day Covers

5.6 67	4d.1s., 1s.9d. (*731, 742, 744*)	3·00
8.8.67	3d., 9d., 1s.6d. (*729, 740, 743*)	3·00
5.2.68	½d., 1d., 2d., 6d. (*723/4, 726, 736*)	3·00
1.7.68	5d., 7d., 8d., 10d. (*735, 737/8, 741*)	3·00

283 "Master Lambton" (Sir Thomas Lawrence)

284 "Mares and Foals in a Landscape" (George Stubbs)

285 "Children Coming Out of School" (L. S. Lowry)

(Des S. Rose)

1967 (10 July). *British Paintings. Chalk-surfaced paper. Two phosphor bands. No wmk.* P 14×15 (4d.) or 15×14 (others).

748	**283**	4d. rose-red, lemon, brown, black, new blue and gold	10	10
		a. Gold (value and Queen's head) omitted	£200	
		b. New blue omitted	£6500	
		Ey. Phosphor omitted	7·00	
749	**284**	9d. Venetian red, ochre, grey-black, new blue, greenish yellow and black	15	15
		a. Black (Queen's head and value) omitted	£450	
		ab. Black (Queen's head only) omitted	£750	
		b. Greenish yellow omitted	£1500	
		Ey. Phosphor omitted	£450	
750	**285**	1s.6d. greenish yellow, grey, rose, new blue, grey-black and gold	25	35
		a. Gold (Queen's head) omitted	£7500	
		b. New blue omitted	£180	
		c. Grey (clouds and shading) omitted	95·00	
		Ey. Phosphor omitted	£300	
Set of 3			30	50
First Day Cover				3·00
Presentation Pack			5·50	

Special First Day of Issue Postmark

G.P.O. Philatelic Bureau, Edinburgh 1 (Type C)	7·00

A First Day of Issue handstamp was provided at Bishop Auckland, Co. Durham, for this issue.

286 *Gypsy Moth IV*

(Des M. and Sylvia Goaman)

1967 (24 July). *Sir Francis Chichester's World Voyage. Chalk-surfaced paper. Three phosphor bands. No wmk.* P 15×14.

751	**286**	1s.9d. black, brown-red, light emerald and blue	20	20
First Day Cover				1·25

Special First Day of Issue Postmarks

G.P.O. Philatelic Bureau, Edinburgh 1	7·00
Greenwich, London SE10	7·00
Plymouth, Devon	7·00

The Philatelic Bureau and Greenwich postmarks are similar in design to that for Plymouth. A First Day of Issue handstamp was provided at Chichester, Sussex for this issue.

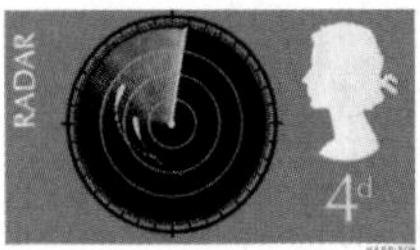

287 Radar Screen

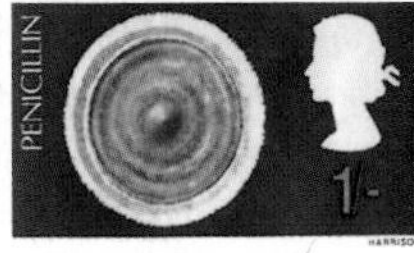

288 *Penicillium notatum*

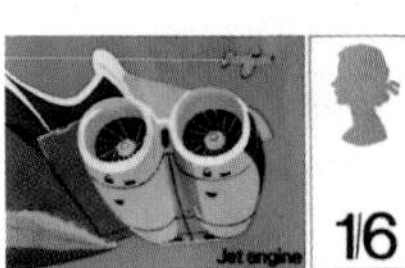

289 Vickers VC-10 Jet Engines

290 Television Equipment

(Des C. Abbott (4d., 1s.), Negus-Sharland team (others))

1967 (19 Sept). *British Discovery and Invention. Chalk-surfaced paper. Three phosphor bands (4d.) or two phosphor bands (others). W* **179** (*sideways on* 1s.9d.). P 14×15 (1s.9d.) or 15×14 (others).

752	**287**	4d. greenish yellow, black and vermilion	10	10
		Ey. Phosphor omitted	5·00	
753	**288**	1s. blue-green, lt greenish blue, slate-purple and bluish violet	10	20
		Wi. Watermark inverted	12·00	
		Ey. Phosphor omitted	9·00	
754	**289**	1s.6d. black, grey, royal blue, ochre and turquoise-blue	20	25
		Wi. Watermark inverted	33·00	
		Ey. Phosphor omitted	£500	
755	**290**	1s.9d. black, grey-blue, pale olive-grey, violet and orange	20	30
		a. Pale olive-grey omitted	£4500	
		b. Orange (Queen's head) omitted		
		Ey. Phosphor omitted	£500	
Set of 4			50	75
First Day Cover				2·50
Presentation Pack			4·00	

Special First of Issue Postmark

G.P.O. Philatelic Bureau, Edinburgh (Type C)........... 4·00

WATERMARK. All issues from this date are on unwatermarked paper *unless otherwise stated*

291 "The Adoration of the Shepherds" (School of Seville)

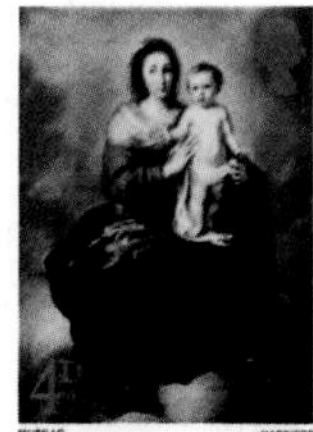

292 "Madonna and Child" (Murillo)

293 "The Adoration of the Shepherds" (Louis le Nain)

(Des S. Rose)

1967. *Christmas. Chalk-surfaced paper. One phosphor band (3d.) or two phosphor bands (others).* P 15×14 (1s.6d.) or 14×15 (others).

No.	Type	Description	Unused	Used
756	**291**	3d. olive-yellow, rose, blue, black and gold (27.11)	10	15
		a. Gold (value and Queen's head) omitted	75·00	
		b. Printed on the gummed side	£400	
		c. Rose omitted	£2750	
		Ey. Phosphor omitted	1·00	
757	**292**	4d. bright purple, greenish yellow, new blue, grey-black and gold (18.10)	10	15
		a. Gold (value and Queen's head) omitted	60·00	
		b. Gold ("4D" only) omitted	£1500	
		c. Greenish yellow (Child, robe and Madonna's face) omitted	£6750	
		d. Greenish yellow and gold omitted	£6500	
		Ey. Phosphor omitted	£125	
758	**293**	1s.6d. bright purple, bistre, lemon, black, orange-red, ultramarine and gold (27.11)	15	10
		a. Gold (value and Queen's head) omitted	£5500	
		ab. Gold (Queen's head only) omitted	£1500	
		b. Ultramarine omitted	£450	
		c. Lemon omitted	£10000	
		Ey. Phosphor omitted	12·00	
Set of 3			30	50
First Day Covers (2)				1·50

Distinct shades exist of the 3d. and 4d. values but are not listable as there are intermediate shades. For the 4d., stamps from one machine show a darker background and give the appearance of the yellow colour being omitted, but this is not so and these should not be confused with the true missing yellow No. 757c.

No. 757b comes from stamps in the first vertical row of a sheet.

The 3d. and 4d. values are known imperforate. They are of proof status.

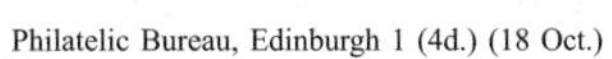

Special First Day of Issue Postmarks

G.P.O. Philatelic Bureau, Edinburgh 1 (4d.) (18 Oct.) (Type C)	1·00
G.P.O. Philatelic Bureau, Edinburgh 1 (3d., 1s.6d.) (27 Nov.) (Type C)	1·00
Bethlehem, Llandeilo, Carms (4d.) (18 Oct.) (Type C)	4·50
Bethlehem, Llandeilo, Carms (3d., 1s.6d.) (27 Nov.) (Type C)	5·00

Gift Pack 1967

1967 (27 Nov). Comprises Nos. 715p/22p and 748/58.

GP758*c* Gift Pack .... 3·00

(Recess Bradbury, Wilkinson)

1967–68. *No wmk. White paper.* P 11×12.

No.	Type	Description	Unused	Used
759	**166**	2s.6d. black-brown (1.7.68)	30	45
760	**167**	5s. red (10.4.68)	70	75
761	**168**	10s. bright ultramarine (10.4.68)	7·75	6·25
762	**169**	£1 black (4.12.67)	7·50	6·00
Set of 4			15·00	12·00

PVA GUM. All the following issues from this date have PVA gum except where footnotes state otherwise.

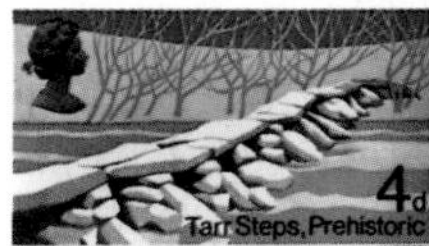

294 Tarr Steps, Exmoor

295 Aberfeldy Bridge

296 Menai Bridge

297 M4 Viaduct

(Des A. Restall (9d.), L. Rosoman (1s.6d.), J. Matthews (others))

1968 (29 Apr). *British Bridges. Chalk-surfaced paper. Two phosphor bands.* P 15×14.

No.	Type	Description	Unused	Used
763	**294**	4d. black, bluish violet, turquoise-blue and gold	10	10
		a. Printed on gummed side	25·00	
		Ey. Phosphor omitted		
764	**295**	9d. red-brown, myrtle-green, ultramarine, olive-brown, black and gold	10	15
		a. Gold (Queen's head) omitted	£160	
		b. Ultramarine omitted	†	£4250
		Ey. Phosphor omitted	15·00	
765	**296**	1s.6d. olive-brown, red-orange, brt green, turquoise-green and gold	15	25
		a. Gold (Queen's head) omitted	£180	
		b. Red-orange (rooftops) omitted	£200	
		Ey. Phosphor omitted	50·00	
766	**297**	1s.9d. olive-brown, greenish yellow, dull green, dp ultramarine and gold	20	30
		a. Gold (Queen's head) omitted	£180	
		Ey. Phosphor omitted	10·00	
Set of 4			50	70
First Day Cover				1·50
Presentation Pack			3·00	

No. 764b is only known on First Day Covers posted from Canterbury, Kent, or the Philatelic Bureau, Edinburgh.

Used examples of the 1s.6d. and 1s.9d. are known with both the gold and the phosphor omitted.

Special First Day of Issue Postmarks

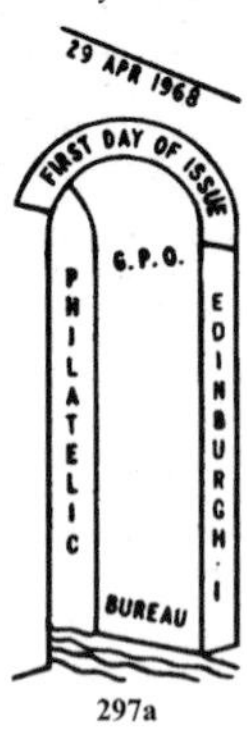

297a

G.P.O.Philatelic Bureau, Edinburgh 1	6·00
Bridge, Canterbury, Kent	7·00
Aberfeldy, Perthshire (Type A) (9d. value only)	10·00
Menai Bridge, Anglesey (Type A) (1s.6d. value only)	10·00

The Bridge, Canterbury, postmark is similar in design to that for the Philatelic Bureau.

298 "TUC" and Trades Unionists

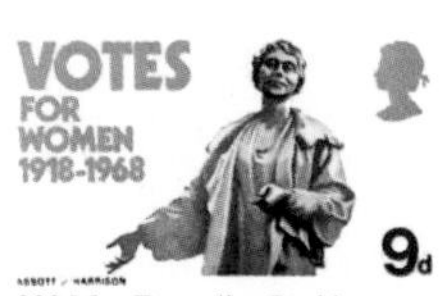

299 Mrs. Emmeline Pankhurst (statue)

300 Sopwith Camel and English Electric Lightning Fighters

301 Captain Cook's Endeavour and Signature

(Des D. Gentleman (4d.), C. Abbott (others))

1968 (29 May). *British Anniversaries. Events described on stamps. Chalk surfaced paper. Two phosphor bands.* P 15×14.

767	**298**	4d. emerald, olive, blue and black	10	10
		Ey. Phosphor omitted	12·00	
768	**299**	9d. reddish violet, bluish grey and black	10	15
		Ey. Phosphor omitted	7·00	
769	**300**	1s. olive-brown, blue, red, slate-blue and black	15	15
		Ey. Phosphor omitted	10·00	
770	**301**	1s.9d. yellow-ochre and blackish brown	35	35
		Ey. Phosphor omitted	£175	
Set of 4			50	50
First Day Cover				4·00
Presentation Pack			3·00	

Special First Day of Issue Postmarks

301a

FIRST DAY OF ISSUE
WOMEN'S SUFFRAGE X
29 MAY 1968
ALDEBURGH
SUFFOLK

301b

301c

FIRST DAY OF ISSUE
29MAY 1968
WHITBY YORKSHIRE

301d

G.P.O. Philatelic Bureau, Edinburgh 1 (Type C)	10·00
Manchester (4d. value only)	3·50
Aldeburgh, Suffolk (9d. value only)	4·00
Hendon, London NW4 (1s. value only)	4·00
Whitby, Yorkshire (1s.9d. value only)	4·00

The Philatelic Bureau postmark was used on sets of four, but the other postmarks were only available on single stamps.

302 "Queen Elizabeth I" (unknown artist)

303 "Pinkie" (Lawrence)

304 "Ruins of St. Mary Le Port" (Piper)

305 "The Hay Wain" (Constable)

(Des S. Rose)

1968 (12 Aug). *British Paintings. Queen's head embossed. Chalk-surfaced paper. Two phosphor bands.* P 15×14 (1s.9d.) or 14×15 (others).

771	**302**	4d. black, vermilion, greenish yellow, grey and gold	10	10
		a. Gold (value and Queen's head) omitted	£180	
		b. Vermilion omitted*	£350	
		Ec. Embossing omitted	80·00	
		Ey. Phosphor omitted	1·50	
		Eya. Gold (value and Queen's head) and phosphor omitted	£180	
772	**303**	1s. mauve, new blue, greenish yellow, black, magenta and gold	10	20
		a. Gold (value and Queen's head) omitted	£3000	
		Eb. Gold (value and Queen's head), embossing and phosphor omitted	£250	
		Ec. Embossing omitted		
		Ey. Phosphor omitted	7·00	
773	**304**	1s.6d. slate, orange, black, mauve, greenish yellow, ultramarine and gold	20	25
		a. Gold (value and Queen's head) omitted	£110	
		Eb. Embossing omitted	£250	
		Ey. Phosphor omitted	10·00	

774	**305**	1s.9d. greenish yellow, black, new blue, red and gold	25	40
		a. Gold (value and Queen's head) and embossing omitted	£500	
		b. Red omitted	£10000	
		Ec. Embossing omitted	£140	
		Ey. Phosphor omitted	20·00	
Set of 4			50	85
First Day Cover				2·00
Presentation Pack			2·00	
Presentation Pack (*German*)			12·00	

No. 774a is only known with the phosphor also omitted.

*The effect of this is to leave the face and hands white and there is more yellow and olive in the costume.

The 4d. also exists with the value only omitted resulting from a colour shift.

Special First Day of Issue Postmark

G.P.O. Philatelic Bureau, Edinburgh 1 (Type C) ...... 5·00

Gift Pack 1968

1968 (16 Sept). Comprises Nos. 763/74.

GP774c	Gift Pack	6·00
GP774d	Gift Pack (German)	28·00

Collectors Pack 1968

1968 (16 Sept). Comprises Nos. 752/8 and 763/74.

CP774e	Collectors Pack	7·00

306 Boy and Girl with Rocking Horse

307 Girl with Doll's House

308 Boy with Train Set

(Des Rosalind Dease. Head printed in gold and then embossed)

1968 (25 Nov). *Christmas. Chalk-surfaced paper. One centre phosphor band (4d.) or two phosphor bands (others).* P 15×14 (4d.) or 14×15 (others).

775	**306**	4d. black, orange, vermilion, ultramarine, bistre and gold	10	15
		a. Gold omitted	£4000	
		b. Vermilion omitted*	£300	
		c. Ultramarine omitted	£250	
		Ed. Embossing omitted	6·00	
		Ey. Phosphor omitted	5·00	
776	**307**	9d. yellow-olive, black, brown, yellow, magenta, orange, turquoise-green and gold	15	25
		a. Yellow omitted	65·00	
		b. Turquoise-green (dress) omitted	£10000	
		Ec. Embossing omitted	6·00	
		Ey. Phosphor omitted	10·00	
		Eya. Embossing and phosphor omitted	10·00	
777	**308**	1s.6d. ultramarine, yellow-orange, bright purple, blue-green, black and gold	15	50
		Ea. Embossing omitted		
		Ey. Phosphor omitted	15·00	
Set of 3			30	50
First Day Cover				1·20
Presentation Pack			5·00	
Presentation Pack (*German*)			14·00	

*The effect of the missing vermilion is shown on the rocking horse, saddle and faces which appear orange instead of red.

A single used example of the 4d. exists with the bistre omitted.

No. 775c is only known with phosphor also omitted.

Two machines were used for printing for the 4d. value:

Stamps from cylinders 1A-1B-2C-1D-1E in combination with 1F, 2F or 3F (gold) were printed entirely on the Rembrandt sheet-fed machine. They invariably have the Queen's head level with the top of the boy's head and the sheets are perforated through the left side margin.

Stamps from cylinders 2A-2B-3C-2D-2E in combination with 1F, 2F, 3F or 4F (gold) were printed on the reel-fed Thrissell machine in five colours (its maximum colour capacity) and subsequently sheet-fed on the Rembrandt machine for the Queen's head and the embossing. The position of the Queen's head is generally lower than on the stamps printed at one operation but it varies in different parts of the sheet and is not, therefore, a sure indication for identifying single stamps. Another small difference is that the boy's grey pullover is noticeably "moth-eaten" in the Thrissell printings and is normal on the Rembrandt. The Thrissell printings are perforated through the top margin.

Special First Day of Issue Postmarks

G.P.O.Philatelic Bureau, Edinburgh 1 (Type C)	4·00
Bethlehem, Llandeilo, Carms (Type C)	7·00

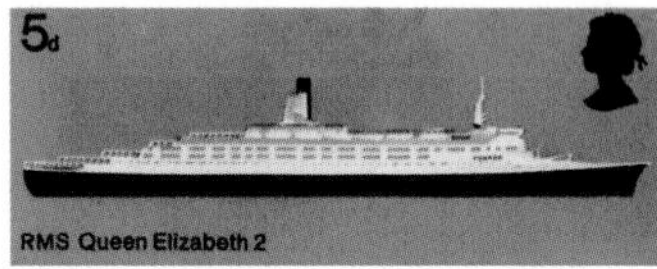

309 *Queen Elizabeth 2*

310 Elizabethan Galleon **311** East Indiaman

312 *Cutty Sark*

313 *Great Britain*

314 *Mauretania I*

(Des D. Gentleman)

1969 (15 Jan). *British Ships. Chalk-surfaced paper. Two vertical phosphor bands at right (1s.), one horizontal phosphor band (5d.) or two phosphor bands (9d.).* P 15×14.

778	**309**	5d. black, grey, red and turquoise	10	15
		a. Black (Queen's head, value, hull and inscr) omitted	£1200	
		b. Grey (decks, etc.) omitted	90·00	
		c. Red (inscription) omitted	50·00	
		Ey. Phosphor omitted	5·00	
		Eya. Red and phosphor omitted		
779	**310**	9d. red, blue, ochre, brown, black and grey	10	25
		a. Strip of 3. Nos. 779/81	1·50	3·00
		ab. Red and blue omitted	£1600	
		ac. Blue omitted	£1600	
		Ey. Phosphor omitted	12·00	
		Eya. Strip of 3. Nos. 779/81. Phosphor omitted	40·00	
780	**311**	9d. ochre, brown, black and grey	10	25
		Ey. Phosphor omitted	12·00	
		ab. Red and blue omitted	£1600	
		ac. Blue omitted	£1600	
		Ey. Phosphor omitted	12·00	
		Eya. Strip of 3. Nos. 779/81. Phosphor omitted	40·00	
781	**312**	9d. ochre, brown, black and grey	10	25
		Ey. Phosphor omitted	12·00	
782	**313**	1s. brown, black, grey, green and greenish yellow	40	35
		a. Pair. Nos. 782/3	1·25	2·50
		ab. Greenish yellow omitted	£2750	
		Ey. Phosphor omitted	28·00	
		Eya. Pair. Nos. 782/3. Phosphor omitted	65·00	
783	**314**	1s. red, black, brown, carmine and grey	40	35
		a. Carmine (hull overlay) omitted	£20000	
		b. Red (funnels) omitted	£14000	
		c. Carmine and red omitted	£14000	
		Ey. Phosphor omitted	30·00	
Set of 6			1·50	1·40
First Day Cover				6·00
Presentation Pack			4·00	
Presentation Pack (*German*)			40·00	

The 9d. and 1s. values were arranged in horizontal strips of three and pairs respectively throughout the sheet. No. 779ab is known only with the phosphor also omitted.

Special First Day of Issue Postmark

G.P.O. Philatelic Bureau, Edinburgh 1 (Type C) .... 10·00

315 Concorde in Flight

316 Plan and Elevation Views

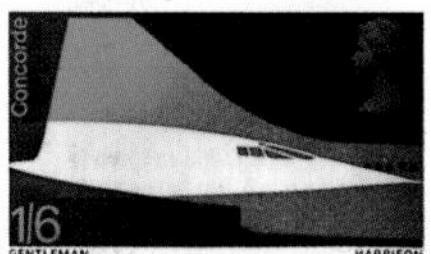

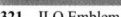

317 Concorde's Nose and Tail

(Des M. and Sylvia Goaman (4d.), D. Gentleman (9d., 1s.6d.))

1969 (3 Mar). *First Flight of Concorde. Chalk-surfaced paper. Two phosphor bands.* P 15×14.

784	**315**	4d. yellow-orange, violet, greenish blue, blue-green and pale green	25	25
		a. Violet (value etc.) omitted	£350	
		b. Yellow-orange omitted	£350	
		Ey. Phosphor omitted	1·00	
		Eya. Yellow-orange and phosphor omitted	£350	
785	**316**	9d. ultramarine, emerald, red and grey-blue	55	75
		a. Face value and inscr omitted	†	£1500
		Ey. Phosphor omitted	£100	
786	**317**	1s.6d. deep blue, silver-grey and light blue	75	1·00
		a. Silver-grey omitted	£350	
		Ey. Phosphor omitted	9·00	
Set of 3			1·00	1·50
First Day Cover				4·00
Presentation Pack			12·00	
Presentation Pack (*German*)			40·00	

No. 785a is caused by a colour shift of the grey-blue. On the only known example the top of the Queen's head appears across the perforations at foot. No. 786a affects the Queen's head which appears in the light blue colour.

G.P.O Philatelic Bureau, Edinburgh (Type C) .... 4·00
Filton, Bristol (Type C) .... 12·00

Special First Day of Issue Postmarks

318 Queen Elizabeth II
(See also Type **357**)

(Des after plaster cast by Arnold Machin. Recess Bradbury, Wilkinson)

1969 (5 Mar). P 12.

787	**318**	2s.6d. brown	35	30
788		5s. crimson-lake	1·75	60
789		10s. deep ultramarine	6·00	7·00
790		£1 bluish black	3·25	1·50
Set of 4			10·00	8·50
First Day Cover				9·50
Presentation Pack			16·00	
Presentation Pack (*German*)			60·00	

Special First Day of Issue Postmarks

G.P.O. Philatelic Bureau (Type C) .... 12·00
Windsor, Berks (Type C) .... 18·00

For decimal issue, see Nos. 829/31*b* and notes after No. 831*b*.

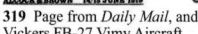

319 Page from *Daily Mail*, and Vickers FB-27 Vimy Aircraft

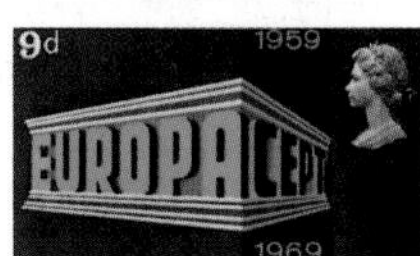

320 Europa and CEPT Emblems

321 ILO Emblem

322 Flags of NATO Countries

323 Vickers FB-27 Vimy Aircraft and Globe showing Flight

(Des P. Sharland (5d., 1s., 1s.6d.), M. and Sylvia Goaman (9d., 1s.9d.))

1969 (2 Apr). *Anniversaries. Events described on stamps. Chalk-surfaced paper. Two phosphor bands.* P 15×14.

791	**319**	5d. black, pale sage-green, chestnut and new blue	10	15
		Ey. Phosphor omitted		
792	**320**	9d. pale turquoise, dp blue, lt emerald-green and black	15	25
		Ey. Phosphor omitted		
		a. Uncoated paper*	£1500	
		Ey. Phosphor omitted	18·00	
793	**321**	1s. brt purple, dp blue and lilac	15	25
		Ey. Phosphor omitted	10·00	
794	**322**	1s.6d. red, royal blue, yellowgreen, black, lemon and new blue	15	30
		e. Black omitted	60·00	
		f. Yellow-green (from flags) omitted	50·00	
		g. Lemon (from flags) omitted	†	£3500
		Ey. Phosphor omitted	9·00	
		Eya. Yellow-green and phosphor omitted	55·00	
795	**323**	1s.9d. yellow-olive, greenish yellow and pale turquoise-green	20	40
		a. Uncoated paper*	£200	
		Ey. Phosphor omitted	6·00	
Set of 5			50	1·00
First Day Cover				3·00
Presentation Pack			3·50	
Presentation Pack (German)			55·00	

*Uncoated paper. The second note after No. 744 also applies here.

No. 794g is only known used on First Day Cover from Liverpool.

Special First Day of Issue Postmark

G.P.O. Philatelic Bureau, Edinburgh (Type C) .... 6·50

324 Durham Cathedral **325** York Minster

326 St. Giles' Cathedral, Edinburgh **327** Canterbury Cathedral

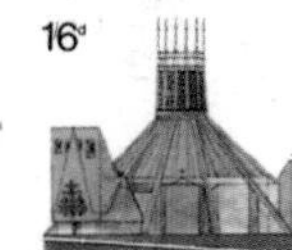

328 St. Paul's Cathedral **329** Liverpool Metropolitan Cathedral

(Des P. Gauld)

1969 (28 May). *British Architecture. Cathedrals. Chalk-surfaced paper. Two phosphor bands.* P 15×14.

796	**324**	5d. grey-black, orange, pale bluish violet and black	10	20
		a. Block of 4. Nos. 796/9	1·10	2·50
		ab. Block of 4. Uncoated paper†	£1000	
		b. Pale bluish violet omitted	£3750	
797	**325**	5d. grey-black, pale bluish violet, new blue and black	10	20
		b. Pale bluish violet omitted	£3750	
798	**326**	5d. grey-black, purple, green and black	10	20
		c. Green omitted*	55·00	
799	**327**	5d. grey-black, green, new blue and black	10	20
800	**328**	9d. grey-black, ochre, pale drab, violet and black	25	50
		a. Black (value) omitted	£100	
		Ey. Phosphor omitted	45·00	
		Eya. Black and phosphor omitted	£150	
801	**329**	1s.6d. grey-black, pale turquoise, pale reddish violet, pale yellow-olive and black	25	30
		a. Black (value) omitted	£2000	
		b. Black (value) double		
		Ey. Phosphor omitted	20·00	
Set of 6			1·10	1·30
First Day Cover				3·00
Presentation Pack			3·25	
Presentation Pack (German)			30·00	

*The missing green on the roof top is known on R. 2/5, R. 8/5 and R. 10/5 but all are from different sheets and it only occurred in part of the printing, being "probably caused by a batter on the impression cylinder". Examples are also known with the green partly omitted.

†Uncoated paper. The second note after No. 744 also applies here.

The 5d. values were issued together *se-tenant* in blocks of four throughout the sheet.

Special First Day of Issue Postmark

G.P.O. Philatelic Bureau, Edinburgh (Type C) .... 4·00

330 The King's Gate, Caernarvon Castle

331 The Eagle Tower, Caernarvon Castle

332 Queen Eleanor's Gate, Caernarvon Castle

333 Celtic Cross, Margam Abbey

334 H.R.H. The Prince of Wales (after photo by G. Argent)

(Des D. Gentleman)

1969 (1 July). *Investiture of H.R.H. The Prince of Wales. Chalk-surfaced paper. Two phosphor bands.* P 14×15.

802	**330**	5d. dp olive-grey, lt olive-grey, dp grey, light grey, red, pale turquoise-green, black and silver	10	15

		a. Strip of 3. Nos. 802/4	30	1·50
		b. Black (value and inscr) omitted	£250	
		c. Red omitted*	£400	
		d. Dp grey omitted**	£180	
		e. Pale turquoise-green omitted	£400	
		Ey. Phosphor omitted	5·00	
		Eya. Strip of 3. Nos. 802/4. Phosphor omitted	15·00	
803	331	5d. dp olive-grey, lt olive-grey, dp grey, light grey, red, pale turquoise-green, black and silver	10	15
		b. Black (value and inscr) omitted	£250	
		c. Red omitted*	£400	
		d. Deep grey omitted**	£180	
		e. Pale turquoise-green omitted	£400	
		f. Light grey (marks on walls, window frames, etc) omitted	†	£7500
		Ey. Phosphor omitted	5·00	
804	332	5d. dp olive-grey, lt olive-grey, dp grey, lt grey, red, pale turquoise-green, black and silver	10	15
		b. Black (value and inscr) omitted	£250	
		c. Red omitted*	£400	
		d. Deep grey omitted**	£180	
		e. Pale turquoise-green omitted	£400	
		Ey. Phosphor omitted	5·00	
805	333	9d. dp grey, lt grey, black and gold	15	30
		Ey. Phosphor omitted	22·00	
806	334	1s. blackish yellow-olive and gold	15	30
		Ey. Phosphor omitted	15·00	
Set of 5			50	1·00
First Day Cover				1·50
Presentation Pack†			2·50	
Presentation Pack (*German*)			28·00	

The 5d. values were issued together se-tenant in strips of three throughout the sheet.

*The 5d. value is also known with the red misplaced downwards and where this occurs the red printing does not take very well on the silver background and in some cases is so faint it could be mistaken for a missing red. However, the red can be seen under a magnifying glass and caution should therefore be exercised when purchasing copies of Nos. 802/4c.

**The deep grey affects the dark portions of the windows and doors.

†In addition to the generally issued Presentation Pack a further pack in different colours and with all texts printed in both English and Welsh was made available exclusively through Education Authorities for free distribution to all schoolchildren in Wales and Monmouthshire (Price £6).

No. 803f is only known commercially used on cover.

Special First Day of Issue Postmarks

G.P.O.Philatelic Bureau, Edinburgh 1 (Type C).	3·00
Day of Investiture, Caernarvon .	5·00

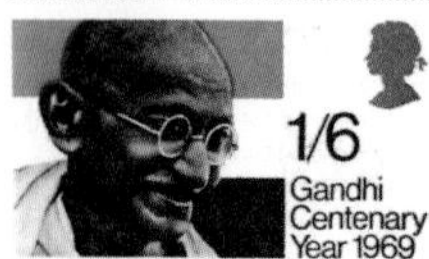

335 Mahatma Gandhi

(Des B. Mullick)

1969 (13 Aug). *Gandhi Centenary Year. Chalk-surfaced paper. Two phosphor bands.* P 15×14.

807	335	1s.6d. black, green, red-orange and grey	30	30
		a. Printed on the gummed side	£400	
		Ey. Phosphor omitted	4·00	
First Day Cover				1·00

Special First Day of Issue Postmark

G.P.O.Philatelic Bureau, Edinburgh (Type C).	1·50

Collectors Pack 1969

1969 (15 Sept). Comprises Nos. 775/86 and 791/807.

CP807*b* Collectors Pack 25·00

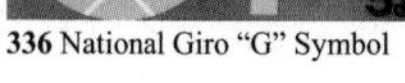

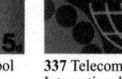

336 National Giro "G" Symbol

337 Telecommunications—International Subscriber Dialling

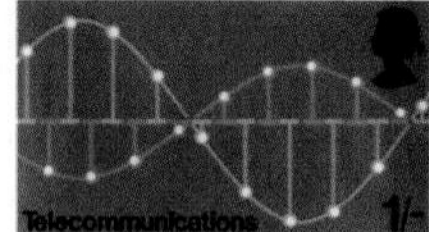

338 Telecommunications—Pulse Code Modulation

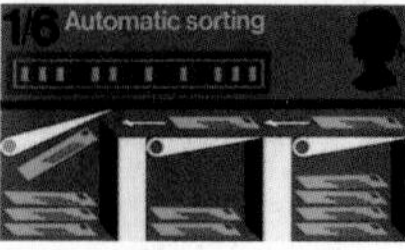

339 Postal Mechanisation—Automatic Sorting

(Des D. Gentleman. Litho De La Rue)

1969 (1 Oct). *Post Office Technology Commemoration. Chalk-surfaced paper. Two phosphor bands.* P 13½×14.

808	336	5d. new blue, greenish blue, lavender and black	10	10
		Ey. Phosphor omitted	5·00	
809	337	9d. emerald, violet-blue and black	15	20
810	338	1s. emerald, lavender and black	15	20
		Ey. Phosphor omitted	£300	
811	339	1s.6d. bright purple, light blue, grey-blue and black	15	35
Set of 4			50	75
First Day Cover				1·50
Presentation Pack			2·75	

Special First Day of Issue Postmark

G.P.O.Philatelic Bureau, Edinburgh (Type C)	2·00

340 Herald Angel

341 The Three Shepherds

342 The Three Kings

(Des F. Wegner. Queen's head (and stars 4d., 5d. and scrollwork 1s.6d.) printed in gold and then embossed)

1969 (26 Nov). *Christmas. Chalk-surfaced paper. Two phosphor bands (5d., 1s.6d.) or one centre band (4d.).* P 15×14.

812	340	4d. vermilion, new blue, orange, brt purple, light green, bluish violet, blackish brown and gold	10	10
		a. Gold (Queen's head etc.) omitted	£4000	
		Eb. Centre band 3½ mm	30	20
813	341	5d. magenta, light blue, royal blue, olive-brown, green, greenish yellow, red and gold	15	15
		a. Lt blue (sheep, etc.) omitted	60·00	
		b. Red omitted*	£675	
		c. Gold (Queen's head) omitted	£450	
		d. Green omitted	£200	
		e. Olive-brown, red and gold omitted	£9000	
		Ef. Embossing omitted	22·00	
		Ey. Phosphor omitted	5·00	
814	342	1s.6d. greenish yellow, brt purple, bluish violet, dp slate, orange, green, new blue and gold	20	20
		a. Gold (Queen's head etc.) omitted	90·00	
		b. Deep slate (value) omitted	£250	
		c. Greenish yellow omitted	£250	
		e. New blue omitted	60·00	
		Ef. Embossing omitted	10·00	
		Ey. Phosphor omitted	6·00	
		Eya. Embossing and phosphor omitted	10·00	
Set of 3			30	30
First Day Cover				1·00
Presentation Pack			2·50	

*The effect of the missing red is shown on the hat, leggings and purse which appear as dull orange.

No. 812 has one centre band 8mm. wide but this was of no practical use in the automatic facing machines and after about three-quarters of the stamps had been printed the remainder were printed with a 3½mm. band (No. 812Eb).

No. 813e was caused by a paper fold and also shows the phosphor omitted.

Used copies of the 5d. have been seen with the olive-brown or greenish yellow (tunic at left) omitted.

Special First Day of Issue Postmarks

P.O. Philatelic Bureau, Edinburgh (Type C)	3·00
Bethlehem, Llandeilo, Carms (Type C)	3·00

343 Fife Harling

344 Cotswold Limestone

345 Welsh Stucco

346 Ulster Thatch

(Des D. Gentleman (5d., 9d.), Sheila Robinson (1s., 1s.6d.))

1970 (11 Feb). *British Rural Architecture. Chalk-surfaced paper. Two phosphor bands.* P 15×14.

No.	Type		Description	Mint	Used
815	**343**	5d.	grey, grey-black, black, lemon, greenish blue, orange-brown, ultramarine and green	10	10
		a.	Lemon omitted	80·00	
		b.	Grey (Queen's head and cottage shading) omitted	£5000	
		c.	Greenish blue (door) omitted	†	£3500
		Ey.	Phosphor omitted	2·00	
816	**344**	9d.	orange-brown, olive-yellow, bright green, black, grey-black and grey	10	25
		Ey.	Phosphor omitted	10·00	
817	**345**	1s.	deep blue, reddish lilac, drab and new blue	15	25
		a.	New blue omitted	80·00	
		Ey.	Phosphor omitted	15·00	
818	**346**	1s.6d.	greenish yellow, black, turquoise-blue and lilac	20	40
		a.	Turquoise-blue omitted	£5000	
		Ey.	Phosphor omitted	5·00	
Set of 4				50	75
First Day Cover					1·50
Presentation Pack				3·25	

Used examples of the 5d. exist, one of which is on piece, with the greenish blue colour omitted.

Special First Day of Issue Postmark

British Philatelic Bureau, Edinburgh (Type C)	3·00

347 Signing the Declaration of Arbroath

348 Florence Nightingale attending Patients

349 Signing of International Co-operative Alliance

350 Pilgrims and *Mayflower*

351 Sir William Herschel, Francis Baily, Sir John Herschel and Telescope

(Des F. Wegner (5d., 9d. and 1s.6d.), Marjorie Saynor (1s., 1s.9d.). Queen's head printed in gold and then embossed)

1970 (1 Apr). *Anniversaries. Events described on stamps. Chalk-surfaced paper. Two phosphor bands.* P 15×14.

No.	Type		Description	Mint	Used
819	**347**	5d.	black, yellow-olive, blue, emerald, greenish yellow, rose-red, gold and orange-red	10	10
		a.	Gold (Queen's head) omitted	£700	
		b.	Emerald omitted	£225	
		Ey.	Phosphor omitted	£300	
820	**348**	9d.	ochre, deep blue, carmine, black, blue-green, yellow-olive, gold and blue	15	15
		a.	Ochre omitted	£180	
		Eb.	Embossing omitted	15·00	
		Ey.	Phosphor omitted	5·00	
821	**349**	1s.	green, greenish yellow, brown, black, cerise, gold and lt blue	20	25
		a.	Gold (Queen's head) omitted	50·00	
		Eb.	Green and embossing omitted	80·00	
		c.	Green omitted	85·00	
		d.	Brown omitted	£150	
		Ee.	Embossing omitted	12·00	
		Ey.	Phosphor omitted	5·00	
		Eya.	Brown and phosphor omitted	£150	
		Eyb.	Embossing and phosphor omitted	22·00	
822	**350**	1s.6d.	greenish yellow, carmine, deep yellow-olive, emerald, black, blue, gold and sage-green	20	30
		a.	Gold (Queen's head) omitted	£140	
		b.	Emerald omitted	75·00	
		Ec.	Embossing omitted	6·00	
		Ey.	Phosphor omitted	5·00	
823	**351**	1s.9d.	black, slate, lemon, gold and bright purple	25	30
		a.	Lemon (trousers and document) omitted	£7500	
		Eb.	Embossing omitted	75·00	
		Ey.	Phosphor omitted	5·00	
Set of 5				75	1·00
First Day Cover					2·00
Presentation Pack				3·00	

No. 823a is known mint, or used on First Day Cover postmarked London WC.

Special First Day of Issue Postmark

British Philatelic Bureau, Edinburgh (Type C)	2·50

First Day of Issue handstamps were provided at Arbroath, Angus, Billericay, Essex; Boston, Lincs and Rochdale, Lancs for this issue.

HAVE YOU READ THE NOTES AT THE BEGINNING OF THIS CATALOGUE?

These often provide answers to the enquiries we receive

352 "Mr. Pickwick and Sam" (*Pickwick Papers*)

353 "Mr. and Mrs. Micawber" (*David Copperfield*)

354 "David Copperfield and Betsy Trotwood" (*David Copperfield*)

355 "Oliver asking for more" (*Oliver Twist*)

356 "Grasmere" (from engraving by J. Farrington, R.A.)

T **352/5** were issued together *se-tenant* in blocks of four throughout the sheet.

(Des Rosalind Dease. Queen's head printed in gold and then embossed)

1970 (3 June). *Literary Anniversaries. Death Centenary of Charles Dickens (novelist) (5d.×4) and Birth Bicentenary of William Wordsworth (poet) (1s.6d.). Chalk-surfaced paper. Two phosphor bands.* P 14×15.

824	**352**	5d. black, orange, silver, gold and magenta	10	25
		a. Block of 4. Nos. 824/7	75	2·00
		ab. Imperf (block of four)	£850	
		ac. Silver (inscr) omitted (block of four)	£20000	
825	**353**	5d. black, magenta, silver, gold and orange	10	25
826	**354**	5d. black, light greenish blue, silver, gold and yellow-bistre	10	25
		b. Yellow-bistre (value) omitted	£2000	
827	**355**	5d. black, yellow-bistre, silver, gold and light greenish blue	10	25
		b. Yellow-bistre (background) omitted	£4250	
		c. Lt greenish blue (value) omitted*	£500	
		d. Lt greenish blue and silver (inscr at foot) omitted	£8000	
828	**356**	1s.6d. yellow-olive, black, silver, gold and bright blue	25	50
		a. Gold (Queen's head) omitted	£2700	
		b. Silver ("Grasmere") omitted	£110	
		c. Bright blue (face value) omitted	£8000	
		d. Bright blue and silver omitted	£12000	
		Ee. Embossing omitted	6·00	
		Ey. Phosphor omitted	5·00	
		Eya. Embossing and phosphor omitted	22·00	
Set of 5			1·00	1·50
First Day Cover				2·00
Presentation Pack			3·00	

*No. 827c (unlike No. 826b) comes from a sheet on which the colour was only partially omitted so that, although No. 827 was completely without the light greenish blue colour, it was still partially present on No. 826.

Essays exist of Nos. 824/7 showing the Queen's head in silver and with different inscriptions.

Special First Day of Issue Postmarks

British Philatelic Bureau, Edinburgh (Type C)	5·00
Cockermouth, Cumberland (Type C) (No. 828 only)	7·00
Rochester, Kent (Type C) (Nos. 824/7)	6·00

A First Day of Issue handstamp was provided at Broadstairs, Kent, for this issue.

356a

357 (Value redrawn)

(Des after plaster cast by Arnold Machin. Recess B.W.)

1970 (17 June)–**72**. *Decimal Currency. Chalk-surfaced paper or phosphorised paper (10p.).* P 12.

829	**356a**	10p. cerise	50	75
830		20p. olive-green	60	25
		Ea. Thinner uncoated paper*		
831		50p. deep ultramarine	1·25	40
		Ea. Thinner uncoated paper*	45·00	
831*b*	**357**	£1 bluish black (6.12.72)	3·50	80
Set of 4			5·25	2·00
First Day Cover (829/31)				2·75
First Day Cover (831b)				3·00
Presentation Pack No. 18 (829/31)			9·00	
Presentation Pack No. 38 (790 (or 831b), 830/1)			10·00	

*These are not as apparent as uncoated photogravure issues where there is normally a higher degree of chalk-surfacing. The 20p. is known only as a block of four with Plate No. 5. The 50p. comes from Plate No. 9.

The 10p. on phosphorised paper continued the experiments which started with the Machin 1s.6d. When the experiment had ended a quantity of the 50p. value was printed on the phosphorised paper to use up the stock. These stamps were issued on 1 February 1973, but they cannot be distinguished from No. 831 by the naked eye. (*Price* £2).

A £1 was also issued in 1970, but it is difficult to distinguish it from the earlier No. 790. In common with the other 1970 values it was issued in sheets of 100.

A whiter paper was introduced in 1973. The £1 appeared on 27 Sept. 1973, the 20p. on 30 Nov. 1973 and the 50p. on 20 Feb. 1974.

Imperforate examples of No. 831b are believed to be printer's waste.

Special First Day of Issue Postmarks

British Philatelic Bureau, Edinburgh (Type C) (Nos. 829/31)	6·00
Windsor, Berks (Type C) (Nos. 829/31)	12·00
Philatelic Bureau, Edinburgh (Type E) (No. 831*b*)	6·00
Windsor, Berks (Type E) (No. 831*b*)	9·00

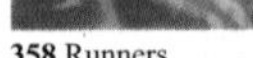

358 Runners

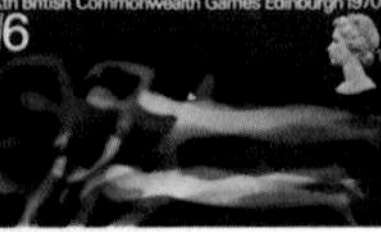

359 Swimmers

360 Cyclists

(Des A. Restall. Litho D.L.R.)

1970 (15 July). *Ninth British Commonwealth Games. Chalk-surfaced paper. Two phosphor bands.* P 13½×14.

No.	Type	Description	Unused	Used
832	**358**	5d. pink, emerald, greenish yellow and deep yellow-green	25	25
		a. Greenish yellow omitted	£7500	
		Ey. Phosphor omitted	£200	
833	**359**	1s.6d. light greenish blue, lilac, bistre-brown and Prussian blue	50	50
		Ey. Phosphor omitted	60·00	
834	**360**	1s.9d. yellow-orange, lilac, salmon and deep red-brown	50	50
Set of 3			75	75
First Day Cover				1·20
Presentation Pack			3·00	

Special First Day of Issue Postmark

British Philatelic Bureau, Edinburgh (Type C). .... 8·00

Collectors Pack 1970

1970 Sept 14 Comprises Nos. 808/28 and 832/4.
CP834*a* Collectors Pack .... 25·00

361 1d. Black (1840)

362 1s. Green (1847)

363 4d. Carmine (1855)

(Des D. Gentleman)

1970 (18 Sept). *"Philympia 70" Stamp Exhibition. Chalk-surfaced paper. Two phosphor bands.* P 14×14½.

No.	Type	Description	Unused	Used
835	**361**	5d. grey-black, brownish bistre, black and dull purple	25	10
		a. Grey-black (Queen's head) omitted	£12000	
		Ey. Phosphor omitted	5·00	
836	**362**	9d. light drab, bluish green, stone, black and dull purple	25	30
		Ey. Phosphor omitted	11·00	
837	**363**	1s.6d. carmine, light drab, black and dull purple	25	45
		Ey. Phosphor omitted	4·00	
Set of 3			50	75
First Day Cover				1·50
Presentation Pack			2·75	

Special First Day of Issue Postmark

British Post Office Philatelic Bureau, Edinburgh (Type D) .... 2·50

364 Shepherds and Apparition of the Angel

365 Mary, Joseph and Christ in the Manger

366 The Wise Men bearing gifts

(Des Sally Stiff after De Lisle Psalter. Queen's head printed in gold and then embossed)

1970 (25 Nov). *Christmas. Chalk-surfaced paper. One centre phosphor band (4d.) or two phosphor bands (others).* P 14×15.

No.	Type	Description	Unused	Used
838	**364**	4d. brown-red, turquoise-green, pale chestnut, brown, grey-black, gold and vermilion	15	10
		Ea. Embossing omitted	50·00	
		Ey. Phosphor omitted	60·00	
839	**365**	5d. emerald, gold, blue, brown-red, ochre, grey-black and violet	15	15
		a. Gold (Queen's head) omitted	†	£3500
		b. Emerald omitted	60·00	
		c. Imperf (pair)	£275	
		Ed. Embossing omitted	15·00	
		Ey. Phosphor omitted	5·00	
840	**365**	1s.6d. gold, grey-black, pale turquoise-green, salmon, ultramarine, ochre and yellow-green	25	30
		a. Salmon omitted	80·00	
		b. Ochre omitted	55·00	
		Ec. Embossing omitted	35·00	
		Ey. Phosphor omitted	5·00	
		Eya. Embossing and phosphor omitted		
Set of 3			50	50
First Day Cover				1·50
Presentation Pack			2·75	

Special First Day of Issue Postmarks

British Post Office Philatelic Bureau, Edinburgh (Type D) .... 2·50
Bethlehem, Llandeilo, Carms .... 3·50

(New Currency. 100 new pence = £1)

"X" NUMBERS. The following definitive series has been allocated "X" prefixes to the catalogue numbers to avoid renumbering all subsequent issues.

NO VALUE INDICATED. Stamps as Types **367/a** inscribed "2nd" or "1st" are listed as Nos. 1445/52, 1511/16, 1663a/6, 1979 and 2039/40.

ELLIPTICAL PERFORATIONS. These were introduced in 1993 and stamps showing them will be found listed as Nos. Y1667 etc.

367

367a

Printing differences

Litho

Photo

(Illustrations enlarged ×6)

Litho. Clear outlines to value and frame of stamp.
Photo. Uneven lines to value and frame formed by edges of screen.

Two types of the 3p., 10p. and 26p. (Nos. X930/c, X886/b and X971/b)

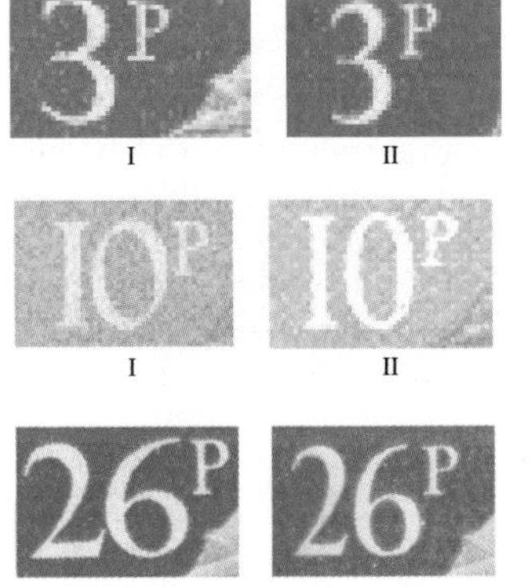

I II

I II

I II

Figures of face value as I (all ptgs of 3p. bright magenta except the multi-value coil No. 930cl and sheets from 21.1.92 onwards, 10p. orange-brown except 1984 "Christian Heritage" £4 booklet and 26p. rosine except 1987 £1.04 barcode booklet).

Figures of face value narrower as in II (from coil No. X930cl and in sheets from 21.1.92 (3p.), 1984 "Christian Heritage" £4 booklet (10p.) or 1987 £1.04 barcode booklet (26p.)). This catalogue includes changes of figure styles on these stamps where there is no other listable difference. Similar changes have also taken place on other values, but only in conjuction with listed colour, paper or perforation changes.

1971 (15 Feb)–**96.** *Decimal Currency. T* **367**. *Chalk-surfaced paper.*

(a) Photo Harrison (except for some printings of Nos. X879 and X913 in sheets produced by Enschedé and issued on 12 Dec 1979 (8p.) and 19 Nov 1991 (18p.)). With phosphor bands. P 15×14.

No.		Description	Mint	Used
X841	½p.	turquoise-blue (2 bands)	10	10
	a.	Imperf (pair)†	£1500	
	l.	Booklet pane. No. X841×2 *se-tenant* vert with X849×2	6·00	
	lEy.	Booklet pane. Phosphor omitted	£200	
	la.	Booklet pane. No. X841×2 *se-tenant* horiz with X849×2 (14.7.71)	1·00	
	laEy.	Booklet pane. Phosphor omitted	£350	
	m.	Booklet pane. No. X841×5 plus label	2·75	
	mEy.	Booklet pane. Phosphor omitted	£110	
	n.	Coil strip. No. X849Eg, X841Eg×2 and X844Eg×2	1·75	
	nEy.	Coil strip. Phosphor omitted	40·00	
	nEv.	Coil strip. PVA gum. No. X849, X841×2 and X844×2 (4.74)	45	
	nEvy.	Coil strip. Phosphor omitted	15·00	
	o.	Booklet pane. No. X841, X851, X852, X852Ea, each×3 (24.5.72)	13·00	
	oEy.	Booklet pane. Phosphor omitted	£1500	
	p.	Booklet pane. No. X841×3, X842 and X852×2 (24.5.72)	60·00	
	pEy.	Booklet pane. Phosphor omitted		
	q.	Coil strip. No. X870, X849, X844 and X841×2 (3.12.75)	1·00	
	r.	Booklet pane. No. X841×2, X844×3 and X870 (10.3.76)	75	
	s.	Booklet pane. No. X841×2, X844×2, X873×2 and X881×4 (8½p. values at right) (26.1.77)	2·00	
	sa.	Ditto, but No. X873Ea and 8½p. values at left	2·00	
	t.	Booklet pane. No. X841, X844, X894×3 and X902 (14p. value at right) (26.1.81)	2·00	
	tEy.	Booklet pane. Phosphor omitted	60·00	
	ta.	Booklet pane. No. X841, X844, X894Ea×3 and X902 (14p. value at left)	1·90	
	taEy.	Booklet pane. Phosphor omitted	60·00	
	u.	Booklet pane. No. X841, X857×4 and X899×3 (12½p. values at left) (1.2.82)	3·00	
	ua.	Ditto, but No. X899Ea and 12½p. values at right	3·00	
	Eg.	Gum arabic (from coil strip, and on 22.9.72 from sheets)	40	
	Egy.	Phosphor omitted	45·00	
X842	½p.	turquoise-blue (1 side band at left) (24.5.72)	55·00	25·00
X843	½p.	turquoise-blue (1 centre band) (14.12.77)	40	25
	l.	Coil strip. No. X843×2, X875 and X845×2 (14.12.77)	85	
	m.	Booklet pane. No. X843×2, X845×2 and X875 plus label (8.2.78)	60	
	mEy.	Booklet pane. Phosphor omitted	40·00	
X844	1p.	crimson (2 bands)	10	15
	a.	Imperf (vert coil)		
	b.	Pair, one imperf 3 sides (vert coil)		
	c.	Imperf (pair)	£1000	
	l.	Booklet pane. No. X844×2 *se-tenant* vert with X848×2	6·00	
	m.	Ditto, but *se-tenant* horiz (14.7.71)	1·00	
	mEy.	Booklet pane. Phosphor omitted	£150	
	n.	Booklet pane. No. X844×2, X876×3 and X883×3 (9p. values at right) (13.6.77)	4·75	
	na.	Ditto, but No. X876Ea and 9p. values at left	2·75	
	Eg.	Gum arabic (from coil strip)	50	
	Egy.	Phosphor omitted	45·00	
X845	1p.	crimson (1 centre band) (14.12.77)	25	20
	l.	Booklet pane. No. X879 and X845×2 plus label (17.10.79)	60	
	m.	Coil strip. No. X879 and X845×2 plus 2 labels (16.1.80)	85	
	n.	Booklet pane. No. X845×2, X860 and X898 each×3 (5.4.83)	6·50	
	nEy.	Booklet pane. Phosphor omitted	20·00	
	p.	Booklet pane. No. X845×3, X863×2 and X900×3 (3.9.84)	4·00	
	pEy.	Booklet pane. Phosphor omitted	£225	
	q.	Booklet pane. No. X845×2 and X896×4 (29.7.86)	9·00	
	s.	Booklet pane. No. X845, X867×2 and X900×3 (20.10.86)	6·00	
	sa.	Ditto, but with vertical edges of pane imperf (29.9.87)	3·00	
	saEy.	Booklet pane. Phosphor omitted	£200	
X846	1p.	crimson ("all-over") (10.10.79)	15	25
X847	1p.	crimson (1 side band at left) (20.10.86)	1·00	1·25

No.	Description	Unused	Used
	Ea. Band at right (3.3.87)	3·50	3·00
	l. Booklet pane. No. X847, X901 and X912×2 (20.10.86)	3·00	
	lEy. Booklet pane. Phosphor omitted	£100	
	m. Booklet pane. No. X847Ea, X901×2, X912×5 and X918 with margins all round (3.3.87)	16·00	
X848	1½p. black (2 bands)	15	25
	a. Uncoated paper*	£130	
	b. Imperf (pair)		
	c. Imperf 3 sides (horiz pair)		
	Ey. Phosphor omitted	55·00	
X849	2p. myrtle-green (2 bands)	15	20
	a. Imperf (horiz pair)	£1750	
	l. Booklet pane. No. X849×2, X880×2 and X886×3 plus label (10p. values at right) (28.8.79)	2·50	
	la. Ditto, but No. X880Ea and 10p. values at left	2·50	
	m. Booklet pane. No. X849×3, X889×2 and X895×2 plus label (12p. values at right) (4.2.80)	2·50	
	mEy. Booklet pane. Phosphor omitted	50·00	
	ma. Booklet pane. No. X849×3, X889Ea×2 and X895×2 plus label (12p. values at left)	2·50	
	maEy. Booklet pane. Phosphor omitted	50·00	
	n. Booklet pane. No. X849, X888×3, X889Ea and X895×4 with margins all round (16.4.80)	4·25	
	nEy. Booklet pane. Phosphor omitted	50·00	
	o. Booklet pane. No. X849×6 with margins all round (16.4.80)	1·40	
	oEy. Booklet pane. Phosphor omitted	55·00	
	p. Booklet pane. No. X849, X857, X898, X899×3 and X899Ea×3 with margins all round (19.5.82)	6·00	
	pEy. Booklet pane. Phosphor omitted	£150	
	Eg. Gum arabic (from coil strip)	2·25	
	Egy. Phosphor omitted	£200	
X850	2p. myrtle-green ("all-over") (10.10.79)	25	30
X851	2½p. magenta (1 centre band)	20	15
	a. Imperf (pair)†	£275	
	Ey. Phosphor omitted	10·00	
	l. Booklet pane. No. X851×5 plus label	4·50	
	lEy. Booklet pane. Phosphor omitted	35·00	
	m. Booklet pane. No. X851×4 plus two labels	5·00	
	mEy. Booklet pane. Phosphor omitted	£150	
	n. Booklet pane. No. X851×3, X852Ea×3 and X855×6 (24.5.72)	8·00	
	nEy. Booklet pane. Phosphor omitted		
	Eg. Gum arabic (13.9.72)	30	
X852	2½p. magenta (1 band at left)	1·50	1·75
	l. Booklet pane. No. X852×2 and X855×4 .	6·00	
	lEy. Booklet pane. Phosphor omitted	£150	
	Ea. Band at right (24.5.72)	1·50	1·75
X853	2½p. magenta (2 bands) (21.5.75)	25	50
X854	2½p. rose-red (2 bands) (26.8.81)	40	60
	l. Booklet pane. No. X854×3, X862×2 and X894×3 (11½p. values at left)	5·25	
	la. Ditto, but No. X894Ea and 11½p. values at right	7·00	
X855	3p. ultramarine (2 bands)	20	25
	a. Imperf (coil strip of 5)	£1750	
	b. Imperf (pair)†	£275	
	c. Uncoated paper*	45·00	
	Ey. Phosphor omitted	2·00	
	l. Booklet pane. No. X855×5 plus label	2·50	
	lEy. Booklet pane. Phosphor omitted	£375	
	n. Booklet pane. No. X855×12 (24.5.72)	5·00	
	nEy. Booklet pane. Phosphor omitted	£250	
	Eg. Gum arabic (23.8.72)	50	
	Egy. Phosphor omitted	10·00	
X856	3p. ultramarine (1 centre band) (10.9.73)	15	20
	a. Imperf (pair)†	£275	
	b. Imperf between (vert pair)†	£375	
	c. Imperf horiz (vert pair)†	£225	
	Eg. Gum arabic	50	
X857	3p. bright magenta (Type I) (2 bands) (1.2.82)	35	35
X858	3½p. olive-grey (2 bands) (*shades*)	25	30
	a. Imperf (pair)	£400	
	Ey. Phosphor omitted	10·00	
	Eb. *Bronze-green* (18.7.73)	25	30
	Eby. Phosphor omitted	10·00	
X859	3½p. olive-grey (1 centre band) (24.6.74)	30	35
X860	3½p. purple-brown (1 centre band) (5.4.83)	1·25	1·25
X861	4p. ochre-brown (2 bands)	20	25
	a. Imperf (pair)†	£1500	
	Ey. Phosphor omitted	35·00	
	Eg. Gum arabic (1.11.72)	40	
X862	4p. greenish blue (2 bands) (26.8.81)	1·75	2·00
X863	4p. greenish blue (1 centre band) (3.9.84)	1·50	1·90
X864	4p. greenish blue (1 band at right) (8.1.85)	1·75	1·75
	Ea. Band at left	1·60	1·75
	l. Booklet pane. No. X864, X864Ea, X901×2, X901Ea×2, X909×2 and X920 with margins all round (8.1.85)	14·00	
	lEy. Booklet pane. Phosphor omitted	£1400	
X865	4½p. grey-blue (2 bands) (24.10.73)	25	30
	a. Imperf (pair)	£325	
	Ey. Phosphor omitted	8·00	
X866	5p. pale violet (2 bands)	20	20
X867	5p. claret (1 centre band) (20.10.86)	2·00	2·25
	Ey. Phosphor omitted	80·00	
X868	5½p. violet (2 bands) (24.10.73)	25	30
X869	5½p. violet (1 centre band) (17.3.75)	25	30
	a. Uncoated paper*	£400	
	Ey. Phosphor omitted	18·00	
X870	6p. light emerald (2 bands)	25	20
	a. Uncoated paper*	20·00	
	Ey. Phosphor omitted	70·00	
	Eg. Gum arabic (6.6.73)	2·50	
X871	6½p. greenish blue (2 bands) (4.9.74)	30	35
X872	6½p. greenish blue (1 centre band) (24.9.75)	25	20
	a. Imperf (vert pair)	£325	
	b. Uncoated paper*	£175	
	Ey. Phosphor omitted	13·00	
X873	6½p. greenish blue (1 band at right) (26.1.77)	70	75
	Ea. Band at left	55	55
X874	7p. purple-brown (2 bands) (15.1.75)	30	35
	a. Imperf (pair)	£750	
	Ey. Phosphor omitted	1·50	
X875	7p. purple-brown (1 centre band) (13.6.77)	25	30
	a. Imperf (pair)	£140	
	l. Booklet pane. No. X875 and X883, each×10 (15.11.78)	4·50	
X876	7p. purple-brown (1 band at right) (13.6.77)	50	50
	Ea. Band at left	45	50
X877	7½p. pale chestnut (2 bands)	25	35
	Ey. Phosphor omitted	20·00	
X878	8p. rosine (2 bands) (24.10.73)	25	30
	a. Uncoated paper*	15·00	
X879	8p. rosine (1 centre band) (20.8.79)	25	30
	a. Uncoated paper*	£850	
	b. Imperf (pair)	£650	
	Ey. Phosphor omitted	£450	
	l. Booklet pane. No. X879 and X886, each×10 (14.11.79)	5·00	
X880	8p. rosine (1 band at right) (28.8.79)	60	75
	Ea. Band at left	60	75
X881	8½p. light yellowish green (2 bands) (*shades*) (24.9.75)	30	25
	a. Imperf (pair)	£1000	
	Eb. *Yellowish green* (24.3.76)	35	35
X882	9p. yellow-orange and black (2 bands)	45	55
	Ey. Phosphor omitted	£100	
X883	9p. deep violet (2 bands) (25.2.76)	35	25
	a. Imperf (pair)	£275	
	Ey. Phosphor omitted	4·00	
X884	9½p. purple (2 bands) (25.2.76)	35	45
	Ey. Phosphor omitted	20·00	
X885	10p. orange-brown and chestnut (2 bands) (11.8.71)	35	30
	a. Orange-brown omitted	£180	
	b. Imperf (horiz pair)	£1750	
	Ey. Phosphor omitted	10·00	
X886	10p. orange-brown (Type I) (2 bands) (25.2.76)	35	25
	a. Imperf (pair)	£275	
	b. Type II (4.9.84)	22·00	22·00
	bl. Booklet pane. No. X886b, X901Ea and X909×7 with margins all round	32·00	
	blEy. Booklet pane. Phosphor omitted	£2000	
X887	10p. orange-brown (Type I) ("all-over") (3.10.79)	35	45
X888	10p. orange-brown (Type I) (1 centre band) (4.2.80)	35	25

No.	Description	Unused	Used
	a. Imperf (pair)	£300	
	l. Booklet pane. No. X888×9 with margins all round (16.4.80)	3·75	
	lEy. Booklet pane. Phosphor omitted	50·00	
	m. Booklet pane. No. X888 and X895, each×10 (12.11.80)	5·50	
X889	10p. orange-brown (Type I) (1 band at right) (4.2.80)	70	80
	Ea. Band at left	70	80
X890	10½p. yellow (2 bands) (25.2.76)	40	45
X891	10½p. deep dull blue (2 bands) (26.4.78)	45	50
X892	11p. brown-red (2 bands) (25.2.76)	40	30
	a. Imperf (pair)	£2250	
X893	11½p. drab (1 centre band) (14.1.81)	40	35
	a. Imperf (pair)	£300	
	Ey. Phosphor omitted	6·00	
	l. Booklet pane. No. X893 and X902, each×10 (11.11.81)	8·50	
X894	11½p. drab (1 band at right) (26.1.81)	55	70
	Ea. Band at left	55	70
	l. Booklet pane. No. X894/Ea, each×2 & X902×6 (6.5.81)	6·50	
X895	12p. yellowish green (2 bands) (4.2.80)	45	45
	l. Booklet pane. No. X895×9 with margins all round (16.4.80)	4·00	
	lEy. Booklet pane. Phosphor omitted	40·00	
X896	12p. bright emerald (1 centre band) (29.10.85)	45	45
	a. Imperf (pair)	£1000	
	Eu. Underprint Type 4 (29.10.85)	55	
	Ey. Phosphor omitted	10·00	
	l. Booklet pane. No. X896×9 with margins all round (18.3.86)	4·75	
	lEy. Booklet pane. Phosphor omitted	£200	
X897	12p. bright emerald (1 band at right) (14.1.86)	80	85
	Ea. Band at left	80	85
	l. Booklet pane. No. X897/Ea, each×2 and X909×6 (12p. values at left) (14.1.86)	6·00	
	la. Ditto, but 12p. values at right	6·00	
	m. Booklet pane. No. X897/Ea, each×3, X909×2 and X919 with margins all round (18.3.86)	23·00	
	mEy. Booklet pane. Phosphor omitted	£1250	
X898	12½p. light emerald (1 centre band) (27.1.82)	45	40
	a. Imperf (pair)	£100	
	Eu. Underprint Type 1 (10.11.82)	60	
	Euy. Phosphor omitted	70·00	
	Ev. Underprint Type 2 (9.11.83)	60	
	Ey. Phosphor omitted	5·50	
	l. Booklet pane. No. X898Eu and X907Eu, each×10 (10.11.82)	8·50	
X899	12½p. light emerald (1 band at right) (1.2.82)	70	75
	Ea. Band at left	70	75
	l. Booklet pane. No. X899/Ea, each×2 and X907×6 (1.2.82)††	5·00	
	lEy. Booklet pane. Phosphor omitted		
	m. Booklet pane. No. X899/Ea, each×3 with margins all round (19.5.82)	3·25	
	mEy. Booklet pane. Phosphor omitted	40·00	
	n. Booklet pane. No. X899/Ea, each×2, and X908×6 (12½p. values at left) (5.4.83)	8·50	
	na. Ditto, but 12½p. values at right	8·00	
X900	13p. pale chestnut (1 centre band) (28.8.84)	40	40
	a. Imperf (pair)	£550	
	Eu. Underprint Type 2 (2.12.86)	90	
	Ey. Phosphor omitted	5·50	
	l. Booklet pane. No. X900×9 with margins all round (8.1.85)	4·50	
	lEy. Booklet pane. Phosphor omitted	£400	
	m. Booklet pane. No. X900×6 with margins all round (3.3.87)	3·75	
	n. Booklet pane. No. X900×4 with margins all round (4.8.87)	3·00	
	o. Booklet pane. No. X900×10 with margins all round (4.8.87)	5·00	
X901	13p. pale chestnut (1 band at right) (3.9.84)	50	60
	Ea. Band at left	50	60
	l. Booklet pane. No. X901/Ea, each×2, and X909×6 (13p. values at left)††	5·00	
	la. Ditto, but 13p. values at right	5·00	
	m. Booklet pane. No. X901/Ea, each×3 with margins all round (4.9.84)	4·50	
	mEy. Booklet pane. Phosphor omitted	£300	
	n. Booklet pane. No. X901Ea and X912×5 (20.10.86)	4·50	
	na. Ditto, but with vertical edges of pane imperf (29.9.87)	4·75	
X902	14p. grey-blue (2 bands) (26.1.81)	75	80
X903	14p. deep blue (1 centre band) (23.8.88)	40	50
	a. Imperf (pair)	£375	
	Ey. Phosphor omitted	7·00	
	l. Booklet pane. No. X903×4 with margins all round	6·00	
	lEy. Booklet pane. Phosphor omitted	£100	
	m. Booklet pane. No. X903×10 with margins all round	9·50	
	n. Booklet pane. No. X903×4 with horizontal edges of pane imperf (11.10.88)	6·50	
	p. Booklet pane. No. X903×10 with horizontal edges of pane imperf (11.10.88)	9·00	
	pEy. Booklet pane. Phosphor omitted	£150	
	q. Booklet pane. No. X903×4 with three edges of pane imperf (24.1.89)	32·00	
	qEy. Booklet pane. Phosphor omitted	35·00	
X904	14p. deep blue (1 band at right) (5.9.88)	4·00	4·00
	l. Booklet pane. No. X904 and X914×2 plus label	8·00	
	lEy. Booklet pane. Phosphor omitted	12·00	
	m. Booklet pane. No. X904×2 and X914×4 with vertical edges of pane imperf	6·50	
	mEy. Booklet pane. Phosphor omitted	£800	
X905	15p. bright blue (1 centre band) (26.9.89)	65	65
	a. Imperf (pair)	£475	
	Ey. Phosphor omitted	10·00	
X906	15p. brt blue (1 band at left) (2.10.89)	3·50	3·50
	Ea. Band at right (20.3.90)	3·00	3·00
	l. Booklet pane. No. X906×2 and X916 plus label	9·50	
	lEy. Booklet pane. Phosphor omitted	£500	
	m. Booklet pane. No. X906Ea, X916, X922, 1446, 1448, 1468Ea, 1470 and 1472 plus label with margins all round (20.3.90)	20·00	
X907	15½p. pale violet (2 bands) (1.2.82)	60	65
	Eu. Underprint Type 1 (10.11.82)	60	
	l. Booklet pane. No. X907×6 with margins all round (19.5.82)	4·00	
	lEy. Booklet pane. Phosphor omitted	80·00	
	m. Booklet pane. No. X907×9 with margins all round (19.5.82)	5·25	
	mEy. Booklet pane. Phosphor omitted	45·00	
X908	16p. olive-drab (2 bands) (5.4.83)	1·25	1·40
X909	17p. grey-blue (2 bands) (3.9.84)	60	60
	Eu. Underprint Type 4 (4.11.85)	70	
	l. Booklet pane. No. X909Eu×3 plus label (4.11.85)	2·50	
	lEy. Booklet pane. Phosphor omitted	60·00	
	Ela. Booklet pane. No. X909×3 plus label (12.8.86)	3·00	
X910	17p. deep blue (1 centre band) (4.9.90)	80	85
	a. Imperf (pair)	£1250	
	Ey. Phosphor omitted	8·00	
X911	17p. deep blue (1 band at right) (4.9.90)	3·25	3·25
	Ea. Band at left	1·25	1·25
	l. Booklet pane. No. X911 and X911Ea×2 plus label	4·75	
	lEy. Booklet pane. Phosphor omitted	60·00	
	m. Booklet pane. No. X911×2 and X917×3 plus three labels with vertical edges of pane imperf	4·25	
	mEy. Booklet pane. Phosphor omitted	70·00	
X912	18p. deep olive-grey (2 bands) (20.10.86)	70	80
X913	18p. bright green (1 centre band) (10.9.91)	60	50
	a. Imperf (pair)	£425	
	Ey. Phosphor omitted	20·00	
X914	19p. brt orange-red (2 bands) (5.9.88)	1·50	1·50
X915	20p. dull purple (2 bands) (25.2.76)	1·20	90
X916	20p. brownish black (2 bands) (2.10.89)	1·50	1·60
X917	22p. brt orange-red (2 bands) (4.9.90)	1·50	1·25
X917*a*	25p. rose-red (2 bands) (6.2.96)	7·00	7·00
X918	26p. rosine (Type I) (2 bands) (3.3.87)	7·00	7·50
X919	31p. purple (2 bands) (18.3.86)	15·00	15·00
X920	34p. ochre-brown (2 bands) (8.1.85)	7·00	7·50
X921	50p. ochre-brown (2 bands) (2.2.77)	2·00	75
X922	50p. ochre (2 bands) (20.3.90)	4·50	4·50

(b) Photo Harrison. On phosphorised paper. P 15×14.

No.	Description	Unused	Used
X924	½p. turquoise-blue (10.12.80)	10	15

	a. Imperf (pair)	£130	
	l. Coil strip. No. X924 and X932×3 (30.12.81)	75	
X925	1p. crimson (12.12.79)	10	15
	a. Imperf (pair)	£1000	
	l. Coil strip. No. X925 and X932Ea×3 (14.8.84)	90	
	m. Booklet pane. No. X925 and X969, each×2 (10.9.91)	2·00	
X926	2p. myrtle-green (face value as T **367**) (12.12.79)	15	20
	a. Imperf (pair)	£1200	
X927	2p. deep green (face value as T **367a**) (26.7.88)	15	20
	a. Imperf (pair)	£1750	
	l. Booklet pane. No. X927×2 and X969×4 plus 2 labels with vert edges of pane imperf (10.9.91)	3·25	
X928	2p. myrtle-green (face value as T **367a**) (5.9.88)	3·25	3·25
	l. Coil strip. No. X928 and X932Ea×3	4·50	
X929	2½p. rose-red (14.1.81)	15	20
	l. Coil strip. No. X929 and X930×3 (6.81)	1·00	
X930	3p. brt magenta (Type I) (22.10.80)	20	25
	a. Imperf (horiz pair)	£1000	
	b. Booklet pane. No. X930, X931×2 and X949×6 with margins all round (14.9.83)	6·50	
	c. Type II (10.10.89)	90	70
	cl. Coil strip. No. X930c and X933×3	2·25	
X931	3½p. purple-brown (30.3.83)	50	60
X932	4p. greenish blue (30.12.81)	25	40
	Ea. Pale greenish blue (14.8.84)	25	40
X933	4p. new blue (26.7.88)	20	25
	a. Imperf (pair)	£1500	
	l. Coil strip. No. X933×3 and X935 (27.11.90)	1·40	
	m. Coil strip. No. X933 and X935, each×2 (1.10.91)	1·00	
	n. Coil strip. No. X933 and X935×3 (31.1.95)	1·00	
X934	5p. pale violet (10.10.79)	30	35
X935	5p. dull red-brown (26.7.88)	25	30
	a. Imperf (pair)	£2500	
X936	6p. yellow-olive (10.9.91)	30	30
X937	7p. brownish red (29.10.85)	1·10	1·25
X938	8½p. yellowish green (24.3.76)	40	50
X939	10p. orange-brown (Type I) (11.79)	35	35
X940	10p. dull orange (Type II) (4.9.90)	40	35
X941	11p. brown-red (27.8.80)	70	80
X942	11½p. ochre-brown (15.8.79)	55	55
X943	12p. yellowish green (30.1.80)	45	45
X944	13p. olive-grey (15.8.79)	45	50
X945	13½p. purple-brown (30.1.80)	60	60
X946	14p. grey-blue (14.1.81)	50	50
X947	15p. ultramarine (15.8.79)	60	60
X948	15½p. pale violet (14.1.81)	60	50
	a. Imperf (pair)	£250	
X949	16p. olive-drab (30.3.83)	55	55
	a. Imperf (pair)	£180	
	Eu. Underprint Type 3 (10.8.83)	80	
	l. Booklet pane. No. X949×9 with margins all round (14.9.83)	5·00	
X950	16½p. pale chestnut (27.1.82)	80	75
X951	17p. light emerald (30.1.80)	60	60
X952	17p. grey-blue (30.3.83)	60	60
	a. Imperf (pair)	£350	
	Eu. Underprint Type 3 (5.3.85)	80	
	l. Booklet pane. No. X952×6 with margins all round (4.9.84)	4·50	
	m. Booklet pane. No. X952×9 with margins all round (8.1.85)	6·00	
X953	17½p. pale chestnut (30.1.80)	70	75
X954	18p. deep violet (14.1.81)	70	70
X955	18p. deep olive-grey (28.8.84)	75	60
	a. Imperf (pair)	£150	
	l. Booklet pane. No. X955×9 with margins all round (3.3.87)	7·50	
	m. Booklet pane. No. X955×4 with margins all round (4.8.87)	3·50	
	n. Booklet pane. No. X955×10 with margins all round (4.8.87)	8·00	
X956	19p. bright orange-red (23.8.88)	80	60
	a. Imperf (pair)	£400	
	l. Booklet pane. No. X956×4 with margins all round	7·00	
	m. Booklet pane. No. X956×10 with margins all round	12·00	
	n. Booklet pane. No. X956×4 with horizontal edges of pane imperf (11.10.88)	8·50	
	o. Booklet pane. No. X956×10 with horizontal edges of pane imperf (11.10.88)	12·00	
	q. Booklet pane. No. X956×4 with three edges of pane imperf (24.1.89)	32·00	
X957	19½p. olive-grey (27.1.82)	2·00	2·00
X958	20p. dull purple (10.10.79)	1·00	75
X959	20p. turquoise-green (23.8.88)	75	70
X960	20p. brownish black (26.9.89)	1·00	1·00
	a. Imperf (pair)	£800	
	l. Booklet pane. No. X960×5 plus label with vertical edges of pane imperf (2.10.89)	6·25	
X961	20½p. ultramarine (30.3.83)	1·25	1·25
	a. Imperf (pair)	£1000	
X962	22p. blue (22.10.80)	90	75
	a. Imperf (pair)	£250	
X963	22p. yellow-green (28.8.84)	90	80
	a. Imperf (horiz pair)	£1400	
X964	22p. bright orange-red (4.9.90)	90	80
	a. Imperf (pair)	£600	
X965	23p. brown-red (30.3.83)	1·25	1·00
	a. Imperf (horiz pair)	£1100	
X966	23p. bright green (23.8.88)	1·10	1·10
X967	24p. violet (28.8.84)	1·40	1·50
X968	24p. Indian red (26.9.89)	2·00	1·60
	a. Imperf (horiz pair)	£2400	
X969	24p. chestnut (10.9.91)	80	80
	a. Imperf (pair)	£225	
X970	25p. purple (14.1.81)	1·00	1·00
X971	26p. rosine (Type I) (27.1.82)	1·10	60
	a. Imperf (horiz pair)	£750	
	b. Type II (4.8.87)	3·50	4·00
	bl. Booklet pane. No. X971b×4 with margins all round	17·00	
X972	26p. drab (Type II) (4.9.90)	1·50	1·25
X973	27p. chestnut (23.8.88)	1·25	1·25
	l. Booklet pane. No. X973×4 with margins all round	12·50	
	m. Booklet pane. No. X973×4 with horizontal edges of pane imperf (11.10.88)	30·00	
X974	27p. violet (4.9.90)	1·50	1·25
X975	28p. deep violet (30.3.83)	1·25	1·25
	a. Imperf (pair)	£1200	
X976	28p. ochre (23.8.88)	1·40	1·25
X977	28p. deep bluish grey (10.9.91)	1·40	1·25
	a. Imperf (pair)	£1600	
X978	29p. ochre-brown (27.1.82)	1·75	1·75
X979	29p. deep mauve (26.9.89)	1·75	1·75
X980	30p. deep olive-grey (26.9.89)	1·25	1·25
X981	31p. purple (30.3.83)	1·25	1·25
	a. Imperf (pair)	£1100	
X982	31p. ultramarine (4.9.90)	1·60	1·50
X983	32p. greenish blue (23.8.88)	1·90	1·75
	a. Imperf (pair)	£1400	
X984	33p. light emerald (4.9.90)	1·75	1·60
X985	34p. ochre-brown (28.8.84)	1·75	1·75
X986	34p. deep bluish grey (26.9.89)	2·00	1·90
X987	34p. deep mauve (10.9.91)	1·75	1·75
X988	35p. sepia (23.8.88)	1·60	1·60
	a. Imperf (pair)	£1350	
X989	35p. yellow (10.9.91)	1·75	1·60
X990	37p. rosine (26.9.89)	2·00	1·75
X991	39p. bright mauve (10.9.91)	1·75	1·75

(c) Photo Harrison. On ordinary paper. P 15×14.

X992	50p. ochre-brown (21.5.80)	1·75	70
	a. Imperf (pair)	£600	
X993	75p. grey-black (face value as T **367a**) (26.7.88)	3·25	1·50

(d) Photo Harrison. On ordinary or phosphorised paper. P 15×14.

X994	50p. ochre (13.3.90)	2·00	70
	a. Imperf (pair)	£1250	

(e) Litho J.W. P 14.

X996	4p. greenish blue (2 bands) (30.1.80)	25	35

X997	4p. greenish blue (phosphorised paper) (11.81)	45	40
X998	20p. dull purple (2 bands) (21.5.80)	1·25	1·20
X999	20p. dull purple (phosphorised paper) (11.81).	1·75	1·20

(f) Litho Questa. P 14 (Nos. X1000, X1003/4 and X1023) or 15×14 (others).

X1000	2p. emerald-green (face value as T **367**) (phosphorised paper) (21.5.80)	20	25
	a. Perf 15×14 (10.7.84)	35	35
X1001	2p. brt green and dp green (face value as T **367a**) (phosphorised paper) (23.2.88)	75	70
X1002	4p. greenish blue (phosphorised paper) (13.5.86)	70	75
X1003	5p. light violet (phosphorised paper) (21.5.80)	40	40
X1004	5p. claret (phosphorised paper) (27.1.82)	50	50
	a. Perf 15×14 (21.2.84)	65	60
X1005	13p. pale chestnut (1 centre band) (9.2.88)	70	75
	l. Booklet pane. No. X1005×6 with margins all round	4·75	
X1006	13p. pale chestnut (1 side band at right) (9.2.88)	75	75
	Ea. Band at left	75	75
	l. Booklet pane. No. X1006/Ea each×3, X1010, X1015 and X1021 with margins all round	30·00	
	lEa. Grey-green (on 18p.) ptg double	£1200	
X1007	14p. deep blue (1 centre band) (11.10.88)	2·00	2·00
X1008	17p. deep blue (1 centre band) (19.3.91)	80	80
	Ey. Phosphor omitted	£180	
	l. Booklet pane. No. X1008×6 with margins all round	5·00	
	lEy. Booklet pane. Phosphor omitted	£750	
X1009	18p. deep olive-grey (phosphorised paper) (9.2.88)	90	95
	l. Booklet pane. No. X1009×9 with margins all round	8·00	
	m. Booklet pane. No. X1009×6 with margins all round	5·50	
X1010	18p. deep olive-grey (2 bands) (9.2.88)	7·50	7·50
X1011	18p. bright green (1 centre band) (27.10.92)	75	75
	l. Booklet pane. No. X1011×6 with margins all round	5·00	
X1012	18p. bright green (1 side band at right) (27.10.92)	1·25	1·40
	Ea. Band at left (10.8.93)	1·75	2·00
	l. Booklet pane. No. X1012×2, X1018×2, X1022×2, 1451a, 1514a and centre label with margins all round	12·00	
	lEa. Bright blue (on 2nd) ptg treble		
	m. Booklet pane. No. X1012Ea, X1020, X1022 and 1451aEb, each×2, with centre label and margins all round (10.8.93)	13·00	
	mEy. Booklet pane. Phosphor omitted	£1600	
X1013	19p. bright orange-red (phosphorised paper) (11.10.88)	2·20	2·00
X1014	20p. dull purple (phosphorised paper) (13.5.86)	1·40	1·40
X1015	22p. yellow-green (2 bands) (9.2.88)	9·00	9·00
X1016	22p. bright orange-red (phosphorised paper) (19.3.91)	1·00	90
	l. Booklet pane. No. X1016×9 with margins all round	9·00	
	m. Booklet pane. No. X1016×6, X1019×2 and centre label with margins all round	9·00	
X1017	24p. chestnut (phosphorised paper) (27.10.92)	90	1·10
	l. Booklet pane. No. X1017×6 with margins all round	5·50	
X1018	24p. chestnut (2 bands) (27.10.92)	1·40	1·40
X1019	33p. light emerald (phosphorised paper) (19.3.91)	2·50	2·50
X1020	33p. lt emerald (2 bands) (25.2.92)	1·50	1·50
X1021	34p. bistre-brown (2 bands) (9.2.88)	7·50	7·50
X1022	39p. brt mauve (2 bands) (27.10.92)	1·50	1·60
X1023	75p. black (face value as T **367**) (ordinary paper) (30.1.80)	3·00	1·50
	a. Perf 15×14 (21.2.84)	3·50	2·25
X1024	75p. brownish grey and black (face value as T **367a**) (ordinary paper) (23.2.88)	9·00	8·50

(g) Litho Walsall. P 14.

X1050	2p. deep green (phosphorised paper) (9.2.93)	1·10	1·10
	l. Booklet pane. No. X1050×2 and X1053×4 plus 2 labels with vert edges of pane imperf	6·75	
X1051	14p. deep blue (1 side band at right) (25.4.89)	4·50	4·50
	Ey. Phosphor omitted	£275	
	l. Booklet pane. No. X1051×2 and X1052×4 with vertical edges of pane imperf	10·00	
	lEy. Booklet pane. Phosphor omitted	£950	
X1052	19p. bright orange-red (2 bands) (25.4.89)	3·00	3·00
	Ey. Phosphor omitted	£225	
X1053	24p. chestnut (phosphorised paper) (9.2.93)	1·10	1·25
X1054	29p. dp mauve (2 bands) (2.10.89)	3·00	3·00
	l. Booklet pane. No. X1054×4 with three edges of pane imperf	15·00	
X1055	29p. deep mauve (phosphorised paper) (17.4.90)	4·50	4·50
	l. Booklet pane. No. X1055×4 with three edges of pane imperf	17·00	
X1056	31p. ultramarine (phosphorised paper) (17.9.90)	1·40	1·40
	l. Booklet pane. No. X1056×4 with horizontal edges of pane imperf	6·00	
X1057	33p. light emerald (phosphorised paper) (16.9.91)	1·25	1·25
	l. Booklet pane. No. X1057×4 with horiz edges of pane imperf	5·00	
X1058	39p. bright mauve (phosphorised paper) (16.9.91)	1·60	1·60
	l. Booklet pane. No. X1058×4 with horiz edges of pane imperf	6·00	

*See footnote after No. 744.

†These come from sheets with gum arabic.

††Examples of Booklet panes Nos. X899l, X901l and X901la are known on which the phosphor bands were printed on the wrong values in error with the result that the side bands appear on the 15½p. or 17p. and the two bands on the 12½p. or 13p. Similarly examples of the 1p. with phosphor band at right instead of left and of the 13p. with band at left instead of right, exist from 50p. booklet pane No. X847l.

Nos. X844a/b come from a strip of eight of the vertical coil. It comprises two normals, one imperforate at sides and bottom, one completely imperforate, one imperforate at top, left and bottom and partly perforated at right due to the bottom three stamps being perforated twice. No. X844b is also known from another strip having one stamp imperforate at sides and bottom.

Nos. X848b/c come from the same sheet, the latter having perforations at the foot of the stamps only.

Multi-value coil strips Nos. X924l, X925l, X928l, X929l, X930cl and X933l/n were produced by the Post Office for use by a large direct mail marketing firm. From 2 September 1981 No. X929l was available from the Philatelic Bureau, Edinburgh, and, subsequently from a number of other Post Office counters. Later multi-value coil strips were sold at the Philatelic Bureau and Post Office philatelic counters.

In addition to booklet pane No. X1012m No. X1020 also comes from the *se-tenant* pane in the Wales £6 booklet. This pane is listed under No. W49a in the Wales Regional section.

PANES OF SIX FROM STITCHED BOOKLETS. Nos. X841m, X851l/m and X855l include one or two printed labels showing commercial advertisements. These were originally perforated on all four sides, but from the August 1971 editions of the 25p. and 30p. booklets (Nos. DH42, DQ59) and December 1971 edition of the 50p. (No. DT4) the line of perforations between the label and the binding margin was omitted. Similar panes, with the line of perforations omitted, exist for the 3p., 3½p. and 4½p. values (Nos. X856, X858 and X865), but these are outside the scope of this listing as the labels are blank.

PART-PERFORATED SHEETS. Since the introduction of the "Jumelle" press in 1972 a number of part perforated sheets, both definitives and commemoratives, have been discovered. It is believed that these occur when the operation of the press is interrupted. Such sheets invariably show a number of "blind" perforations, where the pins have failed to cut the paper. Our listings of imperforate errors from these sheets are for pairs showing no traces whatsoever of the perforations. Examples showing "blind" perforations are outside the scope of this catalogue.

In cases where perforation varieties affect *se-tenant* stamps, fuller descriptions will be found in Vols. 4 and 5 of the *G.B. Specialised Catalogue.*

WHITE PAPER. From 1972 printings appeared on fluorescent white paper giving a stronger chalk reaction than the original ordinary cream paper.

PHOSPHOR OMITTED ERRORS. These are listed for those stamps or booklet panes which were not subsequently issued on phosphorised paper. The following phosphor omitted errors also exist, but can only be identified by the use of an ultra-violet lamp. Prices quoted are for mint examples:

½p. X841 (£1)	8½p. X881 (£1·75)	18p. X912 (£27)
1p. X844 (£3)	10p. X886 (£1)	19p. X914 (£4)
2p. X849 (£5)	11p. X892 (£4)	20p. X916 (£25)
3p. X857 (£100)	12p. X895 (£6)	22p. X917 (£20)
3½p. X860 (£5·50)	14p. X902 (£28)	31p. X919 (£650)
4p. X863 (£85)	15½p. X907 (£4)	33p. X1020 (£375)
4p. X996	16p. X908 (£100)	34p. X920 (£750)
5p. X866 (£225)	17p. X909 (£150)	

No. X909Eu with underprint Type 4 also exists without phosphor (*price* £10).

"ALL-OVER" PHOSPHOR. To improve mechanised handling most commemoratives from the 1972 Royal Silver Wedding 3p. value to the 1979 Rowland Hill Death Centenary set had the phosphor applied by printing cylinder across the entire surface of the stamp, giving a matt effect. Printings of the 1, 2 and 10p. definitives, released in October 1979, also had "all-over" phosphor, but these were purely a temporary expedient pending the adoption of phosphorised paper. Nos. X883, X890 and X921 have been discovered with "all-over" phosphor in addition to the normal phosphor bands. These errors are outside the scope of this catalogue.

PHOSPHORISED PAPER. Following the experiments on Nos. 743c and 829 a printing of the 4½p. definitive was issued on 13 November 1974, which had, in addition to the normal phosphor bands, phosphor included in the paper coating. Because of difficulties in identifying this phosphorised paper with the naked eye this printing is not listed separately in this catalogue.

No. X938 was the first value printed on phosphorised paper without phosphor bands and was a further experimental issue to test the efficacy of this system. From 15 August 1979 phosphorised paper was accepted for use generally, this paper replacing phosphor bands on values other than those required for the second-class rate.

Stamps on phosphorised paper show a shiny surface instead of the matt areas of those printed with phosphor bands.

DEXTRIN GUM. From 1973 printings in photogravure appeared with PVA gum to which dextrin had been added. Because this is virtually colourless a bluish green colouring matter was added to distinguish it from the earlier pure PVA.

The 4p., 5p. (light violet), 20p. and 75p. printed in lithography exist with PVA and PVAD gum. From 1988 Questa printings were with PVAD gum, but did not show the bluish green additive.

VARNISH COATING. Nos. X841 and X883 exist with and without a varnish coating. This cannot easily be detected without the use of an ultra-violet lamp as it merely reduces the fluorescent paper reaction.

POSTAL FORGERIES. In mid-1993 a number of postal forgeries of the 24p. chestnut were detected in the London area. These forgeries, produced by lithography, can be identified by the lack of phosphor in the paper, screening dots across the face value and by the perforations which were applied by a line machine gauging 11.

First Day Covers

15.2.71	½p., 1p., 1½p., 2p., 2½p., 3p., 3½p., 4p., 5p., 6p., 7½p., 9p. (*X841, X844, X848/9, X851, X855, X858, X861, X866, X870, X877, X882*) (Covers carry "POSTING DELAYED BY THE POST OFFICE STRIKE 1971" cachet)	2·50
11.8.71	10p. (*X885*)	1·50
24.5.72	Wedgwood *se-tenant* pane ½p., 2½p. (*X841p*)	25·00
24.10.73	4½p., 5½p., 8p. (*X865, X868, X878*)	1·50
4.9.74	6½p. (*X871*)	1·50
15.1.75	7p. (*X874*)	1·00
24.9.75	8½p. (*X881*)	1·50
25.2.76	9p., 9½p., 10p., 10½p., 11p., 20p. (*X883/4, X886, X890, X892, X915*)	3·50
2.2.77	50p. (*X921*)	1·75
26.4.78	10½p. (*X891*)	1·20
15.8.79	11½p., 13p., 15p. (*X942, X944, X947*)	1·75
30.1.80	4p., 12p., 13½p., 17p., 17½p., 75p. (*X996, X943, X945, X951, X953, X1023*)	3·25
16.4.80	Wedgwood *se-tenant* pane 2p., 10p., 12p. (*X849n*)	2·25
22.10.80	3p., 22p. (*X930, X962*)	1·50
14.1.81	2½p., 11½p., 14p., 15½p., 18p., 25p. (*X929, X893, X946, X948, X954, X970*)	2·00
27.1.82	5p., 12½p., 16½p., 19½p., 26p., 29p. (*X1004, X898, X950, X957, X971, X978*)	3·50
19.5.82	Stanley Gibbons *se-tenant* pane 2p., 3p., 12½p. (*X849p*)	3·00
30.3.83	3½p., 16p., 17p., 20½p., 23p., 28p., 31p. (*X931, X949, X952, X961, X965, X975, X981*)	5·00
14.9.83	Royal Mint *se-tenant* pane 3p., 3½p., 16p. (*X930b*)	4·00
28.8.84	13p., 18p., 22p., 24p., 34p. (*X900, X955, X963, X967, X985*)	3·00
4.9.84	Christian Heritage *se-tenant* pane 10p., 13p., 17p. (*X886bl*)	20·00
8.1.85	*The Times se-tenant* pane 4p., 13p., 17p., 34p. (*X864l*)	9·50
29.10.85	7p., 12p. (*X937, X896*)	3·00
18.3.86	British Rail *se-tenant* pane 12p., 17p., 31p. (*X897m*)	12·00
3.3.87	P & O *se-tenant* pane 1p., 13p., 18p., 26p. (*X847m*)	9·00
9.2.88	*Financial Times se-tenant* pane 13p., 18p., 22p., 34p. (*X1006l*)	15·00
23.8.88	14p., 19p., 20p., 23p., 27p., 28p., 32p., 35p. (*X903, X956, X959, X966, X973, X976, X983, X988*)	6·00
26.9.89	15p., 20p., 24p., 29p., 30p., 34p., 37p. (*X905, X960, X968, X979/80, X986, X990*)	5·00
20.3.90	London Life *se-tenant* pane 15p., (2nd), 20p., (1st), 15p., 20p., 29p. (*X906m*)	10·00
4.9.90	10p., 17p., 22p., 26p., 27p., 31p., 33p. (*X910, X940, X964, X972, X974, X982, X984*)	5·50
19.3.91	Alias Agatha Christie *se-tenant* pane 22p., 33p. (*X1016m*)	8·00
10.9.91	6p., 18p., 24p., 28p., 34p., 35p., 39p. (*X936, X913, X969, X977, X987, X989, X991*)	6·00
27.10.92	Tolkien *se-tenant* pane 18p., (2nd), 24p., (1st), 39p. (*X1012l*)	8·00
10.8.93	Beatrix Potter *se-tenant* pane 18p., (2nd), 33p., 39p. (*X1012m*)	12·00

Post Office Presentation Packs

15.2.71	P.O. Pack No. 26½p. (2 bands), 1p. (2 bands), 1½p. (2 bands), 2p. (2 bands), 2½p. magenta (1 centre band), 3p. ultramarine (2 bands), 3½p. olive-grey (2 bands), 4p. ochre-brown (2 bands), 5p. pale violet (2 bands), 6p. light emerald (2 bands), 7½p. (2 bands), 9p. yellow-orange and black (2 bands). (*Nos.* X841, X844, X848/9, X851, X855, X858, X861, X866, X870, X877, X882)	5·00
15.4.71**	"Scandinavia 71". Contents as above	30·00
25.11.71	P.O. Pack No. 37½p. (2 bands), 1p. (2 bands), 1½p., (2 bands), 2p. (2 bands), 2½p. magenta (1 centre band), 3p. ultramarine (2 bands) or (1 centre band), 3½p. olive-grey (2 bands) or (1 centre band) 4p. ochre-brown (2 bands), 4½p. (2 bands), 5p. pale violet (2 bands), 5½p. (2 bands) or (1 centre band), 6p. (2 bands), 6½p. (2 bands) or (1 centre band), 7p. (2 bands), 7½p. (2 bands), 8p (2 bands), 9p. yellow-orange and black (2 bands), 10p. orange-brown and chestnut (2 bands). (*Nos.* X841, X844, X848/9, X851, X855 or X856, X858 or X859, X861, X865/6, X868 or X869, X870, X871 or X872, X874, X877/8, X882, X885).	
	Later issues of this Pack contained the alternatives	8·00
2.2.77	P.O. Pack No. 90½p. (2 bands), 1p. (2 bands), 1½p (2 bands), 2p. (2 bands), 2½p. magenta (1 centre band), 3p. ultramarine (1 centre band), 5p. pale violet (2 bands), 6½p. (1 centre band), 7p. (2 bands) or (1 centre band), 7½p. (2 bands), 8p. (2 bands), 8½p. (2 bands), 9p. deep violet (2 bands), 9½p. (2 bands), 10p. orange-brown (2 bands), 10½p. yellow (2 bands), 11p. (2 bands), 20p. dull purple (2 bands), 50p. ochre-brown (2 bands) (*Nos.* X841, X844, X848/9, X851, X856, X866, X872, X874 or X875, X877/8, X881, X883/4, X886, X890, X892, X915, X921)	5·00
28.10.81	P.O. Pack No. 129a. 10½p. deep dull blue (2 bands), 11½p. (1 centre band), 2½p. (phos paper), 3p. (phos paper), 11½p. (phos paper), 12p. (phos paper), 13p. (phos paper), 13½p. (phos paper), 14p. (phos paper), 15p. (phos paper), 15½p. (phos paper), 17p. light emerald (phos paper), 17½p. (phos paper), 18p. deep violet (phos paper), 22p. blue (phos paper), 25p. (phos paper), 4p. greenish blue (litho, 2 bands), 75p. (litho) (Nos. X891, X893, X929/30, X942/8, X951, X953/4, X962, X970, X996, X1023)	20·00

3.8.83	P.O. Pack No. 110p. orange-brown (1 centre band), 12½p. (1 centre band), ½p. (phos paper), 1p. (phos paper), 3p. (phos paper), 3½p. (phos paper), 16p. (phos paper), 16½p. (phos paper), 17p. grey-blue (phos paper), 20½p. (phos paper), 23p. brown-red (phos paper), 26p. prosine (phos paper), 28p. deep violet (phos paper), 31p. purple (phos paper), 50p (ord paper), 2p. (litho phos paper), 4p. (litho phos paper), 5p. claret (litho phos paper), 20p. (litho phos paper), 75p. (litho) (*Nos.* X888, X898, X924/5, X930/1, X949/50, X952, X961, X965, X971, X975, X981, X992, X997, X999, X1000, X1004, X1023)	40·00
23.10.84	P.O. Pack No. 5. 13p. (1 centre band), ½p. (phos paper), 1p. (phos paper), 3p. (phos paper), 10p. orange-brown (phos paper), 16p. (phos paper), 17p. grey-blue (phos paper), 18p. dp olive-grey (phos paper), 22p. yellow-green (phos paper), 24p. violet (phos paper), 26p. rosine (phos paper), 28p. deep violet (phos paper), 31p. purple (phos paper), 34p. ochre-brown (phos paper), 50p. (ord paper), 2p. (litho phos paper), 4p. (litho phos paper), 5p. claret (litho phos paper), 20p. (litho phos paper), 75p. (litho) (*Nos.* X900, X924/5, X930, X939, X949, X952, X955, X963, X967, X971, X975, X981, X985, X992, X1000a, X997, X1004a, X999, X1023a)	34·00
3.3.87	P.O. Pack No. 9. 12p. (1 centre band), 13p. (1 centre band), 1p. (phos paper), 3p. (phos paper), 7p. (phos paper), 10p. orange-brown (phos paper), 17p. grey-blue (phos paper), 18p. dp olive-grey (phos paper), 22p. yellow-green (phos paper), 24p. violet (phos paper), 26p. rosine (phos paper), 28p. deep violet (phos paper), 31p. purple (phos paper), 34p. ochre-brown (phos paper), 50p. (ord paper), 2p. (litho phos paper), 4p. (litho phos paper), 5p. claret (litho phos paper), 20p. (litho phos paper), 75p. (litho) (*Nos.* X896, X900, X925, X930, X937, X939, X952, X955, X963, X967, X971, X975, X981, X985, X992, X1000a, X997, X1004a, X999, X1023a)	34·00
23.8.88	P.O. Pack No. 15. 14p. (1 centre band), 19p. (phos paper), 20p. turquoise-green (phos paper), 23p. bright green (phos paper), 27p. chestnut (phos paper), 28p. ochre (phos paper), 32p. (phos paper), 35p. sepia (phos paper) (*Nos.* X903, X956, X959, X966, X973, X976, X983, X988)..	12·00
26.9.89	P.O. Pack No. 19. 15p. (centre band), 20p. brownish black (phos paper), 24p. Indian red (phos paper), 29p. deep mauve (phos paper), 30p. (phos paper), 34p. deep bluish grey (phos paper), 37p. (phos paper) (*Nos.* X905, X960, X968, X979/80, X986, X990)	10·00
4.9.90	P.O. Pack No. 22. 10p. dull orange (phos paper), 17p. (centre band), 22p. bright orange-red (phos paper), 26p. drab (phos paper), 27p. violet (phos paper), 31p. ultramarine (phos paper), 33p. (phos paper) (*Nos.* X940, X910, X964, X972, X974, X9 82, X984)	9·00
14.5.91	P.O. Pack No. 2. 41p. (phos paper), 2p. (phos paper), 3p. (phos paper), 4p. new blue (phos paper), 5p. dull red-brown (phos paper), 10p. dull orange (phos paper), 17p. (centre band), 20p. turquoise-green (phos paper), 22p. bright orange-red (phos paper), 26p. drab (phos paper), 27p. violet (phos paper), 30p. (phos paper), 31p. ultramarine (phos paper), 32p. (phos paper), 33p. (phos paper), 37p. (phos paper), 50p. (ord paper), 75p. (ord paper). (*Nos.* X925, X927, X930, X933, X935, X940, X910, X959, X964, X972, X974, X980, X982/4, X990, X994, X993).............	25·00
10.9.91	P.O. Pack No. 25. 6p (phos paper), 18p. (centre band), 24p. chestnut (phos paper), 28p. deep bluish grey (phos paper), 34p. deep mauve (phos paper), 35p. yellow (phos paper), 39p. (phos paper) (*Nos.* X913, X936, X969, X977, X987, X989, X991)................	9·00

**The "Scandinavia 71" was a special pack produced for sale during a visit to six cities in Denmark, Sweden and Norway by a mobile display unit between 15 April and 20 May 1971. The pack gives details of this tour and also lists the other stamps which were due to be issued in 1971, the text being in English. A separate insert gives translations in Danish, Swedish and Norwegian. The pack was also available at the Philatelic Bureau, Edinburgh.

DECIMAL MACHIN INDEX

Those booklet stamps shown below with an * after the catalogue number do not exist with perforations on all four sides, but show one or two sides imperforate.

Value. Process	*Colour*	*Phosphor*	*Cat. No.*	*Source*
½p. photo	turquoise-blue	2 bands	X841/Eg	(a) with P.V.A. gum–sheets, 5p. m/v coil (X841nEv), 10p.m/v coil (X841q), 10p. booklets (DN46/75, FA1/3), 25p. booklets (DH39/52), 50p. booklets (DT1/12, FB1, FB14/16, FB19/23), £1 Wedgwood booklet (DX1) (b) with gum arabic—sheets, 5p. m/v coil (X841n)
½p. photo	turquoise-blue	1 band at left	X842	£1 Wedgwood booklet (DX1)
½p. photo	turquoise-blue	1 centre band	X843	10p. m/v coil (X843l), 10p. booklets (FA4/9)
½p. photo	turquoise-blue	phos paper	X924	sheets, 12½p. m/v coil (X924l)
1p. photo	crimson	2 bands	X844/Eg	(a) with P.V.A. gum—sheets, vertical coils, 5p. m/v coil (X841nEv), 10p. m/v coil (X841q), 10p. booklets (DN46/75, FA1/3), 50p. booklets (FB1/8, FB14/16) (b) with gum arabic—vertical coils, 5p. m/v coil (X841n)
1p. photo	crimson	1 centre band	X845	10p. m/v coils (X843l, X845m), 10p. booklets (FA4/11), 50p. booklets (FB24/30, 34/36, 43/6, 48, 50)
1p. photo	crimson	"all-over"	X846	sheets
1p. photo	crimson	phos paper	X925	sheets, horizontal and vertical coils, 13p. m/v coil (X925l), 50p. booklet (FB59/66)
1p. photo	crimson	1 band at left	X847	50p. booklets (FB37/42, 47, 49)
1p. photo	crimson	1 band at right	X847Ea	£5 P. & O. booklet (DX8)
1½p. photo	black	2 bands	X848	sheets, 10p. booklets (DN46/75)
2p. photo	myrtle-green	2 bands	X849/Eg	(a) with P.V.A. gum—sheets, 5p. m/v coil (X841nEv), 10p. m/v coil (X841q), 10p. booklets (DN46/75), 50p. booklets (FB9/13), £3 Wedgwood booklet (DX2), £4 SG booklet (DX3) (b) with gum arabic—5p. m/v coil (X841n)
2p. photo	myrtle-green	"all-over"	X850	sheets
2p. photo	myrtle-green	phos paper	X926	sheets
2p. photo	myrtle-green	phos paper	X928	14p. m/v coil (X928l)
2p. litho	emerald-green	phos paper	X1000/a	sheets
2p. litho	brt grn and dp grn	phos paper	X1001	sheets
2p. photo	dp green	phos paper	X927	sheets, £1 booklets (FH23/7)
2p. litho	dp green	phos paper	X1050*	£1 booklets (FH28/30)
2½p. photo	magenta	1 centre band	X851/Eg	(a) with P.V.A. gum—sheets, horizontal and vertical coils, 25p. booklets (DH39/52), 50p. booklets (DT1/12), £1 Wedgwood booklet (DX1) (b) with gum arabic—sheets, horizontal coils
2½p. photo	magenta	1 side band	X852/Ea	(a) band at left—50p. booklets (DT1/12), £1 Wedgwood booklet (DX1) (b) band at right—£1 Wedgwood booklet (DX1)
2½p. photo	magenta	2 bands	X853	sheets
2½p. photo	rose-red	phos paper	X929	sheets, 11½p. m/v coil (X929l)
2½p. photo	rose-red	2 bands	X854	50p. booklets (FB17/18)
3p. photo	ultramarine	2 bands	X855/Eg	(a) with P.V.A. gum—sheets, horizontal and vertical coils, 30p. booklets (DQ56/72), 50p. booklets (DT1/12), £1 Wedgwood booklet (DX1) (b) with gum arabic—sheets, horizontal coils
3p. photo	ultramarine	1 centre band	X856/Eg	(a) with P.V.A. gum—sheets, horizontal and vertical coils, 30p. booklets (DQ73/4), 50p. booklets (DT13/14) (b) with gum arabic—sheets
3p. photo	brt magenta	phos paper	X930	Type I. sheets, 11½p. m/v coil (X929l), £4 Royal Mint booklet (DX4)
3p. photo	brt magenta	phos paper	X930c	Type II. sheets (from 21.1.92), 15p. m/v coil (X930cl)
3p. photo	brt magenta	2 bands	X857	Type I. 50p. booklets (FB19/23), £4 SG booklet (DX3)
3½p. photo	olive-grey	2 bands	X858/Eb	sheets, horizontal and vertical coils, 35p. booklets (DP1/3), 50p. booklets (DT13/14)
3½p. photo	olive-grey	1 centre band	X859	sheet, horizontal coils, 35p. booklet (DP4), 85p. booklet (DW1)
3½p. photo	purple-brown	phos paper	X931	sheets, £4 Royal Mint booklet (DX4)
3½p. photo	purple-brown	1 centre band	X860	50p. booklets (FB24/6)
4p. photo	ochre-brown	2 bands	X861/Eg	(a) with P.V.A. gum—sheets. (b) with gum arabic—sheets
4p. litho	greenish blue	2 bands	X996	sheets
4p. photo	greenish blue	2 bands	X862	50p. booklets (FB17/18)
4p. litho	greenish blue	phos paper	X997	sheets J.W. ptg.
			X1002	sheets Questa ptg.
4p. photo	greenish blue	phos paper	X932	12½p. m/v coil (X924l)
			X932Ea	13p. m/v coil (X925l), 14p. m/v coil (X928l)
4p. photo	greenish blue	1 centre band	X863	50p. booklets (FB27/30)
4p. photo	greenish blue	1 side band	X864/Ea	(a) band at right—£5 Times booklet (DX6) (b) band at left—£5 Times booklet (DX6)
4p. photo	new blue	phos paper	X933	sheets, 15p. m/v coil (X930cl), 17p. m/v coil (X933l), 18p. m/v coil (X933m), 19p m/v coil (X933n)

Value.	*Process*	*Colour*	*Phosphor*	*Cat. No.*	*Source*
4½p.	photo	grey-blue	2 bands	X865	sheets, horizontal coils, 45p. booklets (DS1/2), 85p. booklet (DW1)
5p.	photo	pale violet	2 bands	X866	sheets
5p.	photo	pale violet	phos paper	X934	sheets
5p.	litho	lt violet	phos paper	X1003	sheets
5p.	litho	claret	phos paper	X1004/a	sheets
5p.	photo	claret	1 centre band	X867	50p. booklets (FB35/36, 43/6, 48, 50)
5p.	photo	dull red-brown	phos paper	X935	sheets, 17p. m/v coil (X933l), 18p. m/v coil (X933m), 19p m/v coil (X933n)
5½p.	photo	violet	2 bands	X868	sheets
5½p.	photo	violet	1 centre band	X869	sheets
6p.	photo	lt emerald	2 bands	X870/Eg	(a) with P.V.A. gum—sheets, 10p. m/v coil (X841q), 10p. booklets (FA1/3) (b) with gum arabic—sheets
6p.	photo	yellow-olive	phos paper	X936	sheets
6½p.	photo	greenish blue	2 bands	X871	sheets
6½p.	photo	greenish blue	1 centre band	X872	sheets, horizontal and vertical coils, 65p. booklet (FC1)
6½p.	photo	greenish blue	1 side band	X873/Ea	(a) band at right—50p. booklet (FB1A). (b) band at left—50p. booklet (FB1B)
7p.	photo	purple-brown	2 bands	X874	sheets
7p.	photo	purple-brown	1 centre band	X875	sheets, horizontal and vertical coils, 10p. m/v coil (X843l), 10p. booklets (FA4/9), 70p. booklets (FD1/7), £1.60 Christmas booklet (FX1)
7p.	photo	purple-brown	1 side band	X876/Ea	(a) band at right—50p. booklets (FB2A/8A) (b) band at left—50p. booklets (FB2B/8B)
7p.	photo	brownish red	phos paper	X937	sheets
7½p.	photo	pale chestnut	2 bands	X877	sheets
8p.	photo	rosine	2 bands	X878	sheets
8p.	photo	rosine	1 centre band	X879	sheets, vertical coils, 10p. m/v coil (X845m), 10p. booklets (FA10/11), 80p. booklet (FE1), £1.80 Christmas booklet (FX2)
8p.	photo	rosine	1 side band	X880/Ea	(a) band at right—50p. booklets (FB9A/10A) (b) band at left—50p. booklets (FB9B/10B)
8½p	photo	lt yellowish green	2 bands	X881	sheets, horizontal and vertical coils, 50p. booklet (FB1), 85p. booklet (FF1)
8½p.	photo	yellowish green	phos paper	X938	sheets
9p.	photo	yellow-orange and black	2 bands	X882	sheets
9p.	photo	dp violet	2 bands	X883	sheets, horizontal and vertical coils, 50p. booklet (FB2/8), 90p. booklets (FG1/8), £1.60 Christmas booklet (FX1)
9½p	photo	purple	2 bands	X884	sheets
10p.	recess	cerise	phos paper	829	sheets
10p.	photo	orange-brown and chestnut	2 bands	X885	sheets
10p.	photo	orange-brown	2 bands	X886	Type I. sheets, 50p. booklets (FB9/10), £1.80 Christmas booklet (FX2)
10p.	photo	orange-brown	2 bands	X886b	Type II. £4 Christian Heritage booklet (DX5)
10p.	photo	orange-brown	"all-over"	X887	Type I. sheets, vertical coils, £1 booklet (FH1)
10p.	photo	orange-brown	phos paper	X939	Type I. sheets
10p.	photo	orange-brown	1 centre band	X888	Type I. sheets, vertical coils, £1 booklets (FH2/4), £2.20 Christmas booklet (FX3), £3 Wedgwood booklet (DX2)
10p.	photo	orange-brown	1 side band	X889/Ea	Type I. (a) band at right—50p. booklets (FB11A/13A) (b) band at left—50p. booklets (FB11B/13B), £3 Wedgwood booklet (DX2)
10p.	photo	dull orange	phos paper	X940	sheets
10½p.	photo	yellow	2 bands	X890	sheets
10½p.	photo	dp dull blue	2 bands	X891	sheets
11p.	photo	brown-red	2 bands	X892	sheets
11p.	photo	brown-red	phos paper	X941	sheets
11½p	photo	ochre-brown	phos paper	X942	sheets
11½p	photo	drab	1 centre band	X893	sheets, vertical coils, £1.15 booklets (F1/4), £2.55 Christmas booklet (FX4)
11½p.	photo	drab	1 side band	X894/Ea	(a) band at right—50p. booklets (FB14A/18A), £1.30 booklets (FL1/2) (b) band at left—50p. booklets FB14B/18B), £1.30 booklets (FL1/2)
12p.	photo	yellowish green	phos paper	X943	sheets, vertical coils, £1.20 booklets (FJ1/3)
12p.	photo	yellowish green	2 bands	X895	50p. booklets (FB11/13), £2.20 Christmas booklet (FX3), £3 Wedgwood booklet (DX2)
12p.	photo	brt emerald	1 centre band	X896	sheets, horizontal and vertical coils, 50p. booklet (FB34), £1.20 booklets (FJ4/6), £5 British Rail booklet (DX7)
12p.	photo	brt emerald	1 side band	X897/ Ea	(a) band at right—£1.50 booklets (FP1/2), £5 British Rail booklet (DX7) (b) band at left—£1.50 booklets (FP1/2), £5 British Rail booklet (DX7)
12p.	photo	brt emerald	1 centre band Underprint T.4	X896Eu	sheets

Value.	Process	Colour	Phosphor	Cat. No.	Source
12½p.	photo	lt emerald	1 centre band	X898	sheets, vertical coils, 50p. booklets (FB24/6), £1.25 booklets (FK1/8), £4 SG booklet (DX3)
12½p.	photo	lt emerald	1 centre band Underprint T.1	X898Eu	£2.80 Christmas booklet (FX5)
12½p.	photo	lt emerald	1 centre band Underprint T.2	X898Ev	£2.50 Christmas booklet (FX6)
12½p.	photo	lt emerald	1 side band	X899/Ea	(a) band at right—50p. booklets (FB19A/23A), £1.43 booklets (FN1/6), £1.46 booklets (FO1/3), £4 SG booklet (DX3), £4 Royal Mint booklet (DX4) (b) band at left—50p. booklets (FB19B/23B), £1.43 booklets (FN1/6), £1.46 booklets (FO1/3), £4 SG booklet (DX3), £4 Royal Mint booklet (DX4)
13p.	photo	olive-grey	phos paper	X944	sheets
13p.	photo	pale chestnut	1 centre band	X900	sheets, horizontal and vertical coils, 50p. booklets (FB27/30, 35/6, 43/6, 48, 50), 52p. booklet (GA1), £1.30 booklets (FL3/14, GI1), £5 Times booklet (DX6), £5 P & O booklet (DX8)
13p.	photo	pale chestnut	1 centre band Underprint T.2	X900Eu	£1.30 Christmas booklet (FX9)
13p.	photo	pale chestnut	1 side band	X901/Ea	(a) band at right—50p. booklets (FB37/42, 47, 49), £1.54 booklets (FQ1/4), £4 Christian Heritage booklet (DX5), £5 Times booklet (DX6), £5 P & O booklet (DX8) (b) band at left—£1 booklets (FH6/13), £1.54 booklets (FQ1/4), £4 Christian Heritage booklet (DX5), £5 Times booklet (DX6)
13p.	litho	pale chestnut	1 centre band	X1005	£5 Financial Times booklet (DX9)
13p.	litho	pale chestnut	1 side band	X1006/Ea	£5 Financial Times booklet (DX9)
13½p.	photo	purple-brown	phos paper	X945	sheets
14p.	photo	grey-blue	phos paper	X946	sheets, vertical coils, £1.40 booklets (FM1/4)
14p.	photo	grey-blue	2 bands	X902	50p. booklets (FB14/16), £1.30 booklets (FL1/2), £2.55 Christmas booklet (FX4)
14p.	photo	dp blue	1 centre band	X903	sheets, horizontal and vertical coils, 56p. booklets (GB1/4), £1.40 booklets (FM5/6, GK1, 3)
14p.	photo	dp blue	1 band at right	X904	50p. booklets (FB51/4), £1 booklets (FH14/15)
14p.	litho	dp blue	1 centre band	X1007	£1.40 booklets (GK2, 4)
14p.	litho	dp blue	1 band at right	X1051*	£1 booklet (FH16)
15p.	photo	ultramarine	phos paper	X947	sheets
15p.	photo	brt blue	1 centre band	X905	sheets, horizontal and vertical coils
15p.	photo	brt blue	1 side band	X906/Ea	(a) band at left—50p. booklet (FB55) (b) band at right—£5 London Life booklet (DX11)
15½p.	photo	pale violet	phos paper	X948	sheets, vertical coils, £1.55 booklets (FR1/6)
15½p.	photo	pale violet	2 bands	X907	£1.43 booklets (FN1/6), £4 SG booklet (DX3)
15½p.	photo	pale violet	2 bands Underprint T.1	X907Eu	£2.80 Christmas booklet (FX5)
16p.	photo	olive-drab	phos paper	X949	sheets, vertical coils, £1.60 booklets (FS1, 3/4), £4 Royal Mint booklet (DX4)
16p.	photo	olive-drab	phos paper Underprint T.3	X949Eu	£1.60 booklet (FS2)
16p.	photo	olive-drab	2 bands	X908	£1.46 booklets (FO1/3)
16½p.	photo	pale chestnut	phos paper	X950	sheets
17p.	photo	lt emerald	phos paper	X951	sheets
17p.	photo	grey-blue	phos paper	X952	sheets, vertical coils, £1 booklet (FH5), £1.70 booklets (FT1, 3 & 5/7), £4 Christian Heritage booklet (DX5), £5 Times booklet (DX6), £5 British Rail booklet (DX7)
17p.	photo	grey-blue	phos paper Underprint T.3	X952Eu	£1.70 booklet (FT2)
17p.	photo	grey-blue	2 bands	X909	50p. booklet (FB33), £1.50 booklets (FP1/3), £1.54 booklets (FQ1/4), £4 Christian Heritage booklet (DX5), £5 Times booklet (DX6), £5 British Rail booklet (DX7)
17p.	photo	grey-blue	2 bands Underprint T.4	X909Eu	50p. booklets (FB31/3)
17p.	photo	dp blue	1 centre band	X910	sheets, vertical coils
17p.	photo	dp blue	1 side band	X911/Ea	(a) band at right—50p. booklet (FB57/8), £1 booklet (FH21/2) (b) band at left—50p. booklet (FB57/8)
17p.	litho	dp blue	1 centre band	X1008	£6 Alias Agatha Christie booklet (DX12)
17½p	photo	pale chestnut	phos paper	X953	sheets
18p.	photo	dp violet	phos paper	X954	sheets
18p.	photo	dp olive-grey	phos paper	X955	sheets, vertical coils, 72p. booklet (GC1), £1.80 booklets (FU1/8, GO1), £5 P & O booklet (DX8)
18p.	photo	dp olive-grey	2 bands	X912	50p. booklets (FB37/42, 47, 49), £1 booklet (FH6/13), £5 P & O booklet (DX8)
18p.	litho	dp olive-grey	phos paper	X1009	£5 Financial Times booklet (DX9)
18p.	litho	dp olive-grey	2 bands	X1010	£5 Financial Times booklet (DX9)
18p.	photo	brt green	1 centre band	X913	sheets, vertical coils
18p.	litho	brt green	1 centre band	X1011	£6 Tolkien booklet (DX14)
18p.	litho	brt green	1 side band	X1012/Ea	(a) band at right—£6 Tolkien booklet (DX14). (b) band at left—£6 (£5.64) Beatrix Potter booklet (DX15)).
19p.	photo	brt orange-red	phos paper	X956	sheets, vertical coils, 76p. booklets (GD1/4), £1.90 booklets (FV1/2, GP1, 3)

Value.	*Process*	*Colour*	*Phosphor*	*Cat. No.*	*Source*
19p.	photo	brt orange-red	2 bands	X914	50p. booklets (FB51/4), £1 booklets (FH14/15, 17)
19p.	litho	brt orange-red	phos paper	X1013	£1.90 booklets (GP2, 4)
19p.	litho	brt orange-red	2 bands	X1052*	£1 booklet (FH16)
19½p	photo	olive-grey	phos paper	X957	sheets
20p.	recess	olive-green	none	830	sheets
20p.	photo	dull purple	2 bands	X915	sheets
20p.	photo	dull purple	phos paper	X958	sheets
20p.	litho	dull purple	2 bands	X998	sheets
20p.	litho	dull purple	phos paper	X999	sheets J.W. ptg.
				X1014	sheets Questa ptg.
20p.	photo	turquoise-green	phos paper	X959	sheets
20p.	photo	brownish black	phos paper	X960	sheets, horizontal and vertical coils, £1 booklet (FH18)
20p.	photo	brownish black	2 bands	X916	50p. booklet (FB55), £5 London Life booklet (DX11)
20½p.	photo	ultramarine	phos paper	X961	sheets
22p.	photo	blue	phos paper	X962	sheets
22p.	photo	yellow-green	phos paper	X963	sheets
22p.	litho	yellow-green	2 bands	X1015	£5 Financial Times booklet (DX9)
22p.	photo	brt orange-red	2 bands	X917*	£1 booklet (FH21/2)
22p.	photo	brt orange-red	phos paper	X964	sheets, vertical coils
22p.	litho	brt orange-red	phos paper	X1016	£6 Alias Agatha Christie booklet (DX12)
23p.	photo	brown-red	phos paper	X965	sheets
23p.	photo	brt green	phos paper	X966	sheets
24p.	photo	violet	phos paper	X967	sheets
24p.	photo	Indian red	phos paper	X968	sheets
24p.	photo	chestnut	phos paper	X969	sheets, vertical coils, 50p. booklets (FB59/66), £1 booklets (FH23/7)
24p.	litho	chestnut	phos paper	X1017	£6 Tolkien booklet (DX14) (Questa ptg)
				X1053*	£1 booklet (FH28/30) Walsall ptg
24p.	litho	chestnut	2 bands	X1018	£6 Tolkien booklet (DX14)
25p.	photo	purple	phos paper	X970	sheets
25p.	photo	rose-red	2 bands	X917*a*	horizontal coils
26p.	photo	rosine	phos paper	X971	Type I. sheets
26p.	photo	rosine	2 bands	X918	Type I. £5 P & O booklet (DX8)
26p.	photo	rosine	phos paper	X971b	Type II. £1.04 booklet (GE1)
26p.	photo	drab	phos paper	X972	sheets
27p.	photo	chestnut	phos paper	X973	sheets, £1.08 booklets (GF1/2)
27p.	photo	violet	phos paper	X974	sheets
28p.	photo	dp violet	phos paper	X975	sheets
28p.	photo	ochre	phos paper	X976	sheets
28p.	photo	dp bluish grey	phos paper	X977	sheets
29p.	photo	ochre-brown	phos paper	X978	sheets
29p.	photo	dp mauve	phos paper	X979	sheets
29p.	litho	dp mauve	2 bands	X1054*	£1.16 booklet (GG1)
29p.	litho	dp mauve	phos paper	X1055*	£1.16 booklet (GG2)
30p.	photo	dp olive-grey	phos paper	X980	sheets
31p.	photo	purple	phos paper	X981	sheets
31p.	photo	purple	2 bands	X919	£5 British Rail booklet (DX7)
31p.	photo	ultramarine	phos paper	X982	sheets
31p.	litho	ultramarine	phos paper	X1056*	£1.24 booklet (GH1)
32p.	photo	greenish blue	phos paper	X983	sheets
33p.	photo	lt emerald	phos paper	X984	sheets, vertical coils
33p.	litho	lt emerald	phos paper	X1019	£6 Alias Agatha Christie booklet (DX12)
33p.	litho	lt emerald	phos paper	X1057*	£1.32 booklet (GJ1)
33p.	litho	lt emerald	2 bands	X1020	£6 Wales booklet (DX13), £6 (£5.64) Beatrix Potter booklet (DX15)
34p.	photo	ochre-brown	phos paper	X985	sheets
34p.	photo	ochre-brown	2 bands	X920	£5 Times booklet (DX6)
34p.	litho	bistre-brown	2 bands	X1021	£5 Financial Times booklet (DX9)
34p.	photo	dp bluish grey	phos paper	X986	sheets
34p.	photo	dp mauve	phos paper	X987	sheets
35p.	photo	sepia	phos paper	X988	sheets
35p.	photo	yellow	phos paper	X989	sheets
37p.	photo	rosine	phos paper	X990	sheets
39p.	photo	brt mauve	phos paper	X991	sheets, vertical coils
39p.	litho	brt mauve	phos paper	X1058*	78p. booklet (GD4*a*), £1.56 booklet (GM1)
39p.	litho	brt mauve	2 bands	X1022	£6 Tolkien booklet (DX14), £6 (£5.64) Beatrix Potter booklet (DX15)
50p.	recess	dp ultramarine	none or phos paper	831/Ea	sheets
50p.	photo	ochre-brown	2 bands	X921	sheets
50p.	photo	ochre-brown	none	X992	sheets
50p.	photo	ochre	2 bands	X922	£5 London Life (DX11)
50p.	photo	ochre	none or phos paper	X994	sheets
75p.	litho	black	none	X1023/a	sheets
75p.	litho	brownish grey and black	none	X1024	sheets
75p.	photo	grey-black	none	X993	sheets

Value.	*Process*	*Colour*	*Phosphor*	*Cat. No.*	*Source*
£1	recess	bluish black	none	831*b*	sheets
£1	photo	brt yellow-green and blackish olive	none	1026	sheets
£1.30	photo	drab and dp greenish blue	none	1026*b*	sheets
£1.33	photo	pale mauve and grey-black	none	1026*c*	sheets
£1.41	photo	drab and dp greenish blue	none	1026*d*	sheets
£1.50	photo	pale mauve and grey-black	none	1026*e*	sheets
£1.60	photo	pale drab and dp greenish blue	none	1026*f*	sheets
£2	photo	lt emerald and purple-brown	none	1027	sheets
£5	photo	salmon and chalky blue	none	1028	sheets

For 1st and 2nd class no value indicated (NVI) stamps, see Nos. 1445/52, 1511/16 and 1663a/6.

For table covering Machin stamps with elliptical perforations see after Nos. Y1667, etc, in 1993.

DECIMAL MACHIN MULTI-VALUE COIL INDEX

The following is a simplified checklist of horizontal multi-value coils, to be used in conjunction with the main listing as details of stamps listed there are not repeated.

Strip Value	*Date*	*Contents*	*Cat No.*
5p.	15.2.71	½p. × 2, 1p. × 2, 2p.	X841n
10p.	3.12.75	½p. × 2, 1p., 2p., 6p.	X841q
10p.	14.12.77	½p. × 2, 1p. × 2, 7p.	X843l
10p.	16.1.80	1p. × 2, 8p. plus 2 labels	X845m
11½p.	6.81	2½p., 3p. × 3	X929l
12½p.	30.12.81	½p., 4p. × 3	X924l
13p.	14.8.84	1p., 4p. × 3	X925l
14p.	5.9.88	2p., 4p. × 3	X928l
15p.	10.10.89	3p., 4p. × 3	X930cl
17p.	27.11.90	4p. × 3, 5p.	X933l
18p.	1.10.91	4p. × 2, 5p. × 2	X933m
19p.	31.1.95	4p., 5p. × 3	X933n

Abbreviations used in the diagrams: 2B = 2 bands, CB = centre band, LB = left band and RB = right band. The shaded squares represent printed labels.

Panes completed by unprinted white labels are outside the scope of this catalogue.

Unless otherwise stated the panes were printed in photogravure. Some panes exist in photogravure and lithography and these are separately identified and listed. **Imperforate or straight edges.** These are described under the appropriate illustration and listed as complete panes.

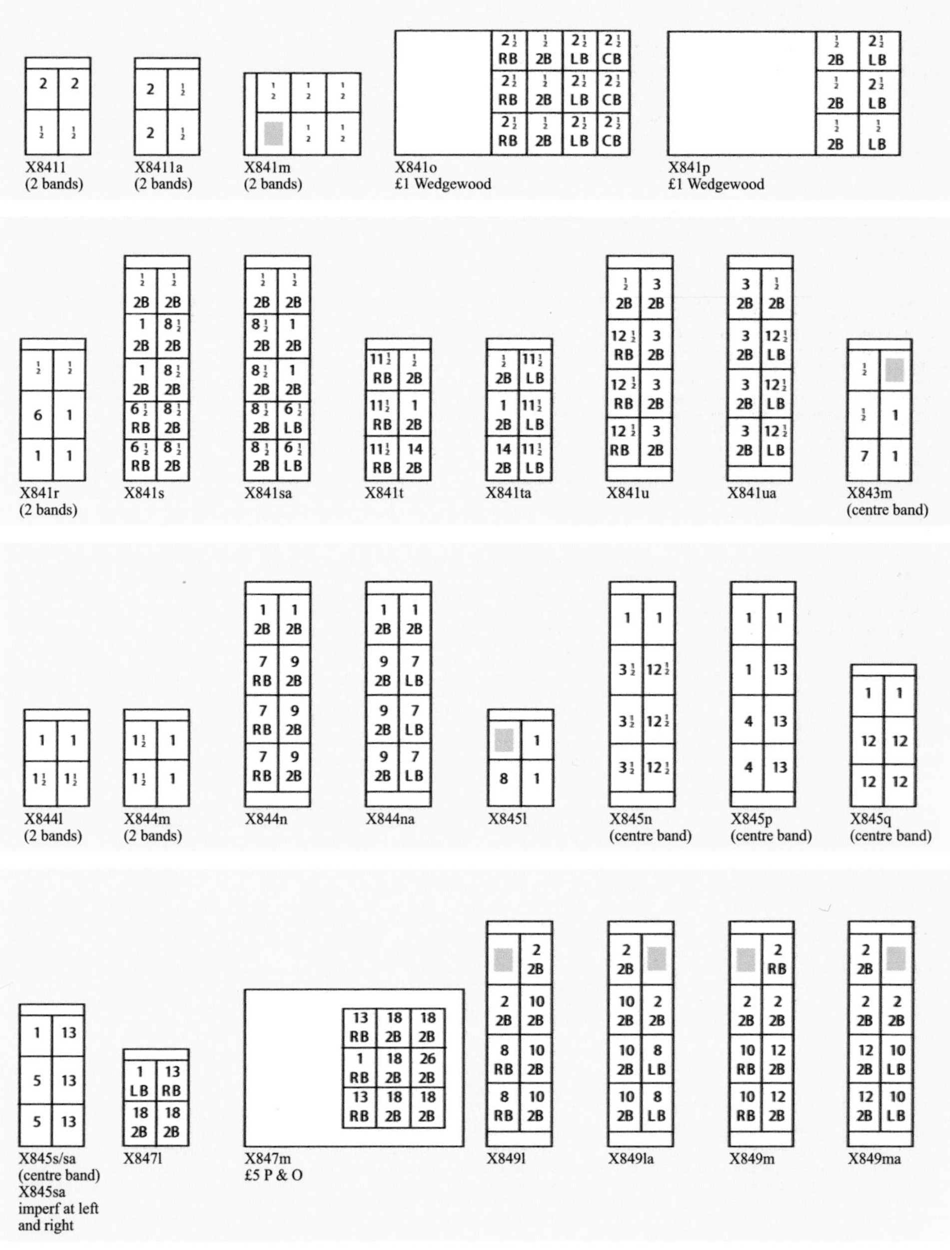

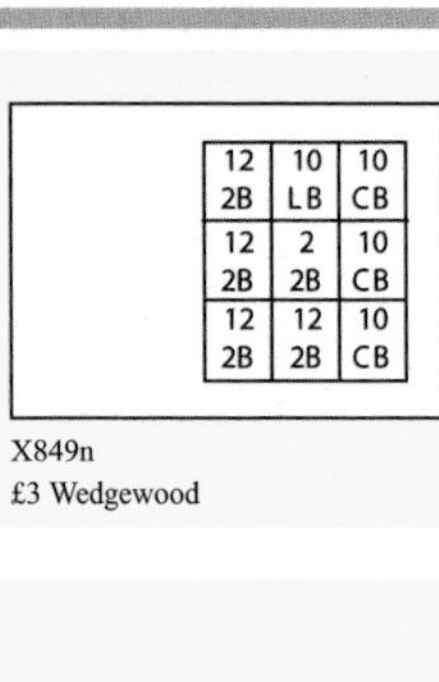

12 2B | 10 LB | 10 CB
12 2B | 2 2B | 10 CB
12 2B | 12 2B | 10 CB

X849n
£3 Wedgewood

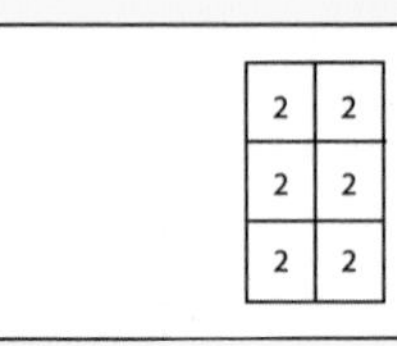

X849o (2 bands)
£3 Wedgewood

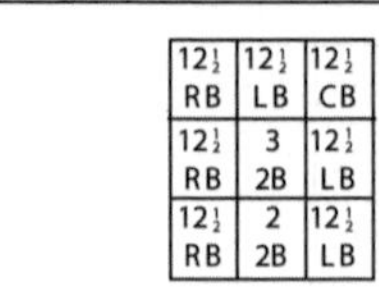

12½ RB | 12½ LB | 12½ CB
12½ RB | 3 2B | 12½ LB
12½ RB | 2 2B | 12½ LB

X849p
£4 Stanley Gibbons

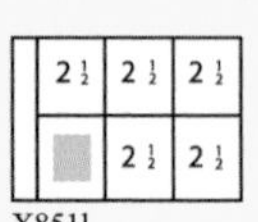

X851l
(centre band)

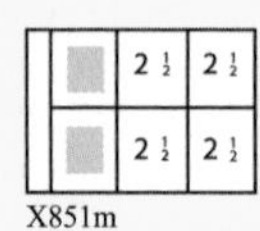

X851m
(centre band)

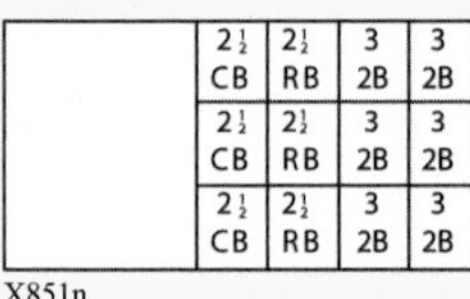

X851n
£1 Wedgewood

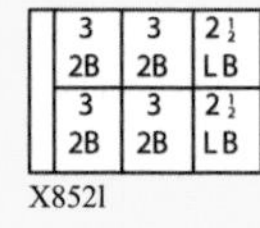

X852l

4 2B	4 2B
11½ RB	2½ 2B
11½ RB	2½ 2B
11½ RB	2½ 2B

X854l

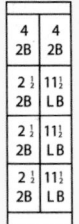

4 2B	4 2B
2½ 2B	11½ LB
2½ 2B	11½ LB
2½ 2B	11½ LB

X854la

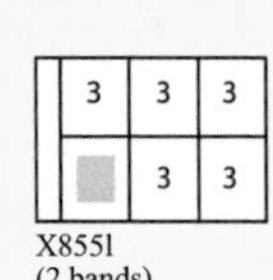

X855l
(2 bands)

13 RB	17 2B	13 LB
4 RB	34 2B	4 LB
13 RB	17 2B	13 LB

X864l
£5 The Times

9 2B	9 2B	9 2B	9 2B	9 2B	9 2B	9 2B	9 2B	9 2B	9 2B
7 CB	7 CB	7 CB	7 CB	7 CB	7 CB	7 CB	7 CB	7 CB	7 CB

X875l
Christmas 1978

10 2B	10 2B	10 2B	10 2B	10 2B	10 2B	10 2B	10 2B	10 2B	10 2B
8 CB	8 CB	8 CB	8 CB	8 CB	8 CB	8 CB	8 CB	8 CB	8 CB

X879l
Christmas 1979

17 2B	17 2B	17 2B
10 2B	17 2B	13 LB
17 2B	17 2B	17 2B

X886bl
£4 Christian Heritage

10	10	10
10	10	10
10	10	10

X888l (centre band)
£3 Wedgewood

12 2B	12 2B	12 2B	12 2B	12 2B	12 2B	12 2B	12 2B	12 2B	12 2B
10 CB	10 CB	10 CB	10 CB	10 CB	10 CB	10 CB	10 CB	10 CB	10 CB

X888m
Christmas 1980

14 2B	14 2B	14 2B	14 2B	14 2B	14 2B	14 2B	14 2B	14 2B	14 2B
11½ CB	11½ CB	11½ CB	11½ CB	11½ CB	11½ CB	11½ CB	11½ CB	11½ CB	11½ CB

X893l
Christmas 1981

14 2B	14 2B	14 2B	14 2B	14 2B
14 2B	11½ LB	11½ RB	11½ LB	11½ RB

X894l
Margin at left or right

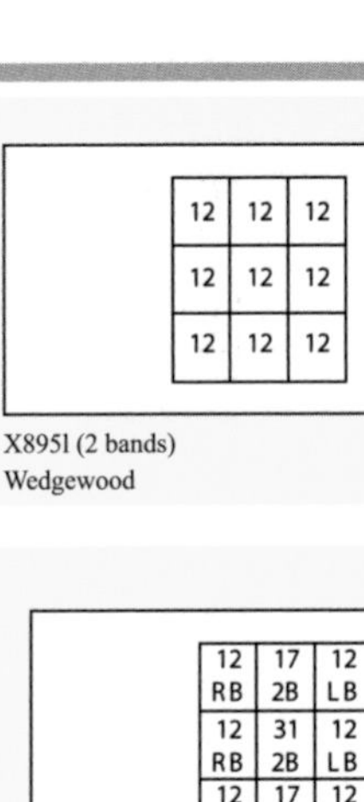

X895l (2 bands)
Wedgewood

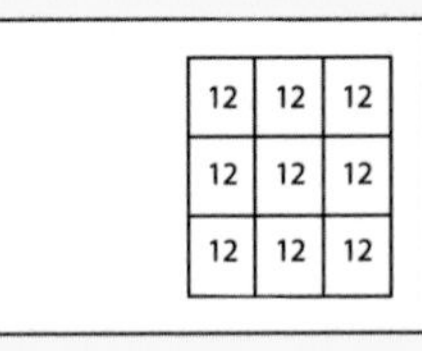

X896l (centre band)
£5 British Rail

	17 2B	17 2B	17 2B	17 2B	17 2B
	12 LB	12 RB	12 LB	12 RB	17 2B

X897l

17 2B	17 2B	17 2B	17 2B	17 2B	
17 2B	12 LB	12 RB	12 LB	12 RB	

X897la

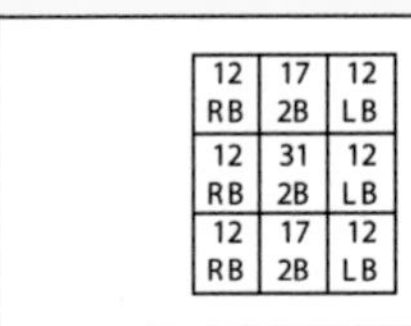

12 RB 17 2B 12 LB
12 RB 31 2B 12 LB
12 RB 17 2B 12 LB

X897m
£5 British Rail

	15½ 2B	15½ 2B	15½ 2B	15½ 2B	15½ 2B	15½ 2B	15½ 2B	15½ 2B	15½ 2B	15½ 2B
	12½ CB	12½ CB	12½ CB	12½ CB	12½ CB	12½ CB	12½ CB	12½ CB	12½ CB	12½ CB

X898l
Christmas 1982

	15½ 2B	15½ 2B	15½ 2B	15½ 2B	15½ 2B
	15½ 2B	12½ LB	12½ RB	12½ LB	12½ RB

X899l
Margin at left or right

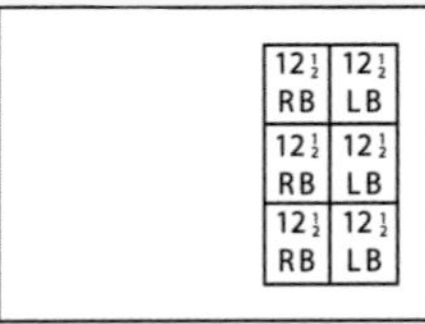

X899m
£4 Stanley Gibbons
£4 Royal Mint

	16 2B	16 2B	16 2B	16 2B	16 2B
	12½ LB	12½ RB	12½ LB	12½ RB	16 2B

X899n

16 2B	16 2B	16 2B	16 2B	16 2B	
16 2B	12½ LB	12½ RB	12½ LB	12½ RB	

X899na

13	13	13
13	13	13
13	13	13

X900l (centre band)
£5 The Times
£5 P & O

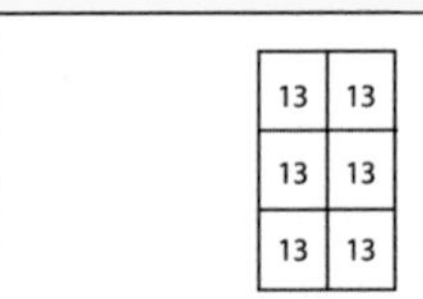

X900m, (photo), X1005l (litho)
(centre band)
£5 P & O (X900m)
£5 Financial times (X 1005l)

13	13
13	13

X900n (centre band)
52p. Barcode booklet

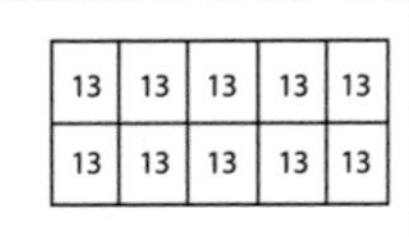

X900o (centre band)
£1.30 Barcode Booklet

	17 2B	17 2B	17 2B	17 2B	17 2B
	13 LB	13 RB	13 LB	13 RB	17 2B

X901l

17 2B	17 2B	17 2B	17 2B	17 2B	
17 2B	13 LB	13 RB	13 LB	13 RB	

X901la

13 RB	13 LB
13 RB	13 LB
13 RB	13 LB

X901m
£4 Christian heritage

13 LB	18 2B
18 2B	18 2B
18 2B	18 2B

X901n/na
901na imperf
at left and right

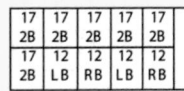

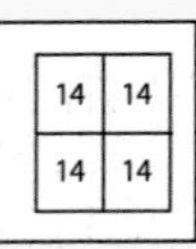

X903l
(centre band)
56p. Barcode Booklet

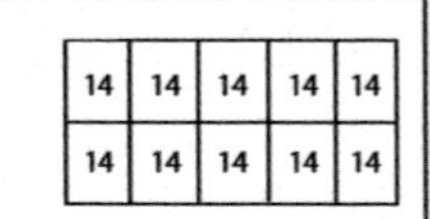

X903m
(centre band)
£1.40 Barcode Booklet

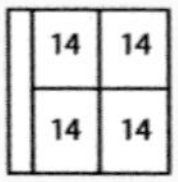

X903n, X903q
(centre band)
56p. Barcode Booklet
X903n imperf at top and bottom
X903q imperf 3 sides

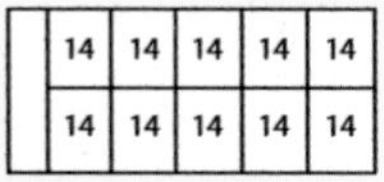

X903p (centre band)
£1.40 Barcode Booklet
Imperf at top and bottom

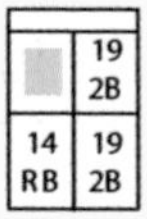

X904l

X904m (photo)
X1051l (litho)
Imperf at left and right

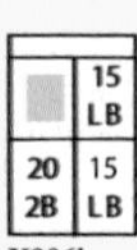

X906l

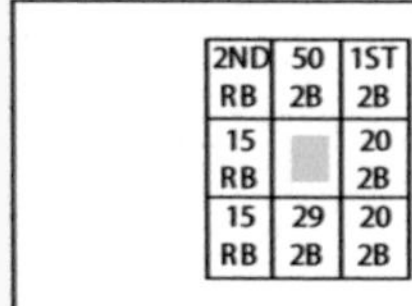

X906m
£5 London Life
The stamps in the bottom row are Penny Black Anniversary definitives (Nos 1468Ea,1470 and 1472)

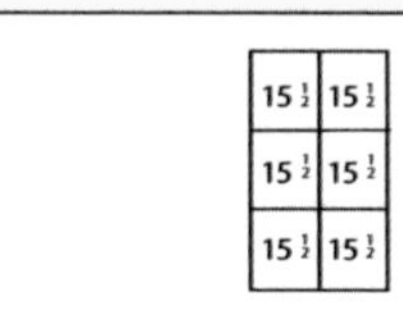

X907l
(2 bands)
£4 Stanley Gibbons

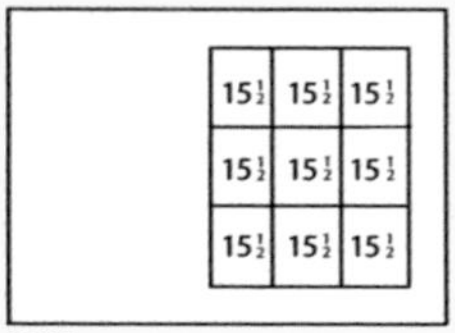

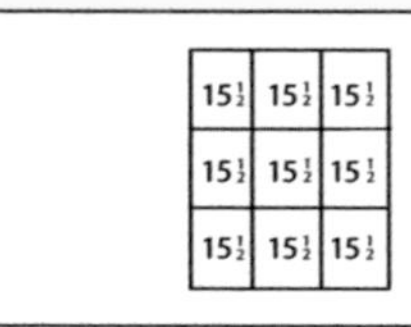

X907m
(2 bands)
£4 Stanley Gibbons

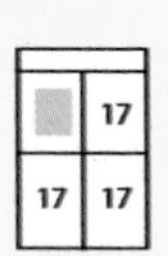

X909l
(2 bands) and underprint X909Ela
(as X909l but without underprint)

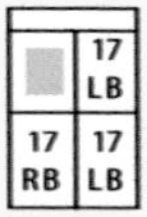

X911l

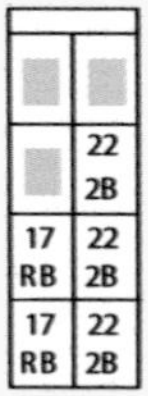

X911m
Imperf at left and right

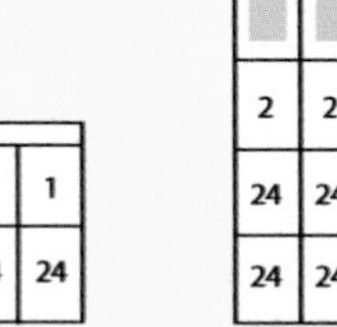

X925m
(phosphorised paper)

X927l (photo)
X1050l (litho)
(phosphorised paper) Imperf at left and right

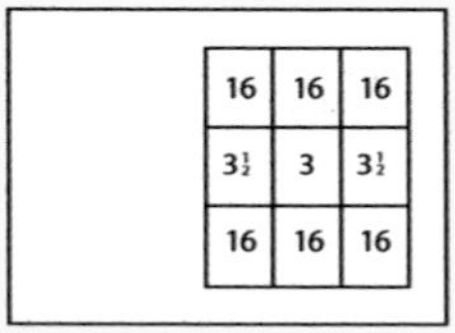

X930b
(phosphorised paper)
£4 Royal mint

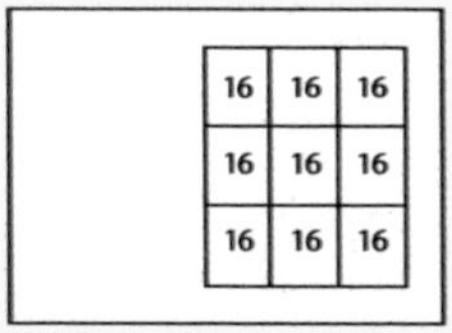

X949l
(phosphorised paper)
£4 Royal Mint

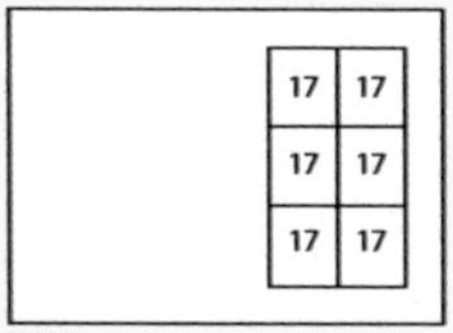

X952l
(phosphorised paper)
£4 Christian Heritage
£5 The Times £5 British Rail
X1008l (centre band)
£6 Agatha Christie

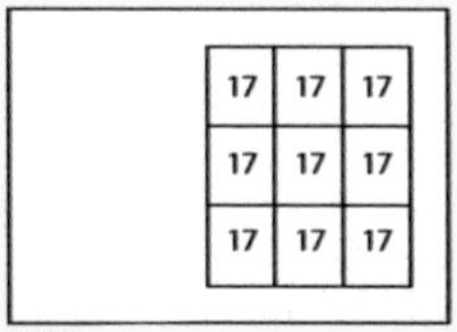

X952m
(phosphorised paper)
£5 The Times
£5 British Rail

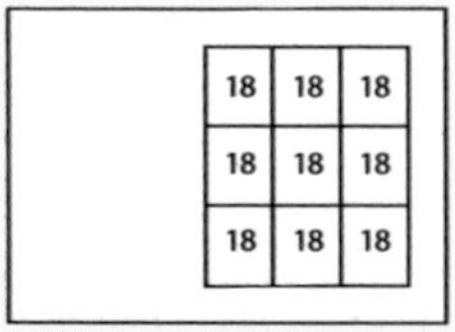

X955l (photo), X1009l (litho)
(phosphorised paper)
£5 P & O (X955l)
£5 Financial Times (X1009l)

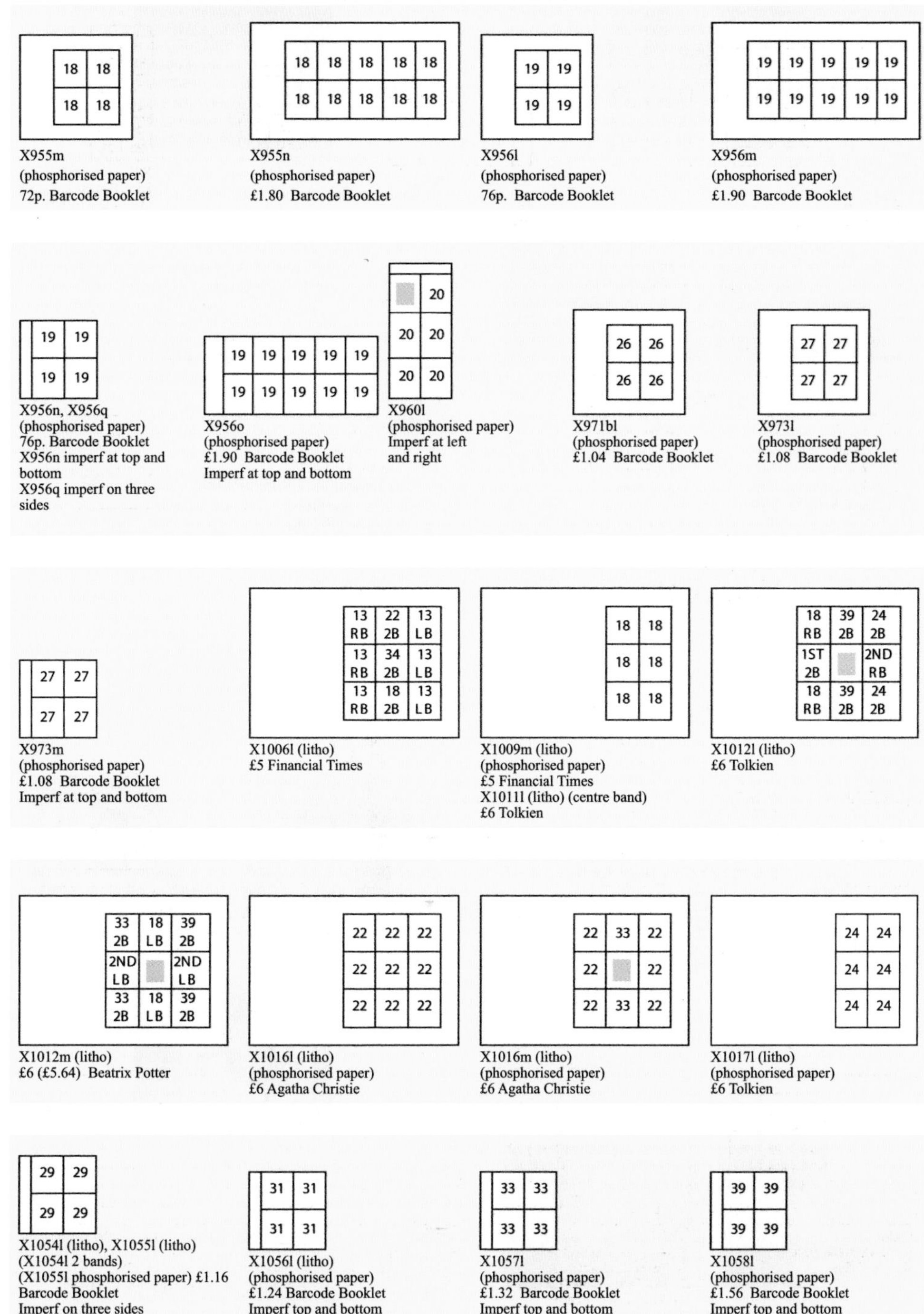

X955m
(phosphorised paper)
72p. Barcode Booklet

X955n
(phosphorised paper)
£1.80 Barcode Booklet

X956l
(phosphorised paper)
76p. Barcode Booklet

X956m
(phosphorised paper)
£1.90 Barcode Booklet

X956n, X956q
(phosphorised paper)
76p. Barcode Booklet
X956n imperf at top and bottom
X956q imperf on three sides

X956o
(phosphorised paper)
£1.90 Barcode Booklet
Imperf at top and bottom

X960l
(phosphorised paper)
Imperf at left and right

X971bl
(phosphorised paper)
£1.04 Barcode Booklet

X973l
(phosphorised paper)
£1.08 Barcode Booklet

X973m
(phosphorised paper)
£1.08 Barcode Booklet
Imperf at top and bottom

X1006l (litho)
£5 Financial Times

X1009m (litho)
(phosphorised paper)
£5 Financial Times
X1011l (litho) (centre band)
£6 Tolkien

X1012l (litho)
£6 Tolkien

X1012m (litho)
£6 (£5.64) Beatrix Potter

X1016l (litho)
(phosphorised paper)
£6 Agatha Christie

X1016m (litho)
(phosphorised paper)
£6 Agatha Christie

X1017l (litho)
(phosphorised paper)
£6 Tolkien

X1054l (litho), X1055l (litho)
(X1054l 2 bands)
(X1055l phosphorised paper) £1.16
Barcode Booklet
Imperf on three sides

X1056l (litho)
(phosphorised paper)
£1.24 Barcode Booklet
Imperf top and bottom

X1057l
(phosphorised paper)
£1.32 Barcode Booklet
Imperf top and bottom

X1058l
(phosphorised paper)
£1.56 Barcode Booklet
Imperf top and bottom

368 "A Mountain Road" (T. P. Flanagan)

369 "Deer's Meadow" (Tom Carr)

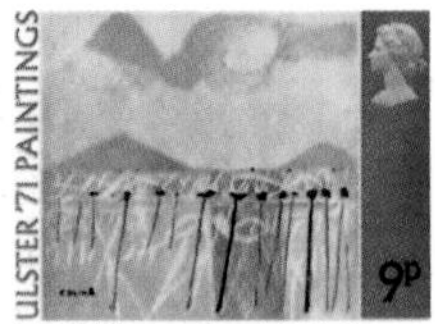

370 "Slieve na brock" (Colin Middleton)

(Colin Middleton)

1971 (16 June). *"Ulster 1971" Paintings. Chalk-surfaced paper. Two phosphor bands.* P 15×14.

881	**368**	3p. yellow-buff, pale yellow, Venetian red, black, blue and drab	25	25
		Ey. Phosphor omitted	6·00	
		a. Venetian red omitted		—
882	**369**	7½p. olive-brown, brownish grey, pale olive-grey, deep blue, cobalt and grey-blue	50	50
		Ey. Phosphor omitted	6·00	
		a. Pale olive-grey omitted*	£110	
		Ey. Phosphor omitted	22·00	
883	**370**	9p. greenish yellow, orange, grey, lavender- grey, bistre, black, pale ochre-brown and ochre-brown	50	50
		a. Orange (flowers) omitted	£1800	
		Ey. Phosphor omitted	22·00	
Set of 3			1·00	1·00
First Day Cover				1·75
Presentation Pack			6·00	

*This only affects the boulder in the foreground, which appears whitish and it only applied to some stamps in the sheet.

Special First Day of Issue Postmarks

British Post Office Philatelic Bureau, Edinburgh
(Type D, see Introduction) ....3·50
Belfast ....8·00

First Day of Issue handstamps, in the same design as that for Belfast, were provided at Armagh, Ballymena, Coleraine, Cookstown, Enniskillen, Londonderry, Newry, Omagh and Portadown for this issue.

371 John Keats (150th Death Anniv)

372 Thomas Gray (Death Bicentenary)

373 Sir Walter Scott (Birth Bicentenary)

(Des Rosalind Dease. Queen's head printed in gold and then embossed)

1971 (28 July). *Literary Anniversaries. Chalk-surfaced paper. Two phosphor bands.* P 15×14.

884	**371**	3p. black, gold and greyish blue	25	10
		a. Gold (Queen's head) omitted	£110	
		Ey. Phosphor omitted	5·00	
885	**372**	5p. black, gold and yellow-olive	45	50
		a. Gold (Queen's head) omitted	£375	
		Ey. Phosphor omitted	32·00	
886	**373**	7½p. black, gold and yellow-brown	45	45
		Eb. Embossing omitted	40·00	
		Ey. Phosphor omitted	22·00	
Set of 3			1·00	1·10
First Day Cover				2·00
Presentation Pack			5·50	

Special First Day of Issue Postmarks

British Post Office Philatelic Bureau, Edinburgh
(Type D, see Introduction) ....5·00
London EC ....8·00

374 Servicemen and Nurse of 1921

375 Roman Centurion

376 Rugby Football, 1871

(Des F. Wegner)

1971 (25 Aug). *British Anniversaries. Events described on stamps. Chalk-surfaced paper. Two phosphor bands.* P 15×14.

887	**374**	3p. red-orange, grey, dp blue, olive-green, olive-brown, black, rosine and violet-blue	25	25
		a. Deep blue omitted*	£675	
		b. Red-orange (nurse's cloak) omitted	£325	
		c. Olive-brown (faces, etc.) omitted	£300	
		d. Black omitted	£14000	

368 "A Mountain Road" (T. P. Flanagan)

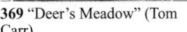

369 "Deer's Meadow" (Tom Carr)

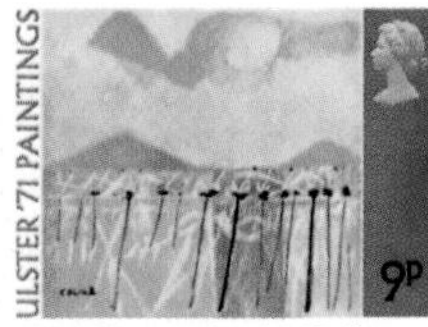

370 "Slieve na brock" (Colin Middleton)

(Colin Middleton)

1971 (16 June). *"Ulster 1971" Paintings. Chalk-surfaced paper. Two phosphor bands.* P 15×14.

881	**368**	3p. yellow-buff, pale yellow, Venetian red, black, blue and drab	25	25
		Ey. Phosphor omitted	6·00	
		a. Venetian red omitted		—
882	**369**	7½p. olive-brown, brownish grey, pale olive-grey, deep blue, cobalt and grey-blue	50	50
		Ey. Phosphor omitted	6·00	
		a. Pale olive-grey omitted*	£110	
		Ey. Phosphor omitted	22·00	
883	**370**	9p. greenish yellow, orange, grey, lavender- grey, bistre, black, pale ochre-brown and ochre-brown	50	50
		a. Orange (flowers) omitted	£1800	
		Ey. Phosphor omitted	22·00	
Set of 3			1·00	1·00
First Day Cover				1·75
Presentation Pack			6·00	

*This only affects the boulder in the foreground, which appears whitish and it only applied to some stamps in the sheet.

Special First Day of Issue Postmarks

British Post Office Philatelic Bureau, Edinburgh
(Type D, see Introduction) .... 3·50
Belfast .... 8·00

First Day of Issue handstamps, in the same design as that for Belfast, were provided at Armagh, Ballymena, Coleraine, Cookstown, Enniskillen, Londonderry, Newry, Omagh and Portadown for this issue.

371 John Keats (150th Death Anniv)

372 Thomas Gray (Death Bicentenary)

373 Sir Walter Scott (Birth Bicentenary)

(Des Rosalind Dease. Queen's head printed in gold and then embossed)

1971 (28 July). *Literary Anniversaries. Chalk-surfaced paper. Two phosphor bands.* P 15×14.

884	**371**	3p. black, gold and greyish blue	25	10
		a. Gold (Queen's head) omitted	£110	
		Ey. Phosphor omitted	5·00	
885	**372**	5p. black, gold and yellow-olive	45	50
		a. Gold (Queen's head) omitted	£375	
		Ey. Phosphor omitted	32·00	
886	**373**	7½p. black, gold and yellow-brown	45	45
		Eb. Embossing omitted	40·00	
		Ey. Phosphor omitted	22·00	
Set of 3			1·00	1·10
First Day Cover				2·00
Presentation Pack			5·50	

Special First Day of Issue Postmarks

British Post Office Philatelic Bureau, Edinburgh
(Type D, see Introduction) .... 5·00
London EC .... 8·00

374 Servicemen and Nurse of 1921

375 Roman Centurion

376 Rugby Football, 1871

(Des F. Wegner)

1971 (25 Aug). *British Anniversaries. Events described on stamps. Chalk-surfaced paper. Two phosphor bands.* P 15×14.

887	**374**	3p. red-orange, grey, dp blue, olive-green, olive-brown, black, rosine and violet-blue	25	25
		a. Deep blue omitted*	£675	
		b. Red-orange (nurse's cloak) omitted	£325	
		c. Olive-brown (faces, etc.) omitted	£300	
		d. Black omitted	£14000	

		e. Grey omitted		£4000
		Ey. Phosphor omitted	3·00	
888	375	7½p. grey, yellow-brown, vermilion, mauve, grey-black, black, silver, gold and ochre	50	50
		a. Grey omitted	£110	
		Ey. Phosphor omitted	15·00	
889	376	9p. new blue, myrtle-green, grey-black, lemon, olive-brown, magenta and yellow-olive	50	50
		a. Olive-brown omitted	£140	
		b. New blue omitted	£4500	
		c. Myrtle-green omitted	£9500	
		d. Lemon (jerseys) omitted		£4000
		Ey. Phosphor omitted	£400	
Set of 3			1·00	1·00
First Day Cover				2·50
Presentation Pack			5·50	

*The effect of the missing deep blue is shown on the sailor's uniform, which appears as grey.

Special First Day of Issue Postmarks

British Post Office Philatelic Bureau, Edinburgh (Type D, see Introduction)	3·50
Maidstone	16·00
Twickenham	16·00
York	16·00

377 Physical Sciences Building, University College of Wales, Aberystwyth

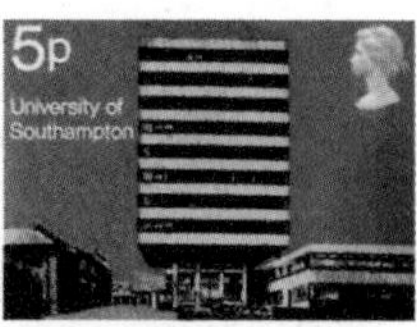

378 Faraday Building, Southampton University

379 Engineering Department, Leicester University

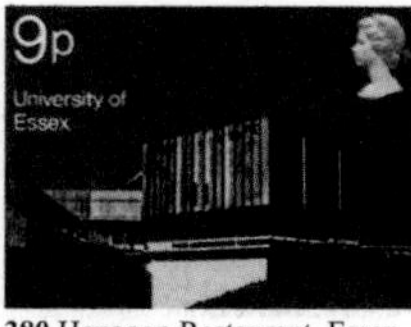

380 Hexagon Restaurant, Essex University

(Des N. Jenkins)

1971 (22 Sept). *British Architecture. Modern University Buildings. Chalk-surfaced paper. Two phosphor bands.* P 15×14.

890	377	3p. olive-brown, ochre, lemon, black and yellow-olive	10	10
		a. Lemon omitted	†	£5250
		b. Black (windows) omitted	£10000	
		Ey. Phosphor omitted	8·00	
891	378	5p. rose, black, chestnut and lilac	25	20
		Ey. Phosphor omitted	70·00	
892	379	7½p. ochre, black and purple-brown	45	55
		Ey. Phosphor omitted	12·00	
893	380	9p. pale lilac, black, sepia-brown and dp blue	75	80
		a. Pale lilac omitted	£3000	
		Ey. Phosphor omitted	18·00	
Set of 4			1·25	1·50
First Day Cover				2·00
Presentation Pack			6·50	

Mint examples of the 5p. exist with a larger "P" following the face value.

No. 890a is only known used on commercial cover from Wantage.

Special First Day of Issue Postmarks

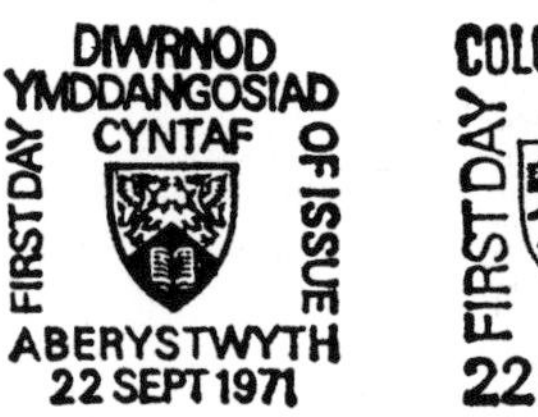

British Post Office Philatelic Bureau, Edinburgh (Type D, see Introduction)	3·00
Aberystwyth	14·00
Colchester	14·00
Leicester	14·00
Southampton	14·00

Collectors Pack 1971

1971 (29 Sept). Comprises Nos. 835/40 and 881/93.

CP893a Collectors Pack	50·00

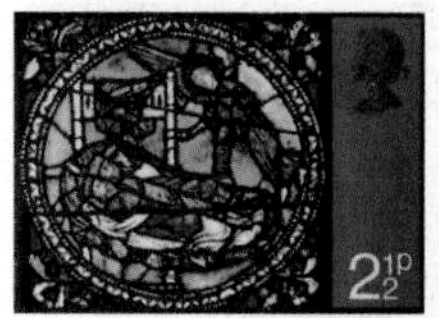

381 "Dream of the Wise Men"

382 "Adoration of the Magi"

383 "Ride of the Magi"

(Des Clarke-Clements-Hughes design team, from stained-glass windows, Canterbury Cathedral. Queen's head printed in gold and then embossed)

1971 (13 Oct). *Christmas. Ordinary paper. One centre phosphor band (2½p.) or two phosphor bands (others).* P 15×14.

No.	Type		Description	Unused	Used
894	**381**	2½p.	new blue, black, lemon, emerald, reddish violet, carmine-red, carmine-rose and gold	10	10
		a.	Imperf (pair)	£450	
		Eb.	Embossing omitted		
895	**382**	3p.	black, reddish violet, lemon, new blue, carmine-rose, emerald, ultramarine and gold	10	10
		a.	Gold (Queen's head) omitted	£650	
		b.	Carmine-rose omitted	£3250	
		c.	Lemon (window panels) omitted	£175	
		d.	New blue omitted	†	£7000
		e.	Reddish violet (tunics etc) omitted	£3500	
		f.	Carmine-rose and lemon omitted		£4000
		g.	Reddish violet and embossing omitted		£4000
		Eh.	Embossing omitted	15·00	
		Ey.	Phosphor omitted	5·00	
		Eya.	Embossing and phosphor omitted	£100	
896	**383**	7½p.	black, lilac, lemon, emerald, new blue, rose, green and gold	55	75
		a.	Gold (Queen's head) omitted	£160	
		b.	Lilac omitted	£650	
		c.	Emerald omitted	£350	
		d.	Lemon omitted		£4000
		Ef.	Embossing omitted	50·00	
		Ef.	Embossing double	50·00	
		Ey.	Phosphor omitted	12·00	
		Eya.	Embossing and phosphor omitted	32·00	
Set of 3				50	75
First Day Cover					2·00
Presentation Pack				4·50	

Special First Day of Issue Postmarks

British Post Office Philatelic Bureau, Edinburgh (Type D, see Introduction) .... 3·50
Bethlehem, Llandeilo, Carms .... 10·00
Canterbury .... 10·00

WHITE CHALK-SURFACED PAPER. From No. 897 all issues, with the exception of Nos. 940/8, were printed on fluorescent white paper, giving a stronger chalk reaction than the original cream paper.

384 Sir James Clark Ross

385 Sir Martin Frobisher

386 Henry Hudson

387 Capt. Scott

(Des Marjorie Saynor. Queen's head printed in gold and then embossed)

1972 (16 Feb). *British Polar Explorers. Two phosphor bands.* P 14×15.

No.	Type		Description	Unused	Used
897	**384**	3p.	yellow-brown, indigo, slate-black, flesh, lemon, rose, brt blue & gold	10	10
		a.	Gold (Queen's head) omitted	£110	
		b.	Slate-black (hair, etc.) omitted	£3500	
		c.	Lemon omitted	£7000	
		Ed.	Embossing omitted	45·00	
		Ee.	Gold (Queen's head) and embossing omitted	£130	
		Ey.	Phosphor omitted	5·00	
		Eya.	Embossing and phosphor omitted	35·00	
898	**385**	5p.	salmon, flesh, purple-brown, ochre, black and gold	15	15
		a.	Gold (Queen's head) omitted	£110	
		Eb.	Embossing omitted	25·00	
		Ey.	Phosphor omitted	12·00	
		Eya.	Gold and phosphor omitted	£140	
		Eyb.	Embossing and phosphor omitted		
899	**386**	7½p.	reddish violet, blue, dp slate, yellow-brown, buff, black and gold	45	50
		a.	Gold (Queen's head) omitted	£325	
		Ey.	Phosphor omitted	20·00	
900	**387**	9p.	dull blue, ultramarine, black, greenish yellow, pale pink, rose-red and gold	70	85
		Ey.	Phosphor omitted	£325	
Set of 4				1·25	1·50
First Day Cover					2·50
Presentation Pack				5·25	

An example of the 3p. is known used on piece with the flesh colour omitted.

Special First Day of Issue Postmarks

Philatelic Bureau, Edinburgh .... 10·00
London WC .... 15·00

388 Statuette of Tutankhamun

389 19th-century Coastguard

390 Ralph Vaughan Williams and Score

(Des Rosalind Dease (3p.), F. Wegner (7½p.), C. Abbott (9p.). Queen's head printed in gold and then embossed (7½p., 9p.))

1972 (26 Apr). *General Anniversaries. Events described on stamps. Two phosphor bands.* P 15×14.

901	**388**	3p. black, grey, gold, dull bistre-brown, blackish brown, pale stone and light brown	25	25
902	**389**	7½p. pale yellow, new blue, slate-blue, violet-blue, slate and gold	50	50
		Ea. Embossing omitted	£200	
		Ey. Phosphor omitted	£250	
903	**390**	9p. bistre-brown, black, sage-green, dp slate, yellow-ochre, brown and gold	50	50
		a. Gold (Queen's head) omitted	£3000	
		b. Brown (facial features) omitted	£1000	
		c. Deep slate omitted	£6000	
		Ed. Embossing omitted		
		Ey. Phosphor omitted	32·00	
Set of 3			1·00	1·00
First Day Cover				2·25
Presentation Pack			4·25	

Special First Day of Issue Postmarks

Philatelic Bureau, Edinburgh .... 3·00
London EC .... 7·00

391 St. Andrew's, Greensted-juxta-Ongar, Essex

392 All Saints, Earls Barton, Northants

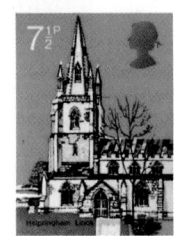

393 St. Andrew's, Letheringsett, Norfolk

394 St. Andrew's, Helpringham, Lincs

395 St. Mary the Virgin, Huish Episcopi, Somerset

(Des R. Maddox. Queen's head printed in gold and then embossed)

1972 (21 June). *British Architecture. Village Churches. Ordinary paper. Two phosphor bands.* P 14×15.

904	**391**	3p. violet-blue, black, lt yellow-olive, emerald-green, orange-vermilion and gold	10	10
		a. Gold (Queen's head) omitted	£110	
		b. Orange-vermilion omitted		£3500
		Ec. Embossing omitted	35·00	
		Ey. Phosphor omitted	6·00	
		Eya. Gold (Queen's head) and phosphor omitted	£140	
		Eyb. Embossing and phosphor omitted	20·00	
905	**392**	4p. deep yellow-olive, black, emerald, violet-blue, orange-vermilion and gold	10	20
		a. Gold (Queen's head) omitted	£4500	
		b. Violet-blue omitted	£150	
		Ec. Embossing omitted	12·00	
		Eya. Phosphor omitted	18·00	
906	**393**	5p. deep emerald, black, royal blue, light yellow-olive, orange-vermilion and gold	15	20
		a. Gold (Queen's head) omitted	£180	
		Eb. Embossing omitted	50·00	
		Ey. Phosphor omitted	25·00	
907	**394**	7½p. orange-red, black, dp yellow-olive, royal blue, lt emerald and gold	50	75
		Ey. Phosphor omitted	18·00	
		Eya. Embossing and phosphor omitted	48·00	

908 **395** 9p. new blue, black, emerald-green, dp yellow-olive, orange-vermilion and gold 50 80
Ea. Embossing omitted........ 20·00
Ey. Phosphor omitted........ 22·00

Set of 5........ 1·25 1·90
First Day Cover........ 2·75
Presentation Pack........ 10·00

Nos. 905a and 906a only exist with the phosphor omitted.

Special First Day of Issue Postmarks

Philatelic Bureau, Edinburgh .... 6·00
Canterbury .... 8·00

"Belgica 72" Souvenir Pack

1972 (24 June). Comprises Nos. 894/6 and 904/8.
CP908b Souvenir Pack .... 10·00

This pack was specially produced for sale at the "Belgica '72" Stamp Exhibition, held in Brussels between 24 June and 9 July. It contains information on British stamps with a religious theme with text in English, French and Flemish, and was put on sale at Philatelic Bureaux in Britain on 26 June.

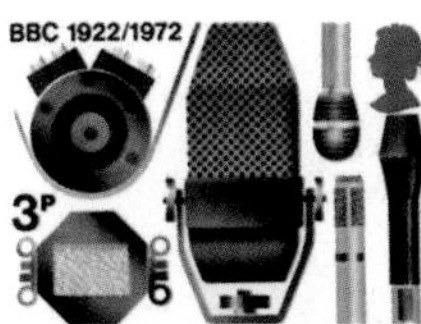

396 Microphones, 1924–69

397 Horn Loudspeaker

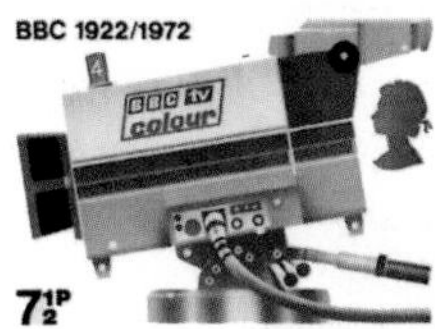

398 T.V. Camera, 1972

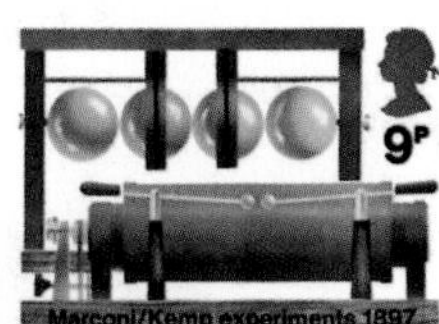

399 Oscillator and Spark Transmitter, 1897

(Des D. Gentleman)

1972 (13 Sept). *Broadcasting Anniversaries. 75th Anniv of Marconi and Kemp's Radio Experiments (9p.), and 50th Anniv of Daily Broadcasting by the B.B.C. (others). Two phosphor bands.* P 15×14.

909 **396** 3p. pale brown, black, grey, greenish yellow and brownish slate........ 10 10
a. Greenish yellow (terminals) omitted £4500

910 **397** 5p. brownish slate, lake-brown, salmon, lt brown, black and red-brown........ 10 20
Ey. Phosphor omitted........ 6·00
Eya. Phosphor on back but omitted on front........ 45·00

911 **398** 7½p. lt grey, slate, brownish slate, magenta and black........ 45 50
a. Brownish slate (Queen's head) omitted........ † £2750
Eya. Phosphor on back but omitted on front........ 45·00

Ey. Phosphor omitted........ 12·00

912 **399** 9p. lemon, brown, brownish slate, deep brownish slate, bluish slate and black........ 50 50
a. Brownish slate (Queen's head) omitted........ £3000
Ey. Phosphor omitted........ 13·00

Set of 4........ 1·00 1·25
First Day Cover........ 2·75
Presentation Pack........ 4·25

In addition to the generally issued Presentation Pack a further pack exists inscribed "1922–1972". This pack of stamps commemorating the 50th Anniversary of the B.B.C. was specially produced as a memento of the occasion for the B.B.C. staff. It was sent with the good wishes of the Chairman and Board of Governors, the Director-General and Board of Management. The pack contains Nos. 909/11 only (Price £35).

No. 911a is only found in first day covers posted from the Philatelic Bureau in Edinburgh.

Special First Day of Issue Postmarks

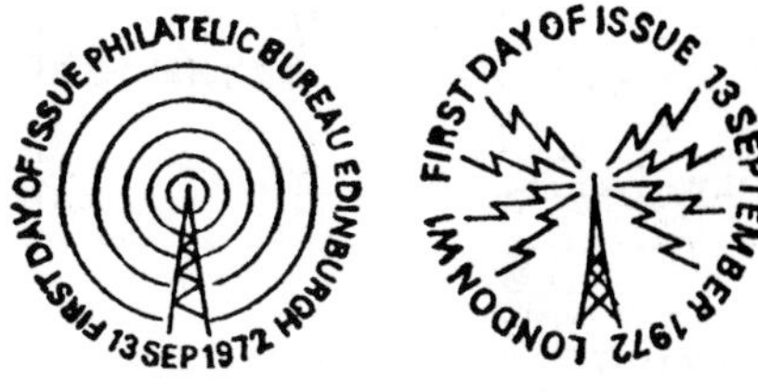

Philatelic Bureau, Edinburgh .... 3·50
London W1 .... 10·00

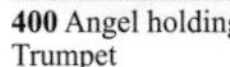

400 Angel holding Trumpet

401 Angel playing Lute

402 Angel playing Harp

(Des Sally Stiff. Photo and embossing)

1972 (18 Oct). *Christmas. One centre phosphor band (2½p.) or two phosphor bands (others).* P 14×15.

913 **400** 2½p. cerise, pale reddish brown, yellow-orange, orange-vermilion, lilac, gold, red-brown and deep grey........ 10 10
a. Gold omitted........ £350
Eb. Embossing omitted........ 15·00
c. Deep grey omitted........ £2000
Ey. Phosphor omitted........ 12·00

914 **401** 3p. ultramarine, lavender, lt turquoise-blue, brt green, gold, red-brown and bluish violet........ 10 10
a. Red-brown omitted........ £650

No.	Type		Description	Unused	Used
			b. Bright green omitted	£160	
			c. Bluish violet omitted	£160	
			d. Lavender omitted	£10000	
			Ee. Embossing omitted	9·00	
			Ey. Phosphor omitted	6·00	
			Eya. Embossing and phosphor omitted	15·00	
915	402	7½p.	dp brown, pale lilac, lt cinnamon, ochre, gold, red-brown and blackish violet	50	45
			a. Ochre omitted	£110	
			b. Blackish violet (shadow) omitted	£7500	
			Ec. Embossing omitted	18·00	
			Ey. Phosphor omitted	12·00	
			Eya. Embossing and phosphor omitted	30·00	
Set of 3				60	45
First Day Cover					1·50
Presentation Pack				4·00	

The gold printing on the 3p. is from two cylinders: 1E and 1F. Examples have been seen with the gold of the 1F cylinder omitted, but these are difficult to detect on single stamps.

Special First Day of Issue Postmarks

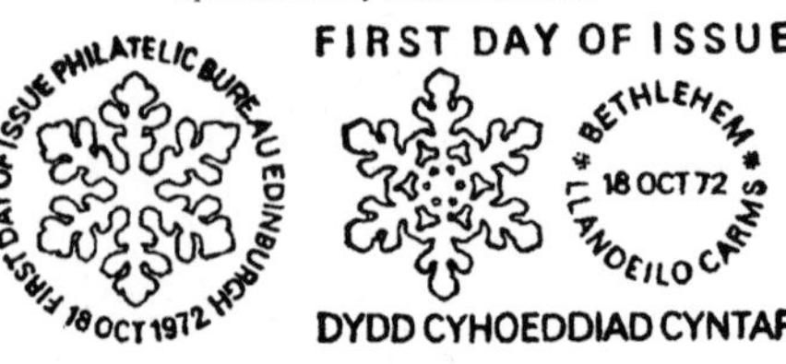

Philatelic Bureau, Edinburgh .... 3·00
Bethlehem, Llandeilo, Carms .... 6·50

403 Queen Elizabeth and Duke of Edinburgh

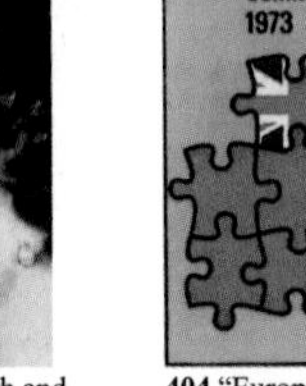

404 "Europe"

(Des J. Matthews from photo by N. Parkinson)

1972 (20 Nov). *Royal Silver Wedding. "All-over" phosphor (3p.) or without phosphor (20p.).* P 14×15.

I. "Rembrandt" Machine

No.	Type		Description	Unused	Used
916	403	3p.	brownish black, dp blue & silver	25	25
			a. Silver omitted	£375	
917		20p.	brownish black, reddish purple and silver	1·00	1·00

II. "Jumelle" Machine

No.	Type		Description	Unused	Used
918	403	3p.	brownish black, dp blue & silver	40	10
Set of 2				1·00	1·00
Gutter Pair (No. 918)				80	
Traffic Light Gutter Pair				20·00	
First Day Cover					1·50
Presentation Pack				4·00	
Presentation Pack (*Japanese*)				9·50	
Souvenir Book				4·00	

The souvenir book is a twelve-page booklet containing photographs of the Royal Wedding and other historic events of the royal family and accompanying information. The 3p. "JUMELLE" has a lighter shade of the brownish black than the 3p. "REMBRANDT". It also has the brown cylinders less deeply etched, which can be distinguished in the Duke's face GB Concise 05 104-145 6/5/05 12:31 am Page 110 which is slightly lighter, and in the Queen's hair where the highlights are sharper.

3p. "REMBRANDT". Cyls. 3A-1B-11C no dot. Sheets of 100 (10×10).

3p. "JUMELLE". Cyls. 1A-1B-3C dot and no dot. Sheets of 100 (two panes 5×10, separated by gutter margin).

Special First Day of Issue Postmarks

Philatelic Bureau, Edinburgh .... 2·50
Windsor, Berks .... 6·00

Collectors Pack 1972

1972 (20 Nov).Comprises Nos. 897/918.
CP918a Collectors Pack .... 27·00

(Des P. Murdoch)

1973 (3 Jan). *Britain's Entry into European Communities. Two phosphor bands.* P 14×15.

No.	Type		Description	Unused	Used
919	404	3p.	dull orange, bright rose-red, ultramarine, lt lilac and black	25	25
920		5p.	new blue, brt rose-red, ultramarine, cobalt-blue and black	25	50
			a. Pair. Nos. 920/1	1·00	1·50
921		5p.	lt emerald-green, brt rose-red, ultramarine, cobalt-blue & black	25	50
Set of 3				1·00	1·00
First Day Cover					2·00
Presentation Pack				3·00	

Nos. 920/1 were printed horizontally *se-tenant* throughout the sheet.

Special First Day of Issue Postmark

Philatelic Bureau, Edinburgh .... 3·00

405 Oak Tree

(Des D. Gentleman)

1973 (28 Feb). *Tree Planting Year. British Trees (1st issue). Two phosphor bands.* P 15×14.

No.	Type		Description	Unused	Used
922	405	9p.	brownish black, apple-green, deep olive, sepia, blackish green and brownish grey	35	40
			a. Brownish black (value and inscr) omitted	£425	
			b. Brownish grey (Queen's head) omitted	£350	
			Ey. Phosphor omitted	90·00	
First Day Cover					1·75
Presentation Pack				2·75	

See also No. 949.

Special First Day of Issue Postmark

Philatelic Bureau, Edinburgh ....3·00

CHALK-SURFACED PAPER. The following issues are printed on chalk-surfaced paper but where "all-over" phosphor has been applied there is no chalk reaction except in the sheet margins outside the phosphor area.

406 David Livingstone

407 H. M. Stanley

T **406/7** were printed together, horizontally *se-tenant* within the sheet.

408 Sir Francis Drake

409 Walter Raleigh

410 Charles Sturt

(Des Marjorie Saynor. Queen's head printed in gold and then embossed)

1973 (18 Apr). *British Explorers. "All-over" phosphor.* P 14×15.

923	**406**	3p. orange-yellow, light orange-brown, grey-black, light turquoise-blue, turquoise-blue and gold	40	25
		a. Pair. Nos. 923/4	80	1·00
		b. Gold (Queen's head) omitted	65·00	
		c. Turquoise-blue (background and inscr) omitted	£425	
		d. Light orange-brown omitted	£400	
		Ee. Embossing omitted	35·00	
924	**407**	3p. orange-yellow, light orange-brown, grey-black, light turquoise-blue, turquoise-blue and gold	40	25
		b. Gold (Queen's head) omitted	65·00	
		c. Turquoise-blue (background and inscr) omitted	£425	
		d. Light orange-brown omitted	£400	
		Ee. Embossing omitted	35·00	
925	**408**	5p. light flesh, chrome-yellow, orange-yellow, sepia, brownish grey, grey-black, violet-blue and gold	40	50
		a. Gold (Queen's head) omitted	£130	
		b. Grey-black omitted	£700	
		c. Sepia omitted	£650	
		Ed. Embossing omitted	9·00	
926	**409**	7½p. light flesh, reddish brown, sepia, ultramarine, grey-black, bright lilac and gold	40	50
		a. Gold (Queen's head) omitted	£3000	
		b. Ultramarine (eyes) omitted		£3000
927	**410**	9p. flesh, pale stone, grey-blue, grey-black, brown-grey, Venetian red, brown-red and gold	40	75
		a. Gold (Queen's head) omitted	£120	
		b. Brown-grey printing double from	£850	
		c. Grey-black omitted	£1400	
		d. Brown-red (rivers on map) omitted	£575	
		Ee. Embossing omitted	40·00	
Set of 5			1·50	1·50
First Day Cover				2·50
Presentation Pack			4·50	

Caution is needed when buying missing gold heads in this issue as they can be removed by using a hard eraser, etc., but this invariably affects the "all-over" phosphor. Genuine examples have the phosphor intact. Used examples off cover cannot be distinguished as much of the phosphor is lost in the course of floating.

In the 5p. value the missing grey-black affects the doublet, which appears as brownish grey, and the lace ruff, which is entirely missing. The missing sepia affects only Drake's hair, which appears much lighter.

The double printing of the brown-grey (cylinder 1F) on the 9p., is a most unusual type of error to occur in a multicoloured photogravure issue. Two sheets are known and it is believed that they stuck to the cylinder and went through a second time. This would result in the following two sheets missing the colour but at the time of going to press this error has not been reported. The second print is slightly askew and more prominent in the top half of the sheets. Examples from the upper part of the sheet showing a clear double impression of the facial features are worth a substantial premium over the price quoted.

Special First Day of Issue Postmark

Philatelic Bureau, Edinburgh ....5·00

First Day of Issue handstamps were provided at Blantyre, Glasgow, and Denbigh for this issue.

411

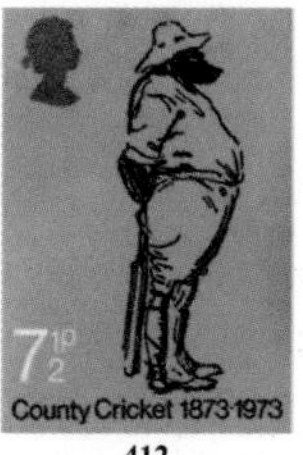

412

413 (T **411/13** show sketches of W.G. Grace by Harry Furniss)

(Des E. Ripley. Queen's head printed in gold and then embossed)

1973 (16 May). *County Cricket 1873–1973. "All-over" phosphor.* P 14×15.

No.	Type	Description	Unused	Used
928	**411**	3p. black, ochre and gold	25	25
		a. Gold (Queen's head) omitted	£2500	
		Eb. Embossing omitted	20·00	
929	**412**	7½p. black, light sage-green and gold	75	75
		a. Gold (Queen's head) omitted	£2500	
		Eb. Embossing omitted	30·00	
930	**413**	9p. black, cobalt and gold	1·25	1·00
		Eb. Embossing omitted	80·00	
Set of 3			1·75	1·50
First Day Cover				3·00
Presentation Pack			4·50	
Souvenir Book			7·00	
P.H.Q. Card (*No.* 928)			70·00	£275

The souvenir book is a 24-page illustrated booklet containing a history of County Cricket with text by John Arlott.

The P.H.Q. card did not become available until mid-July. The used price quoted is for an example used in July or August 1973.

Special First Day of Issue Postmarks

Philatelic Bureau, Edinburgh .... 4·00
Lords, London NW .... 8·00

414 "Self-portrait" (Raeburn)

415 "Self-portrait" (Reynolds)

416 "Nelly O'Brien' (Reynolds)

417 "Rev. R. Walker (The Skater)" (Raeburn)

(Des S. Rose. Queen's head printed in gold and then embossed)

1973 (4 July). *British Paintings. 250th Birth Anniv of Sir Joshua Reynolds and 150th Death Anniv of Sir Henry Raeburn. "All-over" phosphor.* P 14×15.

No.	Type	Description	Unused	Used
931	**414**	3p. rose, new blue, jet-black, magenta, greenish yellow, black, ochre and gold	10	10
		a. Gold (Queen's head) omitted	70·00	
		Ec. Gold (Queen's head) and embossing omitted	75·00	
932	**415**	5p. cinnamon, greenish yellow, new blue, light magenta, black, yellow-olive and gold	30	30
		a. Gold (Queen's head) omitted	80·00	
		b. Greenish yellow omitted	£550	
		Ec. Embossing omitted	30·00	
933	**416**	7½p. greenish yellow, new blue, light magenta, black, cinnamon and gold	30	30
		a. Gold (Queen's head) omitted	£130	
		b. Cinnamon omitted	£6000	
		Ec. Embossing omitted	25·00	
934	**417**	9p. brownish rose, black, dull rose, pale yellow, brownish grey, pale blue and gold	60	60
		b. Brownish rose omitted	75·00	
		Ec. Embossing omitted	£120	
Set of 4			1·20	1·20
First Day Cover				2·00
Presentation Pack			3·25	

Special First Day of Issue Postmark

Philatelic Bureau, Edinburgh .... 3·50

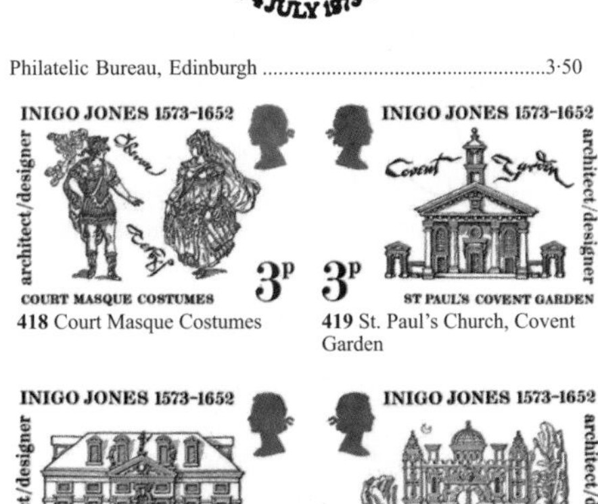

418 Court Masque Costumes

419 St. Paul's Church, Covent Garden

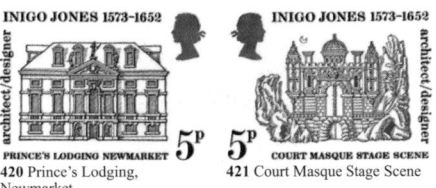

420 Prince's Lodging, Newmarket

421 Court Masque Stage Scene

T **418/19** and T **420/1** were printed horizontally *se-tenant* within the sheet.

(Des Rosalind Dease. Litho and typo B.W.)

1973 (15 Aug). *400th Birth Anniv of Inigo Jones (architect and designer). "All-over" phosphor.* P 15×14.

No.	Type	Description	Unused	Used
935	**418**	3p. deep mauve, black and gold	10	25
		a. Pair. Nos. 935/6	30	50
		ab. Face values omitted	£5500	
		Eac. Deep mauve ptg double (pair)		
		Ec. 9 mm. phosphor band*	15·00	
936	**419**	3p. deep brown, black and gold	10	25

937	**420**	5p. blue, black and gold	35	50
		a. Pair. Nos. 937/8	1·00	1·25
		Ec. 9 mm. phosphor band*	18·00	
938	**421**	5p. grey-olive, black and gold	35	50
Set of 4			1·25	1·25
First Day Cover				2·00
Presentation Pack			3·50	
P.H.Q. Card (*No.* 936)			£200	£200

No. 935ab is caused by the omission of virtually all the black printing from one horizontal row.

*On part of the printings for both values the "all-over" phosphor band missed the first vertical row and a 9 mm. phosphor band was applied to correct this.

Special First Day of Issue Postmark

Philatelic Bureau, Edinburgh . . . . 5·00

422 Palace of Westminster seen from Whitehall

423 Palace of Westminster seen from Millbank

(Des R. Downer. Recess and typo B.W.)

1973 (12 Sept). *19th Commonwealth Parliamentary Conference. "All-over" phosphor.* P 15×14.

939	**422**	8p. black, brownish grey and stone	45	50
940	**423**	10p. gold and black	45	40
Set of 2			75	75
First Day Cover				1·50
Presentation Pack			3·00	
Souvenir Book			7·00	
P.H.Q. Card (*No.* 939)			40·00	£150

The souvenir book is a twelve-page booklet containing a history of the Palace of Westminster.

Special First Day of Issue Postmark

Philatelic Bureau, Edinburgh . . . . 3·50

424 Princess Anne and Capt. Mark Phillips

(Des C. Clements and E. Hughes from photo by Lord Litchfield)

1973 (14 Nov). *Royal Wedding. "All-over" phosphor.* P 15×14.

941	**424**	3½p. dull violet and silver	25	25
		a. Imperf (horiz pair)	£2100	
942		20p. deep brown and silver	1·00	75
		a. Silver omitted	£2000	
Set of 2			1·00	75
Set of 2 *Gutter Pairs*			2·75	
Set of 2 *Traffic Light Gutter Pairs*			£110	
First Day Cover				1·50
Presentation Pack			2·75	
P.H.Q. Card (*No.* 941)			9·00	50·00

Special First Day of Issue Postmarks

Philatelic Bureau, Edinburgh ....2·50
Westminster Abbey, London SW1 ....5·00
Windsor, Berks ....5·00

425

426

427

428

429

T **425/9** depict the carol "Good King Wenceslas" and were printed horizontally *se-tenant* within the sheet.

430 Good King Wenceslas, the Page and Peasant

(Des D. Gentleman)

1973 (28 Nov). *Christmas. One centre phosphor band (3p.) or "all-over" phosphor (3½p.).* P 15×14.

943	**425**	3p. grey-black, violet-blue, slate, brown, rose-red, rosy mauve, turquoise-green, salmon-pink and gold	20	25
		a. Strip of 5. Nos. 943/7	2·25	3·50
		ab. Rosy mauve omitted (strip of 5)	£4500	
		b. Imperf (horiz strip of 5)	£1500	
		Eg. Gum arabic	25	
		Ega. Strip of 5. Nos. 943Eg/7Eg	3·00	
		Egb. Imperf (strip of 5. Nos. 943 Eg/7Eg)	£2750	
944	**426**	3p. grey-black, violet-blue, slate, brown, rose-red, rosy mauve, turquoise-green, salmon-pink and gold	20	25
		a. Rosy mauve omitted	£1750	
		Eg. Gum arabic	25	
945	**427**	3p. grey-black, violet-blue, slate, brown, rose-red, rosy-mauve, turquoise-green, salmon-pink and gold	20	25
		a. Rosy mauve omitted	£1750	
		Eg. Gum arabic	25	
946	**428**	3p. grey-black, violet-blue, slate, brown, rose-red, rosy mauve, turquoise-green, salmon-pink and gold	20	25
		a. Rosy mauve omitted	£1750	
		Eg. Gum arabic	25	
947	**429**	3p. grey-black, violet-blue, slate, brown, rose-red, rosy mauve, turquoise-green, salmon-pink and gold	20	25
		a. Rosy mauve omitted	£1750	
		Eg. Gum arabic	25	
948	**430**	3½p. salmon-pink, grey-black, red-brown, blue, turquoise-green, brt rose-red, rosy mauve, lavendergrey and gold	20	25
		a. Imperf (pair)	£425	
		b. Grey-black (value, inscr, etc.) omitted	80·00	
		c. Salmon-pink omitted	75·00	
		d. Blue (leg, robes) omitted	£140	
		e. Rosy mauve (robe at right) omitted	85·00	
		f. Blue and rosy mauve omitted	£375	
		g. Brt rose-red (King's robe) omitted	80·00	
		h. Red-brown (logs, basket, etc.) omitted		
		i. Turquoise-green (leg, robe, etc.) omitted	£2750	
		j. Gold (background) omitted	†	£750
		Set of 6	2·25	2·50
		First Day Cover		3·50
		Presentation Pack	4·00	

Examples of No. 948j are only known used on covers from Gloucester. The 3½p. has also been seen with the lavender-grey omitted used on piece.

The 3p. and 3½p. are normally with PVA gum with added dextrin, but the 3½p. also exists with normal PVA gum.

Special First Day of Issue Postmarks

Philatelic Bureau, Edinburgh .... 3·00
Bethlehem, Llandeilo, Carms .... 6·00

Collectors Pack 1973

1973 (28 Nov). Comprises Nos. 919/48.
CP948k Collectors Pack .... 27·00

431 Horse Chestnut

(Des D. Gentleman)

1974 (27 Feb). *British Trees (2nd issue). "All-over" phosphor.* P 15×14.

949	**431**	10p. light emerald, bright green, greenish yellow, brown-olive, black and brownish grey	40	35
		Gutter Pair	2·00	
		Traffic Light Gutter Pair	65·00	
		First Day Cover		1·25
		Presentation Pack	2·50	
		P.H.Q. Card	£140	£150

Special First Day of Issue Postmark

Philatelic Bureau, Edinburgh .... 2·00

432 First Motor Fire-engine, 1904

433 Prize-winning Fire-engine, 1863

434 First Steam Fire-engine, 1830

435 Fire-engine, 1766

(Des D. Gentleman)

1974 (24 Apr). *Bicentenary of the Fire Prevention (Metropolis) Act. "All-over" phosphor.* P 15×14.

950	**432**	3½p. grey-black, orange-yellow, greenish yellow, dull rose, ochre and grey	25	10
		a. Imperf (pair)	£825	
951	**433**	5½p. greenish yellow, dp rosy magenta, orange-yellow, lt emerald, grey-black and grey	25	30
952	**434**	8p. greenish yellow, lt blue-green, lt greenish blue, lt chestnut, grey-black and grey	50	50
953	**435**	10p. grey-black, pale reddish brown, lt brown, orange-yellow and grey	50	50
Set of 4			1·25	1·25
Set of 4 *Gutter Pairs*			4·00	
Set of 4 *Traffic Light Gutter Pairs*			65·00	
First Day Cover				3·00
Presentation Pack			2·75	
P.H.Q. Card (*No.* 950)			£140	£150

The 3½p. exists with ordinary PVA gum.

Special First Day of Issue Postmark

Philatelic Bureau, Edinburgh .... 3·50

436 P & O Packet, *Peninsular*, 1888

437 Farman H.F. III Biplane, 1911

438 Airmail-blue Van and Postbox, 1930

439 Imperial Airways Short S.21 Flying Boat *Maia*, 1937

(Des Rosalind Dease)

1974 (12 June). *Centenary of Universal Postal Union. "All over" phosphor.* P 15×14.

954	**436**	3½p. dp brownish grey, brt mauve, grey-black and gold	25	10
955	**437**	5½p. pale orange, lt emerald, grey-black and gold	25	30
956	**438**	8p. cobalt, brown, grey-black & gold	25	35
957	**439**	10p. dp brownish grey, orange, grey-black and gold	50	40
Set of 4			1·00	1·00
Set of 4 *Gutter Pairs*			3·00	
Set of 4 *Traffic Light Gutter Pairs*			45·00	
First Day Cover				2·00
Presentation Pack			2·75	

Special First Day of Issue Postmark

Philatelic Bureau, Edinburgh .... 2·50

440 Robert the Bruce

441 Owain Glyndwr

442 Henry the Fifth

443 The Black Prince

(Des F. Wegner)

1974 (10 July). *Medieval Warriors. "All-over" phosphor.* P 15×14.

958	**440**	4½p. greenish yellow, vermilion, slate-blue, red-brown, reddish brown, lilac-grey and gold	25	10
959	**441**	5½p. lemon, vermilion, slate-blue, red-brown, reddish brown, olive-drab and gold	25	35
960	**442**	8p. dp grey, vermilion, greenish yellow, new blue, red-brown, dp cinnamon and gold	50	50
961	**443**	10p. vermilion, greenish yellow, new blue, red-brown, reddish brown, lt blue and gold	50	50
Set of 4			1·25	1·25
Set of 4 *Gutter Pairs*			4·00	
Set of 4 *Traffic Light Gutter Pairs*			70·00	
First Day Cover				3·00
Presentation Pack			4·00	
P.H.Q. Cards (*set of* 4)			28·00	55·00

Imperforate pairs of SG961 are known and thought to be of proof status (£625 *per pair*).

Special First Day of Issue Postmark

Philatelic Bureau, Edinburgh .... 3·50

444 Churchill in Royal Yacht Squadron Uniform

445 Prime Minister, 1940

446 Secretary for War and Air, 1919

447 War Correspondent, South Africa, 1899

(Des C. Clements and E. Hughes)

1974 (9 Oct). *Birth Centenary of Sir Winston Churchill. "All-over" phosphor.* P 14×15.

962	**444**	4½p. Prussian blue, pale turquoise-green and silver	20	15
963	**445**	5½p. sepia, brownish grey and silver	35	35
964	**446**	8p. crimson, lt claret and silver	60	50
965	**447**	10p. lt brown, stone and silver	60	50
Set of 4			1·60	1·50
Set of 4 Gutter Pairs			4·00	
Set of 4 Traffic Light Gutter Pairs			34·00	
First Day Cover				2·00
Presentation Pack			2·50	
Souvenir Book			3·00	
P.H.Q. Card (*No.* 963)			6·00	32·00

The souvenir book consists of an illustrated folder containing a biography of Sir Winston.

Nos. 962/5 come with PVA gum containing added dextrin, but the 8p. also exists with normal PVA.

Special First Day of Issue Postmarks

Philatelic Bureau, Edinburgh	3·00
Blenheim, Woodstock, Oxford	10·00
House of Commons, London SW	10·00

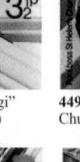

448 "Adoration of the Magi" (York Minster, *circa* 1355)

449 "The Nativity" (St. Helen's Church, Norwich, *circa* 1480)

450 "Virgin and Child" (Ottery St. Mary Church, *circa* 1350)

451 "Virgin and Child" (Worcester Cathedral, *circa* 1224)

(Des Peter Hatch Partnership)

1974 (27 Nov). *Christmas. Church Roof Bosses. One phosphor band (3½p.) or "all-over" phosphor (others).* P 15×14.

966	**448**	3½p. gold, lt new blue, lt brown, grey-black and lt stone	10	10
		a. Light stone (background shading) omitted	£10000	
		Ey. Phosphor omitted	12·00	
967	**449**	4½p. gold, yellow-orange, rose-red, lt brown, grey-black & lt new blue	10	10
968	**450**	8p. blue, gold, lt brown, rose-red, dull green and grey-black	25	50
969	**451**	10p. gold, dull rose, grey-black, lt new blue, pale cinnamon and lt brown	50	50
Set of 4			1·00	1·00
Set of 4 Gutter Pairs			3·50	
Set of 4 Traffic Light Gutter Pairs			36·00	
First Day Cover				2·00
Presentation Pack			2·25	

The phosphor band on the 3½p. was first applied down the centre of the stamp but during the printing this was deliberately placed to the right between the roof boss and the value; however, intermediate positions, due to shifts, are known.

Two used examples of the 3½p. have been reported with the light brown colour omitted.

Special First Day of Issue Postmarks

Philatelic Bureau, Edinburgh	2·50
Bethlehem, Llandeilo, Carms	5·00

Collectors Pack 1974

1974 (27 Nov). Comprises Nos. 949/69.

CP969a Collectors Pack	13·00

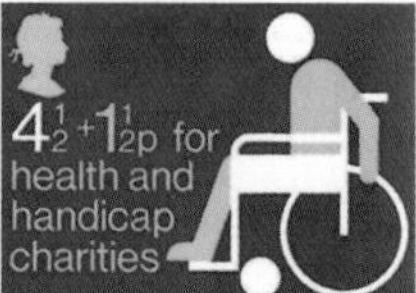

452 Invalid in Wheelchair

(Des P. Sharland)

1975 (22 Jan). *Health and Handicap Funds. "All-over" phosphor.* P 15×14.

970 **452** 4½p.+1½p. azure and grey-blue	25	25
Gutter Pair	50	
Traffic Light Gutter Pair	2·25	
First Day Cover	1·00	

Special First Day of Issue Postmark

Philatelic Bureau, Edinburgh ....1·50

453 "Peace-Burial at Sea"

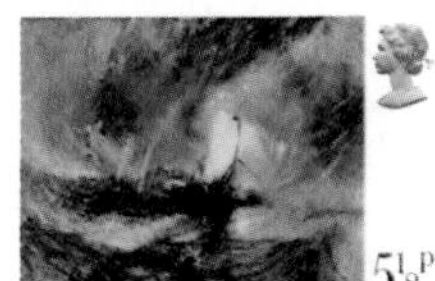

454 "Snowstorm-Steamer off a Harbour's Mouth"

455 "The Arsenal, Venice"

456 "St. Laurent"

(Des S. Rose)

1975 (19 Feb). *Birth Bicentenary of J. M. W. Turner (painter). "All-over" phosphor.* P 15×14.

971	**453**	4½p. grey-black, salmon, stone, blue and grey	25	25
972	**454**	5½p. cobalt, greenish yellow, lt yellow brown, grey-black and rose	25	25
973	**455**	8p. pale yellow-orange, greenish yellow, rose, cobalt and grey-black	25	50
974	**456**	10p. dp blue, lt yellow-ochre, lt brown, dp cobalt and grey-black	50	50
Set of 4			1·00	1·00
Set of 4 Gutter Pairs			2·25	
Set of 4 Traffic Light Gutter Pairs			11·50	
First Day Cover				1·50
Presentation Pack			2·00	
P.H.Q. Card (*No.* 972)			42·00	34·00

Special First Day of Issue Postmarks

London WC ....5·00
Philatelic Bureau, Edinburgh ....2·50

457 Charlotte Square, Edinburgh

458 The Rows, Chester

T **457/8** were printed horizontally *se-tenant* within the sheet.

459 Royal Observatory, Greenwich

460 St. George's Chapel, Windsor

461 National Theatre, London

(Des P. Gauld)

1975 (23 Apr). *European Architectural Heritage Year. "All over" phosphor.* P 15×14.

975	**457**	7p. greenish yellow, brt orange, grey-black, red-brown, new blue, lavender and gold	25	25
		a. Pair. Nos. 975/6	90	1·00
976	**458**	7p. grey-black, greenish yellow, new blue, brt orange, red-brown and gold	25	25
977	**459**	8p. magenta, dp slate, pale magenta, lt yellow-olive, grey-black and gold	40	30
978	**460**	10p. bistre-brown, greenish yellow, dp slate, emerald-green, grey-black and gold	40	30
979	**461**	12p. grey-black, new blue, pale magenta and gold	40	35
Set of 5			1·50	1·25
Set of 5 Gutter Pairs			5·50	
Set of 5 Traffic Light Gutter Pairs			22·00	
First Day Cover				2·50
Presentation Pack			2·50	
P.H.Q. Cards (*Nos.* 975/7)			11·00	40·00

Special First Day of Issue Postmark

Philatelic Bureau, Edinburgh ....7·00

462 Sailing Dinghies

463 Racing Keel Yachts

464 Cruising Yachts

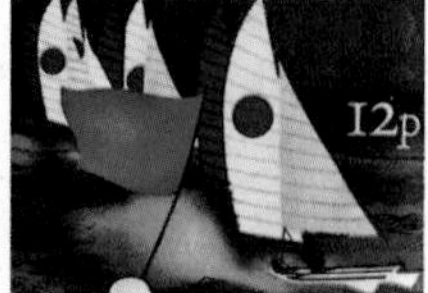

465 Multihulls

(Des A. Restall. Recess and photo)

1975 (11 June). *Sailing. "All-over" phosphor.* P 15×14.

980	**462**	7p. black, bluish violet, scarlet, orange-vermilion, orange and gold	25	20
981	**463**	8p. black, orange-vermilion, orange, lavender, brt mauve, brt blue, dp ultramarine and gold	35	40
		a. Black omitted	70·00	
982	**464**	10p. black, orange, bluish emerald, lt olive-drab, chocolate and gold	35	45
983	**465**	12p. black, ultramarine, turquoise-blue, rose, grey, steel-blue and gold	50	50
Set of 4			1·25	1·25
Set of 4 *Gutter Pairs*			2·50	
Set of 4 *Traffic Light Gutter Pairs*			25·00	
First Day Cover				2·00
Presentation Pack			2·50	
P.H.Q. Card (*No.* 981)			5·75	30·00

On No. 981a the recess-printed black colour is completely omitted.

Special First Day of Issue Postmark

Philatelic Bureau, Edinburgh .... 2·50

A First Day of Issue handstamp was provided at Weymouth for this issue.

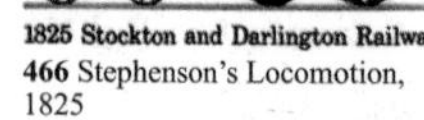

466 Stephenson's Locomotion, 1825

467 *Abbotsford*, 1876

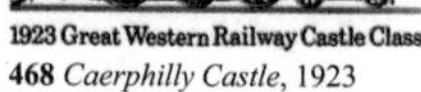

468 *Caerphilly Castle*, 1923

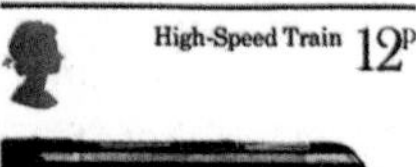

469 High Speed Train, 1975

(Des B. Craker)

1975 (13 Aug). *150th Anniv of Public Railways. "All-over" phosphor.* P 15×14.

984	**466**	7p. red-brown, grey-black, greenish yellow, grey and silver	25	25
985	**467**	8p. brown, orange-yellow, vermilion, grey-black, grey and silver	50	50
986	**468**	10p. emerald-green, grey-black, yellow-orange, vermilion, grey and silver	50	50
987	**469**	12p. grey-black, pale lemon, vermilion, blue, grey and silver	40	50
Set of 4			1·50	1·50
Set of 4 *Gutter Pairs*			3·00	
Set of 4 *Traffic Light Gutter Pairs*			14·00	
First Day Cover				2·50
Presentation Pack			2·50	
Souvenir Book			4·00	
P.H.Q. Cards (*set of* 4)			70·00	72·00

The souvenir book is an eight-page booklet containing a history of the railways.

Special First Day of Issue Postmarks

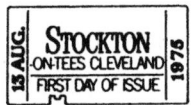

Philatelic Bureau, Edinburgh	3·50
Darlington, Co. Durham	12·00
Shildon, Co. Durham	15·00
Stockton-on-Tees, Cleveland	12·00

470 Palace of Westminster

(Des R. Downer)

1975 (3 Sept). *62nd Inter-Parliamentary Union Conference. "All-over" phosphor.* P 15×14.

988	**470**	12p. lt new blue, black, brownish grey and gold	50	40
Gutter Pair			1·00	
Traffic Light Gutter Pair			4·50	
First Day Cover				80
Presentation Pack			1·25	

Special First Day of Issue Postmark

Philatelic Bureau, Edinburgh .... 1·50

471 Emma and Mr. Woodhouse (*Emma*)

472 Catherine Morland (*Northanger Abbey*)

473 Mr. Darcy (*Pride and Prejudice*)

474 Mary and Henry Crawford (*Mansfield Park*)

(Des Barbara Brown)

1975 (22 Oct). *Birth Bicentenary of Jane Austen (novelist). "All-over" phosphor.* P 14×15.

989	**471**	8½p. blue, slate, rose-red, lt yellow, dull green, grey-black and gold	25	20
990	**472**	10p. slate, brt magenta, grey, lt yellow, grey-black and gold	45	45
991	**473**	11p. dull blue, pink, olive-sepia, slate, pale greenish yellow, grey-black and gold	45	45
992	**474**	13p. brt magenta, lt new blue, slate, buff, dull blue-green, grey-black & gold..	50	50
Set of 4			1·50	1·25
Set of 4 *Gutter Pairs*			2·50	
Set of 4 *Traffic Light Gutter Pairs*			11·00	
First Day Cover				2·50
Presentation Pack			2·50	
P.H.Q. Cards (*set of* 4)			24·00	42·00

Special First Day of Issue Postmarks

Philatelic Bureau, Edinburgh ....3·00
Steventon, Basingstoke, Hants ....6·00

475 Angels with Harp and Lute

476 Angel with Mandolin

477 Angel with Horn

478 Angel with Trumpet

(Des R. Downer)

1975 (26 Nov). *Christmas. One phosphor band (6½p.), phosphor-inked background (8½p.), "all-over" phosphor (others).* P 15×14.

993	**475**	6½p. bluish violet, brt reddish violet, light lavender and gold	25	25
994	**476**	8½p. turquoise-green, brt emerald-green, slate, lt turquoise-green and gold	25	40
995	**477**	11p. vermilion, cerise, pink and gold	50	45
996	**478**	13p. drab, brown, brt orange, buff and gold	50	45
Set of 4			1·25	1·25
Set of 4 *Gutter Pairs*			2·75	
Set of 4 *Traffic Light Gutter Pairs*			11·00	
First Day Cover				1·50
Presentation Pack			2·50	

The 6½p. exists with both ordinary PVA gum and PVA containing added dextrin.

Special First Day of Issue Postmarks

Philatelic Bureau, Edinburgh ....2·00
Bethlehem, Llandeilo, Dyfed ....3·00

Collectors Pack 1975

1975 (26 Nov). Comprises Nos. 970/96.
CP996a Collectors Pack ....9·00

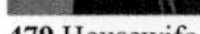
479 Housewife

480 Policeman

481 District Nurse

482 Industrialist

(Des P. Sharland)

1976 (10 Mar). *Telephone Centenary. "All-over" phosphor.* P 15×14.

997	**479**	8½p. greenish blue, deep rose, black and blue	25	20
		a. Deep rose (vase and picture frame) omitted	£2500	
998	**480**	10p. greenish blue, black and yellow-olive	40	40

999	**481**	11p. greenish blue, deep rose, black and brt mauve	50	50
1000	**482**	13p. olive-brown, deep rose, black and orange-red	60	60
Set of 4			1·50	1·50
Set of 4 *Gutter Pairs*			2·75	
Set of 4 *Traffic Light Gutter Pairs*			11·00	
First Day Cover				1·50
Presentation Pack			2·50	

Special First Day of Issue Postmark

Philatelic Bureau, Edinburgh .... 2·00

483 Hewing Coal (Thomas Hepburn)

484 Machinery (Robert Owen)

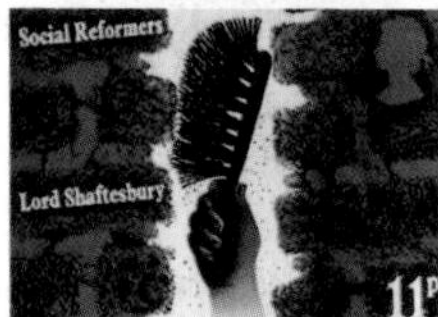

485 Chimney Cleaning (Lord Shaftesbury)

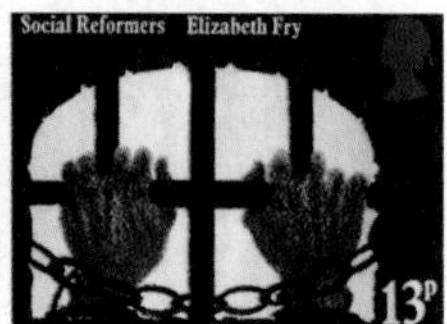

486 Hands clutching Prison Bars (Elizabeth Fry)

(Des D. Gentleman)

1976 (28 Apr). *Social Reformers. "All-over" phosphor.* P 15×14.

1001	**483**	8½p. lavender-grey, grey-black, black and slate-grey	25	20
1002	**484**	10p. lavender-grey, grey-black, grey and slate-violet	40	40
1003	**485**	11p. black, slate-grey and drab	50	50
1004	**486**	13p. slate-grey, black & dp dull green	60	60
Set of 4			1·50	1·50
Set of 4 *Gutter Pairs*			2·75	
Set of 4 *Traffic Light Gutter Pairs*			11·00	
First Day Cover				1·50
Presentation Pack			2·50	
P.H.Q. Card (*No.* 1001)			6·00	20·00

Special First Day of Issue Postmark

Philatelic Bureau, Edinburgh .... 2·00

487 Benjamin Franklin (bust by Jean-Jacques Caffieri)

(Des P. Sharland)

1976 (2 June). *Bicentenary of American Revolution. "All over" phosphor.* P 14×15.

1005	**487**	11p. pale bistre, slate-violet, pale blue-green, black and gold	50	50
Gutter Pair			75	
Traffic Light Gutter Pair			4·00	
First Day Cover				1·50
Presentation Pack			1·25	
P.H.Q. Card			4·25	20·00

Special First Day of Issue Postmark

Philatelic Bureau, Edinburgh .... 2·00

488 "Elizabeth of Glamis"

489 "Grandpa Dickson"

490 "*Rosa Mundi*"

491 "Sweet Briar"

(Des Kristin Rosenberg)

1976 (30 June). *Centenary of Royal National Rose Society. "All-over" phosphor.* P 14×15.

1006	**488**	8½p. brt rose-red, greenish yellow, emerald, grey-black and gold	15	10
1007	**489**	10p. greenish yellow, brt green, reddish brown, grey-black and gold	40	40

1008	**490**	11p. brt magenta, greenish yellow, emerald, grey-blue, grey-black and gold	50	50
1009	**491**	13p. rose-pink, lake-brown, yellowgreen, pale greenish yellow, grey-black and gold	65	65
		a. Value omitted*	£25000	
Set of 4			1·50	1·50
Set of 4 *Gutter Pairs*			3·00	
Set of 4 *Traffic Light Gutter Pairs*			14·00	
First Day Cover				1·50
Presentation Pack			2·50	
P.H.Q. Cards (set of 4)			28·00	35·00

*During repairs to the cylinder the face value on R.1/9 was temporarily covered with copper. This covering was inadvertently left in place during printing, but the error was discovered before issue and most examples were removed from the sheets. Two mint and one used examples have so far been reported, but only one of the mint remains in private hands.

Special First Day of Issue Postmark

Philatelic Bureau, Edinburgh .... 2·00

492 Archdruid

493 Morris Dancing

494 Scots Piper

495 Welsh Harpist

(Des Marjorie Saynor)

1976 (4 Aug). *British Cultural Traditions. "All-over" phosphor.* P 14×15.

1010	**492**	8½p. yellow, sepia, brt rose, dull ultramarine, black and gold	25	20
1011	**493**	10p. dull ultramarine, brt rose-red, sepia, greenish yellow, black and gold	40	40
1012	**494**	11p. bluish green, yellow-brown, yellow-orange, black, brt rose-red and gold.	45	45
1013	**495**	13p. dull violet-blue, yellow-orange, yellow, black, bluish green and gold	60	60
Set of 4			1·50	1·50
Set of 4 *Gutter Pairs*			3·00	
Set of 4 *Traffic Light Gutter Pairs*			13·00	
First Day Cover				2·00
Presentation Pack			2·50	
P.H.Q. Cards (set of 4)			18·00	28·00

The 8½p. and 13p. commemorate the 800th anniversary of the Royal National Eisteddfod.

Special First Day of Issue Postmarks

Philatelic Bureau, Edinburgh .... 2·50
Cardigan, Dyfed .... 5·00

496 Woodcut from *The Canterbury Tales*

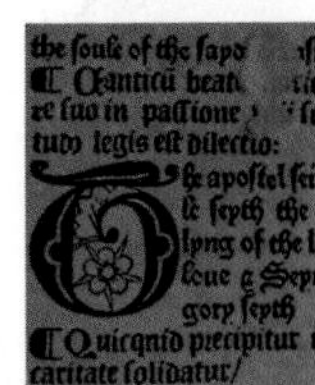

497 Extract from *The Tretyse of Love*

498 Woodcut from *The Game and Playe of Chesse*

499 Early Printing Press

(Des R. Gay. Queen's head printed in gold and then embossed)

1976 (29 Sept). *500th Anniv of British Printing. "All-over" phosphor.* P 14×15.

1014	**496**	8½p. black, lt new blue and gold	25	20
1015	**497**	10p. black, olive-green and gold	40	40
1016	**498**	11p. black, brownish grey and gold	45	45
1017	**499**	13p. chocolate, pale ochre and gold	60	60
Set of 4			1·50	1·50
Set of 4 *Gutter Pairs*			3·00	
Set of 4 *Traffic Light Gutter Pairs*			8·00	
First Day Cover				1·75
Presentation Pack			2·50	
P.H.Q. Cards (set of 4)			10·00	28·00

Special First Day of Issue Postmarks

Philatelic Bureau, Edinburgh .... 2·00
London SW1 .... 3·00

500 Virgin and Child

501 Angel with Crown

502 Angel appearing to Shepherds

503 The Three Kings

(Des Enid Marx)

1976 (24 Nov). *Christmas. English Medieval Embroidery. One phosphor band (6½p.) or "all-over" phosphor (others).* P 15×14.

1018	**500**	6½p. blue, bistre-yellow, brown and orange	25	25
		a. Imperf (pair)	£450	
1019	**501**	8½p. sage-green, yellow, brown-ochre, chestnut and olive-black	35	25
1020	**502**	11p. dp magenta, brown-orange, new blue, black and cinnamon	40	45
		a. Uncoated paper*	75·00	30·00
1021	**503**	13p. bright purple, new blue, cinnamon, bronze-green and olive-grey	45	50
Set of 4			1·25	1·25
Set of 4 Gutter Pairs			2·75	
Set of 4 Traffic Light Gutter Pairs			8·00	
First Day Cover				1·50
Presentation Pack			2·50	
P.H.Q. Cards (set of 4)			4·50	26·00

*See footnote after No. 744.

Special First Day of Issue Postmarks

Philatelic Bureau, Edinburgh ....2·50
Bethlehem, Llandeilo, Dyfed ....3·50

Collectors Pack 1976

1976 (24 Nov). Comprises Nos. 997/1021.
CP1021a Collectors Pack ....13·50

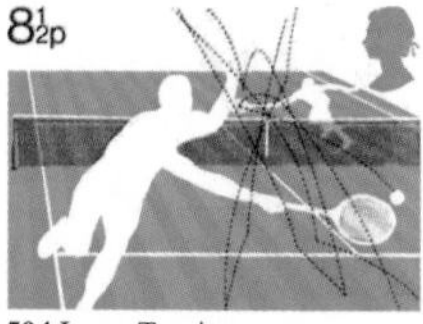

504 Lawn Tennis

505 Table Tennis

506 Squash

507 Badminton

(Des A. Restall)

1977 (12 Jan). *Racket Sports. Phosphorised paper.* P 15×14.

1022	**504**	8½p. emerald-green, black, grey and bluish green	25	20
		a. Imperf (horiz pair)	£950	
1023	**505**	10p. myrtle-green, black, grey-black and dp blue-green	40	40
1024	**506**	11p. orange, pale yellow, black, slate-black and grey	45	40
		a. Imperf (horiz pair)	£2400	
1025	**507**	13p. brown, grey-black, grey and brt reddish violet	45	50
Set of 4			1·25	1·25
Set of 4 Gutter Pairs			3·00	
Set of 4 Traffic Light Gutter Pairs			7·00	
First Day Cover				2·00
Presentation Pack			2·25	
P.H.Q. Cards (set of 4)			8·00	24·00

The only known example of No. 1024a is cut close at left.

Special First Day of Issue Postmark

507a

Philatelic Bureau, Edinburgh ....2·50

508

1977 (2 Feb)–**87**. P 14×15.

1026	**508**	£1 brt yellow-green and blackish olive	3·00	25
		a. Imperf (pair)	£800	
1026*b*		£1.30 pale drab and dp greenish blue (3.8.83)	5·50	6·00
1026*c*		£1.33 pale mauve and grey-black (28.8.84)	7·50	7·00
1026*d*		£1.41 pale drab and dp greenish blue (17.9.85)	8·50	8·50
1026*e*		£1.50 pale mauve and grey-black (2.9.86)	6·00	5·00
1026*f*		£1.60 pale drab and dp greenish blue (15.9.87)	6·50	7·00
1027		£2 light emerald and purple-brown	9·00	50
1028		£5 salmon and chalky blue	22·00	3·00
		a. Imperf (vert pair)	£3750	
Set of 8			55·00	32·00
Set of 8 Gutter Pairs			£150	
Set of 8 Traffic Light Gutter Pairs			£180	
First Day Cover (1026, 1027/8)				8·00

First Day Cover (1026*b*)		6·50
First Day Cover (1026*c*)		8·00
First Day Cover (1026*d*)		8·50
First Day Cover (1026*e*)		5·50
First Day Cover (1026*f*)		8·00
Presentation Pack (*P.O. Pack No.* 91 (small size)) (1026, 1027/8)	48·00	
Presentation Pack (*P.O. Pack No.* 13 (large size)) (1026, 1027/8)	£160	
Presentation Pack (*P.O. Pack No.* 14) (large size) (1026*f*)	12·00	

Special First Day of Issue Postmarks
(for illustrations see Introduction)

Philatelic Bureau, Edinburgh (Type F) (£1, £2, £5)	14·00
Windsor, Berks (Type F) (£1, £2, £5)	20·00
Philatelic Bureau, Edinburgh (Type F) (£1.30)	6·50
Windsor, Berks (Type F) (£1.30)	10·00
British Philatelic Bureau, Edinburgh (Type F) (£1.33)	8·00
Windsor, Berks (Type F) (£1.33)	10·00
British Philatelic Bureau, Edinburgh (Type G) (£1.41)	9·00
Windsor, Berks (Type G) (£1.41)	9·00
British Philatelic Bureau, Edinburgh (Type G) (£1.50)	6·50
Windsor, Berks (Type G) (£1.50)	6·50
British Philatelic Bureau, Edinburgh (Type G) (£1.60)	8·50
Windsor, Berks (Type G) (£1.60)	8·50

509 Steroids—Conformational Analysis

510 Vitamin C—Synthesis

511 Starch—Chromatography

512 Salt—Crystallography

(Des J. Karo)

1977 (2 Mar). *Royal Institute of Chemistry Centenary. "All over" phosphor.* P 15×14.

1029	**509**	8½p. rosine, new blue, olive-yellow, brt mauve, yellow-brown, black and gold	25	20
		a. Imperf (horiz pair)	£1400	
1030	**510**	10p. brt orange, rosine, new blue, brt blue, black and gold	45	45
1031	**511**	11p. rosine, greenish yellow, new blue, dp violet, black and gold	45	45
1032	**512**	13p. new blue, brt green, black and gold	45	45
Set of 4			1·25	1·25
Set of 4 *Gutter Pairs*			3·00	
Set of 4 *Traffic Light Gutter Pairs*			8·00	
First Day Cover				1·50
Presentation Pack			2·25	
P.H.Q. Cards (*set of* 4)			8·00	18·00

Special First Day of Issue Postmark

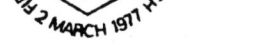

Philatelic Bureau, Edinburgh	2·75

513 **514** **515** **516**

T **513/16** differ in the decorations of "ER".

(Des R. Guyatt)

1977 (11 May). *Silver Jubilee. "All-over" phosphor.* P 15×14.

1033	**513**	8½p. blackish green, black, silver, olive-grey and pale turquoise-green	25	25
		a. Imperf (pair)	£800	
1034		9p. maroon, black, silver, olivegrey and lavender (15 June)	25	25
1035	**514**	10p. blackish blue, black, silver, olive-grey and ochre	25	25
		a. Imperf (horiz pair)	£1700	
1036	**515**	11p. brown-purple, black, silver, olive-grey and rose-pink	50	50
		a. Imperf (horiz pair)	£1700	
1037	**516**	13p. sepia, black, silver, olive-grey and bistre-yellow	50	50
		a. Imperf (pair)	£1100	
Set of 5			1·50	1·25
Set of 5 *Gutter Pairs*			3·50	
Set of 5 *Traffic Light Gutter Pairs*			7·00	
First Day Covers (2)				2·00
Presentation Pack (Nos. 1033, 1035/7)			2·00	
Souvenir Book			3·00	
P.H.Q. Cards (*set of* 5)			14·00	20·00

The Souvenir book is a 16-page booklet containing a history of the Queen's reign.

Special First Day of Issue Postmarks

Philatelic Bureau, Edinburgh (1033, 1035/7) (11 May)	1·50
Philatelic Bureau, Edinburgh (1034) (15 June)	1·00
Windsor, Berks (1033, 1035/7) (11 May)	2·00
Windosr, Berks (1034) (15 June)	1·00

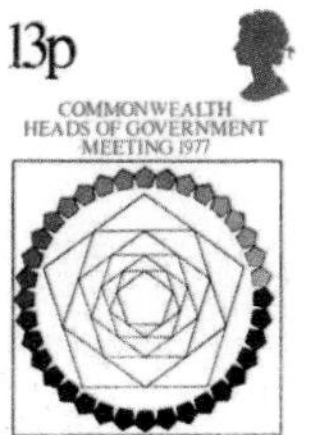

517 "Gathering of Nations"

(Des P. Murdoch. Recess and photo)

1977 (8 June). *Commonwealth Heads of Government Meeting, London. "All-over" phosphor.* P 14×15.

No.	Type	Description	Unused	Used
1038	**517**	13p. black, blackish green, rosecarmine and silver	50	50
Gutter Pair			1·00	
Traffic Light Gutter Pair			2·00	
First Day Cover				1·50
Presentation Pack			1·50	
P.H.Q. Card			3·00	6·00

Special First Day of Issue Postmarks

Philatelic Bureau, Edinburgh .... 1·50
London SW .... 2·00

518 Hedgehog

519 Brown Hare

520 Red Squirrel

521 Otter

522 Badger

T **518/22** were printed horizontally *se-tenant* within the sheet.

(Des P. Oxenham)

1977 (5 Oct). *British Wildlife. "All-over" phosphor.* P 14×15.

No.	Type	Description	Unused	Used
1039	**518**	9p. reddish brown, grey-black, pale lemon, brt turquoise-blue, brt magenta and gold	40	40
		a. Horiz strip of 5. Nos. 1039/43	1·40	2·10
		b. Imperf (vert pair)	£750	
		c. Imperf (horiz pair. Nos. 1039/40)	£1800	
1040	**519**	9p. reddish brown, grey-black, pale lemon, brt turquoise-blue, brt magenta and gold	25	40
1041	**520**	9p. reddish brown, grey-black, pale lemon, brt turquoise-blue, brt . . magenta and gold	25	40
1042	**521**	9p. reddish brown, grey-black, pale lemon, brt turquoise-blue, brt magenta and gold	25	40
1043	**522**	9p. grey-black, reddish brown, pale lemon, brt turquoise-blue, brt magenta and gold	25	40
Set of 5			1·50	1·75
Gutter Strip of 10			2·50	
Traffic Light Gutter Strip of 10			5·00	
First Day Cover				3·00
Presentation Pack			2·50	
P.H.Q. Cards (*set of* 5)			3·00	7·00

Special First Day of Issue Postmark

Philatelic Bureau, Edinburgh .... 3·50

523 "Three French Hens, Two Turtle Doves and a Partridge in a Pear Tree"

524 "Six Geese-a-laying, Five Gold Rings, Four Colly Birds"

525 "Eight Maids-a-milking, Seven Swans a-swimming"

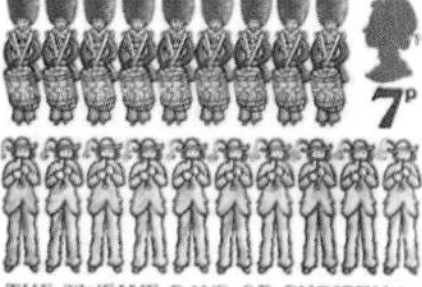

526 "Ten Pipers piping, Nine Drummers drumming"

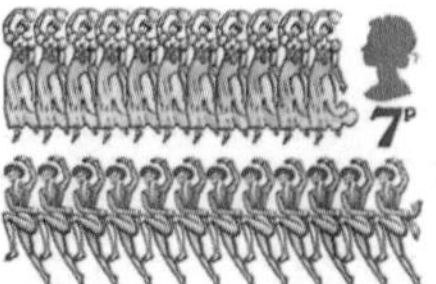

527 "Twelve Lords a-leaping, Eleven Ladies dancing"

T **523/7** depict the carol "The Twelve Days of Christmas" and were printed horizontally *se-tenant* within the sheet.

528 "A Partridge in a Pear Tree"

(Des D. Gentleman)

1977 (23 Nov). *Christmas. One centre phosphor band (7p.) or "all-over" phosphor (9p.).* P 15×14.

1044	**523**	7p.	slate, grey, brt yellow-green, new blue, rose-red and gold	20	15
		a.	Horiz strip of 5. Nos. 1044/8	1·50	2·00
		ab.	Imperf (strip of 5. Nos. 1044/8)	£2000	
1045	**524**	7p.	slate, brt yellow-green, new blue and gold	20	15
1046	**525**	7p.	slate, grey, brt yellow-green, new blue, rose-red and gold	20	15
1047	**526**	7p.	slate, grey, brt yellow-green, new blue, rose-red and gold	20	15
1048	**527**	7p.	slate, grey, brt yellow-green, new blue, rose-red and gold	20	15
1049	**528**	9p.	pale brown, pale orange, brt emerald, pale greenish yellow, slate-black and gold	35	30
		a.	Imperf (pair)	£1200	
Set of 6				1·25	1·10
Set of 6 Gutter Pairs				3·00	
Traffic Light Gutter Pairs				5·00	
First Day Cover					2·25
Presentation Pack				2·25	
P.H.Q. Cards (set of 6)				3·00	6·00

Special First Day of Issue Postmarks

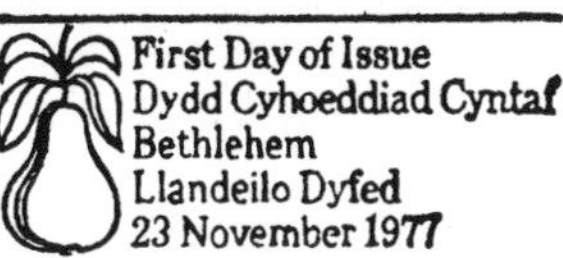

Philatelic Bureau, Edinburgh . . . . 2·50
Bethlehem, Llandeilo, Dyfed . . . . 3·00

Collectors Pack 1977

1977 (23 Nov). Comprises Nos. 1022/5 and 1029/49.
CP1049b Collectors Pack . . . . 9·00

529 Oil–North Sea

530 Coal–Modern Pithead Production Platform

531 Natural Gas- Flame Rising from Sea

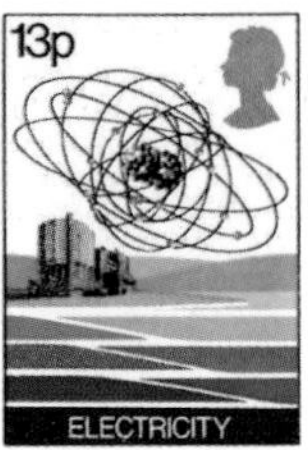

532 Electricity–Nuclear Power Station and Uranium Atom

(Des P. Murdoch)

1978 (25 Jan). *Energy Resources. "All-over" phosphor.* P 14×15.

1050	**529**	9p.	dp brown, orange-vermilion, grey-black, greenish yellow, rose-pink, new blue and silver	25	25
1051	**530**	10½p.	lt emerald-green, grey-black, red-brown, slate-grey, pale apple-green and silver	25	25
1052	**531**	11p.	greenish blue, brt violet, violet-blue, blackish brown, grey-black and silver	50	50
1053	**532**	13p.	orange-vermilion, grey-black, dp brown, greenish yellow, lt brown, lt blue and silver	50	50
Set of 4				1·25	1·25
Set of 4 Gutter Pairs				2·75	
Set of 4 Traffic Light Gutter Pairs				4·50	
First Day Cover					1·50
Presentation Pack				2·00	
P.H.Q. Cards (set of 4)				3·00	6·00

Special First Day of Issue Postmark

Philatelic Bureau, Edinburgh ....2·50

533 The Tower of London

534 Holyroodhouse

535 Caernarvon Castle

536 Hampton Court Palace

(Des R. Maddox (stamps), J. Matthews (miniature sheet))

1978 (1 Mar). *British Architecture. Historic Buildings. "All over" phosphor.* P 15×14.

1054	**533**	9p. black, olive-brown, new blue, brt green, lt yellow-olive and rose-red ..	25	20
1055	**534**	10½p. black, brown-olive, orange-yellow, brt green, lt yellow-olive and violet-blue	25	40
1056	**535**	11p. black, brown-olive, violet-blue, brt green, lt yellow-olive and dull blue .	60	40
1057	**536**	13p. black, orange-yellow, lake-brown, brt green and lt yellow yellow- olive	60	40
Set of 4			1·50	1·25
Set of 4 Gutter Pairs			3·00	
Set of 4 Traffic Light Gutter Pairs			4·50	
First Day Cover				1·50
Presentation Pack			2·00	
P.H.Q. Cards (set of 4)			3·00	6·00
MS1058 121×89 mm. Nos. 1054/7 (sold at 53½p.)			1·25	1·75
		a. Imperforate	£5000	
		b. Lt yellow-olive (Queen's head) omitted	£5000	
		c. Rose-red (Union Jack on 9p.) omitted	£4200	
		d. Orange-yellow omitted	£4200	
		e. New blue (Union Jack on 9p.) omitted	£15000	
First Day Cover				2·00

The premium on No. **MS**1058 was used to support the London 1980 International Stamp Exhibition. No. **MS**1058d is most noticeable on the 10½p. (spheres absent on towers) and around the roadway and arch on the 13p.

Special First Day of Issue Postmarks

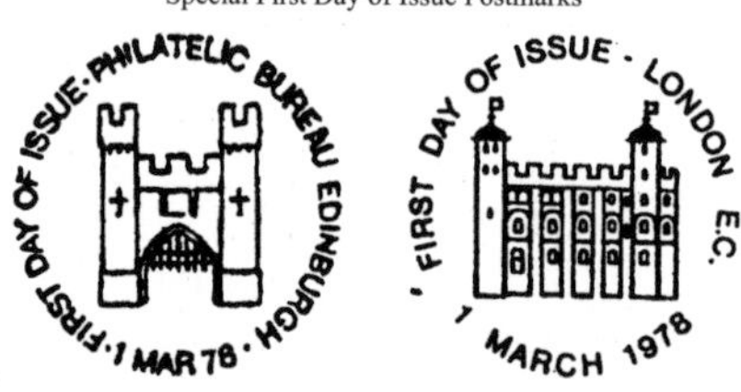

Philatelic Bureau, Edinburgh (stamps)	2.00
Philatelic Bureau, Edinburgh (miniature sheet)	2.50
London EC (stamps)	2.50
London EC (miniature sheet)	3.00

537 State Coach

538 St. Edward's Crown

539 The Sovereign's Orb

540 Imperial State Crown

(Des J. Matthews)

1978 (31 May). *25th Anniv of Coronation. "All-over" phosphor.* P 14×15.

1059	**537**	9p. gold and royal blue	35	25
1060	**538**	10½p. gold and brown-lake	45	45
1061	**539**	11p. gold and dp dull green	45	45
1062	**540**	13p. gold and reddish violet	50	50
Set of 4			1·50	1·50
Set of 4 Gutter Pairs			3·00	
Set of 4 Traffic Light Gutter Pairs			4·25	
First Day Cover				1·50
Presentation Pack			2·00	
Souvenir Book			3·00	
P.H.Q. Cards (set of 4)			3·00	6·00

The souvenir book is a 16-page booklet illustrated with scenes from the Coronation.

Special First Day of Issue Postmarks

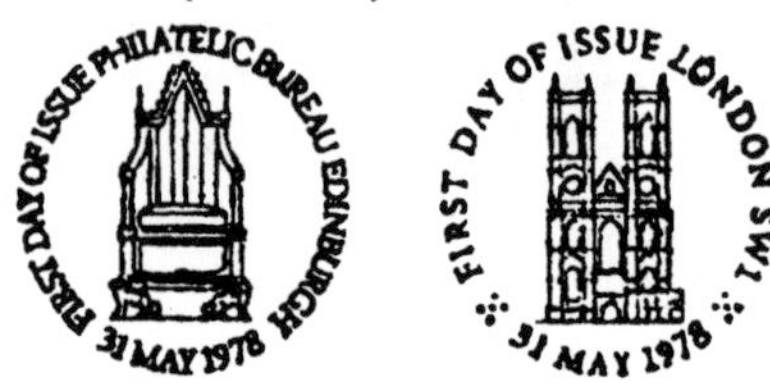

Philatelic Bureau, Edinburgh	2·00
London SW1	2·50

541 Shire Horse

542 Shetland Pony

543 Welsh Pony

544 Thoroughbred

(Des P. Oxenham)

1978 (5 July). *Horses. "All-over" phosphor.* P 15×14.

1063	**541**	9p. black, pale reddish brown, grey-black, greenish yellow, lt blue, vermilion and gold	20	10
1064	**542**	10½p. pale chestnut, magenta, brownish grey, greenish yellow, greenish blue, grey-black and gold	35	40
1065	**543**	11p. reddish brown, black, lt green, greenish yellow, bistre, grey-black and gold	35	45
1066	**544**	13p. reddish brown, pale reddish brown, emerald, greenish yellow, grey-black and gold	45	50
Set of 4			1·25	1·25
Set of 4 Gutter Pairs			3·00	
Set of 4 Traffic Light Gutter Pairs			4·50	
First Day Cover				1·50
Presentation Pack			1·75	
P.H.Q. Cards (set of 4)			2·25	5·75

Special First Day of Issue Postmarks

Philatelic Bureau, Edinburgh	2·00
Peterborough	2·50

545 "Penny-farthing" and 1884 Safety Bicycle

546 1920 Touring Bicycles

547 Modern Small-wheel Bicycles

548 1978 Road-racers

(Des F. Wegner)

1978 (2 Aug). *Centenaries of Cyclists Touring Club and British Cycling Federation. "All-over" phosphor.* P 15×14.

1067	**545**	9p. brown, dp dull blue, rose-pink, pale olive, grey-black and gold	25	20
		a. Imperf (pair)	£400	
1068	**546**	10½p. olive, pale yellow-orange, orange-vermilion, rose-red, lt brown, grey-black and gold	35	40
1069	**547**	11p. orange-vermilion, greenish blue, lt brown, pale greenish yellow, dp grey, grey-black and gold	40	40
1070	**548**	13p. new blue, orange-vermilion, lt brown, olive-grey, grey-black and gold	50	50
		a. Imperf (pair)	£1250	
Set of 4			1·25	1·25
Set of 4 *Gutter Pairs*			2·75	
Set of 4 *Traffic Light Gutter Pairs*			4·50	
First Day Cover				1·50
Presentation Pack			1·75	
P.H.Q. Cards (*set of* 4)			2·25	5·00

Special First Day of Issue Postmarks

Philatelic Bureau, Edinburgh	2·00
Harrogate, North Yorkshire	2·50

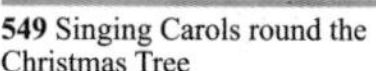

549 Singing Carols round the Christmas Tree

550 The Waits

551 18th-century Carol Singers

552 "The Boar's Head Carol"

(Des Faith Jaques)

1978 (22 Nov). *Christmas. One centre phosphor band (7p.) or "all-over" phosphor (others).* P 15×14.

1071	**549**	7p. brt green, greenish yellow, magenta, new blue, black and gold	25	25
		a. Imperf (pair)	£550	
1072	**550**	9p. magenta, greenish yellow, new blue, sage-green, black and gold	25	25
		a. Imperf (pair)	£950	
1073	**551**	11p. magenta, new blue, greenish yellow, yellow-brown, black and gold	50	50
		a. Imperf (horiz pair)	£1100	
1074	**552**	13p. salmon-pink, new blue, greenish yellow, magenta, black and gold	50	50
Set of 4			1·25	1·25
Set of 4 *Gutter Pairs*			2·50	
Set of 4 Traffic Light *Gutter Pairs*			4·25	
First Day Cover				1·50
Presentation Pack			1·75	
P.H.Q. Cards (set of 4)			2·25	5·00

Special First Day of Issue Postmarks

Philatelic Bureau, Edinburgh	2·00
Bethlehem, Llandeilo, Dyfed	2·50

Collectors Pack 1978

1978 (22 Nov). Comprises Nos. 1050/7 and 1059/74.
CP1074a Collectors Pack .... 9·25

553 Old English Sheepdog

554 Welsh Springer Spaniel

555 West Highland Terrier **556** Irish Setter

(Des P. Barrett)

1979 (7 Feb). *Dogs. "All-over" phosphor.* P 15×14.

1075	**553**	9p.	grey-black, sepia, turquoise-green, pale greenish yellow, pale greenish blue and grey	25	20
1076	**554**	10½p.	grey-black, lake-brown, apple-green, pale greenish yellow, pale greenish blue and grey	40	40
1077	**555**	11p.	grey-black, claret, yellowish green, pale greenish yellow, cobalt and grey	40	40
		a.	Imperf (horiz pair)	£1700	
1078	**556**	13p.	grey-black, lake-brown, green, pale greenish yellow and dp turquoise-blue	40	50
Set of 4				1·25	1·25
Set of 4 Gutter Pairs				7·50	
Set of 4 Traffic Light Gutter Pairs				4·25	
First Day Cover					1·50
Presentation Pack				1·75	
P.H.Q. Cards (set of 4)				2·50	5·00

Special First Day of Issue Postmarks

Philatelic Bureau, Edinburgh ....2·00
London SW ....2·50

557 Primrose

558 Daffodil

559 Bluebell

560 Snowdrop

(Des P. Newcombe)

1979 (21 Mar). *Spring Wild Flowers. "All-over" phosphor.* P 14×15.

1079	**557**	9p.	slate-black, dp brown, pale greenish yellow, dp olive, pale new blue and silver	25	20
		a.	Imperf (pair)	£425	
1080	**558**	10½p.	greenish yellow, grey-green, steel-blue, slate-black, new blue and silver	25	45
		a.	Imperf (vert pair)	£1800	
1081	**559**	11p.	slate-black, dp brown, ultramarine, lt greenish blue, pale greenish yellow and silver	50	45
		a.	Imperf (horiz pair)	£1500	
1082	**560**	13p.	slate-black, indigo, grey-green, sepia, ochre and silver	50	40
		a.	Imperf (horiz pair)	£950	
Set of 4				1·25	1·25
Set of 4 Gutter Pairs				2·50	
Set of 4 Traffic Light Gutter Pairs				4·25	
First Day Cover					1·50
Presentation Pack				1·75	
P.H.Q. Cards (set of 4)				2·50	4·50

Special First Day of Issue Postmark

Philatelic Bureau, Edinburgh ....2·00

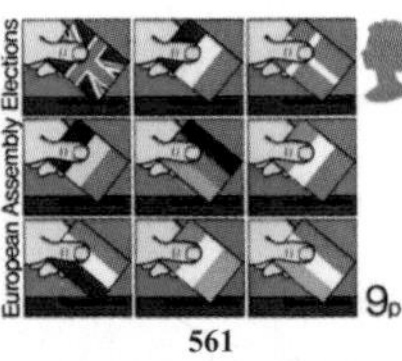

561

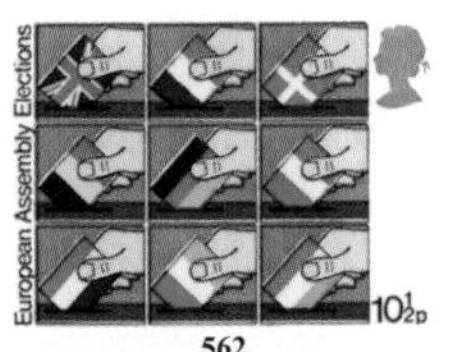

562

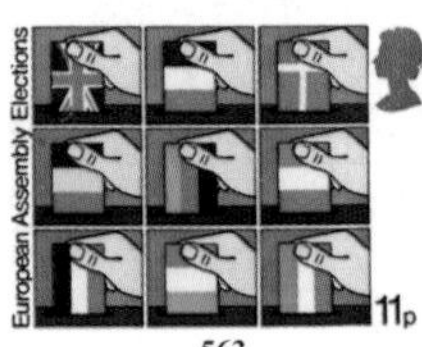

563

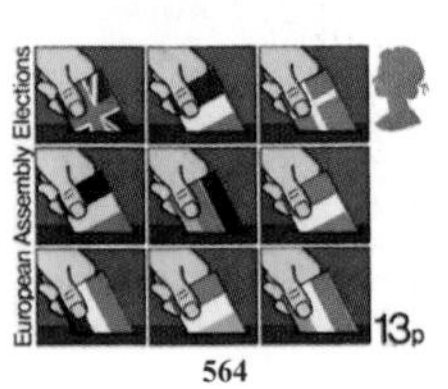

564

T **561/4** show Hands placing National Flags in Ballot Boxes.

(Des S. Cliff)

1979 (9 May). *First Direct Elections to European Assembly. Phosphorised paper.* P 15×14.

1083	**561**	9p.	grey-black, vermilion, cinnamon, pale greenish yellow, pale turquoise-green and dull ultramarine	25	20
1084	**562**	10½p.	grey-black, vermilion, cinnamon, pale greenish yellow, dull ultramarine, pale turquoise-green and chestnut	35	35
1085	**563**	11p.	grey-black, vermilion, cinnamon, pale greenish yellow, dull ultramarine, pale turquoise-green and grey-green	40	40

1086	**564**	13p. grey-black, vermilion, cinnamon, pale greenish yellow, dull ultramarine, pale turquoise-green and brown	45	40
		Set of 4	1·25	1·25
		Set of 4 Gutter Pairs	2·50	
		Set of 4 Traffic Light Gutter Pairs	4·25	
		First Day Cover		1·50
		Presentation Pack	1·75	
		P.H.Q. Cards (set of 4)	2·25	4·50

Special First Day of Issue Postmarks

Philatelic Bureau, Edinburgh .... 2·00
London SW .... 2·50

565 "Saddling 'Mahmoud' for the Derby, 1936" (Sir Alfred Munnings)

566 "The Liverpool Great National Steeple Chase, 1839" (aquatint by F. C. Turner)

567 "The First Spring Meeting, Newmarket, 1793" (J. N. Sartorius)

568 "Racing at Dorsett Ferry, Windsor, 1684" (Francis Barlow)

(Des S. Rose)

1979 (6 June). *Horseracing Paintings. Bicentenary of the Derby (9p.). "All-over" phosphor.* P 15×14.

1087	**565**	9p. lt blue, red-brown, rose-pink, pale greenish yellow, grey-black and gold	25	25
1088	**566**	10½p. bistre-yellow, slate-blue, salmon-pink, lt blue, grey-black and gold	25	25
1089	**567**	11p. rose, vermilion, pale greenish yellow, new blue, grey-black and gold	50	50
1090	**568**	13p. bistre-yellow, rose, turquoise, grey-black and gold	50	50
		Set of 4	1·25	1·25
		Set of 4 Gutter Pairs	2·50	
		Set of 4 Traffic Light Gutter Pairs	4·25	
		First Day Cover		1·50
		Presentation Pack	1·75	
		P.H.Q. Cards (set of 4)	2·25	4·50

Special First Day of Issue Postmarks

Philatelic Bureau, Edinburgh .... 2·00
Epsom, Surrey .... 2·50

569 *The Tale of Peter Rabbit* (Beatrix Potter)

570 *The Wind in the Willows* (Kenneth Grahame)

571 *Winnie-the-Pooh* (A. A. Milne)

572 *Alice's Adventures in Wonderland* (Lewis Carroll)

(Des E. Hughes)

1979 (11 July). *International Year of the Child. Children's Book Illustrations. "All-over" phosphor.* P 14×15.

1091	**569**	9p. dp bluish green, grey-black, bistre-brown, brt rose, greenish yellow and silver	30	25
1092	**570**	10½p. dull ultramarine, grey-black, olive-brown, brt rose, yellow-orange, pale greenish yellow and silver	35	35
1093	**571**	11p. drab, grey-black, greenish yellow, new blue, yellow-orange, agate and silver	40	40
1094	**572**	13p. pale greenish yellow, grey-black, brt rose, dp bluish green, olive-brown, new blue and silver	60	60
		Set of 4	1·50	1·50
		Set of 4 Gutter Pairs	3·00	
		Set of 4 Traffic Light Gutter Pairs	4·25	
		First Day Cover		1·50
		Presentation Pack	2·00	
		P.H.Q. Cards (set of 4)	2·50	4·50

Special First Day of Issue Postmark

Philatelic Bureau, Edinburgh .... 2·00

First Day of Issue handstamps were provided at Hartfield, East Sussex and Stourbridge, West Midlands for this issue.

573 Sir Rowland Hill

574 Postman, circa 1839

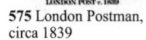

575 London Postman, circa 1839

576 Woman and Young Girl with Letters, 1840

(Des E. Stemp)

1979 (22 Aug–24 Oct). *Death Centenary of Sir Rowland Hill. "All-over" phosphor.* P 14×15.

1095 **573** 10p. grey-black, brown-ochre, myrtle-green, pale greenish yellow, rosine, brt blue and gold 25 20
a. Imperf (horiz pair) £2700
1096 **574** 11½p. grey-black, brown-ochre, brt blue, rosine, bistre-brown, pale greenish yellow and gold 25 35
1097 **575** 13p. grey-black, brown-ochre, brt blue, rosine, bistre-brown, pale greenish yellow and gold 50 45
1098 **576** 15p. grey-black, brown-ochre, myrtle-green, bistre-brown, rosine, pale greenish yellow & gold 75 50
Set of 4 .... 1·50 1·50
Set of 4 *Gutter Pairs* .... 3·00
Set of 4 *Traffic Light Gutter Pairs* .... 4·25
First Day Cover .... 1·50
Presentation Pack .... 1·50
P.H.Q. Cards (*set of* 4) .... 2·25 4·25
MS1099 89×121 mm. Nos. 1095/8 (sold at 59½p.) (24 Oct) .... 1·25 1·50
a. Imperforate £2200
b. Brown-ochre (15p. background, etc.) omitted £1800
c. Gold (Queen's head) omitted £275
d. Brown-ochre, myrtle-green and gold omitted. £6000
e. Brt blue (13p. background, etc.) omitted £6250
f. Myrtle-green (10p. (background), 15p.) omitted £2750
g. Pale greenish yellow omitted £325
h. Rosine omitted £1250
i. Bistre-brown omitted £900
j. Grey-black and pale greenish yellow omitted. £15000
First Day Cover .... 1·50

The premium on No. **MS**1099 was used to support the London 1980 International Stamp Exhibition.

Examples of No. **MS**1099 showing face values on the stamps of 9p., 10½p., 11p. and 13p., with a sheet price of 53½p., were prepared, but not issued. (Price £40,000).

Special First Day of Issue Postmarks

Philatelic Bureau, Edinburgh (stamps) (22 Aug). .... 2·25
Philatelic Bureau, Edinburgh (miniature sheet) (24 Oct) .... 2·00
London EC (stamps) (22 Aug) .... 2·00
London EC (miniature sheet) (24 Oct) .... 2·00

First Day of Issue handstamps were provided at Kidderminster, Worcs on 22 August (pictorial) and 24 October (Type C) and at Sanquhar, Dumfriesshire on 22 August and 24 October (both Type C).

577 Policeman on the Beat

578 Policeman directing Traffic

579 Mounted Policewoman

580 River Patrol Boat

(Des B. Sanders)

1979 (26 Sept). *150th Anniv of Metropolitan Police. Phosphorised paper.* P 15×14.

1100 **577** 10p. grey-black, red-brown, emerald, greenish yellow, brt blue and magenta 30 20
1101 **578** 11½p. grey-black, brt orange, purple-brown, ultramarine, greenish yellow and dp bluish green 35 35
1102 **579** 13p. grey-black, red-brown, magenta, olive-green, greenish yellow and dp dull blue 40 55
1103 **580** 15p. grey-black, magenta, brown, slate-blue, dp brown and greenish black .. 60 55
Set of 4 .... 1·50 1·50
Set of 4 *Gutter Pairs* .... 3·00
Set of 4 *Traffic Light Gutter Pairs* .... 4·25
First Day Cover .... 1·50
Presentation Pack .... 1·75
PHQ Cards (*set of* 4) .... 2·25 4·25

Special First Day of Issue Postmarks

Philatelic Bureau, Edinburgh .... 2·00
London SW .... 2·00

581 The Three Kings

582 Angel appearing to the Shepherds

583 The Nativity

584 Mary and Joseph travelling to Bethlehem

585 The Annunciation

(Des F. Wegner)

1979 (21 Nov). *Christmas. One centre phosphor band (8p.) or phosphorised paper (others).* P 15×14.

1104	**581**	8p.	blue, grey-black, ochre, slate-violet and gold	25	20
			a. Imperf (pair)	£525	
1105	**582**	10p.	brt rose-red, grey-black, chestnut, chrome-yellow, dp violet and gold	25	25
			a. Imperf between (vert pair)	£500	
			b. Imperf (pair)	£900	
1106	**583**	11½p.	orange-vermilion, steel-blue, drab, grey-black, dp blue-green and gold	25	35
1107	**584**	13p.	brt blue, orange-vermilion, bistre, grey-black and gold	50	50
1108	**585**	15p.	orange-vermilion, blue, bistre, grey-black, green and gold	50	50
Set of 5				1·50	1·50
Set of 5 Gutter Pairs				3·50	
Set of 5 Traffic Light Gutter Pairs				4·50	
First Day Cover					1·50
Presentation Pack				2·00	
P.H.Q. Cards (set of 5)				2·50	4·25

Special First Day of Issue Postmarks

Philatelic Bureau, Edinburgh .... 2·00
Bethlehem, Llandeilo, Dyfed .... 2·00

Collectors Pack 1979

1979 (21 Nov). Comprises Nos. 1075/98 and 1100/8.
CP1108a Collectors Pack .... 12·00

586 Common Kingfisher

587 Dipper

588 Moorhen

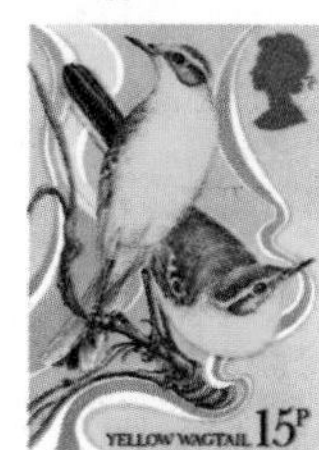

589 Yellow Wagtails

(Des M. Warren)

1980 (16 Jan). *Centenary of Wild Bird Protection Act. Phosphorised paper.* P 14×15.

1109	**586**	10p.	brt blue, brt yellow-green, vermilion, pale greenish yellow, grey-black and gold	20	10
1110	**587**	11½p.	sepia, grey-black, dull ultramarine, vermilion, grey-green, pale greenish yellow and gold	40	35
1111	**588**	13p.	emerald-green, grey-black, brt blue, vermilion, pale greenish yellow and gold	50	55
1112	**589**	15p.	greenish yellow, brown, lt green, slate-blue, grey-black and gold	50	55
Set of 4				1·50	1·50
Set of 4 Gutter Pairs				3·50	
First Day Cover					1·50
Presentation Pack				1·50	
P.H.Q. Cards (set of 4)				2·25	4·50

Special First Day of Issue Postmarks

Philatelic Bureau, Edinburgh .... 2·00
Sandy, Beds .... 2·50

590 *Rocket* approaching Moorish Arch, Liverpool

591 First and Second Class Carriages passing through Olive Mount Cutting

592 Third Class Carriage and Sheep Truck crossing Chat Moss

593 Horsebox and Carriage Truck near Bridgewater Canal

594 Goods Truck and Mail-Coach at Manchester

T **590/4** were printed together, *se-tenant*, in horizontal strips of 5 throughout the sheet.

(Des D. Gentleman)

1980 (12 Mar). *150th Anniv of Liverpool and Manchester Railway. Phosphorised paper.* P 15×14.

1113	**590**	12p. lemon, lt brown, rose-red, pale blue and grey-black	40	40
		a. Strip of 5. Nos. 1113/17	1·75	1·75
		ab. Imperf (horiz strip of 5. Nos. 1113/17)	£1900	
		ac. Lemon omitted (horiz strip of 5. Nos. 1113/17)	£17500	
1114	**591**	12p. rose-red, lt brown, lemon, pale blue and grey-black	40	40
1115	**592**	12p. pale blue, rose-red, lemon, lt brown and grey-black	40	40
1116	**593**	12p. lt brown, lemon, rose-red, pale blue and grey-black	40	40
1117	**594**	12p. lt brown, rose-red, pale blue, lemon and grey-black	40	40
Set of 5			1·75	1·50
Gutter Block of 10			3·75	
First Day Cover				1·75
Presentation Pack			2·00	
P.H.Q. Cards (*set of* 5)			4·25	4·50

Special First Day of Issue Postmarks

Philatelic Bureau, Edinburgh	2·00
Liverpool	2·25
Manchester	2·25

595 Montage of London Buildings

During the printing of No. 1118 the die was re-cut resulting in the following two types:

Type I (original). Top and bottom lines of shading in portrait oval broken. Hatched shading below left arm of Tower Bridge and hull of ship below right arm. Other points: Hatched shading on flag on Westminster Abbey, bottom right of Post Office Tower and archway of entrance to Westminster Abbey.

Type II (re-engraved). Lines in oval unbroken. Solid shading on bridge and ship. Also solid shading on flag, Post Office Tower and archway.

(Des J. Matthews. Eng G. Holt. Recess)

1980 (9 Apr). *"London 1980" International Stamp Exhibition. Phosphorised paper.* P 14½×14.

1118	**595**	50p. agate (I)	1·50	1·50
		Ea. Type II	1·25	1·25
Gutter Pair			3·25	
First Day Cover				1·50
Presentation Pack			1·75	
P.H.Q. Card			2·25	3·00
MS1119 90×123 mm. No. 1118Ea (sold at 75p.) (7 May)			1·50	1·75
		a. Error. Imperf	£1500	
First Day Cover				2·00

Examples of No. 1118 are known in various shades of green.

Such shades result from problems with the drying of the printed sheets on the press, but are not listed as similar colours can be easily faked.

Special First Day of Issue Postmarks

Philatelic Bureau, Edinburgh (stamp) (9 Apr.) 2·00
Philatelic Bureau, Edinburgh (miniature sheet) (7 May) 2·50
London SW (stamp) (9 Apr.) 2·50
London SW (miniature sheet) (7 May) 2·50

596 Buckingham Palace

597 The Albert Memorial

598 Royal Opera House

599 Hampton Court

600 Kensington Palace

(Des Sir Hugh Casson)

1980 (7 May). *London Landmarks. Phosphorised paper.* P 14×15.

1120	**596**	10½p. grey, pale blue, rosine, pale greenish yellow, yellowish green and silver	25	10
1121	**597**	12p. grey-black, bistre, rosine, yellowish green, pale greenish yellow and silver	25	15
		a. Imperf (vert pair)	£1250	
1122	**598**	13½p. grey-black, pale salmon, pale olive-green, slate-blue and silver	40	50
		a. Imperf (pair)	£1250	
1123	**599**	15p. grey-black, pale salmon, slate-blue, dull yellowish green, olive-yellow and silver	50	75
1124	**600**	17½p. grey, slate-blue, red-brown, sepia, yellowish green, pale greenish yellow and silver	75	75
		a. Silver (Queen's head) omitted	£475	
Set of 5			2·00	2·00
Set of 5 Gutter Pairs			4·25	
First Day Cover				2·00
Presentation Pack			2·00	
P.H.Q. Cards (set of 5)			2·25	3·00

No. 1124a shows the Queen's head in pale greenish yellow, this colour being printed beneath the silver for technical reasons.

Special First Day of Issue Postmarks

Philatelic Bureau, Edinburgh 2·25
Kingston-upon-Thames 2·50

T **601/4** show authoresses and scenes from their novels. T **601/2** also include the "Europa" C.E.P.T. emblem.

601 Charlotte Brontë (*Jane Eyre*)

602 George Eliot (*The Mill on the Floss*)

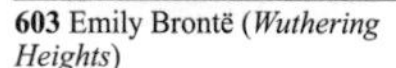

603 Emily Brontë (*Wuthering Heights*)

604 Mrs Gaskell (*North and South*)

(Des Barbara Brown)

1980 (9 July). *Famous Authoresses. Phosphorised paper.* P 15×14.

1125	**601**	12p. red-brown, brt rose, brt blue, greenish yellow, grey and gold	35	20
		Ea. Missing "p" in value (R. 4/6)	25·00	
1126	**602**	13½p. red-brown, dull vermilion, pale blue, pale greenish yellow, grey and gold	40	45
		a. Pale blue omitted	£3500	
1127	**603**	15p. red-brown, vermilion, blue, lemon, grey and gold	40	45
1128	**604**	17½p. dull vermilion, slate-blue, ultramarine, pale greenish yellow, grey and gold	50	50
		a. Imperf and slate-blue omitted (pair)	£850	
Set of 4			1·50	1·50
Set of 4 *Gutter Pairs*			3·75	
First Day Cover				1·50
Presentation Pack			2·00	
P.H.Q. Cards (*set of* 4)			2·50	3·00

Special First Day of Issue Postmarks

Philatelic Bureau, Edinburgh	2·00
Haworth, Keighley, W. Yorks	2·50

605 Queen Elizabeth the Queen Mother

(Des J. Matthews from photograph by N. Parkinson)

1980 (4 Aug). *80th Birthday of Queen Elizabeth the Queen Mother. Phosphorised paper.* P 14×15.

1129	**605**	12p. brt rose, greenish yellow, new blue, grey and silver	75	75
		a. Imperf (horiz pair)	£1750	
Gutter Pair			1·50	
First Day Cover				1·50
P.H.Q. Card			2·25	1·75

Special First Day of Issue Postmarks

Philatelic Bureau, Edinburgh	2·00
Glamis Castle, Forfar	3·00

606 Sir Henry Wood

607 Sir Thomas Beecham

608 Sir Malcolm Sargent

609 Sir John Barbirolli

(Des P. Gauld)

1980 (10 Sept). *British Conductors. Phosphorised paper.* P 14×15.

1130	**606**	12p. slate, rose-red, greenish yellow, bistre and gold	30	10
1131	**607**	13½p. grey-black, vermilion, greenish yellow, pale carmine-rose and gold	45	40
1132	**608**	15p. grey-black, brt rose-red, greenish yellow, turquoise-green and gold	50	55
1133	**609**	17½p. black, brt rose-red, greenish yellow, dull violet-blue and gold	50	55
Set of 4			1·50	1·50
Set of 4 *Gutter Pairs*			3·75	
First Day Cover				1·75
Presentation Pack			2·00	
P.H.Q. cards (*set of* 4)			2·25	3·75

Special First Day of Issues

Postmarks Philatelic Bureau, Edinburgh	2·00
London SW	2·25

610 Running

611 Rugby

612 Boxing

613 Cricket

(Des R. Goldsmith. Litho Questa)

1980 (10 Oct). *Sport Centenaries. Phosphorised paper.* P 14×14½.

No.	Type	Value	Description	Unused	Used
1134	**610**	12p.	pale new blue, greenish yellow, magenta, lt brown, reddish purple and gold	25	20
			a. Gold (Queen's head) omitted	£14000	
1135	**611**	13½p.	pale new blue, olive-yellow, brt purple, orange-vermilion, blackish lilac and gold	50	50
1136	**612**	15p.	pale new blue, greenish yellow, brt purple, chalky blue & gold	50	45
			a. Gold (Queen's head) omitted	£9500	
1137	**613**	17½p.	pale new blue, greenish yellow, magenta, dp olive, grey-brown and gold	50	50
Set of 4				1·50	1·50
Set of 4 *Gutter Pairs*				3·75	
First Day Cover					1·75
Presentation Pack				2·00	
P.H.Q. Cards (*set of* 4)				2·25	3·75

Centenaries:-12p. Amateur Athletics Association; 13½p. Welsh Rugby Union; 15p. Amateur Boxing Association; 17½p. First England-Australia Test Match. Nos. 1134a and 1136a were caused by paper folds.

Special First Day of Issue Postmarks

Philatelic Bureau, Edinburgh	2·00
Cardiff	2·25

614 Christmas Tree

615 Candles

616 Apples and Mistletoe

617 Crown, Chains and Bell

618 Holly

(Des J. Matthews)

1980 (19 Nov). *Christmas. One centre phosphor band (10p.) or phosphorised paper (others).* P 15×14.

No.	Type	Value	Description	Unused	Used
1138	**614**	10p.	black, turquoise-green, greenish yellow, vermilion and blue	20	10
			a. Imperf (horiz pair)	£1250	
1139	**615**	12p.	grey, magenta, rose-red, greenish grey and pale orange	20	20
1140	**616**	13½p.	grey-black, dull yellow-green, brown, greenish yellow and pale olive-bistre	40	40
1141	**617**	15p.	grey-black, bistre-yellow, brt orange, magenta and new blue	55	50
1142	**618**	17½p.	black, vermilion, dull yellowish green and greenish yellow	55	50
Set of 5				1·75	1·50
Set of 5 *Gutter Pairs*				4·50	
First Day Cover					1·75
Presentation Pack				2·00	
P.H.Q. Cards (*set of* 5)				2·25	4·00

Special First Day of Issue Postmarks

Philatelic Bureau, Edinburgh	2·00
Bethlehem, Llandeilo, Dyfed	2·50

Collectors Pack 1980

1980 (19 Nov). Comprises Nos. 1109/18 and 1120/42.

CP1142a Collectors Pack	15·00

619 St. Valentine's Day

620 Morris Dancers

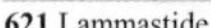
621 Lammastide

622 Medieval Mummers

T **619/20** also include the "Europa" C.E.P.T. emblem.

(Des F. Wegner)

1981 (6 Feb). *Folklore. Phosphorised paper.* P 15×14.

1143	**619**	14p. cerise, green, yellow-orange, salmon-pink, black and gold	25	25
1144	**620**	18p. dull ultramarine, lemon, lake-brown, brt green, black and gold	50	50
1145	**621**	22p. chrome-yellow, rosine, brown, new blue, black and gold	75	80
1146	**622**	25p. brt blue, red-brown, brt rose-red, greenish yellow, black and gold	1·00	1·10
		Set of 4	2·25	2·50
		Set of 4 Gutter Pairs	5·25	
		First Day Cover		2·00
		Presentation Pack	2·25	
		P.H.Q. Cards (set of 4)	2·25	3·25

Special First Day of Issue Postmarks

Philatelic Bureau, Edinburgh .... 2·25
London WC .... 2·50

623 Blind Man with Guide Dog

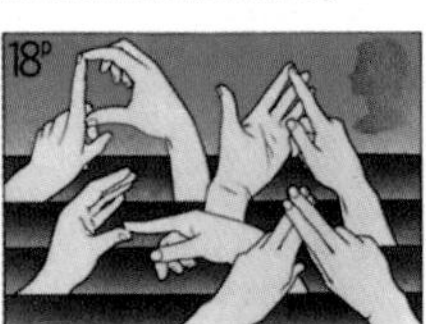

624 Hands spelling "Deaf" in Sign Language

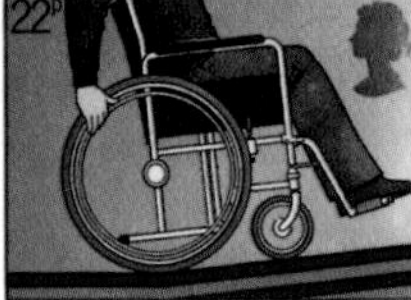

625 Disabled Man in Wheelchair

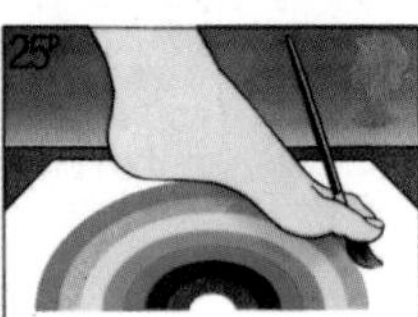

626 Disabled Artist with Foot painting

(Des J. Gibbs)

1981 (25 Mar). *International Year of the Disabled. Phosphorised paper.* P 15×14.

1147	**623**	14p. drab, greenish yellow, brt rose-red, dull purple and silver	50	25
		a. Imperf (pair)	£650	
1148	**624**	18p. dp blue-green, brt orange, dull vermilion, grey-black and silver	50	50
1149	**625**	22p. brown-ochre, rosine, purple-brown, greenish blue, black and silver	75	85
1150	**626**	25p. vermilion, lemon, pale salmon, olive-brown, new blue, black and silver	1·00	1·00
		Set of 4	2·25	2·50
		Set of 4 Gutter Pairs	4·25	
		First Day Cover		2·50
		Presentation Pack	2·25	
		P.H.Q. Cards (set of 4)	2·25	3·25

All known examples of No. 1147a are creased.

Special First Day of Issue Postmarks

Philatelic Bureau, Edinburgh .... 2·25
Windsor .... 2·50

627 *Aglais urticae*

628 *Maculinea arion*

629 *Inachis io*

630 *Carterocephalus palaemon*

(Des G. Beningfield)

1981 (13 May). *Butterflies. Phosphorised paper.* P 14×15.

1151	**627**	14p. greenish yellow, yellow-green, brt rose, brt blue, emerald and gold	25	20
		a. Imperf (pair)	£2500	
1152	**628**	18p. black, greenish yellow, dull yellowish green, brt mauve, brt blue, brt green and gold	75	70
1153	**629**	22p. black, greenish yellow, bronze-green, rosine, ultramarine, lt green and gold	70	85
1154	**630**	25p. black, greenish yellow, bronze-green, brt rose-red, ultramarine, brt emerald and gold	75	85
		Set of 4	2·25	2·50
		Set of 4 Gutter Pairs	4·75	
		First Day Cover		2·50
		Presentation Pack	2·25	
		P.H.Q. Cards (set of 4)	2·25	6·00

Special First Day of Issue Postmarks

Philatelic Bureau, Edinburgh	2·50
London SW	3·00

631 Glenfinnan, Scotland

632 Derwentwater, England

633 Stackpole Head, Wales

634 Giant's Causeway, Northern Ireland

635 St. Kilda, Scotland

(Des M. Fairclough)

1981 (24 June). *50th Anniv of National Trust for Scotland. British Landscapes. Phosphorised paper.* P 15×14.

1155	**631**	14p. lilac, dull blue, reddish brown, bistre-yellow, black and gold	15	25
1156	**632**	18p. bottle green, brt blue, brown, bistre-yellow, black and gold	45	50
1157	**633**	20p. dp turquoise-blue, dull blue, greenish yellow, reddish brown, black and gold	70	75
1158	**634**	22p. chrome-yellow, reddish brown, new blue, yellow-brown, black and gold.	75	1·00
1159	**635**	25p. ultramarine, new blue, olive-green, olive-grey and gold	90	1·00
Set of 5			2·50	3·00
Set of 5 Gutter Pairs			6·00	
First Day Cover				3·25
Presentation Pack			3·00	
P.H.Q. Cards (set of 5)			2·50	5·00

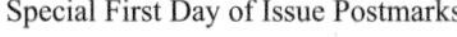

Special First Day of Issue Postmarks

Philatelic Bureau, Edinburgh	2·50
Glenfinnan	3·50
Keswick	3·50

636 Prince Charles and Lady Diana Spencer

(Des J. Matthews from photograph by Lord Snowdon)

1981 (22 July). *Royal Wedding. Phosphorised paper.* P 14×15.

1160	**636**	14p. grey-black, greenish yellow, brt rose-red, ultramarine, pale blue, blue and silver	75	25
1161		25p. drab, greenish yellow, brt rose-red, ultramarine, grey-brown, grey-black and silver	1·50	1·50
Set of 2			2·25	1·50
Set of 2 Gutter Pairs			4·00	6·00
First Day Cover				2·75
Presentation Pack			3·00	
Souvenir Book			3·00	
P.H.Q. Cards (set of 2)			2·50	5·00

The souvenir book is a 12-page illustrated booklet with a set of mint stamps in a sachet attached to the front cover.

Special First Day of Issue Postmarks

Philatelic Bureau, Edinburgh	3·00
Caernarfon, Gwynedd	4·00
London EC	3·50

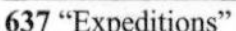

637 "Expeditions"

638 "Skills"

639 "Service"

640 "Recreation"

(Des P. Sharland. Litho J.W.)

1981 (12 Aug). *25th Anniv of Duke of Edinburgh's Award Scheme. Phosphorised paper.* P 14.

1162	**637**	14p. greenish yellow, magenta, pale new blue, black, emerald and silver	25	20
1163	**638**	18p. greenish yellow, magenta, pale new blue, black, cobalt and gold	45	50
1164	**639**	22p. greenish yellow, magenta, pale new blue, black, red-orange and gold	70	70
1165	**640**	25p. brt orange, mauve, pale new blue, black, flesh and bronze	80	80
		Set of 4	2·00	2·00
		Set of 4 Gutter Pairs	5·00	
		First Day Cover		2·00
		Presentation Pack	2·50	
		P.H.Q. Cards (set of 4)	4·25	4·50

Special First Day of Issue Postmarks

Philatelic Bureau, Edinburgh ....2·50
London W2 ....2·75

641 Cockle-dredging from *Linsey II*

642 Hauling in Trawl Net

643 Lobster Potting

644 Hoisting Seine Net

(Des B. Sanders)

1981 (23 Sept). *Fishing Industry. Phosphorised paper.* P 15×14.

1166	**641**	14p. slate, greenish yellow, magenta, new blue, orange-brown, olive-grey and bronze-green	25	25
1167	**642**	18p. slate, greenish yellow, brt crimson, ultramarine, black and greenish slate	50	50
1168	**643**	22p. grey, greenish yellow, brt rose, dull ultramarine, reddish lilac and black	85	85
1169	**644**	25p. grey, greenish yellow, brt rose, cobalt and black	85	85
		Set of 4	2·25	2·50
		Set of 4 Gutter Pairs	5·00	
		First Day Cover		2·50
		Presentation Pack	2·50	
		P.H.Q. Cards (set of 4)	2·25	4·50

Nos. 1166/9 were issued on the occasion of the centenary of the Royal National Mission to Deep Sea Fishermen.

Special First Day of Issue Postmarks

Philatelic Bureau, Edinburgh ....2·50
Hull ....2·75

645 Father Christmas

646 Jesus Christ

647 Flying Angel

648 Joseph and Mary arriving at Bethlehem

649 Three Kings approaching Bethlehem

(Des Samantha Brown (11½p.), Tracy Jenkins (14p.), Lucinda Blackmore (18p.), Stephen Moore (22p.), Sophie Sharp (25p.))

1981 (18 Nov). *Christmas. Children's Pictures. One phosphor band (11½p.) or phosphorised paper (others).* P 15×14.

1170	**645**	11½p. ultramarine, black, red, olive-bistre, brt green and gold	25	20
1171	**646**	14p. bistre-yellow, brt magenta, blue, greenish blue, brt green, black and gold	35	20

1172	**647**	18p. pale blue-green, bistre-yellow, brt magenta, ultramarine, black and gold	50	60
1173	**648**	22p. dp turquoise-blue, lemon, magenta, black and gold	75	75
1174	**649**	25p. royal blue, lemon, brt magenta, black and gold	85	85
		Set of 5	2·50	2·50
		Set of 5 Gutter Pairs	5·50	
		First Day Cover		2·75
		Presentation Pack	3·00	
		P.H.Q. Cards (set of 5)	2·25	5·50

Special First Day of Issue Postmarks

Philatelic Bureau, Edinburgh ....2·25
Bethlehem, Llandeilo, Dyfed ....2·50

Collectors Pack 1981

1981(18 Nov). Comprises Nos. 1143/74.
CP1174a Collectors Pack ....17·50

650 Charles Darwin and Giant Tortoises

651 Darwin and Marine Iguanas

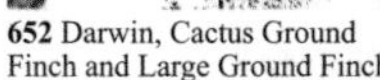

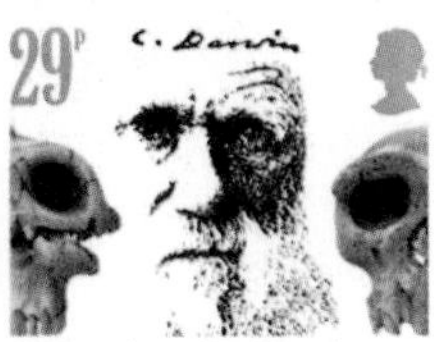

652 Darwin, Cactus Ground Finch and Large Ground Finch

653 Darwin and Prehistoric Skulls

(Des D. Gentleman)

1982 (10 Feb). *Death Centenary of Charles Darwin. Phosphorised paper.* P 15×14.

1175	**650**	15½p. dull purple, drab, bistre, black and grey-black	50	20
1176	**651**	19½p. violet-grey, bistre-yellow, slate-black, red-brown, grey-black and black	50	60
1177	**652**	26p. sage green, bistre-yellow, orange, chalky blue, grey-black, red-brown and black	75	85
1178	**653**	29p. grey-brown, yellow-brown, brown-ochre, black and grey-black	95	90
		Set of 4	2·50	2·50
		Set of 4 Gutter Pairs	5·25	
		First Day Cover		2·75
		Presentation Pack	3·00	
		P.H.Q. Cards (set of 4)	2·50	6·00

Special First Day of Issue Postmarks

Philatelic Bureau, Edinburgh ....2·50
Shrewsbury ....3·00

654 Boys' Brigade

655 Girls' Brigade

656 Boy Scout Movement

657 Girl Guide Movement

(Des B. Sanders)

1982 (24 Mar). *Youth Organizations. Phosphorised paper.* P 15×14.

1179	**654**	15½p. gold, greenish yellow, pale orange, mauve, dull blue and grey-black	25	15
1180	**655**	19½p. gold, greenish yellow, pale orange, brt rose, dp ultramarine, olive-bistre and grey-black	50	50
1181	**656**	26p. gold, greenish yellow, olive-sepia, rosine, dp blue, dp dull green and grey-black	85	85
1182	**657**	29p. gold, yellow, dull orange, cerise, dull ultramarine, chestnut and grey-black	1·00	1·10
		Set of 4	2·50	2·50
		Set of 4 Gutter Pairs	5·50	
		First Day Cover		2·75
		Presentation Pack	3·00	
		P.H.Q. Cards (set of 4)	2·50	6·00

Nos. 1179/82 were issued on the occasion of the 75th anniversary of the Boy Scout Movement; the 125th birth anniversary of Lord Baden-Powell and the centenary of the Boys' Brigade (1983).

Special First Day of Issue Postmarks

Edinburgh Philatelic Bureau	2·50
Glasgow	3·00
London SW	3·00

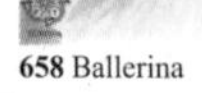

658 Ballerina

659 Harlequin

660 Hamlet

661 Opera Singer

(Des A. George)

1982 (28 Apr). *Europa. British Theatre. Phosphorised paper.* P 15×14.

1183	**658**	15½p.	carmine-lake, greenish blue, greenish yellow, grey-black, bottle green and silver	25	15
1184	**659**	19½p.	rosine, new blue, greenish yellow, black, ultramarine and silver	50	50
1185	**660**	26p.	carmine-red, brt rose-red, greenish yellow, black, dull ultramarine, lake-brown and silver	1·25	1·00
1186	**661**	29p.	rose-red, greenish yellow, brt blue, grey-black and silver	1·50	1·00
Set of 4				3·25	2·50
Set of 4 *Gutter Pairs*				8·00	
First Day Cover					2·75
Presentation Pack				3·00	
P.H.Q. Cards (*set of* 4)				2·50	6·00

Special First Day of Issue Postmarks

Philatelic Bureau, Edinburgh	2·50
Stratford-upon-Avon	3·00

662 Henry VIII and *Mary Rose*

663 Admiral Blake and *Triumph*

664 Lord Nelson and H.M.S. *Victory*

665 Lord Fisher and H.M.S. *Dreadnought*

666 Viscount Cunningham and H.M.S. *Warspite*

(Des Marjorie Saynor. Eng C. Slania. Recess and photo)

1982 (16 June). *Maritime Heritage. Phosphorised paper.* P 15×14.

1187	**662**	15½p.	black, lemon, brt rose, pale orange, ultramarine and grey	35	25
		a.	Imperf (pair)	£1400	
1188	**663**	19½p.	black, greenish yellow, brt rose-red, pale orange, ultramarine and grey	50	50
1189	**664**	24p.	black, orange-yellow, brt rose-red, lake-brown, dp ultramarine and grey	75	85
1190	**665**	26p.	black, orange-yellow, brt rose, lemon, ultramarine and grey	75	85
		a.	Imperf (pair)	£2500	
1191	**666**	29p.	black, olive-yellow, brt rose, orange-yellow, ultramarine and grey	1·00	1·00
Set of 5				3·00	3·50
Set of 5 *Gutter Pairs*				7·00	
First Day Cover					3·75
Presentation Pack				3·50	
P.H.Q. Cards (*set of* 5)				2·50	6·00

Nos. 1187/91 were issued on the occasion of Maritime England Year, the Bicentenary of the Livery Grant by the City of London to the Worshipful Company of Shipwrights and the raising of the Mary Rose from Portsmouth Harbour.

Several used examples of the 15½p. have been seen with the black recess (ship and waves) omitted.

Special First Day of Issue Postmarks

Philatelic Bureau, Edinburgh	3·00
Portsmouth	3·50

667 "Strawberry Thief" (William Morris)

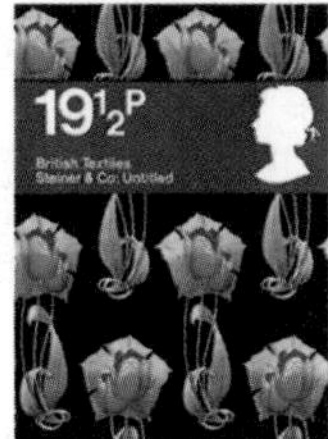

668 Untitled (Steiner and Co)

669 "Cherry Orchard" (Paul Nash)

670 "Chevron" (Andrew Foster)

(Des Peter Hatch Partnership)

1982 (23 July). *British Textiles. Phosphorised paper.* P 14×15.

1192	**667**	15½p.	blue, olive-yellow, rosine, dp blue-green, bistre and Prussian blue	25	25
		a.	Imperf (horiz pair)	£1200	
1193	**668**	19½p.	olive-grey, greenish yellow, brt magenta, dull green, yellow-brown and black	75	75
		a.	Imperf (vert pair)	£1600	
1194	**669**	26p.	brt scarlet, dull mauve, dull ultramarine and brt carmine	75	1·00
1195	**670**	29p.	bronze-green, orange-yellow, turquoise-green, stone, chestnut and sage-green	1·00	1·25
Set of 4				2·50	2·75
Set of 4 *Gutter Pairs*				5·50	
First Day Cover					3·00
Presentation Pack				2·75	
P.H.Q. Cards (*set of* 4)				2·50	6·00

Nos. 1192/5 were issued on the occasion of the 250th birth anniversary of Sir Richard Arkwright (inventor of spinning machine).

Special First Day of Issue Postmarks

Philatelic Bureau, Edinburgh .... 2·75
Rochdale .... 3·00

671 Development of Communications

672 Modern Technological Aids

(Des Delaney and Ireland)

1982 (8 Sept). *Information Technology. Phosphorised paper.* P 14×15.

1196	**671**	15½p.	black, greenish yellow, brt rose-red, bistre-brown, new blue and lt ochre	75	25
		a.	Imperf (pair)	£350	
1197	**672**	26p.	black, greenish yellow, brt rose-red, olive-bistre, new blue and lt olive-grey	50	1·00
		a	Imperf (pair)	£1500	
Set of 2				1·25	1·25
Set of 2 *Gutter Pairs*				2·75	
First Day Cover					1·75
Presentation Pack				1·50	
P.H.Q. cards (*set of* 2)				2·00	5·25

Special First Day of Issue Postmarks

Philatelic Bureau, Edinburgh .... 2·00
London WC .... 2·50

673 Austin "Seven" and "Metro"

674 Ford "Model T" and "Escort"

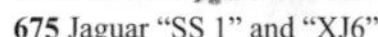

675 Jaguar "SS 1" and "XJ6"

676 Rolls-Royce "Silver Ghost" and "Silver Spirit"

(Des S. Paine. Litho Questa)

1982 (13 Oct). *British Motor Cars. Phosphorised paper.* P 14½×14.

1198	**673**	15½p.	slate, orange-vermilion, brt orange, drab, yellow-green, olive-yellow, bluish grey and black	50	25
1199	**674**	19½p.	slate, brt orange, olive-grey, rose-red, dull vermilion, grey and black	75	75
		Ea.	Rose-red, grey and black ptgs double	£750	
1200	**675**	26p.	slate, red-brown, brt orange, turquoise-green, myrtle-green, dull blue-green, grey and olive	75	75
1201	**676**	29p.	slate, brt orange, carmine-red, reddish purple, grey and black	1·00	1·00
		Ea	Black ptg quadruple	£450	

Eb Brt orange, carmine-red, grey and black ptgs double £850

Set of 4	2·50	2·50
Set of 4 *Gutter Pairs*	6·25	
First Day Cover		2·50
Presentation Pack	3·00	
P.H.Q. cards (*set of* 4)	2·50	6·00

Special First Day of Issue Postmarks

Philatelic Bureau, Edinburgh .... 3·00
Birmingham .... 3·75
Crewe .... 3·75

677 "While Shepherds Watched"

678 "The Holly and the Ivy"

679 "I Saw Three Ships"

680 "We Three Kings"

681 "Good King Wenceslas"

(Des Barbara Brown)

1982 (17 Nov). *Christmas. Carols. One phosphor band (12½p.) or phosphorised paper (others).* P 15×14.

1202	**677**	12½p. black, greenish yellow, brt scarlet, steel blue, red-brown and gold		25	20
1203	**678**	15½p. black, bistre-yellow, brt rose-red, brt blue, brt green and gold		50	20
		a. Imperf (pair)		£1600	
1204	**679**	19½p. black, bistre-yellow, brt rose-red, dull blue, dp brown and gold		65	75
		a Imperf (pair)		£1600	
1205	**680**	26p. black, bistre-yellow, brt magenta, brt blue, chocolate, gold and orange-red		75	80
1206	**681**	29p. black, bistre-yellow, magenta, brt blue, chestnut, gold and brt magenta		1·00	90
Set of 5				3·00	2·50
Set of 5 *Gutter Pairs*				5·25	
First Day Cover					2·50
Presentation Pack				3·25	
P.H.Q. cards (*set of* 5)				2·50	6·00

Special Day of Issue Postmarks

Philatelic Bureau, Edinburgh .... 2·75
Bethlehem, Llandeilo, Dyfed .... 3·00

Collectors Pack 1982

1982 (Nov 17). Comprises Nos. 1175/1206.
CP1206a Collectors Pack .... 26·00

682 Atlantic Salmon

683 Northern Pike

684 Brown Trout

685 Eurasian Perch

(Des A. Jardine)

1983 (26 Jan). *British River Fishes. Phosphorised paper.* P 15×14.

1207	**682**	15½p. grey-black, bistre-yellow, brt purple, new blue and silver	30	10
		a Imperf (pair)	£2000	
1208	**683**	19½p. black, bistre-yellow, olive-bistre, dp claret, silver and dp bluish green	60	60
1209	**684**	26p. grey-black, bistre-yellow, chrome-yellow, magenta, silver and pale blue	75	85
		a. Imperf (pair)	£1200	
1210	**685**	29p. black, greenish yellow, brt carmine, new blue and silver	1·00	1·10
Set of 4			2·50	2·50
Set of 4 *Gutter Pairs*			5·00	
First Day Cover				2·50
Presentation Pack			2·75	
P.H.Q. Cards (*set of* 4)			3·00	7·00

All known examples of No. 1209a are creased.

Special First Day of Issue Postmarks

Philatelic Bureau, Edinburgh ....2·75
Peterborough ....3·00

686 Tropical Island

687 Desert

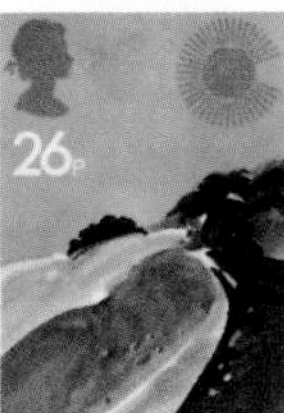

688 Temperate Farmland

689 Mountain Range

(Des D. Fraser)

1983 (9 Mar). *Commonwealth Day. Geographical Regions. Phosphorised paper.* P 14×15.

1211	**686**	15½p.	greenish blue, greenish yellow, brt rose, lt brown, grey-black, dp claret and silver	40	25
1212	**687**	19½p.	brt lilac, greenish yellow, magenta, dull blue, grey-black, dp dull blue and silver	75	75
1213	**688**	26p.	lt blue, greenish yellow, brt magenta, new blue, grey-black, violet and silver	75	75
1214	**689**	29p.	dull violet-blue, reddish violet, slate-lilac, new blue, myrtlegreen, black and silver	1·00	1·00
Set of 4				2·50	2·50
Set of 4 *Gutter Pairs*				6·00	
First Day Cover					2·50
Presentation Pack				3·00	
P.H.Q. Cards (*set of* 4)				2·50	6·50

Special First Day of Issue Postmarks

Philatelic Bureau, Edinburgh ....2·75
London SW ....3·00

690 Humber Bridge

691 Thames Flood Barrier

692 *Iolair* (oilfield emergency support vessel)

(Des M. Taylor)

1983 (25 Mar). *Europa. Engineering Achievements. Phosphorised paper.* P 15×14.

1215	**690**	16p.	silver, orange-yellow, ultramarine, black and grey	50	25
1216	**691**	20½p.	silver, greenish yellow, brt purple, blue, grey-black and grey	1·00	1·00
1217	**692**	28p.	silver, lemon, brt rose-red, chestnut, dull ultramarine, black and grey	1·00	1·00
Set of 3				2·25	2·00
Set of 3 *Gutter Pairs*				7·00	
First Day Cover					2·25
Presentation Pack				2·50	
P.H.Q. Cards (*set of* 3)				2·50	5·75

Special First Day of Issue Postmarks

Philatelic Bureau, Edinburgh ....2·50
Hull ....2·75

693 Musketeer and Pikeman

694 Fusilier and Ensign, The Royal Scots (1633) The Royal Welch Fusiliers (mid-18th century)

695 Riflemen, 95th Rifles (The Royal Green Jackets) (1805)

696 Sergeant (khaki service) and Guardsman (full dress), The Irish Guards (1900)

697 Paratroopers, The Parachute Regiment (1983)

(Des E. Stemp)

1983 (6 July). *British Army Uniforms. Phosphorised paper.* P 14×15.

1218	**693**	16p. black, buff, dp brown, slate-black, rose-red, gold and new blue	50	10
1219	**694**	20½p. black, buff, greenish yellow, slate-black, brown-rose, gold and brt blue	50	60
1220	**695**	26p. black, buff, slate-purple, green, bistre and gold	75	90
		a. Imperf (pair)	£2200	
1221	**696**	28p. black, buff, lt brown, grey, dull rose, gold and new blue	75	90
		a. Imperf (pair)	£1800	
1222	**697**	31p. black, buff, olive-yellow, grey, dp magenta, gold and new blue	75	85
Set of 5			3·00	3·25
Set of 5 Gutter Pairs			7·50	
First Day Cover				3·25
Presentation Pack			3·50	
P.H.Q. Cards (set of 5)			3·50	6·50

Nos. 1218/22 were issued on the occasion of the 350th anniversary of the Royal Scots, the senior line regiment of the British Army.

Special First Day of Issue Postmarks

Philatelic Bureau, Edinburgh .... 3·50
Aldershot .... 3·75

698 20th-century Garden Sissinghurst

699 19th-century Garden, Biddulph Grange

700 18th-century Garden Blenheim

701 17th-century Garden, Pitmedden

(Des Liz Butler. Litho J.W.)

1983 (24 Aug). *British Gardens. Phosphorised paper.* P 14.

1223	**698**	16p. greenish yellow, brt purple, new blue, black, brt green and silver	50	10
1224	**699**	20½p. greenish yellow, brt purple, new blue, black, brt green and silver	50	55
1225	**700**	28p. greenish yellow, brt purple, new blue, black, brt green and silver	75	90
1226	**701**	31p. greenish yellow, brt purple, new blue, black, brt green and silver	1·00	90
Set of 4			2·50	2·25
Set of 4 Gutter Pairs			6·00	
First Day Cover				2·25
Presentation Pack			3·00	
P.H.Q. Cards (set of 4)			3·00	6·25

Nos. 1223/6 were issued on the occasion of the death bicentenary of "Capability" Brown (landscape gardener).

Special First Day of Issue Postmarks

Philatelic Bureau, Edinburgh .... 3·00
Oxford .... 3·50

702 Merry-go-round

703 Big Wheel, Helter-skelter and Performing Animals

704 Side Shows

705 Early Produce Fair

(Des A. Restall)

1983 (5 Oct). *British Fairs. Phosphorised paper.* P 15×14.

No.	Type		Description	Unused	Used
1227	**702**	16p.	grey-black, greenish yellow, orange-red, ochre and turquoise-blue	35	25
1228	**703**	20½p.	grey-black, yellow-ochre, yellow-orange, brt magenta, violet and black	75	75
1229	**704**	28p.	grey-black, bistre-yellow, orange-red, violet and yellow-brown	75	1·00
1230	**705**	31p.	grey-black, greenish yellow, red, dp turquoise-green, slate-violet and brown	1·00	1·00
			Set of 4	2·50	2·75
			Set of 4 *Gutter Pairs*	6·00	
			First Day Cover		3·00
			Presentation Pack	3·00	
			P.H.Q. Cards (*set of* 4)	3·00	6·25

Special First Day of Issue Postmarks

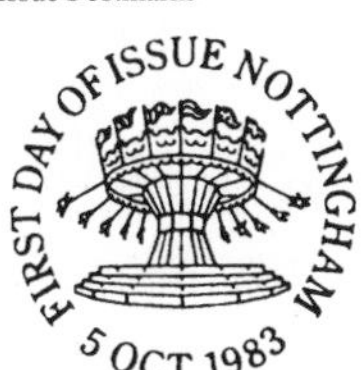

Philatelic Bureau, Edinburgh .... 2·75
Nottingham .... 3·00

706 "Christmas Post" (pillar-box)

707 "The Three Kings" (chimney-pots)

708 "World at Peace" (Dove and Blackbird)

709 "Light of Christmas"(street lamp)

710 "Christmas Dove" (hedge sculpture)

(Des T. Meeuwissen)

1983 (16 Nov). *Christmas. One phosphor band (12½p.) or phosphorised paper (others).* P 15×14.

No.	Type		Description	Unused	Used
1231	**706**	12½p.	black, greenish yellow, brt rose-red, brt blue, gold & grey-black	25	25
			a. Imperf (horiz pair)	£1400	
1232	**707**	16p.	black, greenish yellow, brt rose, pale new blue, gold and brown-purple	50	25
			a. Imperf (pair)	£1100	
1233	**708**	20½p.	black, greenish yellow, brt rose, new blue, gold and blue	75	1·00
1234	**709**	28p.	black, lemon, brt carmine, bluish violet, gold, dp turquoise-green and purple	75	1·00
1235	**710**	31p.	black, greenish yellow, brt rose, new blue, gold, green and brown-olive	1·25	1·25
			Set of 5	3·25	3·25
			Set of 5 *Gutter Pairs*	6·50	
			First Day Cover		3·50
			Presentation Pack	3·50	
			P.H.Q. Cards (*set of* 5)	3·00	6·25

Special First Day of Issue Postmarks

Philatelic Bureau, Edinburgh .... 3·00
Bethlehem, Llandeilo, Dyfed .... 3·25

Collectors Pack 1983

1983 (Nov 16). Comprises Nos. 1207/35.
CP1235a Collectors Pack .... 32·00

711 Arms of the College of Arms

712 Arms of King Richard III (founder)

713 Arms of the Earl Marshal of England

714 Arms of the City of London

(Des J. Matthews)

1984 (17 Jan). *500th Anniv of College of Arms. Phosphorised paper.* P 14½.

No.	Type		Description	Unused	Used
1236	**711**	16p.	black, chrome-yellow, reddish brown, scarlet-vermillion, brt blue and grey-black	50	15
1237	**712**	20½p.	black, chrome-yellow, rosine, brt blue and grey-black	50	65
1238	**713**	28p.	black, chrome-yellow, rosine, brt blue, dull green and grey-black	1·00	1·10

1239	**714**	31p. black, chrome-yellow, rosine, brt blue and grey-black	1·25	1·25
		a. Imperf (horiz pair)	£2500	
Set of 4			3·00	3·00
Set of 4 Gutter Pairs			6·25	
First Day Cover				3·00
Presentation Pack			3·25	
P.H.Q. Cards			3·00	6·50

Special First Day of Issue Postmarks

Philatelic Bureau, Edinburgh ....3·00
London EC ....3·50

715 Highland Cow

716 Chillingham Wild Bull

717 Hereford Bull

718 Welsh Black Bull

719 Irish Moiled Cow

(Des B. Driscoll)

1984 (6 Mar). *British Cattle. Phosphorised paper.* P 15×14.

1240	**715**	16p. grey-black, bistre-yellow, rosine, yellow-orange, new blue and pale drab	35	15
		a. Imperf (vert pair)	£3800	
1241	**716**	20½p. grey-black, greenish yellow, magenta, bistre, dull blue-green, pale drab and lt green	55	60
1242	**717**	26p. black, chrome-yellow, rosine, reddish brown, new blue and pale drab	75	75
1243	**718**	28p. black, greenish yellow, brt carmine, orange-brown, dp dull blue and pale drab	75	85
1244	**719**	31p. grey-black, bistre-yellow, rosine, red-brown, lt blue and pale drab	1·00	90
Set of 5			3·00	3·00
Set of 5 Gutter Pairs			7·25	
First Day Cover				3·00
Presentation Pack			4·00	
P.H.Q. Cards (set of 5)			3·00	6·50

Nos. 1240/4 were issued on the occasion of the centenary of the Highland Cattle Society and the bicentenary of the Royal Highland and Agricultural Society of Scotland.

Special First Day of Issue Postmarks

Philatelic Bureau, Edinburgh ....3·50
Oban, Argyll ....4·50

720 Garden Festival Hall, Liverpool

721 Milburngate Centre, Durham

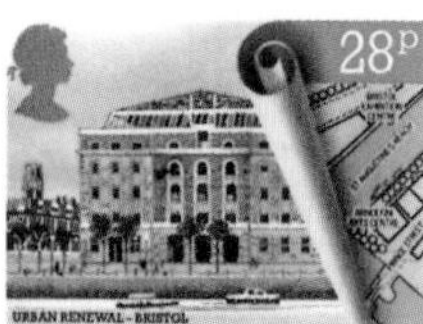

722 Bush House, Bristol

723 Commercial Street Development, Perth

(Des R. Maddox and Trickett and Webb Ltd)

1984 (10 Apr). *Urban Renewal. Phosphorised paper.* P 15×14.

1245	**720**	16p. brt emerald, greenish yellow, cerise, steel-blue, black, silver and flesh	30	10
1246	**721**	20½p. brt orange, greenish yellow, dp dull blue, yellowish green, azure, black and silver	50	60
		a. Imperf (horiz pair)	£2250	
1247	**722**	28p. rosine, greenish yellow, Prussian blue, pale blue-green, black and silver	1·00	1·00
1248	**723**	31p. blue, greenish yellow, cerise, grey-blue, bright green, black and silver	1·00	1·00
		a. Imperf (pair)	£2250	
Set of 4			2·50	2·50
Set of 4 Gutter Pairs			6·50	
First Day Cover				2·50
Presentation Pack			3·00	
P.H.Q. Cards (set of 4)			3·00	6·25

Nos. 1245/8 were issued on the occasion of 150th anniversaries of the Royal Institute of British Architects and the Chartered Institute of Building, and to commemorate the first International Gardens Festival, Liverpool.

Special First Day of Issue Postmarks

Philatelic Bureau, Edinburgh ....3·00
Liverpool ....3·50

724 C.E.P.T. 25th Anniversary Logo

725 Abduction of Europa

(Des J. Larrivière (T **724**), F. Wegner (T **725**))

1984 (15 May). *25th Anniv of C.E.P.T. ("Europa") (T* **724***) and Second Elections to European Parliament (T* **725***). Phosphorised paper.* P 15×14.

1249	**724**	16p. greenish slate, dp blue and gold	50	25
		a. Horiz pair. Nos. 1249/50	1·50	1·25
		ab Imperf (horiz pair)	£2200	
1250	**725**	16p. greenish slate, dp blue, black and gold	50	25
1251	**724**	20½p. Venetian red, dp magenta and gold	1·25	1·25
		a. Horiz pair. Nos. 1251/2	2·50	2·50
		ab. Imperf (horiz pair)	£2200	
1252	**725**	20½p. Venetian red, dp magenta, black and gold	1·25	1·25
Set of 4			3·00	2·75
Set of 2 Gutter Blocks of 4			8·00	
First Day Cover				3·50
Presentation Pack			4·00	
P.H.Q. Cards (set of 4)			3·00	6·25

Nos. 1249/50 and 1251/2 were each printed together, *se-tenant*, in horizontal pairs throughout the sheets.

Special First Day of Issue Postmarks

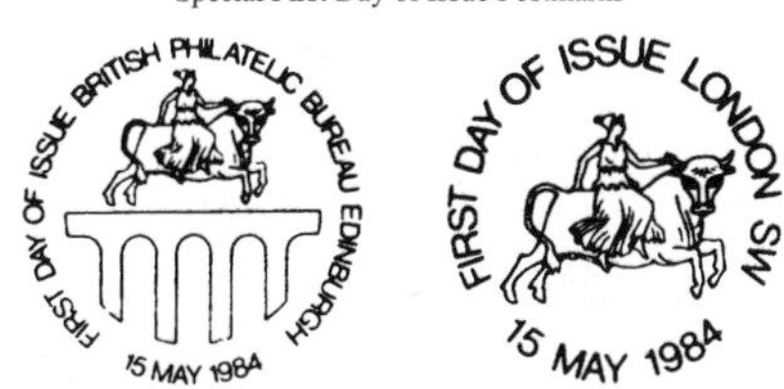

Philatelic Bureau, Edinburgh .... 4·00
London SW .... 4·50

726 Lancaster House

(Des P. Hogarth)

1984 (5 June). *London Economic Summit Conference. Phosphorised paper.* P 14×15.

1253	**726**	31p. silver, bistre-yellow, brown-ochre, black, rosine, brt blue and reddish lilac	1·25	1·25
Gutter Pair			2·50	
First Day Cover				2·25
P.H.Q. Card			1·00	3·50

Special First Day of Issue Postmarks

Philatelic Bureau, Edinburgh .... 2·50
London SW .... 2·50

727 View of Earth from "Apollo 11"

728 Navigational Chart of English Channel

729 Greenwich Observatory

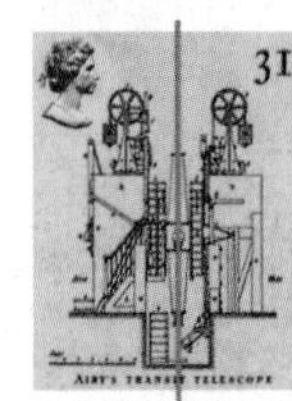

730 Sir George Airy's Transit Telescope

(Des H. Waller. Litho Questa)

1984 (26 June). *Centenary of the Greenwich Meridian. Phosphorised paper.* P 14×14½.

1254	**727**	16p. new blue, greenish yellow, magenta, black, scarlet and blue-black	50	25
		Ea. Black ptg double	†	£1900
1255	**728**	20½p. olive-sepia, lt brown, pale buff, black and scarlet	75	75
1256	**729**	28p. new blue, greenish yellow, scarlet, black and brt purple	1·00	75
1257	**730**	31p. dp blue, cobalt, scarlet & black	1·00	1·00
Set of 4			3·00	2·50
Set of 4 *Gutter Pairs*			6·50	
First Day Cover				2·50
Presentation Pack			3·50	
P.H.Q. Cards (set of 4)			3·00	6·25

On Nos. 1254/7 the Meridian is represented by a scarlet line.

Special First Day of Issue Postmarks

Philatelic Bureau, Edinburgh .... 3·00
London SE10 .... 3·25

731 Bath Mail Coach, 1784

732 Attack on Exeter Mail, 1816

733 Norwich Mail in Thunderstorm, 1827

734 Holyhead and Liverpool Mails leaving London, 1828

735 Edinburgh Mail Snowbound, 1831

(Des K. Bassford and S. Paine. Eng C. Slania. Recess and photo)

1984 (31 July). *Bicentenary of First Mail Coach Run, Bath and Bristol to London. Phosphorised paper.* P 15×14.

1258	**731**	16p. pale stone, black, grey-black and brt scarlet	40	35
		a. Horiz strip of 5. Nos. 1258/62	2·50	2·75
		ab. Imperf (horiz pair. Nos. 1261/1)	£2700	
1259	**732**	16p. pale stone, black, grey-black and brt scarlet	40	35
1260	**733**	16p. pale stone, black, grey-black and brt scarlet	40	35
1261	**734**	16p. pale stone, black, grey-black and brt scarlet	40	35
1262	**735**	16p. pale stone, black, grey-black and brt scarlet	40	35
Set of 5			2·50	1·60
Gutter Block of 10			6·50	
First Day Cover				3·00
Presentation Pack			3·00	
Souvenir Book			7·50	
P.H.Q. Cards (set of 5)			3·00	6·50

Nos. 1258/62 were printed together, se-tenant, in horizontal strips of 5 throughout the sheet.

No. 1258ab shows No. 1260 perforated at left only.

The souvenir book is a 24-page illustrated booklet with a set of mint stamps in a sachet attached to the front cover.

Special First Day of Issue Postmarks

Philatelic Bureau, Edinburgh ......3·50
Bristol ......4·00

736 Nigerian Clinic

737 Violinist and Acropolis, Athens

738 Building Project Sri Lanka

739 British Council Library, Middle East

(Des F. Newell and J. Sorrell)

1984 (25 Sept). *50th Anniv of the British Council. Phosphorised paper.* P 15×14.

1263	**736**	17p. grey-green, greenish yellow, brt purple, dull blue, black, pale green and yellow-green	50	25
1264	**737**	22p. crimson, greenish yellow, brt rose-red, dull green, black, pale drab and slate-purple	85	1·00
1265	**738**	31p. sepia, olive-bistre, red, black, pale stone and olive-brown	85	1·00
1266	**739**	34p. steel blue, yellow, rose-red, new blue, black, azure and pale blue	1·00	1·00
Set of 4			3·00	3·00
Set of 4 Gutter Pairs			6·50	
First Day Cover				3·00
Presentation Pack			3·25	
P.H.Q. Cards (set of 4)			3·00	6·25

Special First Day of Issue Postmarks

London SW . ...3·50
Philatelic Bureau, Edinburgh ......3·50

740 The Holy Family

741 Arrival in Bethlehem

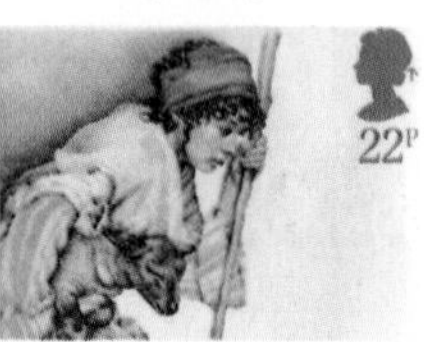

742 Shepherd and Lamb

743 Virgin and Child

744 Offering of Frankincense

(Des Yvonne Gilbert)

1984 (20 Nov). *Christmas. One phosphor band (13p.) or phosphorised paper (others).* P 15×14.

1267	**740**	13p. pale cream, grey-black, bistre-yellow, magenta, red-brown and lake-brown	25	25
		Eu. Underprint Type 4	50	
1268	**741**	17p. pale cream, grey-black, yellow, magenta, dull blue and dp dull blue	50	50
		a. Imperf (pair)	£2200	
1269	**742**	22p. pale cream, grey-black, olive-yellow, brt magenta, brt blue and brownish grey	75	75
1270	**743**	31p. pale cream, grey-black, bistre-yellow, magenta, dull blue and lt brown	1·00	1·00
1271	**744**	34p. pale cream, olive-grey, bistre-yellow, magenta, turquoise-green and brown-olive	1·00	1·00
Set of 5			3·25	3·25
Set of 4 Gutter Pairs			7·00	
First Day Cover				3·25
Presentation Pack			3·75	
P.H.Q. Cards (set of 5)			3·00	6·25

Examples of No. 1267Eu from the 1984 Christmas booklet (No. FX7) show a random pattern of blue double-lined stars printed on the reverse over the gum.

Special First Day of Issue Postmarks

Philatelic Bureau, Edinburgh .... 3·50
Bethlehem, Llandeilo, Dyfed .... 3·50

Collectors Pack 1984

1984 (Nov 20). Comprises Nos. 1236/71.
CP1271a Collectors Pack .... 37·00

Post Office Yearbook

1984. Comprises Nos. 1236/71 in 24-page hardbound book with slip case, illustrated in colour .... 90·00

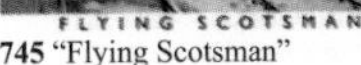
745 "Flying Scotsman"

746 "Golden Arrow"

747 "Cheltenham Flyer"

748 "Royal Scot"

749 "Cornish Riviera"

(Des T. Cuneo)

1985 (22 Jan). *Famous Trains. Phosphorised paper.* P 15×14.

1272	**745**	17p. black, lemon, magenta, dull blue, grey-black and gold	75	25
		a. Imperf (pair)	£2000	
1273	**746**	22p. black, greenish yellow, brt rose, dp dull blue, grey-black and gold	75	1·00
1274	**742**	29p. black, greenish yellow, magenta, blue, grey-black and gold	1·00	1·25
1275	**748**	31p. black, bistre-yellow, brt magenta, new blue, slate-black and gold	1·25	1·50
1276	**749**	34p. black, greenish yellow, brt rose, blue, slate-black and gold	2·50	2·50
Set of 5			6·00	6·00
Set of 5 Gutter Pairs			11·00	
First Day Cover				6·00
Presentation Pack			6·00	
P.H.Q. Cards (set of 5)			6·00	15·00

Nos. 1272/6 were issued on the occasion of the 150th anniversary of the Great Western Railway Company.

Special First Day of Issue Postmarks

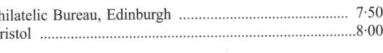

Philatelic Bureau, Edinburgh .... 7·50
Bristol .... 8·00

750 *Bombus terrestris* (bee)

751 *Coccinella septempunctata* (ladybird)

752 *Decticus verrucivorus* (bush-cricket)

753 *Lucanus cervus* (stag beetle)

754 *Anax imperator* (dragonfly)

(Des G. Beningfield)

1985 (12 Mar). *Insects. Phosphorised paper.* P 14×15.

1277	**750**	17p. black, greenish yellow, magenta, blue, azure, gold and slate-black	40	10
1278	**751**	22p. black, greenish yellow, brt rose-red, dull blue-green, slate-black and gold	60	55
1279	**752**	29p. black, greenish yellow, brt rose, greenish blue, grey-black, gold and bistre-yellow	85	90
1280	**753**	31p. black, greenish yellow, rose, pale new blue and gold	1·00	1·00
1281	**754**	34p. black, greenish yellow, magenta, greenish blue, grey-black & gold	1·00	90
Set of 5			3·25	3·25
Set of 5 Gutter Pairs			8·75	
First Day Cover				3·50
Presentation Pack			4·50	
P.H.Q. Cards (set of 5)			3·00	7·50

Nos. 1277/81 were issued on the occasion of the centenaries of the Royal Entomological Society of London's Royal Charter, and of the Selborne Society.

Special First Day of Issue Postmarks

Philatelic Bureau, Edinburgh	4·00
London SW	4·50

755 "Water Music" (George Frederick Handel)

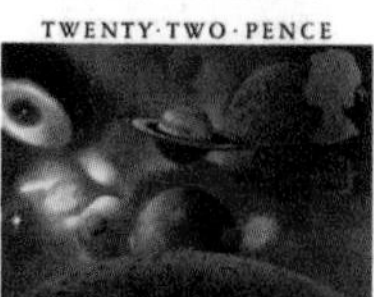

756 "The Planets Suite" (Gustav Holst)

THIRTY·ONE·PENCE
THE·FIRST·CUCKOO
Frederick Delius

757 "The First Cuckoo" (Frederick Delius)

758 "Sea Pictures" (Edward Elgar)

(Des W. McLean)

1985 (14 May). *Europa. European Music Year. British Composers. Phosphorised paper.* P 14×14½.

1282	**755**	17p. black, brt yellow-green, dp magenta, new blue, grey & gold	55	10
		a. Imperf (vert pair)	£1700	
1283	**756**	22p. black, greenish yellow, brt magenta, new blue, grey-black and gold	75	90
		a. Imperf (pair)	£1700	
1284	**757**	31p. black, greenish yellow, magenta, greenish blue, grey-black & gold	1·50	1·25
1285	**758**	34p. black, olive-yellow, bistre, turquoise-blue, slate and gold	1·50	1·25
Set of 4			4·00	3·25
Set of 4 Gutter Pairs			10·00	
First Day Cover				4·00
Presentation Pack			4·75	
P.H.Q. Cards (set of 4)			3·00	7·00

Nos. 1282/5 were issued on the occasion of the 300th birth anniversary of Handel.

Special First Day of Issue Postmarks

Philatelic Bureau, Edinburgh	4·50
Worcester	4·75

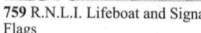

759 R.N.L.I. Lifeboat and Signal Flags

760 Beachy Head Lighthouse and Chart

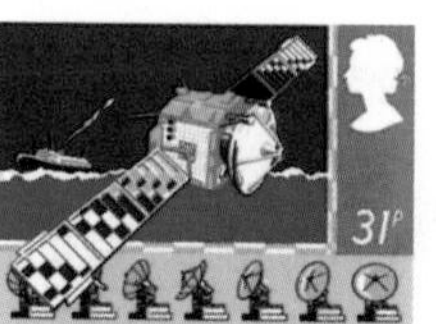

761 "Marecs A" Communications Satellite and Dish Aerials

762 Buoys

(Des F. Newell and J. Sorrell. Litho J.W.)

1985 (18 June). *Safety at Sea. Phosphorised paper.* P 14.

No.	Type	Description	Unused	Used
1286	**759**	17p. black, azure, emerald, ultramarine, orange-yellow, vermilion, brt blue and chrome-yellow	40	25
1287	**760**	22p. black, azure, emerald, ultramarine, orange-yellow, vermilion, brt blue and chrome-yellow	60	75
1288	**761**	31p. black, azure, emerald, ultramarine, orange-yellow, vermilion and brt blue	90	1·00
1289	**762**	34p. black, azure, emerald, ultramarine, orange-yellow, vermilion, brt blue and chrome-yellow	1·00	1·25
		Set of 4	2·75	3·00
		Set of 4 *Gutter Pairs*	7·00	
		First Day Cover		3·00
		Presentation Pack	3·75	
		P.H.Q. Cards (*set of* 4)	3·00	7·00

Nos. 1286/9 were issued on the occasion of the bicentenary of the unimmersible lifeboat and the 50th anniversary of radar.

Special First Day of Issue Postmarks

Philatelic Bureau, Edinburgh .... 3·50
Eastbourne .... 3·50

763 Datapost Motorcyclist, City of London

764 Rural Postbus

765 Parcel Delivery in Winter

766 Town Letter Delivery

(Des P. Hogarth)

1985 (30 July). *350 Years of Royal Mail Public Postal Service. Phosphorised paper.* P 14×15.

No.	Type	Description	Unused	Used
1290	**763**	17p. black, greenish yellow, brt carmine, greenish blue, yellow-brown, grey-black and silver	50	10
		a. Imperf on 3 sides (vert pair)	£1800	
		Eu. Underprint Type **5**	1·00	
1291	**764**	22p. black, greenish yellow, cerise, steel-blue, lt green, grey-black and silver	75	70
1292	**765**	31p. black, greenish yellow, brt carmine, dull blue, drab, grey-black and silver	1·00	1·00
		a. Imperf (vert pair)	£1800	
1293	**766**	34p. black, greenish yellow, cerise, ultramarine, lt brown, grey-black and silver	1·00	1·00
		a. Imperf between (vert pair)	£800	
		Set of 4	2·75	2·50
		Set of 4 *Gutter Pairs*	7·00	
		First Day Cover		3·25
		Presentation Pack	3·75	
		P.H.Q. Cards (*set of* 4)	3·00	7·00

No. 1290a shows perforation indentations at right, but is imperforate at top, bottom and on the left-hand side.

Examples of No. 1290Eu from the 1985 £1.70 booklet (sold at £1.53) (No. FT4) show a blue double-lined D in a random pattern, on the reverse over the gum.

Special First Day of Issue Postmarks

Philatelic Bureau, Edinburgh .... 3·50
Bagshot, Surrey .... 3·75

767 King Arthur and Merlin

768 Lady of the Lake

769 Queen Guinevere and Sir Lancelot

770 Sir Galahad

(Des Yvonne Gilbert)

1985 (3 Sept). *Arthurian Legends. Phosphorised paper.* P 15×14.

No.	Type	Description	Unused	Used
1294	**767**	17p. grey-black, lemon, brown-lilac, ultramarine, grey-black & silver	50	25
		a. Imperf (pair)	£2700	
1295	**768**	22p. black, lemon, brown-lilac, pale blue, grey-black, silver and grey-black	75	75
1296	**769**	31p. black, lemon, magenta, turquoise-blue, grey-black, silver and grey-black	1·25	1·25
1297	**770**	34p. grey, lemon, magenta, new blue, grey-black, silver and grey-black	1·25	1·25
		Set of 4	3·50	3·00
		Set of 4 *Gutter Pairs*	7·00	
		First Day Cover		3·50
		Presentation Pack	3·00	
		P.H.Q. Cards (*set of* 4)	3·00	7·00

Nos. 1294/7 were issued on the occasion of the 500th anniversary of the printing of Sir Thomas Malory's *Morte d'Arthur*.

Special First Day of Issue Postmarks

Philatelic Bureau, Edinburgh	4·00
Tintagel, Cornwall	4·00

771 Peter Sellers (from photo by Bill Brandt)

772 David Niven (from photo by Cornell Lucas)

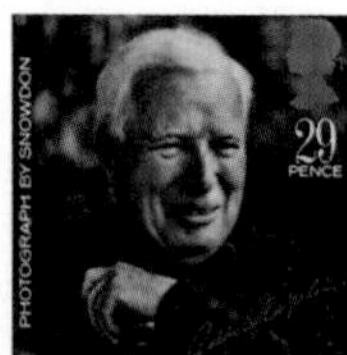

773 Charlie Chaplin (from photo by Lord Snowdon)

774 Vivien Leigh (from photo by Angus McBean)

775 Alfred Hitchcock (from photo by Howard Coster)

(Des K. Bassford)

1985 (8 Oct). *British Film Year. Phosphorised paper.* P 14½.

1298	**771**	17p. grey-black, olive-grey, gold and silver	45	25
1299	**772**	22p. black, brown, gold and silver	60	75
1300	**773**	29p. black, lavender, gold and silver	1·00	1·25
1301	**774**	31p. black, pink, gold and silver	1·10	1·50
1302	**775**	34p. black, greenish blue, gold and silver	1·40	1·50
Set of 5			4·00	4·50
Set of 5 Gutter Pairs			10·50	
First Day Cover				5·00
Presentation Pack			5·50	
Souvenir Book			11·50	
P.H.Q. Cards (*set of 5*)			3·00	8·50

The souvenir book is a 24-page illustrated booklet with a set of mint stamps in a sachet attached to the front cover.

Special First Day of Issue Postmarks

Philatelic Bureau, Edinburgh	5·50
London WC	5·50

776 Principal Boy

777 Genie

778 Dame

779 Good Fairy

780 *Pantomime* Cat

(Des A. George)

1985 (19 Nov). *Christmas. Pantomine Characters. One phosphor band (12p.) or phosphorised paper (others).* P 15×14.

1303	**776**	12p. new blue, greenish yellow, brt rose, gold, grey-black and silver	50	15
		a. Imperf (pair)	£1500	
		Eu. Underprint Type 4	1·00	
1304	**777**	17p. emerald, greenish yellow, brt rose, new blue, black, gold and silver	50	25
		a. Imperf (pair)	£2200	
1305	**778**	22p. brt carmine, greenish yellow, pale new blue, grey, gold and silver	75	1·10
1306	**779**	31p. brt orange, lemon, rose, slate-purple, silver and gold	1·25	1·40
1307	**780**	34p. brt reddish violet, brt blue, brt rose, black, grey-brown, gold & silver	1·25	1·40
Set of 5			4·00	4·00
Set of 5 Gutter Pairs			8·00	
First Day Cover				4·50
Presentation Pack			4·25	
P.H.Q. Cards (*set of 5*)			3·00	7·00
Christmas Folder (*contains No.* 1303×50)			20·00	

Examples of No. 1303Eu from the 1985 Christmas booklet (No. FX8) show a random pattern of blue double-lined stars printed on the reverse over the gum.

Special First Day of Issue Postmarks

Philatelic Bureau, Edinburgh	4·75
Bethlehem, Llandeilo, Dyfed	5·00

Collectors Pack 1985

1985 Nov 19 Comprises Nos. 1272/1307.
CP1307a Collectors Pack .... 35·00

Post Office Yearbook

1985. Comprises Nos. 1272/1307 in 32-page hardbound book with slip case, illustrated in colour .... 80·00

781 Light Bulb and North Sea Oil Drilling Rig (Energy)

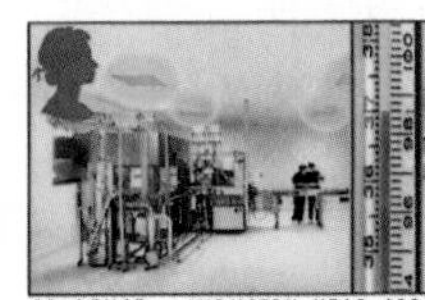

782 Thermometer and Pharmaceutical Laboratory (Health)

783 Garden Hoe Steelworks (Steel)

784 Loaf of Bread and Cornfield (Agriculture)

(Des K. Bassford. Litho Questa)

1986 (14 Jan). *Industry Year. Phosphorised paper.* P 14½×14.

1308	**781**	17p. gold, black, magenta, greenish yellow and new blue	75	25
1309	**782**	22p. gold, pale turquoise-green, black, magenta, greenish yellow & blue	50	75
1310	**783**	31p. gold, black, magenta, greenish yellow and new blue	1·25	1·40
1311	**784**	34p. gold, black, magenta, greenish yellow and new blue	1·25	1·40
Set of 4			3·50	3·50
Set of 4 *Gutter Pairs*			7·00	
First Day Cover				3·50
Presentation Pack			3·75	
P.H.Q. Cards (*set of* 4)			3·50	6·50

Special First Day of Issue Postmarks

Philatelic Bureau, Edinburgh	3·50
Birmingham	4·00

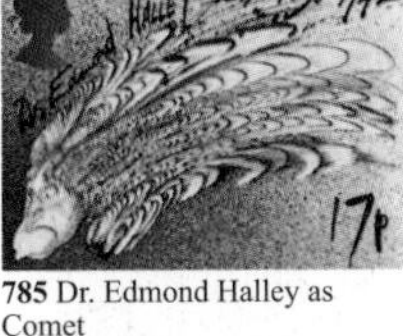
785 Dr. Edmond Halley as Comet

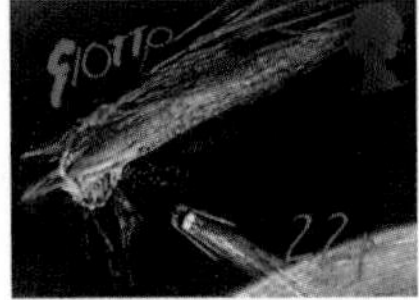
786 *Giotto* Spacecraft approaching Comet

787 "Maybe Twice in a Lifetime"

788 Comet orbiting Sun and Planets

(Des R. Steadman)

1986 (18 Feb). *Appearance of Halley's Comet. Phosphorised paper.* P 15×14.

1312	**785**	17p. black, bistre, rosine, blue, grey-black, gold and dp brown	50	25
1313	**786**	22p. orange-vermilion, greenish yellow, brt purple, new blue, black and gold	75	75
1314	**787**	31p. black, greenish yellow, brt purple, dp turquoise-blue, grey-black and gold	1·25	1·25
1315	**788**	34p. blue, greenish yellow, magenta, dp turquoise-blue, black & gold	1·25	1·40
Set of 4			3·50	3·50
Set of 4 *Gutter Pairs*			7·00	
First Day Cover				3·50
Presentation Pack			3·75	
P.H.Q. Cards (*set of* 4)			4·00	6·50

Special First Day of Issue Postmarks

Philaelic Bureau, Edinburgh	4·00
London SE10	4·50

789 Queen Elizabeth in 1928, 1942 and 1952

790 Queen Elizabeth in 1958, 1973 and 1982

T **789/90** were printed horizontally se-tenant within the sheet

(Des J. Matthews)

1986 (21 Apr). *60th Birthday of Queen Elizabeth II. Phosphorised paper.* P 15×14.

1316	**789**	17p. grey-black, turquoise-green, brt green, green and dull blue	60	50
		a. Pair. Nos. 1316/17	1·50	1·50

1317	**790**	17p. grey-black, dull blue, greenish blue and indigo	60	50
1318	**789**	34p. grey-black, dp dull purple, yellow-orange and red	1·40	1·75
		a. Pair. Nos. 1318/19	3·00	4·00
1319	**790**	34p. grey-black, olive-brown, yellow-brown, olive-grey and red	1·40	1·75
Set of 4			4·50	4·00
Set of Gutter Blocks of 4			11·00	
First Day Cover				4·00
Presentation Pack			5·50	
Souvenir Book			8·50	
P.H.Q. Cards (*set of* 4)			5·00	6·50

The souvenir book is a special booklet, fully illustrated and containing a mint set of stamps.

Special First Day of Issue Postmarks

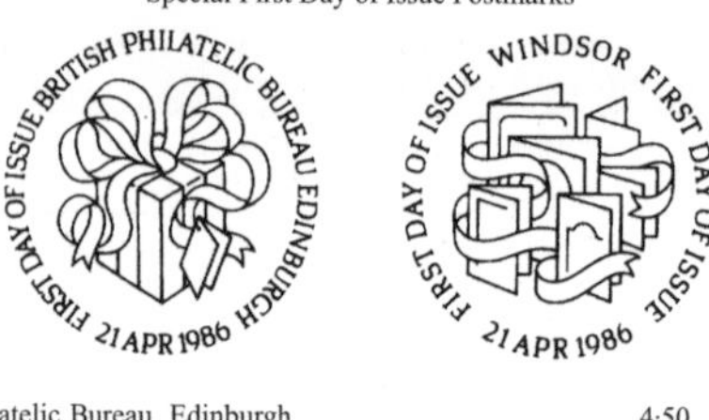

Philatelic Bureau, Edinburgh .... 4·50
Windsor .... 5·00

791 Barn Owl

792 Pine Marten

793 Wild Cat

794 Natterjack Toad

(Des K. Lilly)

1986 (20 May). *Europa. Nature Conservation—Endangered Species. Phosphorised paper.* P 14½×14.

1320	**791**	17p. gold, greenish yellow, rose, yellow-brown, olive-grey, new blue and black	40	10
1321	**792**	22p. gold, greenish yellow, reddish brown, olive-yellow, turquoise-blue, grey-black and black	80	1·00
1322	**793**	31p. gold, brt yellow-green, magenta, lt brown, ultramarine, olive-brown and black	1·50	1·25
1323	**794**	34p. gold, greenish yellow, brt rose-red, brt green, grey-black and black	1·65	1·40
Set of 4			4·00	3·50
Set of Gutter Pairs			10·00	
First Day Cover				4·00
Presentation Pack			4·00	
P.H.Q. Cards (*set of* 4)			3·50	6·50

Special First Day of Issue Postmarks

Philatelic Bureau, Edinburgh .... 4·50
Lincoln .... 4·75

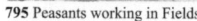

795 Peasants working in Fields

796 Freemen working at Town Trades

797 Knight and Retainers

798 Lord at Banquet

(Des Tayburn Design Consultancy)

1986 (17 Jun). *900th Anniv of Domesday Book. Phosphorised paper.* P 15×14.

1324	**795**	17p. yellow-brown, vermilion, lemon, brt emerald, orange-brown, grey and brownish grey	40	10
1325	**796**	22p. yellow-ochre, red, greenish blue, chestnut, grey-black and brownish grey	85	85
1326	**797**	31p. yellow-brown, vermilion, green, Indian red, grey-black and brownish grey	1·25	1·40
1327	**798**	34p. yellow-ochre, bright scarlet, grey-brown, new blue, lake-brown, grey-black and grey	1·25	1·40
Set of 4			3·50	3·50
Set of Gutter Pairs			7·00	
First Day Cover				4·00
Presentation Pack			4·00	
P.H.Q. Cards (*set of* 4)			3·50	6·50

Special First Day of Issue Postmarks

Philatelic Bureau, Edinburgh .... 4·50
Gloucester .... 4·50

799 Athletics

800 Rowing

801 Weightlifting

802 Rifle Shooting

803 Hockey

(Des N. Cudworth)

1986 (15 July). *Thirteenth Commonwealth Games, Edinburgh and World Hockey Cup for Men, London (34p.). Phosphorised paper.* P 15×14.

1328	**799**	17p. black, greenish yellow, orange-vermilion, ultramarine, chestnut and emerald	40	25
1329	**800**	22p. black, lemon, scarlet, new blue, royal blue, chestnut and dp ultramarine	55	75
		a. Imperf (pair)		—
1330	**801**	29p. grey-black, greenish yellow, scarlet, new blue, brown-ochre, brown-rose and pale chestnut	75	1·00
1331	**802**	31p. black, greenish yellow, rose, blue, dull yellow-green, chestnut and yellow-green	1·00	1·25
1332	**803**	34p. black, lemon, scarlet, brt blue, brt emerald, red-brown and vermilion	1·25	1·25
		a. Imperf (pair)	£2000	
Set of 5			3·50	3·50
Set ofGutter Pairs			8·75	
First Day Cover				3·50
Presentation Pack			2·75	
P.H.Q. Cards (set of 5)			4·00	7·50

No. 1332 also commemorates the centenary of the Hockey Association.

Special First Day of Issue Postmarks

Philatelic Bureau, Edinburgh	5·00
Head Post Office, Edinburgh	5·00

804 Prince Andrew and Miss Sarah Ferguson (from photo by Gene Nocon)

805 Prince Andrew and Miss Sarah Ferguson (from photo by Gene Nocon)

(Des J. Matthews)

1986 (22 July). *Royal Wedding. One phosphor band (12p.) or phosphorised paper (17p.).* P 14×15.

1333	**804**	12p. lake, greenish yellow, cerise, ultramarine, black and silver	50	30
1334	**805**	17p. steel blue, greenish yellow, cerise, ultramarine, black & gold	1·00	1·25
		a. Imperf (pair)	£950	
Set of 2			1·50	1·50
Set of Gutter Pairs			3·00	
First Day Cover				2·00
Presentation Pack			1·75	
P.H.Q. Cards (set of 2)			2·25	5·00

Special First Day of Issue Postmarks

Philatelic Bureau, Edinburgh	2·50
London, SW1	2·75

806 Stylized Cross on Ballot Paper

(Des J. Gibbs. Litho Questa)

1986 (19 Aug). *32nd Commonwealth Parliamentary Association Conference. Phosphorised paper.* P 14×14½.

1335	**806**	34p. pale grey-lilac, black, vermilion, yellow and ultramarine	1·25	1·25
Gutter Pair			2·75	
First Day Cover				1·75
P.H.Q. Card			1·00	3·00

Special First Day of Issue Postmarks

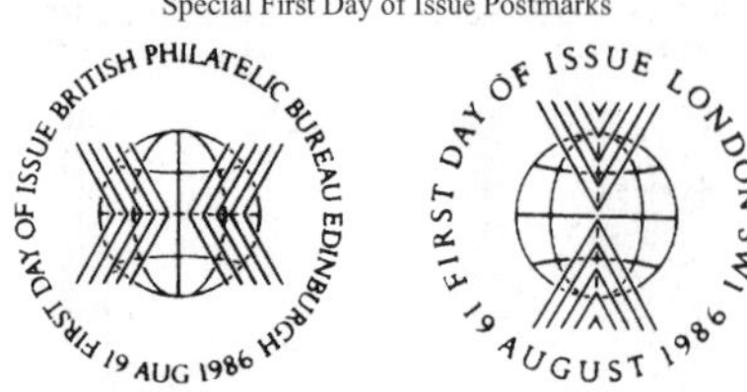

Philatelic Bureau, Edinburgh .... 2·00
London, SW1 .... 2·00

807 Lord Dowding and Hawker Hurricane Mk I

808 Lord Tedder and Hawker Typhoon IB

809 Lord Trenchard and De Havilland D.H.9A

810 Sir Arthur Harris and Avro Type 683 Lancaster

811 Lord Portal and De Havilland D.H.98 Mosquito

(Des B. Sanders)

1986 (16 Sept). *History of the Royal Air Force. Phosphorised paper.* P 14½.

No.	Type	Description	Mint	Used
1336	**807**	17p. pale blue, greenish yellow, brt rose, blue, black and grey-black	50	10
		a. Imperf (pair)	£1250	
1337	**808**	22p. pale turquoise-green, greenish yellow, magenta, new blue, black and grey-black	75	95
		a. Face value omitted*	£500	
		b. Queen's head omitted*	£500	
1338	**809**	29p. pale drab, olive-yellow, magenta, blue, grey-black and black	1·25	1·10
1339	**810**	31p. pale flesh, greenish yellow, magenta, ultramarine, black and grey-black	1·75	1·40
1340	**811**	34p. buff, greenish yellow, magenta, blue, grey-black and black	1·75	1·90
Set of 5			5·00	5·50
Set of 5 Gutter Pairs			12·00	
First Day Cover				5·50
Presentation Pack			5·50	
P.H.Q. Cards (set of 5)			4·50	10·00

Nos. 1336/40 were issued to celebrate the 50th anniversary of the first R.A.F. Commands.

*Nos. 1337a/b come from three consecutive sheets on which the stamps in the first vertical row are without the face value and those in the second vertical row the Queen's head.

Special First Day of Issue Postmarks

Philatelic Bureau, Edinburgh .... 6·00
Farnborough .... 6·00

812 The Glastonbury Thorn

813 The Tanad Valley Plygain

814 The Hebrides Tribute

815 The Dewsbury Church Knell

816 The Hereford Boy Bishop

(Des Lynda Gray)

1986 (18 Nov–2 Dec). *Christmas. Folk Customs. One phosphor band (12p., 13p.) or phosphorised paper (others).* P 15×14.

No.	Type	Description	Mint	Used
1341	**812**	12p. gold, greenish yellow, vermilion, dp brown, emerald and dp blue (2.12)	50	50
		a. Imperf (pair)	£1500	
1342		13p. dp blue, greenish yellow, vermilion, dp brown, emerald and gold	25	15
		Eu. Underprint Type 4 (2.12)	1·00	
1343	**813**	18p. myrtle-green, yellow, vermilion, dp blue, black, reddish brown and gold	50	15
1344	**814**	22p. vermilion, olive-bistre, dull blue, dp brown, dp green and gold	1·00	1·00
1345	**815**	31p. dp brown, yellow, vermilion, violet, dp dull green, black and gold	1·25	1·00
1346	**816**	34p. violet, lemon, vermilion, dp dull blue, reddish brown and gold	1·25	1·10
Set of 6			3·75	3·50
Set of 6 Gutter Pairs			9·00	
First Day Covers (2)				3·75
Presentation Pack (Nos. 1342/6)			3·75	
P.H.Q. Cards (*Nos.* 1342/6) (*set of* 5)			3·50	7·00
Christmas Folder (*contains No.* 1342Eu×36)			17·00	

No. 1341 represented a discount of 1p., available between 2 and 24 December 1986, on the current second class postage rate.

Special First Day of Issue Postmarks

Philatelic Bureau, Edinburgh (Nos. 1342/6) (18 Nov) ......4·00
Bethlehem, Llandeilo, Dyfed (Nos. 1342/6) (18 Nov) ......4·00
Philatelic Bureau, Edinburgh (No. 1341) (2 Dec) ....2·00

Collectors Pack 1986

1986 Nov 18 Comprises Nos. 1308/40 and 1342/6.
CP1346a Collectors Pack .... 37·00

Post Office Yearbook

1986 Nov 18 Comprises Nos. 1308/46 in 32-page hardbound book with slip case, illustrated in colour ....70·00

817 North American Blanket Flower

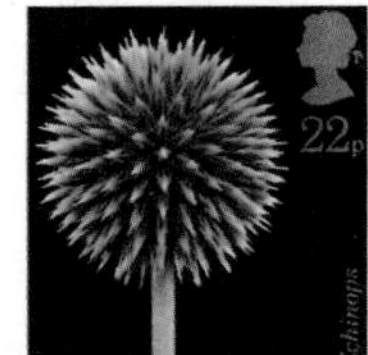

818 Globe Thistle

819 Echeveria

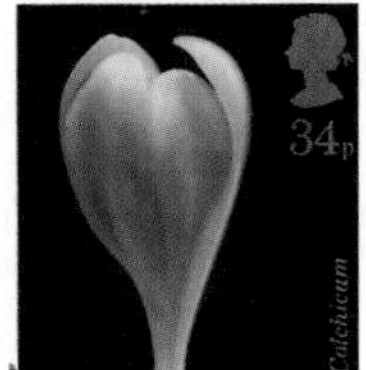

820 Autumn Crocus

(Adapted J. Matthews)

1987 (20 Jan–2 Dec). *Flower Photographs by Alfred Lammer. Phosphorised paper.* P 14½×14.

1347	**817**	18p. silver, greenish yellow, rosine, dp green and black	40	10
1348	**818**	22p. silver, greenish yellow, new blue, greenish blue and black	70	85
1349	**819**	31p. silver, greenish yellow, scarlet, blue-green, dp green and black	1·10	1·25
		a. Imperf (pair)	£2200	
1350	**820**	34p. silver, greenish yellow, magenta, dull blue, dp green and black	1·10	1·25
Set of 4			3·25	3·25
Set of 4 *Gutter Pairs*			7·50	
First Day Cover				3·50
Presentation Pack			4·00	
P.H.Q. Cards (*set of* 4)			3·00	7·00

Special First Day of Issue Postmarks

Philatelic Bureau, Edinburgh ....4·00
Richmond, Surrey ....4·50

821 *The Principia Mathematica*

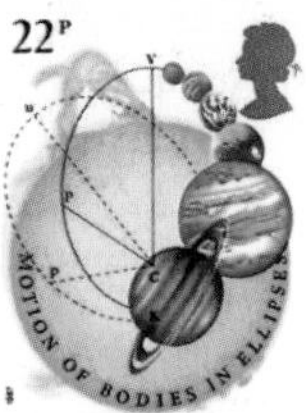

822 Motion of Bodies in *Ellipses*

823 *Optick Treatise*

824 *The System of the World*

(Des Sarah Godwin)

1987 (24 Mar–2 Dec). *300th Anniv of "The Principia Mathematica" by Sir Isaac Newton. Phosphorised paper.* P 14×15.

1351	**821**	18p. black, greenish yellow, cerise, blue-green, grey-black and silver	50	15
1352	**822**	22p. black, greenish yellow, brt orange, blue, brt emerald, silver and bluish violet	75	75
1353	**823**	31p. black, greenish yellow, scarlet, new blue, bronze-green, silver and slate-green	1·25	1·50
1354	**824**	34p. black, greenish yellow, red, brt blue, grey-black and silver	1·25	1·25
Set of 4			3·50	3·25
Set of 4 *Gutter Pairs*			8·00	
First Day Cover				3·75
Presentation Pack			4·00	
P.H.Q. Cards (*set of* 4)			3·00	6·50

Special First Day of Issue Postmarks

Philatelic Bureau, Edinburgh .... 4·00
Woolsthorpe, Lincs .... 4·25

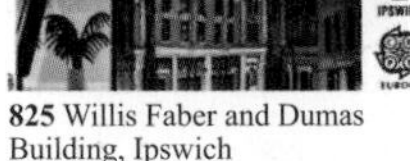

825 Willis Faber and Dumas Building, Ipswich

826 Pompidou Centre, Paris

827 Staatsgalerie, Stuttgart

828 European Investment Bank, Luxembourg

(Des B. Tattersfield)

1987 (12 May). *Europa. British Architects in Europe. Phosphorised paper.* P 15×14.

1355	**825**	18p. black, bistre-yellow, cerise, brt blue, dp grey and grey-black	50	15
1356	**826**	22p. black, greenish yellow, carmine, brt blue, dp grey and grey-black	75	75
1357	**827**	31p. grey-black, bistre-yellow, cerise, brt blue, brt green, black and dull violet	1·25	1·25
		a. Imperf (horiz pair)	£2000	
1358	**828**	34p. black, greenish yellow, cerise, brt blue, grey-black and dp grey	1·75	1·25
Set of 4			4·00	3·25
Set of 4 *Gutter Pairs*			9·50	
First Day Cover				3·75
Presentation Pack			4·00	
P.H.Q. Cards (*set of* 4)			3·00	6·50

Special First Day of Issue Postmarks

Philatelic Bureau, Edinburgh .... 4·00
Ipswich .... 4·00

829 Brigade Members with Ashford Litter, 1887

830 Bandaging Blitz Victim, 1940

831 Volunteer with fainting Girl, 1965

832 Transport of Transplant Organ by Air Wing, 1987

(Des Debbie Cook. Litho Questa)

1987 (16 June). *Centenary of St. John Ambulance Brigade. Phosphorised paper.* P 14×14½.

1359	**829**	18p. new blue, greenish yellow, magenta, black, silver and pink	40	25
		Ea. Black ptg double	†	£950
		Eb. Black ptg triple	†	£1700
1360	**830**	22p. new blue, greenish yellow, magenta, black, silver and cobalt	60	75
1361	**831**	31p. new blue, greenish yellow, magenta, black, silver and bistre-brown	1·25	1·25
1362	**832**	34p. new blue, greenish yellow, magenta, black, silver and greenish grey	1·25	1·25
Set of 4			3·25	3·25
Set of 4 *Gutter Pairs*			7·50	
First Day Cover				3·75
Presentation Pack			4·00	
P.H.Q. Cards (*set of* 4)			3·00	6·50

Special First Day of Issue Postmarks

Philatelic Bureau, Edinburgh .... 4·00
London, EC1 .... 4·00

833 Arms of the Lord Lyon King of Arms

834 Scottish Heraldic Banner of Prince Charles

835 Arms of Royal Scottish Academy of Painting, Sculpture and Architecture

836 Arms of Royal Society of Edinburgh

(Des J. Matthews)

1987 (21 July). *300th Anniv of Revival of Order of the Thistle. Phosphorised paper.* P 14½.

1363	**833**	18p. black, lemon, scarlet, blue, dp green, slate and brown	50	10
1364	**834**	22p. black, greenish yellow, carmine, new blue, dp green, grey and lake-brown	75	90
1365	**835**	31p. black, greenish yellow, scarlet, new blue, dull green, grey and grey-black	1·40	1·40
1366	**836**	34p. black, greenish yellow, scarlet, dp ultramarine, dull green, grey & yellow-brown	1·50	1·40
Set of 4			3·75	3·50
Set of 4 *Gutter Pairs*			8·00	
First Day Cover				3·75
Presentation Pack			4·00	
P.H.Q. Cards (*set of* 4)			3·00	6·50

Special First Day of Issue Postmarks

Philatelic Bureau, Edinburgh	4·00
Rothesay, Isle of Bute	4·50

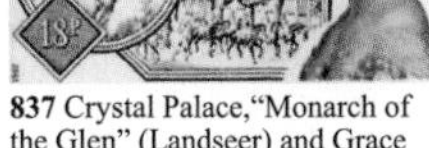

837 Crystal Palace, "Monarch of the Glen" (Landseer) and Grace Darling

838 *Great Eastern, Beeton's Book of Household Management* and Prince Albert

839 Albert Memorial, Ballot Box and Disraeli

840 Diamond Jubilee Emblem, Newspaper Placard for Relief of Mafeking and Morse Key

(Des M. Dempsey. Eng C. Slania. Recess and photo)

1987 (8 Sept). *150th Anniv of Queen Victoria's Accession. Phosphorised paper.* P 15×14.

1367	**837**	18p.	pale stone, dp blue, lemon, rose, greenish blue, brown-ochre and grey-black	50	10
1368	**838**	22p.	pale stone, dp brown, lemon, rose, grey-black & brown-ochre	80	75
1369	**839**	31p.	pale stone, dp lilac, lemon, cerise, brown-ochre, greenish blue and grey-black	1·25	1·50
1370	**840**	34p.	pale stone, myrtle-green, yellow-ochre, reddish brown and brown-ochre	1·35	1·60
Set of 4				3·50	3·50
Set of 4 *Gutter Pairs*				9·00	
First Day Cover					3·75
Presentation Pack				4·25	
P.H.Q. Cards (*set of* 4)				3·00	6·50

Special First Day of Issue Postmarks

Philatelic Bureau, Edinburgh	4·00
Newport, Isle of Wight	4·50

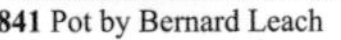

841 Pot by Bernard Leach

842 Pot by Elizabeth Fritsch

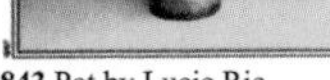

843 Pot by Lucie Rie

844 Pot by Hans Coper

(Des T. Evans)

1987 (13 Oct). *Studio Pottery. Phosphorised paper.* P 14½×14.

1371	**841**	18p.	gold, lemon, lt red-brown, chestnut, lt grey and black	50	25
1372	**842**	26p.	blue over silver, yellow-orange, brt purple, lavender, bluish violet, grey-brown and black	70	75
1373	**843**	31p.	rose-lilac over silver, greenish yellow, cerise, new blue, grey-lilac and black	1·25	1·25
1374	**844**	34p.	copper, yellow-brown, reddish brown, grey-lilac and black	1·40	1·50
Set of 4				3·50	3·50
Set of 4 *Gutter Pairs*				8·50	
First Day Cover					3·75
Presentation Pack				3·50	
P.H.Q. Cards (*set of* 4)				3·00	6·50

Special First Day of Issue Postmarks

Philatelic Bureau, Edinburgh	4·00
St. Ives, Cornwall	4·00

845 Decorating the Christmas Tree

846 Waiting for Father Christmas

847 Sleeping Child and Father Christmas in Sleigh

848 Child reading

849 Child playing Recorder and Snowman

(Des M. Foreman)

1987 (17 Nov). *Christmas. One phosphor band (13p.) or phosphorised paper (others).* P 15×14.

1375	**845**	13p. gold, greenish yellow, rose, greenish blue and black	30	10
		Eu. Underprint Type 4	95	
1376	**846**	18p. gold, greenish yellow, brt purple, greenish blue, brt blue and black	40	20
1377	**847**	26p. gold, greenish yellow, brt purple, new blue, brt blue and black	80	1·00
1378	**848**	31p. gold, greenish yellow, scarlet, brt magenta, dull rose, greenish blue and black	1·10	1·25
1379	**849**	34p. gold, greenish yellow, dull rose, greenish blue, brt blue and black	1·25	1·50
Set of 5			3·50	3·75
Set of 5 *Gutter Pairs*			8·50	
First Day Cover				3·75
Presentation Pack			3·50	
P.H.Q. Cards (*set of* 5)			3·00	6·50
Christmas Folder (*contains No.* 1375Eu×36)			17·00	

Examples of the 13p. value from special folders, containing 36 stamps and sold for £4.60, show a blue underprint of doublelined stars printed on the reverse over the gum.

Special First Day of Issue Postmarks

Philatelic Bureau, Edinburgh .... 4·00
Bethlehem, Llandeilo, Dyfed .... 4·50

Collectors Pack 1987

1987 Nov 17 Comprises Nos. 1347/79.
CP1379a Collectors Pack .... 37·00

Post Office Yearbook

1987 Nov 17 Comprises Nos. 1347/79 in 32-page hardbound book with slip case, illustrated in colour .... 35·00

850 Short-spined Seascorpion ("Bull-rout") (Jonathan Couch)

851 Yellow Waterlily (Major Joshua Swatkin)

852 Whistling ("Bewick's") Swan (Edward Lear)

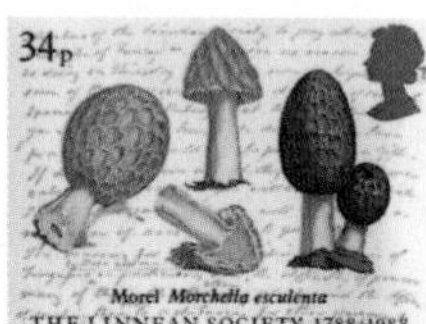

853 *Morchella esculenta* (James Sowerby)

(Des. E. Hughes)

1988 (19 Jan). *Bicentenary of Linnean Society. Archive Illustrations. Phosphorised paper.* P 15×14.

1380	**850**	18p. grey-black, stone, orange-yellow, brt purple, olive-bistre and gold	55	10
1381	**851**	26p. black, stone, bistre-yellow, dull orange, greenish blue, gold and pale bistre	85	10
1382	**852**	31p. black, stone, greenish yellow, rose-red, dp blue, gold and olive-bistre	1·10	1·25
		a. Imperf (horiz pair)	£1700	
1383	**853**	34p. black, stone, yellow, pale bistre, olive-grey, gold and olive-bistre	1·25	1·40
Set of 4			3·25	3·25
Set of 4 *Gutter Pairs*			8·00	
First Day Cover				3·75
Presentation Pack			4·00	
P.H.Q. Cards (*set of* 4)			3·00	6·50

Special First Day of Issue Postmarks

Philatelic Bureau, Edinburgh .... 4·00
London, W1 .... 4·50

854 Revd William Morgan (Bible translator, 1588)

855 William Salesbury (New Testament translator, 1567)

856 Bishop Richard Davies (New Testament translator, 1567)

857 Bishop Richard Parry (editor of Revised Welsh Bible, 1620)

(Des K. Bowen)

1988 (1 Mar). *400th Anniv of Welsh Bible. Phosphorised paper.* P 14½×14.

1384	**854**	18p. grey-black, greenish yellow, cerise, blue, black and emerald	40	10
		a. Imperf (pair)	£1700	
1385	**855**	26p. grey-black, yellow, brt rose-red, turquoise-blue, black and orange	70	95
1386	**856**	31p. black, chrome-yellow, carmine, new blue, grey-black and blue	1·25	1·25
1387	**857**	34p. grey-black, greenish yellow, cerise, turquoise-green, black and brt violet	1·40	1·25
Set of 4			3·25	3·25
Set of 4 *Gutter Pairs*			8·00	
First Day Cover				3·75
Presentation Pack			4·00	
P.H.Q. Cards (*set of* 4)			3·00	6·50

Special First Day of Issue Postmarks

Philatelic Bureau, Edinburgh	4·00
Ty Mawr, Wybrnant, Gwynedd	4·50

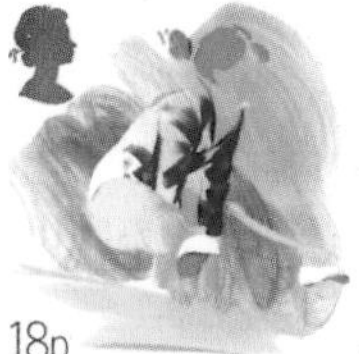

858 Gymnastics (Centenary of British Amateur Gymnastics Association)

859 Downhill Skiing (Ski Club of Great Britain)

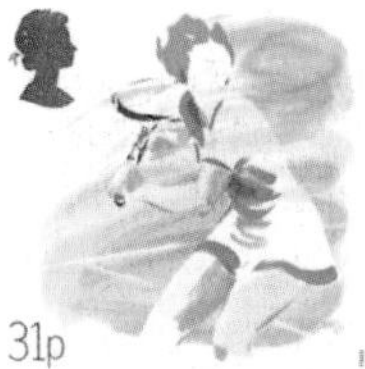

860 Tennis (Centenary of Lawn Tennis Association)

861 Football (Centenary of Football League)

(Des J. Sutton)

1988 (22 Mar). *Sports Organizations. Phosphorised paper.* P 14½.

1388	**858**	18p. violet-blue, greenish yellow, rosine, brt rose, new blue and silver	40	15
		a. Imperf (pair)	£1700	
1389	**859**	26p. violet-blue, greenish yellow, vermilion, carmine, yellow-orange and silver	70	80
1390	**860**	31p. violet-blue, greenish yellow, rose, blue, pale greenish blue, silver and brt orange	1·10	1·25
1391	**861**	34p. violet-blue, greenish yellow, vermilion, blue, brt emerald, silver and pink	1·25	1·25
Set of 4			3·25	3·25
Set of 4 *Gutter Pairs*			8·00	
First Day Cover				3·50
Presentation Pack			4·00	
P.H.Q. Cards (*set of* 2)			2·50	6·00

Special First Day of Issue Postmarks

Philatelic Bureau, Edinburgh	4·00
Wembley	5·00

862 *Mallard* and Mailbags on Pick-up Arms

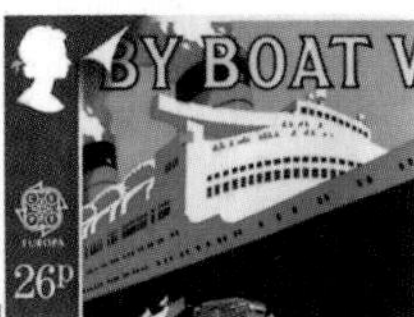

863 Loading Transatlantic Mail on Liner *Queen Elizabeth*

864 Glasgow Tram No. 1173 and Pillar Box

865 Imperial Airways Handley Page H.P.45 *Horatius* and Airmail Van

(Des M. Dempsey)

1988 (10 May). *Europa. Transport and Mail Services in 1930s. Phosphorised paper.* P 15×14.

1392	**862**	18p. brown, yellow, rose-red, dull blue, dp brown, reddish violet and black	50	15
1393	**863**	26p. brown, yellow, orange-vermilion, dull blue, violet-blue, brt emerald and black	1·00	1·00
1394	**864**	31p. brown, yellow-orange, carmine, dull purple, violet-blue, brt green and black	1·25	1·25
1395	**865**	34p. brown, orange-yellow, carmine-rose, bluish violet, brt blue, sepia and black	1·60	1·50
Set of 4			4·00	3·50
Set of 4 *Gutter Pairs*			11·00	
First Day Cover				3·75
Presentation Pack			4·25	
P.H.Q. Cards (*set of* 4)			2·25	6·00

Special First Day of Issue Postmarks

Philatelic Bureau, Edinburgh . ... 4·00
Glasgow . ... 4·50

866 Early Settler and Sailing Clipper

867 Queen Elizabeth II with British and Australian Parliament Buildings

868 W. G. Grace (cricketer) and Tennis Racquet

869 Shakespeare, John Lennon (entertainer) and Sydney Opera House

(Des G. Emery. Litho Questa)

1988 (21 June). *Bicentenary of Australian Settlement. Phosphorised paper.* P 14½.

1396	**866**	18p. dp ultramarine, orange-yellow, scarlet, black, bluish grey and emerald	60	50
		a. Horiz pair. Nos. 1396/7	1·25	1·50
1397	**867**	18p. dp ultramarine, orange-yellow, black, bluish grey and emerald	60	50
1398	**868**	34p. dp ultramarine, orange-yellow, scarlet, black, bluish grey and emerald	1·25	1·25
		a. Horiz pair. Nos. 1398/9	2·25	2·75
1399	**869**	34p. dp ultramarine, orange-yellow, black, bluish grey and emerald	1·25	1·25
Set of 4			3·50	1·90
Set of 2 *Gutter Blocks of* 4			8·25	
First Day Cover				3·75
Presentation Pack			4·00	
Souvenir Book			15·00	
P.H.Q. Cards (*set of* 4)			2·25	6·00

Nos. 1396/7 and 1398/9 were each printed together, *se-tenant*, in horizontal pairs throughout the sheets, each pair showing a background design of the Australian flag.

The 40 page souvenir book contains the British and Australian sets which were issued on the same day in similar designs.

Special First Day of Issue Postmarks

Philatelic Bureau, Edinburgh . ... 3·50
Portsmouth .... 4·00

870 Spanish Galeasse off The Lizard

871 English Fleet leaving Plymouth

872 Engagement off Isle of Wight

873 Attack of English Fire-ships, Calais

874 Armada in Storm, North Sea

(Des G. Evernden)

1988 (19 July). *400th Anniv of Spanish Armada. Phosphorised paper.* P 15×14.

1400	**870**	18p. slate-black, yellow-orange, brt carmine, brt blue, turquoise-blue, yellow-green and gold	70	65
		a. Horiz strip of 5. Nos. 1400/4	3·50	3·75
1401	**871**	18p. slate-black, yellow-orange, brt carmine, brt blue, turquoise-blue, yellow-green and gold	70	65
1402	**872**	18p. slate-black, yellow-orange, brt carmine, brt blue, turquoise-blue, yellow-green and gold	70	65
1403	**873**	18p. slate-black, yellow-orange, brt carmine, brt blue, turquoise-blue, yellow-green and gold	70	65
1404	**874**	18p. slate-black, yellow-orange, brt carmine, brt blue, turquoise-blue, yellow-green and gold	70	65
Set of 5			3·00	3·00
Gutter block of 10			8·00	8·25
First Day Cover				3·75
Presentation Pack			3·75	
P.H.Q. Cards (*set of* 5)			2·75	7·00

Nos. 1400/4 were printed together, *se-tenant*, in horizontal strips of 5 througout the sheet, forming a composite design.

Special First Day of Issue Postmarks

Philatelic Bureau, Edinburgh .... 5·00
Plymouth ....5·50

875 "The Owl and the Pussy-cat"

876 "Edward Lear as a Bird" (self-portrait)

877 "Cat" (from alphabet book)

878 "There was a Young Lady whose Bonnet . . ." (limerick)

(Des M. Swatridge and S. Dew)

1988 (6–27 Sept). *Death Centenary of Edward Lear (artist and author). Phosphorised paper.* P 15×14.

1405	**875**	19p. black, pale cream and carmine.........	65	20
1406	**876**	27p. black, pale cream and yellow...........	1·00	1·00
1407	**877**	32p. black, pale cream and emerald.........	1·25	1·40
1408	**878**	35p. black, pale cream and blue..............	1·40	1·40
Set of 4			4·00	3·50
Set of 4 *Gutter Pairs*			9·00	
First Day Cover				3·75
Presentation Pack			4·25	
P.H.Q. Cards (*set of* 4)			2·25	6·00
P.H.Q. Cards (*set of* 5)			2·75	7·00
MS1409 22×90 mm. Nos. 1405/8 (sold at £1.35) (27 Sept)			7·00	8·50
First Day Cover				8·50

The premium on No. **MS**1409 was used to support the "Stamp World London 90" International Stamp Exhibition.

Special First Day of Issue Postmarks

Philatelic Bureau, Edinburgh (stamps) (6 Sept) .. ..4·00
Philatelic Bureau, Edinburgh (miniature sheet) (27 Sept)..9·00
London N7 (stamps) (6 Sept) .. ..5·00
London N22 (miniature sheet) (27 Sept) . ... 9·50

879 Carrickfergus Castle

CAERNARFON CASTLE

880 Caernarfon Castle

881 Edinburgh Castle

882 Windsor Castle

(Des from photos by Prince Andrew, Duke of York. Eng C. Matthews. Recess Harrison)

1988 (18 Oct). *Ordinary paper.* P 15×14.

1410	**879**	£1 dp green..	4·25	60
1411	**880**	£1.50 maroon	4·50	1·25
1412	**881**	£2 indigo	8·00	1·50
1413	**882**	£5 dp brown	21·00	5·50
Set of 4			35·00	8·00
Set of 4 *Gutter Pairs*			70·00	
First Day Cover				35·00
Presentation Pack			35·00	

For similar designs, but with silhouette of Queen's head see Nos. 1611/14 and 1993/6.

Special First Day of Issue Postmarks

(For illustrations see Introduction)

Philatelic Bureau Edinburgh (Type H) ....40·00
Windsor, Berkshire (Type 1)...45·00

883 Journey to Bethlehem

884 Shepherds and Star

885 Three Wise Men

886 Nativity

887 The Annunciation

(Des L. Trickett)

1988 (15 Nov). *Christmas. Christmas Cards. One phosphor band (14p.) or phosphorised paper (others).* P 15×14.

1414	**883**	14p. gold, orange-yellow, brt mauve, bluish violet, brt blue and grey-black	45	25
		a. Error. "13p" instead of "14p"	£7000	
		b. Imperf (pair)	£1100	
1415	**884**	19p. gold, yellow-orange, brt violet, ultramarine, rose-red, grey-black and brt blue	50	25
		a. Imperf (pair)	£800	
1416	**885**	27p. gold, red, dp lavender, dp lilac, emerald, grey-black and brt blue	90	1·00
1417	**886**	32p. gold, orange-yellow, brt rose, dp mauve, violet, grey-black and brt blue	1·10	1·25
1418	**887**	35p. gold, green, reddish violet, brt blue, brt purple and grey-black	1·40	1·25
Set of 5			4·00	3·75
Set of 5 Gutter Pairs			9·50	
First Day Cover				3·75
Presentation Pack			4·00	
P.H.Q. Cards (set of 5)			3·00	6·00

Examples of No. 1414a were found in some 1988 Post Office Yearbooks.

Special First Day of Issue Postmarks

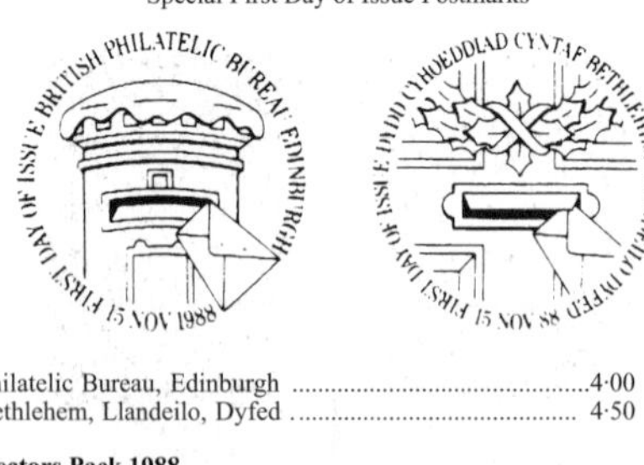

Philatelic Bureau, Edinburgh ....4·00
Bethlehem, Llandeilo, Dyfed ....4·50

Collectors Pack 1988

1988 Nov 15 Comprises Nos. 1380/1408, 1414/18.
CP1418a Collectors Pack ....35·00

Post Office Yearbook

1988 Nov 15 Comprises Nos. 1380/1404, MS1409, 1414/18 in 32-page hardbound book with slip case, illustrated in colour .... 37·00

888 Atlantic Puffin

889 Avocet

890 Oystercatcher

891 Northern Gannet

(Des D. Cordery)

1989 (17 Jan). *Centenary of Royal Society for the Protection of Birds. Phosphorised paper.* P 14×15.

1419	**888**	19p. grey, orange-yellow, orange-red, dull ultramarine, grey-black and silver	25	20
1420	**889**	27p. grey, bistre, rose, steel-blue, lavender, silver and grey-black	1·25	1·25
1421	**890**	32p. grey, bistre, scarlet, orange-red, lavender, silver and black	1·25	1·25
1422	**891**	35p. grey, lemon, rose-carmine, green, new blue, silver and black	1·25	1·25
Set of 4			3·50	3·50
Set of 4 Gutter Pairs			9·50	
First Day Cover				4·00
Presentation Pack			4·00	
P.H.Q. Cards (set of 4)			3·00	7·00

Special First Day of Issue Postmarks

Philatelic Bureau, Edinburgh ....4·00
Sandy, Bedfordshire....5·00

892 Rose

893 Cupid

894 Yachts

895 Fruit

896 Teddy Bear

(Des P. Sutton)

1989 (31 Jan). *Greetings Stamps. Phosphorised paper.* P 15×14.

1423	**892**	19p. black, greenish yellow, brt rose, red, new blue, lt green and gold	3·50	3·00
		a. Booklet pane. Nos. 1423/7×2 plus 12 half stamp-size labels	50·00	
		b. Horiz strip of 5. Nos. 1423/7	25·00	25·00
1424	**893**	19p. black, greenish yellow, brt rose, red, new blue, lt green and gold	3·50	3·00
1425	**894**	19p. black, greenish yellow, brt rose, red, new blue, lt green and gold	3·50	3·00
1426	**895**	19p. black, greenish yellow, brt rose, red, new blue, lt green and gold	3·50	3·00
1427	**896**	19p. black, greenish yellow, brt rose, red, new blue, lt green and gold	3·50	3·00
Set of 5			17·00	12·00
First Day Cover				25·00

Nos. 1423/7 were only issued in £1.90 booklets.

Special First Day of Issue Postmarks

Philatelic Bureau, Edinburgh ....25·00
Lover, Salisbury, Wilts ....25·00

897 Fruit and Vegetables

898 Meat Products

899 Dairy Products

900 Cereal Products

(Des Sedley Place Ltd)

1989 (7 Mar). *Food and Farming Year. Phosphorised paper.* P 14×14½.

1428	**897**	19p. brownish grey, greenish yellow, rose, new blue, black, pale grey and emerald	45	15
1429	**898**	27p. brownish grey, greenish yellow, brt carmine, new blue, black, pale grey and brt orange	90	85
1430	**899**	32p. brownish grey, greenish yellow, rose-red, new blue, black, pale grey and bistre-yellow	1·25	1·40
1431	**900**	35p. brownish grey, greenish yellow, brt carmine, new blue, black, pale grey and brown-red	1·40	1·50
Set of 4			3·50	3·50
Set of 4 Gutter Pairs			8·50	
First Day Cover				3·75
Presentation Pack			4·00	
P.H.Q. Cards (*set of* 4)			2·25	6·50

Special First Day of Issue Postmarks

Philatelic Bureau, Edinburgh ....4·00
Stoneleigh, Kenilworth, Warwicks ....4·50

901 Mortar Board (150th Anniv of Public Education in England)

902 Cross on Ballot Paper (3rd Direct Elections to European Parliament)

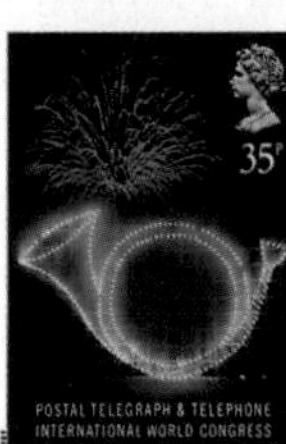

903 Posthorn (26th Postal, Telegraph and Telephone International Congress, Brighton)

904 Globe (Inter-Parliamentary Union Centenary Conference, London)

(Des Lewis Moberly from firework set-pieces. Litho Questa)

1989 (11 Apr). *Anniversaries. Phosphorised paper.* P 14×14½.

1432	**901**	19p. new blue, greenish yellow, magenta and black	1·00	50
		a. Horiz pair. Nos. 1432/3	2·00	2·00
1433	**902**	19p. new blue, greenish yellow, magenta and black	1·00	50
1434	**903**	35p. new blue, greenish yellow, magenta and black	1·50	1·75
		a. Horiz pair. Nos. 1434/5	3·00	4·00
1435	**904**	35p. new blue, greenish yellow, magenta and black	1·50	1·50
Set of 4			3·50	3·50
Set of 2 Gutter Strips of 4			9·00	
First Day Cover				6·00
Presentation Pack			4·00	
P.H.Q. Cards (*set of* 4)			2·25	6·50

Nos. 1432/3 and 1434/5 were each printed together, se-tenant, in horizontal pairs throughout the sheets. Stamps as No. 1435, but inscribed "ONE HUNDREDTH CONFERENCE" were prepared, but not issued.

Special First Day of Issue Postmarks

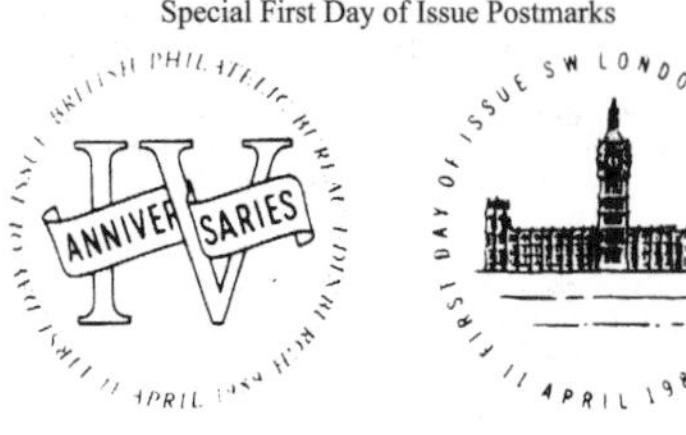

Philatelic Bureau, Edinburgh	5·00
London SW	6·00

905 Toy Train and Aeroplanes

906 Building Bricks

907 Dice and Board Games

908 Toy Robot, Boat and Doll's House

(Des D. Fern)

1989 (16 May). *Europa. Games and Toys. Phosphorised paper.* P 14×15.

1436	**905**	19p. black, greenish yellow, vermilion, blue-green, blue, gold and pale ochre	65	25
1437	**906**	27p. black, greenish yellow, reddish orange, blue-green, blue and gold	95	1·00
1438	**907**	32p. black, greenish yellow, orange-red, blue-green, blue, gold and pale ochre	1·40	1·25
1439	**908**	35p. black, greenish yellow, reddish orange, blue-green, blue, gold and stone	1·50	1·25
Set of 4			4·00	3·50
Set of 4 *Gutter Strips*			10·50	
First Day Cover				3·75
Presentation Pack			4·25	
P.H.Q. Cards (*set of* 4)			2·25	6·50

Special First Day of Issue Postmarks

Philatelic Bureau, Edinburgh	4·00
Leeds	5·00

909 Ironbridge, Shropshire

910 Tin Mine, St. Agnes Head, Cornwall

911 Cotton Mills, New Lanark, Strathclyde

912 Pontcysyllte Aqueduct, Clwyd

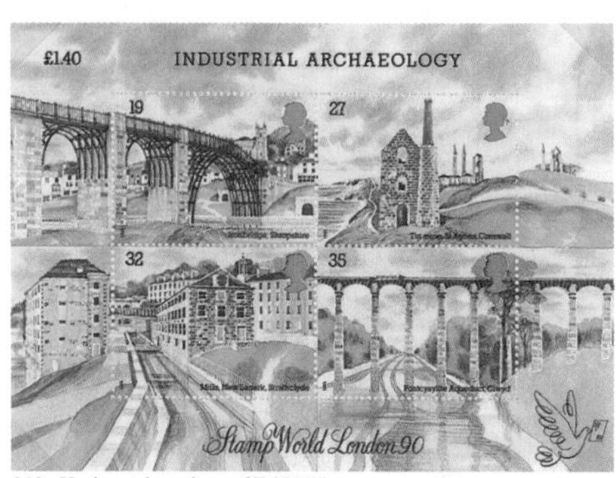

912a Horizontal versions of T **909/12**

(Des R. Maddox)

1989 (4–25 July). *Industrial Archaeology. Phosphorised paper.* P 14×15.

1440	**909**	19p. black, bistre-yellow, rose-red, apple-green, lt blue, grey-black and emerald	60	15
1441	**910**	27p. black, bistre-yellow, rose-red, apple-green, lt blue, grey-black and dull blue	1·00	1·10
1442	**911**	32p. black, yellow-orange, apple-green, yellow, dull blue, grey-black and dp reddish violet	1·10	1·25
1443	**912**	35p. black, yellow, brt rose, apple-green, dull blue, grey-black and vermilion.	1·25	1·50
Set of 4			3·50	3·50
Set of 4 *Gutter Pairs*			8·50	
First Day Cover				3·75
Presentation Pack			4·00	
P.H.Q. Cards (*set of* 4)			2·25	6·50
MS1444	**912a**	122×90 mm. As Nos. 1440/3, but horizontal. Each black, olive-yellow, brt rose-red, dull blue, apple-green, grey-black and vermilion (*sold at* £1.40) (25 July)	6·00	6·50
First Day Cover				6·50

The premium on No. **MS**1444 was used to support the "Stamp World London 90" International Stamp Exhibition.

Special First Day of Issue Postmarks

Philatelic Bureau, Edinburgh (stamps) (4 July) ....4·00
Philatelic Bureau, Edinburgh (miniature sheet) (25 July) . 7·00
Telford (stamps) (4 July) ....5·00
New Lanark (miniature sheet) (25 July) . ...7·50

913

914

1989 (22 Aug). *Booklet Stamps.*

(a) Photo Harrison. P 15×14.

1445	**913**	(2nd) brt blue (1 centre band)..................	1·00	1·00
		b. Booklet pane. No. 1445×4 with three edges of pane imperf (28.11.89)..	22·00	
1446		(2nd) brt blue (1 band at right) (20.3.90)...	3·00	3·25
1447	**914**	(1st) brownish black (phosphorised paper)	1·75	1·00
		a. Booklet pane. No. 1447×10 with horizontal edges of pane imperf.......	15·00	
		b. Booklet pane. No. 1447×4 with three edges of pane imperf (5.12.89)	35·00	
1448		(1st) brownish black (2 phosphor bands) (20.3.90)...	3·25	3·00
First Day Cover (Nos. 1445, 1447)		....		5·00

(b) Litho Walsall. P 14.

1449	**913**	(2nd) brt blue (1 centre band)....................	1·00	90
		a. Imperf between (vert pair)		
		b. Booklet pane. No. 1449×4 with three edges of pane imperf..............	7·00	
		c. Booklet pane. No. 1449×4 with horiz edges of pane imperf (6.8.91).	3·50	
		d. Booklet pane. No. 1449×10 with horiz edges of pane imperf (6.8.91).	6·00	
1450	**914**	(1st) blackish brown (2 phosphor bands).	2·50	2·40
		a. Booklet pane. No. 1450×4 with three edges of pane imperf..............	8·50	
		Ey. Phosphor omitted	£600	

(c) Litho Questa. P 15×14.

1451	**913**	(2nd) brt blue (1 centre band) (19.9.89)	1·00	1·00
		Ey. Phosphor omitted	£150	
1451*a*		(2nd) brt blue (1 band at right) (25.2.92)...	3·00	3·00
		aEb. Band at left (10.8.93)	2·00	2·00
		al. Booklet pane. Nos. 1451aEb and 1514a, each×3, with margins all round (10.8.93)................................	10·00	
1451	**914**	(1st) brownish black (phosphorised paper) (19.9.89)................................	2·50	2·50

Nos. 1445, 1447 and 1449/52 were initially sold at 14p. (2nd) and 19p. (1st), but these prices were later increased to reflect new postage rates.

Nos. 1446 and 1448 come from the *se-tenant* pane in the London Life £5 Booklet. This pane is listed under No. X906m in the Decimal Machin section.

No. 1451a comes from the *se-tenant* panes in the Wales and Tolkien £6 booklet. These panes are listed under Nos. X1012l and W49a (Wales Regionals). No. 1451aEb comes from the £6 (£5.64) Beatrix Potter booklet.

Nos. 1445, 1447 and 1449/50 do not exist perforated on all four sides, but come with either one or two adjacent sides imperforate.

No. 1450Ey comes from a pane in which one stamp was without phosphor bands due to a dry print.

For illustrations showing the differences between photogravure and lithography see above Type **367**.

For similar designs, but in changed colours, see Nos. 1511/16, for those with elliptical perforations, Nos. 1663a/6, and for self-adhesive versions Nos. 2039/40 and 2295.

Special First Day of Issue Postmarks
(for illustrations see Introduction)

Philatelic Bureau Edinburgh (Type G) (in red).. ....6·00
Windsor, Berks (Type G) in red..6·00

915 Snowflake (×10)

916 *Calliphora erythrocephala* (×5) (fly)

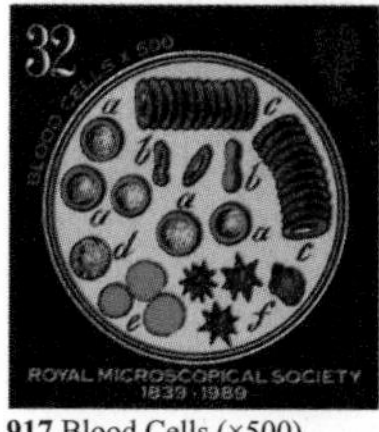

917 Blood Cells (×500)

918 Microchip (×600)

(Des K. Bassford. Litho Questa)

1989 (5 Sept). *150th Anniv of Royal Microscopical Society. Phosphorised paper.* P 14½×14.

1453	**915**	19p. gold, lemon, pale blue, grey, black and grey-black................................	45	25
1454	**916**	27p. gold, lemon, drab, black and grey-black	95	1·00
1455	**917**	32p. gold, lemon, orange-vermilion, flesh, black and grey-black	1·10	1·25
1456	**918**	35p. gold, lemon, black, brt green and grey-black	1·25	1·25
Set of 4		....	3·50	3·50
Set of 4 *Gutter Pairs*		....	8·50	
First Day Cover		....		3·50
Presentation Pack		....	4·00	
P.H.Q. Cards (*set of* 4)		....	2·25	6·50

Special First Day of Issue Postmarks

Philatelic Bureau, Edinburgh . ...4·00
Oxford ....4·50

919 Royal Mail Coach

920 Escort of Blues and Royals

921 Lord Mayor's Coach

922 Passing St. Paul's

923 Blues and Royals Drum Horse

(Des P. Cox)

1989 (17 Oct). *Lord Mayor's Show, London. Phosphorised paper.* P 14×15.

1457	**919**	20p. gold, lemon, rose, orange, pale blue and black	70	40
		a. Horiz strip of 5. Nos. 1457/61	3·25	3·50
		ab. Imperf (horiz strip of 5. Nos. 1457/61)	£8000	
		ac. Imperf (horiz strip of 4. Nos. 1457/60)	£4750	
		ad. Imperf (horiz strip of 3. Nos. 1457/9)	£3750	
1458	**920**	20p. gold, lemon, rose, orange, pale blue and black	70	40
1459	**921**	20p. gold, lemon, rose, orange, pale blue and black	70	40
1460	**922**	20p. gold, lemon, rose, orange, pale blue and black	70	40
1461	**923**	20p. gold, lemon, rose, orange, pale blue and black	70	40
Set of 5			2·75	2·00
Gutter Strip of 10			8·00	
First Day Cover				3·50
Presentation Pack			3·00	
P.H.Q. Cards (set of 5)			3·00	6·50

Nos. 1457/61 were printed together, *se-tenant*, in horizontal strips of 5 throughout the sheet. This issue commemorates the 800th anniversary of the installation of the first Lord Mayor of London.

Nos. 1457ab/ad come from a sheet partly imperf at left. Stamps of Types **919/23**, but each with face value of 19p., were prepared but not issued. One mint *se-tenant* strip has been recorded.

Special First Day of Issue Postmarks

Philatelic Bureau, Edinburgh	4·00
London, EC4	4·50

924 14th-century Peasants from Stained-glass Window

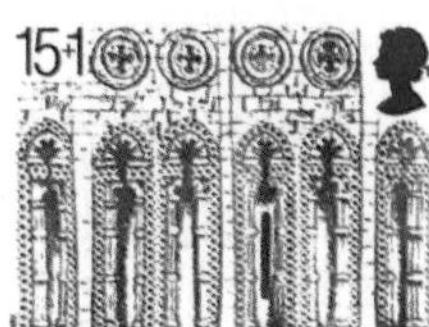

925 Arches and Roundels, West Front

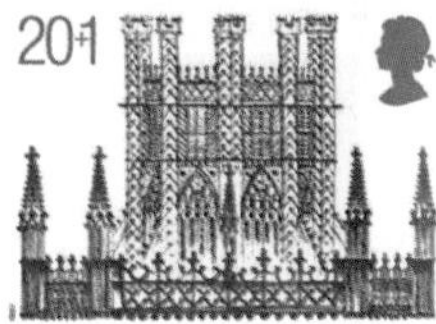

926 Octagon Tower

927 Arcade from West Transept

928 Triple Arch from West Front

(Des D. Gentleman)

1989 (14 Nov). *Christmas. 800th Anniv of Ely Cathedral. One phosphor band (15p., 15p.+1p.) or phosphorised paper (others).* P 15×14.

1462	**924**	15p. gold, silver and blue	40	15
1463	**925**	15p.+1p. gold, silver and blue	50	40
		a. Imperf (pair)	£1400	
1464	**926**	20p.+1p. gold, silver and rosine	65	80
		a. Imperf (pair)	£1400	
1465	**927**	34p.+1p. gold, silver and emerald	1·25	1·75
1466	**928**	37p.+1p. gold, silver and yellow-olive	1·40	1·90
Set of 5			3·75	4·50
Set of 5 Gutter Pairs			9·00	
First Day Cover				4·50
Presentation Pack			4·50	
P.H.Q. Cards (set of 5)			3·00	6·00

Special First Day of Issue Postmarks

Philatelic Bureau, Edinburgh ....4·00
Bethlehem, Llandeilo, Dyfed ....4·50
Ely .... 5·00

Collectors Pack 1989

1989 Nov 14 Comprises Nos. 1419/22, 1428/43 and 1453/66.
CP1466a Collectors Pack ....38·00

Post Office Yearbook

1989 (14 Nov). Comprises Nos. 1419/22, 1428/44 and 1453/66 in hardbound book with slip case, illustrated in colour .... 42·00

929 Queen Victoria and Queen Elizabeth II

(Des J. Matthews (after Wyon and Machin)

1990 (10 Jan–12 June). *150th Anniv of the Penny Black.*

(a) Photo Harrison. P 15×14.

1467	**929**	15p. brt blue (1 centre band)	80	80
		a. Imperf (pair)	£1500	
		l. Booklet pane. No. 1467×10 with horizontal edges of pane imperf (30.1.90)	10·00	
1468		15p. brt blue (1 side band at left) (30.1.90)	3·75	3·75
		Ea. Band at right (20.3.90)	3·25	3·25
		l. Booklet pane. No. 1468×2 and 1470 plus label	9·50	
1469		20p. brownish black and cream (phosphorised paper)	1·00	1·00
		a. Imperf (pair)	£1250	
		l. Booklet pane. No. 1469×5 plus label with vertical edges of pane imperf (30.1.90)	8·00	
		m. Booklet pane. No. 1469×10 with horizontal edges of pane imperf (30.1.90)	11·00	
		n. Booklet pane. No. 1469×6 with margins all round (20.3.90)	5·00	
		r. Booklet pane. No. 1469×4 with three edges of pane imperf (17.4.90)	8·00	
1470		20p. brownish black and cream (2 bands) (30.1.90)	2·75	2·75
1471		29p. dp mauve (phosphorised paper)	1·75	1·75
1472		29p. dp mauve (2 bands) (20.3.90)	9·00	9·00
1473		34p. dp bluish grey (phosphorised paper)	2·00	2·00
1474		37p. rosine (phosphorised paper)	2·25	2·25

(b) Litho Walsall. P 14 (from booklets).

1475	**929**	15p. brt blue (1 centre band) (30.1.90)	1·50	1·75
		l. Booklet pane. No. 1475×4 with three edges of pane imperf	7·00	
		m. Booklet pane. No. 1475×10 with three edges of pane imperf (12.6.90)	12·00	
1476		20p. brownish black and cream (phosphorised paper) (30.1.90)	1·60	1·75
		l. Booklet pane. No. 1476×5 plus label with vertical edges of pane imperf	10·00	
		m. Booklet pane. No. 1476×4 with three edges of pane imperf	10·00	
		n. Booklet pane. No. 1476×10 with three edges of pane imperf (12.6.90)	15·00	

(c) Litho Questa. P 15×14

1477	**929**	15p. brt blue (1 centre band) (17.4.90)	2·25	2·25
1478		20p. brownish black (phosphorised paper) (17.4.90)	2·00	2·25
Set of 5 (Nos. 1467, 1469, 1471, 1473/4)			7·00	7·00
First Day Cover (Nos. 1467, 1469, 1471, 1473/4)				7·00
Presentation Pack (Nos. 1467, 1469, 1471, 1473/4)			9·00	

Nos. 1475/6 do not exist perforated on all four sides, but come with either one or two adjacent sides imperforate.

Nos. 1468, 1468Ea, 1470, 1472 and 1475/8 were only issued in stamp booklets. Nos. 1468Ea, 1470 and 1472 occur in the *se-tenant* pane from the 1990 London Life £5 booklet. This pane is listed as No. X906m.

For illustrations showing the difference between photogravure and lithography see beneath Type **367**.

For No. 1469 in miniature sheet see No. **MS**1501.

For Type **929** redrawn with "1st" face value see No. 2133.

Special First Day of Issue Postmark

Philatelic Bureau, Edinburgh (in red) ....7·50
Windsor, Berks (Type G, see Introduction) (in red) ....8·00

930 Kitten

931 Rabbit

932 Duckling

933 Puppy

(Des T. Evans. Litho Questa)

1990 (23 Jan). *150th Anniv of Royal Society for Prevention of Cruelty to Animals. Phosphorised paper.* P 14×14½.

1479	**930**	20p. new blue, greenish yellow, brt magenta, black and silver	75	50
		a. Silver (Queen's head and face value) omitted	£275	
1480	**931**	29p. new blue, greenish yellow, brt magenta, black and silver	1·25	1·25
		a. Imperf (horiz pair)	£2500	
1481	**932**	34p. new blue, greenish yellow, brt magenta, black and silver	1·25	1·50
		a. Silver (Queen's head and face value) omitted	£550	

1482	**933**	37p. new blue, greenish yellow, brt magenta, black and silver	1·50	1·50
Set of 4			4·50	4·25
Set of 4 *Gutter Pairs*			9·50	
First Day Cover				4·25
Presentation Pack			4·50	
P.H.Q. Cards (*set of* 4)			3·00	7·50

Special First Day of Issue Postmarks

Philatelic Bureau, Edinburgh	4·00
Horsham	5·00

934 Teddy Bear

935 Dennis the Menace

936 Punch

937 Cheshire Cat

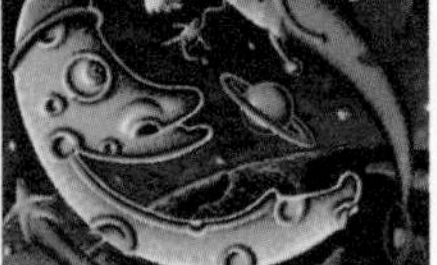

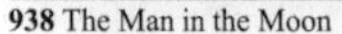

938 The Man in the Moon

939 The Laughing Policeman

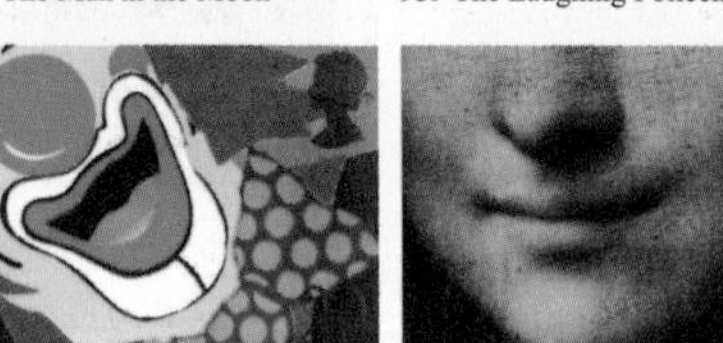

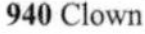

940 Clown

941 Mona Lisa

942 Queen of Hearts

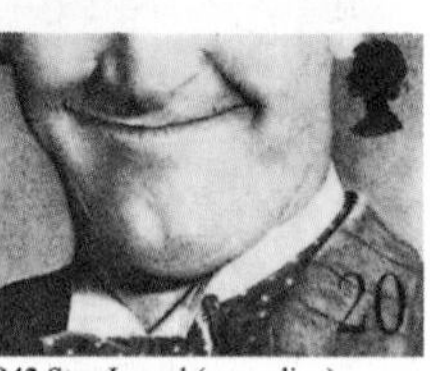

943 Stan Laurel (comedian)

(Des Michael Peters and Partners Ltd)

1990 (6 Feb). *Greetings Stamps. "Smiles". Two phosphor bands.* P 15×14.

1483	**934**	20p. gold, greenish yellow, brt rose-red, new blue and grey-black	3·50	2·50
		a. Booklet pane. Nos. 1483/92 with margins all round	30·00	
1484	**935**	20p. gold, greenish yellow, brt rose-red, new blue, dp blue and grey-black	3·50	2·50
1485	**936**	20p. gold, greenish yellow, brt rose-red, new blue, dp blue and grey-black	3·50	2·50
1486	**937**	20p. gold, greenish yellow, brt rose-red, new blue and grey-black	3·50	2·50
1487	**938**	20p. gold, greenish yellow, brt rose-red, new blue and grey-black	3·50	2·50
1488	**939**	20p. gold, greenish yellow, brt rose-red, new blue and grey-black	3·50	2·50
1489	**940**	20p. gold, greenish yellow, brt rose-red, new blue and grey-black	3·50	2·50
1490	**941**	20p. gold, greenish yellow, brt rose-red, new blue and grey-black	3·50	2·50
1491	**942**	20p. gold, greenish yellow, brt rose-red, new blue and grey-black	3·50	2·50
1492	**943**	20p. gold and grey-black	3·50	2·50
Set of 10			30·00	22·00
First Day Cover				26·00

Nos. 1483/92 were only issued in £2 booklets. The design of Nos. 1483, 1485/7, 1489 and 1492 extend onto the pane margin.

For Types **934/43** inscribed (1st), see Nos. 1550/59.

Special First Day of Issue Postmarks

Philatelic Bureau, Edinburgh	27·00
Giggleswick, North Yorkshire	28·00

20
ALEXANDRA PALACE
STAMP WORLD EXHIBITION
LONDON 1990

944 Alexandra Palace ("Stamp World London 90" Exhibition)

945 Glasgow School of Art

946 British Philatelic Bureau, Edinburgh

947 Templeton Carpet Factory, Glasgow

(Des P. Hogarth)

1990 (6–20 Mar). *Europa (Nos. 1493 and 1495) and "Glasgow 1990 European City of Culture" (Nos. 1494 and 1496). Phosphorised paper.* P 14×15.

1493	**944**	20p. silver, lemon, flesh, grey-brown, blue, grey-black and black	50	25
		a. Booklet pane. No. 1493×4 with margins all round (20 Mar)	3·50	
1494	**945**	20p. silver, greenish yellow, dull orange, blue, grey-black and black	50	25
1495	**946**	29p. silver, stone, orange, olive-sepia, grey-blue, grey-black and black	1·25	1·75
1496	**947**	37p. silver, greenish-yellow, brt emerald, salmon, olive-sepia, brt blue and black	1·50	1·75
Set of 4			3·50	3·50
Set of 4 *Gutter Pairs*			10·00	
First Day Cover				3·50
Presentation Pack			4·25	
P.H.Q. Cards (*set of* 4)			3·00	6·00

Special First Day of Issue Postmarks

Philatelic Bureau, Edinburgh .... 4·00
Glasgow .... 5·00

948 Export Achievement Award

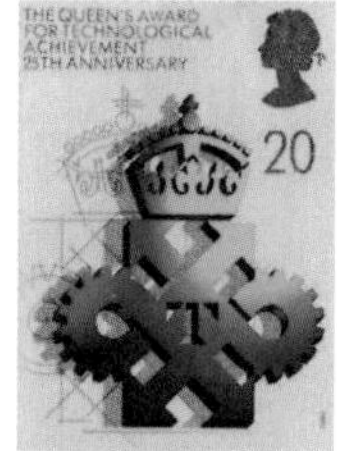

949 Technological Achievement Award

(Des S. Broom. Litho Questa)

1990 (10–20 Apr). *25th Anniv of Queen's Awards for Export and Technology.* P 14×14½.

1497	**948**	20p. new blue, greenish yellow, magenta, black and silver	70	50
		a. Horiz pair. Nos. 1497/8	1·40	1·60
1498	**949**	20p. new blue, greenish yellow, magenta, black and silver	70	50
1499	**948**	37p. new blue, greenish yellow, magenta, black and silver	1·25	1·50
		a. Horiz pair. Nos. 1499/500	3·00	3·25
1500	**949**	37p. new blue, greenish yellow, magenta, black and silver	1·25	1·50
Set of 4			3·50	3·50
Set of 2 *Gutter Strips of* 4			8·50	
First Day Cover				5·00
Presentation Pack			4·50	
P.H.Q. Cards (*set of* 4)			3·00	6·00

Nos. 1497/8 and 1499/1500 were each printed together, *se-tenant*, in horizontal pairs throughout the sheets.

Special First Day of Issue Postmarks

Philatelic Bureau, Edinburgh .... 4·00
London, SW .... 5·00

949a

(Des Sedley Place Design Ltd. Eng C. Matthews. Recess and photo Harrison)

1990 (3 May). *"Stamp World London '90" International Stamp Exhibition. Sheet 122×89 mm containing No. 1469. Phosphorised paper.* P 15×14.

MS1501 **949a** 20p. brownish black and cream (sold at £1)	5·50	5·50
a. Error. Imperf.	£6500	
b. Black (recess-printing) omitted	£15000	
c. Black (recess-printing) inverted	£8000	
First Day Cover		5·75
Souvenir Book (*Nos.* 1467, 1469, 1471, 1473/4 *and* **MS**1501)	20·00	

The premium on No. **MS**1501 was used to support the "Stamp World London '90" International Stamp Exhibition. In No. **MS**1501 only the example of the 20p. is perforated.

No. **MS**1501b shows an albino impression on the reverse. The 1d. black and Seahorse background are omitted due to one sheet becoming attached to the underside of another prior to recessprinting. No. **MS**1501c shows the recess part of the design inverted in relation to the photogravure of Type **929**.

Special First Day of Issue Postmarks

Philatelic Bureau, Edinburgh (in red) .... 6·00
City of London (in red) .... 6·00

A First Day of Issue handstamp as Type B was provided at Alexandra Palace, London N22 for this issue.

950 Cycad and Sir Joseph Banks Building

951 Stone Pine and Princess of Wales Conservatory

KEW GARDENS 1840-1990

952 Willow Tree and Pagoda

953 Cedar Tree and Palm House

(Des P. Leith)

1990 (5–20 June). *150th Anniv of Kew Gardens. Phosphorised paper.* P 14×15.

1502	**950**	20p. black, brt emerald, pale turquoise-green, lt brown and lavender	50	15
1503	**951**	29p. black, brt emerald, turquoise-green, reddish-orange and grey-black	75	1·00
1504	**952**	34p. Venetian red, brt green, cobalt, dull purple, turquoise-green and yellow-green	1·25	1·60
1505	**953**	37p. pale violet-blue, brt emerald, red-brown, steel-blue and brown-rose	1·50	1·50
Set of 4			3·50	3·75
Set of 4 *Gutter Pairs*			9·00	
First Day Cover				3·75
Presentation Pack			4·00	
P.H.Q. Cards (*set of* 4)			3·00	6·00

Special First Day of Issue Postmarks

Philatelic Bureau, Edinburgh	4·00
Kew, Richmond	5·00

954 Thomas Hardy and Clyffe Clump, Dorset

(Des J. Gibbs)

1990 (10–20 July). *150th Birth Anniv of Thomas Hardy (author). Phosphorised paper.* P 14×15.

1506	**954**	20p. vermilion, greenish yellow, pale lake-brown, dp brown, lt red-brown and black	80	75
		a. Imperf (pair)	£1700	
Gutter Pair			1·75	
First Day Cover				1·50
Presentation Pack			1·50	
P.H.Q. Card			1·00	2·25

Special First Day of Issue Postmarks

Philatelic Bureau, Edinburgh	2·00
Dorchester	2·50

955 Queen Elizabeth the Queen Mother

956 Queen Elizabeth

957 Elizabeth, Duchess of York

958 Lady Elizabeth Bowes-Lyon

(Des J. Gorham from photographs by N. Parkinson (20p.), Dorothy Wilding (29p.), B. Park (34p.), Rita Martin (37p.))

1990 (2 Aug). *90th Birthday of Queen Elizabeth the Queen Mother. Phosphorised paper.* P 14×15.

1507	**955**	20p. silver, greenish yellow, magenta, turquoise-blue and grey-black	95	25
1508	**956**	29p. silver, indigo and grey-blue	1·40	1·50
1509	**957**	34p. silver, lemon, red, new blue and grey-black	2·00	2·50
1510	**958**	37p. silver, sepia and stone	2·25	2·50
Set of 4			6·00	6·25
Set of 4 *Gutter Pairs*			15·00	
First Day Cover				6·25
Presentation Pack			7·00	
P.H.Q. Cards (*set of* 4)			5·50	8·00

For these designs with Queen's head and frame in black see Nos. 2280/3.

Special First Day of Issue Postmarks

Philatelic Bureau, Edinburgh	6·00
Westminster, SW1	7·00

1990 (7 Aug)–**92**. *Booklet stamps. As T* **913/14**, *but colours changed.*

(a) Photo Harrison. P 15×14.

1511	**913**	(2nd) dp blue (1 centre band)	1·50	1·50
		a. Booklet pane. No. 1511×10 with horiz edges of pane imperf	12·00	
1512	**914**	(1st) brt orange-red (phosphorised paper)	1·50	1·50
		a. Booklet pane. No. 1512×10 with horiz edges of pane imperf	10·00	

(b) Litho Questa. P 15×14.

1513	**913**	(2nd) dp blue (1 centre band)	2·50	2·50
1514	**914**	(1st) brt orange-red (phosphorised paper)	1·00	1·00
1514*a*		(1st) brt orange-red (2 bands) (25.2.92)	2·25	2·25

(c) Litho Walsall. P 14.

1515	**913**	(2nd) dp blue (1 centre band)	1·00	1·00
		a. Booklet pane. No. 1515×4 with horiz edges of pane imperf	3·75	
		b. Booklet pane. No. 1515×10 with horiz edges of pane imperf	8·50	
1516	**914**	(1st) brt orange-red (phosphorised paper)	1·25	1·25
		a. Booklet pane. No. 1516×4 with horiz edges of pane imperf	4·00	
		b. Booklet pane. No. 1516×10 with horiz edges of pane imperf	8·00	
		c. Perf 13	2·75	3·00
		ca. Booklet pane. No. 1516c×4 with horiz edges of pane imperf	11·00	
First Day Cover (Nos. 1515/16)				5·00

Nos. 1511/14 and 1515/16 were initially sold at 15p. (2nd) and 20p. (1st), but these prices were later increased to reflect new postage rates.

No. 1514a comes from the *se-tenant* panes in the £6 Wales, £6 Tolkien and £5.64 Beatrix Potter booklets. These panes are listed under Nos. X1012l, 1451al and W49a (Wales Regionals). No. 1514a exists with phosphor omitted (*Price* £700 *unused*).

No. 1516c was caused by the use of an incorrect perforation comb.

Nos. 1511/12 and 1515/16 do not exist with perforations on all four sides, but come with either the top or the bottom edge imperforate.

For similar stamps with elliptical perforations see Nos. 1663a/6.

Special First Day of Issue Postmarks

(For illustration see Introduction)

Philatelic Bureau, Edinburgh (Type G)	5·50
Windsor, Berks (Type G)	7·00

959 Victoria Cross

960 George Cross

961 Distinguished Service Cross and Distinguished Service Medal

962 Military Cross and Military Medal

963 Distinguished Flying Cross and Distinguished Flying Medal

(Des J. Gibbs and J. Harwood)

1990 (11 Sept). *Gallantry Awards. Phosphorised paper.* P 14×15 (vert) or 15×14 (horiz).

1517	**959**	20p. grey-black, pale stone, stone, bistre-brown and brt carmine	80	75
1518	**960**	20p. grey-black, pale stone, flesh, grey and ultramarine	80	75
1519	**961**	20p. grey-black, pale stone, flesh, pale blue and ultramarine	80	75
		a. Imperf (pair)	£1400	
1520	**962**	20p. grey-black, pale stone, ochre, pale blue, ultramarine, scarlet and violet	80	75
1521	**963**	20p. grey-black, pale stone, yellow-brown, bluish grey and purple	80	75
Set of 5			3·75	3·50
Set of 5 *Gutter Pairs*			9·25	
First Day Cover				3·75
Presentation Pack			4·00	
P.H.Q. Cards (set of 5)			3·00	8·00

Special First Day of Issue Postmarks

Philatelic Bureau, Edinburgh	4·00
Westminster, SW1	4·75

964 Armagh Observatory, Jodrell Bank Radio Telescope and La Palma Telescope

965 Newton's Moon and Tides Diagram and Early Telescopes

966 Greenwich Old Observatory and Early Astronomical Equipment

967 Stonehenge, Gyroscope and Navigation by Stars

(Des J. Fisher. Litho Questa)

1990 (16 Oct). *Astronomy. Phosphorised paper.* P 14×14½.

No.	Type	Description	Unused	Used
1522	**964**	22p. cream, grey, dull blue-green, slate-blue, blue-green, orange-red, gold & black	65	15
		a. Gold (Queen's head) omitted	£375	
1523	**965**	26p. black, yellow, dull purple, pale cream, brown-rose, new blue, greenish yellow, vermilion and gold	1·00	1·10
1524	**966**	31p. black, cream, pale cream, yellow-orange, salmon, lemon, vermilion and gold	1·25	1·40
1525	**967**	37p. black, pale buff, olive-bistre, pale cream, pale flesh, flesh, grey, rose-red and gold	1·50	1·40
Set of 4			3·75	3·75
Set of 4 Gutter Pairs			9·25	
First Day Cover				4·00
Presentation Pack			4·50	
P.H.Q. Cards (set of 4)			3·00	7·00

Special First Day of Issue Postmarks

Philatelic Bureau, Edinburgh .... 4·50
Armagh .... 5·25

968 Building a Snowman

969 Fetching the Christmas Tree

970 Carol Singing

971 Tobogganing

972 Ice-skating

(Des J. Gorham and A. Davidson)

1990 (13 Nov). *Christmas. One phosphor band (17p.) or phosphorised paper (others).* P 15×14.

No.	Type	Description	Unused	Used
1526	**968**	17p. gold, greenish yellow, rose, new blue and grey-black	50	15
		a. Booklet pane of 20	10·00	
1527	**969**	22p. gold, greenish yellow, magenta, new blue and black	70	20
		a. Imperf (horiz pair)	£450	
1528	**970**	26p. gold, olive-yellow, pale magenta, agate, new blue, dull violet-blue and black	70	1·10
1529	**971**	31p. gold, greenish yellow, brt rose-red, dull mauve, new blue, turquoise-blue and grey-black	1·25	1·50
1530	**972**	37p. gold, greenish yellow, rose, new blue and slate-green	1·25	1·50
Set of 5			4·00	4·00
Set of 5 Gutter Pairs			10·00	
First Day Cover				4·00
Presentation Pack			4·50	
P.H.Q. Cards (set of 5)			3·00	7·00

Booklet pane No. 1526a has the horizontal edges of the pane imperforate.

Special First Day of Issue Postmarks

Philatelic Bureau, Edinburgh .... 4·50
Bethlehem, Llandeilo, Dyfed .... 5·00

Collectors Pack 1990

1990 (13 Nov). Comprises Nos. 1479/82, 1493/1510 and 1517/30.

CP1530a Collectors Pack .... 40·00

Post Office Yearbook

1990 (13 Nov). Comprises Nos. 1479/82, 1493/1500, 1502/10, 1517/30 in hardbound book with slip case, illustrated in colour

YB1530a Yearbook .... 45·00

973 "King Charles Spaniel"

974 "A Pointer"

975 "Two Hounds in a Landscape"

976 "A Rough Dog"

977 "Fino and Tiny"

(Des Carroll, Dempsey and Thirkell Ltd)

1991 (8 Jan). *Dogs. Paintings by George Stubbs. Phosphorised paper.* P 14×14½.

1531	**973**	22p. gold, greenish yellow, magenta, new blue, black and drab	50	15
		a. Imperf (pair)	£950	
1532	**974**	26p. gold, greenish yellow, magenta, new blue, black and drab	75	1·25
1533	**975**	31p. gold, greenish yellow, magenta, new blue, black and drab	1·00	1·25
		a. Imperf (pair)	£1000	
1534	**976**	33p. gold, greenish yellow, magenta, new blue, black and drab	1·25	1·25
1535	**977**	37p. gold, greenish yellow, magenta, new blue, black and drab	1·25	1·25
Set of 5			4·50	4·50
Set of 5 Gutter Pairs			11·00	
First Day Cover				5·00
Presentation Pack			5·00	
P.H.Q. Cards (*set of* 5)			3·50	7·00

Special First Day of Issue Postmarks

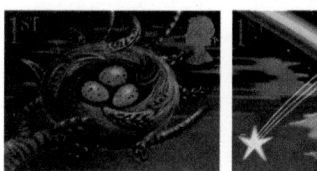

Philatelic Bureau, Edinburgh .... 5·50
Birmingham .... 5·50

978 Thrush's Nest

979 Shooting Star and Rainbow

980 Magpies and Charm Bracelet

981 Black Cat

982 Common Kingfisher with Key

983 Mallard and Frog

984 Four-leaf Clover in Boot and Match Box

985 Pot of Gold at End of Rainbow

986 Heart-shaped Butterflies

987 Wishing Well and Sixpence

(Des T. Meeuwissen)

1991 (5 Feb). *Greetings Stamps. "Good Luck". Two phosphor bands.* P 15×14.

1536	**978**	(1st) silver, greenish yellow, magenta, new blue, olive-brown and black	1·75	1·90
		a. Booklet pane. Nos. 1536/45 plus 12 half stamp-size labels with margins on 3 sides	15·00	
1537	**979**	(1st) silver, greenish yellow, magenta, new blue, olive-brown and black	1·75	1·90
1538	**980**	(1st) silver, greenish yellow, magenta, new blue, olive-brown and black	1·75	1·90
		a. Imperf (pair)	£950	
1539	**981**	(1st) silver, greenish yellow, magenta, new blue, olive-brown and black	1·75	1·90
1540	**982**	(1st) silver, greenish yellow, magenta, new blue, olive-brown and black	1·75	1·90
1541	**983**	(1st) silver, greenish yellow, magenta, new blue, olive-brown and black	1·75	1·90
1542	**984**	(1st) silver, greenish yellow, magenta, new blue, olive-brown and black	1·75	1·90
1543	**985**	(1st) silver, greenish yellow, magenta, new blue, olive-brown and black	1·75	1·90
1544	**986**	(1st) silver, greenish yellow, magenta, new blue, olive-brown and black	1·75	1·90
1545	**987**	(1st) silver, greenish yellow, magenta, new blue, olive-brown and black	1·75	1·90
Set of 10			15·00	17·00
First Day Cover				19·00

Nos. 1536/45 were only issued in £2.20 booklets (sold at £2.40 from 16 September 1991).

The backgrounds of the stamps form a composite design.

Special First Day of Issue Postmarks

Philatelic Bureau, Edinburgh ....19·00
Greetwell, Lincs .... 19·00

988 Michael Faraday (inventor of electric motor) (Birth Bicentenary)

989 Charles Babbage (computer science pioneer) (Birth Bicentenary)

990 Radar Sweep of East Anglia (50th Anniv of Operational Radar Network)

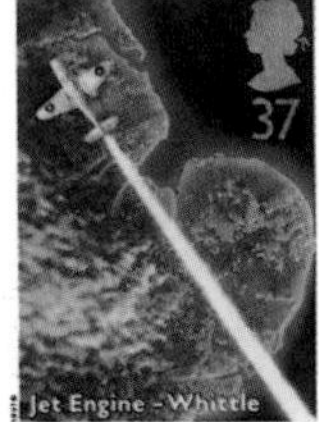

991 Gloster Whittle E28/39 Airplane over East Anglia (50th Anniv of First Flight of Sir Frank Whittle's Jet Engine)

(Des P. Till (Nos. 1546/7), J. Harwood (Nos. 1548/9))

1991 (5 Mar). *Scientific Achievements. Phosphorised paper.* P 14×15.

1546	**988**	22p. silver, olive-brown, greenish yellow, magenta, slate-blue, grey and black.	60	50
		a. Imperf (pair)	£400	
1547	**989**	22p. silver, chrome-yellow, red, grey-black, brownish grey and sepia	60	50
1548	**990**	31p. silver, dp turquoise-green, violet-blue, steel-blue and dp dull blue	1·20	1·50
1549	**991**	37p. silver, olive-bistre, rose-red, turquoise-blue, new blue and grey-black	1·35	1·75
Set of 4			3·50	4·00
Set of 4 *Gutter Pairs*			8·50	
First Day Cover				4·00
Presentation Pack			4·25	
P.H.Q. Cards (*set of* 4)			3·50	7·00

Special First Day of Issue Postmarks

Philatelic Bureau, Edinburgh ....4·00
South Kensington, London, SW7 .... 4·75

992 Teddy Bear

(Des J.-M. Folon)

1991 (26 Mar). *Greeting Stamps. "Smiles". As Nos. 1483/92, but inscribed "1st" as T* **992**. *Two phosphor bands.* P 15×14.

1550	**992**	(1st) gold, greenish yellow, brt rose-red, new blue and grey-black	1·50	1·50
		a. Booklet pane. Nos. 1550/9 plus 12 half stamp-size labels with margins on 3 sides	12·00	
1551	**935**	(1st) gold, greenish yellow, brt rose-red, new blue, dp blue and grey-black	1·50	1·50
1552	**936**	(1st) gold, greenish yellow, brt rose-red, new blue, dp blue and grey-black	1·50	1·50
1553	**937**	(1st) gold, greenish yellow, bright rose-red, new blue and grey-black	1·50	1·50
1554	**938**	(1st) gold, greenish yellow, brt rose-red, new blue and grey-black	1·50	1·50
1555	**939**	(1st) gold, greenish yellow, brt rose-red, new blue and grey-black	1·50	1·50
1556	**940**	(1st) gold, greenish yellow, brt rose-red, new blue and grey-black	1·50	1·50
1557	**941**	(1st) gold, greenish yellow, brt rose-red, new blue and grey-black	1·50	1·50
1558	**942**	(1st) gold, greenish yellow, brt rose-red, new blue and grey-black	1·50	1·50
1559	**943**	(1st) gold and grey-black	1·50	1·50
Set of 10			12·00	13·00
First Day Cover				13·00

Nos. 1550/9 were originally issued in £2.20 booklets (sold at £2.40 from 16 September 1991 and at £2.50 from 1 November 1993). The designs of Nos. 1550, 1552/4, 1556 and 1559 extend onto the pane margin.

The stamps were re-issued in sheets of 10, printed in photogravure by Questa, each with *se-tenant* label on 22 May 2000 in connection with "customised" stamps available at "Stamp Show 2000". The labels show either a pattern of ribbons at £2.95, or a personal photograph for £5.95.

A similar sheet, but printed in lithography by Questa instead of in photogravure, appeared on 3 July 2001. Stamps from this sheet were perforated 14½×14 instead of the previous 15×14. Sheets showing greetings on the labels were available from the Bureau or Postshops at £2.95 each or with personal photographs at £12.95 for two. Similar sheets each containing ten examples of Nos. 1550/1 and 1555/7 were only available with personal photograph. From 29 October 2001 sheets with personal photographs could also be purchased, on an experimental basis, from photo-booths situated at six post offices.

On 1 October 2002 three further sheets appeared printed in lithography by Questa. One contained Nos. 1550/1 each ×10 with greetings labels and cost £5.95. Both designs were also available in sheets of 20 with personal photographs at £14.95 a sheet.

Special First Day of Issue Postmarks

Philatelic Bureau, Edinburgh ....14·00
Laugherton, Lincs ....14·00

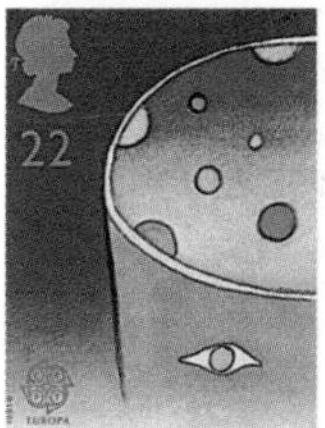

993 Man Looking at Space

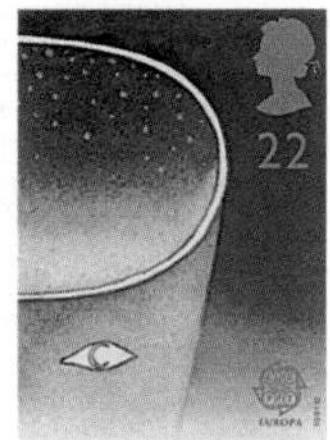

994 Man Looking at Space

995 Space Looking at Man

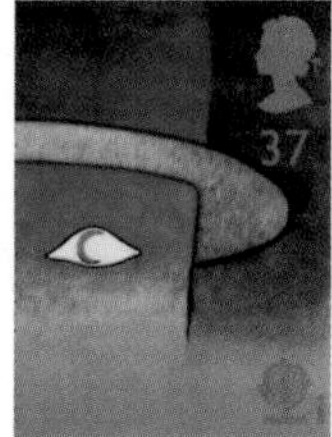

996 Space Looking at Man

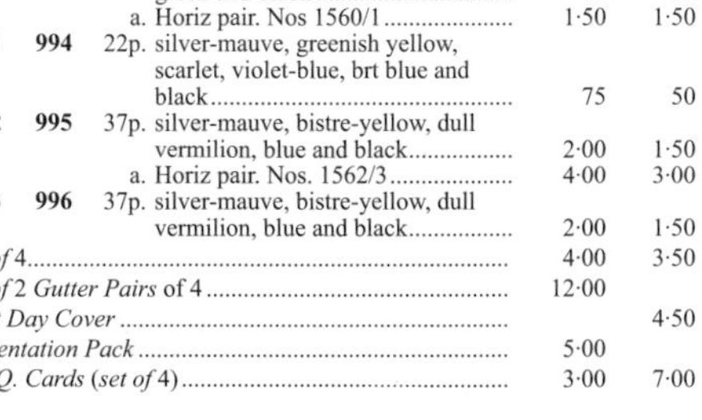

1991 (23 Apr). *Europa. Europe in space. Phosphorised paper.* P 14½×14.

1560	**993**	22p. silver-mauve, greenish yellow, scarlet, violet-blue, brt blue, brt green and black	75	50
		a. Horiz pair. Nos 1560/1	1·50	1·50
1561	**994**	22p. silver-mauve, greenish yellow, scarlet, violet-blue, brt blue and black	75	50
1562	**995**	37p. silver-mauve, bistre-yellow, dull vermilion, blue and black	2·00	1·50
		a. Horiz pair. Nos. 1562/3	4·00	3·00
1563	**996**	37p. silver-mauve, bistre-yellow, dull vermilion, blue and black	2·00	1·50
Set of 4			4·00	3·50
Set of 2 *Gutter Pairs* of 4			12·00	
First Day Cover				4·50
Presentation Pack			5·00	
P.H.Q. Cards (*set of* 4)			3·00	7·00

Special First Day of Issue Postmarks

Philatelic Bureau, Edinburgh ....4·25
Cambridge ....5·50

997 Fencing

998 Hurdling

999 Diving

1000 Rugby

(Des Huntley Muir Partners)

1991 (11 June). *World Student Games, Sheffield (Nos. 1564/6) and World Cup Rugby Championship, London (No. 1567). Phosphorised paper.* P 14½×14.

1564	**997**	22p. black, greenish yellow, vermilion, brt orange, ultramarine and grey	60	20
1565	**998**	26p. pale blue, greenish yellow, red, brt blue and black	1·00	1·00
1566	**999**	31p. brt blue, bistre-yellow, rose, vermilion, new blue and black	1·25	1·25
1567	**1000**	37p. yellow-orange, greenish yellow, rose, brt blue, emerald and black	1·50	1·50
Set of 4			3·50	3·50
Set of 4 *Gutter Pairs*			9·00	
First Day Cover				4·00
Presentation Pack			4·50	
P.H.Q. Cards (*set of* 4)			3·00	7·00

Special First Day of Issue Postmarks

Philatelic Bureau, Edinburgh ....4·25
Sheffield ....4·75

1001 "Silver Jubilee"

1002 "Mme Alfred Carrière"

1003 *Rosa moyesii*

1004 "Harvest Fayre"

1005 "Mutabilis"

(Des Yvonne Skargon. Litho Questa)

1991 (16 July). *Ninth World Congress of Roses, Belfast. Phosphorised paper.* P 14½×14.

1568	**1001**	22p. new blue, greenish yellow, magenta, black and silver	50	20
		a. Silver (Queen's head) omitted	£1250	
		Eb. Black printing double	—	£3000
1569	**1002**	26p. new blue, greenish yellow, magenta, black and silver	75	1·25
1570	**1003**	31p. new blue, greenish yellow, magenta, black and silver	1·00	1·25
1571	**1004**	33p. new blue, greenish yellow, magenta, black and silver	1·25	1·50
1572	**1005**	37p. new blue, greenish yellow, magenta, black and silver	1·50	1·50
Set of 5			4·50	5·00
Set of 5 Gutter Pairs			11·00	
First Day Cover				5·00
Presentation Pack			5·00	
P.H.Q. Cards (set of 5)			3·00	9·00

Special First Day of Issue Postmarks

Philatelic Bureau, Edinburgh .... 6·00
Belfast .... 7·00

1006 Iguanodon

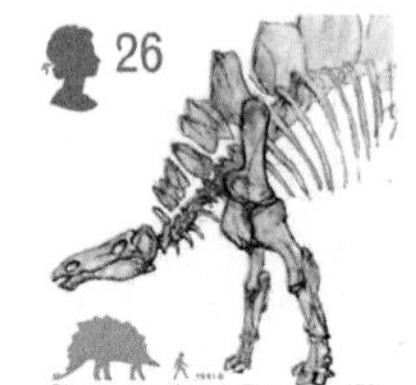

1007 Stegosaurus

1008 Tyrannosaurus

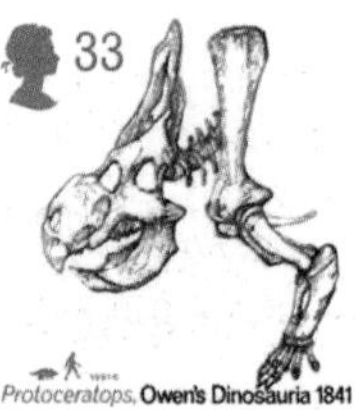

1009 Protoceratops

1010 Triceratops

(Des B. Kneale)

1991 (20 Aug). *150th Anniversary of Dinosaurs' Identification by Owen. Phosphorised paper.* P 14½×14.

1573	**1006**	22p. grey, pale blue, magenta, brt blue, dull violet and grey-black	60	20
		a. Imperf (pair)	£1700	
1574	**1007**	26p. grey, greenish yellow, pale emerald, brt blue-green, pale brt blue, grey-black and black	1·10	1·25
1575	**1008**	31p. grey, lt blue, magenta, brt blue, pale blue, brown and grey-black	1·25	1·25
1576	**1009**	33p. grey, dull rose, pale brt blue, brt rose-red, yellow-orange, grey-black and black	1·50	1·50
1577	**1010**	37p. grey, greenish yellow, turquoise-blue, dull violet, yellow-brown and black	1·60	1·50
Set of 5			5·75	5·00
Set of 5 Gutter Pairs			12·00	
First Day Cover				5·50
Presentation Pack			6·00	
P.H.Q. Cards (set of 5)			3·00	9·00

Special First Day of Issue Postmarks

Philatelic Bureau, Edinburgh .... 6·00
Plymouth .... 7·00

1011 Map of 1816

1012 Map of 1906

1013 Map of 1959

1014 Map of 1991

(Des H. Brown. Recess and litho Harrison (24p.), litho Harrison (28p.), Questa (33p., 39p.))

1991 (17 Sept). *Bicentenary of Ordnance Survey. Maps of Hamstreet, Kent. Phosphorised paper.* P 14½×14.

1578	**1011**	24p. black, magenta and cream	60	20
		Ea. Black (litho) printing treble and magenta printing double	£1200	
		Eb. Black (litho) and magenta printing double	£1750	
		Ec. Black (litho) printing double	£2000	
1579	**1012**	28p. black, brt yellow-green, new blue, reddish orange, magenta, olive-sepia and cream	1·00	95
1580	**1013**	33p. dull blue-green, orange-brown, magenta, olive-grey, greenish yellow, vermilion, greenish grey, pale blue, blue, dull orange, apple green and black	1·25	1·40
1581	**1014**	39p. black, magenta, greenish yellow and new blue	1·50	1·40
Set of 4			3·50	3·50
Set of 4 Gutter Pairs			10·00	
First Day Cover				4·25
Presentation Pack			4·50	
P.H.Q. Cards (set of 4)			3·00	7·00

Mint examples of Type **1012** exist with a face value of 26p. (*Price* £4250).

Special First Day of Issue Postmarks

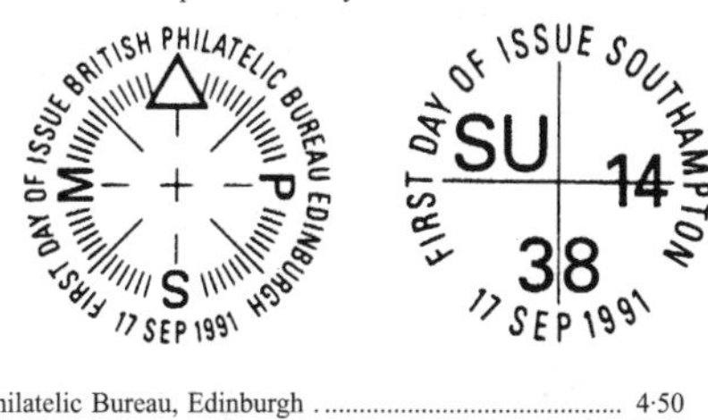

Philatelic Bureau, Edinburgh .... 4·50
Southampton .... 5·50

1015 Adoration of the Magi

1016 Mary and Jesus in Stable

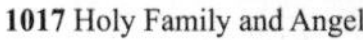

1017 Holy Family and Angel

1018 The Annunciation

1019 The Flight into Egypt

(Des D. Driver)

1991 (12 Nov). *Christmas. Illuminated Letters from "Acts of Mary and Jesus" Manuscript in Bodleian Library, Oxford. One phosphor band (18p.) or phosphorised paper (others).* P 15×14.

1582	**1015**	18p. steel-blue, greenish yellow, rose-red, orange-red, black and gold	75	10
		a. Imperf (pair)	£2200	
		b. Booklet pane of 20	8·25	
1583	**1016**	24p. brt rose-red, greenish yellow, vermilion, slate-blue, yellow-green, grey-black and gold	90	10
1584	**1017**	28p. reddish brown, bistre-yellow, orange-vermilion, orange-red, dp dull blue, grey-black & gold	95	1·25
1585	**1018**	33p. green, greenish yellow, red, orange-red, blue, grey and gold	1·10	1·50
1586	**1019**	39p. orange-red, greenish yellow, orange-vermilion, dp dull blue, olive-sepia, black and gold	1·25	1·75
Set of 5			4·50	4·50
Set of 5 Gutter Pairs			11·00	
First Day Cover				4·50
Presentation Pack			4·50	
P.H.Q. Cards (set of 5)			3·00	7·50

Booklet pane No. 1582b has margins at left, top and bottom.

Special First Day of Issue Postmarks

Philatelic Bureau, Edinburgh .... 5·50
Bethlehem, Landeilo, Dyfed .... 5·50

Collectors Pack 1991

1991 (12 Nov). Comprises Nos. 1531/5, 1546/9 and 1560/86.
CP1586*a* Collectors Pack .... 40·00

Post Office Yearbook

1991 (13 Nov). Comprises Nos. 1531/5, 1546/9 and 1560/86 in hardbound book with slip case, illustrated in colour. .... 45·00

1020 Fallow Deer in Scottish Forest

1021 Hare on North Yorkshire Moors

1022 Fox in the Fens

1023 Redwing and Home Counties Village

1024 Welsh Mountain Sheep in Snowdonia

(Des J. Gorham and K. Bowen)

1992 (14 Jan). *The Four Seasons. Wintertime. One phosphor band (18p.) or phosphorised paper (others).* P 15×14.

1587	**1020**	18p. silver, greenish yellow, grey, dull rose, new blue and black	55	25
1588	**1021**	24p. silver, lemon, rose, blue and grey-black	75	25
		a. Imperf (pair)	£425	
1589	**1022**	28p. silver, greenish yellow, bright rose, steel-blue and grey-black	1·00	1·25
1590	**1023**	33p. silver, greenish yellow, brt orange, brt purple, greenish blue and grey	1·25	1·50
1591	**1024**	39p. silver, yellow, yellow-orange, grey, vermilion, new blue and black	1·40	1·75
		a. Booklet pane. No. 1591×4 with margins all round (25 Feb)	4·75	
Set of 5			4·50	4·50
Set of 5 *Gutter Pairs*			11·00	
First Day Cover				4·50
Presentation Pack			4·50	
P.H.Q. Cards (*set of* 5)			3·00	8·00

Booklet pane No. 1591a comes from the £6 "Cymru-Wales" booklet.

Special First Day of Issue Postmarks

Philatelic Bureau, Edinburgh .... 4·75
Brecon .... 5·50

1025 Flower Spray

1026 Double Locket

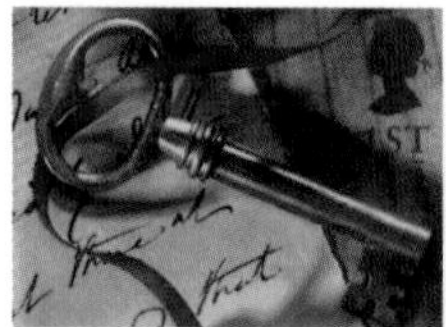

1027 Key

1028 Model Car and Cigarette Cards

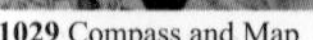

1029 Compass and Map

1030 Pocket Watch

1031 1854 1d. Red Stamp and Pen

1032 Pearl Necklace and Pen

1033 Marbles

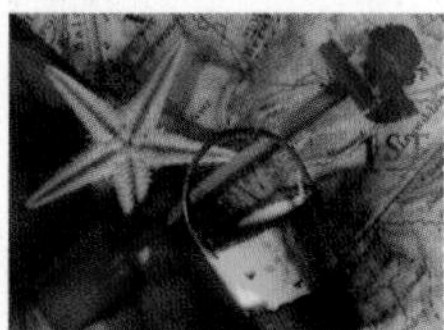

1034 Bucket, Spade and Starfish

(Des Trickett and Webb Ltd)

1992 (28 Jan). *Greetings Stamps. "Memories". Two phosphor bands.* P 15×14.

1592	**1025**	(1st) gold, greenish yellow, magenta, ochre, lt blue and grey-black	1·50	1·50
		a. Booklet pane. Nos. 1592/1601 plus 12 half stamp-size labels with margins on 3 sides	13·00	
1593	**1026**	(1st) gold, greenish yellow, magenta, ochre, lt blue and grey-black	1·50	1·50
1594	**1027**	(1st) gold, greenish yellow, magenta, ochre, lt blue and grey-black	1·50	1·50
1595	**1028**	(1st) gold, greenish yellow, magenta, ochre, lt blue and grey-black	1·50	1·50
1596	**1029**	(1st) gold, greenish yellow, magenta, ochre, lt blue and grey-black	1·50	1·50
1597	**1030**	(1st) gold, greenish yellow, magenta, ochre, lt blue and grey-black	1·50	1·50
1598	**1031**	(1st) gold, greenish yellow, magenta, ochre, lt blue and grey-black	1·50	1·50
1599	**1032**	(1st) gold, greenish yellow, magenta, ochre, lt blue and grey-black	1·50	1·50
1600	**1033**	(1st) gold, greenish yellow, magenta, ochre, lt blue and grey-black	1·50	1·50
1601	**1034**	(1st) gold, greenish yellow, magenta, ochre, lt blue and grey-black	1·50	1·50
Set of 10			13·00	13·00
First Day Cover				13·00
Presentation Pack			17·00	

Nos. 1592/1601 were only issued in £2.40 booklets (sold at £2.50 from 1 November 1993 and at £2.60 from 8 July 1996).

The backgrounds of the stamps form a composite design.

Special First Day of Issue Postmarks

Philatelic Bureau, Edinburgh .... 13·50
Whimsey, Gloucestershire .... 14·00

1035 Queen Elizabeth in Coronation Robes and Parliamentary Emblem

1036 Queen Elizabeth in Garter Robes and Archiepiscopal Arms

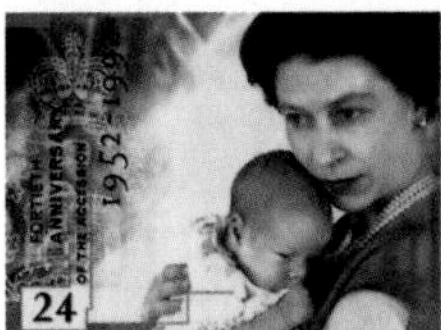

1037 Queen Elizabeth with Baby Prince Andrew and Royal Arms

1038 Queen Elizabeth at Trooping the Colour and Service Emblems

1039 Queen Elizabeth and Commonwealth Emblem

(Des Why Not Associates. Litho Questa)

1992 (6 Feb). *40th Anniv of Accession. Two phosphor bands.* P 14½×14.

1602	**1035**	24p. new blue, greenish yellow, magenta, black, silver and gold	1·10	1·10
		a. Horiz strip of 5. Nos. 1602/6	6·00	7·00
1603	**1036**	24p. new blue, greenish yellow, magenta, black, silver and gold	1·10	1·10
1604	**1037**	24p. new blue, greenish yellow, magenta, black and silver	1·10	1·10
1605	**1038**	24p. new blue, greenish yellow, magenta, black, silver and gold	1·10	1·10
1606	**1039**	24p. new blue, greenish yellow, magenta, black, silver and gold	1·10	1·10
Set of 5			6·00	5·00
Gutter Block of 10			15·00	
First Day Cover				7·00
Presentation Pack			7·00	
P.H.Q. Cards (*set of* 5)			3·00	7·50

Nos. 1602/6 were printed together, *se-tenant*, in horizontal strips of five throughout the sheet.

Special First Day of Issue Postmarks

Philatelic Bureau, Edinburgh ....7·50
Buckingham Palace, London SW1 . ....7·50

1040 Tennyson in 1888 and "The Beguiling of Merlin" (Sir Edward Burne-Jones)

1041 Tennyson in 1856 and "April Love" (Arthur Hughes)

1042 Tennyson in 1864 and "I am Sick of the Shadows" (John Waterhouse)

1043 Tennyson as a Young Man and "Mariana" (Dante Gabriel Rossetti)

(Des Irene von Treskow)

1992 (10 Mar). *Death Centenary of Alfred, Lord Tennyson (poet). Phosphorised paper.* P 14½×14.

1607	**1040**	24p. gold, greenish yellow, magenta, new blue and black	60	20
1608	**1041**	28p. gold, greenish yellow, magenta, new blue and black	85	85
1609	**1042**	33p. gold, greenish yellow, magenta, new blue, bistre and black	1·40	1·60
1610	**1043**	39p. gold, greenish yellow, magenta, new blue, bistre and black	1·50	1·60
Set of 4			4·00	3·75
Set of 4 *Gutter Pairs*			10·00	
First Day Cover				4·25
Presentation Pack			4·50	
P.H.Q. Cards (*Set of* 4)			3·00	7·00

Special First Day of Issue Postmarks

Philatelic Bureau, Edinburgh ....4·50
Isle of Wight... ....4·50

1044 Carrickfergus Castle

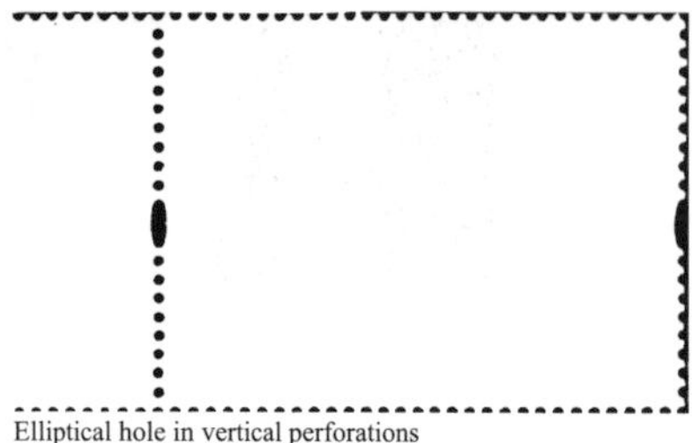
Elliptical hole in vertical perforations

CASTLE
Harrison Plates (Nos. 1611/14)

CASTLE
Enschedé Plates (Nos. 1993/6)

(Des from photos by Prince Andrew, Duke of York. Eng C. Matthews. Recess Harrison)

1992 (24 Mar)–**95**. *Designs as Nos. 1410/13, but showing Queen's head in silhouette as T* **1044**. P 15×14 (with one elliptical hole on each vertical side).

1611	**1044**	£1 bottle green and gold†	5·50	1·00
1612	**880**	£1.50 maroon and gold†	5·50	1·00
1613	**881**	£2 indigo and gold†	7·50	1·00
1613*a*	**1044**	£3 reddish violet and gold† (22.8.95)	18·50	3·00
1614	**882**	£5 dp brown and gold†	17·00	3·00
		a. Gold† (Queen's head) omitted	£400	
Set of 5			48·00	8·00
Set of 5 *Gutter Pairs*			98·00	
First Day Cover (*Nos*. 1611/13, 1614)				35·00
First Day Cover (*No*. 1613a)				10·00
Presentation Pack (*P.O. Pack No*. 27) (*Nos*. 1611/13, 1614)			38·00	
Presentation Pack (*P.O. Pack No*. 33) (*No*. 1613a)			30·00	
P.H.Q. Cards†† (*Nos*. 1611/13, 1614)			12·00	
P.H.Q. Cards (*No*. 1613a)			6·00	22·00

†The Queen's head on these stamps is printed in optically variable ink which changes colour from gold to green when viewed from different angles.

††The P.H.Q. cards for this issue did not appear until 16 February 1993. They do not exist used on the first day of issue of Nos. 1611/13 and 1614.

The £1.50 (5 March 1996), £2 (2 May 1996), £3 (February 1997) and £5 (17 September 1996) subsequently appeared on PVA (white gum) instead of the tinted PVAD previously used.

See also Nos. 1993/6.

Special First Day of Issue Postmarks

(for illustrations see Introduction)

Philatelic Bureau, Edinburgh (Type H) (£1, £1.50, £2, £5) ......35·00
Windsor, Berkshire (Type I) (£1, £1.50, £2, £5) ....35·00
Philatelic Bureau, Edinburgh (Type H) (£3) ....12·00
Carrickfergus, Antrim (as Type I) (£3) ....15·00

1045 British Olympic Association Logo (Olympic Games, Barcelona)

1046 British Paralympic Association Symbol (Paralympics '92, Barcelona)

1047 *Santa Maria* (500th Anniv of Discovery of America by Columbus)

1048 *Kaisei* (Japanese cadet brigantine) (Grand Regatta Columbus, 1992)

1049 British Pavilion, "EXPO '92", Seville

(Des K. Bassford (Nos. 1615/16, 1619), K. Bassford and S. Paine. Eng C. Matthews (Nos. 1617/18). Litho Questa (Nos. 1615/16, 1619) or recess and litho Harrison (Nos. 1617/18))

1992 (7 Apr). *Europa. International Events. Phosphorised paper.* P 14×14½.

1615	**1045**	24p. new blue, lemon, magenta & black..	1·00	75
		a. Horiz pair. Nos. 1615/16	2·25	1·75
1616	**1046**	24p. new blue, lemon, magenta & black..	1·00	75
1617	**1047**	24p. black, grey, carmine, cream & gold.	1·00	75
		a. Cream omitted		£500
1618	**1048**	39p. black, grey, carmine, cream & gold.	1·40	1·50
1619	**1049**	39p. new blue, lemon, magenta & black..	1·40	1·50
Set of 5			5·00	4·50
Set of 3 *Gutter Pairs and a Gutter Strip of* 4			13·00	
First Day Cover				5·00
Presentation Pack			5·25	
PHQ Cards (*set of* 5)			3·00	7·00

Nos. 1615/16 were printed together, *se-tenant*, throughout the sheet.

Special First Day of Issue Postmarks

Philatelic Bureau, Edinburgh ....5·50
Liverpool..5·50

1050 Pikeman

1051 Drummer

1052 Musketeer

1053 Standard Bearer

(Des J. Sancha)

1992 (16 June). *350th Anniv of the Civil War. Phosphorised paper.* P 14½×14.

1620	**1050**	24p. black, stone, bistre, scarlet, indigo, grey-green and yellow-ochre		60	20
		a. Imperf (pair)		£275	
1621	**1051**	28p. black, yellow-ochre, ochre, rose-pink, blue, dull yellow-green and slate-lilac		85	85
1622	**1052**	33p. black, ochre, pale orange, lemon, reddish orange, new blue and olive-green		1·40	1·50
1623	**1053**	39p. black, yellow-ochre, yellow, greenish yellow, vermilion, indigo and orange-brown		1·50	1·75
Set of 4				4·00	4·00
Set of 4 Gutter Pairs				10·50	
First Day Cover					4·00
Presentation Pack				4·50	
P.H.Q. Cards (set of 4)				3·00	7·00

Special First Day of Issue Postmarks

Philatelic Bureau, Edinburgh ....4·50
Banbury, Oxfordshire ....4·50

1058 *Iolanthe*

(Des Lynda Gray)

1992 (21 July). *150th Birth Anniv of Sir Arthur Sullivan (composer). Gilbert and Sullivan Operas. One phosphor band (18p.) or phosphorised paper (others).* P 14½×14.

1624	**1054**	18p. bluish violet, bistre-yellow, scarlet, stone, blue and grey-black	50	20
1625	**1055**	24p. purple-brown, lemon, scarlet, stone, blue, olive-bistre and black	80	20
		a. Imperf (pair)	£275	
1626	**1056**	28p. rose-red, lemon, stone, new blue, bluish violet, brt emerald and black	95	1·00
1627	**1057**	33p. blue-green, orange-yellow, scarlet, olive-bistre, blue, brown-purple and black	1·50	1·60
1628	**1058**	39p. dp blue, lemon, scarlet, stone, lavender, olive-bistre and lake-brown	1·60	1·60
Set of 5			4·50	4·25
Set of 5 Gutter Pairs			10·50	
First Day Cover				4·50
Presentation Pack			4·50	
P.H.Q. Cards (set of 5)			3·00	6·25

Special First Day of Issue Postmarks

Philatelic Bureau, Edinburgh ....5·00
Birmingham ....5·25

1054 *The Yeomen of the Guard*

1055 *The Gondoliers*

1059 "Acid Rain Kills"

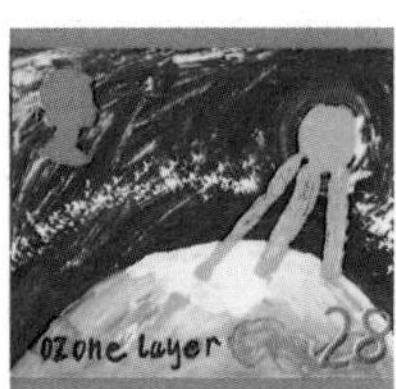

1060 "Ozone Layer"

1056 *The Mikado*

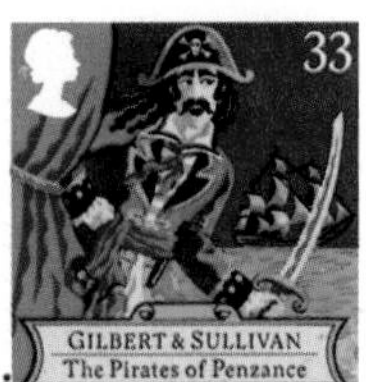

1057 *The Pirates of Penzance*

1061 "Greenhouse Effect"

1062 "Bird of Hope"

(Des Christopher Hall (24p.), Lewis Fowler (28p.), Sarah Warren (33p.), Alice Newton-Mold (39p.). Adapted Trickett and Webb Ltd)

1992 (15 Sept). *Protection of the Environment. Children's Paintings. Phosphorised paper.* P 14×14½.

1629	**1059**	24p.	emerald, greenish yellow, pale olive-yellow, brt carmine and black	70	25
1630	**1060**	28p.	vermilion, lemon, brt blue, new blue, brt green, ultramarine and black	1·10	1·25
1631	**1061**	33p.	greenish blue, greenish yellow, brt rose-red, brt green, emerald, blue and black	1·25	1·50
1632	**1062**	39p.	emerald, greenish yellow, brt magenta, brt orange, brt blue and black	1·40	1·50
Set of 4				4·00	3·75
Set of 4 *Gutter Pairs*				10·00	
First Day Cover					4·00
Presentation Pack				4·50	
P.H.Q. Cards (*set of* 4)				3·00	6·25

Special First Day of Issue Postmarks

Philatelic Bureau, Edinburgh (in green) ....4·50
Torridon (in green) ....5·00

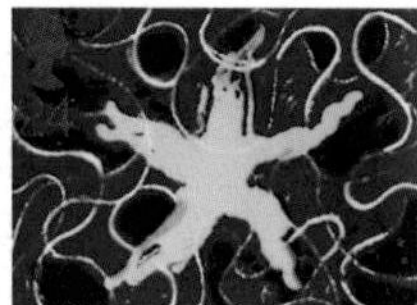

1063 European Star

(Des D. Hockney)

1992 (13 Oct). *Single European Market. Phosphorised paper.* P 15×14.

1633	**1063**	24p.	gold, greenish yellow, brt magenta, dull ultramarine and black	1·00	1·00
Gutter Pair				2·25	
First Day Cover					1·50
Presentation Pack				1·50	
P.H.Q. Card				1·50	4·00

Special First Day of Issue Postmarks

Philatelic Bureau, Edinburgh ....1·75
Westminster ....2·50

1064 "Angel Gabriel", St. James's, Pangbourne

1065 "Madonna and Child", St. Mary's, Bibury

1066 "King with Gold", Our Lady and St. Peter, Leatherhead

1067 "Shepherds", All Saints, Porthcawl

1068 "Kings with Frankincense and Myrrh", Our Lady and St. Peter, Leatherhead

(Des Carroll, Dempsey and Thirkell Ltd from windows by Karl Parsons (18, 24, 33p.) and Paul Woodroffe (28p. 39p.))

1992 (10 Nov). *Christmas. Stained Glass Windows. One centre band (18p.) or phosphorised paper (others).* P 15×14.

1634	**1064**	18p.	black, greenish yellow, mauve, ultramarine, brt emerald and gold	50	15
			a. Booklet pane of 20	7·50	
1635	**1065**	24p.	black, greenish yellow, brt purple, ultramarine, new blue, brt greenish yellow and gold	75	15
1636	**1066**	28p.	black, lemon, rosine, ultramarine, reddish lilac, red-orange and gold	1·00	1·10
1637	**1067**	33p.	brt ultramarine, greenish yellow, rosine, brown, yellow-orange, black and gold	1·25	1·50
1638	**1068**	39p.	black, lemon, rosine, brt blue, dp violet, yellow-orange and gold	1·25	1·50
Set of 5				4·25	4·25
Set of 5 *Gutter Pairs*				10·00	
First Day Cover					4·50
Presentation Pack				4·50	
P.H.Q. Cards (*set of* 5)				3·00	7·50

Booklet pane No. 1634a comes from a special £3 Christmas booklet and has margins at left, top and bottom.

Special First Day of Issue Postmarks

Philatelic Bureau, Edinburgh ....4·75
Bethlehem, Llandeilo, Dyfed ....5·00
Pangbourne ....5·50

Collectors Pack 1992

1992 (10 Nov). Comprises Nos. 1587/91, 1602/10 and 1615/38.
CP1638a Collectors Pack ....45·00

Post Office Yearbook

1992 (11 Nov). Comprises Nos. 1587/91, 1602/10 and 1615/38 in hardbound book with slip case, illustrated in colour ....55·00

1069 Mute Swan Cob and St. Catherine's Chapel, Abbotsbury

1070 Cygnet and Decoy

1071 Swans and Cygnet

1072 Eggs in Nest and Tithe Barn, Abbotsbury

1073 Young Swan and the Fleet

(Des D. Gentleman)

1993 (19 Jan). *600th Anniv of Abbotsbury Swannery. One phosphor band (18p.) or phosphorised paper (others).* P 14×15.

1639	**1069**	18p. gold, greenish yellow, bistre, green, vermilion and black	1·25	25
1640	**1070**	24p. gold, cream, brt green, grey-brown, dull blue and grey-black	1·10	25
1641	**1071**	28p. gold, greenish grey, yellow-brown, myrtle-green, brown, vermilion and black	1·40	2·25
1642	**1072**	33p. gold, ochre, apple-green, olive-brown, brt orange and grey-black	1·75	2·50
1643	**1073**	39p. gold, cream, brt green, cobalt, lt brown and black	1·90	2·50
		Set of 5	6·50	7·50
		Set of 5 *Gutter Pairs*	15·00	
		First Day Cover		7·50
		Presentation Pack	7·00	
		P.H.Q. Cards (*set of* 5)	4·25	8·50

Special First Day of Issue Postmarks

Philatelic Bureau, Edinburgh ....6·50
Abbotsbury, Dorset ....7·50

1074 Long John Silver and Parrot (*Treasure Island*)

1075 Tweedledum and Tweedledee (*Alice Through the Looking-Glass*)

1076 William (*William* books)

1077 Mole and Toad (*The Wind in the Willows*)

1078 Teacher and Wilfrid (*"The Bash Street Kids"*)

1079 Peter Rabbit and Mrs. Rabbit (*The Tale of Peter Rabbit*)

1080 Snowman (*The Snowman*) and Father Christmas (*Father Christmas*)

1081 The Big Friendly Giant and Sophie (*The BFG*)

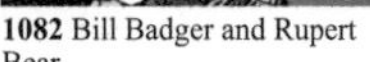

1082 Bill Badger and Rupert Bear

1083 Aladdin and the Genie

(Des Newell and Sorell)

1993 (2 Feb–10 Aug). *Greetings Stamps. "Gift Giving". Two phosphor bands.* P 15×14 (with one elliptical hole in each horizontal side).

No.	Type	Description	Unused	Used
1644	**1074**	(1st) gold, greenish yellow, magenta, pale brown, lt blue and black	1·25	1·25
		a. Booklet pane. Nos. 1644/53	11·00	12·00
1645	**1075**	(1st) gold, cream and black	1·25	1·25
1646	**1076**	(1st) gold, greenish yellow, magenta, cream, new blue and black	1·25	1·25
1647	**1077**	(1st) gold, greenish yellow, magenta, cream, new blue and black	1·25	1·25
1648	**1078**	(1st) gold, greenish yellow, magenta, cream, new blue and black	1·25	1·25
1649	**1079**	(1st) gold, greenish yellow, magenta, cream, new blue and black	1·25	1·25
		a. Booklet pane. No. 1649×4 with margins all round (10 Aug)	4·75	
1650	**1080**	(1st) gold, greenish yellow, magenta, cream, new blue and black	1·25	1·25
1651	**1081**	(1st) gold, greenish yellow, magenta, cream, new blue and black	1·25	1·25
1652	**1082**	(1st) gold, greenish yellow, magenta, cream, new blue and black	1·25	1·25
1653	**1083**	(1st) gold, greenish yellow, magenta, cream, new blue and black	1·25	1·25
Set of 10			11·00	11·00
First Day Cover				12·00
Presentation Pack			16·00	
P.H.Q. Cards (*set of* 10)			13·50	28·00

Nos. 1644/53 were issued in £2.40 booklets (sold at £2.50 from 1 November 1993), together with a pane of 20 half stamp-sized labels. The stamps and labels were affixed to the booklet cover by a common gutter margin.

Booklet pane No. 1649a comes from the £6 (£5.64) Beatrix Potter booklet.

Special First Day of Issue Postmarks

Philatelic Bureau, Edinburgh (No. 1644a) (2 Feb)..........12·00
Greetland (No. 1644a) (2 Feb)..........12·00
Philatelic Bureau, Edinburgh (No. 1649a) (10 Aug)..........6·00
Keswick (No. 1649a) (10 Aug)..........6·00

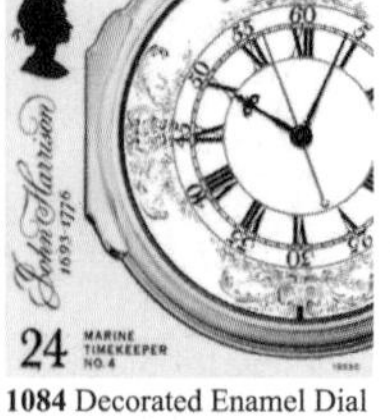

1084 Decorated Enamel Dial

1085 Escapement, Remontoire and Fusée

1086 Balance, Spring and Temperature Compensator

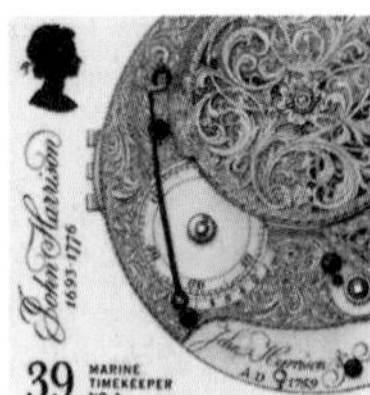

1087 Back of Movement

(Des H. Brown and D. Penny. Litho Questa)

1993 (16 Feb). *300th Birth Anniv of John Harrison (inventor of the marine chronometer). Details of "H4" Clock. Phosphorised paper.* P 14½×14.

No.	Type	Description	Unused	Used
1654	**1084**	24p. new blue, greenish yellow, magenta, black, grey-black and pale cream	60	25
1655	**1085**	28p. new blue, greenish yellow, magenta, black, grey-black and pale cream	1·00	1·25
1656	**1086**	33p. new blue, greenish yellow, magenta, black, grey-black and pale cream	1·40	1·25
1657	**1087**	39p. new blue, greenish yellow, magenta, black, grey-black and pale cream	1·50	1·50
Set of 4			4·00	4·00
Set of 4 *Gutter Pairs*			10·00	
First Day Cover				4·00
Presentation Pack			4·25	
P.H.Q. Cards (*set of* 4)			4·25	7·00

Special First Day of Issue Postmarks

Philatelic Bureau, Edinburgh..........4·25
Greenwich..........4·75

1088 Britannia

(Des B. Craddock, adapted Roundel Design Group. Litho (silver die-stamped, Braille symbol for "10" embossed) Questa)

1993 (2 Mar). *Granite paper.* P 14×14½ (with two elliptical holes on each horizontal side).

1658	**1088**	£10 greenish grey, rosine, yellow, new blue, reddish violet, vermilion, violet, brt green and silver	30·00	12·00
		a. Silver omitted	£1500	
		b. Braille symbol for "10" omitted		
First Day Cover				25·00
Presentation Pack			36·00	
P.H.Q. Card			5·00	35·00

The paper used for No. 1658 contains fluorescent coloured fibres which, together with the ink used on the shield, react under U.V. light.

Special First Day of Issue Postmarks

Philatelic Bureau, Edinburgh .... 26·00
Windsor .... 28·00

1089 *Dendrobium hellwigianum*

1090 *Paphiopedilum Maudiae* "Magnificum"

1091 *Cymbidium lowianum*

1092 *Vanda Rothschildiana*

1093 *Dendrobium vexillarius var albiviride*

(Des Pandora Sellars)

1993 (16 Mar). *14th World Orchid Conference, Glasgow. One phosphor band (18p.) or phosphorised paper (others).* P 15×14.

1659	**1089**	18p. green, greenish yellow, magenta, pale blue, apple-green and slate	45	25
		a. Imperf (pair)	£2200	
1660	**1090**	24p. green, greenish yellow, brt green and grey-black	75	25
1661	**1091**	28p. green, greenish yellow, red, brt turquoise-blue and drab	1·00	1·25
1662	**1092**	33p. green, greenish yellow, pale magenta, brt violet, brt green and grey	1·25	1·50
		a. Copyright logo and "1993" omitted (R. 10/6, dot pane)	15·00	15·00
1663	**1093**	39p. green, greenish yellow, red, pale olive-yellow, brt green, violet and grey-black	1·60	1·40
Set of 5			4·50	4·50
Set of 5 Gutter Pairs			10·00	
First Day Cover				4·50
Presentation Pack			5·00	
P.H.Q. Cards (set of 5)			4·50	7·00

Special First Day of Issue Postmarks

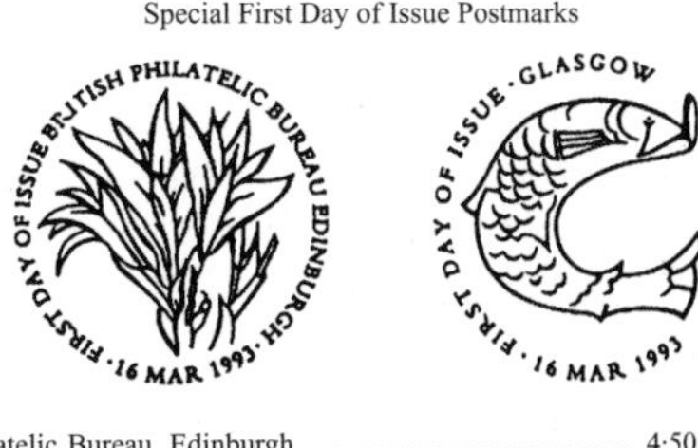

Philatelic Bureau, Edinburgh .... 4·50
Glasgow .... 5·50

FLUORESCENT PHOSPHOR BANDS. Following the introduction of new automatic sorting machinery in 1991 it was found necessary to substantially increase the signal emitted by the phosphor bands. This was achieved by adding a fluorescent element to the phosphor which appears yellow under U.V. light. This combination was first used on an experimental sheet printing of the 18p., No. X913, produced by Enschedé in 1991. All values with phosphor bands from the elliptical perforations issue, including the No Value Indicated design, originally showed this yellow fluor.

From mid-1995 printings of current sheet and booklet stamps began to appear with the colour of the fluorescent element changed to blue. As such differences in fluor colour can only be identified by use of a U.V. lamp they are outside the scope of this catalogue, but full details will be found in the *Great Britain Specialised Catalogue Volume 4.*

The first commemorative/special stamp issue to show the change to blue fluor was the Centenary of Rugby League set, Nos. 1891/5.

COMPUTER-ENGRAVED CYLINDERS. In 1991 Enschedé introduced a new method of preparing photogravure cylinders for Great Britain stamps. This new method utilised computer-engraving instead of the traditional acid-etching and produced cylinders without the minor flaws which had long been a feature of the photogravure process. Such cylinders were first used on Great Britain stamps for the printing of the 18p. released on 19 November 1991 (see No. X913).

Harrison and Sons continued to use the acid-etching method until mid-1996 after which most Machin values, including N.V.I.'s, were produced from computer-engraved cylinders using a very similar process to that of Enschedé. Some values exist in versions from both cylinder production methods and can often be identified by minor differences. Such stamps are, however, outside the scope of this listing, but full details can be found in the current edition of the *Great Britain Specialised Catalogue Volume 4.*

For commemorative stamps the first Harrison issue to use computer-engraved cylinders was the Centenary of Cinema set (Nos. 1920/4).

When Walsall introduced photogravure printing in 1997 their cylinders were produced using a similar computer-engraved process.

1093a

1993 (6 Apr)–**2005**. *Booklet Stamps. As T* **913/14**, *and* **1093a**. P 14 (No. 1665) or 15 × 14 (others) (both with one elliptical hole on each vertical side).

(a) *Photo*
Harrison – No. 1666
Questa – Nos. 1664ab, 1667ab
Walsall – No. 1665
Harrison/De La Rue, Questa or Walsall – No. 1667
Harrison/De La Rue, Enschedé, Questa or Walsall – Nos. 1664, 1668, 1669

No.	Type	Description	Mint	Used
1664	**913**	(2nd) brt blue (1 centre band) (7.9.93)	1·00	1·00
		a. Perf 14 (1.12.98)	1·10	1·10
		l. Booklet pane. Nos. 1664 and 1667 × 3 plus 4 labels ("postcode" on top right label) (27.4.00)	4·50	
		la. As No. 1664al, but inscr "postcodes" on top right label (17.4.01)...	4·50	
		m. Booklet pane. Nos. 1664 × 2 and 1667 × 6 (27.4.00)............................	6·50	
		n. Booklet pane. Nos. 1664 and 1669, each × 4, with central label and margins all round (6.2.02)................	6·00	
		o. Booklet pane. Nos. 1664 and 1668, each × 4, with central label and margins all round (2.6.03)................	3·50	
		p. Booklet pane. Nos. 1664 × 4, Y1703 × 2 and Y1709 × 2, with central label and margins all round (24.2.05)...	3·75	
1665		(2nd) bright blue (1 band at right) (13.10.98)...	1·10	1·10
		Ec. Band at left...	1·00	1·00
		l. Booklet pane. Nos. 1665 × 3 and N181b, S91a and W80a with margins all round	7·50	
1666	**914**	(1st) brt orange-red (phosphorised paper).	1·50	1·25
1667		(1st) brt orange-red (2 phosphor bands) (4.4.95)...	1·10	1·10
		a. Perf 14 (1.12.98)	1·50	1·50
		l. Booklet pane. No. 1667 × 8 with centre label and margins all round (16.2.99)...	6·50	
		m. Booklet pane. No. 1667 × 4 plus commemorative label at right (12.5.99)...	4·50	
1668		(1st) gold (2 phosphor bands) (21.4.97)....	1·00	1·00
		a. Imperf (pair)...	£250	
		l. Booklet pane. Nos. 1668 and Y1686, each × 4, and centre label with margins all round (23.9.97)..............	9·00	
		m. Booklet pane. Nos. 1668/9, each × 4, with centre label and margins all round (24.9.02).................................	9·00	
		n. Booklet pane. Nos. 1668/9, each × 4, with centre label and margins all round (25.2.03).................................	9·00	
		o. Booklet pane. Nos. 1668 and Y1698, each × 4, with centre label and margins all round (16.3.04)..............	8·50	
		p. Booklet pane. Nos. 1668 × 4, Y1709 × 2 and Y1717 × 2, with centre label and margins all round (25.5.04)........	9·25	
		q. Booklet pane. Nos. 1668 × 4, Y1719 × 2 and Y1723 × 2, with centre label and margins all round (18.10.05)......	5·25	
		r. Booklet pane. Nos. 1668 x4, Y1695 × 2 and Y1705 × 2, with centre label and margins all round (23.2.06)........	4·00	
1669	**1093a**	(E) deep blue (2 phosphor bands) (19.1.99)...	1·25	1·25

(b) Litho Questa or Walsall (2nd), *Enschedé, Questa or Walsall* (1st).

No.	Type	Description	Mint	Used
1670	**913**	(2nd) brt blue (1 centre band).....................	90	90
		Ey. Phosphor omitted		
1671	**914**	(1st) brt orange-red (2 phosphor bands)....	1·00	1·00
		Ey. Phosphor omitted..............................	£190	
		l. Booklet pane. No. 1671 × 4 plus commemorative label at left (27.7.94)...	8·50	
		la. Ditto, but with commemorative label at right (16.5.95)	6·00	
		lEy. Phosphor omitted		
		m. Pane. No. 1671 with margins all round (roul 8 across top corners of pane) (Boots logo on margin) (17.8.94)...	2·50	
		mEy. Phosphor omitted.............................		
		ma. Without Boots logo above stamp (11.9.95)...	1·25	
		mb. Ditto, but roul 10 across top corners of pane (20.2.97)..............................	1·40	
		n. Booklet pane. No. 1671 × 9 with margins all round (16.2.99)..............	9·00	

For details of sheets, booklets, etc containing these stamps see Decimal Machin Index following the "Y" numbers.

Nos. 1664/71 were issued in booklet panes showing perforations on all four edges.

On 6 September 1993 Nos. 1670/71 printed in lithography by Questa were made available in sheets from post offices in Birmingham, Coventry, Falkirk and Milton Keynes. These sheet stamps became available nationally on 5 October 1993. On 29 April 1997 No. 1664 printed in photogravure by Walsall became available in sheets. On the same date Nos. 1664 and 1667 were issued in coils printed by Harrison. Sheets of No. 1667 were printed by Walsall from 18 November 1997.

No. 1665 exists with the phosphor band at the left or right of the stamp from separate panes of the £6.16 Speed stamp booklet No. DX21. For pane containing No. 1665bEc see No. Y1676al.

No. 1668 was originally printed by Harrisons in booklets and Walsall in sheets and booklets for The Queen's Golden Wedding and issued on 21 April 1997. It was printed in coils by Enschedé (5.10.02), when gold became the accepted colour for 1st class definitives, and later in sheets and coils by De La Rue.

No. 1669 was intended for the basic European air mail rate, initially 30p., and was at first only available from Barcode booklet No. HF1, printed by Walsall. It appeared in sheets printed by De La Rue on 5 October 1999.

No. 1671m, printed by Questa, was provided by the Royal Mail for inclusion in single pre-packed greetings cards. The pane shows large margins at top and sides with lines of roulette gauging 8 stretching from the bottom corners to the mid point of the top edge. Examples included with greetings cards show the top two corners of the pane folded over. Unfolded examples were available from the British Philatelic Bureau and from other Post Office philatelic outlets. The scheme was originally limited to Boots and their logo appeared on the pane margin. Other card retailers subsequently participated and later supplies omitted the logo.

A further printing by Enschedé in 1997 showed the roulettes gauging 10 (No. 1671mb). Blank pieces of gummed paper have been found showing the perforation and rouletting of No. 1671mb, but no printing.

In mid-1994 a number of postal forgeries of the 2nd bright blue printed in lithography were detected after having been rejected by the sorting equipment. These show the Queen's head in bright greenish blue, have a fluorescent, rather than a phosphor, band and show matt, colourless gum on the reverse. These forgeries come from booklets of ten which also have forged covers.

For self-adhesive versions in these colours see Nos. 2039/40 and 2295/6.

COMMEMORATIVE BOOKLET PANES. Booklets of four 1st Class stamps with *se-tenant* commemorative label were issued for the following anniversaries or events:

300th Anniversary of the Bank of England (No. 1671l)
Birth Centenary of R. J. Mitchell (No. 1671la)
70th Birthday of Queen Elizabeth II (No. 1671la)
"Hong Kong '97" International Stamp Exhibition (No. 1671la)
Commonwealth Heads of Government Meeting, Edinburgh (No. 1671la)
50th Birthday of Prince of Wales (No. 1671la)
50th Anniversary of Berlin Airlift (No. 1667am)
Rugby World Cup (No. 1667am)

First Day Covers

Date	Cover	Price
21.4.97	1st (No. 1668), 26p. (Y1686) (Type G) (Philatelic Bureau or Windsor)...	3·50
23.9.97	B.B.C. label pane 1st × 4, 26p × 4 (No. 1668bl), (Philatelic Bureau or London W1)...........................	15·00
19.1.99	E (No. 1669) (Type G) (Philatelic Bureau or Windsor)..	3·50
16.2.99	"Profile on Print" label pane 1st × 8 (No. 1671n) (see Nos. 2077/9) (Philatelic Bureau or London SW1)..	5·50
6.2.02	"A Gracious Accession" label pane 2nd × 4 and E × 4 (No. 1664an) (see Nos. 2253/7) (Tallents House or Windsor)	5·00
24.9.02	"Across the Universe" label pane 1st × 4, E × 4 (No. 1668bm) (Tallents House or Star, Glenrothes)	5·00
25.2.03	"Microcosmos" label pane 1st × 4, E × 4 (No. 1668bn) (Tallents House or Cambridge)	5·00
2.6.03	"A Perfect Coronation" label pane 2nd × 4, 1st × 4 (No. 1664ao) (Tallents House or London SW1)	4·00
16.3.04	"Letters by Night: A Tribute to the Travelling Post Office" label pane 1st × 4, 37p × 4 (No. 1668bo) (Tallents House or London NW10)	11·00
25.5.04	"The Glory of the Garden" label pane 1st × 4, 42p × 2, 47p × 2 (No. 1668bp) (Tallents House or Wisley, Woking	11·00

24.2.05 The Brontë Sisters label pane 2nd × 4, 39p. × 2, 42p. × 2 (No. 1664ap) (Tallents House or Haworth, Keighley) .... 5·00
18.10.05 Bicentenary of the Battle of Trafalgar label pane 1st × 4, 50p. × 2 and 68p. × 2 (No. 1668bq) (Tallents House and Portsmouth .... 8·50
23.2.06 Birth Bicentenary of Isambard Kingdom Brunel label pane 1st × 4, 35p. × 2 and 40p. × 2 (No. 1668br) (Tallents House or Bristol) .... 7·00

Special First Day of Issue Postmarks

1993 (27 Apr)–**2006**. *As Nos.* X841, *etc, but* P 15 × 14 (with one elliptical hole on each vertical side).

(a) Photo

Enschedé: – 20*p.* (Y1679), 29*p.*, 35*p.* (Y1692), 36*p.*, 38*p.* (Y1700), 41*p.* (Y1706), 43*p.* (Y1710)
Harrison: – 20*p.* (Y1681), 25*p.* (Y1683), 26*p.* (Y1686), 35*p.* (Y1693), 41*p.* (Y1707), 43*p.* (Y1711)
Walsall: – 10*p.* (Y1676a), 19*p.* (Y1678), 38*p.* (Y1701a), 43*p.* (Y1711a).
Enschedé or Harrison/De La Rue: – 4*p.*, 5*p.*, 6*p.*, 10*p.* (Y1676), 25*p.* (Y1684), 31*p.*, 39*p.* (Y1702), 47*p.*, £1
Enschedé, Harrison/De La Rue or Questa: – 1*p.*, 2*p.*
Enschedé, Harrison/De La Rue or Walsall: – 30*p.*, 37*p.* (Y1697), 42*p.*, 50*p.*, 63*p.*
Harrison/De La Rue or Questa: – 19*p.* (Y1677), 20*p.* (Y1680), 26*p.* (Y1685)
De La Rue or Walsall: – 38*p.* (Y1701), 39*p.* (Y1703), 40*p.* (Y1704), 64*p.*, 65*p.*, 68*p.*
De La Rue: – 7*p.*, 8*p.*, 9*p.*, 20*p.* (Y1682), 33*p.*, 34*p.*, 35*p.* (Y1694), 37*p.* (Y1698/9), 41*p.* (1708), 43*p.* (Y1712), 44*p.*, 45*p.*, 46*p.*, 49*p.*, 72*p.*, £1.50, £2, £3, £5
Enschedé or De La Rue: – 35*p.* (Y1695), 40*p.* (Y1705), 47*p.*

No.	Type	Description	Unused	Used
Y1667	**367**	1p. crimson (2 bands) (8.6.93)	25	25
		l. Booklet pane. Nos. Y1667 × 2, Y1680 and Y1685 × 3 plus 2 labels (1.12.98)	8·50	
		m. Booklet pane. Nos. Y1667/8, Y1677 and Y1685 × 3 plus 2 labels (26.4.99)	6·50	
		n. Booklet pane. Nos. Y1667 × 4, Y1677 × 3 and Y1685 with central label and margins all round (21.9.99)	4·50	
Y1668		2p. dp green (2 bands) (11.4.95)	25	25
Y1669		4p. new blue (2 bands) (14.12.93)	25	25
Y1670		5p. dull red-brown (2 bands) (8.6.93)	25	25
Y1671		6p. yellow-olive (2 bands)	25	30
		Ey. Phosphor omitted		
Y1672		7p. grey (2 bands) (20.4.99)	35	35
Y1673		7p. bright magenta 2 (bands) (1.4.04)	25	25
Y1674		8p. yellow (2 bands) (25.4.00)	35	35
Y1675		9p. yellow-orange (2 bands) (5.4.05)	15	20
Y1676		10p. dull orange (2 bands) (8.6.93)	35	35
		a. Perf 14 (13.10.98)	2·00	2·00
		al. Booklet pane. Nos. Y1676a × 2, 1663Ec and Y1711a, each × 3, with centre label and margins all round	12·00	
Y1677		19p. bistre (1 centre band) (26.10.93)	75	75
		a. Imperf (pair)	£400	
		l. Booklet pane. Nos. Y1677 and Y1685 × 7 (26.4.99)	13·00	
		Ey. Phosphor omitted	75·00	
Y1678		19p. bistre (1 band at right) (*p* 14) (15.2.00)	2·00	2·00
		l. Booklet pane. Nos. Y1678 × 4 and Y1701a × 2 with margins all round	22·00	
Y1679		20p. turquoise-green (2 bands) (14.12.93)	90	90
Y1680		20p. brt green (1 centre band) (25.6.96)	70	70
		a. Imperf (horiz pair)	£300	
		l. Booklet pane. Nos. Y1680 and Y1685 × 7 (1.12.98)	14·00	
Y1681		20p. brt green (1 band at right) (23.9.97)	1·50	1·50
		l. Booklet pane. Nos. Y1681 and Y1685, each × 3 with margins all round	6·50	
Y1682		20p. brt green (2 bands) (20.4.99)	75	75
Y1683		25p. rose-red (phosphorised paper) (26.10.93)	1·10	1·10
		a. Imperf (pair)	£450	
		l. Booklet pane. No. Y1683 × 2 plus 2 labels (1.11.93)	2·25	
Y1684		25p. rose-red (2 bands) (20.12.94)	1·10	1·10
		l. Booklet pane. No. Y1684 × 2 plus 2 labels (6.6.95)	3·50	
Y1685		26p. red-brown (2 bands) (25.6.96)	1·10	1·10
		a. Imperf (pair)		
Y1686		26p. gold (2 bands) (21.4.97)	1·10	1·10
		ba. Imperf (horiz pair)	£2250	
Y1687		29p. grey (2 bands) (26.10.93)	1·25	1·25
Y1688		30p. dp olive-grey (2 bands) (27.7.93)	1·10	1·10
		a. Imperf (pair)		
Y1689		31p. dp mauve (2 bands) (25.6.96)	1·20	1·20
Y1690		33p. grey-green (2 bands) (25.4.00)	1·50	1·50
Y1691		34p. yellow-olive (2 bands) (6.5.03)	1·25	1·00
Y1692		35p. yellow (2 bands) (17.8.93)	1·50	1·50
Y1693		35p. yellow (phosphorised paper) (1.11.93)	7·50	7·50
Y1694		35p. sepia (2 bands) (1.4.04)	1·10	1·10
Y1695		35p. yellow-olive (5.4.05) (1 centre band)	50	55
Y1696		36p. brt ultramarine (2 bands) (26.10.93)	1·50	1·50
Y1697		37p. brt mauve (2 bands) (25.6.96)	1·40	1·40
Y1698		37p. grey-black (2 bands) (4.7.02)	1·40	1·40
Y1699		37p. brown-olive (1 centre band) (23.3.06)	60	65
Y1700		38p. rosine (2 bands) (26.10.93)	1·50	1·50
		a. Imperf (pair)	£275	
Y1701		38p. ultramarine (2 bands) (20.4.99)	2·00	2·00
		a. Perf 14 (15.2.00)	7·50	7·50
Y1702		39p. brt magenta (2 bands) (25.6.96)	1·50	1·50
		a. Imperf (pair)		
Y1703		39p. grey (2 bands) (1.4.04)	1·20	1·20
Y1704		40p. dp azure (2 bands) (25.4.00)	1·40	1·40
Y1705		40p. turquoise-blue (2 bands) (1.4.04)	1·30	1·30
Y1706		41p. grey-brown (2 bands) (26.10.93)	1·75	1·75
Y1707		41p. drab (phosphorised paper) (1.11.93)	7·50	7·50
Y1708		41p. rosine (2 bands) (25.4.00)	1·40	1·40
Y1709		42p. dp olive-grey (2 bands) (4.7.02)	1·40	1·40
Y1710		43p. dp olive-brown (2 bands) (25.6.96)	1·75	1·75
Y1711		43p. sepia (2 bands) (8.7.96)	2·50	2·50
		a. Perf 14 (13.10.98)	2·50	2·50
Y1712		43p. emerald (2 bands) (1.4.04)	1·40	1·40
Y1713		44p. grey-brown (2 bands) (20.4.99)	4·25	4·25
Y1714		44p. bright blue (2 bands) (28.3.06)	70	75
Y1715		45p. brt mauve (2 bands) (25.4.00)	1·50	1·50
Y1716		46p. yellow (2 bands) (5.4.05)	70	75
Y1717		47p. turquoise-green (2 bands) (4.7.02)	1·75	1·75
Y1718		49p. red-brown (2 bands) (28.3.06)	75	80
Y1719		50p. ochre (2 bands) (14.12.93)	1·75	1·20
		a. Imperf (pair)		
Y1720		63p. lt emerald (2 bands) (25.6.96)	2·00	2·00
Y1721		64p. turquoise-green (2 bands) (20.4.99)	2·25	2·25
Y1722		65p. greenish blue (2 bands) (25.4.00)	2·10	2·10
Y1723		68p. grey-brown (2 bands) (4.7.02)	2·10	2·10
Y1724		72p. rosine (2 bands) (28.3.06)	1·10	1·20
Y1725		£1 bluish violet (2 bands) (22.8.95)	3·25	3·00
		a. Imperf (horiz pair)	£1100	
Y1726		£1.50 brown-red (2 bands) (1.7.03)	3·50	3·50
Y1727		£2 deep blue-green (2 bands) (1.7.03)	5·00	5·00
		a. Missing "£" in value (R. 18/1, Cyl D1 no dot)		
Y1728		£3 deep mauve (2 bands) (1.7.03)	7·50	5·00
Y1729		£5 azure (2 bands) (1.7.03)	12·00	6·00

(b) Litho Walsall (37p., 60p., 63p.), Questa or Walsall (25p.,35p., 41p.), Questa (others).

No.	Type	Description	Unused	Used
Y1743	**367**	1p. lake (2 bands) (8.7.96)	40	40
		Ey. Phosphor omitted	£350	
		l. Booklet pane. Nos. Y1743 × 2, Y1751 and Y1753 × 3 plus 2 labels	5·00	
		lEy. Booklet pane. Phosphor omitted		
Y1748		6p. yellow-olive (2 bands) (26.7.94)	12·00	13·00
		l. Booklet pane. Nos. Y1748, Y1750 and Y1752 × 4 with margins all round	15·00	
		la. 6p. value misplaced		
Y1749		10p. dull orange (2 bands) (25.4.95)	5·00	5·00
		l. Booklet pane. Nos. Y1749, Y1750/Ea, Y1752 × 2, Y1754/5, Y1757*Ea* and centre label with margins all round	18·00	
		lEy. Booklet pane. Phosphor omitted		
Y1750		19p. bistre (1 band at left) (26.7.94)	1·90	1·75
		Ea. Band at right (25.4.95)	2·50	2·50
		l. Booklet pane. Nos. Y1750/Ea, each × 3 with margins all round (25.4.95)	14·00	
Y1751		20p. brt yellow-green (1 centre band) (8.7.96)	2·25	2·25
		lEy. Phosphor omitted	£200	
		l. Booklet pane. Nos. Y1751 and Y1753 × 7	8·00	
		lEy. Booklet pane. Phosphor omitted		
Y1752		25p. red (2 bands) (1.11.93)	1·10	1·10
		l. Booklet pane. Nos. Y1752, NI72, S84 and W73, each × 2, with centre label and margins all round (14.5.96)	7·50	
Y1753		26p. chestnut (2 bands) (8.7.96)	1·00	1·00
		Ey. Phosphor omitted	50·00	
Y1754		30p. olive-grey (2 bands) (25.4.95)	4·25	4·25
Y1755		35p. yellow (2 bands) (1.11.93)	1·60	1·60
Y1756		37p. brt mauve (2 bands) (8.7.96)	2·40	2·40
Y1757		41p. drab (2 bands) (1.11.93)	1·75	1·75
		Ea. Grey-brown (25.4.95)	3·50	3·50
		Ey. Phosphor omitted		
Y1758		60p. dull blue-grey (2 bands) (9.8.94)	2·50	2·50
Y1759		63p. lt emerald (2 bands) (8.7.96)	3·00	3·00
		Ey. Phosphor omitted		

(c) Eng C. Slania. Recess Enschedé (until Mar 2000) or De La Rue (from 11 Apr 2000)

No.	Type	Description	Unused	Used
Y1800	**367**	£1.50 red (9.3.99)	4·25	2·00
Y1801		£2 dull blue (9.3.99)	6·00	2·25
Y1802		£3 dull violet (9.3.99)	9·00	3·00
Y1803		£5 brown (9.3.99)	15·00	5·00
		P.H.Q. Card (No. Y1725)	40	3·00

No. Y1684 exists with the phosphor bands omitted, but can only be identified by the use of a u.v. lamp (*Price £24 unused*).

Nos. Y1725/9 are printed in Iriodin ink which gives a shiny effect to the solid part of the background behind the Queen's head.

No. Y1748la shows the 6p. value printed 22 mm to the left so that its position on the booklet pane is completely blank except for the phosphor bands. Other more minor misplacements exist.

The De La Rue printings of the high values, Nos. Y1800/3 cannot easily be identified from the original Enschedé issue as single stamps.

For self-adhesive versions of the 42p. and 68p. see Nos. 2297/8.

First Day Covers

Date	Description	Price
26.10.93	19p., 25p., 29p., 36p., 38p., 41p. (Y1677, Y1683, Y1687, Y1696, Y1700, Y1706)	6·00
9.8.94	60p. (Y1758)	4·00
25.4.95	National Trust *se-tenant* pane 10p., 19p., 25p., 30p., 35p., 41p. (Y1749l)	5·00
22.8.95	£1 (Y1725)	3·50
14.5.96	European Football Championship *se-tenant* pane 25p. × 8 (Y1752l)	7·50
25.6.96	20p., 26p., 31p., 37p., 39p., 43p., 63p. (Y1680, Y1685, Y1689, Y1697, Y1702, Y1710, Y1720)	8·00
13.10.98	Speed *se-tenant* pane 10p., 2nd, 43p. (Y1676al)	6·50
9.3.99	£1·50, £2, £3, £5 (Y1800/3) (Type G) (Philatelic Bureau or Windsor)	27·00
20.4.99	7p., 38p., 44p., 64p. (Y1672, Y1701, Y1713, Y1721) (Type G) (Philatelic Bureau or Windsor)	5·00
21.9.99	World Changers *se-tenant* pane 1p.,19p., 26p. (Y1667n) (Philatelic Bureau or Downe, Orpington)	4·00
25.4.00	8p., 33p., 40p., 41p., 45p., 65p. (Y1674, Y1690, Y1704, Y1708, Y1715, Y1722) (Type G) (Philatelic Bureau or Windsor)	5·00
4.7.02	37p., 42p., 47p., 68p. (Y1698, Y1709, Y1717, Y1723) (Type K) (Tallents House or Windsor)	4·00
6.5.03	34p., (Y1691) (Type K) (Tallents House or Windsor)	1·20
1.7.03	£1·50, £2, £3, £5 (*Nos.* Y1726/9) (Type K) (Tallents House or Windsor)	21·00
1.4.04	7p., 35p., 39p., 40p., 43p. Worldwide postcard (Y1673, Y1694, Y1703, Y1705, Y1712, 2357*a*) (Type K) (Tallents House or Windsor)	9·00
5.4.05	9p., 35p., 46p. (*Nos.* Y1675, Y1695, Y1716) (Type K) (Tallents House or Windsor)	2·20
28.3.06	37p., 44p., 49p., 72p. (Y1699, Y1714, Y1718, Y1724 (Type K) (Tallents House or Windsor)	4·25

Post Office Presentation Packs

Date	Description	Price
26.10.93	P.O. Pack No. 30. 19p. (1 centre band), 25p. (phos paper), 29p., 36p., 38p. rosine, 41p. grey-brown (*Nos.* Y1677, Y1683, Y1687, Y1696, Y1700, Y1706)	7·00
21.11.95	P.O. Pack No. 34. 1p. (photo), 2p., 4p., 5p., 6p. (photo), 10p. (photo), 19p. (1 centre band), 20p. turquoise-green, 25p. (photo) (2 bands), 29p., 30p. (photo), 35p. (photo) (2 bands), 36p., 38p. rosine, 41p. grey-brown, 50p., 60p., £1 (*Nos.* Y1667/71, Y1676/7, Y1679, Y1684, Y1687/8, Y1692, Y1696, Y1700, Y1706, Y1719, Y1758, Y1725)	30·00
25.6.96	P.O. Pack No. 35. 20p. brt green (1 centre band), 26p. (photo), 31p., 37p. (photo), 39p., 43p. deep olive brown, 63p. (photo) (*Nos.* Y1680, Y1685, Y1689, Y1697, Y1702, Y1710, Y1720)	9·50
21.4.97	P.O. Pack No. 38. 1st, 26p. gold (*Nos.* 1668, Y1686)	7·50
20.10.98	P.O. Pack No. 41. 2nd brt blue (1 centre band), 1st brt orange-red (2 phosphor bands), 1p., 2p., 4p., 5p., 6p., 10p., 20p. brt green (1 centre band), 26p., 30p., 31p., 37p., 39p., 43p. sepia, 50p., 63p., £1 (*Nos.* 1664, 1667, Y1667/71, Y1676, Y1680, Y1685, Y1688/9, Y1697, Y1702, Y1711, Y1719/20, Y1725)	16·00
9.3.99	P.O. Pack No. 43 or 43a. £1·50, £2, £3, £5 (*Nos.* Y1800/3)	55·00
20.4.99	P.O. Pack No. 44. 7p., 19p., 38p. ultramarine, 44p., 64p. (*Nos.* Y1672, Y1677, Y1701, Y1713, Y1721)	11·00
25.4.00	P.O. Pack No. 49. 8p., 33p., 40p., 41p. rosine, 45p., 65p. (*Nos.* Y1674, Y1690, Y1704, Y1708, Y1715, Y1722)	10·00
12.3.02	P.O. Pack No. 57. 2nd, 1st, E, 1p., 2p., 4p., 5p., 8p., 10p., 20p., 33p., 40p., 41p., 45p., 50p., 65p., £1 (*Nos.* Y1664, Y1667, Y1669, Y1667/70, Y1674, Y1676, Y1682, Y1690, Y1704, Y1708, Y1715, Y1719, Y1722, Y1725)	16·00
4.7.02	P.O. Pack No. 58. 37p., 42p., 47p., 68p. (*Nos.* Y1698, Y1709, Y1717, Y1723)	7·50
1.7.03	P.O. Pack No. 62. £1·50, £2, £3, £5 (*Nos.* Y1726/9)	23·00
1.4.04	P.O. Pack No. 67. 1st gold (DLR ptg), 7p., 35p., 39p., 40p., 43p. Worldwide postcard (*Nos.* 1668, Y1673, Y1694, Y1703, Y1705, Y1712, 2357*a*)	6·00
6.9.05	P.O. Pack No. 69. 1p., 2p., 5p., 9p., 10p., 20p., 35p., 40p., 42p., 46p., 47p., 50p., 68p., £1., 2nd, 1st, Worldwide postcard, Europe, Worldwide (*Nos.* Y1667/8, Y1670, Y1675/6, Y1682, Y1695, Y1705, Y1709, Y1716/17, Y1719, Y1723, Y1725, 2039, 2295, 2357a/9)	11·50
28.3.06	P.O. Pack No. 72. 37p., 44p., 49p., 72p. (*Nos.* Y1699, Y1714, Y1718, Y1724)	3·50

DECIMAL MACHIN, INCLUDING N.V.Is., WITH ELLIPTICAL PERFORATIONS INDEX

Value	*Process*	*Colour*	*Phosphor*	*Cat. No.*	*Source*
2nd	litho Questa or Walsall	brt blue	1 centre band	1670	sheets (Questa), booklets of 4 (Walsall–HA6, Walsall HA9/11), booklets of 10 (Questa–HC11, HC13, HC16, HC18, HC20, Walsall–HC12)
2nd	photo Harrison/De La Rue), Enschedé, Questa or Walsall	brt blue	1 centre band	1664	sheets (Walsall), horizontal coil (Harrison/De La Rue), vertical coils (Harrison/De La Rue or Enschedé) booklets of 4 (Harrison–HA7/8, Walsall–HA12), booklets of 10 (Harrison/De La Rue–HC14/15, HC17, HC19, HC21), £1 booklet (Questa–FH44/a), £2 booklet (Questa–FW12), £7.29 "A Gracious Accession" booklet (Enschedé–DX28), £7.46 "A Perfect Coronation" booklet (Walsall–DX31), £7.43 The Brontë Sisters booklet (Walsall–DX34)
2nd	photo Walsall (*p* 14)	brt blue	1 band at right	1665	£6.16 British Land Speed Record Holders booklet (DX21)
2nd	photo Walsall (*p* 14)	brt blue	1 band at left	1665Ec	£6.16 British Land Speed Record Holders booklet (DX21)
2nd	photo Questa (*p* 14)	brt blue	1 centre band	1664ab	booklets of 10 (HC22)
1st	litho Enschedé, Questa or Walsall	brt orange-red	2 bands	1671	sheets (Questa), greetings card panes Questa–Y1671m/ma, Enschedé–Y1671mb), booklets of 4 (Walsall–HB6, HB8/13, HB15/16, Questa–HB7), booklets of 10 Wallsall–HD10, HD12/19, HD22/3, HD25, HD28, HD34, HD36/8, HD40, Questa–HD11, HD21, HD26, HD50), £7.54 "Profile on Print" booklet (Questa–DX22)
1st	photo Harrison	brt orange-red	phos paper	1666	booklets of 4 (HB5), booklets of 10 (HD9, HD20)
1st	photo Harrison/ De La Rue, Questa or Walsall	brt orange-red	2 bands	1667	sheets (Walsall), horizontal and vertical coils (Harrison, De La Rue), booklets of 4 (Walsall–HB14, HB17/18),booklets of 8 with 2 Millennium commems (Walsall–HBA1/2), booklets of 10 (Harrison/De La Rue–HD24, HD27, HD29/33, HD35, HD39, HD45/9, Walsall–HD44), £1 booklet (Questa–FH44/a), £2 booklet (Questa–FW12), £7.54 "Profile on Print" booklet (De La Rue–DX22)
1st	photo Questa (*p* 14)	brt orange-red	2 bands	1667ab	booklets of 10 (HD51)
1st	photo De La Rue, Enschedé, Harrison, Questa or Walsall	gold	2 bands	1668	sheets (Walsall, De La Rue), vertical coils (Enschedé, De La Rue), booklets of 10 (Harrison–HD41, HD43, Walsall–HD42), £6.15 B.B.C. booklet (Harrison–DX19), £6.83 "Across the Universe" booklet (Questa–DX29, £6.99 "Microcosmos" booklet (Enschedé–DX30), £7.46 "A Perfect Coronation" booklet (Walsall–DX31), £7.44 "Letters by Night" booklet (De La Rue–DX32), £7.23 "The Glory of the Garden" booklet (Enschedé–DX33)
E	photo De La Rue, Enschedé, Questa or Walsall	deep blue	2 bands	1669	sheets (De La Rue), booklets of 4 (Walsall–HF1), £7.29 "A Gracious Accession" booklet (Enschedé–DX28), £6.83 "Across the Universe" booklet (Questa–DX29), £6.99 "Microcosmos" booklet (Enschedé–DX30
lp.	photo De La Rue, Enschedé, Harrison or Questa	crimson	2 bands	Y1667	sheets, £1 booklets (Questa–FH42/3), £6.91 World Changers booklet (Questa–DX23)
lp.	litho Questa	lake	2 bands	Y1743	£1 booklet (FH41)
2p.	photo De La Rue, Enschedé, Harrison or Questa	dp green	2 bands	Y1668	sheets, £1 booklet (Questa–FH43)
4p.	photo De La Rue, Enschedé or Harrison	new blue	2 bands	Y1669	sheets
4p.	photo De La Rue	new blue	phos paper	**MS**2146	Jeffrey Matthews Colour Palette miniature sheet
5p.	photo De La Rue, Enschedé or Harrison	dull red-brown	2 bands	Y1670	sheets
5p.	photo De La Rue	dull red-brown	phos paper	**MS**2146	Jeffrey Matthews Colour Palette miniature sheet
6p.	photo Enschedé or Harrison	yellow-olive	2 bands	Y1671	sheets
6p.	litho Questa	yellow-olive	2 bands	Y1748	£6.04 Northern Ireland booklet (DX16)
6p.	photo De La Rue	yellow-olive	phos paper	**MS**2146	Jeffrey Matthews Colour Palette miniature sheet
7p.	photo De La Rue	grey	2 bands	Y1672	sheets
7p.	photo De La Rue	bright magenta	2 bands	Y1673	sheets
8p.	photo De La Rue	yellow	2 bands	Y1674	sheets
9p.	photo De La Rue	yellow-orange	2 bands	Y1675	sheets
10p.	photo De La Rue, Enschedé or Harrison	dull orange	2 bands	Y1676	sheets
10p.	litho Questa	dull orange	2 bands	Y1749	£6 National Trust booklet (DX17)
10p.	photo Walsall (*p* 14)	dull orange	2 bands	Y1676a	£6.16 British Land Speed Record Holders booklet (DX21)
10p.	photo De La Rue	dull orange	phos paper	**MS**2146	Jeffrey Matthews Colour Palette miniature sheet

Value	*Process*	*Colour*	*Phosphor*	*Cat. No.*	*Source*
19p.	photo Harrison or Questa	bistre	1 centre band	Y1677	sheets, vertical coils, £1 booklet (Questa–FH43), £2 booklet (Questa–FW11), £6.99 World Changers booklet (Questa–DX23)
19p.	litho Questa	bistre	1 band at left	Y1750	£6.04 Northern Ireland booklet (DX16), £6 National Trust booklet (DX17)
19p.	litho Questa	bistre	1 band at right	Y1750Ea	£6 National Trust booklet (DX17)
19p.	photo Walsall (*p* 14)	bistre	1 band at right	Y1678	£7.50 "Special by Design" booklet (DX24)
20p.	photo Enschedé	turquoise-green	2 bands	Y1679	sheets
20p.	photo Harrison or Questa	brt green	1 centre band	Y1680	sheets, £1 booklet (Questa–FH42), £2 booklet (Questa–FW10)
20p.	litho Questa	brt yellow-green	1 centre band	Y1751	£1 booklet (FH41), £2 booklet (FW9)
20p.	photo Harrison	brt green	1 band at right	Y1681	£6.15 B.B.C. booklet (DX19)
20p.	photo De La Rue	brt green	2 bands	Y1682	sheets
25p.	photo Harrison	rose-red	phos paper	Y1683	sheets, vertical coils, 50p booklets (FB67/73), £1 booklets (FH33/7), £2 booklets (FW1/5)
25p.	litho Walsall or Questa	red	2 bands	Y1752	£1 booklets (Walsall–FH31/2), (Questa–FH40), £2 booklet (Questa–FW8), £6.04 Northern Ireland booklet (Questa–DX16), £6 National Trust booklet (Questa–DX17), £6.84 European Football Championship (Questa–DX18)
25p.	photo Harrison or Enschedé	rose-red	2 bands	Y1684	sheets (Harrison or Enschedé), vertical coils (Harrison), 50p booklets (Harrison–FB74/5), £1 booklets (Harrison–FH38/9)), £2 booklets (Harrison–FW6/7)
26p.	photo Harrison or Questa	red-brown	2 bands	Y1685	sheets, £1 booklets (Questa–FH42/3), £2 booklets (Questa–FW10/11), £6.15 B.B.C. booklet (Harrison–DX19), £6.99 World Changers booklet (Questa–DX23)
26p.	litho Questa	chestnut	2 bands	Y1753	£1 booklet (FH41), £2 booklet (FW9)
26p.	photo Harrison	gold	2 bands	Y1686	sheets, £6.15 B B.C. booklet (Harrison–DX19)
29p.	photo Enschedé	grey	2 bands	Y1687	sheets
30p.	photo Enschedé, Harrison or Walsall	dp olive-grey	2 bands	Y1688	sheets, £1.20 booklets (Walsall–GGAl/2)
30p.	litho Questa	olive-grey	2 bands	Y1754	£6 National Trust booklet (DX17)
31p.	photo Enschedé or Harrison	dp mauve	2 bands	Y1689	sheets
31p.	photo De La Rue	dp mauve	phos paper	**MS**2146	Jeffrey Matthews Colour Palette miniature sheet
33p.	photo De La Rue	grey-green	2 bands	Y1690	sheets
34p.	photo De La Rue	yellow-olive	2 bands	Y1691	sheets
35p.	photo Enschedé	yellow	2 bands	Y1692	sheets
35p.	photo Harrison	yellow	phos paper	Y1693	vertical coils
35p.	litho Walsall or Questa	yellow	2 bands	Y1755	£1.40 booklets (Walsall–GK5/7), £6 National Trust booklet (Questa–DX17)
35p.	photo De La Rue	sepia	2 bands	Y1694	sheets
35p.	photo Enschedé or De La Rue	yellow-olive	1 centre band	Y1695	sheets, £7.40 Brunel booklet (Enschedé–DX36)
36p.	photo Enschedé	brt ultramarine	2 bands	Y1696	sheets
37p.	photo Enschedé, Harrison or Walsall	brt mauve	2 bands	Y1697	sheets (Enschedé or Harrison), vertical coils (Harrison), £1.48 booklets (Walsall–GL3/4)
37p.	litho Walsall	brt mauve	2 bands	Y1756	£1.48 booklets (GL1/2)
37p.	photo De La Rue	grey-black	2 bands	Y1698	sheets, £7.44 "Letters by Night" booklet (De La Rue–DX32)
37p.	photo De La Rue	brown-olive	1 centre band	Y1699	sheets
38p.	photo Enschedé	rosine	2 bands	Y1700	sheets
38p.	photo De La Rue or Walsall	ultramarine	2 bands	Y1701	sheets (D.L.R.), £1.52 booklet (Walsall–GLAl)
38p.	photo Walsall (*p* 14)	ultramarine	2 bands	Y1701a	£7.50 "Special by Design" booklet (DX24)
39p.	photo Enschedé or Harrison	brt magenta	2 bands	Y1702	sheets
39p.	photo De La Rue	brt magenta	phos paper	**MS**2146	Jeffrey Matthews Colour Palette miniature sheet
39p.	photo De La Rue or Walsall	grey	2 bands	Y1703	sheets (De La Rue), £7.43 The Brontë Sisters booklet (Walsall–DX34)
40p.	photo De La Rue or Walsall	deep azure	2 bands	Y1704	sheets (D.L.R.), £1.60 booklet (Walsall–GMA1)
40p.	photo De La Rue or Enschedé	turquoise-blue	2 bands	Y1705	sheets (D.L.R.), £7.40 Brunel booklet (Enschedé–DX36)
41p.	photo Enschedé	grey-brown	2 bands	Y1706	sheets
41p.	photo Harrison	drab	phos paper	Y1707	vertical coils
41p.	photo De La Rue	rosine	2 bands	Y1708	sheets
41p.	litho Walsall	drab	2 bands	Y1757	£1.64 booklets (GN1/3)
41p.	litho Questa	grey-brown	2 bands	Y1757*Ea*	£6 National Trust booklet (DX17)

Value	*Process*	*Colour*	*Phosphor*	*Cat. No.*	*Source*
42p.	photo De La Rue, Enschedé or Walsall	dp olive-grey	2 bands	Y1709	sheets (De La Rue), £7.23 "The Glory of the Garden" booklet (Enschedé–DX33), £7.43 The Brontë Sisters booklet (Walsall–DX34)
43p.	photo Enschedé	dp olive-brown	2 bands	Y1710	sheets
43p.	photo Harrison	sepia	2 bands	Y1711	sheets, vertical coils
43p.	photo Walsall (*p* 14)	sepia	2 bands	Y1711*a*	£6.16 British Land Speed Record Holders booklet (DX21)
43p.	photo De La Rue	emerald	2 bands	Y1712	sheets
44p.	photo De La Rue	grey-brown	2 bands	Y1713	sheets
44p.	photo De La Rue	bright blue	2 bands	Y1714	sheets
45p.	photo De La Rue	brt mauve	2 bands	Y1715	sheets
46p.	photo De La Rue	yellow	2 bands	Y1716	sheets
47p.	photo De La Rue or Enschedé	turquoise-green	2 bands	Y1717	sheets (De La Rue), £7.23 "The Glory of the Garden" booklet (Enschedé–DX33)
49p.	photo De La Rue	red-brown	2 bands	Y1718	sheets
50p.	photo Enschedé, Harrison or Walsall	ochre	2 bands	Y1719	sheets (Enschedé or Harrison), £7.26 Trafalgar booklet (Walsall-DX35)
60p.	litho Walsall	dull blue-grey	2 bands	Y1758	£2.40 booklets (GQ1/4)
63p.	photo Enschedé, Harrison or Walsall	lt emerald	2 bands	Y1720	sheets (Enschedé or Harrison), vertical coils (Harrison) £2.52 booklets (Walsall–GR3/4)
63p.	litho Walsall	lt emerald	2 bands	Y1759	£2.52 booklets (GR1/2)
64p.	photo De La Rue or Walsall	turquoise-green	2 bands	Y1721	sheets (D.L.R.), £2.56 booklet (Walsall–GS1)
64p.	photo De La Rue	turquoise-green	phos paper	**MS**2146	Jeffrey Matthews Colour Palette miniature sheet
65p.	photo De La Rue or Walsall	greenish blue	2 bands	Y1722	sheets (D.L.R.), £2.60 booklet (Walsall–GT1)
68p.	photo De La Rue or Walsall	grey-brown	2 bands	Y1723	sheets (D.L.R.), £7.26 Trafalgar booklet (Walsall–DX35)
72p.	photo De La Rue	rosine	2 bands	Y1724	sheets
£1	photo Enschedé or Harrison	bluish violet	2 bands	Y1725	sheets
£1	photo De La Rue	bluish violet	phos paper	**MS**2146	Jeffrey Matthews Colour Palette miniature sheet
£1.50	recess	red	—	Y1800	sheets (Enschedé then D.L.R.)
£1.50	photo De La Rue	brown-red	2 bands	Y1726	sheets
£2	recess	dull blue	—	Y1801	sheets (Enschedé then D.L.R.)
£2	photo De La Rue	deep blue-green	2 bands	Y1727	sheets
£3	recess	dull violet	—	Y1802	sheets (Enschedé then D.L.R.)
£3	photo De La Rue	deep mauve	2 bands	Y1728	sheets
£5	recess	brown	—	Y1803	sheets (Enschedé then D.L.R.)
£5	photo De La Rue	azure	2 bands	Y1729	sheets

Note. Harrison and Sons became De La Rue Security Print on 8 September 1997.

1094 "Family Group" (bronze sculpture) (Henry Moore)

1095 "Kew Gardens" (lithograph) (Edward Bawden)

1096 "St. Francis and the Birds" (Stanley Spencer)

1097 "Still Life: Odyssey I" (Ben Nicholson)

(Des. A. Dastor)

1993 (11 May). *Europa. Contemporary Art. Phosphorised paper.* P 14×14½.

1767	**1094**	24p.	brownish grey, lemon, magenta, turquoise-blue and grey-black	60	20
1768	**1095**	28p.	brownish grey, buff, lt green, yellow-brown, brt orange, new blue and grey-black	90	1·00
1769	**1096**	33p.	brownish grey, cream, greenish yellow, magenta, new blue and grey-black	1·25	1·40
1770	**1097**	39p.	brownish grey, cream, yellow-ochre, rose-lilac, red, lt blue and grey-black	1·75	1·75
Set of 4				4·00	4·00
Set of 4 Gutter Pairs				10·00	
First Day Cover					4·50
Presentation Pack				4·50	
PHQ Cards (set of 4)				4·00	7·00

Special First Day of Issue Postmarks

British Philatelic Bureau, Edinburgh	4·75
London SW	5·00

1098 Emperor Claudius (from gold coin)

1099 Emperor Hadrian (bronze head)

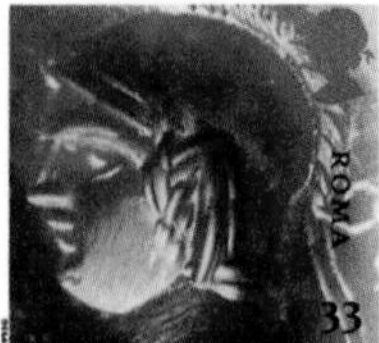

1100 Goddess Roma (from gemstone)

1101 Christ (Hinton St. Mary mosaic)

(Des J. Gibbs)

1993 (15 June). *Roman Britain. Phosphorised paper with two phosphor bands.* P 14×14½.

1771	**1098**	24p.	black, pale orange, lt brown and silver	60	20
1772	**1099**	28p.	black, greenish yellow, brt rose-red, silver, brt blue and grey-black	90	1·00
1773	**1100**	33p.	black, greenish yellow, brt rose-red, silver and grey	1·25	1·40
1774	**1101**	39p.	black, greenish yellow, rosine, silver, pale violet and grey	1·40	1·50
Set of 4				3·75	3·75
Set of 4 Gutter Pairs				10·00	
First Day Cover					3·75
Presentation Pack				4·50	
PHQ Cards (set of 4)				4·25	7·00

Special First Day of Issue Postmarks

British Philatelic Bureau, Edinburgh	4·50
Caerllion	4·50

1102 *Midland Maid* and other Narrow Boats,Grand Junction Canal

1103 *Yorkshire Lass* and other Humber Keels, Stainforth and Keadby Canal

1104 *Valley Princess* and other Horse-drawn Barges, Brecknock and Abergavenny Canal

1105 Steam Barges, including *Pride of Scotland*, and Fishing Boats, Crinan Canal

(Des T. Lewery. Litho Questa)

1993 (20 July). *Inland Waterways. Two phosphor bands.* P 14½×14.

1775	**1102**	24p.	new blue, greenish yellow, brt magenta, black, blue, vermilion, brownish grey and sage-green	50	20

1776	**1103**	28p. new blue, greenish yellow, brt magenta, black, blue, bluish grey, vermilion and sage-green	1·00	1·00
1777	**1104**	33p. new blue, greenish yellow, brt magenta, black, blue, vermilion, greenish grey and sage-green	1·25	1·25
1778	**1105**	39p. new blue, greenish yellow, brt magenta, black, blue, vermilion, sage-green and dull mauve	1·50	1·40
Set of 4			3·75	3·50
Set of 4 *Gutter Pairs*			9·00	
First Day Cover				3·75
Presentation Pack			4·50	
PHQ Cards (*set of* 4)			4·25	7·00

Nos. 1775/8 commemorate the bicentenary of the Acts of Parliament authorising the canals depicted.

Special First Day of Issue Postmarks

British Philatelic Bureau, Edinburgh .... 4·00
Gloucester .... 4·50

1106 Horse Chestnut

1107 Blackberry

1108 Hazel

1109 Rowan

1110 Pear (Des Charlotte Knox)

1993 (14 Sept). *The Four Seasons. Autumn. Fruits and Leaves. One phosphor band (18p.) or phosphorised paper (others).* P 15×14.

1779	**1106**	18p. black, greenish yellow, cerise, brt green, gold and chestnut	50	20
1780	**1107**	24p. black, lemon, cerise, myrtle-green, gold, brt green and brown	75	20
1781	**1108**	28p. grey, lemon, emerald, lake-brown and gold	1·10	1·25
1782	**1109**	33p. grey-black, greenish yellow, rosine, lt green, gold and brown	1·40	1·50
1783	**1110**	39p. myrtle-green, greenish yellow, rosine, olive-sepia, gold, apple-green and dp myrtle-green	1·50	1·50
Set of 5			4·75	4·50
Set of 5 *Gutter Pairs*			10·50	
First Day Cover				4·50
Presentation Pack			4·75	
PHQ Cards (*set of* 5)			4·50	7·00

Special First Day of Issue Postmarks

British Philatelic Bureau, Edinburgh .... 5·00
Taunton .... 5·25

1111 *The Reigate Squire*

1112 *The Hound of the Baskervilles*

1113 *The Six Napoleons*

1114 *The Greek Interpreter*

1115 *The Final Problem*

(Des A. Davidson. Litho Questa)

1993 (12 Oct). *Sherlock Holmes. Centenary of the Publication of "The Final Problem". Phosphorised paper.* P 14×14½.

1784	**1111**	24p. new blue, greenish yellow, magenta, black and gold	1·10	1·10
		a. Horiz strip of 5. Nos. 1784/8	5·00	5·25
1785	**1112**	24p. new blue, greenish yellow, magenta, black and gold	1·10	1·10

1786	**1113**	24p. new blue, greenish yellow, magenta, black and gold	1·10	1·10
1787	**1114**	24p. new blue, greenish yellow, magenta, black and gold	1·10	1·10
1788	**1115**	24p. new blue, greenish yellow, magenta, black and gold	1·10	1·10
Set of 5			5·00	5·00
Gutter strip of 10			11·00	
First Day Cover				5·50
Presentation Pack			5·00	
PHQ Cards (*set of* 5)			4·50	8·00

Nos. 1784/8 were printed together, *se-tenant*, in horizontal strips of 5 throughout the sheet.

Special First Day of Issue Postmarks

British Philatelic Bureau, Edinburgh .... 7·25
London NW1 .... 7·50

A First Day of Issue handstamp was provided at Autumn Stampex, London SW1, for this issue.

1116

(Des J. Matthews. Litho Walsall)

1993 (19 Oct). *Self-adhesive. Two phosphor bands.* Die-cut P 14×15 (with one elliptical hole on each vertical side).

1789	**1116**	(1st) orange-red	1·25	1·40
		Ey. Phosphor omitted		
		a. Booklet pane. No. 1789×20	20·00	
		aEy. Booklet pane. Phosphor omitted		
First Day Cover (*No.* 1789)				4·50
Presentation Pack (*No.* 1789a)			20·00	
PHQ Card			4·00	8·00

No. 1789 was initially sold at 24p. which was increased to 25p. from November 1993.

It was only issued in booklets containing 20 stamps, each surrounded by die-cut perforations.

For similar 2nd and 1st designs printed in photogravure by Enschedé see Nos. 1976/7.

Special First Day of Issue Postmarks

British Philatelic Bureau, Edinburgh 5.00
Newcastle upon Tyne 5.00

1117 Bob Cratchit and Tiny Tim **1118** Mr. and Mrs. Fezziwig

1119 Scrooge

1120 The Prize Turkey

1121 Mr. Scrooge's Nephew

(Des Q. Blake)

1993 (9 Nov). *Christmas. 150th Anniv of Publication of "A Christmas Carol" by Charles Dickens. One phosphor band (19p.) or phosphorised paper (others).* P 15×14.

1790	**1117**	19p. new blue, yellow, magenta, salmon, brt emerald and grey-black	60	15
		a. Imperf (pair)	£1900	
1791	**1118**	25p. yellow-orange, brown-lilac, steel-blue, lake-brown, lt green, grey-black and black	90	15
1792	**1119**	30p. cerise, bistre-yellow, dull blue, brown-rose, pale green, grey-black and black	1·25	1·50
1793	**1120**	35p. dp turquoise-green, lemon, vermilion, dull ultramarine, Indian red, bluish grey and black	1·40	1·60
1794	**1121**	41p. reddish purple, lemon, purple, lt blue, salmon, brt green and black	1·40	1·60
Set of 5			4·50	4·50
Set of 5 *Gutter Pairs*			11·00	
First Day Cover				5·00
Presentation Pack			5·00	
PHQ Cards (*set of* 5)			4·50	8·00

Special First Day of Issue Postmarks

British Philatelic Bureau, Edinburgh ....5·25
Bethlehem, Llandeilo .... 5·50

A First Day of Issue handstamp (pictorial) was provided at the City of London for this issue.

Collectors Pack 1993

1993 (9 Nov). *Comprises Nos.* 1639/43, 1654/7, 1659/63, 1767/88 *and* 1790/4.

CP1794a Collectors Pack ....45·00

Post Office Yearbook

1993 (9 Nov). *Comprises Nos.* 1639/43, 1654/7, 1659/63, 1767/88 *and* 1790/4 *in hardbound book with slip case, illustrated in colour*.......65·00

1122 Class 5 No. 44957 and Class B1 No. 61342 on West Highland Line

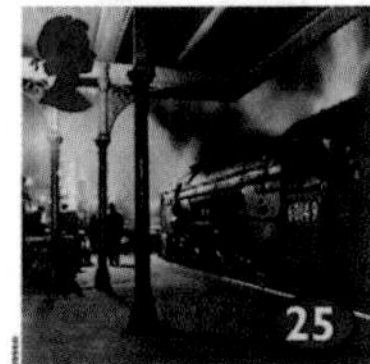

1123 Class A1 No. 60149 *Amadis* at Kings Cross

1124 Class 4 No. 43000 on Turntable at Blyth North

1125 Class 4 No. 42455 near Wigan Central

1126 Class "Castle" No. 7002 *Devizes Castle* on Bridge crossing Worcester and Birmingham Canal

(Des B. Delaney)

1994 (18 Jan). *The Age of Steam. Railway Photographs by Colin Gifford. One phosphor band (19p.) or phosphorised paper with two bands (others).* P 14½.

1795	**1122**	19p. dp blue-green, grey-black & black...	55	25
1796	**1123**	25p. slate-lilac, grey-black and black......	90	95
1797	**1124**	30p. lake-brown, grey-black & black......	1·40	1·40
1798	**1125**	35p. dp claret, grey-black and black........	1·75	1·80
1799	**1126**	41p. indigo, grey-black and black...........	1.80	1·75
Set of 5			6·00	5·50
Set of 5 Gutter Pairs			12·00	
First Day Cover				5·50
Presentation Pack			5·75	
PHQ Cards (set of 5)			5·75	11·00

Nos. 1796/9 are on phosphorised paper and also show two phosphor bands.

Special First Day of Issue Postmarks

Philatelic Bureau, Edinburgh ....5·75
York ....5·75

A First Day of Issue handstamp (pictorial) was provided at Bridge of Orchy for this issue.

1127 Dan Dare and the Mekon

1128 The Three Bears

1129 Rupert Bear

1130 Alice (*Alice in Wonderland*)

1131 Noggin and the Ice Dragon

1132 Peter Rabbit posting Letter

1133 Red Riding Hood the and Wolf

1134 Orlando Marmalade Cat

1135 Biggles

1136 Paddington Bear on Station

(Des Newell and Sorrell)

1994 (1 Feb). *Greetings Stamps. "Messages". Two phosphor bands.* P 15×14 (with one elliptical hole on each vertical side).

1800	**1127**	(1st) gold, greenish yellow, brt purple, bistre-yellow, new blue and black....	1·00	90
		a. Booklet pane. Nos. 1800/9..............	13·00	12·00
1801	**1128**	(1st) gold, greenish yellow, brt purple, bistre-yellow, new blue and black....	1·00	90
1802	**1129**	(1st) gold, greenish yellow, brt purple, bistre-yellow, new blue and black....	1·00	90
1803	**1130**	(1st) gold, bistre-yellow and black...........	1·00	90
1804	**1131**	(1st) gold, greenish yellow, brt purple, bistre-yellow, new blue and black....	1·00	90
1805	**1132**	(1st) gold, greenish yellow, brt purple, bistre-yellow, new blue and black....	1·00	90
1806	**1133**	(1st) gold, greenish yellow, brt purple, bistre-yellow, new blue and black....	1·00	90
1807	**1134**	(1st) gold, greenish yellow, brt purple, bistre-yellow, new blue and black....	1·00	90

1808	**1135**	(1st) gold, greenish yellow, brt purple, bistre-yellow, new blue and black....	1·00	90
1809	**1136**	(1st) gold, greenish yellow, brt purple, bistre-yellow, new blue and black....	1·00	90
Set of 10			11·00	8·00
First Day Cover				12·00
Presentation Pack			18·00	
PHQ Cards (*set of* 10)			16·00	28·00

Nos. 1800/9 were issued in £2.50 stamp booklets (sold at £2.60 from 8 July 1996), together with a pane of 20 half stampsized labels.

The stamps and labels were attached to the booklet cover by a common gutter margin.

Special First Day of Issue Postmarks

British Philatelic Bureau, Edinburgh .... 15·00
Penn, Wolverhampton .... 15·00

Castell Y Waun /Chirk Castle, Clwyd, Cymru/Wales

1137 Castell Y Waun (Chirk Castle), Clwyd, Wales

Ben Arkle, Sutherland, Scotland

1138 Ben Arkle, Sutherland, Scotland

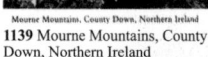

Mourne Mountains, County Down, Northern Ireland

1139 Mourne Mountains, County Down, Northern Ireland

Dersingham, Norfolk, England

1140 Dersingham, Norfolk, England

Dolwyddelan, Gwynedd, Cymru /Wales

1141 Dolwyddelan, Gwynedd, Wales

1994 (1 Mar). *25th Anniv of Investiture of the Prince of Wales. Paintings by Prince Charles. One phosphor band (19p.) or phosphorised paper (others).* P 15×14.

1810	**1137**	19p. grey-black, greenish yellow, magenta, new blue, black & silver...	55	20
1811	**1138**	25p. grey-black, orange-yellow, brt magenta, new blue, silver & black...	1·00	20
1812	**1139**	30p. grey-black, greenish yellow, magenta, new blue, silver & black...	1·10	1·50
		a. Booklet pane. No. 1812×4 with margins all round (26 July)	5·00	
1813	**1140**	35p. grey-black, greenish yellow, magenta, new blue, silver & black...	1·40	1·75
1814	**1141**	41p. grey-black, lemon, magenta, new blue, silver & black	1·50	1·75
Set of 5			5·00	5·00
Set of 5 *Gutter Pairs*			11·00	
First Day Cover				5·00
Presentation Pack			5·00	
PHQ Cards (*set of* 5)			5·75	11·50

Booklet pane No. 1812a comes from the £6.04 "Northern Ireland" booklet.

Special First Day of Issue Postmarks

British Philatelic Bureau, Edinburgh .... 5·50
Caernarfon .... 5·50

1142 Bather at Blackpool

1143 "Where's my Little Lad?"

1144 "Wish You were Here!"

1145 Punch and Judy Show

1146 "The Tower Crane" Machine

(Des M. Dempsey and B. Dare. Litho Questa)

1994 (12 Apr). *Centenary of Picture Postcards. One side band (19p.) or two phosphor bands (others).* P 14×14.

1815	**1142**	19p. new blue, greenish yellow, magenta & black	60	20
1816	**1143**	25p. new blue, greenish yellow, magenta & black	90	20
1817	**1144**	30p. new blue, greenish yellow, magenta & black	1·10	1·50
1818	**1145**	35p. new blue, greenish yellow, magenta & black	1·40	1·75

1819	**1146**	41p. new blue, greenish yellow, magenta & black	1·50	1·75
Set of 5			5·00	5·00
Set of 5 Gutter Pairs			11·00	
First Day Cover				5·00
Presentation Pack			5·00	
PHQ Cards (*set of 5*)			5·75	11·50

Special First Day of Issue Postmarks

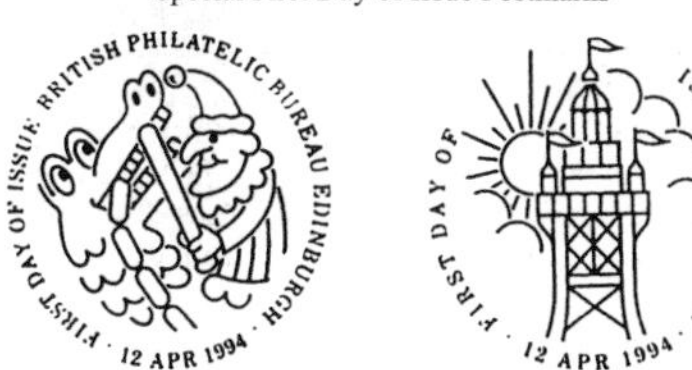

British Philatelic Bureau, Edinburgh	5·00
Blackpool	5·00

1147 British Lion and French Cockerel over Tunnel

1148 Symbolic Hands over Train

(Des G. Hardie (T **1147**), J.-P. Cousin (T **1148**))

1994 (3 May). *Opening of Channel Tunnel. Phosphorised paper.* P 14×14½

1820	**1147**	25p. ultramarine, brt orange, scarlet, new blue, emerald, turquoise-blue & silver	80	70
		a. Horiz pair. Nos. 1820/1	1·75	2·00
1821	**1148**	25p. ultramarine, scarlet, new blue, emerald & silver	80	70
1822	**1147**	41p. new blue, brt orange, scarlet, turquoise-blue, emerald, ultramarine & silver	1·50	1·50
		a. Horiz pair. Nos. 1822/3	3·25	3·25
		ab. Imperf (horiz pair)	£1600	
1823	**1148**	41p. ultramarine, scarlet, new blue, emerald & silver	1·50	1·50
Set of 4			4·50	4·50
First Day Cover				5·25
Presentation Pack			5·00	
Souvenir Book			47·00	
PHQ Cards (*set of 4*)			5·75	9·00

Nos. 1820/1 and 1822/3 were printed together, *se-tenant*, in horizontal pairs throughout the sheets.

Stamps in similar designs were also issued by France. These are included in the souvenir book.

Special First Day of Issue Postmarks

British Philatelic Bureau, Edinburgh	7·50
Folkestone	8·00

1149 Groundcrew replacing Smoke Canisters on Douglas Boston of 88 Sqn

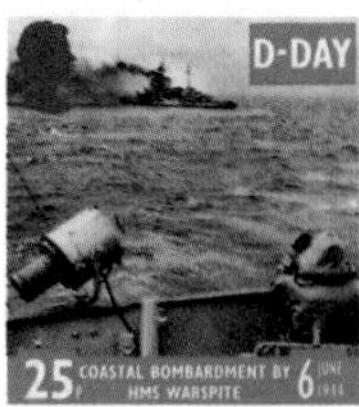

1150 H.M.S. *Warspite* (battleship) shelling Enemy Positions

1151 Commandos landing on Gold Beach

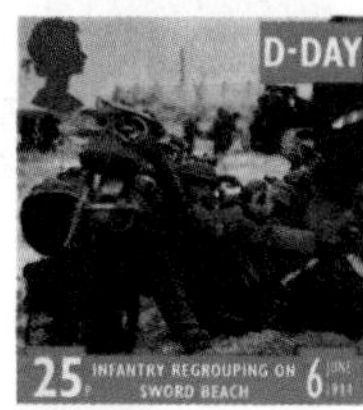

1152 Infantry regrouping on Sword Beach

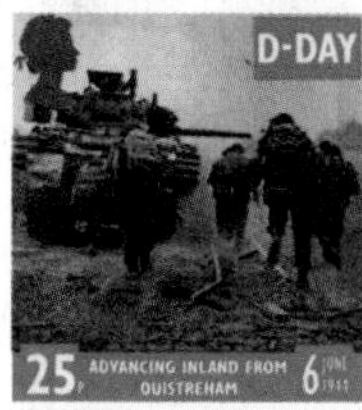

1153 Tank and Infantry advancing, Ouistreham

(Des K. Bassford from contemporary photographs. Litho Questa)

1994 (6 June). *50th Anniv of D-Day. Two phosphor bands.* P 14½×14.

1824	**1149**	25p. pink, greenish yellow, blackish lilac, slate-black, brt scarlet & silver-grey	1·10	1·10
		a. Horiz strip of 5. Nos. 1824/8	5·00	5·50
1825	**1150**	25p. pink. greenish yellow, blackish lilac, slate-black, brt scarlet & silver-grey	1·10	1·10
1826	**1151**	25p. pink, greenish yellow, blackish lilac, slate-black, brt scarlet & silver-grey	1·10	1·10
1827	**1152**	25p. pink. greenish yellow, blackish lilac, slate-black, brt scarlet & silver-grey	1·10	1·10
1828	**1153**	25p. pink, greenish yellow, blackish lilac, slate-black, brt scarlet & silver-grey	1·10	1·10
Set of 5			4·25	5·00
Gutter block of 10			11·00	
First Day Cover				5·50
Presentation Pack			5·50	
PHQ Cards (*set of 5*)			5·00	9·00

Nos. 1824/8 were printed together, *se-tenant*, in horizontal strips of 5 throughout the sheet.

Special First Day of Issue Postmarks

British Philatelic Bureau, Edinburgh	5·00
Portsmouth	5·50

1154 The Old Course, St. Andrews

1155 The 18th Hole, Muirfield

1156 The 15th Hole ("Luckyslap"), Carnoustie

1157 The 8th Hole ("The Postage Stamp"), Royal Troon

1158 The 9th Hole, Turnberry

(Des P. Hogarth)

1994 (5 July). *Scottish Golf Courses. One phosphor band (19p.) or phosphorised paper (others).* P 14½×14.

1829	**1154**	19p. yellow-green, olive-grey, orange-vermilion, apple-green, blue & grey-black	50	20
1830	**1155**	25p. yellow-green, lemon, brt orange, apple-green, blue, magenta & grey-black	75	20
1831	**1156**	30p. yellow-green, yellow, rosine, emerald, blue-green, new blue & grey-black	1·10	1·40
1832	**1157**	35p. yellow-green, yellow, rosine, apple-green, new blue, dull blue & grey-black	1·25	1·40
1833	**1158**	41p. yellow-green, lemon, magenta, apple-green, dull blue, new blue & grey-black	1·40	1·40
Set of 5			4·50	4·25
Set of 5 Gutter Pairs			11·50	
First Day Cover				4·75
Presentation Pack			5·00	
PHQ Cards (set of 5)			5·75	11·50

Nos. 1829/33 commemorate the 250th anniversary of golf's first set of rules produced by the Honourable Company of Edinburgh Golfers.

Special First Day of Issue Postmarks

British Philatelic Bureau, Edinburgh	5·00
Turnberry	5·50

AMSER HAF/SUMMERTIME Llanelwedd
1159 Royal Welsh Show, Llanelwedd

SUMMERTIME Wimbledon
1160 All England Tennis Championships, Wimbledon

SUMMERTIME Cowes
1161 Cowes Week

SUMMERTIME Lord's
1162 Test Match, Lord's

SUMMERTIME Braemar
1163 Braemar Gathering

(Des M. Cook)

1994 (2 Aug). *The Four Seasons. Summertime. One phosphor band (19p.) or phosphorised paper (others).* P 15×14.

1834	**1159**	19p. black, greenish yellow, brt magenta, brown, yellow-brown & new blue	50	20
1835	**1160**	25p. black, greenish yellow, magenta, reddish violet, yellow-green, myrtle-green & new blue	75	20
1836	**1161**	30p. black, greenish yellow, brt magenta, yellow-ochre, dp slate-blue, blue-green & blue	1·10	1·25
1837	**1162**	35p. black, greenish yellow, magenta, slate-lilac, yellow-green, dp bluish green & brt blue	1·25	1·60
1838	**1163**	41p. black, greenish yellow, brt magenta, dp claret, lt brown, myrtle-green & brt blue	1·40	1·60
Set of 5			4·50	4·25
Set of 5 Gutter Pairs			11·50	
First Day Cover				4·75
Presentation Pack			4·75	
PHQ Cards (set of 5)			5·75	11·50

Special First Day of Issue Postmarks

British Philatelic Bureau, Edinburgh	5·00
Wimbledon	5·00

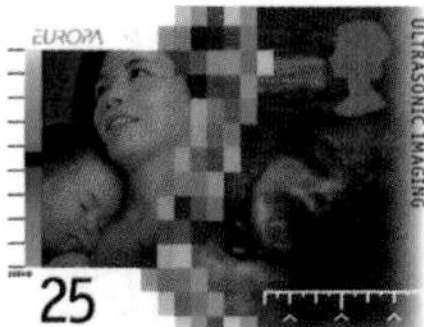

1164 Ultrasonic Imaging

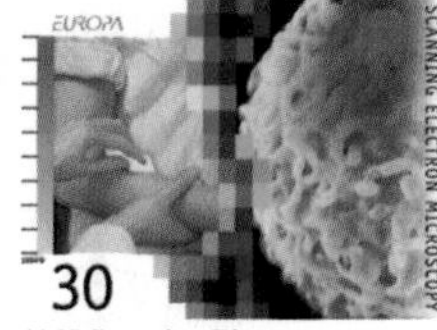

1165 Scanning Electron Microscopy

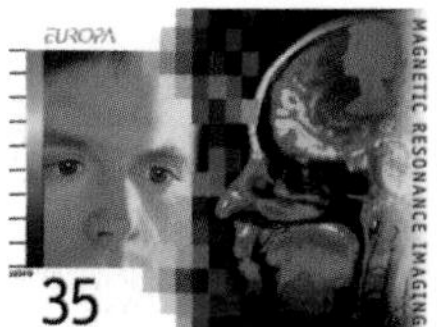

1166 Magnetic Resonance Imaging

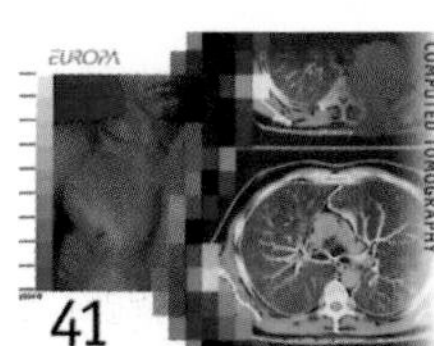

1167 Computed Tomography

(Des P. Vermier and J.-P. Tibbles. Photo Enschedé)

1994 (27 Sept). *Europa. Medical Discoveries. Phosphorised paper.* P 14×14½.

1839 **1164**	25p. greenish yellow, brt magenta, new blue, black & silver		75	25
	a. Imperf (vert pair)		£2000	
1840 **1165**	30p. greenish yellow, brt magenta, new blue, black & silver		1·00	1·25
1841 **1166**	35p. greenish yellow, brt magenta, new blue, black & silver		1·50	1·75
1842 **1167**	41p. greenish yellow, brt magenta, new blue, black & silver		1·75	1·75
Set of 4			4·50	4·50
Set of 4 *Gutter Pairs*			11·00	
First Day Cover				4·75
Presentation Pack			4·75	
PHQ Cards (*set of* 4)			5·75	10·00

Special First Day of Issue Postmarks

British Philatelic Bureau, Edinburgh	5·00
Cambridge	5·00

1168 Mary and Joseph

1169 Three Wise Men

1170 Mary with Doll

1171 Shepherds

1172 Angels

(Des Yvonne Gilbert)

1994 (1 Nov). *Christmas. Children's Nativity Plays. One phosphor band (19p.) or phosphorised paper (others).* P 15×14.

1843 **1168**	19p. turquoise-green, greenish yellow, brt magenta, new blue, dull blue & grey-black	50	15
	a. Imperf (pair)	£175	
1844 **1169**	25p. orange-brown, greenish yellow, brt magenta, new blue, lt blue, bistre & grey-black	75	15
1845 **1170**	30p. lt brown, greenish yellow, brt magenta, blue, turquoise-blue, new blue & brownish grey	1·00	1·50
	a. Imperf (pair)		
1846 **1171**	35p. dp grey-brown, greenish yellow, brt magenta, turquoise-blue, dull violet-blue, ochre & brown	1·25	1·50
1847 **1172**	41p. blue, greenish yellow, brt magenta, turquoise-blue, lt blue & dp grey	1·50	1·75
Set of 5		4·50	4·75
Set of 5 *Gutter Pairs*		10·50	
First Day Cover			4·75
Presentation Pack		4·75	
PHQ Cards (*set of* 5)		5·75	11·50

Special First Day of Issue Postmarks

British Philatelic Bureau, Edinburgh	5·00
Bethlehem, Llandeilo	5·00

Collectors Pack 1994

1994 (14 Nov). *Comprises Nos.* 1795/1847.

CP1847*a* Collectors Pack .... 55·00

Post Office Yearbook

1994 (14 Nov). *Comprises Nos.* 1795/9 *and* 1810/47 *in hardbound book with slip case, illustrated in colour* .... 55·00

1173 Sophie (black cat)

1174 Puskas (Siamese) and Tigger (tabby)

1175 Chloe (ginger cat)

1176 Kikko (tortoiseshell) and Rosie (Abyssinian)

1177 Fred (black and white cat)

(Des Elizabeth Blackadder. Litho Questa)

1995 (17 Jan). *Cats. One phosphor band (19p.) or two phosphor bands (others).* P 14½×14.

1848	**1173**	19p. new blue, greenish yellow, magenta, black & brown-red	75	20
1849	**1174**	25p. new blue, greenish yellow, magenta, black & dull yellowgreen	75	25
1850	**1175**	30p. new blue, greenish yellow, magenta, black & yellow-brown	1·00	1·50
1851	**1176**	35p. new blue, greenish yellow, magenta, black & yellow	1·25	1·50
1852	**1177**	41p. new blue, greenish yellow, magenta, black & reddish orange	1·50	1·50
Set of 5			4·75	4·75
Set of 5 *Gutter Pairs*			11·00	
First Day Cover				4·75
Presentation Pack			5·50	
PHQ Cards (*set of* 5)			6·00	11·50

Special First Day of Issue Postmarks

British Philatelic Bureau, Edinburgh ... 5·50
Kitts Green ... 5·50

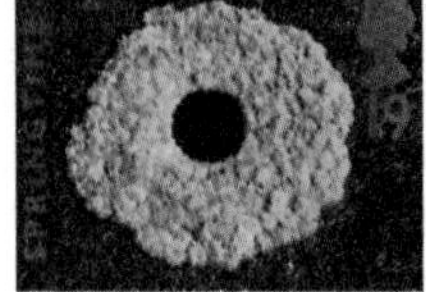

1178 Dandelions

1179 Chestnut Leaves

1180 Garlic Leaves

1181 Hazel Leaves

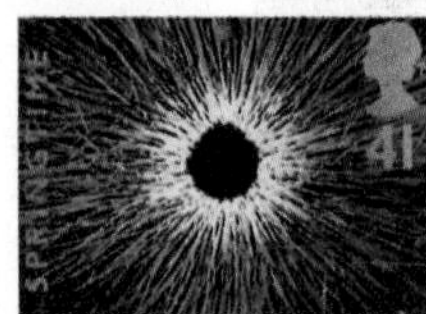

1182 Spring Grass

1995 (14 Mar). *The Four Seasons. Springtime. Plant Sculptures by Andy Goldsworthy. One phosphor band (19p.) or two phosphor bands (others).* P 15×14.

1853	**1178**	19p. silver, greenish yellow, magenta, green & grey-black	75	15
1854	**1179**	25p. silver, greenish yellow, magenta, new blue & black	75	15
1855	**1180**	30p. silver, greenish yellow, magenta, new blue & black	1·00	1·50
1856	**1181**	35p. silver, greenish yellow, magenta, new blue & black	1·25	1·50
1857	**1182**	41p. silver, greenish yellow, magenta, new blue, blue-green & black	1·50	1·75
Set of 5			4·75	4·75
Set of 5 *Gutter Pairs*			11·50	
First Day Cover			4·75	
Presentation Pack			5·00	
PHQ Cards (*set of* 5)			6·00	11·50

Special First Day of Issue Postmarks

British Philatelic Bureau, Edinburgh ... 5·00
Springfield ... 5·50

1183 "La Danse a la Campagne" (Renoir)

1184 "Troilus and Criseyde" (Peter Brookes)

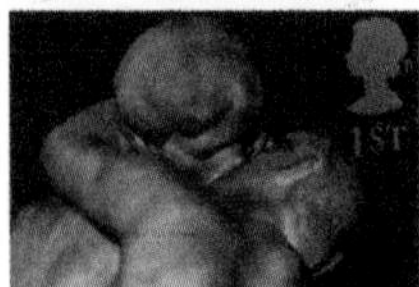

1185 "The Kiss" (Rodin)

1186 "Girls on the Town" (Beryl Cook)

1187 "Jazz" (Andrew Mockett)

1188 "Girls performing a Kathak Dance" (Aurangzeb period)

1189 "Keppel with her Daughter" (Alice Hughes)

1190 "Children Playing" (L. S. Lowry)

1191 "Circus Clowns" (Emily Firmin and Justin Mitchell)

1192 Decoration from "All the Love Poems of Shakespeare" (Eric Gill)

(Des Newell and Sorrell. Litho Walsall)

1995 (21 Mar). *Greetings Stamps. "Greetings in Art". Two phosphor bands.* P 14½×14 (with one elliptical hole on each vertical side).

1858	**1183**	(1st) greenish yellow, new blue, magenta, black & silver	1·00	80
		a. Booklet pane. Nos. 1858/67	11·50	11·00
		ab. Silver (Queen's head and "1ST") and phosphor omitted	£10000	
1859	**1184**	(1st) greenish yellow, new blue, magenta, black & silver	1·00	80
1860	**1185**	(1st) greenish yellow, new blue, magenta, black & silver	1·00	80
1861	**1186**	(1st) greenish yellow, new blue, magenta, black & silver	1·00	80
1862	**1187**	(1st) greenish yellow, new blue, magenta, black & silver	1·00	80
1863	**1188**	(1st) greenish yellow, new blue, magenta, black & silver	1·00	80
1864	**1189**	(1st) purple-brown & silver	1·00	80
1865	**1190**	(1st) greenish yellow, new blue, magenta, black & silver	1·00	80
1866	**1191**	(1st) greenish yellow, new blue, magenta, black & silver	1·00	80
1867	**1192**	(1st) black, greenish yellow & silver	1·00	80
Set of 10			11·00	7·00
First Day Cover				11·50
Presentation Pack			12·00	
PHQ Cards (*set of* 10)			16·00	28·00

Nos. 1858/67 were issued in £2.50 stamp booklets (sold at £2.60 from 8 July 1996), together with a pane of 20 half stampsized labels.

The stamps and labels were attached to the booklet cover by a common gutter margin.

Special First Day of Issue Postmarks

British Philatelic Bureau, Edinburgh	12·00
Lover	13·00

1193 Fireplace Decoration, Attingham Park, Shropshire

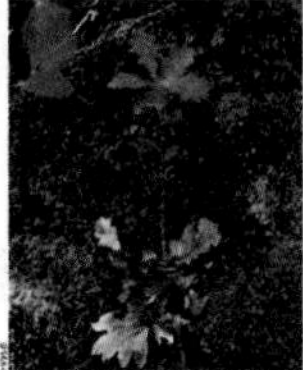

1194 Oak Seedling

1195 Carved Table Leg, Attingham Park

1196 St. David's Head, Dyfed, Wales

1197 Elizabethan Window, Little Moreton Hall, Cheshire

(Des T. Evans)

1995 (11 Apr). *Centenary of The National Trust. One phosphor band (19p.), two phosphor bands (25p., 35p.) or phosphorised paper (30p., 41p.).* P 14×15.

1868	**1193**	19p.	grey-green, stone, grey-brown, grey-black & gold	60	20
1869	**1194**	25p.	grey-green, greenish yellow, magenta, new blue, gold & black	80	20
			a. Booklet pane. No. 1869×6 with margins all round (25 Apr)	4·50	
1870	**1195**	30p.	grey-green, greenish yellow, magenta, new blue, gold, black & slate-black	1·00	1·50
1871	**1196**	35p.	grey-green, greenish yellow, magenta, blue, gold & black	1·25	1·50
1872	**1197**	41p.	grey-green, greenish yellow, brt green, slate-green, gold, blackish brown & black	1·40	1·75
Set of 5				4·50	4·75
Set of 5 *Gutter Pairs*				11·00	
First Day Cover					4·75
Presentation Pack				4·75	
PHQ Cards (*set of* 5)				6·00	11·50

Booklet pane No. 1869a comes from the £6 "National Trust" booklet.

Special First Day of Issue Postmarks

British Philatelic Bureau, Edinburgh .... 5·00
Alfriston .... 5·25

1198 British Troops and French Civilians celebrating

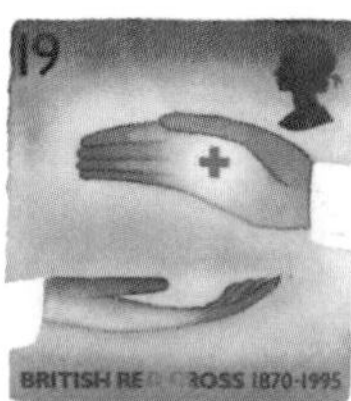

1199 Symbolic Hands and Red Cross

1200 St. Paul's Cathedral and Searchlights

1201 Symbolic Hand releasing Peace Dove

1202 Symbolic Hands

(Des J. Gorham (Nos. 1873, 1875), J-M. Folon (others))

1995 (2 May). *Europa. Peace and Freedom. One phosphor band (Nos. 1873/4) or two phosphor bands (others).* P 14½×14.

1873	**1198**	19p. silver, bistre-brown & grey-black	70	40
1874	**1199**	19p. silver, bistre-yellow, brt rose-red, vermilion, brt blue & slate-blue	70	40
1875	**1200**	25p. silver, blue & grey-black	1·00	1·00
1876	**1201**	25p. silver, vermilion, brt blue & grey-black	1·00	1·00
		a. Imperf (vert pair)	£3500	
1877	**1202**	30p. silver, bistre-yellow, brt magenta, pale greenish blue, grey-black & flesh	1·25	2·25
Set of 5			4·25	4·25
Set of 5 Gutter Pairs			10·50	
First Day Cover				4·75
Presentation Pack			5·00	
PHQ Cards (set of 5)			6·00	11·50

Nos. 1873 and 1875 commemorate the 50th anniversary of the end of the Second World War, No. 1874 the 125th anniversary of the British Red Cross Society and Nos. 1876/7 the 50th anniversary of the United Nations.

Nos. 1876/7 include the "EUROPA" emblem.

For No. 1875 with the face value expressed as "1st" see No. **MS**2547.

Special First Day of Issue Postmarks

British Philatelic Bureau, Edinburgh .... 5·00
London SW .... 5·50

A First Day of Issue handstamp (pictorial) was provided at London EC4 for this issue.

1203 *The Time Machine*

1204 *The First Men in the Moon*

1205 *The War of the Worlds*

1206 *The Shape of Things to Come*

(Des Siobhan Keaney. Litho Questa)

1995 (6 June). *Science Fiction. Novels by H. G. Wells. Two phosphor bands.* P 14½×14.

1878	**1203**	25p. new blue, greenish yellow, magenta, black & rosine	75	25
1879	**1204**	30p. new blue, greenish yellow, black, rosine & violet	1·25	1·50
1880	**1205**	35p. rosine, greenish yellow, violet, black & lt blue-green	1·25	1·60
1881	**1206**	41p. new blue, greenish yellow, magenta, black & rosine	1·50	1·60
Set of 4			4·25	4·50
Set of 4 Gutter Pairs			10·00	
First Day Cover				4·75
Presentation Pack			5·00	
PHQ Cards (set of 4)			5·00	10·00

Nos. 1878/81 commemorate the centenary of publication of Wells's *The Time Machine.*

Special First Day of Issue Postmarks

British Philatelic Bureau, Edinburgh .... 5·00
Wells .... 5·50

1207 The Swan, 1595

1208 The Rose, 1592

1209 The Globe, 1599

1210 The Hope, 1613

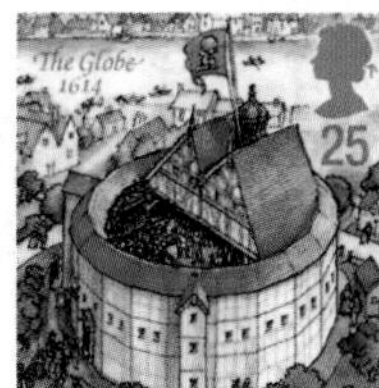

1211 The Globe, 1614

(Des C. Hodges. Litho Walsall)

1995 (8 Aug). *Reconstruction of Shakespeare's Globe Theatre. Two phosphor bands.* P 14½.

1882	**1207**	25p. brownish grey, black, magenta, new blue & greenish yellow	90	90
		a. Horiz strip of 5. Nos. 1882/6	4·50	4·75
1883	**1208**	25p. brownish grey, black, magenta, new blue & greenish yellow	90	90
1884	**1209**	25p. brownish grey, black, magenta, new blue & greenish yellow	90	90
1885	**1210**	25p. brownish grey, black, magenta, new blue & greenish yellow	90	90
1886	**1211**	25p. brownish grey, black, magenta, new blue & greenish yellow	90	90
Set of 5			4·25	4·75
Gutter Strip of 10			10·50	
First Day Cover				5·50
Presentation Pack			5·00	
PHQ Cards (*set of* 5)			6·00	11·50

Nos. 1882/6 were issued together, *se-tenant*, in horizontal strips of 5 throughout the sheet with the backgrounds forming a composite design.

Special First Day of Issue Postmarks

British Philatelic Bureau, Edinburgh .... 5·75
Stratford-upon-Avon .... 5·75

1212 Sir Rowland Hill and Uniform Penny Postage Petition

1213 Hill and Penny Black

1214 Guglielmo Marconi and Early Wireless

1215 Marconi and Sinking of *Titanic* (liner)

(Des The Four Hundred, Eng C. Slania. Recess and litho Harrison)

1995 (5 Sept). *Pioneers of Communications. One phosphor band (19p.) or phosphorised paper (others).* P 14×14.

1887	**1212**	19p. silver, red & black	75	30
1888	**1213**	25p. silver, brown & black	1·00	50
		a. Silver (Queen's head and face value) omitted	£400	
1889	**1214**	41p. silver, grey-green & black	1·50	1·75
1890	**1215**	60p. silver, dp ultramarine & black	1·75	2·25
Set of 4			4·50	4·50
Set of 4 *Gutter Pairs*			11·00	
First Day Cover				4·75
Presentation Pack			5·00	
PHQ Cards (*set of* 4)			5·75	11·50

Nos. 1887/8 mark the birth bicentenary of Sir Rowland Hill and Nos. 1889/90 the centenary of the first radio transmissions.

Special First Day of Issue Postmarks

British Philatelic Bureau, Edinburgh .... 5·00
London EC .... 5·00

1216 Harold Wagstaff

1217 Gus Risman

1218 Jim Sullivan

1219 Billy Batten

1220 Brian Bevan

(Des C. Birmingham)

1995 (3 Oct). *Centenary of Rugby League. One phosphor band (19p.) or two phosphor bands (others).* P 14½×14.

1891	**1216**	19p. blue, greenish yellow, magenta, new blue, grey-black & black	75	25
1892	**1217**	25p. slate-purple, greenish yellow, magenta, new blue, grey-black & black	75	30
1893	**1218**	30p. slate-green, greenish yellow, brt purple, new blue, grey-black & black	1·00	1·50
1894	**1219**	35p. slate-black, greenish yellow, magenta, new blue & black	1·00	1·60
1895	**1220**	41p. bluish grey, orange-yellow, magenta, new blue, grey-black & black	1·50	1·60
		Set of 5	4·75	4·75
		Set of 5 Gutter Pairs	11·00	
		First Day Cover		4·75
		Presentation Pack	5·50	
		PHQ Cards (*set of 5*)	6·00	11·50

Special First Day of Issue Postmarks

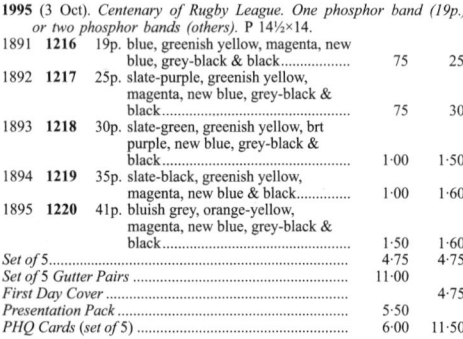

British Philatelic Bureau, Edinburgh .... 5·00
Huddersfield .... 5·75

A First Day of Issue handstamp (pictorial) was provided at Headingly, Leeds for this issue.

1221 European Robin in Mouth of Pillar Box

1222 European Robin on Railings and Holly

1223 European Robin on Snow-covered Milk Bottles

1224 European Robin on Road Sign

1225 European Robin on Door Knob and Christmas Wreath

(Des K. Lilly)

1995 (30 Oct). *Christmas. Christmas Robins. One phosphor band (19p.) or two phosphor bands (others).* P 15×14.

1896	**1221**	19p. silver, greenish yellow, vermilion, orange-vermilion, bistre & black	60	20
1897	**1222**	25p. silver, greenish yellow, scarlet, pale blue, ochre & black	85	30
1898	**1223**	30p. silver, greenish yellow, rose-carmine, lt green, olive-brown & grey	1·25	1·50
1899	**1224**	41p. silver, greenish yellow, rose-red, dull blue, bistre & black	1·60	1·75
1900	**1225**	60p. silver, orange-yellow, red-orange, bistre & black	1·75	1·90
		Set of 5	5·50	5·50
		Set of 5 Gutter Pairs	12·00	
		First Day Cover		5·50
		Presentation Pack	5·75	
		PHQ Cards (*set of 5*)	6·00	11·50

The 19p. value was re-issued on 3 October 2000 in sheets of 20, each with a *se-tenant* label showing Christmas greetings (sold for £3.99) or a personal photograph (sold for £7.99). These sheets were printed in photogravure by Questa and were sold by the Philatelic Bureau and selected philatelic outlets. Similar sheets were available from 9 October 2001 when the price for a personalised version was increased to £8.75. These could also be purchased, on an experimental basis, from photo-booths at six post offices.

Special First Day of Issue Postmarks

British Philatelic Bureau, Edinburgh .... 5·50
Bethlehem, Llandeilo .... 5·50

Collectors Pack 1995

1995 (30 Oct). *Comprises Nos.* 1848/1900.
CP1900*a* Collectors Pack .... 55·00

Post Office Yearbook

1995 (30 Oct). *Comprises Nos.* 1848/57 *and* 1868/1900 *in hardback book with slip case, illustrated in colour* .... 55·00

1226 Opening Lines of "To a Mouse" and Fieldmouse

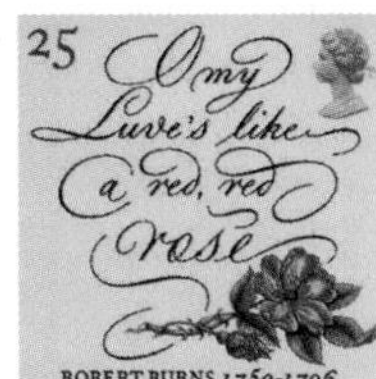
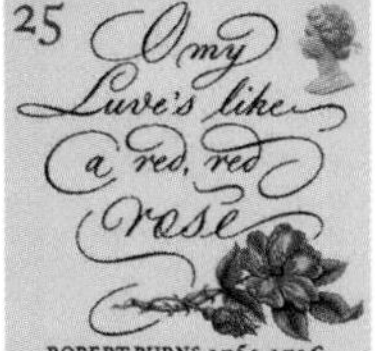

1227 "O my Luve's like a red, red rose" and Wild Rose

1228 "Scots, wha hae wi Wallace bled" and Sir William Wallace

1229 "Auld Lang Syne" and Highland Dancers

(Des Tayburn Design Consultancy. Litho Questa)

1996 (25 Jan). *Death Bicentenary of Robert Burns (Scottish poet). One phosphor band (19p.) or two phosphor bands (others).* P 14½.

1901	**1226**	19p. cream, bistre-brown & black	75	25
1902	**1227**	25p. cream, bistre-brown, black, magenta, bistre-yellow & new blue	1·00	30
1903	**1228**	41p. cream, bistre-brown, black, magenta, bistre-yellow & new blue	1·50	2·00
1904	**1229**	60p. cream, bistre-brown, black, magenta, bistre-yellow & new blue	1·75	2·50
		Set of 4	4·50	4·50
		Set of 4 *Gutter Pairs*	10·50	
		First Day Cover		4·75
		Presentation Pack	5·00	
		PHQ Cards (*set of* 4)	6·00	11·50

Special First Day of Issue Postmarks

British Philatelic Bureau, Edinburgh	5·00
Dumfries	5·25

1230 "MORE! LOVE" (Mel Calman)

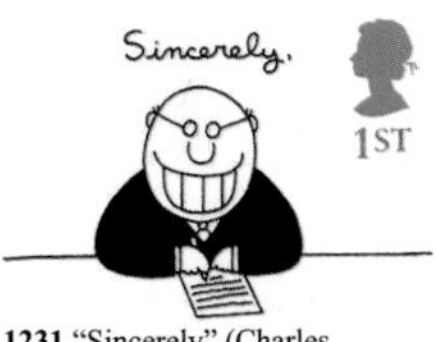

1231 "Sincerely" (Charles Barsotti)

1232 "Do you have something for the HUMAN CONDITION?" (Leo Cullum)

1233 "MENTAL FLOSS" (Mel Calman)

1234 "4.55 P.M." (Charles Barsotti)

1235 "Dear lottery prize winner" (Larry)

1236 "I'm writing to you because...." (Mel Calman)

1237 "FETCH THIS, FETCH THAT" (Charles Barsotti)

1238 "My day starts before I'm ready for it" (Mel Calman)

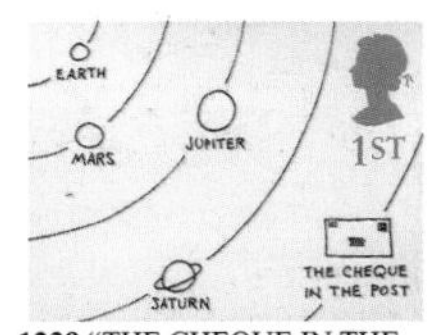

1239 "THE CHEQUE IN THE POST" (Jack Ziegler)

(Des M. Wolff. Litho Walsall)

1996 (26 Feb–11 Nov). *Greetings Stamps. Cartoons. "All over" phosphor.* P 14½×14 (with one elliptical hole on each vertical side).

1905	**1230**	(1st) black & bright mauve	80	75
		a. Booklet pane. Nos. 1905/14	10·00	11·00
		p. Two phosphor bands (11 Nov)	1·25	1·25
		pa. Booklet pane. Nos. 1905p/14p	28·00	26·00
1906	**1231**	(1st) black & blue-green	80	75
		p. Two phosphor bands (11 Nov)	1·25	1·25
1907	**1232**	(1st) black & new blue	80	75
		p. Two phosphor bands (11 Nov)	1·25	1·25
1908	**1233**	(1st) black & brt violet	80	75
		p. Two phosphor bands (11 Nov)	1·25	1·25
1909	**1234**	(1st) black & vermilion	80	75
		p. Two phosphor bands (11 Nov)	1·25	1·25
1910	**1235**	(1st) black & new blue	80	75
		p. Two phosphor bands (11 Nov)	1·25	1·25
1911	**1236**	(1st) black & vermilion	80	75
		p. Two phosphor bands (11 Nov)	1·25	1·25
1912	**1237**	(1st) black & brt violet	80	75
		p. Two phosphor bands (11 Nov)	1·25	1·25
1913	**1238**	(1st) black & blue-green	80	75
		p. Two phosphor bands (11 Nov)	1·25	1·25
1914	**1239**	(1st) black & brt mauve	80	75
		p. Two phosphor bands (11 Nov)	1·25	1·25
		Set of 10 (*Nos.* 1905/14)	9·00	6·75
		Set of 10 (*Nos.* 1905p/14p)	13·00	11·00
		First Day Cover (1905/14)		11·00
		Presentation Pack (1905/14)	16·00	
		PHQ Cards (*set of* 10)	16·00	28·00

Nos. 1905/14 were issued in £2.50 stamp booklets (sold at £2.60 from

Nos. 1905/14 were issued in £2.50 stamp booklets (sold at £2.60 from 8 July 1996), together with a pane of twenty half stamp-sized labels. The stamps and labels were attached to the booklet cover by a common gutter margin.

These designs were re-issued on 18 December 2001 in sheets of 10, each with a *se-tenant* label showing cartoon comments (sold for £2.95). They were re-issued again on 29 July 2003 in sheets of 20 sold for £6.15 containing two of each design, each stamp accompanied by a half stamp-size label showing a crossword grid (clues printed on the bottom sheet margin). Sheets of 20 with personal photographs on the labels and a crossword puzzle in the bottom sheet margin were also available, at £14.95 a sheet from Royal Mail, Edinburgh and Post Office philatelic outlets, or £15 a sheet from photo booths.

All these sheets were printed in lithography by Questa with two phosphor bands and perforated 14½×14 (without elliptical holes), and were available from the bureau and other selected philatelic outlets.

Special First Day of Issue Postmarks

British Philatelic Bureau, Edinburgh .... 9·00
Titterhill, Haytons Bent, Ludlow .... 9·00

1240 "Muscovy Duck"

1241 "Lapwing"

1242 "White-fronted Goose"

1243 "Bittern"

1244 "Whooper Swan"

(Des Moseley Webb)

1996 (12 Mar). *50th Anniv of the Wildfowl and Wetlands Trust. Bird Paintings by C. F. Tunnicliffe. One phosphor band (19p.) or phosphorised paper (others).* P 14×14½.

1915	**1240**	19p. sepia, orange-yellow, brown, pale buff, grey & gold	70	25
1916	**1241**	25p. bistre-brown, greenish yellow, magenta, new blue, pale buff, gold & black	90	30
1917	**1242**	30p. bistre-brown, greenish yellow, magenta, new blue, pale buff, gold & grey-black	1·00	1·25
1918	**1243**	35p. sepia, pale orange, lake-brown, brown-olive, pale buff, gold & grey-black	1·10	1·50
1919	**1244**	41p. sepia, greenish yellow, magenta, new blue, pale buff, gold & grey-black	1·50	1·60
Set of 5			4·75	4·50
Set of 5 Gutter Pairs			10·50	
First Day Cover				5·75
Presentation Pack			5·00	
PHQ Cards (set of 5)			6·00	11·50

Special First Day of Issue Postmarks

British Philatelic Bureau, Edinburgh .... 6·00
Slimbridge, Gloucester ....6·50

1245 The Odeon, Harrogate

1246 Laurence Olivier and Vivien Leigh in *Lady Hamilton* (film)

1247 Old Cinema Ticket

1248 Pathé News Still

1249 Cinema Sign, The Odeon, Manchester

(Des The Chase)

1996 (16 Apr). *Centenary of Cinema. One phosphor band (19p.) or two phosphor bands (others).* P 14×14½.

1920	**1245**	19p. black, greenish yellow, silver, brt magenta & new blue	50	25

1921	**1246**	25p. black, greenish yellow, silver, brt magenta & new blue	70	30
1922	**1247**	30p. black, greenish yellow, silver, brt magenta & new blue	1·00	1·75
1923	**1248**	35p. black, red & silver	1·25	2·00
1924	**1249**	41p. black, greenish yellow, silver, brt magenta & new blue	1·50	2·25
Set of 5			4·75	4·75
Set of 5 Gutter Pairs			11·00	
First Day Cover				5·75
Presentation Pack			5·50	
PHQ Cards (set of 5)			6·00	11·50

Special First Day of Issue Postmarks

British Philatelic Bureau, Edinburgh	6·00
London, WC2	6·50

1250 Dixie Dean

1251 Bobby Moore

1252 Duncan Edwards

1253 Billy Wright

1254 Danny Blanchflower

(Des H. Brown. Litho Questa)

1996 (14 May). *European Football Championship. One phosphor band (19p.) or two phosphor bands (others).* P 14½×14.

1925	**1250**	19p. vermilion, black, pale grey & grey	50	20
		a. Booklet pane. No. 1925×4 with margins all round	3·25	
1926	**1251**	25p. brt emerald, black, pale grey & grey	75	20
		a. Booklet pane. No. 1926×4 with margins all round	3·25	
1927	**1252**	35p. orange-yellow, black, pale grey & grey	1·25	1·75
		a. Booklet pane. Nos. 1927/9, each ×2, with margins all round	8·00	
1928	**1253**	41p. new blue, black, pale grey & grey	1·50	1·75
1929	**1254**	60p. brt orange, black, pale grey & grey	1·75	2·00
Set of 5			5·50	5·75
Set of 5 Gutter Pairs			12·00	
First Day Cover				5·75
Presentation Pack			5·75	
PHQ Cards (set of 5)			6·00	11·50

Special First Day of Issue Postmarks

British Philatelic Bureau, Edinburgh	6·00
Wembley	6·00

1255 Athlete on Starting Blocks

1256 Throwing the Javelin

1257 Basketball

1258 Swimming

1259 Athlete celebrating and Olympic Rings

(Des N. Knight. Litho Questa)

1996 (9 July). *Olympic and Paralympic Games, Atlanta. Two phosphor bands.* P 14½×14.

1930	**1255**	26p. greenish grey, silver, rosine, black, magenta, bistre-yellow & new blue	1·10	1·00
		a. Horiz strip of 5. Nos. 1930/4	5·00	5·50
1931	**1256**	26p. greenish grey, silver, rosine, black, magenta, bistre-yellow & new blue	1·10	1·00
1932	**1257**	26p. greenish grey, silver, rosine, black, magenta, bistre-yellow & new blue	1·10	1·00
1933	**1258**	26p. greenish grey, silver, rosine, black, magenta, bistre-yellow & new blue	1·10	1·00
1934	**1259**	26p. greenish grey, silver, rosine, black, magenta, bistre-yellow & new blue	1·10	1·00
Set of 5			4·50	4·50
Gutter Strip of 10			11·00	
First Day Cover				5·50
Presentation Pack			4·50	
PHQ Cards (set of 5)			6·00	11·50

Nos. 1930/4 were printed together, *se-tenant*, in horizontal strips of 5 throughout the sheet.

For these designs with face value expressed as "1st" see **MS**2554.

Special First Day of Issue Postmarks

British Philatelic Bureau, Edinburgh .... 5·50
Much Wenlock .... 6·00

1260 Prof. Dorothy Hodgkin (scientist)

1261 Dame Margot Fonteyn (ballerina)

1262 Dame Elisabeth Frink (sculptress)

1263 Dame Daphne du Maurier (novelist)

1264 Dame Marea Hartman (sports administrator)

(Des Stephanie Nash)

1996 (6 Aug). *Europa. Famous Women. One phosphor band (20p.) or two phosphor bands (others).* P 14½.

1935	**1260**	20p. dull blue-green, brownish grey & black	60	25
1936	**1261**	26p. dull mauve, brownish grey & black	75	25
		a. Imperf (horiz pair)	£325	
1937	**1262**	31p. bronze, brownish grey & black	1·10	1·10
1938	**1263**	37p. silver, brownish grey & black	1·25	1·40
1939	**1264**	43p. gold, brownish grey & black	1·50	1·50
Set of 5			4·75	4·50
Set of 5 Gutter Pairs			12·00	
First Day Cover				5·00
Presentation Pack			4·75	
PHQ Cards (set of 5)			6·00	11·50

Nos. 1936/7 include the "EUROPA" emblem.

Special First Day of Issue Postmarks

British Philatelic Bureau, Edinburgh .... 5·50
Fowey .... 6·00

1265 *Muffin the Mule*

1266 *Sooty*

1267 *Stingray*

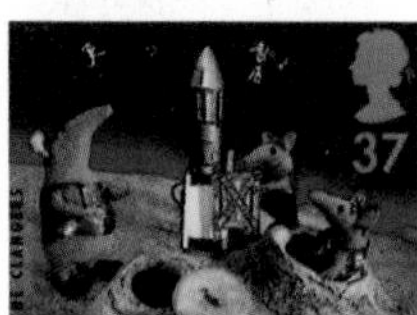

1268 *The Clangers*

1269 *Dangermouse*

(Des Tutssels. Photo Harrison (No. 1940a) or Enschedé (others))

1996 (3 Sept)–**97**. *50th Anniv of Children's Television. One phosphor band (20p.) or two phosphor bands (others).* P 14½×14.

1940	**1265**	20p. dp claret, black, magenta, rosine & greenish yellow	55	20
		a. Perf 15×14 (23.9.97)	2·00	2·00
		ab. Booklet pane. No. 1940a×4 with margins all round	8·00	
1941	**1266**	26p. brt blue, black, dp grey-blue, magenta & greenish yellow	80	20
1942	**1267**	31p. greenish blue, black, new blue, magenta & greenish yellow	1·00	1·50
1943	**1268**	37p. dull violet-blue, black, new blue, magenta & greenish yellow	1·40	1·75
1944	**1269**	43p. brt purple, black, new blue, magenta & greenish yellow	1·60	2·00
Set of 5			4·75	4·75
Set of 5 Gutter Pairs			10·50	
First Day Cover				4·75
Presentation Pack			4·75	
PHQ Cards (set of 5)			6·00	11·50

No. 1940a comes from the 1997 £6.15 B.B.C. stamp booklet.

Special First Day of Issue Postmarks

British Philatelic Bureau, Edinburgh	5·50
Alexandra Palace, London	6·00

1270 Triumph TR3

1271 MG TD

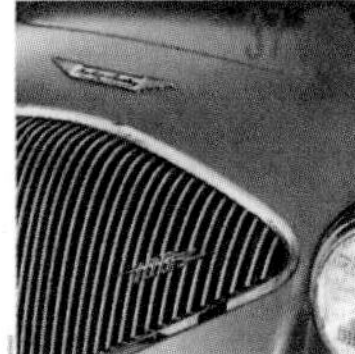
1272 Austin-Healey 100

1273 Jaguar XK120

1274 Morgan Plus 4

(Des S. Clay)

1996 (1 Oct). *Classic Sports Cars. One phosphor band (20p.) or two phosphor bands (others).* P 14½.

1945	**1270**	20p.	silver, greenish yellow, brt scarlet, vermilion, new blue & black	55	20
1946	**1271**	26p.	silver, greenish yellow, magenta, greenish blue & black	1·10	20
			a. Imperf (pair)	£650	
1947	**1272**	37p.	silver, greenish yellow, brt magenta, dp turquoise-blue, new blue & black	1·40	1·90
			a. Imperf (pair)	£800	
1948	**1273**	43p.	silver, greenish yellow, magenta, greenish blue & black	1·60	1·90
			a. Imperf (horiz pair)	£1500	
1949	**1274**	63p.	silver, greenish yellow, magenta, greenish blue, stone & black	1·75	2·00
Set of 5				5·75	6·00
Set of 5 *Gutter Pairs*				13·00	
First Day Cover					6·00
Presentation Pack				6·00	
PHQ Cards (*set of* 5)				6·00	11·50

On Nos. 1946/9 the right-hand phosphor band on each stamp is three times the width of that on the left.

Special First Day of Issue Postmarks

British Philatelic Bureau, Edinburgh	6·00
Beaulieu, Brockenhurst	6·25

A pictorial First Day of Issue handstamp was provided at London E1 for this issue.

1275 The Three Kings

1276 The Annunciation

1277 The Journey to Bethlehem

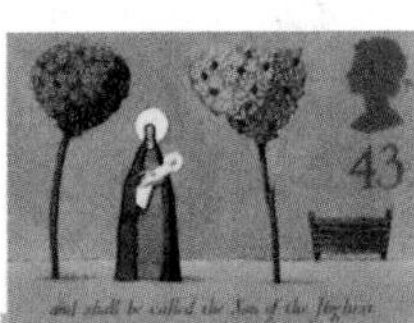
1278 The Nativity

1279 The Shepherds

(Des Laura Stoddart)

1996 (28 Oct). *Christmas. One phosphor band (2nd) or two phosphor bands (others).* P 15×14.

1950	**1275**	(2nd)	gold, greenish yellow, magenta, blue, black & lt brown	75	20
1951	**1276**	(1st)	gold, yellow, cerise, new blue, black & lt brown	1·00	35
1952	**1277**	31p.	gold, orange-yellow, cerise, blue, black & lt brown	1·25	1·75
1953	**1278**	43p.	gold, greenish yellow, magenta, new blue, grey-black & lt brown	1·25	1·75
1954	**1279**	63p.	gold, greenish yellow, magenta, new blue, black & lt brown	1·50	2·00
Set of 5				5·50	5·50
Set of 5 *Gutter Pairs*				13·00	
First Day Cover					6·00
Presentation Pack				5·75	
PHQ Cards (*set of* 5)				6·00	11·50

Special First Day of Issue Postmarks

British Philatelic Bureau, Edinburgh .... 6·25
Bethlehem, Llandeilo .... 6·25

Collectors Pack 1996

1996 (28 Oct). *Comprises Nos.* 1901/4 *and* 1915/54.
CP1954*a* Collectors Pack ....55·00

Post Office Yearbook

1996 (28 Oct). *Comprises Nos.* 1901/4 *and* 1915/54 *in hardback book with slip case, illustrated in colour* ....60·00

1280 *Gentiana acaulis* (Georg Ehret)

1281 *Magnolia grandiflora* (Ehret)

1282 *Camellia japonica* (Alfred Chandler)

1283 *Tulipa* (Ehret)

1284 *Fuchsia "Princess of Wales"* (Augusta Withers)

1285 *Tulipa gesneriana* (Ehret)

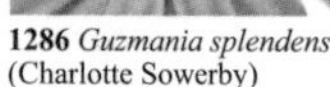
1286 *Guzmania splendens* (Charlotte Sowerby)

1287 *Iris latifolia* (Ehret)

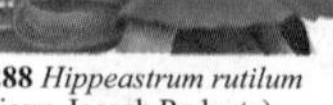
1288 *Hippeastrum rutilum* (Pierre-Joseph Redoute)

1289 *Passiflora coerulea* (Ehret)

(Des Tutssels. Litho Walsall)

1997 (6 Jan). *Greeting Stamps. 19th-century Flower Paintings. Two phosphor bands.* P 14½×14 (with one elliptical hole on each vertical side).

1955	**1280**	(1st)	greenish yellow, new blue, magenta, black, blue-green & gold.................	85	90
		a.	Booklet pane. Nos. 1955/64.............	11·25	11·25
		ab.	Gold, blue-green and phosphor omitted	£15000	
1956	**1281**	(1st)	greenish yellow, new blue, magenta, black, blue-green & gold.................	85	90
1957	**1282**	(1st)	greenish yellow, new blue, magenta, black, blue-green & gold.................	85	90
1958	**1283**	(1st)	greenish yellow, new blue, magenta, black, blue-green & gold.................	85	90
1959	**1284**	(1st)	greenish yellow, new blue, magenta, black, blue-green & gold.................	85	90
1960	**1285**	(1st)	greenish yellow, new blue, magenta, black, blue-green & gold.................	85	90
1961	**1286**	(1st)	greenish yellow, new blue, magenta, black, blue-green & gold.................	85	90
1962	**1287**	(1st)	greenish yellow, new blue, magenta, black, blue-green & gold.................	85	90
1963	**1288**	(1st)	greenish yellow, new blue, magenta, black, blue-green & gold.................	85	90
1964	**1289**	(1st)	greenish yellow, new blue, magenta, black, blue-green & gold.................	85	90
Set of 10			....	9·00	8·00
First Day Cover			....		11·50
Presentation Pack			....	16·00	
PHQ Cards (*set of* 10)			....	16·00	28·00

Nos. 1955/64 were issued in £2.60 stamp booklets together with a pane of twenty half-sized labels. The stamps and labels were attached to the booklet cover by a common gutter margin. Nos. 1955/64 were re-issued on 21 January 2003 in *se-tenant* sheets of 20, each accompanied by a label showing further flowers (sold at £5.95) or personal photographs (sold at £14.95). These stamps were printed in lithography by Questa and are without elliptical holes in the perforations. For booklet stamps in designs as Nos. 1955, 1958 and 1962 printed by Enschedé see Nos. 2463/5.

For Nos. 1995, 1958 and 1962 perf 15x14 see Nos. 2463/5.

Special First Day of Issue Postmarks

British Philatelic Bureau, Edinburgh .... 12·00
Kew, Richmond, Surrey .... 13·00

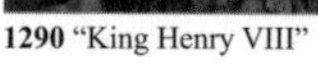
1290 "King Henry VIII"

1291 "Catherine of Aragon"

1292 "Anne Boleyn"

1293 "Jane Seymour"

1294 "Anne of Cleves"

1295 "Catherine Howard"

1296 "Catherine Parr"

(Des Kate Stephens from contemporary paintings)

1997 (21 Jan). *450th Death Anniv of King Henry VIII. Two phosphor bands.* P 15 (No. 1965) or 14×15 (others).

1965	**1290**	26p. gold, greenish yellow, brt purple, new blue and black	1·00	90
		a. Imperf (pair)	£1200	
1966	**1291**	26p. gold, greenish yellow, brt carmine, new blue and black	1·25	1·00
		a. Horiz strip of 6. Nos. 1966/71	8·00	8·50
1967	**1292**	26p. gold, greenish yellow, brt carmine, new blue and black	1·25	1·00
1968	**1293**	26p. gold, greenish yellow, brt carmine, new blue and black	1·25	1·00
1969	**1294**	26p. gold, greenish yellow, brt carmine, new blue and black	1·25	1·00
1970	**1295**	26p. gold, greenish yellow, brt carmine, new blue and black	1·25	1·00
1971	**1296**	26p. gold, greenish yellow, brt carmine, new blue and black	1·25	1·00
Set of 7			7·75	6·50
Set of 1 *Gutter Pair and a Gutter Strip of* 12			17·00	
First Day Cover				9·50
Presentation Pack			10·00	
PHQ Cards (*set of* 7)			10·00	18·00

Nos. 1966/71 were printed together, *se-tenant*, in horizontal strips of 6 throughout the sheet.

Special First Day of Issue Postmarks

British Philatelic Bureau, Edinburgh	10·00
Hampton Court, East Molesey	11·00

1297 St. Columba in Boat

1298 St. Columba on Iona

1299 St. Augustine with King Ethelbert

1300 St. Augustine with Model of Cathedral

(Des Claire Melinsky. Photo Enschedé)

1997 (11 Mar). *Religious Anniversaries. Two phosphor bands.* P 14½.

1972	**1297**	26p. greenish yellow, magenta, new blue, grey-black and gold	75	35
		a. Imperf (pair)	£500	
1973	**1298**	37p. greenish yellow, magenta, new blue, grey-black and gold	1·10	1·50
1974	**1299**	43p. greenish yellow, magenta, new blue, grey-black and gold	1·50	1·50
1975	**1300**	63p. greenish yellow, magenta, new blue, grey-black and gold	2·00	2·10
Set of 4			4·75	5·00
Set of 4 *Gutter Pairs*			11·50	
First Day Cover				5·75
Presentation Pack			5·25	
PHQ Cards (*set of* 4)			5·75	11·50

Nos. 1972/3 commemorate the 1400th death anniversary of St. Columba and Nos. 1974/5 the 1400th anniversary of the arrival of St. Augustine of Canterbury in Kent.

Special First Day of Issue Postmarks

British Philatelic Bureau, Edinburgh	6·00
Isle of Iona	6·00

1301

1302

(Des J. Matthews. Photo Enschedé)

1997 (18 Mar). *Self-adhesive. One centre phosphor band (2nd) or two phosphor bands (1st).* P 14×15 die-cut (with one elliptical hole on each vertical side).

1976	**1301**	(2nd) bright blue	2·75	2·50
1977	**1302**	(1st) bright orange-red	2·75	2·75
Set of 2			4·50	5·25
First Day Cover				5·50
Presentation Pack (P.O. Pack No. 37)			6·50	

Nos. 1976/7, which were sold at 20p. and 26p., were in rolls of 100 with the stamps separate on the backing paper.

Special First Day of Issue Postmarks

British Philatelic Bureau, Edinburgh	5·50
Glasgow	5·50

1303 *Dracula*

1304 *Frankenstein*

1305 *Dr. Jekyll and of Mr. Hyde*

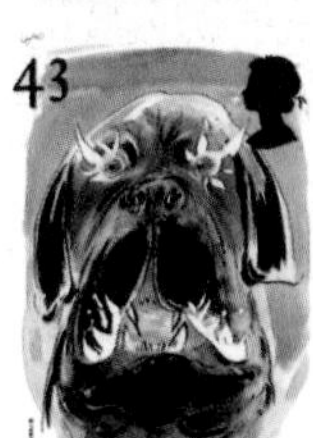

1306 *The Hound the Baskervilles*

(Des I. Pollock. Photo Walsall)

1997 (13 May). *Europa. Tales and Legends. Horror Stories. Two phosphor bands.* P 14×15.

1980	**1303**	26p. grey-black, black, new blue, magenta and greenish yellow	1·00	40
1981	**1304**	31p. grey-black, black, new blue, magenta and greenish yellow	1·10	1·50
1982	**1305**	37p. grey-black, black, new blue, magenta and greenish yellow	1·30	1·75
1983	**1306**	43p. grey-black, black, new blue, magenta and greenish yellow	2·00	1·95
Set of 4			5·00	5·50
Set of 4 *Gutter Pairs*			12·00	
First Day Cover				5·50
Presentation Pack			5·25	
PHQ Cards (*set of* 4)			5·75	11·50

Nos. 1980/3 commemorate the birth bicentenary of Mary Shelley (creator of Frankenstein) with the 26p. and 31p. values incorporating the "EUROPA" emblem. Each value has features printed in fluorescent ink which are visible under ultra-violet light.

Special First Day of Issue Postmarks

British Philatelic Bureau, Edinburgh	6·00
Whitby	6·00

1307 Reginald Mitchell and Supermarine Spitfire MkIIA

1308 Roy Chadwick and Avro Lancaster MkI

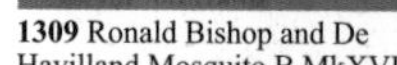

1309 Ronald Bishop and De Havilland Mosquito B MkXVI

1310 George Carter and Gloster Meteor T Mk7

1311 Sir Sidney Camm and Hawker Hunter FGA Mk9

(Des Turner Duckworth)

1997 (10 June). *British Aircraft Designers. One phosphor band (20p.) or two phosphor bands (others).* P 15×14.

1984	**1307**	20p. silver, greenish yellow, magenta, new blue, black and grey	75	40
1985	**1308**	26p. silver, greenish yellow, magenta, new blue, black and grey	1·10	1·25
1986	**1309**	37p. silver, greenish yellow, magenta, new blue, black and grey	1·40	1·25
1987	**1310**	43p. silver, greenish yellow, magenta, new blue, black and grey	1·50	1·60

1988	**1311**	63p. silver, greenish yellow, magenta, new blue, black and grey	2·00	2·00
Set of 5			6·00	6·50
Set of 5 *Gutter Pairs*			15·00	
First Day Cover				6·50
Presentation Pack			6·50	
PHQ Cards (*set of* 5)			6·00	13·00

Special First Day of Issue Postmarks

British Philatelic Bureau, Edinburgh .... 6·50
Duxford, Cambridge .... 6·50

1312 Carriage Horse and Coachman

1313 Lifeguards Horse and Trooper

1314 Blues and Royals Drum Horse and Drummer

1315 Duke of Edinburgh's Horse and Groom

(Des J.-L. Benard. Litho Walsall)

1997 (8 July). *"All the Queen's Horses". 50th Anniv of the British Horse Society. One phosphor band (20p.) or two phosphor bands (others).* P 14½.

1989	**1312**	20p. scarlet-vermilion, black, magenta, new blue and greenish yellow	80	45
1990	**1313**	26p. scarlet-vermilion, black, magenta, new blue and greenish yellow	1·10	1·50
1991	**1314**	43p. scarlet-vermilion, black, magenta, new blue and greenish yellow	1·50	1·50
1992	**1315**	63p. scarlet-vermilion, black, magenta, new blue and greenish yellow	2·00	2·00
Set of 4			5·00	5·25
Set of 4 *Gutter Pairs*			12·00	
First Day Cover				5·75
Presentation Pack			5·50	
PHQ Cards (*set of* 4)			5·75	11·50

Special First Day of Issue Postmarks

British Philatelic Bureau, Edinburgh .... 6·00
Windsor, Berks . ... 6·00

CASTLE

Harrison plates (Nos. 1611/14)

CASTLE

Enschedé plates (Nos. 1993/6)

Differences between Harrison and Enschedé:
Harrison- "C" has top serif and tail of letter points to right. "A" has flat top. "S" has top and bottom serifs.
Enschedé- "C" has no top serif and tail of letter points upwards. "A" has pointed top. "S" has no serifs.

Harrison plates (Nos. 1611/14) Enschedé plates (Nos. 1993/6)

(Des from photos by Prince Andrew, Duke of York. Eng Inge Madle Recess (Queen's head by silk screen process) Enschedé)

1997 (29 July). *Designs as Nos. 1611/14 with Queen's head in silhouette as T* **1044**, *but re-engraved with differences in inscription as shown above.* P 15×14 (with one elliptical hole on each vertical side).

1993	**880**	£1.50 deep claret and gold†	10·00	6·00
		a. Gold (Queen's head) omitted		£1500
1994	**881**	£2 indigo and gold†	12·00	2·25
		a. Gold (Queen's head) omitted	£600	
1995	**1044**	£3 violet and gold†	26·00	3·50
		a. Gold (Queen's head) omitted	£2000	
1996	**882**	£5 deep brown and gold†	28·00	10·00
		a. Gold (Queen's head) omitted	£3750	
Set of 4			68·00	18·00
Set of 4 *Gutter Pairs*			£140	
Presentation Pack (*P.O. Pack No.* 40)			£150	

†The Queen's head on these stamps is printed in optically variable ink which changes colour from gold to green when viewed from different angles. No. 1996a occurs on R. 5/8 and 6/8 from some sheets.

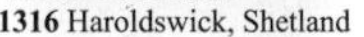

1316 Haroldswick, Shetland

1317 Painswick, Gloucestershire

1318 Beddgelert, Gwynedd

1319 Ballyroney, County Down

(Des T. Millington. Photo Enschedé)

1997 (12 Aug). *Sub-Post Offices. One phosphor band (20p.) or two phosphor bands (others).* P 14½.

1997	**1316**	20p. greenish yellow, bright magenta, new blue, grey-black, rosine and blue-green	75	50
1998	**1317**	26p. greenish yellow, bright magenta, new blue, grey-black, rosine and blue-green	1·00	1·00
1999	**1318**	43p. greenish yellow, bright magenta, new blue, grey-black, rosine and blue-green	1·50	1·50
2000	**1319**	63p. greenish yellow, bright magenta, new blue, grey-black, rosine and blue-green	2·25	2·25
Set of 4			5·50	5·00
Set of 4 *Gutter Pairs*			12·00	
First Day Cover				5·75
Presentation Pack			5·00	
PHQ Cards (*set of* 4)			5·75	11·50

Nos. 1997/2000 were issued on the occasion of the Centenary of the National Federation of Sub-Postmasters.

Special First Day of Issue Postmarks

British Philatelic Bureau, Edinburgh .... 6·00
Wakefield ....6·00

PRINTERS. Harrison and Sons Ltd became De La Rue Security Print on 8 September 1997. This was not reflected in the sheet imprints until mid-1998.

1320 *Noddy*

1321 *Famous Five*

1322 *Secret Seven*

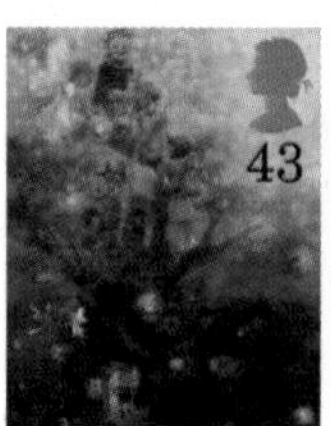

1323 *Faraway Tree*

1324 *Malory Towers*

(Des C. Birmingham. Photo Enschedé)

1997 (9 Sept). *Birth Centenary of Enid Blyton (children's author). One phosphor band (20p.) or two phosphor bands (others).* P 14×14½.

2001	**1320**	20p. greenish yellow, magenta, new blue, grey-black and deep grey-blue	50	45
2002	**1321**	26p. greenish yellow, magenta, new blue, grey-black and deep grey-blue	1·00	1·25
2003	**1322**	37p. greenish yellow, magenta, new blue, grey-black and deep grey-blue	1·25	1·25
2004	**1323**	43p. greenish yellow, magenta, new blue, grey-black and deep grey-blue	1·50	2·00
2005	**1324**	63p. greenish yellow, magenta, new blue, grey-black and deep grey-blue	1·50	2·00
Set of 5			5·25	6·00
Set of 5 *Gutter Pairs*			12·00	
First Day Cover				6·00
Presentation Pack			5·75	
PHQ Cards (*set of* 5)			6·00	13·00

Special First Day of Issue Postmarks

British Philatelic Bureau, Edinburgh .... 6·50
Beaconsfield .... 6·50

1325 Children and Father Christmas pulling Cracker

1326 Father Christmas with Traditional Cracker

1327 Father Christmas riding Cracker

1328 Father Christmas on Snowball

1329 Father Christmas and Chimney

(Des J. Gorham and M. Thomas (1st), J. Gorham (others))

1997 (27 Oct). *Christmas. 150th Anniv of the Christmas Cracker. One phosphor band (2nd) or two phosphor bands (others).* P 15×14.

2006	**1325**	(2nd) gold, greenish yellow, bright magenta, new blue and grey-black...	75	20
		a. Imperf (pair)...	£1500	
2007	**1326**	(1st) gold, greenish yellow, bright magenta, new blue and grey-black...	90	30
2008	**1327**	31p. gold, greenish yellow, bright magenta, new blue, bright blue and grey-black...	1·00	1·50
		a. Imperf (pair)...	£1300	
2009	**1328**	43p. gold, greenish yellow, bright magenta, pale new blue and grey-black...	1·25	1·75
2010	**1329**	63p. gold, greenish yellow, bright magenta, new blue and grey-black...	1·60	2·00
Set of 5			5·50	5·00
Set of 5 *Gutter Pairs*			12·00	
First Day Cover				6·00
Presentation Pack			5·75	
PHQ Cards (*set of* 5)			6·00	13·00

The 1st value was re-issued on 3 October 2000 in sheets of 10, each with a *se-tenant* label showing Christmas greetings (sold for £2.95) or a personal photograph (sold for £5.95). These sheets were printed in photogravure by Questa and were sold by the Philatelic Bureau and selected philatelic outlets. Similar sheets were available from 9 October 2001 when the price for the personalised version was increased to £12.95 for two sheets. These could also be purchased, on an experimental basis, from photo-booths situated at six post offices. From 1 October 2002 the size of the sheet was increased to 20 either with greetings labels (sold at £5.95) or personal photographs (sold at £14.95). These stamps were printed by Questa in lithography and perforated 14½×14.

Special First Day of Issue Postmarks

British Philatelic Bureau, Edinburgh ... 6·25
Bethlehem, Llandeilo ... 6·25

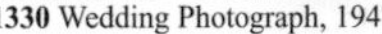

1330 Wedding Photograph, 1947

1331 Queen Elizabeth II and Prince Philip, 1997

(Des D. Driver (20p., 43p.), Lord Snowdon (26p., 63p.))

1997 (13 Nov). *Royal Golden Wedding. One phosphor band (20p.) or two phosphor bands (others).* P 15.

2011	**1330**	20p. gold, yellow-brown and grey-black.	85	45
		a. Imperf (pair)...	£3000	
2012	**1331**	26p. gold, bistre-yellow, magenta, new blue, grey-black and greenish grey..	1·10	70
2013	**1330**	43p. gold, bluish green and grey-black....	1·90	2·25
2014	**1331**	63p. gold, bistre-yellow, magenta, new blue, grey-black and lavender-grey..	2·50	3·00
Set of 4			5·75	5·75
Set of 4 *Gutter Pairs*			12·00	
First Day Cover				8·25
Presentation Pack			6·25	
Souvenir Book (contains Nos. 1668, 1989/92 and 2011/14)			50·00	
PHQ Cards (*set of* 4)			5·75	11·50

For 26p. and (1st) Machin printed in gold, see Nos. 1668 and Y1686.

Special First Day of Issue Postmarks

British Philatelic Bureau, Edinburgh ... 9·00
London, SW1 ... 10·00

Collectors Pack 1997

1997 (13 Nov). *Comprises Nos.* 1965/75, 1980/92 *and* 1997/ 2014.
CP2014*a* Collectors Pack ... 65·00

Post Office Yearbook

1997 (13 Nov). *Comprises Nos.* 1965/75, 1980/92 *and* 1997/ 2014 *in hardback book with slip case* ... 65·00

1332 Common Dormouse

1333 Lady's Slipper Orchid

1334 Song Thrush

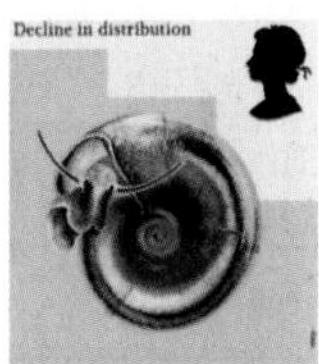

1335 Shining Ram's-horn Snail

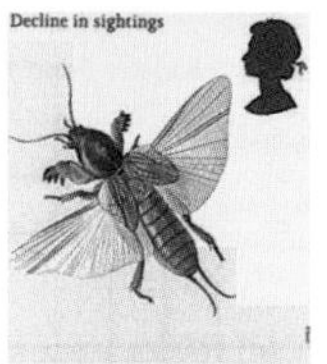

1336 Mole Cricket

1337 Devil's Bolete

(Des R. Maude. Litho Questa)

1998 (20 Jan). *Endangered Species. One side phosphor band (20p.) or two phosphor bands (others).* P 14×14½.

2015	**1332**	20p. black, new blue, magenta, greenish yellow, deep blue and pale lavender-grey	60	40
2016	**1333**	26p. black, new blue, magenta, greenish yellow, deep blue and pale yellow-olive	75	40
2017	**1334**	31p. black, new blue, magenta, greenish yellow, deep blue and pale bluish grey	1·00	2·00
2018	**1335**	37p. black, new blue, magenta, greenish yellow, deep blue and pale greenish grey	1·25	1·25
2019	**1336**	43p. black, new blue, magenta, greenish yellow, deep blue and pale dull mauve	1·40	1·75
2020	**1337**	63p. black, new blue, magenta, greenish yellow, deep blue and pale grey-brown	1·90	2·25
Set of 6			6·25	6·50
Set of 6 *Gutter Pairs*			15·00	
First Day Cover				6·50
Presentation Pack			6·75	
PHQ Cards (*set of* 6)			6·00	14·00

Special First Day of Issue Postmarks

British Philatelic Bureau, Edinburgh . . . . . 6·50
Selborne, Alton . . . . . 7·00

1338 Diana, Princess of Wales (photo by Lord Snowdon)

1339 At British Lung Foundation Function, April 1997 (photo by John Stillwell)

1340 Wearing Tiara, 1991 (photo by Lord Snowdon)

1341 On Visit to Birmingham, October 1995 (photo by Tim Graham)

1342 In Evening Dress, 1987 (photo by Terence Donavan)

(Des B. Robinson)

1998 (3 Feb). *Diana, Princess of Wales Commemoration. Two phosphor bands.* P 14×15.

2021	**1338**	26p. purple, greenish yellow, magenta, new blue and black	90	90
		a. Horiz strip of 5. Nos. 2021/5	4·50	4·50
		ab. Imperf (horiz strip of 5. Nos. 2021/5)	£12500	
		ac. Imperf (horiz strip of 4. Nos. 2021/4)	£6000	
		ad. Imperf (horiz strip of 3. Nos. 2021/3)	£4000	
2022	**1339**	26p. purple, greenish yellow, magenta, new blue and black	90	90
2023	**1340**	26p. purple, greenish yellow, magenta, new blue and black	90	90
2024	**1341**	26p. purple, greenish yellow, magenta, new blue and black	90	90
2025	**1342**	26p. purple, greenish yellow, magenta, new blue and black	90	90
Set of 5			4·50	4·00
Gutter Strip of 10			10·00	
First Day Cover				5·50
Presentation Pack			16·00	
Presentation Pack (Welsh)			£150	

Nos. 2021/5 were printed together, se-tenant, in horizontal strips of 5 throughout the sheet.

No. 2021ac shows No. 2025 perforated at right only. In addition to the generally issued Presentation Pack a further pack with all text printed in English and Welsh was available.

Special First Day of Issue Postmarks

British Philatelic Bureau, Edinburgh . . . . . 6·00
Kensington, London . . . . . 6·00

1343 Lion of England and Griffin of Edward III

1344 Falcon of Plantagenet and Bull of Clarence

1345 Lion of Mortimer and Yale of Beaufort

1346 Greyhound of Richmond and Dragon of Wales

1347 Unicorn of Scotland and Horse of Hanover

(Des J. Matthews. Recess and litho Harrison)

1998 (24 Feb). *650th Anniv of the Order of the Garter. The Queen's Beasts. Two phosphor bands.* P 15×14.

2026	**1343**	26p. silver, green, bright blue, carmine-red, vermilion, lemon, grey-black and black	90	90
		a. Horiz strip of 5. Nos. 2026/30	4·50	4·50
		ab. Missing green (on Nos. 2026, 2028/9) (horiz strip of 5)	£10000	
		Eay. Horiz strip of 5. Phosphor omitted	25·00	
2027	**1344**	26p. silver, bright blue, carmine-red, vermilion, lemon, grey, grey-black and black	90	90
2028	**1345**	26p. silver, green, bright blue, carmine-red, vermilion, lemon, grey, grey-black and black	90	90
2029	**1346**	26p. silver, green, bright blue, carmine-red, vermilion, lemon, grey, grey-black and black	90	90
2030	**1347**	26p. silver, green, bright blue, vermilion, lemon, grey, grey-black and black	90	90
Set of 5			4·00	4·00
Gutter Block of 10			10·00	
First Day Cover				5·25
Presentation Pack			5·00	
PHQ Cards (*set of* 5)			6·00	13·00

Nos. 2026/30 were printed together, *se-tenant*, in horizontal strips of 5 throughout the sheet. The phosphor bands on Nos. 2026/30 are only half the height of the stamps and do not cover the silver parts of the designs.

Special First Day of Issue Postmarks

British Philatelic Bureau, Edinburgh .... 5·50
London SW1 .... 5·50

1348

(Des G. Knipe, adapted Dew Gibbons Design Group. Photo Walsall)

1998 (10 Mar). *As T* **157** *(Wilding Definitive of 1952–54) but with face values in decimal currency as T* **1348**. *One side phosphor band (20p.) or two phosphor bands (others).* P 14 (with one elliptical hole on each vertical side).

2031	**1348**	20p. light green (1 band at right)	70	75
		Ea. Band at left	70	75
		b. Booklet pane. Nos. 2031/Ea each ×3 with margins all round	4·75	
		c. Booklet pane. Nos. 2031/Ea and 2032/3, all×2, and central label with margins all round	9·50	
2032		26p. red-brown	90	95
		a. Booklet pane. No. 2032×9 with margins all round	9·50	
		b. Booklet pane. Nos. 2032/3, each ×3 with margins all round	9·50	
2033		37p. light purple	2·75	2·75
Set of 3 (*cheapest*)			4·00	4·00
First Day Cover (*No.* 2031c)				7·00

Nos. 2031/3 were only issued in the 1998 £7.49 Wilding Definitives stamp booklet No. DX20.

For further Wilding designs with decimal face values and on paper watermarked W **1565** see Nos. 2258/9, **MS**2326, **MS**2367 and 2378/9.

Special First Day of Issue Postmarks

British Philatelic Bureau, Edinburgh .... 7·00
London SW1 .... 7·00

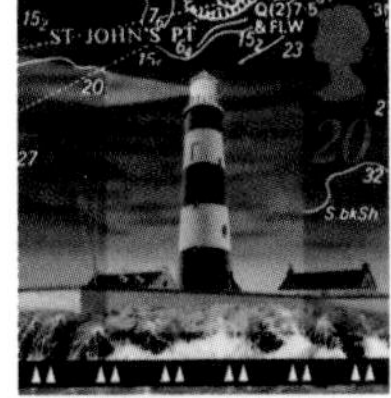

1349 St. John's Point Lighthouse, County Down

1350 Smalls Lighthouse, Pembrokeshire

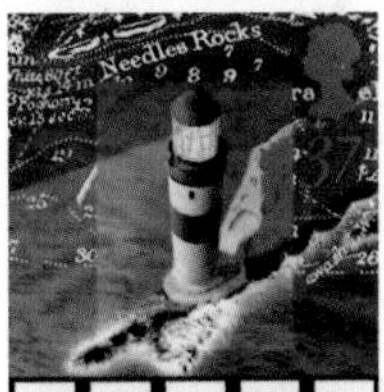

1351 Needles Rock Lighthouse, Isle of Wight, c 1900

1352 Bell Rock Lighthouse, Arbroath, mid-19th-century

1353 Original Eddystone Lighthouse, Plymouth, 1698

(Des D. Davis and J. Boon. Litho Questa)

1998 (24 Mar). *Lighthouses. One side phosphor band (20p.) or two phosphor bands (others).* P 14½×14.

2034	**1349**	20p. gold, greenish yellow, magenta, new blue and black	50	40
2035	**1350**	26p. gold, greenish yellow, magenta, new blue and black	75	50
2036	**1351**	37p. gold, greenish yellow, magenta, new blue and black	1·10	1·50
2037	**1352**	43p. gold, greenish yellow, magenta, new blue and black	1·50	1·75
2038	**1353**	63p. gold, greenish yellow, magenta, new blue and black	2·10	2·50
Set of 5			5·50	6·00
Set of 5 Gutter Pairs			13·50	
First Day Cover				6·00
Presentation Pack			6·00	
PHQ Cards (set of 5)			6·00	13·00

Nos. 2034/8 commemorate the 300th anniversary of the first Eddystone Lighthouse and the final year of manned lighthouses.

Special First Day of Issue Postmarks

British Philatelic Bureau, Edinburgh	6·00
Plymouth	6·00

(Photo Enschedé, Questa or Walsall)

1998 (6 Apr)–**2001**. *Self-adhesive. Designs as T* **913/14**. *One centre phosphor band (2nd), or two phosphor bands (1st).* P 15×14 die-cut (with one elliptical hole on each vertical side).

2039	(2nd) bright blue	30	35
	a. Imperf (pair)	75·00	
	b. Perf 14½×14 die-cut (22.6.98)	£150	
2040	(1st) bright orange-red	40	45
	a. Imperf (pair)	75·00	
	b. Perf 14½×14 die-cut (22.6.98)	£150	
	Ey. Phosphor omitted		
	l. Booklet pane. No. 2040×6 plus commemorative label at left (29.1.01)	9·50	

Nos. 2039/40, initially sold for 20p. and 26p., were in rolls of 200 printed by Enschedé with the surplus self-adhesive paper removed.

2nd and 1st self-adhesive stamps as Nos. 2039/40 were issued in sheets, printed in photogravure by Walsall Security Printers, on 22 June 1998. These are similar to the previous coil printings, but the sheets retain the surplus self-adhesive paper around each stamp. Stamps from these sheets have square perforation tips instead of the rounded versions to be found on the coils.

Nos. 2039b and 2040b come from initial stocks of these Walsall sheet printings sent to the Philatelic Bureau and supplied to collectors requiring single stamps.

A further printing in sheets appeared on 4 September 2000 printed by Walsall (2nd) or Questa (1st). These sheets were slightly re-designed to provide a block of 4, rather than a strip, in the top panel. Individual stamps cannot be identified as coming from these new sheets as they have rounded perforation tips similar to those on the original coil printings.

The sheets of 100 were re-issued on 9 May 2002 printed by Enschedé in the same format as used in September 2000. The individual stamps are similar to the Enschedé coil printings of April 1998. A further printing of No. 2039 in sheets of 100 appeared on 4 July 2002 printed by Enschedé. On this printing the top panel reverted to a strip of 4 with the typography on the label matching that of contemporary stamp booklets.

No. 2039 was issued on 18 March 2003 in stripped matrix sheets of 100, printed by Walsall.

The sheets of 100 were again issued but without the strapline "The Real Network" on 15 June 2004. The stamps in stripped matrix sheets of 100 had rounded perforations and were printed by Walsall.

Both values appeared in stamp booklets from 29 January 2001. No. 2040l comes from self-adhesive booklet No. MB2. The label commemorates the death centenary of Queen Victoria.

See also Nos. 2295/8.

1354 Tommy Cooper **1355** Eric Morecambe **1356** Joyce Grenfell **1357** Les Dawson **1358** Peter Cook

(Des G. Scarfe. Litho Walsall)

1998 (23 Apr). *Comedians. One side phosphor band (20p.) or two phosphor bands (others).* P 14½×14.

2041	**1354**	20p. vermilion, black, rose-pink, new blue and greenish yellow	50	50
		Ea. Vermilion printed double		£1500
		Eb. Vermilion and black both printed quadruple with rose-pink and new blue both printed double	†	£2500
		Ec. Vermilion and black both printed double	†	£2000
2042	**1355**	26p. vermilion, black, rose-pink and new blue	75	85
		Ea. Vermilion printed double	£250	
		Eb. Vermilion printed triple	£550	
		Ec. Black and vermilion printed double.	£2000	
2043	**1356**	37p. vermilion, black, rose-pink, new blue and greenish yellow	1·25	1·25
2044	**1357**	43p. vermilion, black, rose-pink, new blue and pale orange	1·50	1·50
2045	**1358**	63p. vermilion, black, deep rose-pink, new blue and greenish yellow	1·75	2·10
Set of 5			5·25	5·50
Set of 5 Gutter Pairs			13·50	
First Day Cover				6·00
Presentation Pack			6·00	
PHQ Cards (set of 5)			6·00	13·00

Stamps as Type **1356**, but with a face value of 30p., were prepared but not issued. Mint examples and a first day cover have been reported (*Price* £1750).

Special First Day of Issue Postmarks

British Philatelic Bureau, Edinburgh .... 6·50
Morecambe .... 6·50

1359 Hands forming Heart

1360 Adult and Child holding Hands

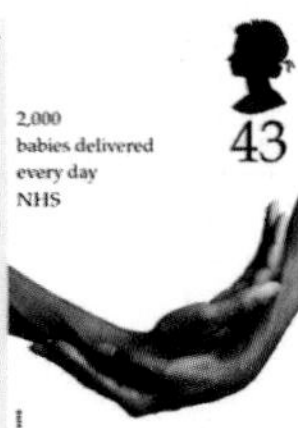

1361 Hands forming Cradle

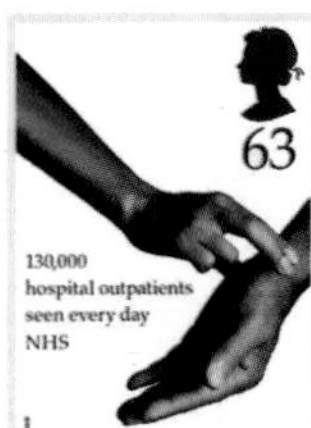

1362 Hand taking Pulse

(Des V. Frost from photos by A. Wilson. Litho Questa)

1998 (23 June). *50th Anniv of the National Health Service. One side phosphor band (20p.) or two phosphor bands (others).* P 14×14½.

2046	**1359**	20p. deep claret, black, grey-brown, pale cream and cream	50	50
2047	**1360**	26p. deep grey-green, black, grey-brown, pale cream and cream	90	90
2048	**1361**	43p. deep lilac, black, grey-brown, pale cream and cream	1·50	1·50
2049	**1362**	63p. deep dull blue, black, grey-brown, pale cream and cream	2·10	2·10
Set of 4			4·50	4·50
Set of 4 *Gutter Pairs*			11·00	
First Day Cover				5·75
Presentation Pack			5·50	
PHQ Cards (*set of* 4)			5·75	11·50

Special First Day of Issue Postmarks

British Philatelic Bureau, Edinburgh .... 5·50
Tredegar, Wales...5·50

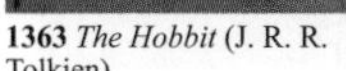

1363 *The Hobbit* (J. R. R. Tolkien)

1364 *The Lion, The Witch and the Wardrobe* (C. S. Lewis)

1365 *The Phoenix and the Carpet* (E. Nesbit)

1366 *The Borrowers* (Mary Norton)

1367 *Through the Looking Glass* (Lewis Carroll)

(Des P. Malone. Photo D.L.R.)

1998 (21 July). *Famous Children's Fantasy Novels. One centre phosphor band (20p.) or two phosphor bands (others).* P 15×14.

2050	**1363**	20p. silver, greenish yellow, bright magenta, new blue, black and gold..	50	45
2051	**1364**	26p. silver, greenish yellow, bright magenta, new blue, black and gold..	75	55
		a. Imperf (pair)	£900	
2052	**1365**	37p. silver, greenish yellow, bright magenta, new blue, black and gold..	1·25	1·50
2053	**1366**	43p. silver, greenish yellow, bright magenta, new blue, black and gold..	1·50	1·50
2054	**1367**	63p. silver, greenish yellow, bright magenta, new blue, black and gold..	2·10	2·00
Set of 5			5·75	5·75
Set of 5 *Gutter Pairs*			13·00	
First Day Cover				5·75
Presentation Pack			6·00	
PHQ Cards (*set of* 5)			6·00	13·00

Nos. 2050/4 commemorate the birth centenary of C. S. Lewis and the death centenary of Lewis Carroll.

Special First Day of Issue Postmarks

British Philatelic Bureau, Edinburgh ....6·00
Oxford ....6·50

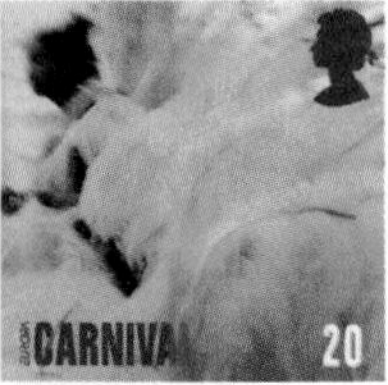

1368 Woman in Yellow Feathered Costume

1369 Woman in Blue Costume and Headdress

1370 Group of Children in White and Gold Robes

1371 Child in "Tree" Costume

(Des T. Hazael. Photo Walsall)

1998 (25 Aug). *Europa. Festivals. Notting Hill Carnival. One centre phosphor band (20p.) or two phosphor bands (others).* P 14×14½.

2055	**1368**	20p. gold, black, new blue, bright magenta and greenish yellow	75	45
2056	**1369**	26p. gold, grey-black, new blue, bright magenta and greenish yellow	95	55
2057	**1370**	43p. gold, grey-black, new blue, bright magenta and bistre-yellow	1·50	2·00
2058	**1371**	63p. gold, grey-black, new blue, bright magenta and greenish yellow	2·00	2·75
Set of 4			4·75	4·75
Set of 4 Gutter Pairs			12·50	
First Day Cover				5·75
Presentation Pack			5·25	
PHQ Cards (*set of* 4)			5·75	11·50

The 20p. and 26p. incorporate the "EUROPA" emblem.

Special First Day of Issue Postmarks

British Philatelic Bureau, Edinburgh	6·00
London W11	6·50

1372 Sir Malcolm Campbell's *Bluebird*, 1925

1373 Sir Henry Segrave's *Sunbeam*, 1926

1374 John G. Parry Thomas's *Babs*, 1926

1375 John R. Cobb's *Railton Mobil Special*, 1947

1376 Donald Campbell's *Bluebird CN7*, 1964

(Des Roundel Design Group. Photo De La Rue)

1998 (29 Sept). *British Land Speed Record Holders. One phosphor band (20p.) or two phosphor bands (others).* P 15×14.

2059	**1372**	20p. rosine, greenish yellow, magenta, new blue, black and silver (1 centre band)	50	25
		a. Perf 14½×13½ (1 side band at right) (13.10.98)	1·40	50
		aEb. Band at left	1·00	1·00
		ac. Booklet pane. Nos. 2059a and 2059aEb, each ×2, with margins all round	5·00	
2060	**1373**	26p. rosine, greenish yellow, magenta, new blue, black and silver	75	30
		a. Rosine (face value) omitted	£2500	
		Eb. "2" from face value omitted	£2000	
		Ec. "6" from face value omitted	£2000	
2061	**1374**	30p. rosine, greenish yellow, magenta, new blue, black and silver	1·25	1·50
2062	**1375**	43p. rosine, greenish yellow, magenta, new blue, black and silver	1·50	1·60
2063	**1376**	63p. rosine, greenish yellow, magenta, new blue, black and silver	2·00	2·40
Set of 5			5·50	5·50
Set of 5 Gutter Pairs			13·00	
First Day Cover				6·00
Presentation Pack			6·25	
PHQ Cards (*set of* 5)			6·00	13·00

Nos. 2059/63 commemorate the 50th death anniversary of Sir Malcolm Campbell.

Nos. 2060a/Ec occur on the fourth vertical row of several sheets. Other examples show one or other of the figures partially omitted. Nos. 2059a/aEb come from the £6.16 British Land Speed Record Holders stamp booklet, No. DX21, and were printed by Walsall. There are minor differences of design between No. 2059 (sheet stamp printed by De La Rue) and Nos. 2059a/aEb (booklet stamps printed by Walsall), which omit the date and copyright symbol.

Special First Day of Issue Postmarks

British Philatelic Bureau, Edinburgh	6·50
Pendine	6·50

1377 Angel with Hands raised in Blessing

1378 Angel praying

1379 Angel playing Flute

1380 Angel playing Lute

1381 Angel praying

(Des Irene von Treskow. Photo De La Rue)

1998 (2 Nov). *Christmas. Angels. One centre phosphor band (20p.) or two phosphor bands (others).* P 15×14.

2064	**1377**	20p. gold, greenish yellow, magenta, new blue and grey-black	50	50
		a. Imperf (pair)	£425	
2065	**1378**	26p. gold, greenish yellow, magenta, new blue and grey-black	75	60
		a. Imperf (pair)	£1600	
2066	**1379**	30p. gold, greenish yellow, magenta, new blue and grey-black	1·25	1·50
2067	**1380**	43p. gold, greenish yellow, magenta, new blue and grey-black	1·50	1·60
		a. Imperf (pair)	£1600	
2068	**1381**	63p. gold, greenish yellow, magenta, new blue and grey-black	2·00	2·25
Set of 5			5·75	5·75
Set of 5 Gutter Pairs			13·00	
First Day Cover				6·00
Presentation Pack			6·50	
PHQ Cards (set of 5)			6·00	13·00

Special First Day of Issue Postmarks

British Philatelic Bureau, Edinburgh ....6·25
Bethlehem ....6·25

Collectors Pack 1998

1998 (2 Nov). *Comprises Nos.* 2015/30, 2034/8 *and* 2041/68.
CP2068*a* Collectors Pack .... 95·00

Post Office Yearbook

1998 (2 Nov). *Comprises Nos.* 2015/30, 2034/8 *and* 2041/68 *in hardback book with slip case* .... 85·00

1382 Greenwich Meridian Clock (John Harrison's andchronometer)

1383 Industrial Worker and Blast Furnace (James Watt's discovery of steam power)

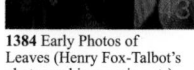

1384 Early Photos of Leaves (Henry Fox-Talbot's photographic experiments)

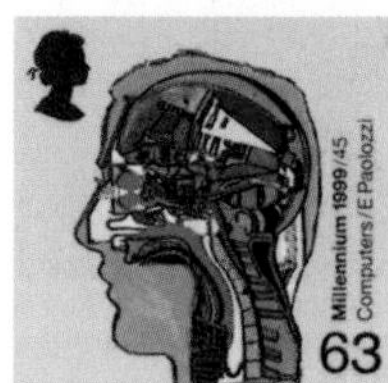

1385 Computer inside Human Head (Alan Turing's work on computers)

(Des D. Gentleman (20p.), P. Howson (26p.), Z. and Barbara Baran (43p.), E. Paolozzi (63p.). Photo Enschedé (26p.), Questa (63p. No. 2072a) or De La Rue (others))

1999 (12 Jan). *Millennium Series. The Inventors' Tale. One centre phosphor band (20p.) or two phosphor bands (others).* P 14×14½.

2069	**1382**	20p. silver, deep grey, pale olive-grey, greenish grey, grey-black and bright rose-red	75	70
		a. Imperf (horiz pair)	£1600	
2070	**1383**	26p. silver, black, new blue, bright magenta and greenish yellow	95	1·00
2071	**1384**	43p. silver, greenish yellow, bright crimson, new blue, black and bright magenta	1·50	1·60
2072	**1385**	63p. greenish blue, greenish yellow, cerise, new blue, black and pale lemon	2·25	2·40
		a. Perf 13½×14 (21 Sept)	3·50	3·50
		ab. Booklet pane. No. 2072a×4 with margins all round	10·00	
Set of 4			5·25	5·25
Set of 4 Gutter Pairs			13·00	
First Day Cover (Philatelic Bureau) (Type J, see Introduction)				10·00
First Day Cover (Greenwich, London SE)				14·00
Presentation Pack			7·50	
PHQ Cards (set of 4)			8·50	13·00

No. 2072a comes from the £6.99 World Changers booklet, No. DX23.

Special First Day of Issue Postmark

1386 Airliner hugging Globe (International air travel)

1387 Woman on Bicycle (Development of the bicycle)

1388 Victorian Railway Station (Growth of public transport)

1389 Captain Cook and Maori (Captain James Cook's voyages)

(Des G. Hardie (20p.), Sara Fanelli (26p.), J. Lawrence (43p.), A. Klimowski (63p.). Photo Enschedé (20p., 63p.) or De La Rue (26p.). Litho Enschedé (43p.))

1999 (2 Feb). *Millennium Series. The Travellers' Tale. One centre phosphor band (20p.) or two phosphor bands (others).* P 14×14½.

2073	**1386**	20p. silver, vermilion, grey-black, bluish violet, greenish blue and pale grey ..	75	70
2074	**1387**	26p. silver, greenish yellow, cerise, new blue, black and vermilion................	95	1·00
2075	**1388**	43p. grey-black, stone and bronze	1·50	1·60
2076	**1389**	63p. silver, grey-black, new blue, bright magenta and greenish yellow..........	2·25	2·40
Set of 4			5·25	5·25
Set of 4 *Gutter Pairs*			13·00	
First Day Cover (Philatelic Bureau) (Type J, see Introduction)				8·00
First Day Cover (Coventry)				8·50
Presentation Pack			7·50	
PHQ Cards (*set of* 4)			8·50	13·00

Special First Day of Issue Postmark

1390

1999 (16 Feb).

(a) Embossed and litho Walsall. Self-adhesive. Die-cut perf 14×15.

2077	**1390**	(1st) grey (face value) (Queen's head in colourless relief) (phosphor background around head)................	3·00	2·25
		l. Booklet pane. No. 2077×4 with margins all round	10·00	

(b) Eng C. Slania. Recess Enschedé. P 14×14½.

2078	**1390**	(1st) grey-black (2 phosphor bands).........	3·00	2·25
		l. Booklet pane. No. 2078×4 with margins all round	10·00	

(c) Typo Harrison. P 14×15.

2079	**1390**	(1st) black (2 phosphor bands)................	3·00	2·25
		Ey. Phosphor omitted		
		l. Booklet pane. No. 2078×4 with margins all round	10·00	
		Ey. Booklet pane.Phosphor omitted.......		
First Day Covers (3 covers with Nos. 2077l, 2078l, 2079l) (Philatelic Bureau)				12·00
First Day Covers (3 covers with Nos. 2077l, 2078l, 2079l) (London SW1)				12·00

Nos. 2077/9 were only issued in the £7.54 "Profile on Print" booklet, No. DX22.

Special First Day of Issue Postmarks

1391 Vaccinating Child (pattern in cow markings) (Jenner's development of smallpox vaccine)

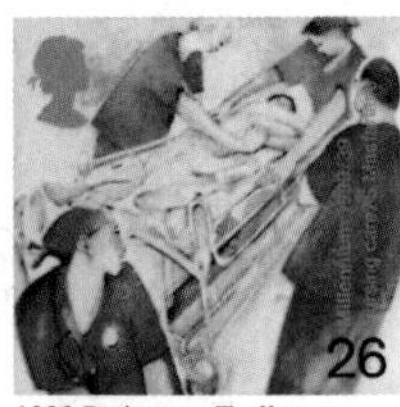

1392 Patient on Trolley (nursing care)

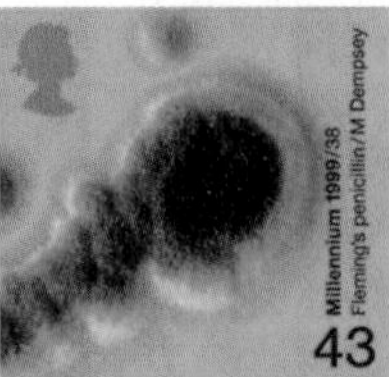

1393 Penicillin Mould (Fleming's discovery of penicillin)

1394 Sculpture of Test-tube Baby (development of in-vitro fertilization)

(Des P. Brookes (20p.), Susan Macfarlane (26p.), M. Dempsey (43p.), A. Gormley (63p.). Photo Questa)

1999 (2 Mar). *Millennium Series. The Patients' Tale. One centre phosphor band (20p.) or two phosphor bands (others). P 13½×14.*

2080	**1391**	20p. greenish yellow, bright magenta, new blue, black and silver................	75	70
		a. Booklet pane. No. 2080×4 with margins all round (21 Sept).............	2·50	

2081	**1392**	26p. greenish yellow, bright magenta, new blue, black, silver and deep turquoise-blue	95	1·00
		a. Imperf (pair)	£1900	
2082	**1393**	43p. greenish yellow, bright magenta, new blue, black, deep bluish green and silver	1·50	1·60
2083	**1394**	63p. greenish yellow, bright magenta, new blue, black, silver and blueblack	2·25	2·40
Set of 4			5·25	5·25
Set of 4 *Gutter Pairs*			13·00	
First Day Cover (Philatelic Bureau) (Type J, see Introduction)				8·00
First Day Cover (Oldham)				8·50
Presentation Pack			7·50	
PHQ Cards (*set of* 4)			8·50	13·00

No. 2080a comes from the £6.99 World Changers booklet, No. DX23.

Special First Day of Issue Postmark

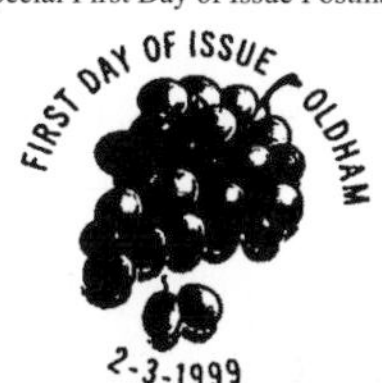

1395 Dove and Norman Settler (medieval migration to Scotland)

1396 Pilgrim Fathers and Red Indian (17th-century migration to America)

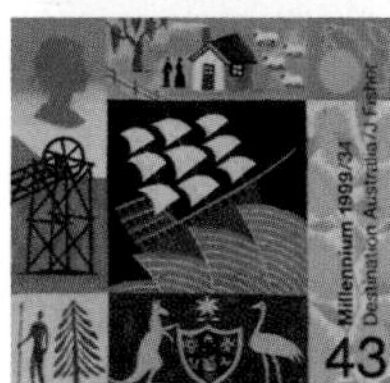

1397 Sailing Ship and Aspects of Settlement (19th-century migration to Australia)

1398 Hummingbird and Superimposed Stylized Face (20th-century migration to Great Britain)

(Des J. Byrne (20p.), W. McLean (26p.), J. Fisher (43p.), G. Powell (63p.). Litho (20p.) or photo (others) Walsall)

1999 (6 Apr). *Millennium Series. The Settlers' Tale. One centre phosphor band (20p.) or two phosphor bands (others).* P 14×14½.

2084	**1395**	20p. gold, silver, black, magenta, blue and greenish yellow	75	70
2085	**1396**	26p. greenish yellow, magenta, new blue, grey-black and silver	95	1·00
		a. Booklet pane. Nos. 2085 and 2089 with margins all round (12 May)	6·00	
2086	**1397**	43p. greenish yellow, magenta, new blue, grey-black, gold and chocolate	2·00	1·75
2087	**1398**	63p. greenish yellow, magenta, new blue, reddish violet, deep reddish violet and gold	3·00	3·00
Set of 4			5·75	5·75
Set of 4 *Gutter Pairs*			13·00	
First Day Cover (Philatelic Bureau) (Type J, see Introduction)				8·00
First Day Cover (Plymouth)				8·50
Presentation Pack			7·50	
PHQ Cards (*set of* 4)			8·50	13·00

No. 2085a comes from the £2.60 booklet, No. HBA1.

Imperf pairs of Nos. 2085 and 2089 are known and believed to be of proof status (Price £750).

Imperf pairs of No. 2085 with silver and phosphor omitted are known and believed to be of proof status (Price £350).

Imperf pairs of No. 2086 are known with gold, chocolate and phosphor omitted and believed to be of proof status (Price £350).

Special First Day of Issue Postmark

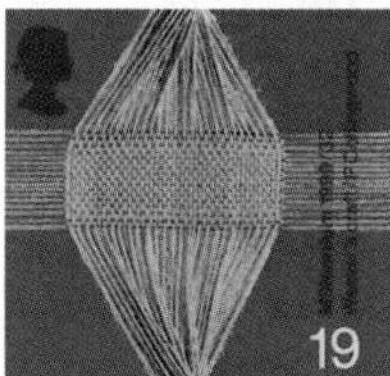

1399 Woven Threads (woollen industry)

1400 Salts Mill, Saltaire (worsted cloth industry)

1401 Hull on Slipway (shipbuilding)

1402 Lloyd's Building (City of London finance centre)

(Des P. Collingwood (19p.), D. Hockney (26p.), B. Sanderson (44p.), B. Neiland (64p.). Litho (19p.) or photo (others) De La Rue)

1999 (4 May). *Millennium Series. The Workers' Tale. One centre phosphor band (19p.) or two phosphor bands (others).* P 14×14½.

2088	**1399**	19p. drab, greenish yellow, cerise, new blue, grey-black and bronze	75	70
		a. Bronze (Queen's head) omitted	£350	
		aEy. Bronze and phosphor omitted	£350	
2089	**1400**	26p. silver, greenish yellow, rosine, new blue and grey-black	95	1·00
2090	**1401**	44p. silver, greenish yellow, orangered, bright blue, yellow-brown and grey-black	1·75	1·60
2091	**1402**	64p. silver, greenish yellow, rosine, new blue and grey-black	2·25	2·40
Set of 4			5·25	5·25
Set of 4 *Gutter Pairs*			13·00	
First Day Cover (Philatelic Bureau) (Type J, see Introduction)				8·00
First Day Cover (Belfast)				8·50
Presentation Pack			7·50	
PHQ Cards (*set of* 4)			8·50	13·00

For No. 2089, printed by Walsall in photogravure, see booklet pane No. 2085a.

Special First Day of Issue Postmark

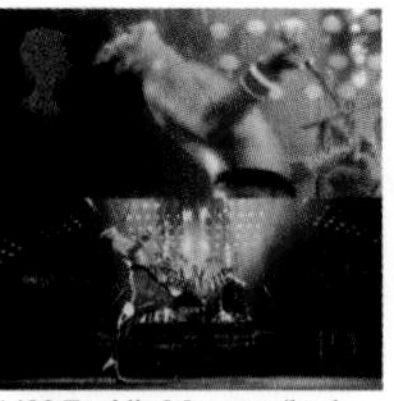
1403 Freddie Mercury (lead singer of Queen) ("Popular Music")

1404 Bobby Moore with World Cup, 1966 ("Sport")

1405 Dalek from Dr. Who (science-fiction series) ("Television")

1406 Charlie Chaplin (film star) ("Cinema")

(Des P. Blake (19p.), M. White (26p.), Lord Snowdon (44p.), R. Steadman (64p.). Photo Enschedé)

1999 (1 June). *Millennium Series. The Entertainers' Tale. One centre phosphor band (19p.) or two phosphor bands (others).* P 14×14½.

2092	**1403**	19p. greenish yellow, bright magenta, new blue, grey-black and gold	75	70
2093	**1404**	26p. greenish yellow, bright magenta, new blue, grey-black, gold and stone	95	1·00
2094	**1405**	44p. greenish yellow, bright magenta, new blue, grey-black and silver	1·50	1·60
2095	**1406**	64p. greenish yellow, bright magenta, new blue, grey-black and silver	2·25	2·40
		Set of 4	5·25	5·25
		Set of 4 *Gutter Pairs*	13·00	
		First Day Cover (Philatelic Bureau) (Type J, see Introduction)		8·00
		First Day Cover (Wembley)		8·50
		Presentation Pack	7·50	
		PHQ Cards (*set of* 4)	8·50	13·00

Special First Day of Issue Postmark

1407 Prince Edward and Miss Sophie Rhys-Jones (from photos by John Swannell)

1408

(Adapted J. Gibbs. Photo De La Rue)

1999 (15 June). *Royal Wedding. Two phosphor bands.* P 15×14.

2096	**1407**	26p. vermilion, black, grey-black and silver	85	85
		a. Imperf (pair)	£850	
2097	**1408**	64p. new blue, black, grey-black and silver	2·50	2·50
		Set of 2	3·00	3·00
		Set of 2 *Gutter Pairs*	7·00	
		First Day Cover (Philatelic Bureau)		4·75
		First Day Cover (Windsor)		5·25
		Presentation Pack	4·00	
		PHQ Cards (*set of* 2)	8·50	6·75

Special First Day of Issue Postmarks

1409 Suffragette behind Prison Window (Equal Rights for Women)

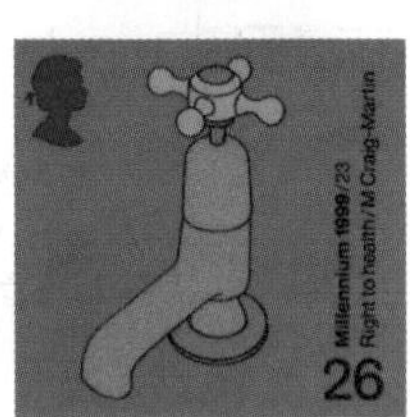

1410 Water Tap (Right to Health)

1411 Generations of School Children (Right to Education)

1412 "MAGNA CARTA" (Human Rights)

(Des Natasha Kerr (19p.), M. Craig-Martin (26p.), A. Drummond (44p.), A. Kitching (64p.). Photo De La Rue)

1999 (6 July). *Millennium Series. The Citizens' Tale. One centre phosphor band (19p.) or two phosphor bands (others).* P 14×14½.

2098	**1409**	19p. silver, greenish yellow, cerise, new blue and grey-black	75	70
2099	**1410**	26p. grey-black, new blue, bright mauve, rosine, turquoise-green and apple-green	95	1·00

			Unused	Used
2100	**1411**	44p. bright blue, greenish yellow, cerise, new blue and grey-black	1·75	1·60
2101	**1412**	64p. gold, greenish yellow, cerise, new blue and grey-black	2·50	2·40
Set of 4			5·75	5·25
Set of 4 *Gutter Pairs*			13·00	
First Day Cover (Philatelic Bureau) (Type J, see Introduction)				8·00
First Day Cover (Newtown, Powis)				8·50
Presentation Pack			7·50	
PHQ Cards (*set of* 4)			8·50	13·00

Special First Day of Issue Postmark

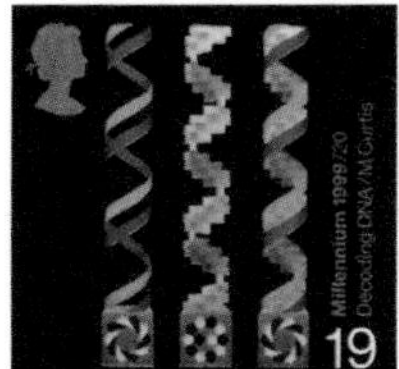

1413 Molecular Structures (DNA Decoding)

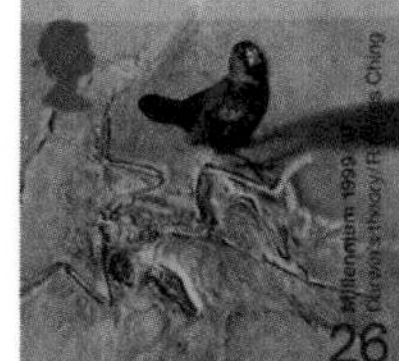

1414 Galapagos Finch and Fossilized Skeleton (Darwin's Theory of Evolution)

1415 Rotation of Polarized Light by Magnetism (Faraday's work on Electricity)

1416 Saturn (development of astronomical telescopes)

(Des M. Curtis (19p.), R. Harris Ching (26p.), C. Gray (44p.), from Hubble Space Telescope photograph (64p.). Photo (19p., 64p.) or litho (26p., 44p.) Questa)

1999 (3 Aug). *Millennium Series. The Scientists' Tale. One centre phosphor band (19p.) or two phosphor bands (others).* P 13½×14 (19p., 64p.) or 14×14½ (26p., 44p.).

			Unused	Used
2102	**1413**	19p. bright magenta, greenish yellow, new blue, black and silver	75	70
2103	**1414**	26p. greenish yellow, bright magenta, new blue, black, bronze and reddish violet	1·50	1·00
		a. Imperf (pair)	£750	
		b. Perf 14½×14 (21 Sept)	2·00	2·00
		ba. Booklet pane. No. 2103b×4 with margins all round	8·00	
2104	**1415**	44p. greenish yellow, bright magenta, new blue, black and gold	1·50	1·60
		a. Perf 14½×14 (21 Sept)	2·75	2·75
		ab. Booklet pane. No. 2104a×4 with margins all round	9·00	
2105	**1416**	64p. bright magenta, greenish yellow, new blue, black and silver	2·25	2·40
Set of 4			5·25	5·25
Set of 4 *Gutter Pairs*			13·00	
First Day Cover (Philatelic Bureau) (Type J, see Introduction)				8·00
First Day Cover (Cambridge)				8·50
Presentation Pack			7·50	
PHQ Cards (*set of* 4)			8·50	13·00

Nos. 2103b and 2104a come from the £6.99 World Changers booklet, No. DX23.

Special First Day of Issue Postmark

(Photo De La Rue)

1999 (11 Aug). *Solar Eclipse. Sheet 89×121 mm. Two phosphor bands.* P 14×14½.

		Unused	Used
MS2106 T **1416**×4 (sold at £2.56)		21·00	21·00
	a. Imperf	£3250	
First Day Cover (Philatelic Bureau)			22·00
First Day Cover (Falmouth)			22·00

Special First Day of Issue Postmarks

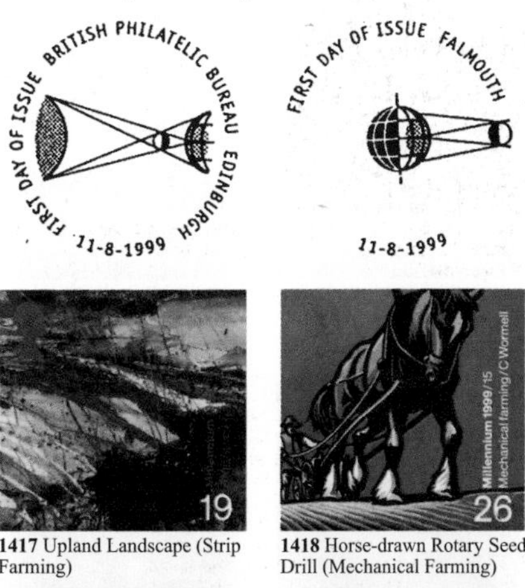

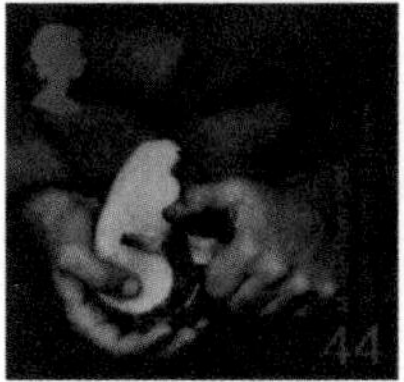

1417 Upland Landscape (Strip Farming)

1418 Horse-drawn Rotary Seed Drill (Mechanical Farming)

1419 Man peeling Potato (Food Imports)

1420 Aerial View of Combine Harvester (Satellite Agriculture)

(Des D. Tress (19p.), C. Wormell (26p.), Tessa Traeger (44p.), R. Cooke (64p.). Photo Walsall (No. 2108a) or De La Rue (others))

1999 (7 Sept). *Millennium Series. The Farmers' Tale. One centre phosphor band (19p.) or two phosphor bands (others).* P 14×14½.

			Unused	Used
2107	**1417**	19p. grey-black, greenish yellow, cerise, new blue and silver	75	70

2108	**1418**	26p. chestnut, orange-brown, violet-blue, grey-black, pale turquoise-green and silver	95	1·00
		a. Booklet pane. No. 2108×2 with margins all round (21 Sept)	6·00	
2109	**1419**	44p. silver, yellow-brown, brown and grey-black	1·50	1·60
2110	**1420**	64p. deep brown, greenish yellow, magenta, new blue and silver	2·25	2·40
Set of 4			5·25	5·25
Set of 4 *Gutter Pairs*			13·00	
First Day Cover (Philatelic Bureau) (Type J, see Introduction)				8·00
First Day Cover (Laxton, Newark)				8·50
Presentation Pack			7·50	
PHQ Cards (*set of* 4)			8·50	13·00

The 19p. includes the "EUROPA" emblem. No. 2108a comes from the £2.60 booklet, No. HBA2.

Special First Day of Issue Postmark

1421 Robert the Bruce (Battle of Bannockburn, 1314)

1422 Cavalier and Horse (English Civil War)

1423 War Graves Cemetery, The Somme (World Wars)

1424 Soldiers with Boy (Peace-keeping)

(Des A. Davidson (19p.), R. Kelly (26p.), D. McCullin (44p.), C. Corr (64p.). Litho (19p.) or photo (others) Walsall)

1999 (5 Oct). *Millennium Series. The Soldiers' Tale. One centre phosphor band (19p.) or two phosphor bands (others).* P 14×14½.

2111	**1421**	19p. black, stone and silver	75	70
2112	**1422**	26p. lemon, black, grey, silver and gold	95	1·00
2113	**1423**	44p. grey-black, black and silver	2·00	1·60
2114	**1424**	64p. greenish yellow, red-orange, bright magenta, pale new blue, black and bright blue	2·50	2·40
Set of 4			5·75	5·25
Set of 4 *Gutter Pairs*			13·00	
First Day Cover (Philatelic Bureau) (Type J, see Introduction)				8·00
First Day Cover (London SW)				8·50
Presentation Pack			7·50	
PHQ Cards (*set of* 4)			8·50	13·00

Special First Day of Issue Postmark

1425 "Hark the herald angels sing" and Hymn book (John Wesley)

1426 King James I and Bible (Authorised Version of Bible)

1427 St. Andrews Cathedral, Fife ("Pilgrimage")

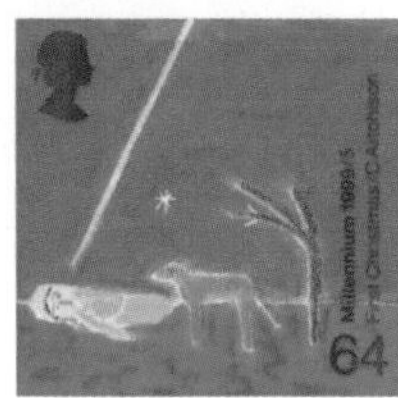

1428 Nativity ("First Christmas")

(Des B. Neuenschwander (19p.), Clare Melinsky (26p.), Catherine Yass (44p.), C. Aitchison (64p.). Photo De La Rue)

1999 (2 Nov). *Millennium Series. The Christians' Tale. One centre phosphor band (19p.) or two phosphor bands (others).* P 14×14½.

2115	**1425**	19p. gold, stone, greenish yellow, bright crimson, deep dull blue, black and yellow-ochre	75	70
		a. Imperf (pair)	£400	
2116	**1426**	26p. gold, greenish yellow, bright scarlet, emerald, dull violet and black	95	1·00
2117	**1427**	44p. gold, greenish yellow, bright magenta, new blue, black and ultramarine	1·50	1·60
2118	**1428**	64p. gold, bistre-yellow, cerise, bright emerald, bistre, slate-blue, pale new blue and black	2·25	2·40
Set of 4			5·25	5·25
Set of 4 *Gutter Pairs*			13·00	
First Day Cover (Philatelic Bureau) (Type J, see Introduction)				8·00
First Day Cover (St. Andrews, Fife)				8·50
Presentation Pack			7·50	
PHQ Cards (*set of* 4)			8·50	13·00

Special First Day of Issue Postmark

1429 "World of the Stage" (Allen Jones)

1430 "World of Music" (Bridget Riley)

1431 "World of Literature" (Lisa Milroy)

1432 "New Worlds" (Sir Howard Hodgkin)

(Photo Walsall)

1999 (7 Dec). *Millennium Series. The Artists' Tale. One centre phosphor band (19p.) or two phosphor bands (others).* P 14×14½.

2119	**1429**	19p. greenish yellow, bright magenta, new blue, black and silver	75	70
2120	**1430**	26p. lemon, orange, pale new blue, violet-blue and black	95	1·00
2121	**1431**	44p. greenish yellow, bright magenta, new blue, black and gold	1·50	1·60
2122	**1432**	64p. greenish yellow, yellow, bright turquoise-green, bright magenta, new blue, black, gold and silver	2·25	2·40
Set of 4			5·25	5·25
Set of 4 *Gutter Pairs*			13·00	
First Day Cover (Philatelic Bureau) (Type J, see Introduction)				8·00
First Day Cover (Stratford -upon- Avon)				8·50
Presentation Pack			7·50	
PHQ Cards (*set of* 4)			8·50	13·00

Special First Day of Issue Postmark

Collectors Pack 1999

1999 (7 Dec). *Comprises Nos.* 2069/76, 2080/105 *and* 2107/22.

CP2122*a* Collectors Pack £135

Post Office Yearbook

1999 (7 Dec). *Comprises Nos.* 2069/76, 2080/105 *and* 2107/22 *in hardback book with slip case* £135

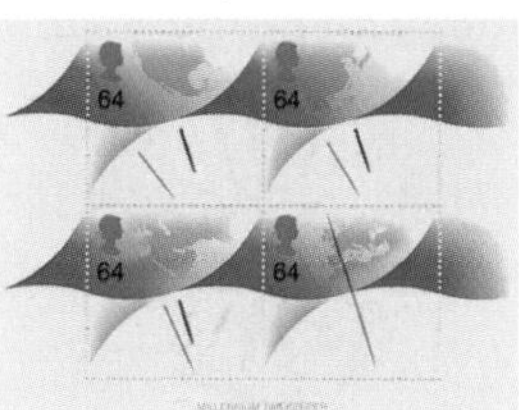

1433a

(Des D. Gentleman. Photo De La Rue)

1999 (14 Dec). *Millennium Series. "Millennium Timekeeper". Sheet 120×89 mm. Each design silver, deep grey, pale olive-grey, greenish grey, grey-black and bright rose-red. Two phosphor bands.* P 14×14½.

MS2123 **1433a** 64p. Clock face and map of North America; 64p. Clock face and map of Asia; 64p. Clock face and map of Middle East; 64p. Clock face and map of Europe	26·00	26.00
First Day Cover (Philatelic Bureau)		26·00
First Day Cover (Greenwich SE)		26·00
Presentation Pack	30·00	
PHQ Cards (*set of* 5)	14·00	32·00

No. **MS**2123 also exists overprinted "EARLS COURT, LONDON 22-28 MAY 2000 THE STAMP SHOW 2000" from Exhibition Premium Passes, costing £10, available from 1 March 2000 (*Price* £35).

Special First Day of Issue Postmarks

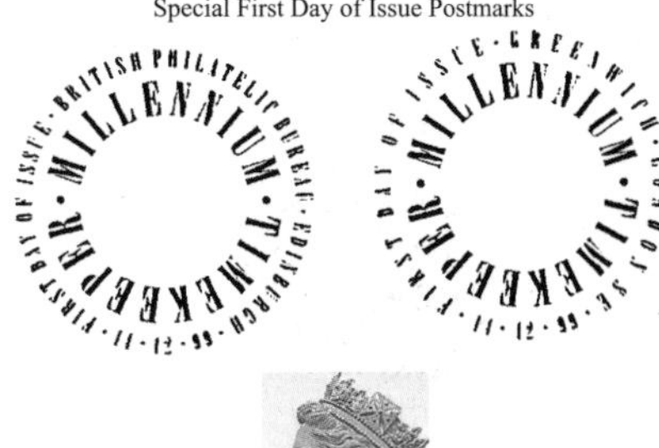

1437 Queen Elizabeth II

(Des A. Machin, adapted R. Scholey. Photo De La Rue, Questa or Walsall (No. 2124), Walsall (Nos. 2124bl, 2124dl), Questa or Walsall (No. 2124d))

2000 (6 Jan–Aug). *New Millennium. Two phosphor bands.* P 15×14 (with one elliptical hole on each vertical side).

2124	**1437**	(1st) olive-brown	1·00	1·00
		a. Imperf (pair)	£700	
		bl. Booklet pane. No. 2124×4 plus commemorative label at right (21.3.00)	6·00	
		bm. Booklet pane. No. 2124×9 with margins all round (4 Aug)	9·00	
		cEy. Phosphor omitted	£500	
		d. Perf 14	1·00	1·00
		dEa. Phosphor omitted		
		dl. Booklet pane. No. 2124d×8 with central label and margins all round (15.2.00)	8·00	
First Day Cover (No. 2124) (Philatelic Bureau) (Type G, see Introduction)				3·00
First Day Cover (No. 2124) (Windsor) (Type G)				3·00
First Day Cover (No. 2124bm) (Philatelic Bureau)				6·00
First Day Cover (No. 2124bm) (London SW1)				6·00
First Day Cover (No. 2124dl) (Philatelic Bureau)				6·00
First Day Cover (No. 2124dl) (London SW5)				6·00
Presentation Pack			6·00	
PHQ Card (23 May)			5·00	16·00

No. 2124d comes from stamp booklets printed by Questa. Similar booklets produced by Walsall have the same perforation as the sheet stamps. The labels on booklet pane No. 2124bl show either Postman Pat, publicising "The Stamp Show 2000", or the National Botanic Garden of Wales.

Special First Day of Issue Postmarks (for use on No. 2124dl only)

For special first day of issue postmarks used on No. 2124bm see below No. **MS**2161.

1438 Barn Owl (World Owl Trust, Muncaster) Science Centre, Leicester)

1439 Night Sky (National Space

1440 River Goyt and Textile Mills (Torrs Walkway, New Mills)

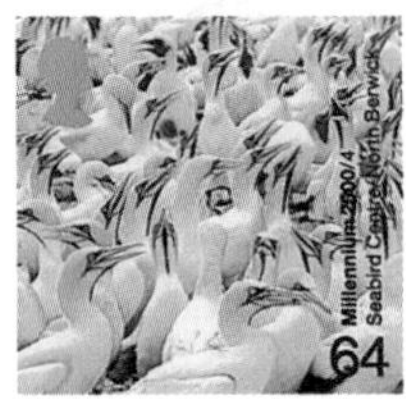

1441 Cape Gannets (Seabird Centre, North Berwick)

(Litho (44p.), photo (others) Walsall (No. 2126a/ab) or Questa (others))

2000 (18 Jan)–**02**. *Millennium Projects (1st series). "Above and Beyond". One centre phosphor band (19p.) or two phosphor bands (others).* P 14×14½ (1st, 44p.) or 13½×14 (others).

2125	**1438**	19p. greenish yellow, magenta, pale new blue, black and silver	1·25	70
		a. Imperf (pair)	£1250	
2126	**1439**	26p. greenish yellow, magenta, pale new blue, black and silver	95	1·00
		a. Imperf (pair)	£1250	
2126*a*		(1st) greenish yellow, magenta, pale new blue, black and silver (26.5.00)	5·25	3·50
		ab. Booklet pane. Nos. 2126a and 2139 with margins all round	7·00	
		ac. Booklet pane. No. 2126a×4 with margins all round (24.9.02)	15·00	
2127	**1440**	44p. black, bistre-brown, buff and silver	1·50	1·75
2128	**1441**	64p. greenish yellow, magenta, blue, black, silver and orange	2·50	2·50
Set of 4 (ex No. 2126a)			5·75	5·75
Set of 4 *Gutter Pairs*			15·00	
First Day Cover (Nos. 2125/8) (Philatelic Bureau) (Type J, see Introduction)				8·00
First Day Cover (Nos. 2125/8) (Muncaster, Ravenglass)				8·50
First Day Cover (No. 2126ab) (Philatelic Bureau)				7·00
First Day Cover (No. 2126ab) (Leicester)				7·00
Presentation Pack			6·50	
PHQ Cards (*set of* 4)			8·50	13·00

No. 2126a comes from the £2.70 Millennium booklet, No. HBA3, and the "Across the Universe" sponsored booklet, No. DX29.

Imperforate pairs of No. 2128 with Queen's head in gold, Nos. 2126 and 2139 with inscriptions in an alternative typeface and No. 2128 with inscriptions in silver are all of proof status (Prices from £200).

Special First Day of Issue Postmarks

1442 Millennium Beacon (Beacons across The Land)

1443 Garratt Steam Locomotive No. 143 pulling Train (Rheilffordd Eryri, Welsh Highland Railway)

1444 Lightning (Dynamic Earth Centre, Edinburgh)

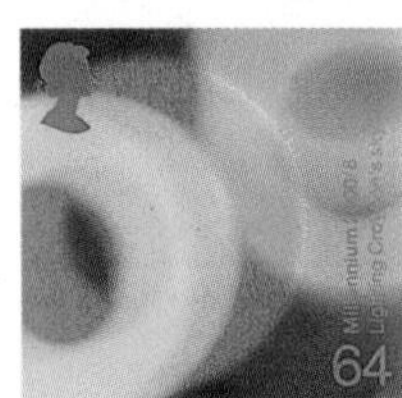

1445 Multicoloured Lights (Lighting Croydon's Skyline)

(Photo De La Rue)

2000 (1 Feb). *Millennium Projects (2nd series). "Fire and Light". One centre phosphor band (19p.) or two phosphor bands (others).* P 14×14½.

2129	**1442**	19p. silver, greenish yellow, bright magenta, new blue and black	75	70
2130	**1443**	26p. silver, greenish yellow, bright magenta, new blue and black	1·25	1·00
2131	**1444**	44p. silver, greenish yellow, bright magenta, new blue and black	1·50	1·50
2132	**1445**	64p. silver, greenish yellow, bright magenta, pale greenish blue and black	2·25	2·50
Set of 4			5·50	5·50
Set of 4 *Gutter Pairs*			15·00	
First Day Cover (Philatelic Bureau) (Type J, see Introduction)				8·00
First Day Cover (Edinburgh 3°10'W)				8·50
Presentation Pack			6·50	
PHQ Cards (*set of* 4)			8·50	13·00

Special First Day of Issue Postmark

1446 Queen Victoria and Queen Elizabeth II

(Des J. Matthews. Photo Walsall)

2000 (15 Feb). *T* **929** *redrawn with "1st" face value as T* **1446**. *Two phosphor bands.* P 14 (with one elliptical hole on each vertical side).

2133	**1446**	(1st) brownish black and cream	1·50	1·25
		l. Booklet pane. No. 2133×6 with margins all round	8·00	
First Day Cover (No. 2133l) (Philatelic Bureau)				4·00
First Day Cover (No. 2133l) (London SW5)				4·00

No. 2133 was only issued in £7 0.50 stamp booklets. For illustrations of first day cover cancellations see below No. 2124.

1447 Beach Pebbles (Turning the Tide, Durham Coast)

1448 Frog's Legs and Water Lilies (National Pondlife Centre, Merseyside)

1449 Cliff Boardwalk (Parc Arfordirol, Llanelli Coast)

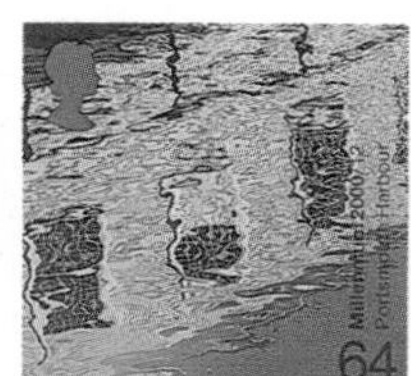

1450 Reflections in Water (Portsmouth Harbour Development)

(Litho (44p.), photo (others) Walsall)

2000 (7 Mar). *Millennium Projects (3rd series). "Water and Coast". One centre phosphor band (19p.) or two phosphor bands (others).* P 14×14½.

2134	**1447**	19p. silver, black, dull blue, sagegreen, olive-grey, orange-yellow and pale grey	75	70
2135	**1448**	26p. new blue, silver, black, greenish yellow and magenta	1·25	1·00
2136	**1449**	44p. black, grey and silver	1·50	1·50
2137	**1450**	64p. black, grey, deep bluish green, greenish blue, cobalt, grey-green and brownish grey	2·25	2·50
Set of 4			5·50	5·50
Set of 4 *Gutter Pairs*			15·00	
First Day Cover (Philatelic Bureau) (Type J, see Introduction)				8·00
First Day Cover (Llanelli)				8·50
Presentation Pack			6·50	
PHQ Cards (*set of* 4)			8·50	13·00

Special First Day of Issue Postmark

1451 Reed Beds, River Braid (ECOS, Ballymena)

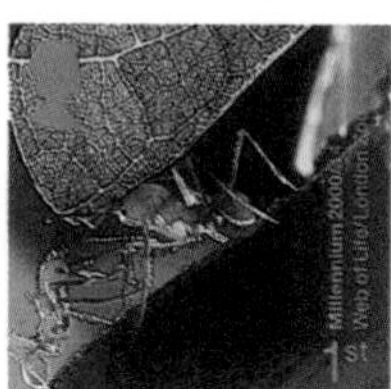

1452 South American Leaf-cutter Ants ("Web of Life" Exhibition, London Zoo)

1453 Solar Sensors (Earth Centre, Doncaster)

1454 Hydroponic Leaves (Project SUZY, Teesside)

(Photo De La Rue)

2000 (4 Apr). *Millennium Projects (4th series). "Life and Earth". One centre phosphor band (2nd) or two phosphor bands (others).* P 14×14½.

2138	**1451**	(2nd) silver, greenish yellow, magenta, new blue, black and grey	75	70
2139	**1452**	(1st) silver, greenish yellow, magenta, new blue and black	1·25	1·00
2140	**1453**	44p. silver, greenish yellow, magenta, new blue and black	1·50	1·50
2141	**1454**	64p. silver, greenish yellow, magenta, new blue and grey-black	2·25	1·50
Set of 4			5·50	5·50
Set of 4 *Gutter Pairs*			15·00	
First Day Cover (Philatelic Bureau) (Type J, see Introduction)				8·00
First Day Cover (Doncaster)				8·50
Presentation Pack			6·50	
PHQ Cards (*set of* 4)			8·50	13·00

For No. 2139 printed by Walsall in photogravure, see booklet pane No. 2126ab.

Types **1453/4** with face values of 45p. and 65p. were prepared, but not issued.

Special First Day of Issue Postmark

1455 Pottery Glaze (Ceramica Museum, Stoke-on-Trent)

1456 Bankside Galleries (Tate Modern, London)

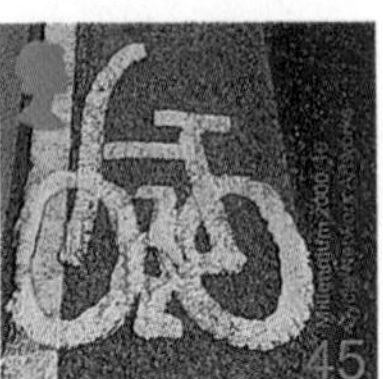

1457 Road Marking (Cycle Network Artworks) (Photo Enschedé)

1458 People of Salford (Lowry Centre, Salford)

2000 (2 May). *Millennium Projects (5th series). "Art and Craft". One centre phosphor band (2nd) or two phosphor bands (others).* P 14×14½.

2142	**1455**	(2nd) greenish yellow, magenta, new blue, black, silver and greybrown	75	70
2143	**1456**	(1st) greenish yellow, magenta, new blue, black and silver	1·25	1·00
2144	**1457**	45p. greenish yellow, magenta, new blue, black and silver	1·50	1·50
2145	**1458**	65p. greenish yellow, magenta, new blue, black, dull silver and silver	2·25	2·50
		Set of 4	5·50	5·50
		Set of 4 *Gutter Pairs*	15·00	
		First Day Cover (Philatelic Bureau) (Type J, see Introduction)		8·00
		First Day Cover (Salford)		8·50
		Presentation Pack	7·50	
		PHQ Cards (*set of* 4)	8·50	13·00

Special First Day of Issue Postmark

(Des J. Matthews. Photo De La Rue)

2000 (22 May). *"Stamp Show 2000" International Stamp Exhibition, London. Jeffrey Matthews Colour Palette. Sheet, 124×70 mm, containing stamps as T* **367** *with two labels. Phosphorised paper.* P 15×14 (with one elliptical hole on each vertical side).

MS2146 4p. new blue; 5p. dull red-brown; 6p. yellow-olive; 10p. dull orange; 31p. deep mauve; 39p. bright magenta; 64p. turquoise-green; £1 bluish violet	18·00	18·00
First Day Cover (Philatelic Bureau)		18·00
First Day Cover (Earls Court, London SW5)		19·00
Exhibition Card (wallet, sold at £4.99, containing one mint sheet and one cancelled on postcard)		30·00

The £1 value is printed in Iriodin ink which gives a shiny effect to the solid part of the background behind the Queen's head.

Special First Day of Issue Postmarks

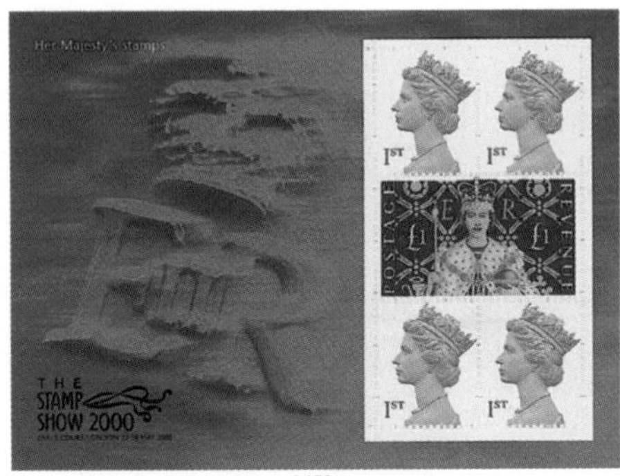

1459a

(Des Delaney Design Consultants. Photo De La Rue)

2000 (23 May). *"Stamp Show 2000" International Stamp Exhibition, London. "Her Majesty's Stamps". Sheet 121×89 mm. Phosphorised paper.* P 15×14 (with one elliptical hole on each vertical side of stamps as T **1437**).

MS2147 **1459a** (1st) olive-brown (Type **1437**)×4; £1 slate-green (as Type **163**)	21·00	21·00
First Day Cover (Philatelic Bureau)		22·00
First Day Cover (City of Westminster, London SW1)		24·00
Presentation Pack	90·00	
PHQ Cards (*set of* 2)	16·00	28·00

The £1 value is an adaptation of the 1953 Coronation 1s.3d. stamp originally designed by Edmund Dulac. It is shown on one of the PHQ cards with the other depicting the complete miniature sheet.

Special First Day of Issue Postmarks

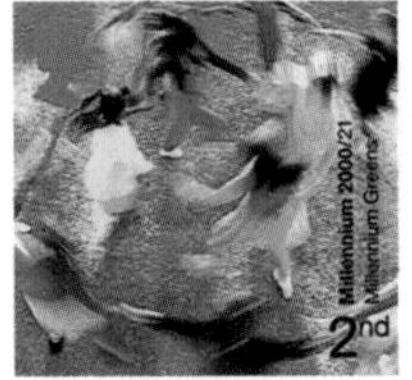

1460 Children playing (Millennium Greens Project)

1461 Millennium Bridge, Gateshead

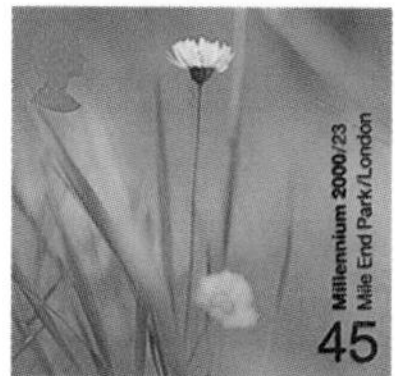

1462 Daisies (Mile End Park, London)

1463 African Hut and Thatched Cottage ("On the Meridian Line" Project)

(Photo (2nd, 45p.) or litho (1st, 65p.) Walsall)

2000 (6 June). *Millennium Projects (6th series). "People and Places". One centre phosphor band (2nd) or two phosphor bands (others).* P 14×14½.

2148	**1460**	(2nd)	bistre-yellow, bright magenta, new blue, grey-black and silver	75	70
2149	**1461**	(1st)	deep ultramarine, silver, black, new blue, bright magenta and greenish yellow	1·25	1·00
2150	**1462**	45p.	greenish yellow, magenta, pale new blue, grey-black, silver and deep turquoise-green	1·50	1·50
2151	**1463**	65p.	silver, black, new blue, bright magenta and greenish yellow	2·25	2·50

Set of 4 ... 5·50 5·50
Set of 4 *Gutter Pairs* ... 15·00
First Day Cover (Philatelic Bureau) (Type J, see Introduction) ... 8·00
First Day Cover (Gateshead) ... 8·50
Presentation Pack ... 7·50
PHQ Cards (*set of* 4) ... 8·50 13·00

Special First Day of Issue Postmark

1464 Raising the Stone (Strangford Stone, Killyleagh)

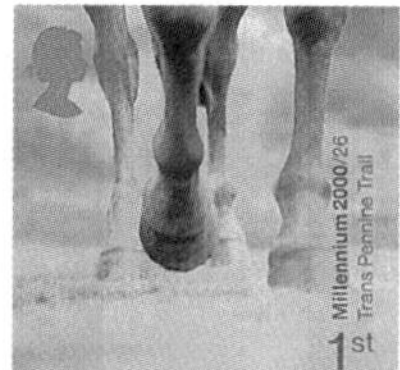

1465 Horse's Hooves (Trans Pennine Trail, Derbyshire)

1466 Cyclist (Kingdom of Fife Cycle Ways, Scotland)

1467 Bluebell Wood (Groundwork's "Changing Places" Project)

(Photo Walsall (Nos. 2153a, 2155a) or Enschedé (others))

2000 (4 July). *Millennium Projects (7th series). "Stone and Soil". One centre phosphor band (2nd) or two phosphor bands (others).* P 14×14½

2152	**1464**	(2nd)	brownish black, grey-black and silver	75	70
2153	**1465**	(1st)	greenish yellow, bright magenta, new blue, grey-black, silver and grey	1·25	1·00
		a.	Booklet pane. Nos. 2153 and 2157 with margins all round (5 Sept)	8·50	
2154	**1466**	45p.	brownish black, grey-black, black and silver	1·50	1·75
2155	**1467**	65p.	greenish yellow, bright magenta, new blue, black and silver	2·50	2·50
		a.	Booklet pane. No. 2155×2 with margins all round (18 Sept)	5·00	

Set of 4 ... 5·50 5·75
Set of 4 *Gutter Pairs* ... 15·00
First Day Cover (Philatelic Bureau) (Type J, see Introduction) ... 8·00
First Day Cover (Killyleagh) ... 8·50
Presentation Pack ... 7·50
PHQ Cards (*set of* 4) ... 8·50 13·00

No. 2155a comes from the £7 Treasury of Trees booklet, No. DX26.

Special First Day of Issue Postmark

1468 Tree Roots ("Yews for the Millennium" Project)

1469 Sunflower ("Eden" Project, St. Austell)

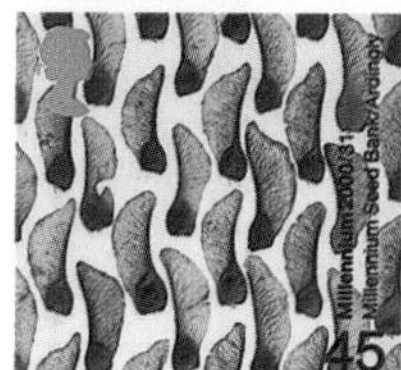

1470 Sycamore Seeds (Millennium Seed Bank, Wakehurst Place, Surrey)

1471 Forest, Doire Dach ("Forest for Scotland")

(Photo Walsall (Nos. 2156a, 2158a, 2159a) or De La Rue (others))

2000 (1 Aug). *Millennium Projects (8th series). "Tree and Leaf". One centre phosphor band (2nd) or two phosphor bands (others)).* P 14×14½.

2156	**1468**	(2nd)	silver, greenish yellow, magenta, new blue and black	75	70
		a.	Booklet pane. No. 2156×4 with margins all round (18 Sept)	4·00	
2157	**1469**	(1st)	greenish yellow, magenta, new blue, black and silver	1·25	1·00
2158	**1470**	45p.	black, greenish yellow, magenta, new blue, grey-black and silver	1·50	1·60

		a. Booklet pane. No. 2158×4 with margins all round (18 Sept)	6·00	
2159	**1471**	65p. silver, greenish yellow, magenta, new blue and black	2·50	2·50
		a. Booklet pane. No. 2159×2 with margins all round (18 Sept)	5·00	
Set of 4			5·50	5·50
Set of 4 Gutter Pairs			15·00	
First Day Cover (Philatelic Bureau) (Type J, see Introduction)				8·00
First Day Cover (St Austell)				8·50
Presentation Pack			7·50	
PHQ Cards (*set of* 4)			8·50	13·00

Nos. 2156a, 2158a and 2159a come from the £7 Treasury of Trees booklet, No. DX26. For No. 2157 printed by Walsall in photogravure, see booklet pane No. 2153a.

Special First Day of Issue Postmark

1472 Queen Elizabeth the Queen Mother

1472a Royal Family on Queen Mother's 99th Birthday

(Des J. Gibbs from photo by J. Swannell. Photo Questa (Nos. 2160, **MS**2161a) or De La Rue (No. **MS**2161))

2000 (4 Aug). *Queen Elizabeth the Queen Mother's 100th Birthday. Phosphorised paper plus two phosphor bands.* P 14½.

2160	**1472**	27p. silver, greenish yellow, magenta, new blue and black	2·50	2·75
		a. Booklet pane. No. 2160×4 with margins all round	9·00	
MS2161		121×89mm. **1472a** 27p.×4, silver, greenish yellow, magenta, new blue and black	11·00	11·00
		a. Booklet pane. As No. **MS**2161, but larger, 150×95 mm, and with additional silver frame	10·00	8·00
First Day Cover (No. 2160a) (Philatelic Bureau)				8·00
First Day Cover (No. 2160a) (London SW1)				8·00
First Day Cover (**MS**2161) (Philatelic Bureau)				12·00
First Day Cover (**MS**2161) (London SW1)				12·00
Presentation Pack (**MS**2161)			28·00	
PHQ Cards (*set of* 5)			11·00	24·00

No. 2160 was only issued in £7.03 stamp booklets and as part of Nos. **MS**2161/a.

The complete miniature sheet is shown on one of the PHQ cards with the others depicting individual stamps.

Special First Day of Issue Postmarks

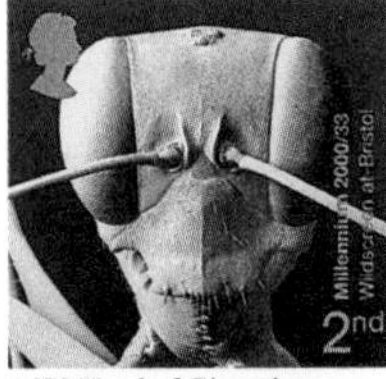

1473 Head of Gigantiops *destructor* (Ant) (Wildscreen at Bristol)

1474 Gathering Water Lilies on Broads (Norfolk and Norwich Project)

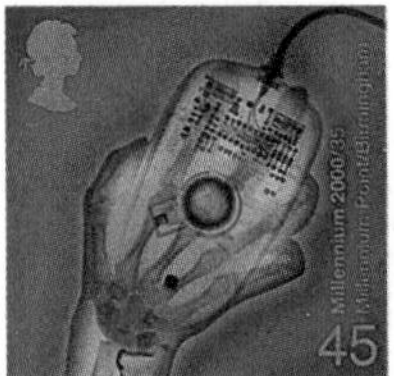

1475 X-ray of Hand holding Computer Mouse (Millennium Point, Birmingham)

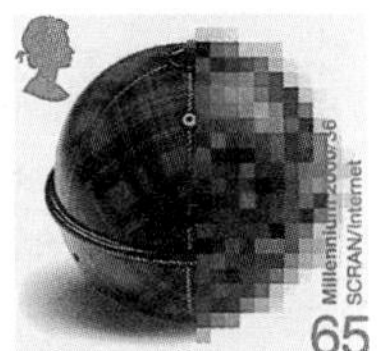

1476 Tartan Wool Holder (Scottish Cultural Resources Access Network)

(Litho Walsall)

2000 (5 Sept). *Millennium Projects (9th series). "Mind and Matter". One centre phosphor band (2nd) or two phosphor bands (others).* P 14×14½.

2162	**1473**	(2nd) black, orange-yellow, slate-green and silver	75	70
2163	**1474**	(1st) black, sage-green, ochre and gold	1·25	1·00
2164	**1475**	45p. silver, black, new blue, magenta and greenish yellow	1·50	1·75
2165	**1476**	65p. silver, black, new blue, magenta and greenish yellow	2·25	2·50
Set of 4			5·50	5·75
Set of 4 Gutter Pairs			15·00	
First Day Cover (Philatelic Bureau) (Type J, see Introduction)				8·00
First Day Cover (Norwich)				8·50
Presentation Pack			7·50	
PHQ Cards (*set of* 4)			8·50	13·00

Special First Day of Issue Postmark

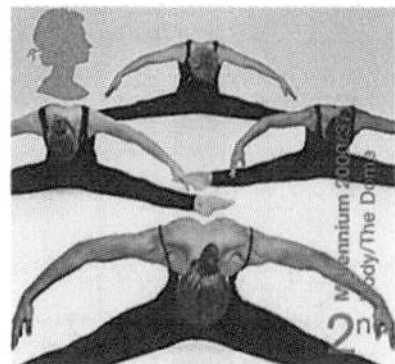

1477 Acrobatic Performers (Millennium Dome)

1478 Football Players (Hampden Park, Glasgow)

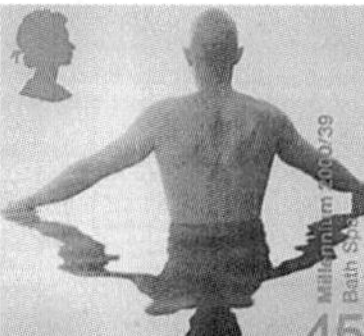

1479 Bather (Bath Spa Project)

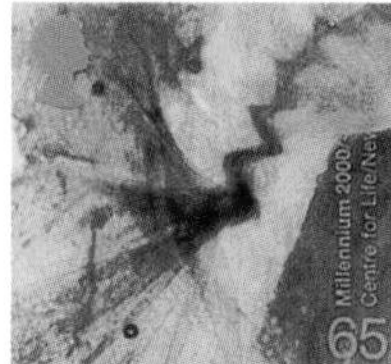

1480 Hen's Egg under Magnification (Centre for Life, Newcastle)

(Litho (2nd) or photo (others) Questa)

2000 (3 Oct). *Millennium Projects (10th series). "Body and Bone". One centre phosphor band (2nd) or two phosphor bands (others).* P 14×14½ (2nd) or 13½×14 (others).

2166 **1477** (2nd) black, slate-blue and silver 75 70
2167 **1478** (1st) magenta, new blue, greenish yellow, black and silver .... 1·25 1·00
2168 **1479** 45p. mauve, olive-grey, greenish yellow, grey-black and silver .... 1·50 1·50
2169 **1480** 65p. magenta, pale new blue, greenish yellow, grey-black and silver .... 2·25 2·50

Set of 4 .... 5·50 5·75
Set of 4 *Gutter Pairs* .... 15·00
First Day Cover (Philatelic Bureau) (Type J, see Introduction) .... 8·00
First Day Cover (Glasgow) .... 8·50
Presentation Pack .... 7·50
PHQ Cards (*set of* 4) .... 8·50 13·00

Special First Day of Issue Postmark

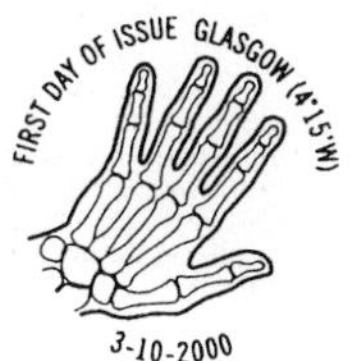

1481 Virgin and Child Stained Glass Window, St. Edmundsbury Cathedral (Suffolk Cathedral Millennium Project)

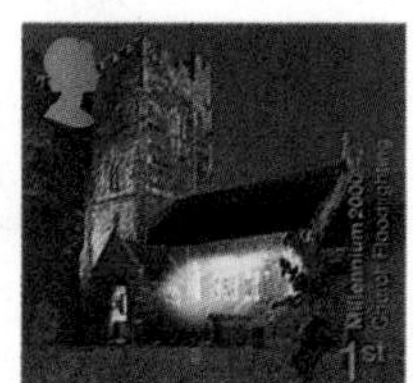

1482 Floodlit Church of St. Peter and St. Paul, Overstowey (Church Floodlighting Trust)

1483 12th-cent Latin Gradual (St. Patrick Centre, Downpatrick)

1484 Chapter House Ceiling, York Minster (York Millennium Mystery Plays)

(Photo De La Rue)

2000 (7 Nov). *Millennium Projects (11th series). "Spirit and Faith". One centre phosphor band (2nd) or two phosphor bands (others).* P 14×14½.

2170 **1481** (2nd) gold, greenish yellow, cerise, new blue and grey-black 75 70
a. Imperf pair £575
2171 **1482** (1st) gold, greenish yellow, cerise, new blue, bright blue, black and grey-black .... 1·25 1·00
a. Imperf (pair) £575
2172 **1483** 45p. deep reddish purple, olive-sepia, red, black and gold .... 1·50 1·50
2173 **1484** 65p. gold, greenish yellow, cerise, new blue, grey-black and black .... 2·25 2·50

Set of 4 .... 5·50 5·50
Set of 4 *Gutter Pairs* .... 15·00
First Day Cover (Philatelic Bureau) (Type J, see Introduction) .... 8·00
First Day Cover (Downpatrick) .... 8·50
Presentation Pack .... 7·50
PHQ Cards (*set of* 4) .... 8·50 13·00

Special First Day of Issue Postmark

Post Office Yearbook

2000 (Nov 7). *Comprises Nos.* 2125/6, 2127/32, 2134/45, 2148/59 *and* **MS** 2161/81 *in hardback book with slip case* £100

The last two issues in the Millennium Projects Series were supplied for insertion into the above at a later date.

1485 Church Bells (Ringing in the Millennium)

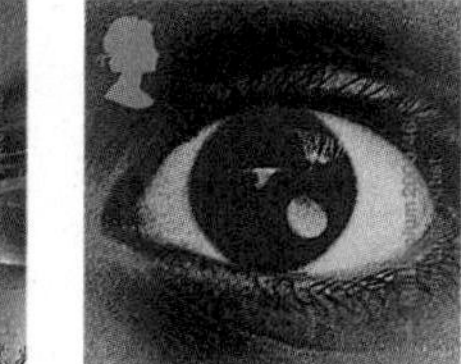

1486 Eye (Year of the Artist)

1487 Top of Harp (Canolfan Mileniwm, Cardiff)

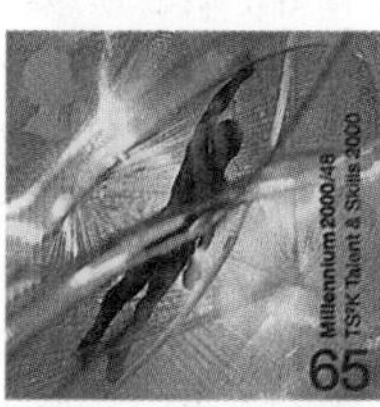

1488 Silhouetted Figure within Latticework (TS2K Creative Enterprise Centres, London)

(Photo De La Rue)

2000 (5 Dec). *Millennium Projects (12th series). "Sound and Vision". One centre phosphor band (2nd) or two phosphor bands (others).* P 14×14½.

2174	**1485**	(2nd) silver, greenish yellow, magenta, new blue and black	75	70
2175	**1486**	(1st) silver, magenta, blue, black and brownish grey	1·25	1·00
2176	**1487**	45p. silver, greenish yellow, magenta, new blue and black	1·50	1·50
2177	**1488**	65p. black, greenish yellow, magenta, new blue, grey-black and silver	2·25	2·50

Set of 4 .... 5·50 5·50
Set of 4 Gutter Pairs .... 15·00
First Day Cover (Philatelic Bureau) (Type J, see Introduction) .... 8·00
First Day Cover (Cardiff) .... 8·50
Presentation Pack .... 7·50
PHQ Cards (*set of* 4) .... 8·50 13·00

Special First Day of Issue Postmark

Collectors Pack 2000

2000 (Dec 5) *Comprises Nos.* 2125/6, 2127/32, 2134/45, 2148/59 *and* **MS** 2161/81.
CP2181a Collectors Pack £120

1489 "Flower" ("Nurture Children")

1490 "Tiger" ("Listen to Children")

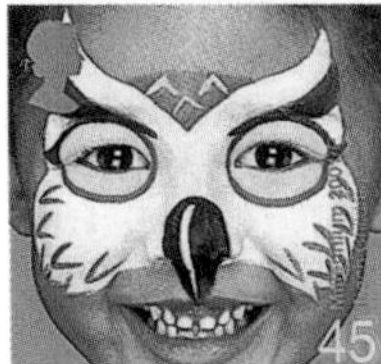

1491 "Owl" ("Teach Children")

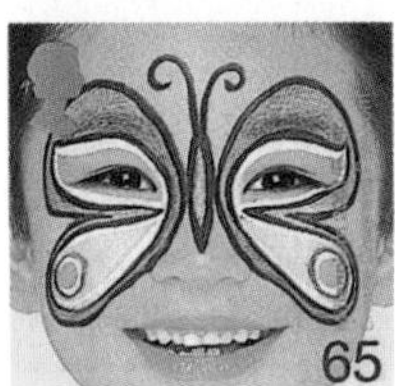

1492 "Butterfly" ("Ensure Children's Freedom")

(Des Why Not Associates. Photo De La Rue)

2001 (16 Jan). *New Millennium. Rights of the Child. Face Paintings. One centre phosphor band (2nd) or two phosphor bands (others).* P 14×14½.

2179	**1489**	(2nd) bright violet, greenish yellow, cerise, new blue, rosine, grey-black and silver	75	75
2179	**1490**	(1st) lemon, greenish yellow, cerise, new blue, emerald, grey-black and silver	1·00	1·10
2180	**1491**	45p. orange-yellow, greenish yellow, cerise, new blue, pale violet-blue, grey-black and silver	1·60	1·75
2181	**1492**	65p. bright violet, greenish yellow, cerise, new blue, lemon, grey-black and silver	2·40	2·50

Set of 4 .... 5·75 5·75
Set of 4 Gutter Pairs .... 14·00
First Day Cover (Philatelic Bureau) .... 7·50
First Day Cover (Hope, Hope Valley) .... 8·00
Presentation Pack .... 7·50
PHQ Cards (*set of* 4) .... 8·50 13·00

Special First Day of Issue Postmarks

1493 "Love"

1494 "THANKS"

1495 "abc" (New Baby)

1496 "WELCOME"

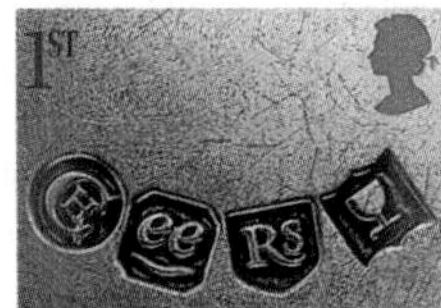

1497 " Cheers"

(Des Springpoint Design. Photo Enschedé)

2001 (6 Feb). *Greetings Stamps. "Occasions". Two phosphor bands.* P 14×14½.

2182	**1493**	(1st) silver, greenish yellow, magenta, pale greenish blue, black and silver-grey	1·10	1·10
2183	**1494**	(1st) silver, greenish yellow, magenta, pale greenish blue, black and silver-grey	1·10	1·10
2184	**1495**	(1st) silver, greenish yellow, magenta, pale greenish blue, black and silver-grey	1·10	1·10
2185	**1496**	(1st) silver, greenish yellow, magenta, pale greenish blue, black and silver-grey	1·10	1·10
2186	**1497**	(1st) silver, greenish yellow, magenta, pale greenish blue, black and silver-grey	1·10	1·10

Set of 5	5·00	4·50
Set of 5 *Gutter Pairs*	13·00	
First Day Cover (Philatelic Bureau)		6·50
First Day Cover (Merry Hill, Wolverhampton)		7·00
Presentation Pack (13 Feb)	6·50	
PHQ Cards (*set of* 5)	8·50	13·00

The silver-grey backgrounds are printed in Iriodin ink which gives a shiny effect.

Further packs of Nos. 2182/6 were sold from 3 July 2001. These comprised the listed stamps in blocks of ten (from sheets) with an insert describing the occasion (*Price* £10 *per pack*).

Nos. 2182/6 were re-issued on 1 May 2001 in sheets of 20 printed by Questa in lithography instead of photogravure, in connection with the "customised" stamps scheme. Such sheets contained twenty examples of either Nos. 2182, 2184 or 2185, or ten each of Nos. 2183 and 2186. Sheets with personal photographs printed on the labels were available from Royal Mail in Edinburgh at £12 each. From 5 June 2001 a similar sheet containing four of each design in horizontal strips, with postal symbols on the labels, was sold at £5.95.

Special First Day of Issue Postmarks

1498 Dog and Owner on Bench

1499 Dog in Bath

1500 Boxer at Dog Show

1501 Cat in Handbag

1502 Cat on Gate

1503 Dog in Car

1504 Cat at Window

1505 Dog Behind Fence

1506 Cat watching Bird

1507 Cat in Washbasin

(Des johnson banks. Photo Walsall)

2001 (13 Feb). *Cats and Dogs. Self-adhesive. Two phosphor bands.* P 15×14 die-cut.

2187	**1498**	(1st) black, grey and silver	1·50	1·50
		a. Sheetlet. Nos. 2187/96	15·00	11·50
		aa. Imperf (sheetlet)	£3800	
		b. Booklet pane. Nos. 2187/96 plus No. 2040×2	15·00	
		ba. Imperf (pane)		
2188	**1499**	(1st) black, grey and silver	1·50	1·50
2189	**1500**	(1st) black, grey and silver	1·50	1·50
2189	**1500**	(1st) black, grey and silver	1·50	1·50
2190	**1501**	(1st) black, grey and silver	1·50	1·50
2191	**1502**	(1st) black, grey and silver	1·50	1·50
2192	**1503**	(1st) black, grey and silver	1·50	1·50
2193	**1504**	(1st) black, grey and silver	1·50	1·50
2194	**1505**	(1st) black, grey and silver	1·50	1·50
2195	**1506**	(1st) black, grey and silver	1·50	1·50
2196	**1507**	(1st) black, grey and silver	1·50	1·50
2187/96 *Set of* 10			14·00	14·00
First Day Cover (Philatelic Bureau)				15·00
First Day Cover (Petts Wood, Orpington)				16·00
Presentation Pack			20·00	
PHQ Cards (*set of* 10)			14·00	30·00

Nos. 2187/96 were printed together in sheetlets of 10 (5×2), with the surplus self-adhesive paper around each stamp retained. The pane has vertical roulettes between rows 2/3 and 4/5 with the design on the reverse of the backing paper similar to Booklet No. PM1.

Special First Day of Issue Postmarks

1508 "RAIN"

1509 "FAIR"

1510 "STORMY"

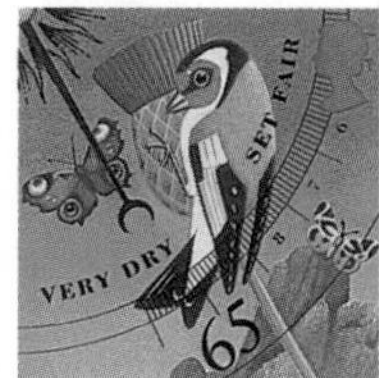

1511 "VERY DRY"

(Des H. Brown and T. Meeuwissen. Photo De La Rue)

2001 (13 Mar). *The Weather. One side phosphor band (19p.) or two phosphor bands (others).* P 14½.

2197	**1508**	19p. black, greenish yellow, bright magenta, new blue and gold	70	75
2198	**1509**	27p. black, greenish yellow, bright magenta, new blue and gold	85	1·00
2199	**1510**	45p. black, greenish yellow, bright magenta, new blue and gold	1·50	1·50

2200 **1511** 65p. black, greenish yellow, bright magenta, new blue and gold .... 2·40 2·50
Set of 4 .... 5·00 5·50
Set of 4 *Gutter Pairs* .... 14·00
First Day Cover (Philatelic Bureau) .... 7·00
First Day Cover (Fraserburgh) .... 8·00
Presentation Pack .... 12·50
MS2201 105×105 mm. Nos. 2197/200 .... 13·00 13·00
First Day Cover (Philatelic Bureau) .... 15·00
First Day Cover (Fraserburgh) .... 16·00
PHQ Cards (*set of* 5) .... 8·50 16·00

Nos. 2197/200 show the four quadrants of a barometer dial which are combined on the miniature sheet. The reddish violet on both the 27p. and the miniature sheet is printed in thermochromic ink which changes from reddish violet to light blue when exposed to heat. The PHQ cards depict the four values and the miniature sheet.

Special First Day of Issue Postmarks

1512 *Vanguard* Class Submarine, 1992

1513 *Swiftsure* Class Submarine, 1973

1514 *Unity* Class Submarine, 1939

1515 "Holland" Type Submarine, 1901

1516 White Ensign

1517 Union Jack

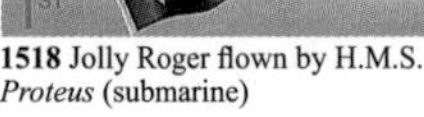

1518 Jolly Roger flown by H.M.S. *Proteus* (submarine)

1519 Flag of Chief of Defence Staff

(Des D. Davis. Photo Questa)

2001 (10 Apr). *Centenary of Royal Navy Submarine Service. One centre phosphor band (2nd) or two phosphor bands (others).* P 15×14.

(a) Submarines. PVA gum.

2202 **1512** (2nd) black, brownish black, dull purple and gold 70 75
a. Perf 15½×15 (22 Oct) .... 3·75 3·00
ab. Booklet pane. Nos. 2202a and 2204a, each ×2, with margins all round .... 12·00
2203 **1513** (1st) black, azure, slate-blue and gold 85 90
a. Perf 15½×15 (22 Oct) .... 3·75 3·00
ab. Booklet pane. Nos. 2203a and 2205a, each ×2, with margins all round .... 12·00
2204 **1514** 45p. magenta, chrome yellow, new blue, black and gold .... 1·75 1·60
a. Perf 15½×15 (22 Oct) .... 3·75 3·00
2205 **1515** 65p. magenta, chrome yellow, new blue, black and gold .... 2·40 2·50
a. Perf 15½×15 (22 Oct) .... 3·75 3·00
Set of 4 .... 5·25 5·25
Set of 4 *Gutter Pairs* .... 13·50
First Day Cover (Philatelic Bureau) .... 7·50
First Day Cover (Portsmouth) .... 8·00
Presentation Pack .... 7·00
PHQ Cards (*set of* 4) .... 8·50 14·00

(b) Flags. PVA gum. P 14½.

MS2206 92×97 mm. **1516** (1st) bright scarlet, blue and silver; **1517** (1st) bright scarlet, blue and silver; **1518** (1st) black, blue and silver; **1519** (1st) bright scarlet, blue, greenish yellow, black and silver (22 Oct) .... 9·00 9·00
a. Booklet pane. As No. **MS**2206 but larger, 152×96 mm .... 9·00 9·00
First Day Cover (Tallents House) .... 11·00
First Day Cover (Rosyth, Dunfermline) .... 12·00
Presentation Pack .... 12·00
PHQ Cards (*set of* 5) .... 5·00 12·00

(c) Self-adhesive. Die-cut P 15½×14 (No. 2207) or 14½ (others).

2207 **1513** (1st) black, azure, slate-blue and gold (17 Apr) .... 40·00 37·00
a. Booklet pane. No. 2207×2 plus No. 2040×4 .... 75·00
ab. Booklet pane. Imperf £1750
2208 **1516** (1st) bright scarlet, blue and silver (22 Oct) .... 12·00 12·00
a. Booklet pane. Nos. 2208/9 plus No. 2040×4 .... 17·00
ab. Booklet pane. Imperf £3500
2209 **1518** (1st) black, blue and silver (22 Oct) .... 12·00 12·00

The five PHQ cards depict the four designs and the complete miniature sheet.

Nos. 2202a/5a were only issued in the £6.76 "Unseen and Unheard" booklet, No. DX27, and Nos. 2207/9 only come from two different £1.62 self-adhesive booklets.

Type **1516** was re-issued on 21 June 2005 in sheets of 20, printed in lithography by Cartor and sold at £6.55, containing four vertical rows of five stamps alternated with half stamp-size printed labels showing signal flags. These sheets with personalised photographs were available at £14.95 from the Royal Mail.

Type **1517** was re-issued on 27 July 2004 in sheets of 20, printed in lithography by Walsall and sold at £6.15, containing vertical strips of five stamps alternated with half stamp-size printed labels. These sheets with personalised photographs were available at £14.95 from the Royal Mail in Edinburgh.

Special First Day of Issue Postmarks

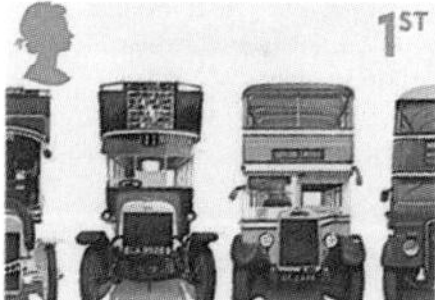

1520 Leyland X2 Open-top, London General B Type, Leyland Titan TD1 and AEC Regent 1

1521 AEC Regent 1, Daimler COG5, Utility Guy Arab Mk II and AEC Regent III RT Type

1522 AEC Regent III RT Type, Bristol KSW5G Open-top, AEC Routemaster and Bristol Lodekka FSF6G

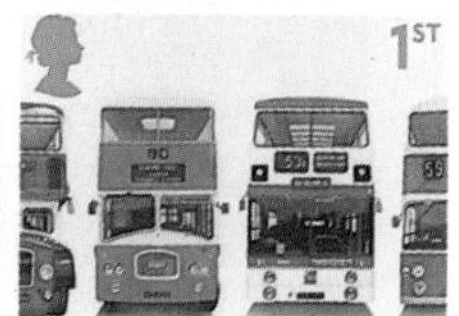

1523 Bristol Lodekka FSF6G, Leyland Titan PD3/4, Leyland Atlantean PDR1/1 and Daimler Fleetline CRG6LX-33

1524 Daimler Fleetline CRG6LX-33, MCW Metrobus DR102/43, Leyland Olympian ONLXB/1R and Dennis Trident

(Des M. English. Litho Questa)

2001 (15 May). *150th Anniv of First Double-decker Bus. "All-over" phosphor.* P 14½×14.

2210	**1520**	(1st) new blue, greenish yellow, magenta, black and grey	1·10	1·10
		a. Horiz strip of 5. Nos. 2210/14	5·50	5·75
		ab. Imperf (horiz strip of 5)	£2200	
2211	**1521**	(1st) new blue, greenish yellow, magenta, black and grey	1·10	1·10
2212	**1522**	(1st) new blue, greenish yellow, magenta, black and grey	1·10	1·10
		a. Grey omitted	£5000	
2213	**1523**	(1st) new blue, greenish yellow, magenta, black and grey	1·10	1·10
2214	**1524**	(1st) new blue, greenish yellow, magenta, black and grey	1·10	1·10
Set of 5			5·25	5·25
Gutter Strip of 10			12·00	
First Day Cover (Philatelic Bureau)				6·50
First Day Cover (Covent Garden, London WC2)				7·00
Presentation Pack			8·00	
PHQ Cards (*set of* 5)			8·50	24·00
First Day Cover (Philatelic Bureau)				15·00
First Day Cover (Covent Garden, London WC2)				8·50
MS2215 120×105 mm. Nos. 2210/14			9·75	9·75

Nos. 2210/14 were printed together, *se-tenant*, in horizontal strips of 5 throughout the sheet. The illustrations of the first bus on No. 2210 and the last bus on No. 2214 continue onto the sheet margins.

In No. **MS**2215 the illustrations of the AEC Regent III RT Type and the Daimler Fleetline CRG6LX-33 appear twice.

Special First Day of Issue Postmarks

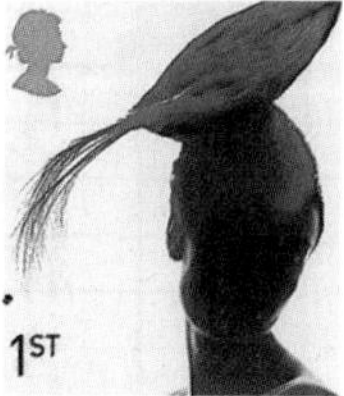

1525 Toque Hat by Pip Hackett

1526 Butterfly Hat by Dai Rees

1527 Top Hat by Stephen Jones

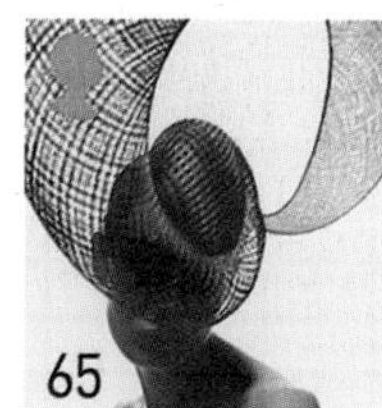

1528 Spiral Hat by Philip Treacy

(Des Rose Design from photos by N. Knight. Litho Enschedé)

2001 (19 June). *Fashion Hats. "All-over" phosphor.* P 14½.

2216	**1525**	(1st) greenish yellow, bright magenta, new blue, grey-black and silver	85	90
2217	**1526**	(E) greenish yellow, bright magenta, new blue, grey-black and silver	1·10	1·25
2218	**1527**	45p. greenish yellow, bright magenta, new blue, grey-black and silver	1·60	1·60
2219	**1528**	65p. greenish yellow, bright magenta, new blue, grey-black and silver	2·50	2·50
Set of 4			5·50	5·50
Set of 4 *Gutter Pairs*			13·00	
First Day Cover (Tallents House)				7·25
First Day Cover (Ascot)				7·50
Presentation Pack			7·50	
PHQ Cards (*set of* 4)			8·50	14·00

Special First Day of Issue Postmarks

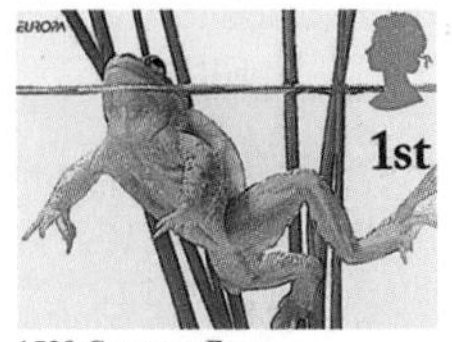

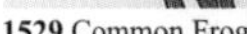
1529 Common Frog

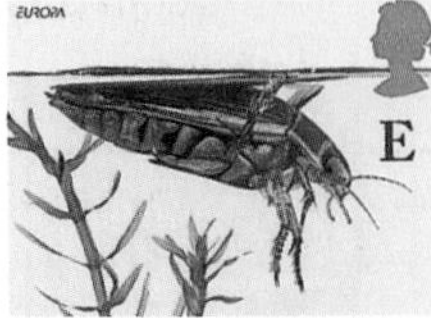

1530 Great Diving Beetle

1531 Three-Spined Stickleback

1532 Southern Hawker Dragonfly

(Des J. Gibbs. Photo De La Rue)

2001 (10 July). *Europa. Pond Life. Two phosphor bands.* P 15×14.

2220	**1529**	(1st)	black, greenish yellow, bright magenta, new blue, bluish silver and silver	1·00	1·00
2221	**1530**	(E)	black, greenish yellow, bright magenta, new blue, bluish silver and silver	1·25	1·25
2222	**1531**	45p.	black, greenish yellow, bright magenta, new blue, bluish silver, dull silver and silver	1·50	1·50
2223	**1532**	65p.	black, greenish yellow, bright magenta, new blue, bluish silver and silver	2·00	2·25
Set of 4				5·50	5·75
Set of 4 *Gutter Pairs*				15·00	
First Day Cover (Tallents House)					11·00
First Day Cover (Oundle, Peterborough)					12·00
Presentation Pack				7·50	
PHQ Cards (*set of* 4)				8·50	14·00

The 1st and E values incorporate the "EUROPA" emblem. The bluish silver on all four values is in Iriodin ink and was used as a background for those parts of the design below the water line.

Special First Day of Issue Postmarks

1533 Policeman

1534 Clown

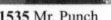

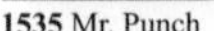
1535 Mr. Punch

1536 Judy

1537 Beadle

1538 Crocodile

(Des K. Bernstein from puppets by Bryan Clarkez)

2001 (4 Sept). *Punch and Judy Show Puppets. Two phosphor bands.* P 14×15.

(a) Photo Walsall. PVA gum.

2224	**1533**	(1st)	greenish yellow, bright magenta, new blue, grey-black, violet, deep magenta, ultramarine and silver	1·00	75
			a. Horiz strip of 6. Nos. 2224/9	5·00	5·25
2225	**1534**	(1st)	greenish yellow, bright magenta, new blue, grey-black, violet, deep magenta, ultramarine and silver	1·00	75
2226	**1535**	(1st)	greenish yellow, bright magenta, new blue, grey-black, violet, deep magenta, ultramarine and silver	1·00	75
2227	**1536**	(1st)	greenish yellow, bright magenta, new blue, grey-black, violet, deep magenta, ultramarine and silver	1·00	75
2228	**1537**	(1st)	greenish yellow, bright magenta, new blue, grey-black, violet, deep magenta, ultramarine and silver	1·00	75
2229	**1538**	(1st)	greenish yellow, bright magenta, new blue, grey-black, violet, deep magenta, ultramarine and silver	1·00	75
Set of 6				5·50	5·50
Gutter Block of 12				13·00	
First Day Cover (Tallents House)					7·00
First Day Cover (Blackpool)					7·50
Presentation Pack				7·00	
PHQ Cards (*set of* 6)				8·50	18·00

(b) Photo Questa. Self-adhesive. Die-cut P 14×15½.

2230	**1535**	(1st)	greenish yellow, bright magenta, new blue, grey-black, violet, deep magenta, ultramarine and silver (4 Sept)	10·00	10·00
			a. Booklet pane. Nos. 2230/1 plus No. 2040×4	16·00	
2231	**1536**	(1st)	greenish yellow, bright magenta, new blue, grey-black, violet, deep magenta, ultramarine and silver (4 Sept)	10·00	10·00

Nos. 2224/9 were printed together, *se-tenant*, as horizontal strips of 6 in sheets of 60 (6×10).

Nos. 2230/1 were only issued in £1.62 stamp booklets.

Imperforate strips of 6 with alternative background colours to 2224, 2228 and 2229 are of proof status (*Price* £2500).

Special First Day of Issue Postmarks

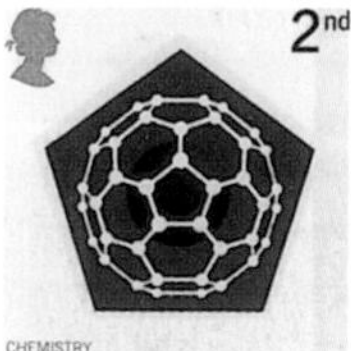

1539 Carbon 60 Molecule (Chemistry)

1540 Globe (Economic Sciences)

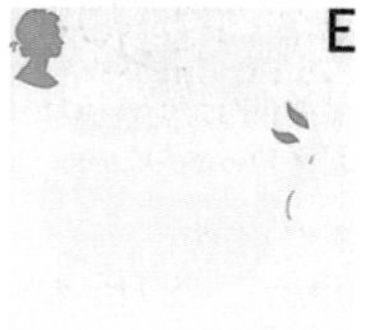

1541 Embossed Dove (Peace)

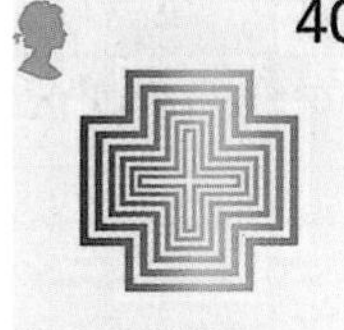

1542 Crosses (Physiology or Medicine)

1543 Poem "The Addressing of Cats" by T. S. Eliot in Open Book (Literature)

1544 Hologram of Boron Molecule (Physics)

(Des P. Vermier. Eng Ing Madle (1st). Litho and silk-screen ptg (2nd), litho and recess (1st), litho and embossed (E), litho (45p.), litho and hologram (65p.) Enschedé)

2001 (2 Oct). *Centenary of Nobel Prizes. One side phosphor band (2nd) or phosphor frame (others).* P 14½.

2232	**1539**	(2nd) black, silver and grey-black		75	65
2233	**1540**	(1st) black, silver, dull mauve, blue and rosine		1·00	90
2234	**1541**	(E) black, silver and bright green		1·00	1·25
2235	**1542**	40p. black, silver, new blue and greenish yellow		1·25	1·25
2236	**1543**	45p. black, silver, yellow-ochre and pale grey		1·50	1·75
2237	**1544**	65p. black and silver		2·25	2·50
Set of 6				7·50	7·50
Set of 6 Gutter Pairs				20·00	
First Day Cover (Tallents House)					9·50
First Day Cover (Cambridge)					10·00
Presentation Pack				10·00	
PHQ Cards (*set of 6*)				10·00	18·00

The grey-black on No. 2232 is printed in thermochromic ink which temporarily changes to pale grey when exposed to heat. The centre of No. 2235 is coated with a eucalyptus scent.

Special First Day of Issue Postmarks

1545 Robins with Snowman

1546 Robins on Bird Table

1547 Robins skating on Bird Bath

1548 Robins with Christmas Pudding

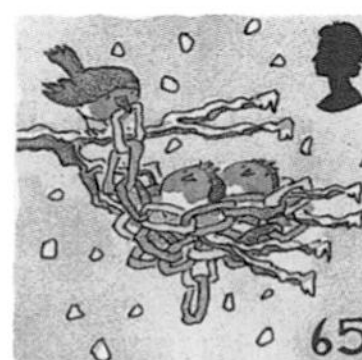

1549 Robins in Paper Chain Nest

(Des A. Robins and H. Brown. Photo De La Rue)

2001 (6 Nov). *Christmas. Robins. Self-adhesive. One centre phosphor band (2nd) or two phosphor bands (others).* Die-cut p 14½.

2238	**1545**	(2nd) new blue, blue, greenish yellow, bright magenta, vermilion and black	75	70
		a. Booklet pane. No. 2238×24	12·00	
		b. Imperf (pair)	£950	
2239	**1546**	(1st) red-orange, blue, greenish yellow, bright magenta, new blue and black	1·00	1·00
		a. Booklet pane. No. 2239×12	8·00	
2240	**1547**	(E) indigo, azure, greenish yellow, bright magenta, new blue, vermilion and black	1·00	1·10
2241	**1548**	45p. bright purple, blue, greenish yellow, bright magenta, new blue, vermilion and black	1·50	1·50
2242	**1549**	65p. greenish blue, blue, greenish yellow, bright magenta, new blue, vermilion and black	2·00	2·25
		a. Imperf (pair) (die-cut perforations and roulettes omitted)	£950	
		b. Imperf backing paper (pair) (roulettes omitted)	£275	
Set of 5			6·00	6·00
First Day Cover (Tallents House)				9·50
First Day Cover (Bethlehem, Llandeilo)				10·00
Presentation Pack			8·00	
PHQ Cards (*set of 5*)			11·00	16·00

Nos. 2238/40 were each printed in sheets of 50 with the surplus backing paper around each stamp retained and separated by gauge 9 roulettes. The 1st value was re-issued on 30 September 2003 in sheets of 20 (sold at £6.15) printed in lithography instead of photogravure, each stamp accompanied by a stamp-size label showing a snowman. Sheets with personal photographs printed on the labels were available from Royal Mail, Edinburgh for £14.95 or photobooths at selected post offices and Safeway stores for £15.

The 2nd and 1st values were re-issued together on 1 November 2005 in sheets of 20, printed in lithography by Cartor, sold at £5.60, containing ten 2nd class and ten 1st class, each stamp accompanied by a label showing a snowman. Separate sheets of 20 2nd class and 20 1st class were available with personalised photographs at £9.95 (2nd) or £14.95 (1st) from Royal Mail.

No. 2238b shows both the die-cut perforations and the roulettes omitted. Stamps from booklet panes Nos. 2238a and 2239a differ from those in sheets by omitting the roulettes in the backing paper between each stamp. Instead there are roulettes after the first and then every alternate horizontal row to assist with the folding of the booklets.

Special First Day of Issue Postmarks

Collectors Pack 2001

2001 (6 Nov). *Comprises Nos.* 2178/2200, 2202/6, 2210/14, 2216/29 *and* 2232/42.

CP2242a Collectors Pack £120

Post Office Yearbook

2001 (6 Nov) *Comprises Nos.* 2178/96, **MS**2201/6, 2210/14, 2216/29 *and* 2232/42 *in hardback book with slip case* £110

1550 "How the Whale got his Throat"

1551 "How the Camel got his Hump"

1552 "How the Rhinoceros got his Skin"

1553 "How the Leopard got his Spots"

1554 "The Elephant's Child"

1555 "The Sing-Song of Old Man Kangaroo"

1556 "The Beginning of the Armadillos"

1557 "The Crab that played with the Sea"

1558 "The Cat that walked by Himself"

1559 "The Butterfly that stamped"

(Des I. Cohen. Photo Walsall)

2002 (15 Jan). *Centenary of Publication of Rudyard Kipling's* Just So *Stories. Self-adhesive. Two phosphor bands.* Die-cut P 15×14.

No.	Design	Description	Mint	Used
2243	**1550**	(1st) new blue, magenta, greenish yellow and black	95	85
		a. Sheetlet. Nos. 2243/52	10·00	10·00
2244	**1551**	(1st) new blue, magenta, greenish yellow and black	95	85
2245	**1552**	(1st) new blue, magenta, greenish yellow and black	95	85
2246	**1553**	(1st) new blue, magenta, greenish yellow and black	95	85
2247	**1554**	(1st) new blue, magenta, greenish yellow and black	95	85
2248	**1555**	(1st) new blue, magenta, greenish yellow and black	95	85
2249	**1556**	(1st) new blue, magenta, greenish yellow and black	95	85
2250	**1557**	(1st) new blue, magenta, greenish yellow and black	95	85
2251	**1558**	(1st) new blue, magenta, greenish yellow and black	95	85
2252	**1559**	(1st) new blue, magenta, greenish yellow and black	95	85
Set of 10			9·00	8·00
First Day Cover (Tallents House)				11·00
First Day Cover (Burwash, Etchingham)				12·00
Presentation Pack			12·00	
PHQ Cards (*set of* 10)			8·50	28·00

Nos. 2243/52 were printed together in sheetlets of 10 (5×2), with the surplus self-adhesive paper around each stamp retained. The pane shows vertical roulettes between rows 2/3 and 4/5 and has illustrations on the reverse of the backing paper.

Special First Day of Issue Postmarks

1560 Queen Elizabeth II, 1952 (Dorothy Wilding)

1561 Queen Elizabeth II, 1968 (Cecil Beaton)

1562 Queen Elizabeth II, 1978 (Lord Snowdon)

1563 Queen Elizabeth II, 1984 (Yousef Karsh)

1564 Queen Elizabeth II, 1996 (Tim Graham)

1565

(Des Kate Stephens. Photo De La Rue)

2002 (6 Feb). *Golden Jubilee. Studio portraits of Queen Elizabeth II by photographers named. One centre phosphor band (2nd) or two phosphor bands (others).* W **1565** (sideways). P 14½×14.

2253	**1560**	(2nd) silver, pale turquoise-green, black and deep grey	75	55
		a. Watermark upright	2·50	70
		b. Booklet pane. Nos. 2253a/6a with margins all round	12·00	
2254	**1561**	(1st) silver, pale turquoise-green, black and grey-black	1·00	80
		a. Watermark upright	1·25	1·00
		b. Booklet pane. Nos. 2254a/7a with margins all round	9·50	
2255	**1562**	(E) silver, pale turquoise-green, black and grey-black	1·25	1·25
		a. Watermark upright	1·75	1·40
2256	**1563**	45p. silver, pale turquoise-green, black and grey-black	1·50	1·50
		a. Watermark upright	2·50	1·50
2257	**1564**	65p. silver, pale turquoise-green, black and grey-black	2·25	2·25
		a. Watermark upright	4·00	2·25
Set of 5			6·00	6·50
Set of 5 Gutter Pairs			16·00	
First Day Cover (Tallents House)				8·00
First Day Cover (Windsor)				8·50
Presentation Pack			7·50	
PHQ Cards (*set of* 5)			4·50	14·00

The turquoise-green is used as an underlay for the black colour on all five values.

Nos. 2253a/7a were only available in £7.29 stamp booklets.

Special First Day of Issue Postmarks

1566

(Des M. Farrar-Bell (2nd), Enid Marx (1st). Photo Enschedé)

2002 (6 Feb). *As T* **154/5** *(Wilding definitive of 1952-54), but with service indicator as T* **1566**. *One centre phosphor band (2nd) or two phosphor bands (1st).* W **1565**. *Uncoated paper.* P 15×14 (with one elliptical hole on each vertical side).

2258	**1566**	(2nd) carmine-red	1·20	1·00
		Ea. Watermark diagonal	4·50	3·25
		b. Booklet pane. Nos. 2258×4, 2258Ea and 2259×4 with centre blank label and margins all round	14·00	
2259	–	(1st) green	1·25	1·25
First Day Cover (No. 2258b) (Tallents House)				10·00
First Day Cover (No. 2258b) (Windsor)				10·00

Nos. 2258/9 were only issued in the £7.29 "A Gracious Accession" booklet, No. DX28.

No. 2258b contains a block of 8, four of each value, with a blank central label, plus an additional 2nd value shown to the left at such an angle so as to produce a diagonal watermark. First day cover postmarks were as Nos. 2253/7.

1567 Rabbits ("a new baby")

1568 "LOVE"

1569 Aircraft Sky-writing "hello"

1570 Bear pulling Potted Topiary Tree (Moving Home)

1571 Flowers ("best wishes")

(Des I. Bilbey (Nos. 2260, 2264), A. Kitching (No. 2261), Hoop Associates (No. 2262) and G. Percy (No. 2263))

2002 (5 Mar)–**02**. *Greetings Stamps. "Occasions". Two phosphor bands.* P 15×14.

(a) Litho Questa.

No.	Type	Description	Unused	Used
2260	**1567**	(1st) greenish yellow, magenta, new blue, black and lilac	1·00	1·00
2261	**1568**	(1st) greenish yellow, magenta, new blue, black and silver	1·00	1·00
2262	**1569**	(1st) greenish yellow, magenta, new blue and black	1·00	1·00
2263	**1570**	(1st) greenish yellow, magenta, new blue and black	1·00	1·00
2264	**1571**	(1st) greenish yellow, magenta, new blue, black and cobalt	1·00	1·00
		Set of 5	4·75	4·75
		Set of 5 *Gutter Pairs*	12·00	
		First Day Cover (Tallents House)		6·75
		First Day Cover (Merry Hill, Wolverhampton)		7·00
		Presentation Pack	6·00	
		PHQ Cards (*set of* 5)	4·50	14·00

(b) Photo Questa. Self-adhesive. Die-cut P 15×14.

No.	Type	Description	Unused	Used
2264*a*	**1569**	(1st) greenish yellow, magenta, new blue and black (4.3.03)	4·00	4·00
		ab. Booklet pane. No. 2264a×2 plus No. 2295×4	10·00	

Nos. 2260/4 were re-issued on 23 April in sheets of 20 with half stamp-size labels, with either the five designs *se-tenant* with greetings on the labels (sold at £5.95) or in sheets of one design with personal photographs on the labels (sold at £12.95). These stamps, printed by Questa in lithography, were perforated 14½×14 instead of 15×14.

Type **1569** was re-issued on 30 January 2004 for Hong Kong Stamp Expo in sheets of 20, each stamp accompanied by a half stamp-size *se-tenant* label, printed in lithography by Walsall. It was issued again on 21 April 2005 for Pacific Explorer 2005 World Stamp Expo in sheets of 20 with half stamp-size *se-tenant* labels, perforated 14½×14.

No. 2264a was only issued in £1.62 stamp booklets, No. PM8, in which the surplus self-adhesive paper around each stamp was removed.

Special First Day of Issue Postmarks

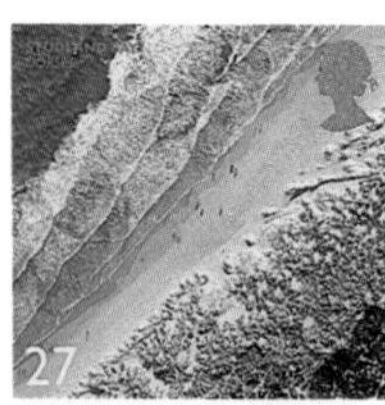

1572 Studland Bay, Dorset

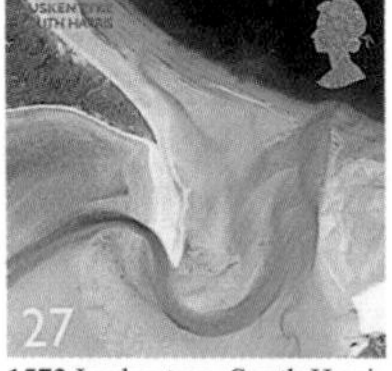

1573 Luskentyre, South Harris

1574 Cliffs, Dover, Kent

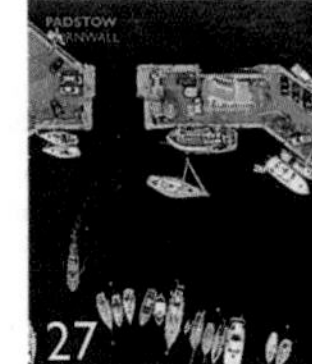

1575 Padstow Harbour, Cornwall

1576 Broadstairs, Kent

1577 St. Abb's Head, Scottish Borders

1578 Dunster Beach, Somerset

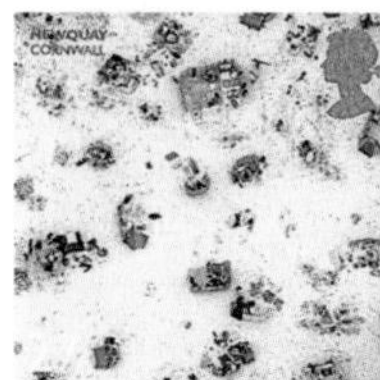
1579 Newquay Beach, Cornwall

1580 Portrush, County Antrim

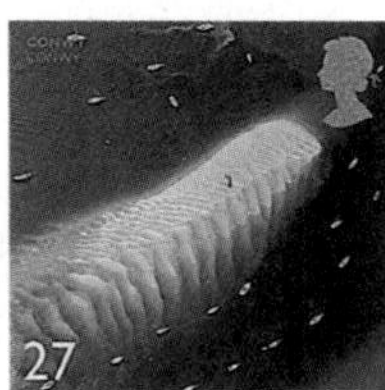

1581 Sand-spit, Conwy

(Des R. Cooke. Litho Walsall)

2002 (19 Mar). *British Coastlines. Two phosphor bands.* P 14½.

No.	Type	Description	Unused	Used
2265	**1572**	27p. silver, black, greenish yellow, bright magenta and new blue	75	80
		a. Block of 10. Nos. 2265/74	8·75	8·75
		b. Silver omitted (block of 10)	£5000	
2266	**1573**	27p. silver, black, greenish yellow, bright magenta and new blue	75	80
2267	**1574**	27p. silver, black, greenish yellow, bright magenta and new blue	75	80
2268	**1575**	27p. silver, black, greenish yellow, bright magenta and new blue	75	80
2269	**1576**	27p. silver, black, greenish yellow, bright magenta and new blue	75	80
2270	**1577**	27p. silver, black, greenish yellow, bright magenta and new blue	75	80
2271	**1578**	27p. silver, black, greenish yellow, bright magenta and new blue	75	80
2272	**1579**	27p. silver, black, greenish yellow, bright magenta and new blue	75	80
2273	**1580**	27p. silver, black, greenish yellow, bright magenta and new blue	75	80
2274	**1581**	27p. silver, black, greenish yellow, bright magenta and new blue	75	80
		Set of 10	7·00	7·25
		Gutter Block of 20	20·00	
		First Day Cover (Tallents House)		11·50
		First Day Cover (Poolewe, Achnasheen)		12·00
		Presentation Pack	10·50	
		PHQ Cards (*set of* 10)	9·25	28·00

Nos. 2265/74 were printed together, *se-tenant*, in blocks of 10 (5×2) throughout the sheet.

Special First Day of Issue Postmarks

1582 Slack Wire Act

1583 Lion Tamer

1584 Trick Tri-cyclists

1585 Krazy Kar

1586 Equestrienne

(Des R. Fuller. Photo Questa)

2002 (10 Apr*). *Europa. Circus. One centre phosphor band (2nd) or two phosphor bands (others).* P 14½.

2275	**1582**	(2nd) greenish yellow, magenta, new blue, black, bright orange, emerald and silver	50	60
2276	**1583**	(1st) greenish yellow, magenta, new blue, black, bright orange, emerald and silver	75	85
2277	**1584**	(E) greenish yellow, magenta, new blue, black, bright orange, emerald and silver	1·00	1·25
		a. Imperf (pair)	£900	
2278	**1585**	45p. greenish yellow, magenta, new blue, black, bright orange, emerald and silver	1·75	1·50
2279	**1586**	65p. greenish yellow, magenta, new blue, black, bright orange, emerald and silver	2·75	2·25
Set of 5			6·00	6·00
Set of 5 *Gutter Pairs*			16·00	
First Day Cover (Tallents House)				8·00
First Day Cover (Clowne, Chesterfield)				9·00
Presentation Pack			7·50	
PHQ Cards (*set of* 5)			4·50	14·00

The 1st and E values incorporate the "EUROPA" emblem.

*Due to the funeral of the Queen Mother, the issue of Nos. 2275/9 was delayed from 9 April, the date which appears on first day covers.

Special First Day of Issue Postmarks

1587 Queen Elizabeth the Queen Mother

(Des J. Gorham from photographs by N. Parkinson (1st), Dorothy Wilding (E), B. Park (45p.), Rita Martin (65p.). Photo De La Rue)

2002 (25 Apr). *Queen Elizabeth the Queen Mother Commemoration. Vert designs as T* **955/8** *with changed face values and showing both the Queen's head and frame in black as in T* **1587**. *Two phosphor bands.* P 14×15.

2280	**1587**	(1st) black, greenish yellow, magenta, new blue and grey-black	1·00	85
2281	**956**	(E) black and indigo	1·25	1·10
2282	**957**	45p. black, greenish yellow, magenta, new blue and grey-black	1·50	1·50
2283	**958**	65p. black, stone and sepia	2·00	2·25
Set of 4			5·50	5·50
Set of 4 *Gutter Pairs*			14·00	
First Day Cover (Tallents House)				8·00
First Day Cover (London SW1)				9·00
Presentation Pack			7·00	

Special First Day of Issue Postmarks

1588 Airbus A340-600 (2002)

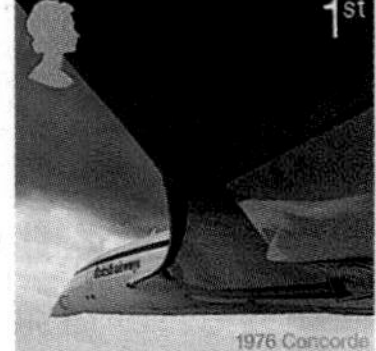

1589 Concorde (1976)

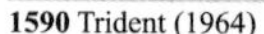
1590 Trident (1964)

1591 VC10 (1964)

1592 Comet (1952)

(Des Roundel)

2002 (2 May). *50th Anniv of Passenger Jet Aviation. Airliners. One centre phosphor band (2nd) or two phosphor bands (others).* P 14½. (a) Photo De La Rue. PVA gum.

2284	**1588**	(2nd)	greenish yellow, bright magenta, new blue, black and silver	75	55
2285	**1589**	(1st)	greenish yellow, bright magenta, new blue, black and silver	1·00	80
2286	**1590**	(E)	greenish yellow, bright magenta, new blue, black and silver	1·25	1·25
2287	**1591**	45p.	greenish yellow, bright magenta, new blue, black and silver	1·50	1·50
2288	**1592**	65p.	greenish yellow, bright magenta, new blue, black and silver	2·00	2·25
Set of 5				6·00	6·00
Set of 5 Gutter Pairs				16·00	
First Day Cover (Tallents House)					8·00
First Day Cover (Heathrow Airport, London)					6·00
Presentation Pack				7·50	
MS2289 120×105 mm. Nos. 2284/8				8·25	8·25
First Day Cover (Tallents House)					8·00
First Day Cover (Heathrow Airport, London)					9·00
PHQ Cards (*set of* 6)				5·25	8·00

(b) Photo Questa. Self-adhesive. Die-cut P 14½.

2290	**1589**	(1st)	greenish yellow, bright magenta, new blue, black and silver	4·00	4·00
			a. Booklet pane. No. 2040×4 and No. 2290×2	10·00	

No. 2290 was only issued in £1.62 stamp booklets.

Special First Day of Issue Postmarks

1593 Crowned Lion with Shield of St. George

1594 Top Left Quarter of English Flag, and Football

1595 Top Right Quarter of English Flag, and Football

1596 Bottom Left Quarter of English Flag, and Football

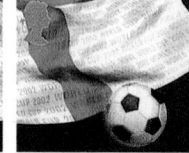

1597 Bottom Right Quarter of English Flag, and Football

(Des Sedley Place (No. 2291), H. Brown (No. **MS**2292). Photo Walsall)

2002 (21 May). *World Cup Football Championship, Japan and Korea. Two phosphor bands.* P 14½×14. (a) PVA gum.

2291	**1593**	(1st)	deep turquoise-blue, scarlet-vermilion and silver	2·50	2·50
			Gutter Pair	11·00	
MS2292 145×74 mm. No. 2291; **1594** (1st) deep turquoise-blue, indigo, deep blue, black, silver, scarlet-vermilion and pale bluish grey; **1595** (1st) deep turquoise-blue, indigo, deep blue, black, silver, scarlet-vermilion and pale bluish grey; **1596** (1st) deep turquoise-blue, indigo, deep blue, black, silver, scarlet-vermilion and pale bluish grey; **1597** (1st) deep turquoise-blue, indigo, deep blue, black, silver, scarlet-vermilion and pale bluish grey. P 14½ (square) or 15×14 (horiz)				5·50	5·75
First Day Cover (**MS**2292) (Tallents House)					5·75
First Day Cover (**MS**2292) (Wembley)					6·00
Presentation Pack (**MS**2292)				6·25	
PHQ Cards (*set of* 6)				5·25	9·00

(b) Self-adhesive. Die-cut P 15×14.

2293	**1594**	(1st)	deep turquoise-blue, indigo, deep blue, black, silver, scarlet-vermilion and pale bluish grey	4·00	4·00
			a. Booklet pane. Nos. 2293/4 plus No. 2040×4	10·00	10·00
2294	**1595**	(1st)	deep turquoise-blue, indigo, deep blue, black, silver, scarlet-vermilion and pale bluish grey	4·00	4·00

The complete minature sheet is shown on one of the PHQ cards with the others depicting individual stamps from No. **MS**2292 and No. 2291.

Nos. 2293/4 were only issued in £1.62 stamp booklets.

Stamps as Type **1597** also exist in sheets of 20 with *se-tenant* labels, printed by lithography instead of photogravure. Such sheets, with the labels showing match scenes or supporters, were available at £5.95 from philatelic outlets, or with personal photographs at £12.95 from Royal Mail in Edinburgh.

Special First Day of Issue Postmarks

(Photo Questa, Walsall, Enschedé or De La Rue (1st), Walsall (others))

2002 (5 June). *Self-adhesive. Two phosphor bands.* P 15×14 die-cut (with one elliptical hole on each vertical side).

2295	**914**	(1st) gold	1·00	1·00
2296	**1093a**	(E) deep blue (4 July)	1·25	1·25
2297	**367a**	42p. deep olive-grey (4 July)	1·25	1·25
2298		68p. grey-brown (4 July)	2·00	2·00
Set of 4			5·00	5·00
PHQ Card (No. 2295) (Walsall) (27.3.03)			45	2·00

No. 2295, sold for 27p., was initially only available in booklets of 6 or 12, printed by Questa or Walsall, with the surplus self-adhesive paper around each stamp removed. Later booklets were also printed by De La Rue. Nos. 2296/8 were only issued in separate booklets, each containing six stamps with the surplus self-adhesive paper around each stamp removed.

A further printing of No. 2295 in sheets of 100 appeared on 4 July 2002 produced by Enschedé and on 18 March 2003 in stripped matrix sheets of 100 printed by Walsall. The top panel shows a strip of four with the typography of the label matching that of booklet Type ME 2.

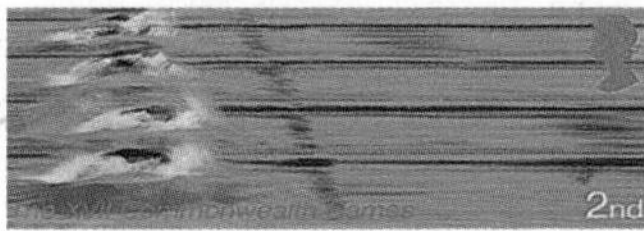

1598 Swimming

1599 Running

1600 Cycling

1601 Long Jumping

1602 Wheelchair Racing

(Des Madeleine Bennett. Photo Enschedé)

2002 (16 July). *17th Commonwealth Games, Manchester. One side phosphor band (2nd) or two phosphor bands (others).* P 14½.

2299	**1598**	(2nd) greenish yellow, magenta, greenish blue, black, silver and new blue	75	55
2300	**1599**	(1st) greenish yellow, magenta, new blue, black and silver	1·00	80
2301	**1600**	(E) greenish yellow, magenta, new blue, black and silver	1·25	1·25
2302	**1601**	47p. greenish yellow, magenta, new blue, black and silver	1·50	1·50
2303	**1602**	68p. greenish yellow, magenta, new blue, black and silver	2·00	2·25
Set of 5			6·00	6·00
Set of 5 *Gutter Pairs*			14·00	
First Day Cover (Tallents House)				8·00
First Day Cover (Manchester)				9·00
Presentation Pack			7·50	
PHQ Cards (*set of* 5)			4·75	15·00

On Nos. 2300/3 the phosphor bands appear at the right and the centre of each stamp.

Special First Day of Issue Postmarks

1603 Tinkerbell

1604 Wendy, John and Michael Darling in front of Big Ben

1605 Crocodile and Alarm Clock

1606 Captain Hook

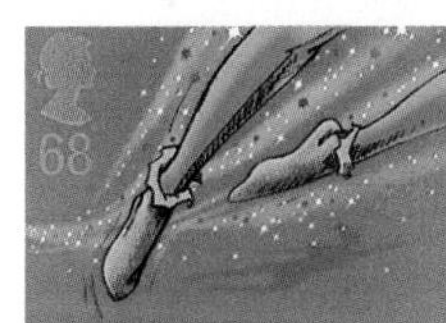

1607 Peter Pan

(Des Tutssels. Photo De La Rue.)

2002 (20 Aug). *150th Anniv of Great Ormond Street Children's Hospital. "Peter Pan" by Sir James Barrie. One centre phosphor band (2nd) or two phosphor bands (others).* P 15×14.

2304	**1603**	(2nd) gold, deep ultramarine, greenish yellow and grey-black	75	55
2305	**1604**	(1st) gold, purple, greenish yellow, deep violet and grey-black	1·00	80
2306	**1605**	(E) gold, blue-green, greenish yellow, bright carmine, new blue grey-black and orange-brown	1·25	1·25
2307	**1606**	47p. gold, pale new blue, greenish yellow, bright carmine and grey-black	1·50	1·50
2308	**1607**	68p. gold, bright rose-red, orange-brown, emerald and grey-black	2·00	2·25
Set of 5			6·00	6·00
Set of 5 *Gutter Pairs*			16·00	
First Day Cover (Tallents House)				8·00
First Day Cover (Hook)				8·50
Presentation Pack			7·50	
PHQ Cards (*set of* 5)			4·75	15·00

Special First Day of Issue Postmarks

1608 Millennium Bridge, 2001

1609 Tower Bridge, 1894

1610 Westminster Bridge, 1864

1611 "Blackfriars Bridge, c1800" (William Marlow)

1612 "London Bridge, c1670" (Wenceslaus Hollar)

(Des Sarah Davies and R. Maude)

2002 (10 Sept). *Bridges of London. One centre phosphor band (2nd) or two phosphor bands (others). (a) Litho Questa. PVA gum.* P 15×14.

2309	**1608**	(2nd)	greenish yellow, magenta, new blue and black	75	55
2310	**1609**	(1st)	grey-brown, black, brown-purple and pale grey-brown	1·00	80
2311	**1610**	(E)	greenish yellow, magenta, new blue, black and reddish brown	1·25	1·25
2312	**1611**	47p.	greenish yellow, magenta, new blue and black	1·50	1·50
2313	**1612**	68p.	greenish yellow, magenta, new blue, black and reddish brown	2·00	2·25
Set of 5				6·50	6·00
Set of 5 Gutter Pairs				16·00	
First Day Cover (Tallents House)					9·00
First Day Cover (London SE1)					10·00
Presentation Pack				8·00	
PHQ Cards (*set of 5*)				4·00	7·00

(b) Photo Questa. Self-adhesive. Die-cut P 15×14.

2314	**1609**	(1st)	grey-brown, black, brown-purple and pale grey-brown	6·00	6·00
			a. Booklet pane. No. 2314×2, and No. 2295×4	14·00	

No. 2314 was only issued in £1.62 stamp booklets in which the surplus self-adhesive paper around each stamp was removed.

Special First Day of Issue Postmarks

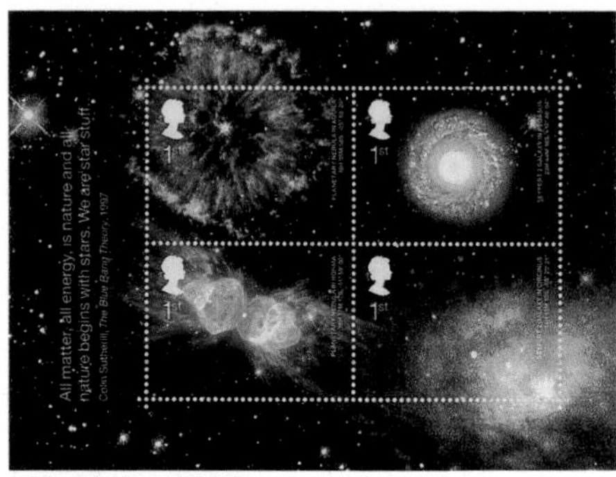

1613a Galaxies and Nebula
(*Illustration reduced. Actual size* 120×89 *mm*)

(Des Rose Design. Photo Questa)

2002 (24 Sept). *Astronomy. Sheet 120×89 mm. Multicoloured. Two phosphor bands.* P 14½×14.

MS2315 **1613a** (1st) Planetary nebula in Aquila; (1st) Seyfert 2 galaxy in Pegasus; (1st) Planetary nebula in Norma; (1st) Seyfert 2 galaxy in Circinus	5·25	5·25
a. Booklet pane. As No. **MS**2315, but larger, 150×95 mm	1·60	
First Day Cover (Tallents House)		5·75
First Day Cover (Star, Glenrothes)		6·00
Presentation Pack	5·50	
PHQ Cards (*set of 5*)	4·75	15·00

The five PHQ cards depict the four designs and the complete miniature sheet.

Special First Day of Issue Postmarks

1614 Green Pillar Box, 1857

1615 Horizontal Aperture Box, 1874

1616 Air Mail Box, 1934

1617 Double Aperture Box, 1939

1618 Modern Style Box, 1980

(Des Silk Pearce. Eng C. Slania. Recess and litho Enschedé)

2002 (8 Oct). *150th Anniv of the First Pillar Box. One centre phosphor band (2nd) or two phosphor bands (others).* P 14×14½.

2316	**1614**	(2nd) greenish black, new blue, bright magenta, greenish yellow, grey and silver	75	55
2317	**1615**	(1st) deep blue, new blue, bright magenta, greenish yellow, grey and silver	1·00	80
2318	**1616**	(E) deep blue, new blue, bright magenta, greenish yellow, grey and silver	1·25	1·25
2319	**1617**	47p. brown-purple, new blue, bright magenta, greenish yellow, grey and silver	1·50	1·50
2320	**1618**	68p. deep brown-red, new blue, bright magenta, greenish yellow, grey and silver	2·00	2·25
Set of 5			6·00	6·00
Set of 5 *Gutter Pairs*			14·00	
First Day Cover (Tallents House)				8·50
First Day Cover (Bishops Caundle, Sherborne)				9·00
Presentation Pack			7·50	
PHQ Cards (*set of* 5)			4·75	16·00

Special First Day of Issue Postmarks

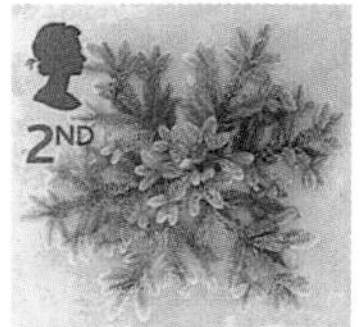

1619 Blue Spruce Star

1620 Holly

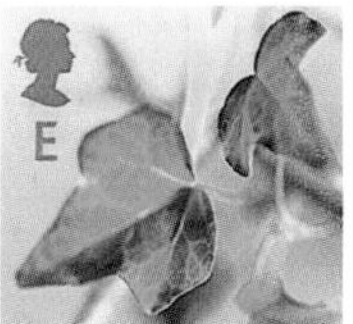

1621 Ivy

1622 Mistletoe

1623 Pine Cone

(Des Rose Design. Photo De La Rue)

2002 (5 Nov). *Christmas. Self-adhesive. One centre phosphor band (2nd) or two phosphor bands (others).* Die-cut p 14½×14.

2321	**1619**	(2nd) lilac, greenish yellow, bright carmine, new blue and black	75	55
		a. Booklet pane. No. 2321×24	6·75	
		b. Imperf (pair)	80·00	
2322	**1620**	(1st) greenish grey, greenish yellow, bright carmine, new blue and black	1·00	80
		a. Booklet pane. No. 2322×12	4·75	
		b. Imperf (pair)	£325	
2323	**1621**	(E) dull mauve, greenish yellow, bright carmine, new blue and black	1·25	1·25
2324	**1622**	47p. silver, greenish yellow, bright carmine, new blue and black	1·50	1·50
2325	**1623**	68p. light blue, greenish yellow, bright carmine, new blue and black	2·00	2·25
Set of 5			6·00	6·00
First Day Cover (Tallents House)				8·50
First Day Cover (Bethlehem, Llandeilo)				9·00
Presentation Pack			7·50	
PHQ Cards (*set of* 5)			4·75	16·00

Nos. 2321/5 were each printed in sheets of 50, with the surplus backing paper around each stamp retained, separated by gauge 9 roulettes. Nos. 2321b and 2322b show both the die-cut perforations and the roulettes omitted.

Special First Day of Issue Postmarks

Collectors Pack 2002

2002 (5 Nov). *Comprises Nos.* 2243/57, 2260/4, 2265/88, 2291/2, 2299/313 *and* **MS**2315/25.

CP2325*a* Collectors Pack £100

Post Office Yearbook

2002 (5 Nov). *Comprises Nos.* 2243/57, 2260/4, 2265/88, 2291/2, 2299/313 *and* **MS**2315/25 *in hardback book with slip case* .... 95·00

(Des Rose Design. Photo De La Rue)

2002 (5 Dec). *50th Anniv of Wilding Definitives (1st issue). Sheet 124×70 mm containing designs as T* **154/5** *and* **157/60** *(1952–54 issue), but with values in decimal currency as T* **1348** *or with service indicator as T* **1566**, *printed on pale cream. One centre phosphor band (2nd) or two phosphor bands (others).* W **1565**. P 15×14 (with one elliptical hole on each vertical side).

MS2326 1p. orange-red; 2p. ultramarine; 5p. red-brown; (2nd) carmine-red; (1st) green; 33p. brown; 37p. magenta; 47p. bistre-brown; 50p. green and label showing national emblems	10·00	10·00

First Day Cover (Tallents House)		10·00
First Day Cover (Windsor)		11·00
Presentation Pack	£100	
PHQ Cards (*set of* 5)	3·00	12·00

The five PHQ cards depict the 1st, 2nd, 33p., 37p. and 47p. stamps.

Special First Day of Issue Postmarks

1624 Barn Owl landing

1625 Barn Owl with folded Wings and Legs down

1626 Barn Owl with extended Wings and Legs down

1627 Barn Owl in Flight with Wings lowered

1628 Barn Owl in Flight with Wings raised

1629 Kestrel with Wings folded

1630 Kestrel with Wings fully extended upwards

1631 Kestrel with Wings horizontal

1632 Kestrel with wings partly extended downwards

1633 Kestrel with wings fully extended downwards

(Des J. Gibbs from photographs by S. Dalton. Litho Walsall)

2003 (14 Jan). *Birds of Prey. Phosphor background.* P 14½.

2327	**1624**	(1st) brownish grey, black, greenish yellow, magenta and new blue	70	80
		a. Block of 10. Nos. 237/36	9·00	8·75
		ab. Brownish grey and phosphor omitted	£2000	
2328	**1625**	(1st) brownish grey, black, greenish yellow, magenta and new blue	70	80
2329	**1626**	(1st) brownish grey, black, greenish yellow, magenta and new blue	70	80
2330	**1627**	(1st) brownish grey, black, greenish yellow, magenta and new blue	70	80
2331	**1628**	(1st) brownish grey, black, greenish yellow, magenta and new blue	70	80
2332	**1629**	(1st) brownish grey, black, greenish yellow, magenta and new blue	70	80
2333	**1630**	(1st) brownish grey, black, greenish yellow, magenta and new blue	70	80
2334	**1631**	(1st) brownish grey, black, greenish yellow, magenta and new blue	70	80
2335	**1632**	(1st) brownish grey, black, greenish yellow, magenta and new blue	70	80
2336	**1633**	(1st) brownish grey, black, greenish yellow, magenta and new blue	70	80
Set of 10			6·25	7·25
Gutter Block of 20			24·00	
First Day Cover (Tallents House)				11·00
First Day Cover (Hawkshead Ambleside)				12·00
Presentation Pack			12·00	
PHQ Cards (*set of* 10)			9·25	28·00

Nos. 2327/36 were printed together, *se-tenant*, in blocks of 10 (5×2) throughtout the sheet.

No. 2327ab shows the owl white on Nos. 2327/31, and the face value with Queen's head omitted on Nos. 2332/6.

Special First Day of Issue Postmarks (applied in silver)

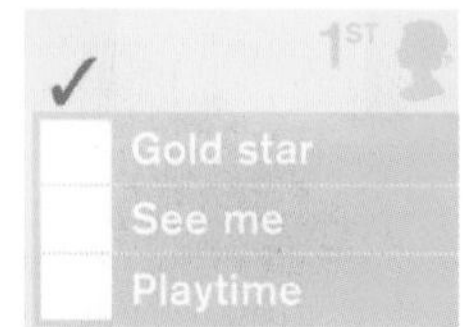
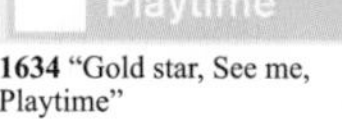

1634 "Gold star, See me, Playtime"

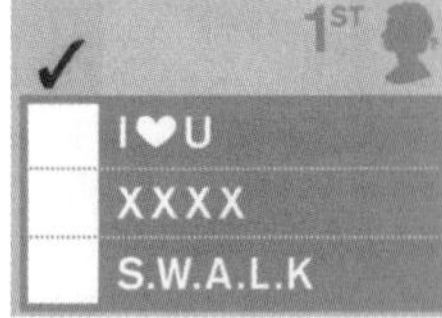

1635 "I♥U, XXXX, S.W.A.L.K."

1636 "Angel, Poppet, Little terror"

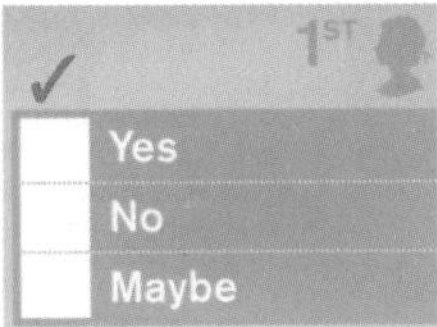

1637 "Yes, No, Maybe"

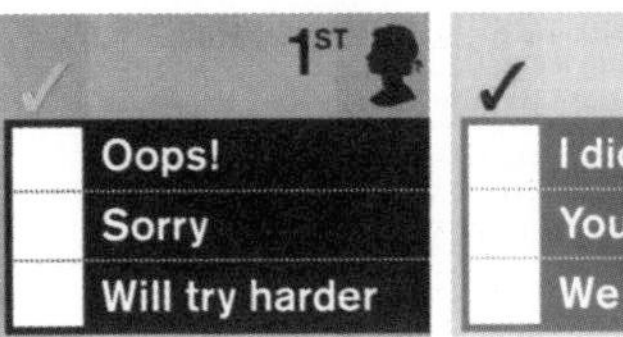

1638 "Oops!, Sorry, Will try harder"

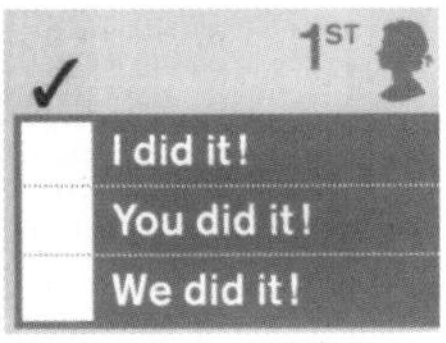

1639 "I did it!, You did it!, We did it!"

(Des UNA, Sara Wiegand and M. Exon. Litho Questa)

2003 (4 Feb). *Greetings Stamps. "Occasions". Two phosphor bands.* P 14½×14.

2337	**1634**	(1st) lemon and new blue	1·00	1·00
		a. Block of 6. Nos. 2337/42	5·50	5·50
		b. Imperf (block of 6)	£1800	
2338	**1635**	(1st) red and deep ultramarine	1·00	1·00
2339	**1636**	(1st) purple and bright yellow-green	1·00	1·00
2340	**1637**	(1st) bright yellow-green and red	1·00	1·00
2341	**1638**	(1st) deep ultramarine and lemon	1·00	1·00
2342	**1639**	(1st) new blue and purple	1·00	1·00
Set of 6			5·50	5·50
Gutter Block of 12			7·00	
First Day Cover (Tallents House)				9·00
First Day Cover (Merry Hill, Wolverhampton)				9·00
Presentation Pack			7·00	
PHQ Cards (*set of* 6)			5·25	18·00

Nos. 2337/42 were printed together, *se-tenant,* in blocks of 6 (3×2) throughout the sheet. Nos. 2337/42 were also issued in sheets of 20 (containing four of Nos. 2338 and 2340 and three each of the others) with *se-tenant* labels. Such sheets with the labels showing printed faces were available at £5.95 from philatelic outlets, or with personalised photographs at £14.95 from Royal Mail in Edinburgh.

Special First Day of Issue Postmarks

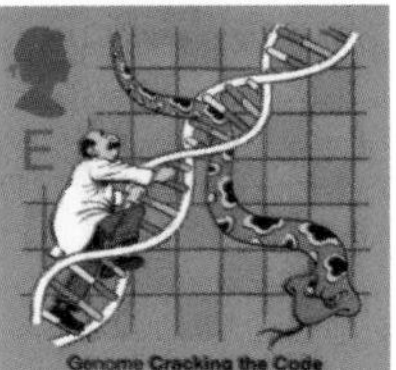

1642 DNA Snakes and Ladders

1643 "Animal Scientists"

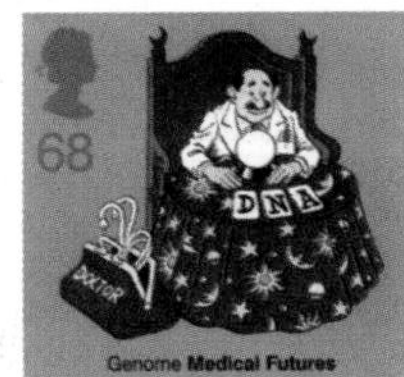

1644 Genome Crystal Ball

(Des Williams Murray Hamm and P. Brookes. Litho Enschedé)

2003 (25 Feb). *50th Anniv of Discovery of DNA. One centre phosphor band (2nd) or two phosphor bands (others).* P 14½.

2343	**1640**	(2nd) azure, black, new blue, magenta and greenish yellow	1·00	55
		a. Booklet pane. Nos. 2343/4, each ×2, with margins all round	2·00	
2344	**1641**	(1st) bright apple-green, black, new blue, magenta and greenish yellow	1·00	80
2345	**1642**	(E) yellow-orange, black, new blue, magenta and greenish yellow	1·25	1·25
		a. Booklet pane. No. 2345×4 with margins all round	3·00	
2346	**1643**	47p. bistre-yellow, black, new blue, magenta and greenish yellow	1·50	1·50
2347	**1644**	68p. lavender, black, new blue, magenta and greenish yellow	2·00	2·25
Set of 5			6·50	6·00
Set of 5 *Gutter Pairs*			15·00	
First Day Cover (Tallents House)				10·00
First Day Cover (Cambridge)				10·00
Presentation Pack			8·00	
PHQ Cards (*set of* 5)			4·75	18·00

Special First Day of Issue Postmarks

1640 Completing the Genome Jigsaw

1641 Ape with Moustache and Scientist

1645 Strawberry

1646 Potato

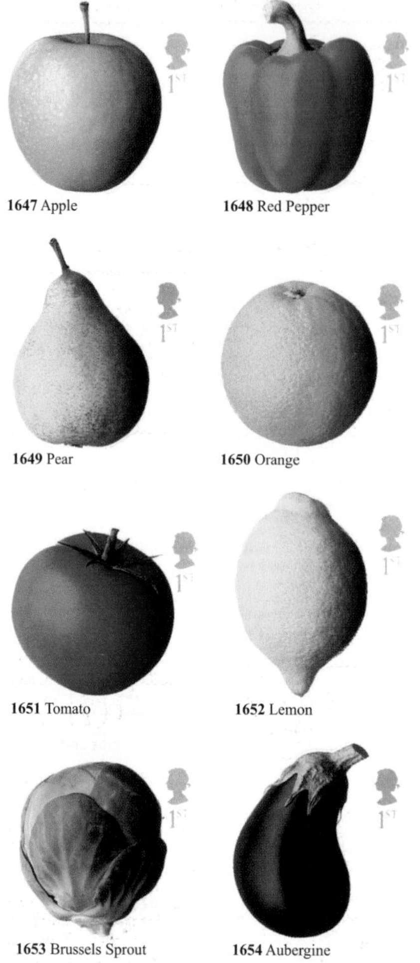

1647 Apple
1648 Red Pepper
1649 Pear
1650 Orange
1651 Tomato
1652 Lemon
1653 Brussels Sprout
1654 Aubergine

(Des Johnson Banks. Photo Walsall)

2003 (25 Mar). *Fruit and Vegetables. Self-adhesive. Two phosphor bands.* P 14½×14 die-cut (without teeth around protruding tops or bottoms of the designs).

2348	**1645**	(1st) greenish yellow, magenta, new blue, black and silver	70	80
		a. Sheetlet. Nos. 2348/57 and pane of decorative labels	9·00	9·00
		ab. Imperf (block of 10)	£1800	
2349	**1646**	(1st) greenish yellow, magenta, new blue, black and silver	70	80
2350	**1647**	(1st) greenish yellow, magenta, new blue, black and silver	70	80
2351	**1648**	(1st) greenish yellow, magenta, new blue, black and silver	70	80
2352	**1649**	(1st) greenish yellow, magenta, new blue, black and silver	70	80
2353	**1650**	(1st) greenish yellow, magenta, new blue, black and silver	70	80
2354	**1651**	(1st) greenish yellow, magenta, new blue, black and silver	70	80
2355	**1652**	(1st) greenish yellow, magenta, new blue, black and silver	70	80
2356	**1653**	(1st) greenish yellow, magenta, new blue, black and silver	70	80
2357	**1654**	(1st) greenish yellow, magenta, new blue, black and silver	70	80
Set of 10			6·25	7·25
First Day Cover (Tallents House)				12·00
First Day Cover (Pear Tree, Derby)				12·00
Presentation Pack			60·00	
PHQ Cards (*set of* 10)			9·25	12·00

Nos. 2348/57 were printed together in sheets of 10 with the surplus self-adhesive paper around each stamp retained. The stamp pane is accompanied by a similar-sized pane of self-adhesive labels showing ears, eyes, mouths, hats etc which are intended for the adornment of fruit and vegetables depicted. This pane is separated from the stamps by a line of roulettes.

Nos. 2348/57 were re-issued on 7th March 2006 in sheets of 20, containing two of each of the ten designs accompanied by *se-tenant* labels with speech bubbles and stickers showing eyes, hats, etc. in the sheet margin. These sheets were printed in lithography by Cartor and sold for £6.55.

Special First Day of Issue Postmarks

1655

(Des Sedley Place. Photo Walsall)

2003 (27 Mar)–**04**. *Overseas Booklet Stamps. Self-adhesive. Two phosphor bands.* P 15×14 die-cut with one elliptical hole on each vertical side.

2357*a*		(Worldwide postcard) grey-black, rosine and ultramarine (1.4.04)	65	70
2358	**1655**	(Europe) new blue and rosine	80	85
2359		(Worldwide) rosine and new blue	1·60	1·70
First Day Cover (Nos. 2358/9) (Tallents House) (Type K, see Introduction)				5·25
First Day Cover (Nos. 2358/9) (Windsor) (Type K)				5·25
Presentation Pack (P.O. Pack No. 60)			3·00	
PHQ Card (No. 2358)			45	2·00

No. 2357*a* was intended to pay postcard rate to foreign destinations (43p.).

Nos. 2358/9 were intended to pay postage on mail up to 40 grams to either Europe (52p.) or to foreign destinations outside Europe (£1.12).

Operationally they were only available in separate booklets of 4 (Nos. MI1, MJ1 and MJA1), initially sold at £1.72, £2.08 and £4.48, with the surplus self-adhesive paper around each stamp removed.

No. 2357*a* was available from philatelic outlets as a single stamp or in P.O. Pack No. 67 together with six definitive stamps. These single stamps had white backing paper.

For listing of first day cover (together with five definitives issued on the same day) and presentation pack for No. 2357*a* see after No. Y1803.

Single examples of Nos. 2358/9 were available from philatelic outlets as sets of two or in P.O. Pack No. 60. These stamps had coloured backing paper showing parts of the booklet covers.

1656 Amy Johnson (pilot) and Bi-plane

1657 Members of 1953 Everest Team

1658 Freya Stark (traveller and writer) and Desert

1659 Ernest Shackleton (Antarctic explorer) and Wreck of *Endurance*

1660 Francis Chichester (yachtsman) and *Gipsy Moth IV*

1661 Robert Falcon Scott (Antarctic explorer) and Norwegian Expedition at the Pole

(Des H. Brown)

2003 (29 Apr). *Extreme Endeavours (British Explorers). One centre phosphor band (2nd) or two phosphor bands (others).* P 15×14½.

(a) Photo Questa. PVA gum.

2360	**1656**	(2nd)	gold, black, magenta, greenish yellow and new blue	50	50
2361	**1657**	(1st)	gold, black, magenta, greenish yellow and new blue	75	75
2362	**1658**	(E)	gold, black, magenta, greenish yellow and new blue	1·25	1·50
2363	**1659**	42p.	gold, black, magenta, greenish yellow and new blue	1·25	1·75
2364	**1660**	47p.	gold, black, magenta, greenish yellow and new blue	1·50	2·00
2365	**1661**	68p.	gold, black, magenta, greenish yellow and new blue	2·00	2·50
Set of 6				7·00	7·75
Set of 6 Gutter Pairs				18·00	
First Day Cover (Tallents House)					12·00
First Day Cover (Plymouth)					12·00
Presentation Pack				9·00	
PHQ Cards (set of 6)				3·25	12·00

(b) Photo De La Rue. Self-adhesive. Die-cut P 14½.

2366	**1657**	(1st)	gold, black, magenta, greenish yellow and new blue	4·00	4·00
			a. Booklet pane. No. 2366×2 plus No. 2295×4	10·00	

The phosphor bands on Nos. 2361/5 are at the centre and right of each stamp.

No. 2366 was only issued in £1.62 stamp booklets, No. PM9, in which the surplus self-adhesive paper around each stamp was removed.

Special First Day of Issue Postmarks

(Des Rose Design. Photo De La Rue)

2003 (20 May). *50th Anniv of Wilding Definitives (2nd issue). Sheet 124×70 mm, containing designs as T* **155/8** *and 160 (1952–54 issue), but with values in decimal currency as T* **1348** *or with service indicator as T* **1566**, *printed on pale cream. One centre phosphor band (20p.) or two phosphor bands (others).* W **1565**. P 15×14 (with one elliptical hole on each vertical side).

MS2367 4p. deep lilac; 8p. ultramarine; 10p. reddish purple; 20p. bright green; 28p. bronze-green; 34p. brown-purple; (E) chestnut; 42p. Prussian blue; 68p. grey-blue and label showing national emblems	10·50	11·25
First Day Cover (Tallents House)		13·00
First Day Cover (Windsor)		14·00
Presentation Pack	15·00	

Special First Day of Issue Postmarks

1662 Guardsmen in Coronation Procession

1663 East End Children reading Coronation Party Poster

1664 Queen Elizabeth II in Coronation Chair with Bishops of Durham and Bath and Wells

1665 Children in Plymouth working on Royal Montage

1666 Queen Elizabeth II in Coronation Robes (photograph by Cecil Beaton)

1667 Children's Race at East End Street Party

1668 Coronation Coach passing through Marble Arch

1669 Children in Fancy Dress

1670 Coronation Coach outside Buckingham Palace

1671 Children eating at London Street Party

(Des Kate Stephens. Photo De La Rue (sheets) or Walsall (booklets))

2003 (2 June). *50th Anniv of Coronation.* W **1565**. *Two phosphor bands.* P 14½×14.

2368	**1662**	(1st) greenish yellow, bright magenta, new blue, grey-black, deep turquoise-blue and gold	45	50
		a. Block of 10. Nos. 2368/77	8·75	8·75
		b. Booklet pane. Nos. 2368, 2370, 2373 and 2375 with margins all round	1·70	
2369	**1663**	(1st) black and gold	45	50
		b. Booklet pane. Nos. 2369, 2372, 2374 and 2377 with margins all round	1·70	
2370	**1664**	(1st) greenish yellow, bright magenta, new blue, grey-black, deep turquoise-blue and gold	45	50
2371	**1665**	(1st) black and gold	45	50
2372	**1666**	(1st) greenish yellow, bright magenta, new blue, grey-black and deep turquoise-blue	45	50
2373	**1667**	(1st) black and gold	45	50
2374	**1668**	(1st) greenish yellow, bright magenta, new blue, grey-black, deep turquoise-blue and gold	45	50
2375	**1669**	(1st) black and gold	45	50
2376	**1670**	(1st) greenish yellow, bright magenta, new blue, grey-black, deep turquoise-blue and gold	45	50
2377	**1671**	(1st) black and gold	45	50

Set of 10	4·50	5·00
Gutter Block of 20	20·00	
First Day Cover (Tallents House)		12·00
First Day Cover (London SW1)		12·00
Presentation Pack	20·00	
PHQ Cards (*set of* 10)	3·75	12·00

Nos. 2368/77 were printed together, *se-tenant*, in blocks of 10 (5×2) throughout sheets of 60. No. 2372 does not show a silhouette of the Queen's head in gold as do the other nine designs.

Special First Day of Issue Postmarks

(Photo Walsall)

2003 (2 June). *50th Anniv of Coronation. Booklet stamps. Designs as T* **160** *(Wilding definitive of 1952) and 163 (Coronation commemorative of 1953), but with values in decimal currency as T* **1348**. W **1565**. *Two phosphor bands.* P 15×14 (with one elliptical hole on each vertical side for Nos. 2378/9).

2378	**160**	47p. bistre-brown	5·00	2·50
		a. Booklet pane. Nos. 2378/9, each ×2, and 2380 with margins all round	65·00	
2379		68p. grey-blue	5·00	2·50
2380	**163**	£1 deep yellow-green	50·00	45·00
Set of 3			55·00	45·00

Nos. 2378/80 were only available in £7.46 stamp booklets, No. DX31. Stamps as Nos. 2378/9, but on pale cream, were also included in the Wilding miniature sheets, Nos. **MS**2326 or **MS**2367. A £1 design as No. 2380, but on phosphorised paper, was previously included in the "Stamp Show 2000" miniature sheet, No. **MS**2147.

1672 Prince William in September 2001 (Brendan Beirne)

1673 Prince William in September 2000 (Tim Graham)

1674 Prince William in September 2001 (Camera Press)

1675 Prince William in September 2001 (Tim Graham)

(Des Madeleine Bennett. Photo Walsall)

2003 (17 June). *21st Birthday of Prince William of Wales. Phosphor backgrounds.* P 14½.

No.	Type	Description	Unused	Used
2381	**1672**	28p. silver, black, grey-black and light green	1·00	50
2382	**1673**	(E) dull mauve, grey-black and light green	1·25	1·50
2383	**1674**	47p. greenish grey, grey-black, black and light green	1·75	2·00
2384	**1675**	68p. sage-green, black and bright green	2·50	2·00
		Set of 4	5·00	6·00
		Set of 4 Gutter Pairs	13·00	
		First Day Cover (Tallents House)		10·00
		First Day Cover (Cardiff)		10·00
		Presentation Pack	18·00	
		PHQ Cards (*set of 4*)	1·50	10·00

Special First Day of Issue Postmarks

1676 Loch Assynt, Sutherland

1677 Ben More, Isle of Mull

1678 Rothiemurchus, Cairngorms

1679 Dalveen Pass, Lowther Hills

1680 Glenfinnan Viaduct, Lochaber

1681 Papa Little, Shetland Islands

(Des Phelan Barker. Photo De La Rue)

2003 (15 July). *A British Journey: Scotland. One centre phosphor band (2nd) or two phosphor bands (others).* P 14½. *(a) PVA gum.*

No.	Type	Description	Unused	Used
2385	**1676**	(2nd) silver, black, bright magenta, greenish yellow and new blue	50	35
2386	**1677**	(1st) silver, black, bright magenta, greenish yellow and new blue	75	50
2387	**1678**	(E) silver, black, bright magenta, greenish yellow and new blue	1·25	1·25
2388	**1679**	42p. silver, black, bright magenta, greenish yellow and new blue	1·25	1·50
2389	**1680**	47p. silver, black, bright magenta, greenish yellow and new blue	1·50	2·00
2390	**1681**	68p. silver, black, bright magenta, greenish yellow and new blue	2·00	2·50
		Set of 6	7·00	7·75
		Set of 6 Gutter Pairs	16·00	
		First Day Cover (Tallents House)		11·00
		First Day Cover (Baltasound, Unst, Shetland)		11·00
		Presentation Pack	9·50	
		PHQ Cards (*set of 6*)	2·25	11·00

(b) Self-adhesive.

No.	Type	Description	Unused	Used
2391	**1677**	(1st) silver, black, bright magenta, greenish yellow and new blue	4·00	4·00
		a. Booklet pane. No. 2391×2, and No. 2295×4	10·00	

No. 2391 was only issued in £1.68 stamp booklets, No. PM10, in which the surplus self-adhesive paper around each stamp was removed.

Special First Day of Issue Postmarks

1682 "The Station" (Andrew Davidson)

1683 "Black Swan" (Stanley Chew)

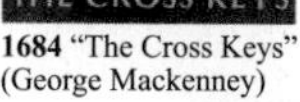

1684 "The Cross Keys" (George Mackenney)

1685 "The Mayflower" (Ralph Ellis)

1686 "The Barley Sheaf" (Joy Cooper)

(Des Elmwood. Photo De La Rue)

2003 (12 Aug). *Europa. British Pub Signs. Two phosphor bands.* P 14×14½.

2392 **1682** (1st) silver, black, magenta, greenish yellow and new blue 75 50
a. Booklet pane. No. 2392×4 with margins all round (16.3.04) .... 3·75
2393 **1683** (E) silver, black, magenta, greenish yellow and new blue .... 2·00 2·00
2394 **1684** 42p. silver, black, magenta, greenish yellow and new blue .... 1·50 1·50
2395 **1685** 47p. silver, black, magenta, greenish yellow and new blue .... 1·75 2·00
2396 **1686** 68p. silver, black, magenta, greenish yellow and new blue .... 2·00 2·25
Set of 5 .... 7·50 7·75
Set of 5 *Gutter Pairs* .... 17·00
First Day Cover (Tallents House) .... 11·00
First Day Cover (Cross Keys, Hereford) .... 11·00
Presentation Pack .... 9·00
PHQ Cards (*set of* 5) .... 1·90 11·00

The 1st and E values include the "EUROPA" emblem. No. 2392a comes from the £7.44 "Letters by Night" booklet, No. DX32.

Special First Day of Issue Postmarks

1687 Meccano Constructor Biplane, c.1931

1688 Wells-Brimtoy Clockwork Double-decker Omnibus, c.1938

1689 Hornby M1 Clockwork Locomotive and Tender, c.1948

1690 Dinky Toys Ford Zephyr, c. 1956

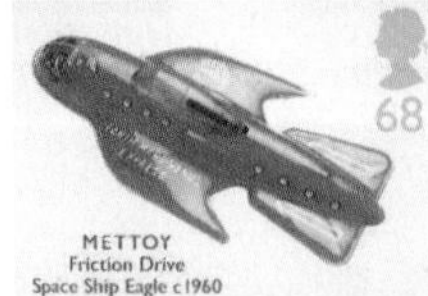

1691 Mettoy Friction Drive Space Ship Eagle, c.1960

(Des Trickett and Webb)

2003 (18 Sept). *Classic Transport Toys. Two phosphor bands. (a) Photo Enschedé. PVA gum.* P 14½×14.

2397 **1687** (1st) silver, blue-black, black, new blue, magenta and greenish yellow 75 50
2398 **1688** (E) silver, blue-black, black, new blue, magenta and greenish yellow .... 1·25 1·25
2399 **1689** 42p. silver, blue-black, black, new blue, magenta and greenish yellow .... 1·50 1·50
2400 **1690** 47p. silver, blue-black, black, new blue, magenta and greenish yellow .... 1·75 1·75
2401 **1691** 68p. silver, blue-black, black, new blue, magenta and greenish yellow .... 2·00 2·50
Set of 5 .... 7·00 7·25
Set of 5 *Gutter Pairs* .... 16·00
First Day Cover (Tallents House) .... 10·00
First Day Cover (Toye, Downpatrick) .... 10·00
Presentation Pack .... 9·00
PHQ Cards (*set of* 6) .... 2·75 10·00
MS2402 115×105mm. Nos. 2397/401 .... 7·00 8·25
First Day Cover .... 10·00

(*b*) *Photo De La Rue. Self-adhesive.* Die-cut P 14½×14.

2403 **1687** (1st) silver, blue-black, black, new blue, magenta and greenish yellow .... 5·00 5·00
a. Booklet pane. No. 2403×2 and No. 2295×4 .... 12·00

The complete miniature sheet is shown on one of the PHQ cards with the others depicting individual stamps.

No. 2403 was only issued in £1.68 stamp booklets, No. PM11, in which the surplus self-adhesive paper around each stamp was removed.

Special First Day of Issue Postmarks

1692 Coffin of Denytenamun, Egyptian, c.900BC

1693 Alexander the Great, Greek, c.200BC

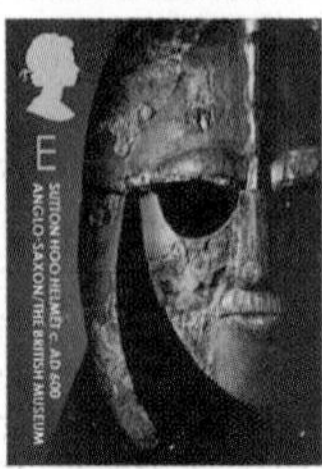

1694 Sutton Hoo Helmet, Anglo-Saxon, c.AD600

1695 Sculpture of Parvati, South Indian, c.AD1550

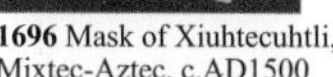

1696 Mask of Xiuhtecuhtli, Mixtec-Aztec, c.AD1500

1697 Hoa Hakananai'a, Easter Island, c.AD1000

(Des Rose Design. Photo Walsall)

2003 (7 Sept). *250th Anniv of the British Museum. One side phosphor band (2nd), two phosphor bands ((1st), (E), 47p.) or phosphor background at left and band at right (42p., 68p.).* P 14×14½.

2404	**1692**	(2nd)	brownish grey, black, greenish yellow, magenta and pale new blue	50	35
2405	**1693**	(1st)	brownish grey, black, greenish yellow, magenta and pale new blue	75	50
2406	**1694**	(E)	brownish grey, black, greenish yellow, magenta and pale new blue	1·25	1·25
2407	**1695**	42p.	brownish grey, black, greenish yellow, magenta and pale new blue	1·25	1·50
2408	**1696**	47p.	brownish grey, black, greenish yellow, magenta and pale new blue	1·50	2·00
2409	**1697**	68p.	brownish grey, black, greenish yellow, magenta and pale new blue	2·00	2·75
Set of 6				7·00	7·75
Set of 6 Gutter Pairs				18·00	
First Day Cover (Tallents House)					11·00
First Day Cover (London WC1)					11·00
Presentation Pack				9·00	
PHQ Cards (*set of 6*)				2·75	11·00

Special First Day of Issue Postmarks

1698 Ice Spiral

1699 Icicle Star

1700 Wall of Ice Blocks

1701 Ice Ball

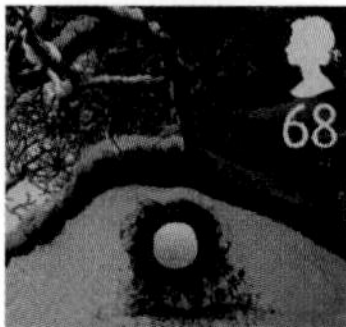

1702 Ice Hole

1703 Snow Pyramids

(Des D. Davis. Photo De La Rue)

2003 (4 Nov). *Christmas. Ice Sculptures by Andy Goldsworthy. Self-adhesive. One side phosphor band (2nd), "all-over" phosphor (1st) or two bands (others).* Die-cut perf 14½×14.

2410	**1698**	(2nd)	magenta, greenish yellow, new blue and black	75	35
			a. Booklet pane. No. 2410×24	7·25	
2411	**1699**	(1st)	magenta, greenish yellow, new blue and black	1·25	50
			a. Booklet pane. No. 2411×12	5·00	
2412	**1700**	(E)	magenta, greenish yellow, new blue and black	1·50	1·50
2413	**1701**	53p.	magenta, greenish yellow, new blue and black	1·75	1·75
2414	**1702**	68p.	magenta, greenish yellow, new blue and black	2·00	2·00
2415	**1703**	£1.12	magenta, greenish yellow, new blue and black	2·00	2·00
Set of 6				9·00	9·00
First Day Cover (Tallents House)					12·50
First Day Cover (Bethlehem, Llandeilo)					12·50
Presentation Pack				11·00	
PHQ Cards (*set of 6*)				4·00	12·50

Nos. 2410/15 were each printed in sheets of 50 with the surplus backing paper around each stamp removed. The 2nd and 1st class were also issued in separate sheets of 20 printed in lithography instead of photogravure, each stamp accompanied by a half stamp-size *se-tenant* label showing either ice sculptures (2nd) or animals (1st). Both sheets have the backing paper around each stamp retained. The 2nd class sheet was sold for £4.20 and the 1st class for £6.15. These sheets were also available with personal photographs instead of labels at £9.95 (2nd) or £14.95 (1st) from Royal Mail, Edinburgh or £15 from photo-booths at selected post offices and Safeway stores.

Special First Day of Issue Postmarks

Collectors Pack 2003

2003 (4 Nov). *Comprises Nos.* 2327/57, 2360/5, 2368/77, 2381/90, 2392/401 *and* 2404/15

CP2415a Collectors Pack £100

Post Office Yearbook

2003 (4 Nov). *Comprises Nos.* 2327/57, 2360/5, 2368/77, 2381/90, 2392/401 *and* 2404/15 *in hardback book with slipcase* £100

1704 (*Illustration reduced. Actual size* 115×88 *mm*)

(Des Why Not Associates. Litho Walsall)

2003 (19 Dec). *England's Victory in Rugby World Cup Championship, Australia. Sheet 115×85 mm. Multicoloured. Two phosphor bands.* P 14.

MS2416 **1704** (1st) England flags and fans; (1st) England team standing in circle before match; 68p. World Cup trophy; 68p. Victorious England players after match ..	6·00	10·00
First Day Cover (Tallents House)		12·00
First Day Cover (Twickenham)		12·00
Presentation Pack	11·00	

Special First Day of Issue Postmarks

1705 *Dolgoch*, Rheilffordd Talyllyn Railway, Gwynedd

1706 CR Class 439, Bo'ness and Kinneil Railway, West Lothian

1707 GCR Class 8K, Leicestershire

1708 GWR Manor Class *Bradley Manor*, Severn Valley Railway, Worcestershire

1709 SR West Country Class *Blackmoor Vale*, Bluebell Railway, East Sussex

1710 BR Standard Class, Keighley and Worth Valley Railway, Yorkshire

(Des Roundel. Litho De La Rue)

2004 (13 Jan–16 Mar). *Classic Locomotives. One side phosphor band (20p.) or two phosphor bands (others).* P 14½.

2417	**1705**	20p. greenish yellow, magenta, new blue, silver and black	65	65
2418	**1706**	28p. greenish yellow, magenta, new blue, silver and black	90	90
		a. Booklet pane. Nos. 2418/20 with margins all round (16 Mar)	3·50	
2419	**1707**	(E) greenish yellow, magenta, new blue, silver and black	1·20	1·20
2420	**1708**	42p. greenish yellow, magenta, new blue, silver and black	1·30	1·30
2421	**1709**	47p. greenish yellow, magenta, new blue, silver and black	1·50	1·50
		a. Imperf.	£1200	
2422	**1710**	68p. greenish yellow, magenta, new blue, silver and black	2·20	2·20
Set of 6			7·00	7·00
Set of 6 *Gutter Pairs*			15·00	
First Day Cover (Tallents House)				12·00
First Day Cover (York)				12·00
Presentation Pack			30·00	
PHQ Cards (*set of* 6)			5·75	12·00
MS2423 190×67 mm. Nos. 2417/22			30·00	25·00
First Day Cover (Tallents House)				27·00
First Day Cover (York)				27·00

No. 2418a comes from the £7.44 "Letters by Night" booklet, No. DX32.

Special First Day of Issue Postmarks

1711 Postman

1712 Face

1713 Duck

1714 Baby

1715 Aircraft

(Des S. Kambayashi. Litho De La Rue)

2004 (3 Feb). *Occasions. Two phosphor bands.* P 14½×14.

2424	**1711**	(1st) bright mauve and black	90	90
		a. Horiz strip of 5. Nos. 2424/8	5·00	5·00
		ab. Imperf strip of 5		
2425	**1712**	(1st) magenta and black	90	90
2426	**1713**	(1st) lemon and black	90	90
2427	**1714**	(1st) pale turquoise-green and black	90	90
2428	**1715**	(1st) bright new blue and black	90	90
Set of 5			4·50	4·50
Gutter Block of 10			9·00	
First Day Cover (Tallents House)				6·50
First Day Cover (Merry Hill, Wolverhampton)				6·50
Presentation Pack			6·25	
PHQ Cards (*set of* 5)			4·75	10·00

Nos. 2424/8 were printed together, *se-tenant*, as horizontal strips of 5 in sheets of 25 (5×5). Nos. 2424/8 were also issued in sheets of 20 containing vertical strips of the five designs alternated with half stamp-size labels. These sheets with printed labels were available at £6.15 from philatelic outlets, or with personalised photographs at £14.95 from Royal Mail in Edinburgh.

Special First Day of Issue Postmarks

1716 Map showing Middle Earth

1717 Forest of Lothlórien in Spring

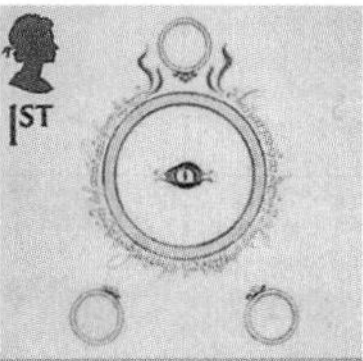

1718 Dust-jacket for *The Fellowship of the Ring*

1719 Rivendell

1720 The Hall at Bag End

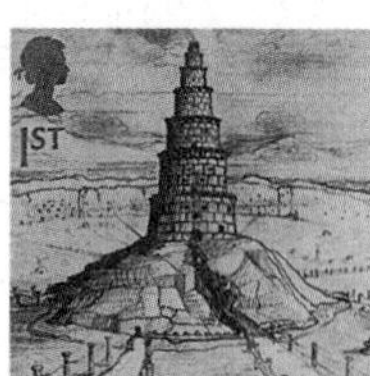

1721 Orthanc

1722 Doors of Durin

1723 Barad-dûr

1724 Minas Tirith

1725 Fangorn Forest

(Des HGV Design. Litho Walsall)

2004 (26 Feb). *50th Anniv of Publication of The Fellowship of the Ring and The Two Towers by J. R. R. Tolkien. Two phosphor bands.* P 14½.

2429	**1716**	(1st) pale stone, sepia, black, greenish yellow, magenta and new blue	90	90
		a. Block of 10. Nos. 2429/38	9·00	10·00
2430	**1717**	(1st) pale stone, sepia, black, greenish yellow, magenta and new blue	90	90
2431	**1718**	(1st) pale stone, sepia, black, greenish yellow, magenta and new blue	90	90
2432	**1719**	(1st) pale stone, sepia, black, greenish yellow, magenta and new blue	90	90
2433	**1720**	(1st) pale stone, sepia, black, greenish yellow, magenta and new blue	90	90
2434	**1721**	(1st) pale stone, sepia, black, greenish yellow, magenta and new blue	90	90
2435	**1722**	(1st) pale stone, sepia, black, greenish yellow, magenta and new blue	90	90
2436	**1723**	(1st) pale stone, sepia, black, greenish yellow, magenta and new blue	90	90
2437	**1724**	(1st) pale stone, sepia, black, greenish yellow, magenta and new blue	90	90

2438 **1725** (1st) pale stone, sepia, black, greenish yellow, magenta and new blue......... 90 90
Set of 10........................ 9·00 9·00
Gutter Block of 20........................ 12·00
First Day Cover (Tallents House)........................ 10·00
First Day Cover (Oxford)........................ 10·00
Presentation Pack........................ 25·00
PHQ Cards (*set of* 10)........................ 9·75 12·00

Nos. 2429/38 were printed together, *se-tenant*, in blocks of 10 (5×2) throughout the sheet.

Special First Day of Issue Postmarks

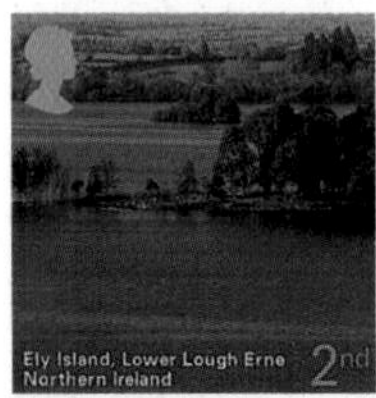

1726 Ely Island, Lower Lough Erne

1727 Giant's Causeway, Antrim Coast

1728 Slemish, Antrim Mountains

1729 Banns Road, Mourne Mountains

1730 Glenelly Valley, Sperrins

1731 Islandmore, Strangford Lough

(Des Phelan Barker. Photo Enschedé)

2004 (16 Mar). *A British Journey: Northern Ireland. One side phosphor band (2nd) or two phosphor bands (others).* P 14½.

(a) PVA gum.

2439 **1726** (2nd) silver, black, new blue, magenta and greenish yellow........................ 65 65
2440 **1727** (1st) silver, black, new blue, magenta and greenish yellow........................ 90 90
2441 **1728** (E) silver, black, new blue, magenta and greenish yellow........................ 1·20 1·20
2442 **1729** 42p. silver, black, new blue, magenta and greenish yellow........................ 1·30 1·30
2443 **1730** 47p. silver, black, new blue, magenta and greenish yellow........................ 1·50 1·50
2444 **1731** 68p. silver, black, new blue, magenta and greenish yellow........................ 2·20 2·20
Set of 6........................ 7·75 7·75
Set of 6 *Gutter Pairs*........................ 12·00
First Day Cover (Tallents House)........................ 12·50
First Day Cover (Garrison, Enniskillen)........................ 12·50
Presentation Pack........................ 12·00
PHQ Cards (*set of* 6)........................ 5·75 12·50

(b) Self-adhesive. Die-cut perf 14½.

2445 **1727** (1st) silver, black, new blue, magenta and greenish yellow........................ 4·50 4·50
a. Booklet pane. No. 2445×2 and No. 2295×4........................ 10·00

No. 2445 was only issued in £1.68 stamp booklets No. PM12 in which the surplus self-adhesive paper around each stamp was removed.

Special First Day of Issue Postmarks

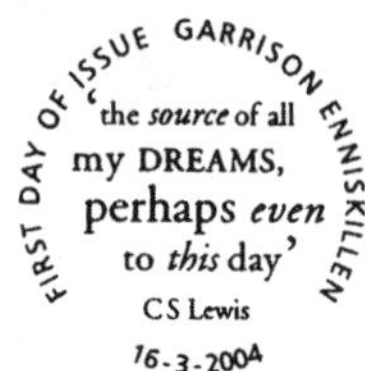

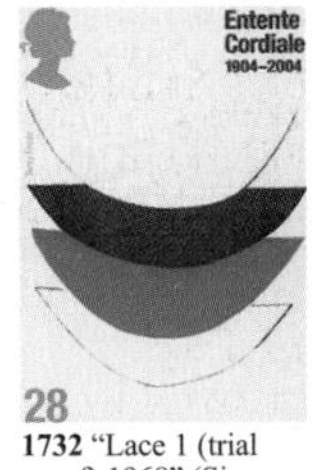

1732 "Lace 1 (trial proof) 1968" (Sir Terry Frost)

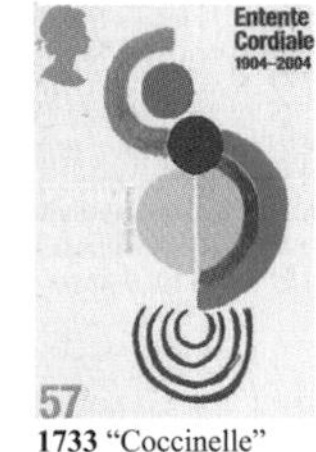

1733 "Coccinelle" (Sonia Delaunay)

(Des Rose Design. Photo Walsall)

2004 (6 Apr). *Centenary of the Entente Cordiale. Contemporary Paintings. Two phosphor bands.* P 14×14½.

2446 **1732** 28p. grey, black and rosine........................ 1·00 85
2447 **1733** 57p. grey, black, grey-brown, rosine, new blue, orange-yellow and bright crimson........................ 2·25 2·00
Set of 2........................ 3·00 2·75
Set of 2 *Gutter Pairs*........................ 6·00
Set of 2 *Traffic Light gutter blocks of* 4........................ 15·00
First Day Cover (Tallents House)........................ 4·50
First Day Cover (London SW1)........................ 4·50
Presentation Pack........................ 30·00
Presentation Pack (UK and French stamps)........................ 30·00
PHQ Cards (*set of* 2)........................ 1·90 5·00

Stamps in similar designs were issued by France and these are included in the joint Presentation Pack.

Special First Day of Issue Postmarks

1734 "RMS *Queen Mary 2*, 2004" (Edward D. Walker)

1735 "SS *Canberra*, 1961" (David Cobb)

1736 "RMS *Queen Mary*, 1936" (Charles Pears)

1737 "RMS *Mauretania*, 1907" (Thomas Henry)

1738 "SS *City of New York*, 1888" (Raphael Monleaon y Torres)

1739 "PS *Great Western*, 1838" (Joseph Walter)

(Des J. Gibbs. Photo De La Rue)

2004 (13 Apr). *Ocean Liners. Two phosphor bands.* P 14½×14.

(a) PVA gum.

2448	**1734**	(1st) gold, black, magenta, greenish yellow and new blue	90	90
2449	**1735**	(E) gold, black, magenta, greenish yellow and new blue	1·30	1·30
2450	**1736**	42p. gold, black, magenta, greenish yellow and new blue	1·30	1·30
2451	**1737**	47p. gold, black, magenta, greenish yellow and new blue	1·50	1·50
2452	**1738**	57p. gold, black, magenta, greenish yellow and new blue	1·80	1·80
2453	**1739**	68p. gold, black, magenta, greenish yellow and new blue	2·20	2·20
Set of 6			9·00	9·00
Set of 6 *Gutter Pairs*			18·00	
First Day Cover (Tallents House)				10·00
First Day Cover (Southampton)				10·00
Presentation Pack			11·00	
PHQ Cards (*set of* 7)			6·75	10·00
MS2454 114×104mm. Nos. 2448/53			18·00	18·00
First Day Cover (Tallents House)				18·00
First Day Cover (Southampton)				18·00

(b) Self-adhesive. Die-cut perf 14½×14.

2455	**1734**	(1st) gold, black, magenta, greenish yellow and new blue	4·50	4·50
		a. Booklet pane. No. 2455×2 and No. 2295×4	10·00	

Nos. 2448/55 commemorate the introduction to service of the *Queen Mary 2*.

The complete miniature sheet is shown on one of the PHQ cards with the others depicting individual stamps. No. 2455 was only issued in £1.68 stamp booklets No. PM13 in which the surplus self-adhesive paper around each stamp was removed.

No. **MS**2454 is known to exist with a face value of "53" on No. 2452.

Special First Day of Issue Postmarks

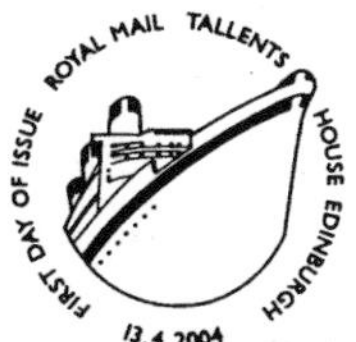

1740 Dianthus Allwoodii Group

1741 Dahlia "Garden Princess"

1742 Clematis "Arabella"

1743 Miltonia "French Lake"

1744 Lilium "Lemon Pixie"

1745 Delphinium "Clifford Sky"

(Des Rose Design. Photo Enschedé)

2004 (25 May). *Bicentenary of the Royal Horticultural Society (1st issue). One side phosphor band (2nd) or "all-over" phosphor (others).* P 14½.

2456	**1740**	(2nd) sage-green, black, new blue, magenta and greenish yellow	70	70
		a. Booklet pane. Nos. 2456, 2458/9 and 2461 with margins all round	5·50	
2457	**1741**	(1st) sage-green, black, new blue, magenta and greenish yellow	90	90
		a. Booklet pane. Nos. 2457 and 2460, each ×2, with margins all round	4·75	
2458	**1742**	(E) sage-green, black, new blue, magenta and greenish yellow	1·30	1·30
2459	**1743**	42p. sage-green, black, new blue, magenta and greenish yellow	1·40	1·50
2460	**1744**	47p. sage-green, black, new blue, magenta and greenish yellow	1·50	2·00
2461	**1745**	68p. sage-green, black, new blue, magenta and greenish yellow	2·20	3·50
Set of 6			8·00	9·50
Set of 6 *Gutter Pairs*			16·00	
First Day Cover (Tallents House)				11·00
First Day Cover (Wisley, Woking)				11·00
Presentation Pack			11·00	
PHQ Cards (*set of* 7)			6·75	12·00

MS2462 115×105 mm.Nos. 2456/61	10·00	10·00
First Day Cover (Tallents House)		11·00
First Day Cover (Wisley, Woking)		11·00

The complete miniature sheet is shown on one of the PHQ cards with the others depicting individual stamps.

The 1st class stamp was also issued in sheets of 20, printed in lithography by Walsall and sold at £6.15, containing vertical strips of five stamps alternated with printed labels giving information about dahlias. These sheets with personalised photographs were available at £14.95 from the Royal Mail in Edinburgh.

Special First Day of Issue Postmarks

(Litho Enschedé)

2004 (25 May). *Bicentenary of the Royal Horticultural Society (2nd issue). Booklet stamps. Designs as Nos. 1955, 1958 and 1962 (1997 Greeting Stamps 19th-century Flower Paintings). Two phosphor bands.* P 15×14 (with one elliptical hole on each vert side.

2463	**1280**	(1st) greenish yellow, new blue, magenta, black, blue-green and gold	1·50	1·50
		a. Booklet pane. Nos. 2463, 2464×2 and 2465 with margins all round	4·00	
2464	**1283**	(1st) greenish yellow, new blue, magenta, black, blue-green and gold	50	50
2465	**1287**	(1st) greenish yellow, new blue, magenta, black, blue-green and gold	1·50	1·50
Set of 3			7·00	7·00

On Nos. 2463/5 the phosphor bands appear at the left and the centre of each stamp. Nos. 2463/5 were only available in £7.23 stamp booklets, No. DX33.

1746 Barmouth Bridge

1747 Hyddgen, Plynlimon

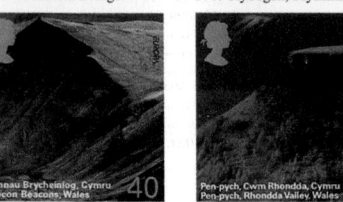

1748 Brecon Beacons

1749 Pen-pych, Rhondda Valley

1750 Rhewl, Dee Valley

1751 Marloes Sands

(Des Phelan Barker. Photo De La Rue)

2004 (15 June). *A British Journey: Wales. One centre phosphor band (2nd), "all-over" phosphor (1st) or two phosphor bands (others).* P 14½.

(a) PVA gum.

2466	**1746**	(2nd) silver, black, magenta, greenish yellow and new blue	70	70
2467	**1747**	(1st) silver, black, magenta, greenish yellow and new blue	90	90
2468	**1748**	40p. silver, black, magenta, greenish yellow and new blue	1·75	1·50
2469	**1749**	43p. silver, black, magenta, greenish yellow and new blue	2·00	2·00
2470	**1750**	47p. silver, black, magenta, greenish yellow and new blue	2·50	3·00
2471	**1751**	68p. silver, black, magenta, greenish yellow and new blue	3·50	4·00
Set of 6			10·00	10·00
Set of 6 *Gutter Pairs*			18·00	
First Day Cover (Tallents House)				11·00
First Day Cover (Llanfair)				11·00
Presentation Pack			11·00	
PHQ Cards (*set of* 6)			5·75	12·00

(b) Self-adhesive. Die-cut perf 14½.

2472	**1747**	(1st) silver, black, magenta, greenish yellow and new blue	5·00	5·00
		a. Booklet pane. No. 2472×2 and No. 2295×4	12·00	

The 1st and 40p. values include the "EUROPA" emblem.

No. 2472 was only issued in £1.68 stamp booklets, No. PM14, in which the surplus self-adhesive paper around each stamp was removed.

Special First Day of Issue Postmarks

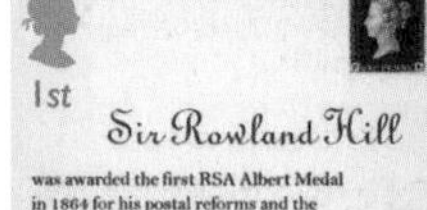

1752 Sir Rowland Hill Award

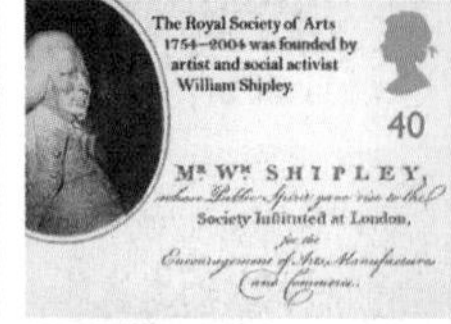

1753 William Shipley (Founder of Royal Society of Arts)

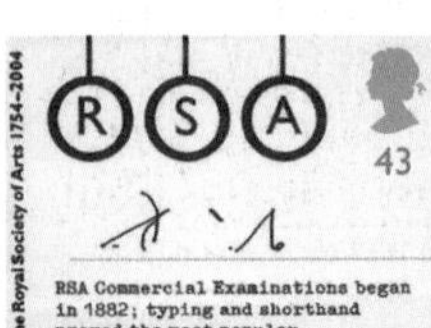

1754 "RSA" as Typewriter Keys and Shorthand

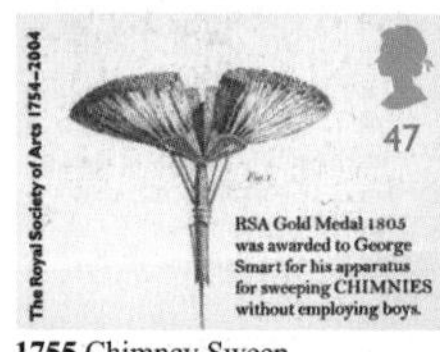

1755 Chimney Sweep

Eric Gill created this famous typeface and was among the very first to be awarded the distinction of Royal Designer for Industry (RDI) by the RSA in 1938. 57

eg: abcdefghijklmnopqrstuvwxyz

The Royal Society of Arts 1754–2004

1756 "Gill Typeface"

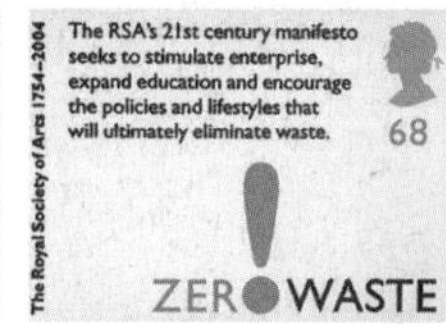

1757 "Zero Waste"

(Des D. Birdsall. Litho Walsall)

2004 (10 Aug). *250th Anniv of the Royal Society of Arts. Two phosphor bands.* P 14.

No.	Type	Description	Unused	Used
2473	**1752**	(1st) silver, vermilion, blackish-brown and black	95	95
2474	**1753**	40p. silver, vermilion, grey-black, blackish-brown and black	1·30	1·30
2475	**1754**	43p. silver, new blue, vermilion and black	1·40	1·40
2476	**1755**	47p. silver, vermilion, blackish-brown and black	1·50	1·50
2477	**1756**	57p. silver, vermilion and black	1·90	1·90
2478	**1757**	68p. silver, vermilion and black	2·20	2·20
Set of 6			9·25	9·25
Set of 6 *Gutter Pairs*			18·00	
First Day Cover (Tallents House)				12·00
First Day Cover (London WC2)				12·00
Presentation Pack			11·00	
PHQ Cards (*set of* 6)			5·75	12·00

Special First Day of Issue Postmarks

1758 Pine Marten

1759 Roe Deer

1760 Badger

1761 Yellow-necked Mouse

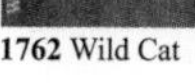
1762 Wild Cat

1763 Red Squirrel

1764 Stoat

1765 Natterer's Bat

1766 Mole

1767 Fox

(Des Kate Stephens. Photo Enschedé)

2004 (16 Sept). *Woodland Animals. Two phosphor bands.* P 14½.

No.	Type	Description	Unused	Used
2479	**1758**	(1st) ochre, black, bright new blue, magenta and lemon	90	90
		a. Block of 10. Nos. 2479/88	9·00	10·00
2480	**1759**	(1st) ochre, black, bright new blue, magenta and lemon	90	90
2481	**1760**	(1st) ochre, black, bright new blue, magenta and lemon	90	90
2482	**1761**	(1st) ochre, black, bright new blue, magenta and lemon	90	90
2483	**1762**	(1st) ochre, black, bright new blue, magenta and lemon	90	90
2484	**1763**	(1st) ochre, black, bright new blue, magenta and lemon	90	90
2485	**1764**	(1st) ochre, black, bright new blue, magenta and lemon	90	90
2486	**1765**	(1st) ochre, black, bright new blue, magenta and lemon	90	90
2487	**1766**	(1st) ochre, black, bright new blue, magenta and lemon	90	90
2488	**1767**	(1st) ochre, black, bright new blue, magenta and lemon	90	90
Set of 10			9·00	9·00
Gutter Block of 20			18·00	
First Day Cover (Tallents House)				12·00
First Day Cover (Woodland, Bishop Auckland)				12·00
Presentation Pack			12·00	
PHQ Cards (*set of* 10)			9·75	14·00

Nos. 2479/88 were printed together, *se-tenant*, in blocks of 10 (5×2) throughout sheets of 30.

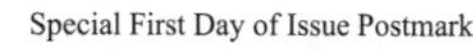
Special First Day of Issue Postmarks

1768 Pte. McNamara, 5th Dragoon Guards, Heavy Brigade charge, Battle of Balaklava

1769 Piper Muir, 42nd Regt of Foot, amphibious assault on Kerch

1770 Sgt. Maj. Edwards, Scots Fusilier Guards, gallant action, Battle of Inkerman

1771 Sgt. Powell, 1st Regt of Foot Guards, Battles of Alma and Inkerman

1772 Sgt. Maj. Poole, Royal Sappers and Miners, defensive line, Battle of Inkerman

1773 Sgt. Glasgow, Royal Artillery, gun battery besieged Sevastopol

Special First Day of Issue Postmarks

1773a

1774 Father Christmas on Snowy Roof

1775 Celebrating the Sunrise

1776 On Roof in Gale

1777 With Umbrella in Rain

1778 On Edge of Roof with Torch

1779 Sheltering behind Chimney

(Des Atelier Works. Litho Walsall)

2004 (12 Oct). *150th Anniv of the Crimean War. One centre phosphor band (2nd) or two phosphor bands (others).* P 14.

2489	**1768**	(2nd)	greyish silver, brownish grey, black and grey-black	70	70
			a. Greyish silver and phosphor omitted	£750	
2490	**1769**	(1st)	greyish silver, brownish grey, black and grey-black	90	90
2491	**1770**	40p.	greyish silver, brownish grey, black and grey-black	2·00	2·00
2492	**1771**	57p.	greyish silver, brownish grey, black and grey-black	2·50	2·50
			a. Imperf	£350	
2493	**1772**	68p.	greyish silver, brownish grey, black and grey-black	2·75	3·00
			a. Imperf	£1000	
2494	**1773**	£1.12	greyish silver, brownish grey, black and grey-black	4·50	5·00
Set of 6				12·00	12·00
Set of 6 *Gutter Pairs*				20·00	
Set of 6 *Traffic Light Gutter Pairs*				25·00	
First Day Cover (Tallents House)					13·50
First Day Cover (London SW3)					13·50
Presentation Pack				12·50	
PHQ Cards (*set of* 6)				5·75	14·00

Nos. 2489/94 show "Crimean Heroes" photographs taken in 1856.

(Des R. Briggs. Photo De La Rue)

2004 (2 Nov). *Christmas. One centre phosphor band (2nd) or two phosphor bands (others).* P 14½×14.

(a) Self-adhesive.

2495	**1774**	(2nd)	magenta, greenish yellow, new blue and black	70	70
			a. Booklet pane. No. 2495×24	16·00	
2496	**1775**	(1st)	magenta, greenish yellow, new blue and black	90	90
			a. Booklet pane. No. 2496×12	11·00	
2497	**1776**	40p.	magenta, greenish yellow, new blue and black	1·30	1·30
2498	**1777**	57p.	magenta, greenish yellow, new blue and black	1·80	1·80
2499	**1778**	68p.	magenta, greenish yellow, new blue and black	2·20	2·20
2500	**1779**	£1.12	magenta, greenish yellow, new blue and black	3·75	3·75
Set of 6				11·00	12·00
First Day Cover (Tallents House)					13·50
First Day Cover (Bethlehem, Llandeilo)					13·50
Presentation Pack				12·50	
PHQ Cards (*set of* 7)				6·75	14·00

(b) PVA gum.

MS2501 115×105 mm. As Nos. 2495/500	10·50	10·50
First Day Cover (Tallents House)		13·50
First Day Cover (Bethlehem, Llandeilo)		13·50

Nos. 2495/500 were each printed in sheets of 50 with the surplus backing paper around each stamp removed.

The seven PHQ cards depict the six individual stamps and the miniature sheet.

The 2nd and 1st class were also issued together in sheets of 20, sold at £5.40, containing ten 2nd class and ten 1st class, each value arranged in vertical rows of five alternated with rows of half stamp-size labels showing Father Christmas. Separate sheets of 20 2nd class and 20 1st class were available with personalised photographs at £9.95 (2nd class) or £14.95 (1st class) from Royal Mail, Edinburgh. These sheets were printed in lithography instead of photogravure and had the backing paper around the stamps retained.

Special First Day of Issue Postmarks

Collectors Pack 2004

2004 (2 Nov). *Comprises Nos.* 2417/22, 2424/44, 2446/53, 2456/61, 2466/71 *and* 2473/500.

CP2500a Collectors Pack .... 65·00

Post Office Yearbook

2004 (2 Nov). *Comprises Nos.* 2417/22, 2424/44, 2446/53, 2456/61, 2466/71 *and* 2473/500 *in hardback book with slipcase* .... 80·00

1780 British Saddleback Pigs

1781 Khaki Campbell Ducks

1782 Clydesdale Mare and Foal

1783 Dairy Shorthorn Cattle

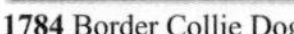

1784 Border Collie Dog

1785 Light Sussex Chicks

1786 Suffolk Sheep

1787 Bagot Goat

1788 Norfolk Black Turkeys

1789 Embden Geese

(Des C. Wormell. Photo Enschedé)

2005 (11 Jan). *Farm Animals. Two phosphor bands.* P 14½.

No.	Type	Description	Unused	Used
2502	**1780**	(1st) grey, grey-black, new blue, magenta and greenish yellow	1·00	1·00
		a. Block of 10. Nos. 2502/11	10·00	12·00
2503	**1781**	(1st) grey, grey-black, new blue, magenta and greenish yellow	1·00	1·00
2504	**1782**	(1st) grey, grey-black, new blue, magenta and greenish yellow	1·00	1·00
2505	**1783**	(1st) grey, grey-black, new blue, magenta and greenish yellow	1·00	1·00
2506	**1784**	(1st) grey, grey-black, new blue, magenta and greenish yellow	1·00	1·00
2507	**1785**	(1st) grey, grey-black, new blue, magenta and greenish yellow	1·00	1·00
2508	**1786**	(1st) grey, grey-black, new blue, magenta and greenish yellow	1·00	1·00
2509	**1787**	(1st) grey, grey-black, new blue, magenta and greenish yellow	1·00	1·00
2510	**1788**	(1st) grey, grey-black, new blue, magenta and greenish yellow	1·00	1·00
2511	**1789**	(1st) grey, grey-black, new blue, magenta and greenish yellow	1·00	1·00
		Set of 10	9·00	9·00
		Gutter Block of 20	16·00	
		Traffic Light Gutter Block of 20	20·00	
		First Day Cover (Tallents House)		12·00
		First Day Cover (Paddock, Huddersfield)		12·00
		Presentation Pack	13·00	
		PHQ Cards (*set of* 10)	7·25	14·00

Nos. 2502/11 were printed together, *se-tenant*, in blocks of 10 (5×2) throughout sheets of 30. Nos. 2502/11 were also issued in sheets of 20, containing two of each of the ten designs, arranged in vertical strips of five alternated with printed labels showing black/white illustrations of farm scenes. These sheets were printed in lithography by Walsall and sold for £6.15.

They were also available with personal photographs on the labels at £14.95 per sheet from Royal Mail, Edinburgh.

Special First Day of Issue Postmarks

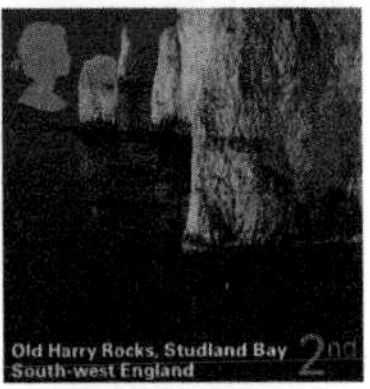

1790 Old Harry Rocks, Studland Bay

1791 Wheal Coates, St. Agnes

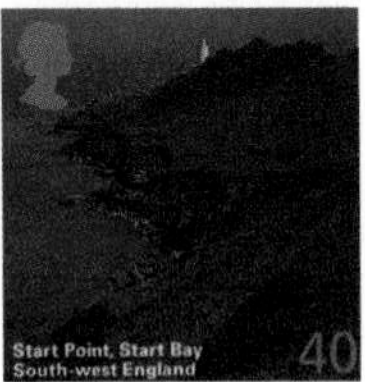

1792 Start Point, Start Bay

1793 Horton Down, Wiltshire

1794 Chiselcombe, Exmoor

1795 St. James's Stone, Lundy

(Des J. Phelan and Lissa Barker. Photo De La Rue)

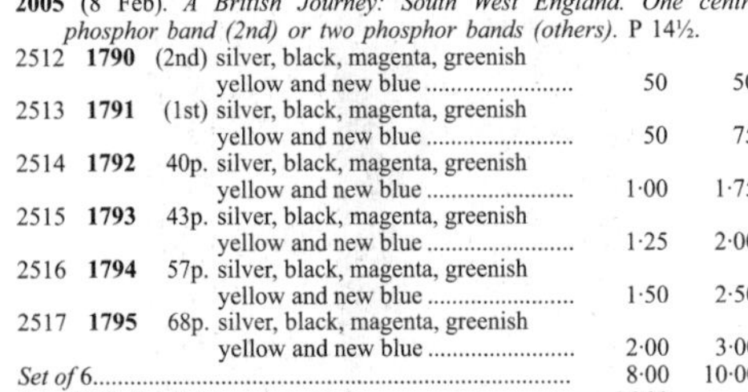

2005 (8 Feb). *A British Journey: South West England. One centre phosphor band (2nd) or two phosphor bands (others).* P 14½.

2512	**1790**	(2nd)	silver, black, magenta, greenish yellow and new blue	50	50
2513	**1791**	(1st)	silver, black, magenta, greenish yellow and new blue	50	75
2514	**1792**	40p.	silver, black, magenta, greenish yellow and new blue	1·00	1·75
2515	**1793**	43p.	silver, black, magenta, greenish yellow and new blue	1·25	2·00
2516	**1794**	57p.	silver, black, magenta, greenish yellow and new blue	1·50	2·50
2517	**1795**	68p.	silver, black, magenta, greenish yellow and new blue	2·00	3·00
Set of 6				8·00	10·00
Set of 6 *Gutter Pairs*				16·00	
First Day Cover (Tallents House)					10·00
First Day Cover (The Lizard, Helston)					10·00
Presentation Pack				8·75	
PHQ Cards (*set of* 6)				4·25	10·00

Special First Day of Issue Postmarks

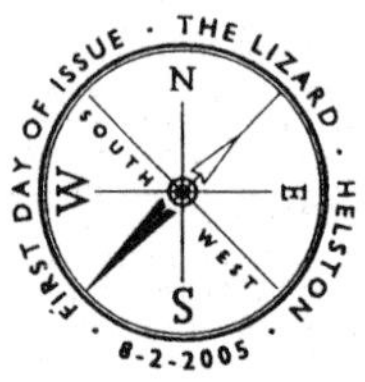

1796 "Mr Rochester"

1797 "Come to Me"

1798 "In the Comfort of her Bonnet"

1799 "La Ligne des Rats"

1800 "Refectory"

1801 "Inspection"

(Des P. Willberg. Litho Walsall)

2005 (24 Feb). *150th Death Anniv of Charlotte Bronte. Illustrations of scenes from Jane Eyre by Paula Rego. One centre phosphor band (2nd), or two phosphor bands (others).* P 14×14½.

2518	**1796**	(2nd)	silver, sage-green, brownish grey and black	30	35
			a. Booklet pane. Nos. 2518/19, both ×2, with margins all round	1·40	
2519	**1797**	(1st)	silver, lemon, magenta, new blue and black	40	45
2520	**1798**	40p.	silver, lemon, magenta, new blue and black	85	65
			a. Booklet pane. Nos. 2520/3 with margins all round	4·25	
2521	**1799**	57p.	silver, brownish grey and black	1·85	90
2522	**1800**	68p.	silver, pale brownish grey, lemon, magenta, new blue and black	2·00	1·10
2523	**1801**	£1.12	silver, brownish grey and black	2·70	1·80
Set of 6				8·00	10·00
Set of 6 *Gutter Pairs*				16·50	
Set of 6 *Traffic Light blocks of* 4				25·00	
First Day Cover (Tallents House)					11·00
First Day Cover (Haworth, Keighley)					11·00
Presentation Pack				9·00	
PHQ Cards (*set of* 7)				11·00	11·00
MS2524 114×105 mm. Nos. 2518/23				8·00	10·00
First Day Cover (Tallents House)					11·00
First Day Cover (Haworth, Keighley)					11·00

The complete miniature sheet is shown on one of the PHQ cards with the others depicting individual stamps.

Special First Day of Issue Postmarks

1802 Spinning Coin

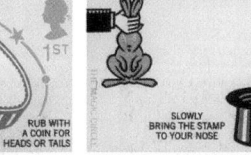

1803 Rabbit out of Hat Trick

1804 Knotted Scarf Trick

1805 Card Trick

1806 Pyramid under Fez Trick

(Des G. Hardie and Tatham Design. Photo Walsall)

2005 (15 Mar). *Centenary of the Magic Circle. Two phosphor bands.* P 14½×14.

2525	**1802**	(1st)	brownish grey, bright blue, yellow-orange and black	65	45
2526	**1803**	40p.	brownish grey, turquoise-green, bright violet, yellow-orange and black	85	65
2527	**1804**	47p.	brownish grey, bright mauve, bright violet, turquoise-green, yellow-orange and black	1·95	1·00
2528	**1805**	68p.	brownish grey, turquoise-green, rosine and black	2·00	1·10
2529	**1806**	£1.12	brownish grey, bright mauve, new blue, lilac, reddish violet and black	2·70	1·80
Set of 5				8·00	10·00
Set of 5 Gutter Pairs				16·50	
First Day Cover (Tallents House)					11·75
First Day Cover (London NW1)					11·75
Presentation Pack				9·00	
PHQ Cards (*set of* 5)				2·25	11·75

Nos. 2525/9 are each printed with instructions for the illusion or trick on the stamp. No. 2525 can be rubbed with a coin to reveal the "head" or "tail" of a coin. The two versions, which appear identical before rubbing, are printed in alternate rows of the sheet, indicated by the letters H and T in the side margins of the sheet. Nos. 2526 and 2528 each show optical illusions. The bright mauve on No. 2527 and the bright mauve, new blue, and lilac on No. 2529 are printed in thermochromic inks which fade temporarily when exposed to heat, making the pyramid under the centre fez visible.

The 1st class stamp was also issued in sheets of 20, printed in lithography instead of photogravure and sold at £6.15, containing vertical rows of five stamps alternated with half stamp-size printed labels illustrating magic tricks. These sheets were also available with personal photographs on the labels at £14.95 per sheet from Royal Mail, Edinbugh.

Special First Day of Issue Postmarks

(Des Sedley Place. Recess and litho Enschedé)

2005 (22 Mar). *50th Anniv of First Castles Definitives. Sheet 127×73 mm, containing horiz designs as T* **166/9** *(Castles definitive of 1955–58) but with values in decimal currency, printed on pale cream. "All-over" phosphor.* P 11×11½.

MS2530 **166** 50p. brownish-black; **169** 50p. black; **167** £1 dull vermilion; 168 $1 royal blue	8·00	10·00
First Day Cover (Tallents House)		12·00
First Day Cover (Windsor)		12·00
Presentation Pack	8·75	
PHQ Cards (*set of* 5)	2·20	12·00

The five PHQ cards depict the whole miniature sheet and the four stamps it contains.

Special First Day of Issue Postmarks

1807 (*Illustration reduced. Actual size* 85×115 *mm*)

(Des Rose Design. Litho Enschedé)

2005 (9 Apr). *Royal Wedding. Sheet 85×115 mm. Multicoloured. "All-over" phosphor.* P 13½×14.

MS2531 30p.×2 Prince Charles and Mrs Camilla Parker Bowles laughing; 68p.×2 Prince Charles and Mrs Camilla Parker Bowles smiling into camera	5·00	5·00
First Day Cover (Tallents House)		5·75
First Day Cover (Windsor)		5·75
Presentation Pack	5·75	

No. **MS**2531 was officially issued on 9th April. It was originally intended for issue on 8th April, and many post offices put it on sale on that day. Royal Mail first day covers were dated 8th April, but could be ordered with a 9th April Windsor handstamp. Our prices cover either date.

Special First Day of Issue Postmarks

1808 Hadrian's Wall, England

1809 Uluru-Kata Tjuta National Park, Australia

1810 Stonehenge, England

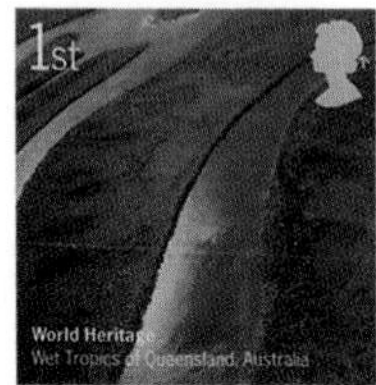

1811 Wet Tropics of Queensland, Australia

1812 Blenheim Palace, England

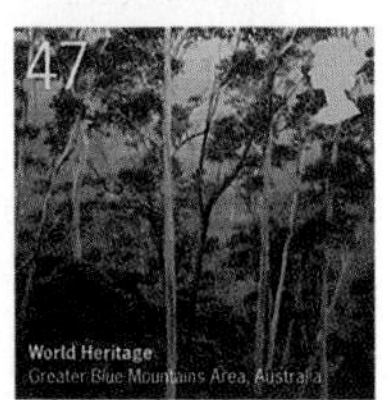

1813 Greater Blue Mountains Area, Australia

1814 Heart of Neolithic Orkney, Scotland

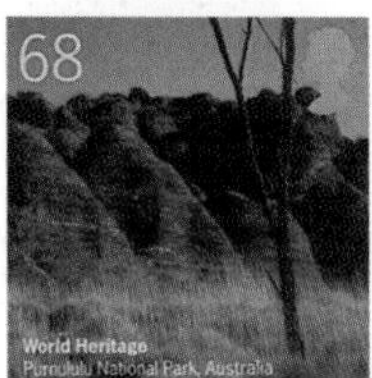

1815 Purnululu National Park, Australia

(Des J. Godfrey. Litho Enschedé)

2005 (21 Apr). *World Heritage Sites. One side phosphor band (2nd) or two phosphor bands (others).* P 14½.

2532	**1808**	2nd silver, black, magenta, new blue and greenish yellow	50	60
		a. Horiz pair. Nos. 2532/3	1·00	1·20
2533	**1809**	2nd silver, black, magenta, new blue and greenish yellow	50	60
2534	**1810**	1st silver, black, magenta, new blue and greenish yellow	70	75
		a. Horiz pair. Nos. 2534/5	1·40	1·50
2535	**1811**	1st silver, black, magenta, new blue and greenish yellow	70	75
2536	**1812**	47p. silver, black, magenta, new blue and greenish yellow	90	95
		a. Horiz pair. Nos. 2536/7	1·80	3·00
2537	**1813**	47p. silver, black, magenta, new blue and greenish yellow	90	95
2538	**1814**	68p. silver, black, magenta, new blue and greenish yellow	2·00	2·20
		a. Horiz pair. Nos. 2538/9	4·00	4·40
2539	**1815**	68p. silver, black, magenta, new blue and greenish yellow	2·00	2·20
		Set of 8	8·00	10·00
		Set of 4 *Gutter Strips of* 4	16·50	
		Set of 4 *Traffic Light Gutter blocks of* 8	35·00	
		First Day Cover (Tallents House)		11·00
		First Day Cover (Blenheim Palace, Woodstock)		11·00
		Presentation Pack	9·00	
		PHQ Cards (*set of* 8)	3·50	11·00

The two designs of each value were printed together, *se-tenant*, in horizontal pairs in sheets of 30 (6×5).

Stamps in these designs were also issued by Australia.

Special First Day of Issue Postmarks

1816 Ensign of the Scots Guards, 2002

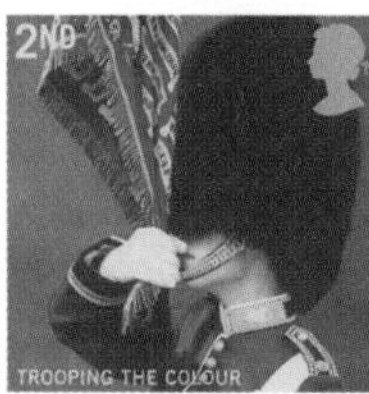

1817 Queen taking the salute as Colonel-in-Chief of the Grenadier Guards, 1983

1818 Trumpeter of the Household Cavalry, 2004

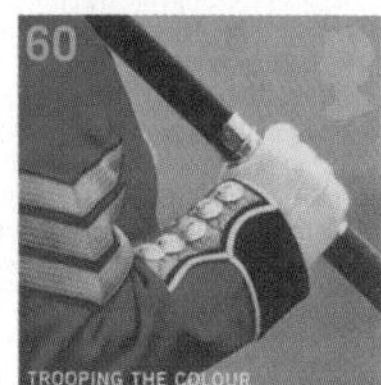

1819 Welsh Guardsman, 1990s

1820 Queen riding side-saddle, 1972

1821 Queen and Duke of Edinburgh in carriage, 2004

(Des A. Altmann. Litho Walsall)

2005 (7 June). *Trooping the Colour. One phosphor band (2nd), two phosphor bands (others).* P 14½.

No.	Type	Description	Unused	Used
2540	**1816**	(2nd) silver, greenish yellow, bright carmine, new blue and black	70	80
2541	**1817**	(1st) silver, greenish yellow, bright carmine, new blue and black	75	90
2542	**1818**	42p. silver, greenish yellow, bright carmine, new blue and black	1·00	1·20
2543	**1819**	60p. silver, greenish yellow, bright carmine, new blue and black	1·50	1·60
2544	**1820**	68p. silver, greenish yellow, bright carmine, new blue and black	1·70	1·80
2545	**1821**	£1.12 silver, greenish yellow, bright carmine, new blue and black	2·20	2·30
		Set of 6	8·00	9·00
		Set of 6 Gutter Pairs	11·00	
		First Day Cover (Tallents House)		10·00
		First Day Cover (London SW1)		10·00
		Presentation Pack	9·00	
		PHQ Cards (set of 6)	2·75	10·00
MS2546		115×105 mm. Nos. 2540/5	8·00	9·00
		First Day Cover (Tallents House)		10·00
		First Day Cover (London SW1)		10·00

Special First Day of Issue Postmarks

1822 (*Illustration reduced. Actual size* 115×105 *mm*)

(Des J. Matthews. Photo Enschedé)

2005 (5 July). *60th Anniv of End of the Second World War. Sheet 115×105 mm containing design as T* **1200** *(1995 Peace and Freedom) but with service indicator and No. 1664b×5. Two phosphor bands.* P 15×14 (with one elliptical hole on each vert side) (1664b) or 14½×14 (other).

No.	Description	Unused	Used
MS2547 **1822**	(1st) gold×5; (1st) silver, blue and grey-black	5·00	5·00
	First Day Cover (Tallents House)		5·75
	First Day Cover (Peacehaven, Newhaven)		5·75

Special First Day of Issue Postmarks

1823 Norton F.1, Road Version of Race Winner (1991)

1824 BSA Rocket 3, Early Three Cylinder "Superbike" (1969)

1825 Vincent Black Shadow, Fastest Standard Motorcycle (1949)

1826 Triumph Speed Twin, Two Cylinder Innovation (1938)

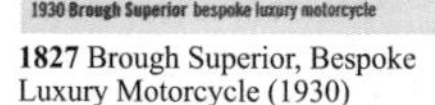

1827 Brough Superior, Bespoke Luxury Motorcycle (1930)

1828 Royal Enfield, Small Engined Motor Bicycle (1914)

(Des I. Chilvers and M. English. Litho Walsall)

2005 (19 July). *Motorcycles. Two phosphor bands.* P 14×14½.

No.	Type	Description	Unused	Used
2548	**1823**	(1st) silver, greenish yellow, bright crimson, new blue and black	75	80
2549	**1824**	40p. silver, greenish yellow, bright crimson, new blue and black	90	1·00
2550	**1825**	42p. silver, greenish yellow, bright crimson, new blue and black	95	1·00
2551	**1826**	47p. silver, greenish yellow, bright crimson, new blue and black	1·20	1·40
2552	**1827**	60p. silver, greenish yellow, bright crimson, new blue and black	1·50	1·80
2553	**1828**	68p. silver, greenish yellow, bright crimson, new blue and black	1·90	2·10
		Set of 6	7·00	7·50
		Set of 6 Gutter Pairs	14·25	
		First Day Cover (Tallents House)		8·25
		First Day Cover (Solihull)		8·25
		Presentation Pack	15·00	
		PHQ Cards (set of 6)	2·75	8·25

Special First Day of Issue Postmarks

1829 (*Illustration reduced. Actual size* 115×105 *mm*)

(Des CDT Design. Litho Walsall)

2005 (5 Aug). *London's Successful Bid for Olympic Games, 2012. Sheet 115×105 mm containing designs as T* **1255/9**, *but with service indicator. Multicoloured. Two phosphor bands.* P 14½.

MS2554 **1829** (1st) Athlete celebrating×2; (1st) Throwing the javelin; (1st) Swimming; (1st) Athlete on starting blocks; (1st) Basketball	5·00	5·00
First Day Cover (Tallents House)		5·75
First Day Cover (London E15)		5·75
Presentation Pack	5·50	

Stamps from **MS**2554 are all inscribed "London 2012—Host City" and have imprint date "2005". The design as Type **1259** omits the Olympic rings.

Special First Day of Issue Postmarks

1830 African Woman eating Rice

1831 Indian Woman drinking Tea

1832 Boy eating Sushi

1833 Woman eating Pasta

1834 Woman eating Chips

1835 Teenage Boy eating Apple

(Des Catell Ronca and Rose Design. Photo Enschedé)

2005 (23 Aug). *Europa. Gastronomy. Changing Tastes in Britain. One side phosphor band (2nd) or two phosphor bands (others).* P 14½.

2555	**1830**	(2nd)	olive-grey, grey-black, new blue, magenta and greenish yellow	60	70
2556	**1831**	(1st)	olive-grey, grey-black, new blue, magenta and greenish yellow	90	1·00
2557	**1832**	42p.	olive-grey, grey-black, new blue, magenta and greenish yellow	1·30	1·40
2558	**1833**	47p.	olive-grey, grey-black, new blue, magenta and greenish yellow	1·50	1·60
2559	**1834**	60p.	olive-grey, grey-black, new blue, magenta and greenish yellow	1·80	1·90
2560	**1835**	68p.	olive-grey, grey-black, new blue, magenta and greenish yellow	2·00	2·20
Set of 6				7·50	8·00
Set of 6 *Gutter Pairs*				15·50	
First Day Cover (Tallents House)					8·25
First Day Cover (Cookstown)					8·25
Presentation Pack				8·25	
PHQ Cards (*set of* 6)				2·75	8·25

Special First Day of Issue Postmarks

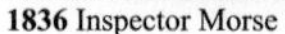

1836 Inspector Morse

1837 Emmerdale

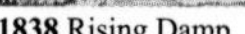

1838 Rising Damp

1839 The Avengers

1840 The South Bank Show

1841 Who Wants to be a Millionaire

(Des Kate Stephens. Litho DLR)

2005 (15 Sept). *50th Anniversary of Independent Television. Classic ITV Programmes. One side phosphor band (2nd) or two phosphor bands (others).* P 14½×14.

2561	**1836**	(2nd) new blue, magenta, greenish yellow and brownish-black	60	70
2562	**1837**	(1st) new blue, magenta, greenish yellow and brownish-black	90	1·00
2563	**1838**	42p. new blue, magenta, greenish yellow and brownish-black	1·30	1·40
2564	**1839**	47p. new blue, magenta, greenish yellow and brownish-black	1·40	1·50
2565	**1840**	60p. new blue, magenta, greenish yellow and brownish-black	1·80	1·90
2566	**1841**	68p. new blue, magenta, greenish yellow and brownish-black	2·00	2·20
Set of 6			7·50	8·00
Set of 6 *Gutter Pairs*			15·50	
First Day Cover (Tallents House)				8·25
First Day Cover (London SE19)				8·25
Presentation Pack			8·25	
PHQ Cards (*set of* 6)			1·80	8·25

The 1st class stamps were also issued in sheets of 20 sold at £6.55, printed in lithography by Walsall, containing four vertical rows of five stamps alternated with half stamp-size labels. These sheets with personalised photographs were available at £14.95 from the Royal Mail.

Special First Day of Issue Postmarks

1842 *Guzmania splendens* (Charlotte Sowerby)

(Photo Walsall)

2005 (4 Oct). *Smilers Booklet stamps. Designs as Types 992, 1221, 1286, 1517 and 1568/9 but smaller, 20×23 mm and inscribed "1st" as T* **1842.** *Self-adhesive. Two phosphor bands.* Die-cut p 15×14½.

2567	**1842**	(1st) multicoloured	90	1·00
		a. Booklet pane. Nos. 2567/72	5·00	
2568	**1569**	(1st) multicoloured	90	1·00
2569	**1568**	(1st) multicoloured	90	1·00
2570	**1517**	(1st) multicoloured	90	1·00
2571	**992**	(1st) multicoloured	90	1·00
2572	**1221**	(1st) multicoloured	90	1·00
Set of 6			5·00	6·00
First Day Cover (Tallents House) (Type K, see Introduction)				6·75
First Day Cover (Windsor) (Type K)				6·75

Nos. 2567/72 were only issued in £1.80 stamp booklets, No. QA1, in which the surplus backing paper around each stamp was removed.

Stamps in these designs in separate sheets printed in lithography by Cartor were available with personal photographs on the labels at £14.95 per sheet from Royal Mail, Edinburgh.

1843 Cricket Scenes (*Illustration reduced. Actual size* 115×90 *mm*)

(Des Why Not Associates. Litho Cartor)

2005 (6 Oct). *England's Ashes Victory. Sheet 115×90 mm. Multicoloured. Two phosphor bands.* P 14½×14.

MS2573 **1843** (1st) England team with Ashes trophy; (1st) Kevin Pieterson, Michael Vaughan and Andrew Flintoff on opening day of First Test, Lords; 68p. Michael Vaughan, Third Test, Old Trafford; 68p. Second Test cricket, Edgbaston	5·00	5·00
First Day Cover (Tallents House)		5·75
First Day Cover (London SE11)		5·75
Presentation Pack	5·75	

Special First Day of Issue Postmarks

1844 *Entrepreante* with dismasted British *Belle Isle*

1845 Nelson wounded on Deck of HMS *Victory*

1846 British Cutter *Entrepreante* attempting to rescue Crew of burning French *Achille*

1847 Cutter and HMS *Pickle* (schooner)

1848 British Fleet attacking in Two Columns

1849 Franco/Spanish Fleet putting to Sea from Cadiz

(Des D. Davis. Litho Cartor)

2005 (18 Oct). *Bicentenary of the Battle of Trafalgar (1st issue). Scenes from "Panorama of the Battle of Trafalgar" by William Heath. Two phosphor bands.* P 15×14½.

2574	**1844**	(1st)	gold, deep bluish-green, greenish yellow, magenta, new blue and black	90	1·00
			a. Horiz pair. Nos. 2574/5	1·75	2·00
			b. Booklet pane. Nos. 2574, 2576 and 2578	4·20	
2575	**1845**	(1st)	gold, deep bluish-green, greenish yellow, magenta, new blue and black	90	1·00
			b. Booklet pane. Nos. 2575, 2577 and 2579	4·25	
2576	**1846**	42p.	gold, deep bluish-green, greenish yellow, magenta, new blue and black	1·30	1·40
			a. Horiz pair. Nos. 2576/7	2·50	2·75
2577	**1847**	42p.	gold, deep bluish-green, greenish yellow, magenta, new blue and black	1·25	1·40
2578	**1848**	68p.	gold, deep bluish-green, greenish yellow, magenta, new blue and black	2·00	2·20
			a. Horiz pair. Nos. 2578/9	4·00	4·40
2579	**1849**	68p.	gold, deep bluish-green, greenish yellow, magenta, new blue and black	2·00	2·20
Set of 6				8·00	9·00
Set of 3 *Gutter Strips of* 4				17·00	
First Day Cover (Tallents House)					9·75
First Day Cover (Portsmouth)					9·75
Presentation Pack				8·50	
PHQ Cards (*set of* 7)				3·00	9·75
MS2580 190×68 mm. Nos. 2574/9				8·00	9·00
First Day Cover (Tallents House)					9·75
First Day Cover (Portsmouth)					9·75

Nos. 2574/5, 2576/7 and 2578/9 were each printed together, *se-tenant*, in horizontal pairs throughout the sheets, each pair forming a composite design.

The phosphor bands are at just left of centre and at right of each stamp.

The seven PHQ cards depict the six individual stamps and the miniature sheet.

Special First Day of Issue Postmarks

(Litho Cartor)

2005 (18 Oct). *Bicentenary of the Battle of Trafalgar (2nd issue). Booklet stamp. Design as Type* **1516** *(2001 White Ensign from Submarine Centenary). Two phosphor bands.* P 14½.

2581	**1516**	(1st)	multicoloured	1·25	1·25
			a. Booklet pane. No. 2581×3 with margins all round	3·50	

1850 Black Madonna and Child from Haiti

1851 "Madonna and Child" (Marianne Stokes)

1852 "The Virgin Mary with the Infant Christ"

1853 Choctaw Virgin Mother and Child (Fr. John Giuliani)

1854 "Madonna and the Infant Jesus" (from India)

1855 "Come let us adore Him" (Dianne Tchumut)

(Des Irene Von Trekow. Photo De La Rue)

2005 (1 Nov). *Christmas. Madonna and Child Paintings. One side phosphor band (2nd) or two phosphor bands (others).* P 14½×14.

(a) Self-adhesive

2582	**1850**	(2nd)	silver, magenta, greenish yellow, new blue and black	60	70
			a. Booklet pane. No. 2582×24	14·00	
2583	**1851**	(1st)	silver, magenta, greenish yellow, new blue and black	90	1·00
			a. Booklet pane. No. 2583×12	10·50	

No.	Type	Description	Unused	Used
2584	**1852**	42p. silver, magenta, greenish yellow, new blue and black	1·30	1·40
2585	**1853**	60p. silver, magenta, greenish yellow, new blue and black	1·80	1·90
2586	**1854**	68p. silver, magenta, greenish yellow, new blue and black	2·00	2·20
2587	**1855**	£1.12 silver, magenta, greenish yellow, new blue and black	3·40	3·60
		Set of 6	9·50	10·00
		First Day Cover (Tallents House)		7·25
		First Day Cover (Bethlehem, Llandeilo)		7·25
		Presentation Pack	10·25	
		PHQ Cards (*set of* 6)	3·00	8·50

The seven PHQ cards depict the six individual stamps and the miniature sheet.

(b) PVA gum

Description	Unused	Used
MS2588 115×102 mm. As Nos. 2582/7	9·50	10·00
First Day Cover (Tallents House)		10·75
First Day Cover (Bethlehem, Llandeilo)		10·75

Special First Day of Issue Postmarks

Collectors Pack

2005 (1 Nov). Comprises Nos. 2502/23, 2525/9. **MS**2531/45, 2548/53, 2555/66, 2574/9 and 2582/7.

Description	Price
CP2587a Collectors Pack	50·00

Post Office Yearbook

2005 (1 Nov). Comprises Nos. 2502/23, 2525/9, **MS**2531/45, 2548/53, 2555/66, MS2574/9 and 2582/7.

Description	Price
YB2587a Yearbook	60·00

Miniature Sheet Collection

2005 (1 Nov). Comprises Nos. **MS**2524, **MS**2530/1, **MS**2546/7, **MS**2554. **MS**2580 and **MS**2588.

Description	Price
MS2588*a* Miniature Sheet Collection	33·00

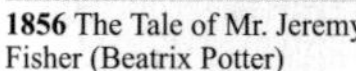

1856 The Tale of Mr. Jeremy Fisher (Beatrix Potter)

1857 Kipper (Mick Inkpen)

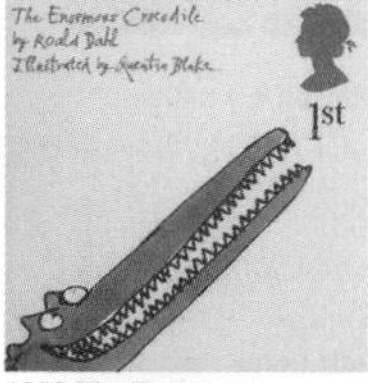

1858 The Enormous Crocodile (Roald Dahl)

1859 More About Paddington (Michael Bond)

1860 Comic Adventures of Boots (Satoshi Kitamura)

1861 Alice's Adventures in Wonderland (Lewis Carroll)

1862 The Very Hungry Caterpillar (Eric Carle)

1863 Maisy's ABC (Lucy Cousins)

(Des Rose Design. Litho DLR)

2006 (10 Jan). *Animal Tales. One side phosphor band (2nd) or two phosphor bands (others).* P 14½.

No.	Type	Description	Unused	Used
2589	**1856**	(2nd) brownish-black, new blue, magenta, greenish yellow and black	30	35
		a. Horiz pair. Nos. 2589/90	60	70
2590	**1857**	(2nd) brownish-black, new blue, magenta, greenish yellow and black	30	35
2591	**1858**	(1st) brownish-black, new blue, magenta, greenish yellow and black	45	50
		a. Horiz pair. Nos. 2591/2	90	1·00
2592	**1859**	(1st) brownish-black, new blue, magenta, greenish yellow and black	45	50
2593	**1860**	42p. brownish-black, new blue, magenta, greenish yellow and black	65	70
		a. Horiz pair. Nos. 2593/4	1·30	1·40
2594	**1861**	42p. brownish-black, new blue, magenta, greenish yellow and black	65	70
2595	**1862**	68p. brownish-black, new blue, magenta, greenish yellow and black	1·00	1·10
		a. Horiz pair. Nos. 2595/6	2·00	2·20
2596	**1863**	68p. brownish-black, new blue, magenta, greenish yellow and black	1·00	1·10
		Set of 8	4·75	5·25
		Set of 4 *Gutter Strips of* 4	9·75	
		Set of 4 *Traffic Light Gutter blocks of* 8	22·00	
		First Day Cover (Tallents House)		6·25
		First Day Cover (Mousehole, Penzance, Cornwall)		6·25
		Presentation Pack	5·50	
		PHQ Cards (*set of* 8)	3·50	7·75

Nos. 2589/90, 2591/2, 2593/4 and 2595/6 were printed together, *se-tenant*, in horizontal pairs in sheets of 30.

A design as No. 2592 but self-adhesive was issued in sheets of 20, sold at £6.55, containing four vertical rows of five stamps alternated with printed labels. This sheet was also available with personal photographs on the labels at £14.95 from Royal Mail.

No. 2595 contains two die-cut holes.

Special First Day of Issue Postmarks

1864 Carding Mill Valley, Shropshire

1865 Beachy Head, Sussex

1866 St. Paul's Cathedral, London

1867 Brancaster, Norfolk

1868 Derwent Edge, Peak District

1869 Robin Hood's Bay, Yorkshire

1870 Buttermere, Lake District

1871 Chipping Campden, Cotswolds

1872 St. Boniface Down, Isle of Wight

1873 Chamberlain Square, Birmingham

(Des Phelan Barker Design Consultants. Photo DLR)

2006 (7 Feb). *A British Journey: England. Two phosphor bands.* P 14½.

2597	**1864**	(1st) silver, black, rosine, greenish yellow and new blue	45	50
		a. Block of 10. Nos. 2597/606	4·50	5·00
2598	**1865**	(1st) silver, black, rosine, greenish yellow and new blue	45	50
2599	**1866**	(1st) silver, black, rosine, greenish yellow and new blue	45	50
2600	**1867**	(1st) silver, black, rosine, greenish yellow and new blue	45	50
2601	**1868**	(1st) silver, black, rosine, greenish yellow and new blue	45	50
2602	**1869**	(1st) silver, black, rosine, greenish yellow and new blue	45	50
2603	**1870**	(1st) silver, black, rosine, greenish yellow and new blue	45	50
2604	**1871**	(1st) silver, black, rosine, greenish yellow and new blue	45	50
2605	**1872**	(1st) silver, black, rosine, greenish yellow and new blue	45	50
2606	**1873**	(1st) silver, black, rosine, greenish yellow and new blue	45	50
Set of 10			4·50	5·00
Gutter Block of 20			9·25	
First Day Cover (Tallents House)				6·00
First Day Cover (Tea Green, Luton)				6·00
Presentation Pack			5·25	
PHQ Cards (*set of* 10)			4·50	9·50

Nos. 2597/606 were printed together, *se-tenant*, in blocks of ten (5×2) throughout the sheets of 30.

First Day of Issue Postmarks

1874 Royal Albert Bridge

1875 Box Tunnel

1876 Paddington Station

1877 *Great Eastern* (paddle steamer)

1878 Clifton Suspension Bridge Design

1879 Maidenhead Bridge

(Des Hat-trick Design. Litho Enschedé)

2006 (23 Feb). *Birth Bicentenary of Isambard Kingdom Brunel (engineer) (1st issue). Phosphor-coated paper (42p.) or two phosphor bands (others).* P 14×13½.

2607	**1874**	(1st) silver, black, new blue, magenta and greenish yellow	45	50
		a. Booklet pane. Nos. 2607, 2609 and 2612	2·10	
2608	**1875**	40p. silver, black, new blue, magenta and greenish yellow	60	65
		a. Booklet pane. Nos. 2608 and 2610/11	2·20	
2609	**1876**	42p. silver, black, new blue, magenta and greenish yellow	65	70
2610	**1877**	47p. silver, black, new blue, magenta and greenish yellow	70	75
		a. Booklet pane. No. 2610 and No. 2614×2	2·75	
2611	**1878**	60p. silver, black, new blue, magenta and greenish yellow	90	95
2612	**1879**	68p. silver, black, new blue, magenta and greenish yellow	1·00	1·10
Set of 6			4·25	4·50
Set of 6 Gutter Pairs			8·75	
First Day Cover (Tallents House)				5·75
First Day Cover (Bristol)				5·75
Presentation Pack			5·00	
PHQ Cards (set of 7)			3·00	8·00
MS2613 190×65 mm. Nos. 2607/12			4·25	4·50
First Day Cover (Tallents House)				5·75
First Day Cover (Bristol)				5·75

The phosphor bands on Nos. 2607/8 and 2610/12 are at just left of centre and at right of each stamp.

The complete miniature sheet is shown on one of the PHQ Cards with the others depicting individual stamps.

First Day of Issue Postmarks

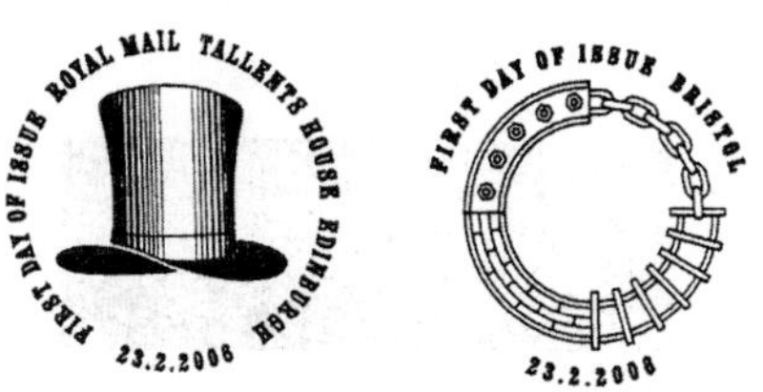

(Litho Enschedé)

2006 (23 Feb). *Birth Bicentenary of Isambard Kingdom Brunel (2nd issue). Booklet stamp. Design as Type* **1739** *("PS Great Western" from 2004 Ocean Liners). Two phosphor bands.* P 14½×14.

2614	**1739**	68p. multicoloured	1·10	1·10

No. 2614 was only available in stamp booklets, No. DX36.

1880 Sabre-tooth Cat

1881 Giant Deer

1882 Woolly Rhino

1883 Woolly Mammoth

1884 Cave Bear

2006 (21 Mar). *Ice Age Animals. Two phosphor bands.* P 14½.

2615	**1880**	(1st) black and silver	45	50
2616	**1881**	42p. black and silver	65	70
2617	**1882**	47p. black and silver	70	75
2618	**1883**	68p. black and silver	1·00	1·10
2619	**1884**	£1.12 black and silver	1·70	1·80
Set of 5			4·50	4·75
Set of 5 Gutter Pairs			9·25	
First Day Cover (Tallents House)				6·00
First Day Cover (Freezywater, Enfield)				6·00
Presentation Pack			5·25	
PHQ Cards (set of 5)			2·20	6·00

Special First Day of Issue Postmarks

ROYAL MAIL POSTAGE LABELS

These imperforate labels were issued as an experiment by the Post Office. Special microprocessor controlled machines were installed at post offices in Cambridge, London, Shirley (Southampton) and Windsor to provide an after-hours sales service to the public. The machines printed and dispensed the labels according to the coins inserted and the buttons operated by the customer. Values were initially available in ½p. steps to 16p. and in addition, the labels were sold at philatelic counters in two packs containing either 3 values (3½, 12½, 16p.) or 32 values (½p. to 16p.).

From 28 August 1984 the machines were adjusted to provide values up to 17p. After 31 December 1984 labels including ½p. values were withdrawn. The machines were taken out of service on 30 April 1985.

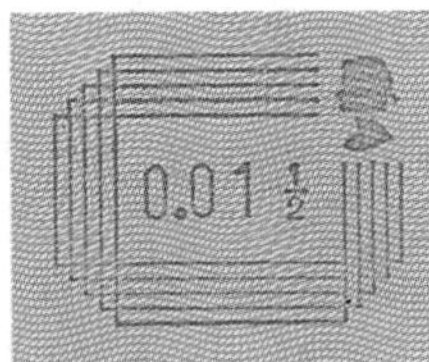

Machine postage-paid impression in red on phosphorised paper with grey-green background design. No watermark. Imperforate.

1984 (1 May–28 Aug).

Set of 32 (*½p. to 16p.*)	15·00	22·00
Set of 3 (*3½p., 12½p., 16p.*)	2·50	3·00
Set of 3 *on First Day Cover* (1.5.84)		6·50
Set of 2 (*16½p., 17p.*) (28.8.84)	4·00	3·00

REGIONAL ISSUES

CHANNEL ISLANDS

GENERAL ISSUE

C **1** Gathering Vraic

C **2** Islanders gathering Vraic

Broken Wheel (R. 20/5)

(Des J. R. R. Stobie (1d.) or from drawing by E. Blampied (2½d.). Photo Harrison)

1948 (10 May). *Third Anniv of Liberation.* W **127** *of Great Britain.* P 15×14.

C1	C **1**	1d. scarlet	25	30
C2	C **2**	2½d. ultramarine	25	30
		a. Broken wheel	15·00	
First Day Cover				35·00

PRINTERS (£.s.d. stamps of all regions):—Photo Harrison & Sons. Portrait by Dorothy Wilding Ltd.

DATES OF ISSUE. Conflicting dates of issue have been announced for some of the regional issues, partly explained by the stamps being released on different dates by the Philatelic Bureau in Edinburgh or the Philatelic Counter in London and in the regions. We have adopted the practice of giving the earliest known dates, since once released the stamps could have been used anywhere in the U.K.

I. ENGLAND

EN **1** Three Lions

EN **2** Crowned Lion with Shield of St. George

EN **3** Oak Tree

EN **4** Tudor Rose

(Des Sedley Place, from sculptures by D. Dathan. Photo Questa (No. EN1b) or De La Rue (others))

2001 (23 Apr)–**02**. *One centre phosphor band (2nd) or two phosphor bands (others).* P 15×14 (with one elliptical hole on each vertical side).

EN1	EN **1**	(2nd) slate-green and silver	60	40
		a. Imperf (pair)		
		b. Booklet pane. Nos. EN1/2, each×4, and No. S95, with margins all round (24.9.02)	6·00	
EN2	EN **2**	(1st) lake-brown and silver	75	60
EN3	EN **3**	(E) olive-green and silver	1·00	75
EN4	EN **4**	65p. deep reddish lilac and silver	2·50	2·25
EN5		68p. deep reddish lilac and silver (4.7.02)	2·00	1·75
Presentation Pack (*Nos.* EN1/4) (*P.O. Pack No.* 54)			7·00	
PHQ Cards (*Nos.* EN1/4) (*set of* 4)			1·50	10·00

Nos. EN1/3 were initially sold at 19p., 27p. and 36p., the latter representing the basic European airmail rate.

First Day Covers

23.4.01	2nd, 1st, E, 65p. (*EN1/4*) Philatelic Bureau (Type G, see Intorduction)	3·25
	Windsor	3·50
4.7.02	68p. (*EN5*) Tallents House (Type K, see Introduction)	1·75
	London (as Windsor)	2·00

Special First Day of Issue Postmark

Combined Presentation Packs for England, Northern Ireland, Scotland and Wales

4.7.02	P.O. Pack No. 59. 68p. from England, Northern Ireland, Scotland and Wales (*Nos.* EN5, NI93, S99, W88)	8·00
11.5.04	P.O. Pack No. 68. 40p from England, Northern Ireland, Scotland and Wales (*Nos.* EN9, NI97, S112, W101)	6·25
5.4.05	P.O Pack No. 69. 42p. from England, Northern Ireland, Scotland and Wales (*Nos.* EN10, NI98, S113, W102)	3·25

28.3.06 P.O. Pack No. 73. 44p. and 72p. from England, Northern Ireland, Scotland and Wales (Nos. EN11, EN13, NI99, NI101, S114, S116, W103, W105) .... 7·50

(Photo Walsall (No. EN6a) or De La Rue (others))

2003 (14 Oct)–**06**. *As Nos. EN1/3 and EN5, and new values, but with white borders. One centre phosphor band (2nd) or two phosphor bands (others).* P 15×14 (with one elliptical hole on each vertical side).

EN6	EN **1**	(2nd) slate-green and silver	65	50
		a. Booklet pane. Nos. EN6 and EN9, each×2, with central label and margins all round (24.2.05)	1·80	
EN7	EN **2**	(1st) lake-brown and silver	75	70
EN8	EN **3**	(E) olive-green and silver	1·00	90
EN9		40p. olive-green and silver (11.5.04)	1·25	1·25
EN10		42p. olive-green and silver (5.4.05)	65	70
EN11		44p. olive-green and silver (28.3.06)	65	70
EN12	EN **4**	68p. deep reddish lilac and silver	2·00	1·75
EN13		72p. deep reddish lilac and silver (28.3.06)	1·10	1·20
Presentation Pack (Nos. EN6/8, EN12) (*P.O. Pack No.* 63)			5·00	
PHQ Cards (Nos. EN6/8, EN12) (*set of* 4)			1·70	4·00

No. EN6a comes from booklet No. DX34.

First Day Covers

14.10.03	2nd, 1st, E, 68p. (*EN6/8, EN12*)	
	Tallents House (Type K, see Introduction)	3·25
	London (as Windsor)	3·50
11.5.04	40p. (*EN9*) Tallents House (Type K)	2·75
	London (as Windsor)	2·75
28.3.06	44p., 72p., (*EN11, EN13*) Tallents House (Type K)	2·75
	London (as Windsor)	2·75

II. NORTHERN IRELAND

N **1**

N **2**

N **3**

(Des W. Hollywood (3d., 4d., 5d.), L. Pilton (6d., 9d.), T. Collins (1s.3d., 1s.6d.))

1958–67. W **179**. P 15×14.

NI1	N **1**	3d. deep lilac (18.8.58)	15	10
		p. One centre phosphor band (9.6.67)	15	15
NI2		4d. ultramarine (7.2.66)	15	15
		p. Two phosphor bands (10.67)	15	15
NI3	N **2**	6d. deep claret (29.9.58)	20	25
NI4		9d. bronze-green (2 phosphor bands) (1.3.67)	30	70
NI5	N **3**	1s.3d. green (29.9.58)	30	70
NI6		1s.6d. grey-blue (2 phosphor bands) (1.3.67)	30	70
		Ey. Phosphor omitted	£200	

First Day Covers

18.8.58	3d. (*NI1*)	30·00
29.9.58	6d., 1s.3d. (*NI3, NI5*)	35·00
7.2.66	4d. (*NI2*)	7·00
1.3.67	9d., 1s.6d. (*NI4, NI6*)	4·00

For Nos. NI1, NI3 and NI5 in Presentation Pack, see below Wales No. W6.

1968–69. *No watermark. Chalk-surfaced paper. One centre phosphor band (Nos. NI8/9) or two phosphor bands (others). Gum arabic (No. NI7) or PVA gum (others).* P 15×14.

NI7	N **1**	4d. dp brt blue (27.6.68)	15	15
		Ev. PVA gum* (23.10.68)	13·00	
NI8		4d. olive-sepia (4.9.68)	15	15
		Ey. Phosphor omitted		
NI9		4d. brt vermilion (26.2.69)	20	20
		Ey. Phosphor omitted	4·50	
NI10		5d. royal blue (4.9.68)	20	20
		Ey. Phosphor omitted	25·00	
NI11	N **3**	1s.6d. grey-blue (20.5.69)	2·25	2·50
		Ey. Phosphor omitted	£500	

4.9.68	*First Day Cover* (NI8, NI10)	3·00
	Presentation Pack (containing Nos. NI1p, NI4/6, NI8/10) (9.12.70)	3·50

*No. NI7Ev was never issued in Northern Ireland. After No. NI7 (gum arabic) had been withdrawn from Northern Ireland but whilst still on sale at the philatelic counters elsewhere, about fifty sheets with PVA gum were sold over the London Philatelic counter on 23 October, 1968, and some were also on sale at the British Philatelic Exhibition Post Office.

N **4**

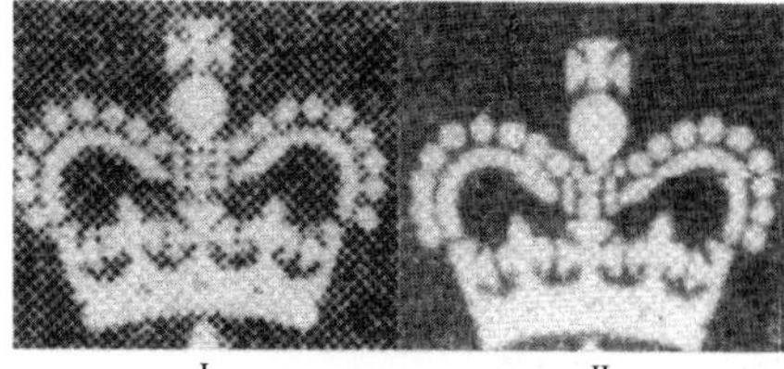
I II

Redrawn design of Type N 4 (litho ptgs.)

Two Types of Crown

Type I:–Crown with all pearls individually drawn.

Type II:–Crown with clear outlines, large pearls and strong white line below them. First 3 pearls at left are joined, except on Nos. NI39 and NI49.

The following stamps printed in lithography show a screened background behind and to the left of the emblem: 11½p., 12½p., 14p. (No. NI38), 15½p., 16p., 18p. (No. NI45), 19½p., 22p. (No. NI53) and 28p. (No. NI62). The 13p. and 17p. (No. NI43) also showed screened backgrounds in Type I, but changed to solid backgrounds for Type II. The 31p. had a solid background in Type I, but changed to a screened background for Type II. All other values printed in lithography have solid backgrounds.

(Des J. Matthews after plaster cast by Arnold Machin)

1971 (7 July)–**93**. *Decimal Currency. Chalk-surfaced paper. Type* N **4**.

(a) Photo Harrison. With phosphor bands. P 15×14.

NI12	2½p. brt magenta (1 centre band)	70	45
NI13	3p. ultramarine (2 bands)	30	25
	Ey. Phosphor omitted	50·00	
NI14	3p. ultramarine (1 centre band) (23.1.74)	20	15
NI15	3½p. olive-grey (2 bands) (23.1.74)	20	25
NI16	3½p. olive-grey (1 centre band) (6.11.74)	20	25
NI17	4½p. grey-blue (2 bands) (6.11.74)	30	25
NI18	5p. reddish violet (2 bands)	1·00	1·00
NI19	5½p. violet (2 bands) (23.1.74)	20	20
	Ey. Phosphor omitted	£250	
NI20	5½p. violet (1 centre band) (21.5.75)	20	25
NI21	6½p. greenish blue (1 centre band) (14.1.76)	20	20
NI22	7p. purple-brown (1 centre band) (18.1.78)	35	25
NI23	7½p. chestnut (2 bands)	1·25	1·25
	Ey. Phosphor omitted	£100	
NI24	8p. rosine (2 bands) (23.1.74)	35	35
	Ey. Phosphor omitted	75·00	
NI25	8½p. yellow-green (2 bands) (14.1.76)	35	40
NI26	9p. dp violet (2 bands) (18.1.78)	40	40
	Ey. Phosphor omitted	25·00	
NI27	10p. orange-brown (2 bands) (20.10.76)	40	50
NI28	10p. orange-brown (1 centre band) (23.7.80)	50	50
NI29	10½p. steel-blue (2 bands) (18.1.78)	40	50
NI30	11p. scarlet (2 bands) (20.10.76)	50	50
	Ey. Phosphor omitted	5·00	

(b) Photo Harrison. On phosphorised paper. P 15×14.

NI31	12p. yellowish green (23.7.80)	50	50
NI32	13½p. purple-brown (23.7.80)	60	70
NI33	15p. ultramarine (23.7.80)	60	70

(c) Litho Questa (Type II, unless otherwise stated). P 14 (11½p., 12½p., 14p. (No. NI38), 15½p., 16p., 18p. (No. NI45), 19½p., 20½p., 22p. (No. NI53), 26p. (No. NI60), 28p. (No. NI62)) or 15×14 (others).

NI34	11½p. drab (Type I) (1 side band) (8.4.81)	85	85

NI35	12p. brt emerald (1 side band) (7.1.86)	70	80
NI36	12½p. lt emerald (Type I) (1 side band) (24.2.82)	60	60
	a. Perf 15×14 (28.2.84)	5·25	5·25
NI37	13p. pale chestnut (Type I) (1 side band) (23.10.84)	80	50
	Ea. Type II (28.11.86)	1·50	75
	Ey. Phosphor omitted (Type I)		
NI38	14p. grey-blue (Type I) (phosphorised paper) (8.4.81)	75	75
NI39	14p. dp blue (1 centre band) (8.11.88)	75	60
NI40	15p. brt blue (1 centre band) (28.11.89)	90	60
NI41	15½p. pale violet (Type I) (phosphorised paper) (24.2.82)	80	80
NI42	16p. drab (Type I) (phosphorised paper) (27.4.83)	1·00	1·00
	a. Perf 15x14 (28.2.84)	8·25	8·50
NI43	17p. grey-blue (Type I) (phosphorised paper) (23.10.84)	90	95
	Ea. Type II (9.9.86)	£140	90·00
NI44	17p. dp blue (1 centre band) (4.12.90)	1·00	80
NI45	18p. dp violet (Type I) (phosphorised paper) (8.4.81)	1·00	1·00
NI46	18p. dp olive-grey (phosphorised paper) (6.1.87)	1·00	90
NI47	18p. brt green (1 centre band) (3.12.91)	1·00	95
	a. Perf 14 (31.12.92*)	2·50	2·50
NI48	18p. brt green (1 side band) (10.8.93)	2·25	2·25
	l. Booklet pane. Nos. NI48, NI59, S61, S71, W49Eb and W60 with margins all round	14·00	
NI49	19p. brt orange-red (phosphorised paper) (8.11.88)	1·00	1·00
NI50	19½p. olive-grey (Type I) (phosphorised paper) (24.2.82)	1·50	1·75
NI51	20p. brownish black (phosphorised paper) (28.11.89)	1·00	80
NI52	20½p. ultramarine (Type I) (phosphorised paper) (27.4.83)	4·50	4·25
NI53	22p. blue (Type I) (phosphorised paper) (8.4.81)	1·10	1·10
NI54	22p. yellow-green (Type I) (phosphorised paper) (23.10.84)	1·10	1·10
NI55	22p. brt orange-red (phosphorised paper) (4.12.90)	1·25	90
NI56	23p. brt green (phosphorised paper) (8.11.88)	1·25	1·10
NI57	24p. Indian red (phosphorised paper) (28.11.89)	1·25	1·25
NI58	24p. chestnut (phosphorised paper) (3.12.91)	1·10	90
NI59	24p. chestnut (2 bands) (10.8.93)	2·25	2·50
NI60	26p. rosine (Type I) (phosphorised paper) (24.2.82)	1·25	1·25
	a. Perf 15×14 (Type II) (27.1.87)	3·00	3·25
NI61	26p. drab (phosphorised paper) (4.12.90)	1·75	1·75
NI62	28p. dp violet-blue (Type I) (phosphorised paper) (27.4.83)	1·50	1·50
	a. Perf 15x14 (Type II) (27.1.87)	1·25	1·25
NI63	28p. dp bluish grey (phosphorised paper) (3.12.91)	1·50	1·50
NI64	31p. brt purple (Type I) (phosphorised paper) (23.10.84)	1·75	2·00
	Ea. Type II (14.4.87)	1·90	1·75
NI65	32p. greenish blue (phosphorised paper) (8.11.88)	1·75	1·75
NI66	34p. dp bluish grey (phosphorised paper) (28.11.89)	1·75	1·75
NI67	37p. rosine (phosphorised paper) (4.12.90)	2·00	2·50
NI68	39p. brt mauve (phosphorised paper) (3.12.91)	2·00	2·25

*Earliest known date of use.

No. NI47a was caused by the use of a reserve perforating machine for some printings in the second half of 1992.

Nos. NI48 and NI59 only come from booklets.

From 1972 printings were made on fluorescent white paper and from 1973 most printings had dextrin added to the PVA gum (see notes after 1971 Decimal Machin issue).

First Day Covers

7.7.71	2½p., 3p., 5p., 7½p. (*NI12/13, NI18, NI23*)	3·50
23.1.74	3p., 3½p., 5½p., 8p. (*NI14/15, NI19, NI24*)	2·40
6.11.74	4½p. (*NI17*)	1·50
14.1.76	6½p., 8½p. (*NI21, NI25*)	1·50
20.10.76	10p., 11p. (*NI27, NI30*)	1·75
18.1.78	7p., 9p., 10½p. (*NI22, NI26, NI29*)	1·75
23.7.80	12p., 13½p., 15p. (*NI31/3*)	3·00
8.4.81	11½p., 14p., 18p., 22p. (*NI34, NI38, NI45, NI53*)	2·50
24.2.82	12½p., 15½p., 19½p., 26p. (*NI36, NI41, NI50, NI60*)	4·00
27.4.83	16p., 20½p., 28p. (*NI42, NI52, NI62*)	4·00
23.10.84	13p., 17p., 22p., 31p. (*NI37, NI43, NI54, NI64*)	4·75
7.1.86	12p. (*NI35*)	2·00
6.1.87	18p. (*NI46*)	2·00
8.11.88	14p., 19p., 23p., 32p. (*NI39, NI49, NI56, NI65*)	4·25
28.11.89	15p., 20p., 24p., 34p. (*NI40, NI51, NI57, NI66*)	5·00
4.12.90	17p., 22p., 26p., 37p. (*NI44, NI55, NI61, NI67*)	5·00
3.12.91	18p., 24p., 28p., 39p. (*NI47, NI58, NI63, NI68*)	5·50

Presentation Packs

7.7.71	P.O. Pack No. 29. 2½p., 3p. (2 bands), 5p., 7½p. (*Nos.* NI12/13, NI18, NI23)	3·50
29.5.74	P.O. Pack No. 61. 3p. (1 centre band), 3½p. (2 bands) or (1 centre band), 5½p. (2 bands) or (1 centre band), 8p. (*Nos.* NI14, NI15 or NI16, NI19 or NI20, NI24). The 4½p. (No. NI17) was added later	2·25
20.10.76	P.O. Pack No. 84. 6½p., 8½p., 10p. (2 bands), 11p. (*Nos.* NI21, NI25, NI27, NI30)	2·00
28.10.81	P.O. Pack No. 129d. 7p., 9p., 10½p., 12p. (photo), 13½p., 15p. (photo), 11½p., 14p. grey-blue, 18p. dp violet, 22p. blue (*Nos.* NI22, NI26, NI29, NI31/4, NI38, NI45, NI53)	9·00
3.8.83	P.O. Pack No. 4. 10p. (1 centre band), 12½p., 16p., 20½p., 26p. rosine, 28p. dp violet-blue (*Nos.* NI28, NI36, NI42, NI52, NI60, NI62)	17·00
23.10.84	P.O. Pack No. 8. 10p. (1 centre band), 13p., 16p., 17p. grey-blue, 22p. yellow-green, 26p. rosine, 28p. dp violet-blue, 31p. (*Nos.* NI28, NI37, NI42a, NI43, NI54, NI60, NI62, NI64)	18·00
3.3.87	P.O. Pack No. 12. 12p. (litho), 13p., 17p. grey-blue, 18p. dp olive-grey, 22p. yellow-green, 26p. rosine, 28p. dp violet-blue, 31p. (*Nos.* NI35, NI37, NI43, NI46, NI54, NI60a, NI62a, NI64)	16·00

Presentation Packs for Northern Ireland, Scotland and Wales

8.11.88	P.O. Pack No. 17. 14p. dp blue, 19p., 23p., 32p. (*Nos.* NI39, NI49, NI56, NI65), 14p. (1 centre band), 19p. (phosphorised paper), 23p. (phosphorised paper), 32p. (*Nos.* S54, S62, S67, S77), 14p. dp blue, 19p., 23p., 32p. (*Nos.* W40, W50, W57, W66)	16·00
28.11.89	P.O. Pack No. 20. 15p. (litho), 20p., 24p. Indian red, 34p. (*Nos.* NI40, NI51, NI57, NI66), 15p. (litho), 20p., 24p. Indian red, 34p. (Nos. S56, S64, S69, S78), 15p. (litho), 20p., 24p. Indian red, 34p. (*Nos.* W41, W52, W58, W67)	15·00
4.12.90	P.O. Pack No. 23. 17p. dp blue, 22p. brt orange-red, 26p. drab, 37p., (Nos. NI44, NI55, NI61, NI67), 17p. dp blue, 22p. brt orange-red, 26p. drab, 37p, (*Nos.* S58, S66, S73, S79), 17p. dp blue, 22p. brt orange-red, 26p. drab, 37p. (*Nos.* W45, W56, W62, W68)	15·00
3.12.91	P.O. Pack No. 26. 18p. brt green, 24p. chestnut, 28p. dp bluish grey, 39p. (*Nos.* NI47, NI58, NI63, NI68), 18p. brt green, 24p. chestnut, 28p. dp bluish grey, 39p. (*Nos.* S60, S70, S75, S80), 18p. brt green, 24p. chestnut, 28p. dp bluish grey, 39p. (Nos. W48, W59, W64, W69)	15·00

(Des J. Matthews after plaster cast by Arnold Machin)

1993 (7 Dec)–**2000**. *Chalk-surfaced paper.*

(*a*) *Litho Questa.* P 15×14 (with one elliptical hole on each vertical side).

NI69	**N 4**	19p. bistre (1 centre band)	90	80
NI70		19p. bistre (1 band at left) (26.7.94)	1·25	1·75
		Ey. Phosphor omitted	£950	
		a. Booklet pane. Nos. NI70×2, NI72×4, NI74, NI76 and centre label with margins all round	8·00	
		b. Booklet pane. Nos. NI70, NI72, NI74 and NI76 with margins all round	6·00	
		bEy. Booklet pane. Phosphor omitted		
		Ec. Band at right (25.4.95)	2·50	2·50

No.	Type	Description	Mint	Used
		d. Booklet pane. Nos. NI70Ec, NI72, S82, S84, W71 and W73 with margins all round (25.4.95)	10·00	
		da. Part perf pane*		
NI71		20p. brt green (1 centre band) (23.7.96)	1·50	1·50
NI72		25p. red (2 bands)	75	75
		Ey. Phosphor omitted	£950	
NI73		26p. red-brown (2 bands) (23.7.96)	1·75	1·75
NI74		30p. dp olive-grey (2 bands)	1·25	1·25
		Ey. Phosphor omitted	£950	
NI75		37p. brt mauve (2 bands) (23.7.96)	2·75	3·00
NI76		41p. grey-brown (2 bands)	1·50	1·75
		Ey. Phosphor omitted	£950	
NI77		63p. lt emerald (2 bands) (23.7.96)	4·75	5·00

(b) Photo Walsall (19p., 20p., 26p. (No. NI81b), 38p., 40p., 63p., 64p., 65p.), Harrison or Walsall (26p. (No. NI81), 37p.). P 14 (No. NI80) or 15×14 (others) (both with one elliptical hole on each vertical side).

No.	Type	Description	Mint	Used
NI78	N **4**	19p. bistre (1 centre band) (8.6.99)	1·25	1·25
NI79		20p. brt green (1 centre band) (1.7.97)	75	70
NI80		20p. brt green (1 side band at right) (13.10.98)	2·75	3·00
		al. Booklet pane. Nos. NI80, S90a, W79a and Y1700a×3 with margins all round	10·00	
NI81		26p. chestnut (2 bands) (1.7.97)	1·25	1·00
		al. Booklet pane. Nos. NI81/2, S91/2 and W80/1 with margins all round (23.9.97)	6·00	
		b. Perf 14 (13.10.98)	2·75	2·75
NI82		37p. brt mauve (2 bands) (1.7.97)	2·25	2·25
NI83		38p. ultramarine (2 bands) (8.6.99)	4·25	4·00
NI84		40p. dp azure (2 bands) (25.4.00)	2·00	2·00
NI85		63p. lt emerald (2 bands) (1.7.97)	4·75	5·00
NI86		64p. turquoise-green (2 bands) (8.6.99)	6·00	6·00
NI87		65p. greenish blue (2 bands) (25.4.00)	2·75	3·00

*No. NI70da, which comes from the 1995 National Trust £6 booklet, shows the top two values in the pane of 6 (Nos. S82, S84) completely imperforate and the two Wales values below partly imperforate.

Nos. NI70, NI80 and NI81b only come from booklets.

The listed booklet panes come from the following Sponsored Booklets:

NI70a/b	–Booklet DX16
NI70d	–Booklet DX17
NI80al	–Booklet DX21
NI81al	–Booklet DX19

First Day Covers

7.12.93	19p., 25p., 30p., 41p. (*NI69, NI72, NI74, NI76*)	6·00
26.7.94	Northern Ireland *se-tenant* pane 19p., 25p., 30p., 41p. (*NI70a*)	8·00
23.7.96	20p., 26p., 37p., 63p. (*NI71, NI73, NI75, NI77*)	8·75
8.6.99	38p., 64p. (*NI83, NI86*)	4·00
25.4.00	1st, 40p., 65p. (*NI84, NI87, NI88b*)	7·00

Presentation Packs

8.6.99	P.O. Pack No. 47. 19p., 26p., 38p., 64p. (*Nos.* NI78, NI81, NI83, NI86)	10·00
25.4.00	P.O. Pack No. 52. 1st, 40p., 65p. (*Nos.* NI88b, NI84, NI87)	10·00

Presentation Packs for Northern Ireland, Scotland and Wales

7.12.93	P.O. Pack No. 31. 19p., 25p., 30p., 41p., eachx3 (*Nos.* NI69, NI72, NI74, NI76, S81, S84, S86, S88, W70, W73, W75, W77)	15·00
23.7.96	P.O. Pack No. 36. 20p., 26p., 37p., 63p., eachx3 (*Nos.* NI71, NI73, NI75, NI77, S83, S85, S87, S89, W72, W74, W76, W78)	24·00
20.10.98	P.O. Pack No. 42. 20p. (*1 centre band*), 26p., 37p., 63p., eachx3 (*Nos.* NI79, NI81/2, NI85, S90/3, W79/82)	24·00

N **5**

(Des J. Matthews. Photo Walsall)

2000 (15 Feb). *Type* N **4** *redrawn with "1st" face value as Type* N **5**. *Two phosphor bands.* P 14 (with one elliptical hole on each vertical side).

No.	Type	Description	Mint	Used
NI88	N **5**	(1st) bright orange-red	2·75	2·75
		al. Booklet pane. Nos. NI88, S108 and W97, each×3 with margins all round	13·00	
		b. Perf 15×14 (25 Apr)	9·00	7·00
		First Day Cover (*se-tenant pane No.* NI88al) (Philatelic Bureau)		13·00
		First Day Cover (*se-tenant pane No.* NI88al) (London SW5)		13·00

No. NI88 was issued in £7.50 stamp booklets (No. DX24) and No. NI88b in sheets.

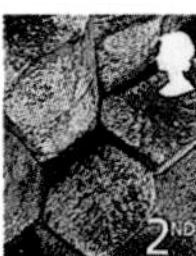

N **6** Basalt Columns, Giant's Causeway

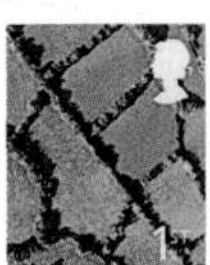

N **7** Aerial View of Patchwork Fields

N **8** Linen Pattern

N **9** Vase Pattern from Belleck

(Des Rodney Miller Associates. Litho De La Rue or Enschedé (1st, 2nd), De La Rue or Walsall (E), Walsall (65p.), De La Rue (68p.))

2001 (6 Mar)–**03**. *One centre phosphor band (2nd) or two phosphor bands (others).* P 15×14 (with one elliptical hole on each vertical side).

No.	Type	Description	Mint	Used
NI89	N **6**	(2nd) black, new blue, bright magenta and greenish yellow	50	35
		a. Booklet pane. No. NI89x5 and No. NI90x4 with margins all round (25.2.03)	5·50	
		Ey. Phosphor omitted	£600	
NI90	N **7**	(1st) black, new blue and greenish yellow	1·00	1·00
		Ey. Phosphor omitted	35·00	
NI91	N **8**	(E) black, new blue and pale orange	1·25	1·25
NI92	N **9**	65p. black, bright magenta and greenish yellow	2·75	2·75
NI93		68p. black, bright magenta and greenish yellow (4.7.02)	2·75	2·75
		Presentation Pack (*Nos.* NI89/92) (*P.O. Pack No.* 53)	7·00	
		PHQ Cards (*Nos.* NI89/92) (*set of* 4)	1·50	10·00

Nos. NI89, NI90 and NI91 were initially sold at 19p., 27p. and 36p., the latter representing the basic European airmail rate. A new printing of No. NI91, produced by De La Rue instead of Walsall, was issued on 15 October 2002. Stamps from this printing do not differ from those produced by Walsall. Booklet pane No. NI89a was printed by Enschedé. For combined presentation pack for all four Regions, see under England.

First Day Covers

6.3.01	2nd, 1st, E, 65p. (*NI89/92*)	
	Philatelic Bureau	4·50
	Belfast	5·00
4.7.02	68p. (NI93)	
	Tallents House (Type K, see Introduction)	2·50
	Belfast	3·00

Special First Day of Issue Postmarks

(Litho Walsall (NI98) or De La Rue (others))

2003 (14 Oct)–**06**. *As Nos. NI89/91 and NI93, and new values, but with white borders. One centre phosphor band (2nd) or two phosphor bands (others).* P 15×14 (with one elliptical hole on each vertical side).

NI94	N **6**	(2nd) black, new blue, bright magenta and greenish yellow	50	35
NI95	N **7**	(1st) black, new blue and greenish yellow	60	50
NI96	N **8**	(E) black and new blue	75	65
NI97		40p. black and new blue (11.5.04)	1·25	1·25
NI98		42p. black, new blue and orange yellow (5.4.05)	65	70
		a. Black, new blue and greenish-yellow (26.7.05)	65	70
NI99		44p. black, new blue and greenish yellow (28.3.06)	65	70
NI100	N **9**	68p. black, bright magenta* and greenish yellow	2·75	2·75
NI101		72p. black, greyish black, bright magenta and greenish yellow (28.3.06)	1·10	1·20
Presentation Pack (*Nos.* NI94/6, NI100) (*P.O. Pack No.* 66)			6·00	
PHQ Cards (*Nos.* NI94/6, NI100) (*set of* 4)			1·50	10·00

No NI98 (Walsall printing) appears bluish grey and No. NI98a (De La Rue printing) appears olive-grey.

*The bright magenta used on the 68p. is fluorescent.

First Day Covers

14.10.03	2nd, 1st, E, 68p. (*NI94/6, NI98*)	
	Tallents House (Type K, see Introduction)	3·25
	Belfast	3·25
11.5.04	40p. (*NI97*)	
	Tallents House (Type K)	2·75
	Belfast	2·75
28.3.06	44p., 72p. (*NI99, NI101*)	
	Tallents House (Type K)	2·75
	Belfast	2·75

III. SCOTLAND

S **1**

S **2**

S **3**

(Des. G. Huntly (3d., 4d., 5d.), J. Fleming (6d., 9d.), A. Imrie (1s.3d., 1s.6d.))

1958–67. W **179**. P 15×14.

S1	S **1**	3d. dp lilac (18.8.58)	15	15
		p. Two phosphor bands (29.1.63)	13·00	2·75
		pa. One phosphor band at right (30.4.65)	20	25
		pb. Band at left	20	25
		pc. Horiz pair. Nos. S1pa/pb	40	1·00
		pd. One centre phosphor band (9.11.67)	15	15
S2		4d. ultramarine (7.2.66)	15	15
		p. Two phosphor bands	15	15
S3	S **2**	6d. dp claret (29.9.58)	20	15
		p. Two phosphor bands (29.1.63)	20	20
S4		9d. bronze-green (2 phosphor bands) (1.3.67)	35	40
S5	S **3**	1s.3d. green (29.9.58)	40	40
		p. Two phosphor bands (29.1.63)	40	40
S6		1s.6d. grey-blue (2 phosphor bands) (1.3.67)	45	50

First Day Covers

18.8.58	3d. (*S1*)	17.00
29.9.58	6d., 1s.3d. (*S3, S5*)	25.00
7.2.66	4d. (*S2*)	7.00
1.3.67	9d., 1s.6d. (*S4, S6*)	6.00

The one phosphor band on No. S1pa was produced by printing broad phosphor bands across alternate vertical perforations. Individual stamps show the band at right or left (same prices either way).

For Nos. S1, S3 and S5 in Presentation Pack, see below Wales No. W6.

1967–70. *No watermark. Chalk-surfaced paper. One centre phosphor band (S7, S9/10) or two phosphor bands (others). Gum arabic (Nos. S7, S8) or PVA gum (others).* P 15×14.

S7	S **1**	3d. dp lilac (16.5.68)	10	15
		Ey. Phosphor omitted	7·00	
		Ev. PVA gum	10	
		Eya. Phosphor omitted (No. S7Ev)	4·00	
S8		4d. dp brt blue (28.11.67)	10	15
		Ey. Phosphor omitted	10·00	
		Ev. PVA gum (25.7.68)	10	
S9		4d. olive-sepia (4.9.68)	10	10
		Ey. Phosphor omitted	3·00	
S10		4d. brt vermilion (26.2.69)	10	10
		Ey. Phosphor omitted	2·50	
S11		5d. royal blue (4.9.68)	20	10
		Ey. Phosphor omitted	55·00	
S12	S **2**	9d. bronze-green (28.9.70)	5·50	5·50
		Ey. Phosphor omitted	£250	
S13	S **3**	1s.6d. grey-blue (12.12.68)	1·75	1·50
		Ey. Phosphor omitted	£125	

4.9.68	First Day Cover (*S9, S11*)	3·00
	Presentation Pack (*containing Nos.* S3, S5p., S7, S9/13) (9.12.70)	8·00

S **4**

I II

Redrawn design of Type S 4 (litho ptgs.)

The introduction of the redrawn lion took place in 1983 when Waddington's had the contract and therefore the 13, 17, 22 and 31p. exist in both types and perforated 14. The Questa printings, perforated 15x14, are all Type II.

The Types of Lion.

Type I:–The eye and jaw appear larger and there is no line across the bridge of the nose.

Type II:–The tongue is thick at the point of entry to the mouth and the eye is linked to the background by a solid line.

The following stamps printed in lithography show a screened background behind and to the left of the emblem: 12½p., 15½p., 16p., 19½p., 28p. (Nos. S50 and S74) and 31p. (Nos. S51 and S76). The 13p. and 17p. (No. S43) also showed screened backgrounds for both Type I and II of the John Waddington printings, but changed to solid backgrounds for the Questa Type II. All other values printed in lithography have solid backgrounds.

(Des J. Matthews after plaster cast by Arnold Machin)

1971 (7 July)–**93**. *Decimal Currency. Chalk-surfaced paper. Type* S **4**.

(a) Photo Harrison. With phosphor bands. P 15×14.

S14	2½p. brt magenta (1 centre band)	25	20
	Ey. Phosphor omitted	8·00	
	Eg. Gum arabic (22.9.72)	30	

	Egy. Phosphor omitted	20·00	
S15	3p. ultramarine (2 bands)	35	15
	Ey. Phosphor omitted	15·00	
	Eg. Gum arabic (14.12.72)	10	
	Ega. Imperf (pair)	£650	
	Egy. Phosphor omitted	50·00	
S16	3p. ultramarine (1 centre band) (23.1.74)	15	15
S17	3½p. olive-grey (2 bands) (23.1.74)	20	25
	Ey. Phosphor omitted	50·00	
S18	3½p. olive-grey (1 centre band) (6.11.74)	20	25
S19	4½p. grey-blue (2 bands) (6.11.74)	30	25
S20	5p. reddish violet (2 bands)	1·00	1·25
S21	5½p. violet (2 bands) (23.1.74)	20	20
S22	5½p. violet (1 centre band) (21.5.75)	20	25
	a. Imperf (pair)	£500	
S23	6½p. greenish blue (1 centre band) (14.1.76)	20	20
S24	7p. purple-brown (1 centre band) (18.1.78)	30	30
S25	7½p. chestnut (2 bands)	1·25	1·25
	Ey. Phosphor omitted	5·00	
S26	8p. rosine (2 bands) (23.1.74)	45	40
S27	8½p. yellow-green (2 bands) (14.1.76)	40	40
S28	9p. dp violet (2 bands) (18.1.78)	40	40
S29	10p. orange-brown (2 bands) (20.10.76)	45	50
S30	10p. orange-brown (1 centre band) (23.7.80)	40	50
S31	10½p. steel-blue (2 bands) (18.1.78)	45	50
S32	11p. scarlet (2 bands) (20.10.76)	50	50
	Ey. Phosphor omitted	2·00	

(b) Photo Harrison. On phosphorised paper. P 15×14.

S33	12p. yellowish green (23.7.80)	50	50
S34	13½p. purple-brown (23.7.80)	70	80
S35	15p. ultramarine (23.7.80)	60	70

(c) Litho J.W. (Type I unless otherwise stated). One side phosphor band (11½p., 12p., 12½p., 13p.) or phosphorised paper (others). P 14.

S36	11½p. drab (8.4.81)	80	80
	Ey. Phosphor omitted	£700	
S37	12p. brt emerald (Type II) (7.1.86)	2·00	2·00
S38	12½p. lt emerald (24.2.82)	60	70
S39	13p. pale chestnut (Type I) (23.10.84)	75	75
	Ey. Phosphor omitted	£700	
	Ea. Type II (1.85)	8·00	4·25
	Eay. Phosphor omitted	£750	
S40	14p. grey-blue (8.4.81)	75	75
S41	15½p. pale violet (24.2.82)	80	80
S42	16p. drab (Type II) (27.4.83)	80	85
S43	17p. grey-blue (Type I) (23.10.84)	2·25	2·25
	Ea. Type II (1.85)	1·25	1·00
S44	18p. dp violet (8.4.81)	80	80
S45	19½p. olive-grey (24.2.82)	1·75	1·75
S46	20½p. ultramarine (Type II) (27.4.83)	3·50	3·50
S47	22p. blue (8.4.81)	1·00	1·00
S48	22p. yellow-green (Type I) (23.10.84)	4·25	4·25
	Ea. Type II (1.86)	50·00	30·00
S49	26p. rosine (24.2.82)	1·25	1·25
S50	28p. dp violet-blue (Type II) (27.4.83)	1·25	1·25
S51	31p. brt purple (Type I) (23.10.84)	2·50	2·50
	Ea. Type II (11.85*)	£120	80·00

(d) Litho Questa (Type II). P 15×14.

S52	12p. brt emerald (1 side band) (29.4.86)	2·00	2·25
S53	13p. pale chestnut (1 side band) (4.11.86)	70	75
S54	14p. dp blue (1 centre band) (8.11.88)	60	70
	l. Booklet pane. No. S54×6 with margins all round (21.3.89)	3·50	
S55	14p. dp blue (1 side band) (21.3.89)	80	90
	l. Booklet pane. No. S55×5, S63×2, S68 and centre label with margins all round	18·00	
	la. Error. Booklet pane imperf	£1750	
S56	15p. brt blue (1 centre band) (28.11.89)	70	70
	a. Imperf (three sides) (block of four)	£275	
S57	17p. grey-blue (phosphorised paper) (29.4.86)	4·00	4·00
S58	17p. dp blue (1 centre band) (4.12.90)	1·00	1·10
S59	18p. dp olive-grey (phosphorised paper) (6.1.87)	1·10	85
S60	18p. brt green (1 centre band) (3.12.91)	1·25	90
	a. Perf 14 (26.9.92*)	1·00	1·00
	aEy. Phosphor omitted	£1250	
S61	18p. brt green (1 side band) (10.8.93)	2·75	3·00
S62	19p. brt orange-red (phosphorised paper) (8.11.88)	70	70
	l. Booklet pane. No. S62×9 with margins all round (21.3.89)	5·50	
	m. Booklet pane. No. S62×6 with margins all round (21.3.89)	4·50	
S63	19p. brt orange-red (2 bands) (21.3.89)	2·25	2·00
S64	20p. brownish black (phosphorised paper) (28.11.89)	95	95
S65	22p. yellow-green (phosphorised paper) (27.1.87)	1·25	1·50
S66	22p. brt orange-red (phosphorised paper) (4.12.90)	1·25	90
S67	23p. brt green (phosphorised paper) (8.11.88).	1·25	1·10
S68	23p. brt green (2 bands) (21.3.89)	14·00	14·00
S69	24p. Indian red (phosphorised paper) (28.11.89)	1·25	1·25
S70	24p. chestnut (phosphorised paper) (3.12.91)	1·40	1·25
	a. Perf 14 (10.92*)	3·00	3·25
S71	24p. chestnut (2 bands) (10.8.93)	2·75	3·00
S72	26p. rosine (phosphorised paper) (27.1.87)	3·75	4·00
S73	26p. drab (phosphorised paper) (4.12.90)	1·25	1·25
S74	28p. dp violet-blue (phosphorised paper) (27.1.87)	1·25	1·25
S75	28p. dp bluish grey (phosphorised paper) (3.12.91)	1·25	1·50
	a. Perf 14 (18.2.93*)	6·50	6·75
S76	31p. brt purple (phosphorised paper) (29.4.86)	2·25	2·25
S77	32p. greenish blue (phosphorised paper) (8.11.88)	1·75	2·00
S78	34p. dp bluish grey (phosphorised paper) (28.11.89)	1·75	1·75
S79	37p. rosine (phosphorised paper) (4.12.90)	2·00	2·25
S80	39p. brt mauve (phosphorised paper) (3.12.91)	2·00	2·25
	a. Perf 14 (11.92)	4·50	4·75

*Earliest known date of use.

Nos. S55, S61, S63, S68 and S71 only come from booklets.

The listed booklet panes come from the following Sponsored Booklets:

S54l –Booklet DX10
S55l –Booklet DX10
S62l/m –Booklet DX10

No. S56a occured in the second vertical row of two sheets. It is best collected as a block of four including the left-hand vertical pair imperforate on three sides.

Nos. S60a, S70a, S75a and S80a were caused by the use of a reserve perforating machine for some printings in the second half of 1992.

From 1972 printings were on fluorescent white paper. From 1973 most printings had dextrin added to the PVA gum (see notes after the 1971 Decimal Machin issue).

First Day Covers

7.7.71	2½p., 3p., 5p., 7½p. (*S14/15, S20, S25*)	3·00
23.1.74	3p., 3½p., 5½p., 8p. (*S16/17, S21, S26*)	2·50
6.11.74	4½p. (*S19*)	1·50
14.1.76	6½p., 8½p. (*S23, S27*)	1·50
20.10.76	10p., 11p. (*S29, S32*)	1·50
18.1.78	7p., 9p., 10½p. (*S24, S28, S31*)	1·75
23.7.80	12p., 13½p., 15p. (*S33/5*)	2·75
8.4.81	11½p., 14p., 18p., 22p. (*S36, S40, S44, S47*)	2·50
24.2.82	12½p., 15½p., 19½p., 26p. (*S38, S41, S45, S49*)	3·50
27.4.83	16p., 20½p., 28p. (*S42, S46, S50*)	4·00
23.10.84	13p., 17p., 22p., 31p. (*S39, S43, S48, S51*)	4·00
7.1.86	12p. (*S37*)	2·00
6.1.87	18p. (*S59*)	1·80
8.11.88	14p., 19p., 23p., 32p. (*S54, S62, S67, S77*)	4·25
21.3.89	Scots Connection *se-tenant* pane 14p., 19p., 23p. (*S55l*)	14·00
28.11.89	15p., 20p., 24p., 34p. (*S56, S64, S69, S78*)	5·00
4.12.90	17p., 22p., 26p., 37p. (*S58, S66, S73, S79*)	5·00
3.12.91	18p., 24p., 28p., 39p. (*S60, S70, S75, S80*)	5·50

Presentation Packs

7.7.71	P.O. Pack No. 27. 2½p., 3p. (*2 bands*), 5p., 7½p. (*Nos.* S14/15, S20, S25).	3·50
29.5.74	P.O. Pack No. 62. 3p. (*1 centre band*), 3½p. (2 bands) or (1 centre band), 5½p. (2 bands) or (1 centre band), 8p. (*Nos.* S16, S17 or S18, S21 or S22, S26). The 4½p. (No. S19) was added later.	2·50
20.10.76	P.O. Pack No. 85. 6½p., 8½p., 10p. (*2 bands*), 11p. (*Nos.* S23, S27, S29, S32)	2·00
28.10.81	P.O. Pack No. 129b. 7p., 9p., 10½p., 12p. (*photo*), 13½p., 15p. (photo), 11½p., 14p. grey-blue, 18p. dp violet, 22p. blue (*Nos.* S24, S28, S31, S33/6, S40, S44, S47)	9·00
3.8.83	P.O. Pack No. 2. 10p. (*1 centre band*), 12½p., 16p., 20½p., 26p. (J.W.), 28p. (J.W.), (Nos. S30, S38, S42, S46, S49/50)	17·00

23.10.84	P.O. Pack No. 6. 10p. (*1 centre band*), 13p. (J.W.), 16p., 17p. (J.W.), 22p. yellow-green, 26p. (J.W.), 28p. (J.W.), 31p. (J.W.), (*Nos.* S30, S39, S42/3, S48/51)	17·00
3.3.87	P.O. Pack No. 10. 12p. (litho), 13p. (Questa), 17p. grey-blue (Questa), 18p. dp olive-grey, 22p. yellow-green, 26p. rosine (Questa), 28p. dp violet-blue (Questa), 31p. (Questa) (*Nos. S52/3, S57, S59, S65, S72, S74, S76*)	16·00

Presentation Packs containing stamps of Northern Ireland, Scotland and Wales are listed after those for Northern Ireland.

1977–78 EXPERIMENTAL MACHINE PACKETS. These are small cartons containing loose stamps for sale in vending machines. The experiment was confined to the Scottish Postal Board area, where six vending machines were installed, the first becoming operational in Dundee about February 1977.

The cartons carry labels inscribed "ROYAL MAIL STAMPS", their total face value (30p. or 60p.) and their contents.

At first the 30p. packet contained two 6½p. and two 8½p. Scottish Regional stamps and the 60p. packet had four of each. The stamps could be in pairs or blocks, but also in strips or singles.

With the change in postal rates on 13 June 1977 these packets were withdrawn on 11 June and on 13 June the contents were changed, giving three 7p. and one 9p. for the 30p. packet and double this for the 60p. packet. However, this time ordinary British Machin stamps were used. Moreover the Edinburgh machine, situated in an automatic sorting area, was supplied with 7p. stamps with two phosphor bands instead of the new centre band 7p. stamps, despite instructions having been given to withdraw the two band stamps. However, the demand for these packets was too great to be filled and by 27 June the machine was closed down. It was brought back into use on 16 August 1977, supplying 7p. stamps with the centre band.

The 6½p. and 8½p. Scottish Regional packets were put on sale at the Edinburgh Philatelic Bureau in June 1977 and withdrawn in April 1978. The packets with the 7p. and 9p. Machin stamps were put on sale at the Bureau in June 1977 and withdrawn in December 1978.

Such machine packets are outside the scope of this catalogue.

(Des J. Matthews after plaster cast by Arnold Machin)

1993 (7 Dec)–**98**. *Chalk-surfaced paper.*

(*a*) *Litho Questa.* P 15×14 (with one elliptical hole on each vertical side).

S81	S **4**	19p. bistre (1 centre band)	80	70
S82		19p. bistre (1 band at right) (25.4.95)	3·00	3·25
S83		20p. brt green (1 centre band) (23.7.96)	1·50	1·50
S84		25p. red (2 bands)	1·10	1·00
S85		26p. red-brown (2 bands) (23.7.96)	1·75	2·00
S86		30p. dp olive-grey (2 bands)	1·25	1·25
S87		37p. brt mauve (2 bands) (23.7.96)	2·75	3·00
S88		41p. grey-brown (2 bands)	1·75	2·00
		Ey. Phosphor omitted	£300	
S89		63p. lt emerald (2 bands) (23.7.96)	4·00	4·25

(*b*) *Photo Walsall (20p., 26p. (No. S91a), 63p.), Harrison or Walsall (26p. (No. S91), 37p.).* P 14 (No. S90a) or 15×14 (others) (both with one elliptical hole on each vertical side).

S90	S **4**	20p. brt green (1 centre band) (1.7.97)	1·00	60
S90*a*		20p. brt green (1 side band at right) (13.10.98)	2·75	2·75
S91		26p. chestnut (2 bands) (1.7.97)	1·00	1·00
		a. Perf 14 (13.10.98)	2·75	2·75
S92		37p. brt mauve (2 bands) (1.7.97)	1·50	1·50
S93		63p. lt emerald (2 bands) (1.7.97)	4·00	4·00

Nos. S82, S90a and S91a only come from booklets. The Harrison printings of Nos. S9½ come from booklet pane No. NI81al.

First Day Covers

7.12.93	19p., 25p., 30p., 41p. (*S81, S84, S86, S88*)	6·00
23.7.96	20p. 26p., 37p., 63p. (*S83, S85, S87, S89*)	8·75

For Presentation Pack containing stamps of Northern Ireland, Scotland and Wales see after No. NI85 of Northern Ireland.

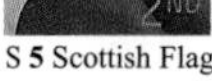

S **5** Scottish Flag

S **6** Scottish Lion

S **7** Thistle

S **8** Tartan

(Des A. Morris (2nd), F. Pottinger and T. Chalk (1st, E). Adapted Tayburn. Photo Questa (Nos. S94a, S95a), De La Rue (No. S99), De La Rue or Walsall (Nos. S94/5), Walsall (others))

1999 (8 June)–**2002**. *One centre phosphor band (2nd) or two phosphor bands (others).* P 15×14 (with one elliptical hole on each vertical side).

S94	S **5**	(2nd) new blue, blue and silver	30	35
		a. Booklet pane. Nos. S94×6 and S98×2 with centre label and margins all round (4.8.00)	7·00	
S95	S **6**	(1st) greenish yellow, dp rose-red, rose-red and silver	40	45
		a. Booklet pane. Nos. S95/6, each×4, with centre label and margins all round (22.10.01)	7·75	
S96	S **7**	(E) brt lilac, dp lilac and silver	1·75	1·75
S97	S **8**	64p. greenish yellow, brt magenta, new blue, grey-black and silver	9·00	7·75
S98		65p. greenish yellow, brt magenta, new blue, grey-black and silver (25.4.00)	3·00	3·25
S99		68p. greenish yellow, bright magenta, new blue, grey-black and silver (4.7.02)	3·25	3·25
Presentation Pack (*P.O. Pack No.* 45) (2nd, 1st, E, 64p.) (Nos. S94/7)			10·00	
Presentation Pack (*P.O. Pack No.* 50) (65p.) (No. S98)			6·50	
Presentation Pack (*P.O. Pack No.* 55) (2nd, 1st, E, 65p.) (Nos. S94/6, S98)			6·00	
PHQ Cards (*set of* 4) (*Nos.* S94/7)			1·50	10·00

Nos. S94, S95 and S96 were initially sold at 19p., 26p. and 30p., the latter representing the basic European airmail rate.

New printings of Nos. S94/5, produced by De La Rue instead of Walsall were issued on 5 June 2002. Stamps from this printing do not differ from those produced by Walsall.

No. S94a comes from booklet No. DX25.

No. S95a comes from booklet No. DX27.

For combined presentation pack for all four Regions, see under England.

First Day Covers

8.6.99	2nd, 1st, E, 64p. (*S94/7*) Philatelic Bureau	6·00
	Edinburgh	6·50
25.4.00	65p. (*S98*) Philatelic Bureau	3·00
	Edinburgh	3·50
4.8.00	Queen Elizabeth the Queen Mother *se-tenant* pane 2nd, 65p. (*S94a*) Philatelic Bureau (as for Nos. 2160/1)	4·75
	London SW1 (*as for Nos. 2160/1*)	4·75
22.10.01	Unseen and Unheard *se-tenant* pane (1st), E, (S95a) Philatelic Bureau (*as for MS2206*)	7·00
	Rosyth, Dunfermline (*as for MS2206*)	7·00
4.7.02	68p. (S99) Tallents House (Type K) (*see Introduction*)	1·75
	Edinburgh	1·75

Special First Day of Issue Postmarks

(for use on Nos. S94, S95/8)

S 9

(Des J. Matthews. Photo Walsall)

2000 (15 Feb). *Type S* **4** *redrawn with "1st" face value as Type* S **9**. *Two phosphor bands.* P 14 (with one elliptical hole on each vertical side).

S108	S **9**	(1st) bright orange-red	3·00	3·25

No. S108 was only issued in £7.50 stamp booklets (No. DX24).

(Photo Walsall or De La Rue (42p.) or De La Rue (others))

2003 (14 Oct)–**06**. *As Nos. S94/6 and S99, and new values, but with white borders. One centre phosphor band (2nd) or two phosphor bands (others).* P 15×14 (with one elliptical hole on each vertical side).

S109	S **5**	(2nd) new blue, blue and silver	30	35
		a. Booklet pane. Nos. S109 and EN10, each×3, with margins all round (16.3.04)	8·50	
S110	S **6**	(1st) rose-red, greenish yellow, deep rose-red and silver	45	50
S111	S **7**	(E) bright lilac, deep lilac and silver	60	65
S112		40p. bright lilac, deep lilac and silver (11.5.04)	1·25	1·25
S113		42p. bright lilac, deep lilac and silver (5.4.05)	65	70
S114		44p. bright lilac, deep lilac and silver (28.3.06)	65	70
S115	S **8**	68p. bright magenta, greenish yellow, new blue, grey-black and silver	1·10	1·20
S116		72p. bright magenta, greenish yellow, new blue, grey-black and silver	1·10	1·20
Presentation Pack (*Nos.* S109/11, S115) (*P.O. Pack No.* 64)			2·75	
PHQ Cards (*Nos.* S109/11, S115) (*set of* 4)			1·70	4·00

No. S109a comes from booklet No. DX32.

The Walsall printing of No. S113 was issued on 5 April 2005, and the De La Rue printing on 24 May 2005.

First Day Covers

14.10.03	2nd, 1st, E, 68p. (*S109/11, S115*) Tallents House (Type K, see Introduction)	3·25
	Edinburgh	3·25
11.5.04	40p. (*S112*) Tallents House (Type K)	2·75
	Edinburgh	2·75
28.3.06	44p., 72p. (*S114, S116*) Tallents House (Type K)	2·75
	Edinburgh	2·75

(Des H. Brown. Photo De La Rue)

2004 (5 Oct). *Opening of New Scottish Parliament Building, Edinburgh. Sheet 123×70 mm. Printed in photogravure by De La Rue. One centre phosphor band (2nd) or two phosphor bands (others).* P 15×14 (with one elliptical hole on each vertical side).

MSS120	Nos. S109, S110×2 and S112×2	5·00	5·00
First Day Cover (Tallents House)			7·25
First Day Cover (Edinburgh)			7·25

Special First Day of Issue Postmarks

IV. WALES

From the inception of the Regional stamps, the Welsh versions were tendered to members of the public at all Post Offices within the former County of Monmouthshire but the national alternatives were available on request. By August 1961 the policy of "dual stocking" of definitive stamps was only maintained at Abergavenny, Chepstow, Newport and Pontypool. Offices with a Monmouthshire postal address but situated outside the County, namely Beachley, Brockweir, Redbrook, Sedbury, Tutshill, Welsh Newton and Woodcroft, were not supplied with the Welsh Regional stamps. With the re-formation of Counties, Monmouthshire became known as Gwent and was also declared to be part of Wales. From 1 July 1974, therefore, except for the offices mentioned above, only Welsh Regional stamps were available at the offices under the jurisdiction of Newport, Gwent.

W 1

W 2

W 3

(Des R. Stone)

1958–67. W **179**. P 15×14.

W1	W **1**	3d. dp lilac (18.8.58)	15	15
		p. One centre phosphor band (16.5.67)	20	15
W2		4d. ultramarine (7.2.66)	20	15
		p. Two phosphor bands (10.67)	20	15
W3	W **2**	6d. dp claret (29.9.58)	35	30
W4		9d. bronze-green (2 phosphor bands) (1.3.67)	40	35
		Ey. Phosphor omitted	£350	
W5	W **3**	1s.3d. green (29.9.58)	40	40
W6		1s.6d. grey-blue (2 phosphor bands) (1.3.67)	40	40
		Ey. Phosphor omitted	50·00	

First Day Covers

18.8.58	3d. (*W1*)	12·00
29.9.58	6d., 1s.3d. (*W3, W5*)	25·00
7.2.66	4d. (*W2*)	7·00
1.3.67	9d., 1s.6d. (*W4, W6*)	4·00
	Presentation Pack*	£100

*This was issued in 1960 and comprises Guernsey No. 7, Jersey No. 10, Isle of Man No. 2, Northern Ireland Nos. NI1, NI3 and NI5, Scotland Nos. S1, S3 and S5 and Wales Nos. W1, W3 and W5 together with a 6-page printed leaflet describing the stamps. There exist two forms: (*a*) inscribed "7s.3d." for sale in the U.K.; and (*b*) inscribed "$1.20" for sale in the U.S.A.

1967–69. *No wmk. Chalk-surfaced paper. One centre phosphor band (W7, W9/10) or two phosphor bands (others). Gum arabic (3d.) or PVA gum (others).* P 15×14.

W7	W **1**	3d. dp lilac (6.12.67)	10	15
		Ey. Phosphor omitted	60·00	
W8		4d. ultramarine (21.6.68)	10	15
W9		4d. olive-sepia (4.9.68)	15	15
W10		4d. brt vermilion (26.2.69)	15	15
		Ey. Phosphor omitted	2·00	
W11		5d. royal blue (4.9.68)	15	15
		Ey. Phosphor omitted	3·00	
W12	W **3**	1s.6d. grey-blue (1.8.69)	3·50	3·50

4.9.68	First Day Cover (*W9, W11*)	3·00
	Presentation Pack (*containing Nos.* W4, W6/7, W9/11) (9.12.70)	4·00

W **4** With "p"

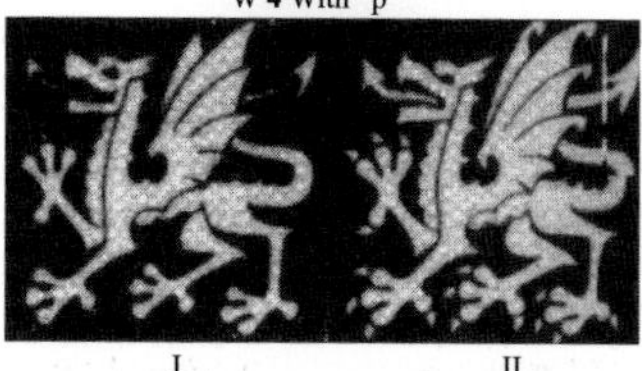

I II

Redrawn design of Type W 4 (litho ptgs.)

Two Types of Dragon

Type I:-The eye is complete with white dot in the centre. Wing-tips, tail and tongue are thin.

Type II:-The eye is joined to the nose by a solid line. Tail, wing-tips, claws and tongue are wider than in Type I.

The following stamps printed in lithography show a screened background behind and to the left of the emblem: 11½p., 12½p., 14p. (No. W39), 15½p., 16p., 18p. (No. W46), 19½p., 22p. (No. W54) and 28p. (No. W63). The 13p. and 17p. (No. W44) also show screened backgrounds in Type I, but changed to solid backgrounds for Type II. All other values printed in lithography have solid backgrounds.

(Des J. Matthews after plaster cast by Arnold Machin)

1971 (7 July)–**93**. *Decimal Currency. Chalk-surfaced paper. Type* W **4**.

(a) Photo Harrison. With phosphor bands. P 15×14.

W13	2½p. brt magenta (1 centre band)	20	20
	Ey. Phosphor omitted	7·50	
	Eg. Gum arabic (22.9.72)	20	
	Ega. Imperf (pair)	£600	
W14	3p. ultramarine (2 bands)	25	20
	Ey. Phosphor omitted	30·00	
	Eg. Gum arabic (6.6.73)	25	
	Eya. Phosphor omitted (No. W14Eg)	12·00	
W15	3p. ultramarine (1 centre band) (23.1.74)	25	25
W16	3½p. olive-grey (2 bands) (23.1.74)	20	30
W17	3½p. olive-grey (1 centre band) (6.11.74)	20	30
W18	4½p. grey-blue (2 bands) (6.11.74)	30	30
W19	5p. reddish violet (2 bands)	1·25	1·25
	Ey. Phosphor omitted	20·00	
W20	5½p. violet (2 bands) (23.1.74)	25	30
	Ey. Phosphor omitted	£180	
W21	5½p. violet (1 centre band) (21.5.75)	25	30
	a. Imperf (pair)	£600	
W22	6½p. greenish blue (1 centre band) (14.1.76)	20	20
W23	7p. purple-brown (1 centre band) (18.1.78)	25	25
W24	7½p. chestnut (2 bands)	1·75	1·75
	Ey. Phosphor omitted	95·00	
W25	8p. rosine (2 bands) (23.1.74)	30	35
	Ey. Phosphor omitted	£800	
W26	8½p. yellow-green (2 bands) (14.1.76)	30	35
W27	9p. dp violet (2 bands) (18.1.78)	40	40
W28	10p. orange-brown (2 bands) (20.10.76)	40	40
W29	10p. orange-brown (1 centre band) (23.7.80)	40	40
W30	10½p. steel-blue (2 bands) (18.1.78)	45	45
W31	11p. scarlet (2 bands) (20.10.76)	45	45

(b) Photo Harrison. On phosphorised paper. P 15×14.

W32	12p. yellowish green (23.7.80)	50	50
W33	13½p. purple-brown (23.7.80)	60	70
W34	15p. ultramarine (23.7.80)	60	70

(c) Litho Questa (Type II unless otherwise stated). P 14 (11½p., 12½p., 14p. (No. W39), 15½p., 16p., 18p. (No. W46), 19½p., 20½p., 22p. (No. W54), 26p. (No. W61), 28p. (No. W63)) or 15×14 (others).

W35	11½p. drab (Type I) (1 side band) (8.4.81)	90	80
W36	12p. brt emerald (1 side band) (7.1.86)	2·00	2·00
W37	12½p. lt emerald (Type I) (1 side band) (24.2.82)	70	70
	a. Perf 15×14 (10.1.84)	4·75	4·25
W38	13p. pale chestnut (Type I) (1 side band) (23.10.84)	60	60
	Ea. Type II (1.87)	1·90	1·75
W39	14p. grey-blue (Type I) (phosphorised paper) (8.4.81)	70	70
W40	14p. dp blue (1 centre band) (8.11.88)	75	75
W41	15p. brt blue (1 centre band) (28.11.89)	80	75
	Ey. Phosphor omitted		
W42	15½p. pale violet (Type I) (phosphorised paper) (24.2.82)	75	75
W43	16p. drab (Type I) (phosphorised paper) (27.4.83)	1·75	1·75
	a. Perf 15×14 (10.1.84)	1·75	1·75
W44	17p. grey-blue (Type I) (phosphorised paper) (23.10.84)	70	80
	Ea. Type II (18.8.86)	50·00	40·00
W45	17p. dp blue (1 centre band) (4.12.90)	90	80
	Ey. Phosphor omitted	18·00	
W46	18p. dp violet (Type I) (8.4.81)	1·00	95
W47	18p. dp olive-grey (phosphorised paper) (6.1.87)	95	90
W48	18p. brt green (1 centre band) (3.12.91)	75	75
	Ey. Phosphor omitted	£200	
	a. Booklet pane. No. W48×6 with margins all round (25.2.92)	3·25	
	aEy. Phosphor omitted		
	b. Perf 14 (12.1.93*)	5·25	5·25
W49	18p. brt green (1 side band at right) (25.2.92)	2·00	2·00
	a. Booklet pane. No. X1020×2, 1451a, 1514a, W49×2, W60×2 and centre label with margins all round	11·00	
	aEy. Phosphor omitted	£200	
	Eb. Band at left (10.8.93)	2·00	2·00
W50	19p. brt orange-red (phosphorised paper) (8.11.88)	1·00	80
W51	19½p. olive-grey (Type I) (phosphorised paper) (24.2.82)	1·75	2·00
W52	20p. brownish black (phosphorised paper) (28.11.89)	90	90
W53	20½p. ultramarine (Type I) (phosphorised paper) (27.4.83)	3·50	3·50
W54	22p. blue (Type I) (phosphorised paper) (8.4.81)	1·10	1·10
W55	22p. yellow-green (Type I) (phosphorised paper) (23.10.84)	95	1·10
W56	22p. brt orange-red (phosphorised paper) (4.12.90)	1·00	1·10
W57	23p. brt green (phosphorised paper) (8.11.88)	1·00	1·10
W58	24p. Indian red (phosphorised paper) (28.11.89)	1·25	1·25
W59	24p. chestnut (phosphorised paper) (3.12.91)	75	75
	a. Booklet pane. No. W59x6 with margins all round (25.2.92)	5·00	
	b. Perf 14 (14.9.92*)	4·75	5·25
W60	24p. chestnut (2 bands) (25.2.92)	1·25	1·50
W61	26p. rosine (Type I) (phosphorised paper) (24.2.82)	1·10	1·10
	a. Perf 15×14 (Type II) (27.1.87)	5·75	6·00
W62	26p. drab (phosphorised paper) (4.12.90)	1·75	1·75
W63	28p. dp violet-blue (Type I) (phosphorised paper) (27.4.83)	1·50	1·50
	a. Perf 15×14 (Type II) (27.1.87)	1·50	1·50
W64	28p. dp bluish grey (phosphorised paper) (3.12.91)	1·50	1·50
W65	31p. brt purple (Type I) (phosphorised paper) (23.10.84)	1·75	1·75
W66	32p. greenish blue (phosphorised paper) (8.11.88)	1·75	1·75
W67	34p. dp bluish grey (phosphorised paper) (28.11.89)	1·75	1·75
W68	37p. rosine (phosphorised paper) (4.12.90)	2·25	2·25
W69	39p. brt mauve (phosphorised paper) (3.12.91)	2·25	2·25

*Earliest known date of use.

Nos. W48b and W59b were caused by the use of a reserve perforating machine for some printings in the second half of 1992.

Nos. W49, W49Eb and W60 only come from booklets.

The listed booklet panes come from the following Sponsored Booklets:

W48a – Booklet DX13
W49a – Booklet DX13
W59a – Booklet DX13

No. W60 exists with the phosphor omitted, but cannot be identified without the use of u.v. light (Price £375 unused).

From 1972 printings were on fluorescent white paper. From 1973 most printings had dextrin added to the PVA gum (see notes after 1971 Decimal Machin issue).

First Day Covers

7.7.71	2½p., 3p., 5p., 7½p., (*W13/14, W19, W24*)	3·00
23.1.74	3p., 3½p., 5½p., 8p. (*W15/16, W20, W25*)	2·50
6.11.74	4½p. (*W18*)	1·50
14.1.76	6½p., 8½p. (*W22, W26*)	1·50
20.10.76	10p., 11p. (*W28, W31*)	1·50
18.1.78	7p., 9p., 10½p. (*W23, W27, W30*)	1·75
23.7.80	12p., 13½p., 15p. (*W32/4*)	3·00
8.4.81	11½p., 14p., 18p., 22p. (*W35, W39, W46, W54*)	2·50
24.2.82	12½p., 15½p., 19½p., 26p. (*W37, W42, W51, W61*)	3·50
27.4.83	16p., 20½p., 28p. (*W43, W53, W63*)	3·50
23.10.84	13p., 17p., 22p., 31p. (*W38, W44, W55, W65*)	4·25
7.1.86	12p. (*W36*)	2·00
6.1.87	18p. (*W47*)	2·00
8.11.88	14p., 19p., 23p., 32p. (*W40, W50, W57, W66*)	4·50
28.11.89	15p., 20p., 24p., 34p. (*W41, W52, W58, W67*)	5·00
4.12.90	17p., 22p., 26p., 37p (*W45, W56, W62, W68*)	5·00

3.12.91	18p., 24p., 28p., 39p. (*W48, W59, W64, W69*)	5·50
25.2.92	Cymru-Wales se-tenant pane 18p. (*2nd*), 24p. (1st), 33p. (W49a)	10·00

Presentation Packs

7.7.71	P.O. Pack No. 28. 2½p., 3p. (*2 bands*), 5p., 7½p. (*Nos.* W13/14, W19, W24)	3·50
29.5.74	P.O. Pack No. 63. 3p. (*1 centre band*), 3½p. (2 bands) or (1 centre band), 5½p. (2 bands) or (1 centre band), 8p. (*Nos.* W15, W16 or W17, W20 or W21, W25). The 4½p. (No. W18) was added later	2·50
20.10.76	P.O. Pack No. 86. 6½p., 8½p., 10p. (*2 bands*), 11p. (*Nos.* W22, W26, W28, W31)	2·00
28.10.81	P.O. Pack No. 129c. 7p., 9p., 10½p., 12p. (*photo*), 13½p., 15p. (photo), 11½p., 14p. grey-blue, 18p. dp violet, 22p. blue (*Nos.* W23, W27, W30, W32/5, W39, W46, W54)	9·00
3.8.83	P.O. Pack No. 3. 10p. (*1 centre band*), 12½p., 16p., 20½p., 26p. rosine, 28p. dp violet-blue (*Nos.* W29, W37, W43, W53, W61, W63)	17·00
23.10.84	P.O. Pack No. 7. 10p. (*1 centre band*), 13p., 16p., 17p. grey-blue, 22p. yellow-green, 26p. rosine, 28p. dp violet-blue, 31p. (*Nos.* W29, W38, W43a, W44, W55, W61, W63, W65)	17·00
3.3.87	P.O. Pack No. 11. 12p. (litho), 13p., 17p. grey-blue, 18p. dp olive-grey, 22p. yellow-green, 26p. rosine, 28p. dp violet-blue, 31p. (*Nos.* W36, W38, W44, W47, W55, W61a, W63a, W65)	16·00

Presentation Packs containing stamps of Northern Ireland, Scotland and Wales are listed after those for Northern Ireland.

(Des J. Matthews after plaster cast by Arnold Machin. Litho Questa)

1993 (7 Dec)–**96**. *Chalk-surfaced paper.* P 15×14 (with one elliptical hole on each vertical side).

W70	W **4**	19p. bistre (1 centre band)	80	70
W71		19p. bistre (1 band at right) (25.4.95)	3·75	4·00
W72		20p. brt green (1 centre band) (23.7.96)	1·75	2·00
W73		25p. red (2 bands)	1·25	1·00
W74		26p. red-brown (2 bands) (23.7.96)	2·00	2·25
W75		30p. dp olive-grey (2 bands)	1·25	1·25
W76		37p. brt mauve (2 bands) (23.7.96)	2·75	3·00
W77		41p. grey-brown (2 bands)	2·00	2·00
W78		63p. lt emerald (2 bands) (23.7.96)	4·50	4·75

No. W71 only comes from booklets.

First Day Covers

7.12.93	19p., 25p., 30p., 41p. (*W70, W73, W75, W77*)	6·00
23.7.96	20p., 26p., 37p., 63p., (*W72, W74, W76, W78*)	7·00

For Presentation Packs containing stamps of Northern Ireland, Scotland and Wales see after No. NI85 of Northern Ireland.

W **5** Without "p"

(Photo Walsall (20p., 26p. (No. W80a), 63p.), Harrison or Walsall (26p. (No. W80), 37p.))

1997 (1 July)–**98**. *Chalk-surfaced paper.* P 14 (No. W79a) or 15×14 (others) (both with one elliptical hole on each vertical side).

W79	W **5**	20p. brt green (1 centre band)	80	80
W79*a*		20p. brt green (1 side band at right) (13.10.98)	2·25	2·00
W80		26p. chestnut (2 bands)	1·00	1·00
		a. Perf 14 (13.10.98)	2·75	2·75
W81		37p. brt mauve (2 bands)	2·75	2·75
W82		63p. lt emerald (2 bands)	4·00	4·50

Nos. W79a and W80a were only issued in booklets.

The Harrison printings of Nos. W80/1 come from booklet pane No. NI81al.

First Day Cover

1.7.97	20p., 26p., 37p., 63p. (*W79, W80/2*)	6·00
	Presentation Pack 1.7.97 P.O. Pack No. 39. 20p., 26p., 37p., 63p. (*Nos. W79, W80/2*)	15·00

W **6** Leek

W **7** Welsh Dragon

W **8** Daffodil

W **9** Prince of Wales Feathers

(Des D. Petersen (2nd), T. & G. Petersen (1st), I. Rees (E), R. Evans (64p., 65p.). Adapted Tutssels. Photo De La Rue or Walsall (2nd, 1st), De La Rue (68p.), Walsall (others))

1999 (8 June)–**2002**. *One phosphor band (2nd) or two phosphor bands (others).* P 14 (No. W83a) or 15×14 (others) (both with one elliptical hole on each vertical side).

W83	W **6**	(2nd) orange-brown, yellow-orange and black (1 centre band)	60	50
W83*a*		(2nd) orange-brown, yellow-orange and black (1 band at right) (p 14) (18.9.00)	3·75	4·00
		al. Booklet pane. No. 2124d and W83a, each×4, with centre label and margins all round	15·00	
W84	W **7**	(1st) blue-green, greenish yellow, silver and black	1·00	60
W85	W **8**	(E) greenish blue, dp greenish blue and grey-black	1·50	1·50
W86	W **9**	64p. violet, gold, silver and black	7·00	7·75
W87		65p. violet, gold, silver and black (25.4.00)	3·00	3·25
W88		68p. violet, gold, silver and black (4.7.02)	2·75	2·75

Presentation Pack (*P.O. Pack No.* 46) (2nd, 1st, E, 64p.) (*Nos.* W83, W84/6))	14·00	
Presentation Pack (*P.O. Pack No.* 51) (65p.) (*No.* W87))	3·00	
Presentation Pack (*P.O. Pack No.* 56) (2nd, 1st, E, 65p.) (*Nos.* W83, W84/5, W87))	8·00	
PHQ Cards (*set of* 4) (*Nos.* W83, W84/6)	1·50	10·00

Nos. W83, W84 and W85 were initially sold at 19p., 26p. and 30p., the latter representing the basic European airmail rate.

New printings of Nos. W83 and W84, produced by De La Rue instead of Walsall, were issued on 28 May 2003 and 4 March 2003. Stamps from these printings do not differ from those produced by Walsall.

No. W83a comes from the £7 Treasury of Trees booklet (No.DX26).

For combined presentation pack for all four Regions, see under England.

First Day Covers

8.6.99	2nd (*centre band*), 1st, E, 64p. (*W83,W84/6*)	
	Philatelic Bureau	6·00
	Cardiff	6·50
25.4.00	65p. (*W87*) Philatelic Bureau	3·00
	Cardiff	3·50
18.9.00	Treasury of Trees *se-tenant* pane 1st (*Millennium*), 2nd (*2124d, W83a*)	
	Philatelic Bureau	5·00
	Llangernyw, Abergele	5·00
4.7.02	68p. (*W88*) Tallents House (Type K) (*see Introduction*)	1·75
	Cardiff	1·75

Special First Day of Issue Postmarks

W **10**

(Des J. Matthews. Photo Walsall)

2000 (15 Feb). *Type* W **4** *redrawn with "1af/st" face value as Type* W **10**. *Two phosphor bands.* P 14 (with one elliptical hole on each vertical side).

W97	W **10**	(1st) bright orange-red	3·00	2·75

No. W97 was only issued in £7.50 stamp booklets (No. DX24).

(Photo Walsall or De La Rue (42p.) or De La Rue (others))

2003 (14 Oct)–**06**. *As Nos. W83, W84/5 and W88, and new values, but with white borders. One centre phosphor band (2nd) or two phosphor bands (others).* P 15×14 (with one elliptical hole on each vertical side).

W98	W **6**	(2nd) orange-brown, deep orange-brown and black	30	35
W99	W **7**	(1st) blue-green, greenish yellow, silver and black	45	50
W100	W **8**	(E) greenish blue, deep greenish blue and grey-black	60	65
W101		40p. greenish blue, deep greenish blue and grey-black (11.5.04)	1·25	1·25
W102		42p. greenish blue, deep greenish blue and grey-black (5.4.05)	65	70
W103		44p. greenish blue, deep greenish blue and grey-black (28.3.06)		
W104	W **9**	68p. violet, gold, silver and black	1·10	1·20
W105		72p. violet, gold, silver and black (28.3.06)	1·10	1·20
Presentation Pack (Nos. W98/ 100, W104). (*P.O. Pack No.* 65)			2·75	
PHQ Cards (Nos. W98/100, W104) (*set of* 4)			1·70	4·00

The Walsall printing of No. W102 was issued on 5 April 2005 and the De La Rue on 24 May 2005.

First Day Covers

14.10.03	2nd, 1st, E, 68p. (*W98/100, W104*) Tallents House (Type K) (see Introduction)	3·25
	Cardiff	3·25
11.5.04	40p. (*W101*) Tallents House (Type K)	2·75
	Cardiff	2·75
28.3.06	44p., 72p. (*W103, W105*) Tallents House (Type K)	2·75
	Cardiff	2·75

(Des Silk Pearce. Photo De La Rue)

2006 (1 Mar). *Opening of New Welsh Assembly Building, Cardiff. Sheet 123×70 mm. One centre phosphor band (2nd) or two phosphor bands (others).* P 15×14 (with one elliptical hole on each vertical side).

MSW109	Nos. W98, W99×2 and W104×2	3·25

First Day Cover (Tallents House)	4·50
First Day Cover (Cardiff)	4·50

V. GUERNSEY

War Occupation Issues

BISECTS. On 24 December 1940 authority was given, by Post Office notice, that prepayment of penny postage could be effected by using half a British 2d. stamp, diagonally bisected. Such stamps were first used on 27 December 1940.

The 2d. stamps generally available were those of the Postal Centenary issue, 1940 (S.G. 482) and the first colour of the King George VI issue (S.G. 465). These are listed under Nos. 482a and 465b. A number of the 2d. King George V, 1912–22, and of the King George V photogravure stamp (S.G. 442) which were in the hands of philatelists, were also bisected and used.

1

1a Loops (*half actual size*)

(Des E. W. Vaudin. Typo Guernsey Press Co Ltd)

1941–44. *Rouletted.*

(a) White paper. No wmk.

1	**1**	½d. light green (7.4.41)	5·25	2·50
		a. Emerald-green (6.41)	6·00	2·00
		b. Bluish green (11.41)	32·00	13·00
		c. Brt green (2.42)	22·00	10·00
		d. Dull green (9.42)	4·00	2·00
		e. Olive-green (2.43)	32·00	16·00
		f. Pale yellowish green (7.43 and later) (*shades*)	3·00	2·00
		g. Imperf (pair)	£200	
		h. Imperf between (horiz pair)	£700	
		i. Imperf between (vert pair)	£800	
2		1d. scarlet (18.2.41)	2·25	1·25
		a. Pale vermilion (7.43)	3·50	1·25
		b. Carmine (1943)	2·00	1·50
		c. Imperf (pair)	£150	75·00
		d. Imperf between (horiz pair)	£700	
		da. Imperf vert (centre stamp of horiz strip of 3)		
		e. Imperf between (vert pair)	£800	
		f. Printed double (scarlet shade)	£100	
3		2½d. ultramarine (12.4.44)	9·75	10·00
		a. Pale ultramarine (7.44)	6·00	5·00
		b. Imperf (pair)	£500	
		c. Imperf between (horiz pair)	£1000	
Set of 3			7·00	6·50

First Day Covers

18.2.41	1d.	15·00
7.4.41	½d.	6·00
12.4.44	2½d.	8·00

(b) Bluish French bank-note paper. W 1a (sideways).

4	**1**	½d. bright green (11.3.42)	27·00	21·00
5		1d. scarlet (9.4.42)	14·00	21·00

First Day Covers

11.3.42	½d.	80·00
9.4.42	1d.	45·00

The dates given for the shades of Nos. 1/3 are the months in which they were printed as indicated on the printer's imprints. Others are issue dates.

2

3

(Des E. A. Piprell. Portrait by Dorothy Wilding Ltd. Photo Harrison & Sons)

1958 (18 Aug)–**67**. W **179** of Great Britain. P 15×14.

6	**2**	2½d. rose-red (8.6.64)	35	40
7	**3**	3d. dp lilac	30	30
		p. One centre phosphor band (24.5.67)	15	20
8		4d. ultramarine (7.2.66)	25	30
		p. Two phosphor bands (24.10.67)	15	20
Set of 3 (*cheapest*)			70	80

First Day Covers

18.8.58	3d.	20·00
8.6.64	2½d.	30·00
7.2.66	4d.	8·00

For No. 7 in Presentation Pack, see Regional Issues below Wales No. W6.

1968–69. *No wmk. Chalk-surfaced paper. PVA gum*. One centre phosphor band (Nos. 10/11) or two phosphor bands (others).* P 15×14.

9	**3**	4d. pale ultramarine (16.4.68)	10	20
		Ey. Phosphor omitted	45·00	
10		4d. olive-sepia (4.9.68)	10	15
		Ey. Phosphor omitted	45·00	
11		4d. brt vermilion (26.2.69)	20	25
12		5d. royal blue (4.9.68)	20	30
Set of 4			50	1·00

First Day Cover

4.9.68	4d., 5d	3·00

No. 9 was not issued in Guernsey until 22 April.

*PVA Gum. See note after No. 722 of Great Britain.

VI. ISLE OF MAN

Although specifically issued for use in the Isle of Man, these issues were also valid for use throughout Great Britain.

DATES OF ISSUE. The note at the beginning of Northern Ireland also applies here.

Nos. 8/11 and current stamps of Great Britain were withdrawn from sale on the island from 5 July 1973 when the independent postal administration was established but remained valid for use there for a time. They also remained on sale at the Philatelic Sales counters in the United Kingdom until 4 July 1974.

1

2

(Des J. Nicholson. Portrait by Dorothy Wilding Ltd. Photo Harrison)

1958 (18 Aug)–**68**. W **179**. P 15×14.

1	**1**	2½d. carmine-red (8.6.64)	50	1·25
2	**2**	3d. dp lilac	50	20
		a. Chalk-surfaced paper (17.5.63)	12·00	10·00
		p. One centre phosphor band (27.6.68)	20	50
3		4d. ultramarine (7.2.66)	1·50	1·50
		p. Two phosphor bands (5.7.67)	20	30
Set of 3 (*cheapest*)			80	1·60

First Day Covers

18.8.58	3d.	32·00
8.6.64	2½d.	45·00
7.2.66	4d.	15·00

No. 2a was released in London sometime after 17 May 1963, this being the date of issue in Douglas.

For No. 2 in Presentation Pack, see Regional Issues below Wales No. W6.

1968–69. *No wmk. Chalk-surfaced paper. PVA gum. One centre phosphor band (Nos. 5/6) or two phosphor bands (others).* P 15×14.

4	**2**	4d. blue (24.6.68)	25	30
5		4d. olive-sepia (4.9.68)	25	40
		Ey. Phosphor omitted	22·00	
6		4d. brt vermilion (26.2.69)	45	75
7		5d. royal blue (4.9.68)	45	75
		Ey. Phosphor omitted	£175	
Set of 4			1·25	2·00

First Day Cover

4.9.68	4d., 5d	4·00

3

(Des J. Matthews. Portrait after plaster cast by Arnold Machin. Photo Harrison)

1971 (7 July). *Decimal Currency. Chalk-surfaced paper. One centre phosphor band (2½p.) or two phosphor bands (others).* P 15×14.

8	**3**	2½p. brt magenta	20	15
		Ey. Phosphor omitted	£1500	
9		3p. ultramarine	20	15
10		5p. reddish violet	40	60
		Ey. Phosphor omitted	£275	
11		7½p. chestnut	40	75
Set of 4			1·10	1·50
Presentation Pack			2·75	

First Day Cover

7.7.71	2½p., 3p., 5p., 7½p.	3·00

All values exist with PVA gum on ordinary cream paper and the 2½p. and 3p. also on fluorescent white paper.

VII. JERSEY

War Occupation Issues

1

(Des Major N. V. L. Rybot. Typo Evening Post, Jersey)

1941–43. *White paper (thin to thick).* No wmk. P 11.

1	**1**	½d. brt green (29.1.42)	5·25	3·75
		a. Imperf between (vert pair)	£800	
		b. Imperf between (horiz pair)	£700	
		c. Imperf (pair)	£250	
		d. On greyish paper (1.43)	5·50	5·50
2		1d. scarlet (1.4.41)	6·25	3·50
		a. Imperf between (vert pair)	£800	
		b. Imperf between (horiz pair)	£700	
		c. Imperf (pair)	£275	
		d. On chalk-surfaced paper	42·00	38·00
		e. On greyish paper (1.43)	5·50	5·75

First Day Covers

1.4.41	1d.	7·00
29.1.42	½d.	7·00

2 Old Jersey Farm

3 Portelet Bay

4 Corbière Lighthouse

5 Elizabeth Castle

6 Mont Orgueil Castle

7 Gathering Vraic (seaweed)

(Des E. Blampied. Eng H. Cortot. Typo French Govt Ptg Works, Paris)

1943–44. No wmk. P 13½.

3	**2**	½d. green (1 June)	9·75	10·00
		a. Rough, grey paper (6.10.43)	9·00	6·50
4	**3**	1d. scarlet (1 June)	2·25	50
		a. On newsprint (28.2.44)	2·50	75
5	**4**	1½d. brown (8 June)	7·00	5·75
6	**5**	2d. orange-yellow (8 June)	6·50	2·00
7	**6**	2½d. blue (29 June)	2·00	1·00
		a. On newsprint (25.2.44)	1·00	1·75
		ba. Thin paper*	£225	
8	**7**	3d. violet (29 June)	1·25	2·75
Set of 6			22·00	15·00
First Day Covers (3)				30·00
Set of 6 Gutter Pairs			45·00	

*On No. 7ba the design shows clearly through the back of the stamp.

8

9

(Des. E. Blampied (T **8**), W. Gardner (T **9**). Portrait by Dorothy Wilding Ltd. Photo Harrison & Sons)

1958 (18 Aug)–**67**. W **179** of Great Britain. P 15×14.

9	**8**	2½d. carmine-red (8.6.64)	30	45
		a. Imperf three sides (pair)	£2000	10
10	**9**	3d. dp lilac	30	25
		p. One centre phosphor band (9.6.67)	15	15
11		4d. ultramarine (7.2.66)	25	30
		p. Two phosphor bands (5.9.67)	15	25
Set of 3 (*cheapest*)			50	75

First Day Covers

18.8.58	3d.	20·00
8.6.64	2½d.	30·00
7.2.66	4d.	10·00

For No. 10 in Presentation Pack, see Regional Issues below Wales No. W6.

1968–69. *No wmk. Chalk-surfaced paper. PVA gum*. One centre phosphor band (4d. values) or two phosphor bands (5d.).* P 15×14.

12	**9**	4d. olive-sepia (4.9.68)	15	25
		Ey. Phosphor omitted	£1000	
13		4d. brt vermilion (26.2.69)	15	25
14		5d. royal blue (4.9.68)	15	50
Set of 3			40	1·10

First Day Cover

4.9.68	4d., 5d	3·00

*PVA Gum. See note after No. 722 of Great Britain.

POSTAGE DUE STAMPS

PERFORATIONS. All postage due stamps to No. D101 are perf 14×15.

WATERMARK. The watermark always appears sideways and this is the "normal" listed in this Catalogue for Nos. D1/D68. Varieties occur as follows. The point of identification is which way the top of the crown points, but (where they occur) the disposition of the letters needs to be noted also. The meaning of the terms is given below: (1) as described and illustrated in the Catalogue, i.e. as read through the front of the stamp, and (2) what is seen during watermark detection when the stamp is face down and the back is under examination.

Watermark	*Crown pointing*	*Letters reading*
	(1) *As described*	
Sideways	left	upwards
Sideways-inverted	right	downwards
Sideways and reversed	left	downwards, back to front
Sideways-inverted and reversed	right	upwards, back to front
	(2) *As detected* (*stamp face down*)	
Sideways	right	upwards, back to front
Sideways-inverted	left	downwards, back to front
Sideways and reversed	right	downwards
Sideways-inverted and reversed	left	upward

D 1

D 2

(Des G. Eve. Typo Somerset House (early trial printings of ½d., 1d., 2d. and 5d.; all printings of 1s.) or Harrison (later printings of all values except 1s.))

1914 (20 Apr)–**22**. W **100** *(Simple Cypher) (sideways).*

D1	**D 1**	½d. emerald	1·50	50	25
		Wi. Watermark sideways-inverted	2·00	1·00	1·00
		Wj. Watermark sideways and reversed	18·00	12·00	15·00
		Wk. Watermark sideways-inverted and reversed			
D2		1d. carmine	1·50	50	25
		a. *Pale carmine*	1·50	75	50
		Wi. Watermark sideways-inverted	2·00	1·00	1·00
		Wj. Watermark sideways and reversed			
		Wk. Watermark sideways-inverted and reversed	15·00	12·00	12·00
D3		1½d. chestnut (1922)	£140	48·00	20·00
		Wi. Watermark sideways-inverted	£175	70·00	20·00
D4		2d. agate	1·50	50	25
		Wi. Watermark sideways-inverted	3·00	2·00	2·00
		Wj. Watermark sideways-inverted and reversed	9·00	6·00	6·00
D5		3d. violet (1918)	24·00	5·00	75
		a. *Bluish violet*	24·00	6·00	2·75

		Wi. Watermark sideways-inverted	24·00	7·50	2·00
		Wj. Watermark sideways-inverted and reversed			
D6		4d. dull grey-green (12.20)	£120	18·00	5·00
		Wi. Watermark sideways-inverted	£140	40·00	5·00
D7		5d. brownish cinnamon	18·00	7·00	3·50
		Wi. Watermark sideways-inverted	40·00	16·00	16·00
D8		1s. brt blue (1915)	£130	40·00	4·75
		a. *Dp brt blue*	£130	40·00	5·00
		Wi. Watermark sideways-inverted	70·00	20·00	20·00
		Wj. Watermark sideways-inverted and reversed			
Set of 8			£395	£100	32·00

Stamps from the above issue are known bisected and used for half their face value at the following sorting offices:

1d. Barrhead (1922), Bristol (1918), Cowes (1923), Elgin (1921), Kidlington (1922, 1923), Kilburn, London NW (1923), Malvern (1915), Palmers Green, London N (1922), Plaistow, London E (1916), River, Dover (1922), Rock Ferry, Birkenhead (1915, 1918), St. Ouens, Jersey (1924), Salford, Manchester (1914), South Tottenham, London N (1921), Warminster (1922), Wavertree, Liverpool (1921), Whitchurch (1922), Winton, Bournemouth (1921), Wood Green, London N (1921)

2d. Anerley, London SE (1921), Bethnal Green, London E (1918), Christchurch (1921), Didcot (1919), Ealing, London W (1921), Hythe, Southampton (1923), Kirkwall (1922), Ledbury (1922), Malvern (1921, 1923), Sheffield (1921), Shipley (1922), Streatham, London SW (1921), Victoria Docks & North Woolwich (1921), West Kensington, London W (1921, 1922)

3d. Malvern (trisected and used for 1d.) (1921), Warminster (1922)

(Typo Waterlow)

1924. *As 1914–22, but on thick chalk-surfaced paper.*

D9	**D 1**	1d. carmine	10·00	6·00	6·00
		Wi. Watermark sideways-inverted			

(Typo Waterlow and (from 1934) Harrison)

1924–31. *W* **111** *(Block Cypher) sideways.*

D10	**D 1**	½d. emerald (6.25)	2·50	1·25	75
		Wi. Watermark sideways-inverted	6·00	3·00	1·50
D11		1d. carmine (4.25)	2·50	60	25
		Wi. Watermark sideways-inverted	—	—	10·00
D12		1½d. chestnut (10.24)	£140	47·00	22·00
		Wi. Watermark sideways-inverted	—	—	30·00
D13		2d. agate (7.24)	9·00	1·00	25
		Wi. Watermark sideways-inverted	—	—	10·00
D14		3d. dull violet (10.24)	10·00	1·50	25
		a. Printed on gummed side	£125	75·00	+0·02
		b. Experimental paper W **111a**	85·00	55·00	35·00
		Wi. Watermark sideways-inverted	10·00	5·00	2·00
D15		4d. dull grey-green (10.24)	50·00	15·00	4·25
		Wi. Watermark sideways-inverted	55·00	16·00	25·00
D16		5d. brownish cinnamon (1.31)	£120	65·00	45·00
D17		1s. dp blue (9.24)	40·00	8·50	50
		Wi. Watermark sideways-inverted			
D18	**D 2**	2s.6d. purple/*yellow* (5.24)	£240	85·00	1·75
		Wi. Watermark sideways-inverted			
Set of 9			£585	£200	60·00

Stamps from the above issue are known bisected and used for half their face value at the following sorting offices:

1d. Ashton under Lyne (1932), Hastings (1930), Penryn, Cornwall (1928), Shenfield (1926), Wimbledon, London SW (1925)

2d. Perranwell Station (1932)

1936–37. W **125** (E 8 R) sideways.

D19	**D 1**	½d. emerald (6.37)	12·00	10·50
D20		1d. carmine (5.37)	2·00	1·75
D21		2d. agate (5.37)	12·00	12·00
D22		3d. dull violet (3.37)	2·00	2·00
D23		4d. dull grey-green (12.36)	40·00	34·00
D24		5d. brownish cinnamon (11.36)	65·00	30·00
		a. Yellow-brown (1937)	28·00	28·00
D25		1s. dp blue (12.36)	11·00	8·50
D26	**D 2**	2s.6d. purple/*yellow* (5.37)	£320	12·00
Set of 8			£390	90·00

The 1d. of the above issue is known bisected and used for half its face value at the following sorting office:

1d. Solihull

(1937)

1937–38. *W* **127** *(G VI R) sideways.*

D27	**D 1**	½d. emerald (5.38)	13·00	3·75
D28		1d. carmine (5.38)	3·00	50
		Wi. Watermark sideways-inverted	£130	
D29		2d. agate (5.38)	2·75	30
		Wi. Watermark sideways-inverted	12·00	
D30		3d. violet (12.37)	10·50	30
		Wi. Watermark sideways-inverted	30·00	
D31		4d. dull grey-green (9.37)	£110	10·00
		Wi. Watermark sideways-inverted	£130	
D32		5d. yellow-brown (11.38)	16·50	75
		Wi. Watermark sideways-inverted	35·00	
D33		1s. dp blue (10.37)	78·00	75
		Wi. Watermark sideways-inverted	65·00	
D34	**D 2**	2s.6d. purple/yellow (9.38)	85·00	1·25
Set of 8			£260	18·00

The 2d. from the above issue is known bisected and used for half its face value at the following sorting offices:

2d. Boreham Wood (1951), Camberley (1951), Harpenden (1951, 1954), St. Albans (1951)

DATES OF ISSUE. The dates for Nos. D35/68 are those on which stanps were first issued by the Supplies Department to postmasters.

1951–52. *Colours changed and new value (1½d.).* W **127** (G VI R) sideways.

D35	**D 1**	½d. yellow-orange (18.9.51)	3·50	3·50
		a. Bright orange (5.54)	25·00	
D36		1d. violet-blue (6.6.51)	1·50	75
		Wi. Watermark sideways-inverted		
D37		1½d. green (11.2.52)	2·00	2·00
		Wi. Watermark sideways-inverted	10·00	
D38		4d. blue (14.8.51)	50·00	22·00
D39		1s. ochre (6.12.51)	28·00	5·25
		Wi. Watermark sideways-inverted		
Set of 5			75·00	28·00

The 1d. of the above issue is known bisected and used for half its face value at the following sorting offices:

1d. Camberley (1954), Capel, Dorking (1952)

1954–55. W **153** (Mult Tudor Crown and E 2 R) sideways.

D40	**D 1**	½d. bright orange (8.6.55)	7·00	5·25
		Wi. Watermark sideways-inverted	12·00	
D41		2d. agate (28.7.55)	26·00	18·00
		Wi. Watermark sideways-inverted		
D42		3d. violet (4.5.55)	62·00	52·00
D43		4d. blue (14.7.55)	26·00	26·00
		a. Imperf (pair)	£250	
D44		5d. yellow-brown (19.5.55)	20·00	15·50
D45	**D 2**	2s.6d. purple/*yellow* (11.54)	£135	5·75
		Wi. Watermark sideways-inverted		
Set of 6			£225	£100

1955–57. W **165** (Mult St. Edward's Crown and E 2 R) sideways.

D46	**D 1**	½d. bright orange (16.7.56)	2·75	3·25
		Wi. Watermark sideways-inverted	12·00	
D47		1d. violet-blue (7.6.56)	5·00	1·50
D48		1½d. green (13.2.56)	8·50	7·00
		Wi. Watermark sideways-inverted	15·00	
D49		2d. agate (22.5.56)	45·00	3·50
D50		3d. violet (5.3.56)	6·00	1·50
		Wi. Watermark sideways-inverted	30·00	
D51		4d. blue (24.4.56)	25·00	6·00
		Wi. Watermark sideways-inverted	35·00	
D52		5d. brown-ochre (23.3.56)	26·00	20·00
D53		1s. ochre (22.11.55)	65·00	2·25
		Wi. Watermark sideways-inverted		
D54	**D 2**	2s.6d. purple/yellow (28.6.57)	£200	8·25
		Wi. Watermark sideways-inverted		
D55		5s. scarlet/yellow (25.11.55)	£150	32·00
		Wi. Watermark sideways-inverted		
Set of 10			£425	65·00

Stamps from the above issue are known bisected and used for half their face value at the following sorting offices:

1d. Beswick, Manchester (1958), Huddersfield (1956), London SE (1957)
2d. Eynsham, Oxford (1956), Garelochhead, Helensburgh (1956), Harpenden (1956), Hull (1956), Kingston on Thames (1956), Leicester Square, London WC (1956), London WC (1956)
3d. London SE (1957) 4d. Poplar, London E (1958)

1959–63. W **179** (Mult St. Edward's Crown) sideways.

No.	Type	Description	Unused	Used
D56	D **1**	½d. bright orange (18.10.61)	15	1·25
		Wi. Watermark sideways-inverted	2·00	
D57		1d. violet-blue (9.5.60)	15	50
		Wi. Watermark sideways-inverted	16·00	
D58		1½d. green (5.10.60)	2·50	2·50
D59		2d. agate (14.9.59)	1·10	50
		Wi. Watermark sideways-inverted	50·00	
D60		3d. violet (24.3.59)	30	30
		Wi. Watermark sideways-inverted	12·00	
D61		4d. blue (17.12.59)	30	30
		Wi. Watermark sideways-inverted	35·00	
D62		5d. yellow-brown (6.11.61)	45	60
		Wi. Watermark sideways-inverted	5·00	
D63		6d. purple (29.3.62)	50	30
		Wi. Watermark sideways-inverted	45·00	
D64		1s. ochre (11.4.60)	90	30
		Wi. Watermark sideways-inverted	10·00	
D65	D **2**	2s.6d. purple/*yellow* (11.5.61)	3·00	50
		Wi. Watermark sideways-inverted	9·00	
D66		5s. scarlet/*yellow* (8.5.61)	8·25	1·00
		Wi. Watermark sideways-inverted	15·00	
D67		10s. blue/*yellow* (2.9.63)	11·50	5·75
		Wi. Watermark sideways-inverted	35·00	
D68		£1 black/*yellow* (2.9.63)	45·00	8·25
Set of 13			68·00	20·00

Whiter paper. The note after No. 586 also applies to Postage Due stamps.

Stamps from the above issue are known bisected and used for half their face value at the following sorting offices:

1d. Chieveley, Newbury (1962, 1963), Henlan, Llandyssil (1961), Mayfield (1962), St. Albans (1964)
2d. Doncaster (?)

1968–69. *Typo. No wmk. Chalk-surfaced paper.*

No.	Type	Description	Unused	Used
D69	D **1**	2d. agate (11.4.68)	75	1·00
		Ev. PVA gum (26.11.68)	75	
D70		3d. violet (9.9.68)	1·00	1·00
D71		4d. blue (6.5.68)	1·00	1·00
		Ev. PVA gum	£1500	
D72		5d. orange-brown (3.1.69)	8·00	11·00
D73		6d. purple (9.9.68)	2·25	1·75
D74		1s. ochre (19.11.68)	4·00	2·50
Set of 6			16·50	20·00

The 2d. and 4d. exist with gum arabic and PVA gum; the remainder with PVA gum only.

Stamps from the above issue are known bisected and used for half their face value at the following sorting offices:

4d. Northampton (1970)
6d. Kilburn, London NW (1968)

1968–69. *Photo. No wmk. Chalk-surfaced paper. PVA gum.*

No.	Type	Description	Unused	Used
D75	D **1**	4d. blue (12.6.69)	7·00	6·75
D76		8d. red (3.10.68)	50	1·00

Nos. D75/6 are smaller, 21½x17½ mm.

D **3**

D **4**

(Des J. Matthews. Photo Harrison)

1970 (17 June)–**75**. *Decimal Currency. Chalk-surfaced paper.*

No.	Type	Description	Unused	Used
D77	D **3**	½p. turquoise-blue (15.2.71)	15	2·50
D78		1p. dp reddish purple (15.2.71)	15	15
D79		2p. myrtle-green (15.2.71)	20	15
D80		3p. ultramarine (15.2.71)	20	15
D81		4p. yellow-brown (15.2.71)	25	15
D82		5p. violet (15.2.71)	25	15
D83		7p. red-brown (21.8.74)	35	1·00
D84	D **4**	10p. carmine	30	30
D85		11p. slate-green (18.6.75)	50	1·00
D86		20p. olive-brown	60	25
D87		50p. ultramarine	2·00	1·25
D88		£1 black	4·00	1·00
D89		£5 orange-yellow and black (2.4.73)	36·00	1·50
Set of 13			40·00	7·75
Presentation Pack (*P.O. Pack No.* 36) (*Nos.* D77/82, D84, D86/8 (3.11.71)			20·00	
Presentation Pack (*P.O. Pack No.* 93) (Nos. D77/88) (30.3.77)			10·00	

Later printings were on fluorescent white paper, some with dextrin added to the PVA gum (see notes after X1058).

The 2p. from the above issue is known bisected and used for half its face value at the following sorting office:

2p. Exeter (1977)

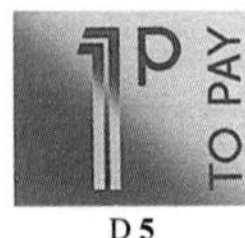

D **5**

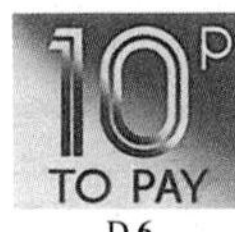

D **6**

(Des Sedley Place Design Ltd. Photo Harrison)

1982 (9 June). *Chalk-surfaced paper.*

No.	Type	Description	Unused	Used
D90	D **5**	1p. lake	10	30
D91		2p. brt blue	30	30
D92		3p. dp mauve	15	30
D93		4p. dp blue	15	25
D94		5p. sepia	20	25
D95	D **6**	10p. lt brown	30	40
D96		20p. olive-green	50	60
D97		25p. dp greenish blue	80	90
D98		50p. grey-black	1·75	1·75
D99		£1 red	3·25	1·25
D100		£2 turquoise-blue	7·00	4·25
D101		£5 dull orange	14·00	2·25
Set of 12			24·00	10·00
Set of 12 *Gutter Pairs*			48·00	
Presentation Pack			48·00	

D **7**

(Des Sedley Place Design Ltd. Litho Questa)

1994 (15 Feb). P 15×14 (with one elliptical hole on each vertical side).

No.	Type	Description	Unused	Used
D102	D **7**	1p. red, yellow & black	10	75
D103		2p. magenta, purple & black	10	75
D104		5p. yellow, red-brown & black	15	50
D105		10p. yellow, emerald & black	30	75
D106		20p. blue-green, violet & black	75	1·50
D107		25p. cerise, rosine & black	1·50	2·00
D108		£1 violet, magenta & black	7·00	10·00
D109		£1.20 greenish blue, blue-green & black	8·00	12·00
D110		£5 greenish black, blue-green & black	30·00	20·00
Set of 9			45·00	45·00
First Day Cover			22·00	
Presentation Pack			50·00	

Special First Day of Issue Postmark

London EC3 .... 22·00

Following changes in the method of collecting money due on unpaid or underpaid mail the use of postage due stamps was restricted from April 1995 to mail addressed to business customers and to Customs/V.A.T. charges levied by the Royal Mail on behalf of the Customs and Excise. The use of postage due stamps ceased on 28 January 2000.

SPECIMEN STAMPS (Postage Dues)

1914–22. *Wmk Simple Cypher Sideways.*

SD1	½d. emerald (No. D1) (23)	35·00
SD2	1d. carmine (No. D2) (23)	35·00
SD3	1½d. chestnut (No. D3) (23)	60·00
SD4	2d. agate (No. D4) (23, 26)	30·00
SD5	3d. violet (No. D5) (23, 26)	35·00
SD6	4d. dull grey-green (No. D6) (23)	35·00
SD7	5d. brownish cinnamon (No. D7) (23)	35·00
SD8	1s. bright blue (No. D8) (23, 26)	35·00

1924–31. *Wmk Block Cypher Sideways.*

SD9	½d. emerald (No. D10) (23, 26, 30)	35·00
SD10	1d. carmine (No. D11) (23, 26, 30)	45·00
SD11	1½d. chestnut (No. D12) (23)	45·00
SD12	2d. agate (No. D13) (23, 30)	35·00
SD13	3d. dull violet (No. D14) (23)	45·00
SD14	4d. dull grey-brown (No. D15) (23, 26)	45·00
SD15	1s. deep blue (No. D17) (23)	45·00
SD16	2s.6d. purple/*yellow* (No. D18) (23, 30)	45·00

1936–37. *Wmk "E8R" sideways.*

SD17	3d. dull violet (No. D22)
SD18	4d. dull grey-green (No. D23)
SD19	5d. brownish cinnamon (No. D24)
SD20	1s. deep blue (No. D25)

1937–38. *Wmk "GVIR" sideways.*

SD21	½d. emerald (No. D27) (9)
SD22	1d. carmine (No. D28) (9)
SD23	2d. agate (No. D29) (9)
SD24	3d. violet (No. D30) (9)
SD25	4d. dull grey-green (No. D31) (9)
SD26	5d. yellow-brown (No. D32) (9)
SD27	1s. deep blue (No. D33) (9)
SD28	2s.6d. purple/*yellow* (No. D34) (9)

OFFICIAL STAMPS

In 1840 the 1d. black (Type **1**), with "V R" in the upper corners, was prepared for official use, but was never issued for postal purposes. Obliterated specimens are those which were used for experimental trials of obliterating inks, or those that passed through the post by oversight.

V 1

1840. *Prepared for use but not issued; "V" "R" in upper corners. Imperf.*

V1	V **1**	1d. black	£15000	£20000

The following Official stamps would be more correctly termed Departmental stamps as they were exclusively for the use of certain government departments. Until 1882 official mail used ordinary postage stamps purchased at post offices, the cash being refunded once a quarter. Later the government departments obtained Official stamps by requisition.

Official stamps were on sale to the public for a short time at Somerset House but they were not sold from post offices. The system of only supplying the Government departments with stamps was open to abuse so that all official stamps were withdrawn on 13 May 1904.

OVERPRINTS, PERFORATIONS, WATERMARKS. All official stamps were overprinted by Thomas De La Rue & Co. and are perf 14. Except for the 5s., and 10s. on Anchor, they are on Crown watermarked paper unless otherwise stated.

INLAND REVENUE

These stamps were used by revenue officials in the provinces, mail to and from Head Office passing without a stamp. The London Office used these stamps only for foreign mail.

I.R. **OFFICIAL**	**I. R.** **OFFICIAL**
(O **1**)	(O **2**)

Optd with Types O **1** (½d. to 1s.) or O **2** (others).

1882–1901. *Stamps of Queen Victoria.*

(a) Issues of 1880–81

		Un	**Used*	*Used on cover*
O1	½d. dp green (1.11.82)	85·00	30·00	75·00
O2	½d. pale green	65·00	25·00	
O3	1d. lilac (Die II) (1.10.82)	4·00	2·00	20·00
	a. Optd in blue-black	£190	70·00	
	b. "OFFICIAL" omitted	—	£7000	
	Wi. Watermark inverted	—	£1250	
O4	6d. grey (Plate 18) (3.11.82)	£400	85·00	

No. O3 with the lines of the overprint transposed is an essay.

(b) Issues of 1884–88

O5	½d. slate-blue (8.5.85)	65·00	22·00	90·00
O6	2½d. lilac (12.3.85)	£300	£100	£950
O7	1s. dull green (12.3.85)	£4000	£1200	
O8	5s. rose (*blued paper*) (wmk Anchor) (12.3.85)	£7500	£2800	
O9	5s. rose (wmk Anchor) (3.90)	£3500	£1200	
	a. Raised stop after "R"	£4000	£1500	
	b. Optd in blue-black	£4500	£1500	
O9*c*	10s. cobalt (*blued paper*) (wmk Anchor) (12.3.85)	£16000	£4500	
	a. Raised stop after "R"			
O9*d*	10s. ultramarine (*blued paper*) (wmk Anchor) (12.3.85)	£12000	£3500	
O10	10s. ultramarine (wmk Anchor) (3.90)	£5000	£1750	
	a. Raised stop after "R"	£5750	£2500	
	b. Optd in blue-black	£5750	£2500	
O11	£1 brown-lilac (wmk Crowns) (12.3.85)	£35000	£18000	
	a. Frame broken	£40000		
O12	£1 brown-lilac (wmk Orbs) (3.90)	£55000	£25000	
	a. Frame broken	£65000		
	b. Optd in blue-black			

Nos. O3, O13, O15 and O16 may be found showing worn impressions of the overprints with thicker letters.

(c) Issues of 1887–92.

O13	½d. vermilion (15.5.88)	8·00	3·00	60·00
	a. Without "I.R."	£3500		
	b. Imperf	£2600		
	c. Opt double (imperf)	£3500		
O14	2½d. purple/*blue* (2.92)	£100	10·00	£300
O15	1s. dull green (9.89)	£550	£175	£2250
O16	£1 green (6.92)	£7500	£1750	
	a. No stop after "R"	—	£2500	
	b. Frame broken	£11000	£2800	

(d) Issues of 1887 and 1900.

O17	½d. blue-green (4.01)	10·00	6·00	£200
O18	6d. purple/rose-red (1.7.01)	£300	80·00	
O19	1s. green and carmine (12.01)	£2400	£850	

*O1/19 For well-centred, lightly used +35%

1902–04. *Stamps of King Edward VII. Ordinary paper.*

O20	½d. blue-green (4.2.02)	22·00	3·00	£110
O21	1d. scarlet (4.2.02)	15·00	2·00	75·00
O22	2½d. ultramarine (19.2.02)	£700	£175	
O23	6d. pale dull purple (14.3.04)	£135000	£80000	
O24	1s. dull green & carmine (29.4.02)	£2250	£500	
O25	5s. brt carmine (29.4.02)	£10000	£6000	
	a. Raised stop after "R"	£11000	£6500	
O26	10s. ultramarine (29.4.02)	£55000	£25000	
	a. Raised stop after "R"	£60000	£28000	
O27	£1 blue-green (29.4.02)	£37000	£18000	

SPECIMEN STAMPS (Inland Revenue)

1882–85. *Stamps of 1880–84.*

SO1	½d. deep green (No. O1) (9)	£200
SO2	½d. slate-blue (No. O5) (9)	£200
SO3	1d. lilac (No. O3) (9, 15)	£125
SO4	2½d. lilac (No. O6) (9)	£200
SO5	6d. grey (No. O4) (9, 15)	£200
SO6	1s. dull green (No. O7) (9)	£800

1885–90. *High value stamps of 1883–91.*

SO7	5s. rose (blued paper) (No. O8) (9, 11)	£1200
SO8	5s. rose (white paper) (No. O9) (9, 11, 13, 16)	£800
SO9	10s. cobalt (blued paper) (No. O9c) (11)	£2250
SO10	10s. ultramarine (blued paper) (No. O9d) (10)	£1800
SO11	10s. ultramarine (white paper) (No. O10) (9, 10, 11, 16)	£1100
SO12	£1 brown-lilac (wmk Crowns) (No. O11) (11)	£3000
SO13	£1 brown-lilac (wmk Orbs) (No. O12) (9, 11)	£5500

1887–1901. *Stamps of 1887–1900.*

SO14	½d. vermilion (No. O13) (9, 15)	80·00
SO15	½d. blue-green (No. O17) (15)	£100
SO16	2½d. purple/*blue* (No. O14) (9, 13, 15)	80·00
SO17	6d. purple/*rose-red* (No. O18) (15, 16)	£175
SO18	1s. dull green (No. O15) (9, 15)	£175
SO19	1s. green and carmine (No. O19) (15)	£700
SO20	£1 green (No. O16) (9, 10, 15)	£950

1902–04. *Stamps of King Edward VII.*

SO21	½d. blue-green (No. O20) (15)	£325
SO22	1d. scarlet (No. O21) (15)	£325
SO23	2½d. ultramarine (No. O22) (15, 16)	£425
SO24	6d. pale dull purple (No. O23) (16)	£18000
SO25	1s. dull green and carmine (No. O24) (16)	£650
SO26	5s. bright carmine (No. O25) (16)	£4200
SO27	10s. ultramarine (No. O26) (16)	£9800
SO28	£1 dull blue-green (No. O27) (16)	£8000

OFFICE OF WORKS

These were issued to Head and Branch (local) offices in London and to Branch (local) offices at Birmingham, Bristol, Edinburgh, Glasgow, Leeds, Liverpool, Manchester and Southampton. The overprints on stamps of value 2d. and upwards were created later in 1902, the 2d. for registration fees and the rest for overseas mail.

O. W.

OFFICIAL

(O **3**)

Optd with Type O **3**

1896 (24 Mar)–**02**. *Stamps of Queen Victoria.*

		Un	**Used*	*Used on Cover*
O31	½d. vermilion	£200	£100	£500
O32	½d. blue-green (2.02)	£300	£150	
O33	1d. lilac (Die II)	£350	£100	£550
O34	5d. dull purple & blue (II) (29.4.02)	£2000	£750	
O35	10d. dull purple & carmine (28.5.02)	£3500	£1000	

1902 (11 Feb)–**03**. *Stamps of King Edward VII. Ordinary paper.*

O36	½d. blue-green (2.02)	£500	£150	£1500
O37	1d. scarlet	£500	£150	£350
O38	2d. yellowish green & carmine-red (27.4.02)	£1500	£375	£2400
O39	2½d. ultramarine (29.4.02)	£2000	£550	£3750
O40	10d. dull purple & carmine (28.5.03)	£20000	£4750	

*O31/40 **For well-centred, lightly used** +25%

SPECIMEN STAMPS

1896–1902. *Stamps of 1887–1900 and 1d. lilac.*

SO46	½d. vermilion (No. O31) (9, 15)	£225
SO47	½d. blue-green (No. O32) (15)	£325
SO48	1d. lilac (No. O33) (9, 15, 16)	£225
SO49	5d. dull purple and blue (No. O34) (16)	£550
SO50	10d. dull purple and carmine (No. O35) (16)	£1200

1902–03. *Stamps of King Edward VII.*

SO51	½d. blue-green (No. O36) (15)	£325
SO52	1d. scarlet (No. O37) (15)	£325
SO53	2d. yellowish green and carmine-red (No. O38) (16)	£600
SO54	2½d. ultramarine (No. O39) (16)	£675
SO55	10d. dull purple and carmine (No. O40) (16)	£5000

ARMY

Letters to and from the War Office in London passed without postage. The overprinted stamps were distributed to District and Station Paymasters nationwide, including Cox and Co., the Army Agents, who were paymasters to the Household Division.

ARMY	ARMY	ARMY
OFFICIAL	OFFICIAL	OFFICIAL
(O **4**)	(O **5**)	(O **6**)

1896 (1 Sept)–**01**. *Stamps of Queen Victoria optd with Type* O **4** *(½d., 1d.) or O* **5** *(2½d., 6d.).*

		Un	**Used*	*Used on cover*
O41	½d. vermilion	3·50	1·50	40·00
	a. "OFFICIAI" (R.13/7)	£200	90·00	
	b. Lines of opt transposed	£2000		
	Wi. Watermark inverted	£500	£200	
O42	½d. blue-green (6.00)	4·00	7·00	
	Wi. Watermark inverted	£500	£175	
O43	1d. lilac (Die II)	3·50	2·50	65·00
	a. "OFFICAI" (R.13/7)	£150	85·00	
O44	2½d. purple/*blue*	30·00	20·00	£450
O45	6d. purple/*rose-red* (20.9.01)	75·00	40·00	£975

Nos. O41a and O43a occur in sheets overprinted by Forme 1.

1902–03. *Stamps of King Edward VII optd with Type* O **4** *(Nos. O48/50) or Type O* **6** *(O52). Ordinary paper.*

O48	½d. blue-green (11.2.02)	5·00	2·00	90·00
O49	1d. scarlet (11.2.02)	5·00	2·00	90·00
	a. "ARMY" omitted	†	—	
O50	6d. pale dull purple (23.8.02)	£150	70·00	
O52	6d. pale dull purple (12.03)	£1800	£750	

SPECIMEN STAMPS

1896–1901. *Stamps of 1887–1900 and 1d. lilac.*

S56	½d. vermilion (No. O41) (9)	£140
S57	½d. blue-green (No. O42) (15)	£180
S58	1d. lilac (No. O43) (9)	£140
S59	2½d. purple/*blue* (No. O44) (9)	£140
S60	6d. purple/*rose-red* (No. O45) (15)	£250

1902. *Stamps of King Edward VII.*

S61	½d. blue-green (No. O48) (15)	£225
S62	1d. scarlet (No. O49) (15)	£225
S63	6d. pale dull purple (No. O50) (16)	£275

GOVERNMENT PARCELS

These stamps were issued to all departments, including Head Office, for use on parcels weighing over 3 lb. Below this weight government parcels were sent by letter post to avoid the 55% of the postage paid from accruing to the railway companies, as laid down by parcel-post regulations. Most government parcels stamps suffered heavy postmarks in use.

GOVT

PARCELS

(O **7**)

Optd as Type O **7**

1883 (1 Aug)–**86**. *Stamps of Queen Victoria.*

O61	1½d. lilac (1.5.86)	£300	60·00
	a. No dot under "T"	£450	£110
	b. Dot to left of "T"	£450	£110
O62	6d. dull green (1.5.86)	£1750	£750
O63	9d. dull green	£1500	£600

		Un	*Used
O64	1s. orange-brown (watermark Crown, Pl 13)	£850	£200
	a. No dot under "T"	£1200	£250
	b. Dot to left of "T"	£1200	£250
O64*c*	1s. orange-brown (Pl 14)	£1800	£300
	ca. No dot under "T"	£2200	£400
	cb. Dot to left of "T"		

1887–90. *Stamps of Queen Victoria.*

O65	1½d. dull purple & pale green (29.10.87)	80·00	7·00
	a. No dot under "T"	£120	18·00
	b. Dot to right of "T"	£120	18·00
	c. Dot to left of "T"	£120	18·00
O66	6d. purple/rose-red (19.12.87)	£150	30·00
	a. No dot under "T"	£150	30·00
	b. Dot to right of "T"	£200	35·00
	c. Dot to left of "T"	£200	35·00
O67	9d. dull purple & blue (21.8.88)	£225	40·00
	Wi. Watermark inverted		
O68	1s. dull green (25.3.90)	£400	£175
	a. No dot under "T"	£475	—
	b. Dot to right of "T"	£475	£250
	c. Dot to left of "T"	£500	£250
	d. Optd in blue-black		

1891–1900. *Stamps of Queen Victoria.*

O69	1d. lilac (Die II) (18.6.97)	70·00	15·00
	a. No dot under "T"	£100	38·00
	b. Dot to left of "T"	£100	38·00
	c. Opt inverted	£3750	£1700
	d. Ditto. Dot to left of "T"	£4000	£2000
	Wi. Watermark inverted	—	£350
O70	2d. grey-green & carmine (24.10.91)	£150	20·00
	a. No dot under "T"	£250	45·00
	b. Dot to left of "T"	£250	45·00
O71	4½d. green & carmine (29.9.92)	£250	£180
	b. Dot to right of "T"		
	Wi. Watermark inverted		
O72	1s. green & carmine (11.00)	£425	£160
	a. Opt inverted	†	£9000

*O61/72 **For well-centred lightly used** +100%

1902. *Stamps of King Edward VII. Ordinary paper.*

O74	1d. scarlet (30.10.02)	30·00	12·00
O75	2d. yellowish green & carmine-red (29.4.02)	£140	35·00
O76	6d. pale dull purple (19.2.02)	£240	35·00
	a. Opt double, one albino	£10000	
O77	9d. dull purple & ultramarine (28.8.02)	£480	£150
O78	1s. dull green & carmine (17.12.02)	£800	£225

The "no dot under T" variety occured on R.12/3 and 20/2. The "dot to left of T" comes four times in the sheet on R.2/7, 6/7, 7/9 and 12/9. The best example of the "dot to right of T" is on R.20/1. All three varieties were corrected around 1897.

SPECIMEN STAMPS

1883–86. *Stamps of 1881–84.*

SO29	1½d. lilac (No. O61) (9)	£120
SO30	6d. dull green (No. O62) (9)	£175
SO31	9d. dull green (No. O63) (9)	£175
SO32	1s. orange-brown (No. O64) (9)	£200

1887–1900. *Stamps of 1887–1900 and 1d. lilac.*

SO33	1d. lilac (No. O69) (15)	£275
SO34	1½d. dull purple and pale green (No. O65) (9, 10, 13, 15)	£175
SO35	2d. green and carmine (No. O70) (9, 11, 13, 15)	£175
SO36	4½d. grey-green and carmine (No. O71) (9, 13, 15)	£175
SO37	6d. purple/*rose-red* (No. O76) (9, 13, 15)	£175
SO38	9d. dull purple and blue (No. O67) (9, 10, 13, 15)	£175
SO39	1s. dull green (No. O68) (9, 13, 15)	£175
SO40	1s. green and carmine (No. O72) (9)	£225

1902. *Stamps of King Edward VII.*

SO41	1d. scarlet (No. O74) (16)	£185
SO42	2d. yellowish green and carmine-red (No. O75) (16)	£185
SO43	6d. pale dull purple (No. O76) (15, 16)	£180
SO44	9d. dull purple and ultramarine (No. O77) (16)	£325
SO45	1s. dull green and carmine (No. O78) (16)	£375

BOARD OF EDUCATION

BOARD

OF

EDUCATION

(O **8**)

Optd with Type O **8**

1902 (19 Feb). *Stamps of Queen Victoria.*

O81	5d. dull purple & blue (II)	£2000	£550
O82	1s. green & carmine	£5500	£8500

1902 (19 Feb)–**04**. *Stamps of King Edward VII. Ordinary paper.*

		Un	**Used*	*Used on cover*
O83	½d. blue-green	£150	35·00	£350
O84	1d. scarlet	£150	35·00	£375
O85	2½d. ultramarine	£3000	£250	
O86	5d. dull purple & ultramarine (6.2.04)	£15000	£4000	
O87	1s. dull green & carmine (23.12.02)	£75000		

SPECIMEN STAMPS

1902. *Stamps of 1887–1900.*

SO64	5d. dull purple and blue (No. O81) (15)	£750
SO65	1s. grey-green and carmine (No. O82) (15)	£1500

1902–04. *Stamps of King Edward VII.*

SO66	½d. blue-green (No. O83) (15)	£225
SO67	1d. scarlet (No. O84) (15)	£225
SO68	2½d. ultramarine (No. O85) (15)	£500
SO69	5d. dull purple and ultramarine (No. O86) (15)	£1800
SO70	1s. dull green and carmine (No. O87) (15)	£12000

ROYAL HOUSEHOLD

R.H.

OFFICIAL

(O **9**)

1902. *Stamps of King Edward VII optd with Type* O **9**. *Ordinary paper.*

		Un	**Used*	*Used on cover*
O91	½d. blue-green (29.4.02)	£350	£180	£1000
O92	1d. scarlet (19.2.02)	£300	£150	£900

SPECIMEN STAMPS

1902. *Stamps of King Edward VII.*

SO71	½d. blue-green (No. O91) (16)	£600
SO72	1d. scarlet (No. O92) (15)	£600

ADMIRALTY

ADMIRALTY

OFFICIAL

(O **10**)

ADMIRALTY

OFFICIAL

(O **11**) (with different "M")

1903 (1 Apr). *Stamps of King Edward VII optd with Type* O **10**. *Ordinary paper.*

		Un	**Used*	*Used on cover*
O101	½d. blue-green	25·00	12·00	
O102	1d. scarlet	15·00	6·00	£275
O103	1½d. dull purple & green	£225	£110	
O104	2d. yellowish green & carminered	£250	£125	

O105	2½d. ultramarine	£375	£110
O106	3d. purple/*yellow*	£300	£120

1903–04. *Stamps of King Edward VII optd with Type* O **11**. *Ordinary paper.*

O107	½d. blue-green (9.03)	50·00	20·00	£450
O108	1d. scarlet (12.03)	50·00	20·00	£125
O109	1½d. dull purple & green (2.04)	£700	£450	
O110	2d. yellowish green & carminered (3.04)	£1100	£500	
O111	2½d. ultramarine (3.04)	£1200	£700	
O112	3d. dull purple/*orange-yellow* (12.03)	£1000	£250	

Stamps of various issues perforated with a Crown and initials ("H. M.O.W.", "O.W.", "B.T." or "S.O.") or with initials only ("H.M.S.O." or "D.S.I.R.") have also been used for official purposes, but these are outside the scope of this catalogue.

SPECIMEN STAMPS

1903. *Stamps of King Edward VII overprinted with Type* O **10**.

SO73	½d. blue-green (No. O101) (16)	£225
SO74	1d. scarlet (No. O102) (16)	£225
SO75	1½d. dull purple and green (No. O103) (16)	£300
SO76	2d. yellowish green and carmine-red (No. O104) (16)	£300
SO77	2d. ultramarine (No. O105) (16)	£300
SO78	3d. dull purple/*orange-yellow* (No. O106) (16)	£300

1903–04. *Stamps of King Edward VII overprinted with Type* O **11**.

SO79	½d. blue-green (No. O107) (16)	£225
SO80	1d. scarlet (No. O108) (16)	£225
SO81	2d. yellowish green and carmine-red (No. O110) (16)	£325
SO82	3d. dull purple/orange-yellow (No. O112) (16)	£325

POSTAL FISCAL STAMPS

PRICES. Prices in the used column are for stamps with genuine postal cancellations dated from the time when they were authorised for use as postage stamps. Beware of stamps with fiscal cancellations removed and fraudulent postmarks applied.

VALIDITY. The 1d. surface-printed stamps were authorised for postal use from 1 June 1881 and at the same time the 1d. postage issue, No. 166, was declared valid for fiscal purposes. The 3d. and 6d. values together with the embossed issues were declared valid for postal purposes by another Act effective from 1 January 1883.

SURFACE-PRINTED ISSUES

(Typo Thomas De La Rue & Co.)

F **1** Rectangular Buckle

F **2**

F **3** Octagonal Buckle

F **4**

F **5** Double-lined Anchor

F **6** Single-lined Anchor

1853–57. P 15½×15.

(a) Wmk F **5** *(inverted) (1853–55).*

			Un	*Used	Used on cover
F1	F **1**	1d. lt blue (10.10.53)	35·00	45·00	£170
		Wi. Watermark upright	£110		
		Wj. Watermark reversed (large loop to right)	£110		
F2	F **2**	1d. ochre (10.53)	£100	£120	£475
		a. *Tête-bêche* (in block of four)	£16000		
		Wj. Watermark reversed (large loop to right)	£250		
F3	F **3**	1d. pale turquoise-blue (12.53)	27·00	42·00	£250
		Wi. Watermark upright	75·00		
F4		1d. lt blue/*blue* (12.53)	70·00	70·00	£400
		Wi. Watermark upright	£120	£190	
F5	F **4**	1d. reddish lilac/*blue glazed paper* (25.3.55)	£100	£110	£350
		Wi. Watermark upright	£150	£200	

Only one example is known of No. F2a outside the National Postal Museum and the Royal Collection.

(b) Wmk F **6** *(1856–57).*

F6	F **4**	1d. reddish lilac (*shades*)	9·25	7·75	£140
		Wi. Watermark inverted	£120		
		Wj. Watermark reversed	£140		
F7		1d. reddish lilac/*bluish* (*shades*) (1857)	9·25	7·75	£140
		Wj. Watermark reversed	£140		

INLAND REVENUE

(F 7)

1860 (3 Apr). *No. F7 optd with Type* F **7**, *in red.*

F8	F **4**	1d. dull reddish lilac/*blue*	£700	£550	£1100
		Wj. Wmk reversed			

BLUE PAPER. In the following issues we no longer distinguish between bluish and white paper. There is a range of papers from white or greyish to bluish.

F **8**

F **9**

F 10

1860–67. *Bluish to white paper.* P 15½×15.

(a) Wmk F **6** *(1860).*

F9	F **8**	1d. reddish lilac (May)	11·00	11·00	£140
		Wi. Watermark inverted	£100		
F10	F **9**	3d. reddish lilac (June)	£350	£225	£400
F11	F **10**	6d. reddish lilac (Oct)	£160	£140	£350
		Wi. Watermark inverted	£200	£160	
		Wj. Watermark reversed	£200	£160	

(b) W **40**. *(Anchor 16 mm high) (1864).*

F12	F **8**	1d. pale reddish lilac (Nov)	9·25	9·25	£140
		Wi. Watermark inverted			
F13	F **9**	3d. pale reddish lilac	£200	£140	£400
F14	F **10**	6d. pale reddish lilac	£160	£140	£350
		Wi. Watermark inverted	£250		

(c) W **40** *(Anchor 18 mm high) (1867).*

F15	F **8**	1d. reddish lilac	18·00	18·00	£200
F16	F **9**	3d. reddish lilac	90·00	90·00	£350
F17	F **10**	6d. reddish lilac	80·00	65·00	£225

For stamps perf 14, see Nos. F24/7.

F 11

F 12

Four Dies of Type F 12

Nos. F19/21 show "O" of "ONE" circular. No. F22 (Die 4) shows a horizontal oval and is the only Die to have this plus heavy shading on hair ribbons.

Die 1. Four lines of shading in left band of ribbon opposite "Y" of "PENNY". Small ornaments and heavy shading under chin

Die 2. Two lines of shading in left band of ribbon. Clear lines of shading under chin. Small ornaments

Die 3. Mid-size ornaments: line shading under chin extended halfway down neck

Die 4. Large size ornaments: straight line of shading continued to bottom of neck

1867–81. *White to bluish paper.* P 14.

(a) W **47** *(Small Anchor).*

F18	F **11**	1d. purple (1.9.67)	16·00	16·00	£110
		Wi. Watermark inverted	£100	£110	
F19	F **12**	1d. purple (Die I) (6.68)	5·00	5·50	£110
		Wi. Watermark inverted	70·00		
F20		1d. purple (Die 2) (6.76)	20·00	14·00	£250
F21		1d. purple (Die 3) (3.77)	10·00	10·00	£160
F22		1d. purple (Die 4) (7.78)	6·50	6·50	£100

(b) W **48** *(Orb).*

F23	F **12**	1d. purple (Die 4) (1.81)	6·50	3·25	90·00
		Wi. Watermark inverted	£100		

1881. *White to bluish paper.* P 14.

(a) W **40** *(Anchor 18 mm high) (Jan).*

F24	F **9**	3d. reddish lilac	£650	£350	£750
F25	F **10**	6d. reddish lilac	£300	£140	£350

(b) W **40** *(Anchor 20 mm high) (May).*

F26	3d. reddish lilac	£500	£275	£550
F27	6d. reddish lilac	£275	£140	£350·0

ISSUES EMBOSSED IN COLOUR

(Made at Somerset House)

The embossed stamps were struck from dies not appropriated to any special purpose on paper which had the words "INLAND REVENUE" previously printed, and thus became available for payment of any duties for which no special stamps had been provided.

The die letters are included in the embossed designs and holes were drilled for the insertion of plugs showing figures indicating dates of striking.

F 13

F 14

INLAND REVENUE (F 15)

INLAND REVENUE (F 16)

1860 (3 Apr)–**71**. *Types* F **13/14** *and similar types embossed on bluish paper. Underprint Type* F **15**. No wmk. Imperf.

F28	2d. pink (Die A) (1.1.71)	£550	
F29	3d. pink (Die C)	£140	
	a. *Tête-bêche* (vert pair)	£1100	
F30	3d. pink (Die D)	£550	
F31	6d. pink (Die T)		
F32	6d. pink (Die U)	£275	
	a. *Tête-bêche* (vert pair)		
F33	9d. pink (Die C) (1.1.71)	£700	
F34	1s. pink (Die E) (28.6.61)	£550	
	a. *Tête-bêche* (vert pair)		
F35	1s. pink (Die F) (28.6.61)	£200	
	a. *Tête-bêche* (vert pair)	£800	
F36	2s. pink (Die K) (6.8.61)	£550	
F37	2s.6d. pink (Die N) (28.6.61)		
F38	2s.6d. pink (Die O) (28.6.61)	£275	

1871 (Aug). *As last but perf 12½.*

F39	2d. pink (Die A)	£350	
F42	9d. pink (Die C)	£800	
F43	1s. pink (Die E)	£550	
F44	1s. pink (Die F)	£475	
F45	2s.6d. pink (Die O)	£275	

1874 (Nov). *Types as before embossed on white paper. Underprint Type F* **16**, *in green.* W **47** (Small Anchor). P 12½.

F46	2d. pink (Die A)		
F47	9d. pink (Die C)		
F48	1s. pink (Die F)	£550	
F49	2s.6d. pink (Die O)		

It is possible that the 2d., 9d. and 2s.6d. may not exist with the thin underprint, Type F **16**, in this shade.

1875 (Nov)–**80**. *As last but colour changed and on white or bluish paper.*

F50	2d. vermilion (Die A) (1880)	£400	
F51	9d. vermilion (Die C) (1876)	£550	
F52	1s. vermilion (Die E)	£350	
F53	1s. vermilion (Die F)	£800	
F54	2s.6d. vermilion (Die O) (1878)	£350	

1882 (Oct). *As last but* W **48** *(Orbs).*

F55	2d. vermilion (Die A)		
F56	9d. vermilion (Die C)		
F57	1s. vermilion (Die E)		
F58	2s.6d. vermilion (Die O)	£700	£550

Although specimen overprints of Nos. F55/7 are known there is some doubt if these values were issued.

The sale of Inland Revenue stamps up to the 2s. value ceased from 30 December 1882 and stocks were called in and destroyed. The 2s.6d. value remained on sale until 2 July 1883 when it was replaced by the 2s.6d. "Postage & Revenue" stamps. Inland Revenue stamps still in the hands of the public continued to be accepted for revenue and postal purposes.

SPECIMEN STAMPS (Postal Fiscals)

(i) Receipt and Draft Stamps

1856. *1d. lilac, Type* F **4**, *Wmk* F **6**, *White paper.*

No.	Description	Price
SF1	1d. reddish lilac (No. F6) (2)	£110

(ii) Surface-printed Inland Revenue Stamps

1860. *Provisional Issue, Wmk* F **6**.

No.	Description	Price
SF2	1d. reddish lilac (No. F9) (2)	£125
SF3	3d. pale reddish lilac (No. F10) (2)	£150
SF4	6d. reddish lilac (No. F11) (2)	£150

1864. *Change to watermark* W **40** *(Anchor 16 mm high).*

No.	Description	Price
SF5	3d. pale reddish lilac (No. F13) (9)	£125

1867. *Change to watermark* W **40** *(Anchor 18 mm high).*

No.	Description	Price
SF6	3d. reddish lilac (No. F16) (9, 10)	£125
SF7	6d. reddish lilac (No. F17) (6, 9, 10)	£125

1867–81. *White to bluish paper.*

No.	Description	Price
SF8	1d. reddish lilac (No. F20) (9)	65·00
SF9	1d. purple (No. F21) (9)	50·00

1881. *Wmk* W **40** *(Anchor 20 mm high).*

No.	Description	Price
SF10	3d. reddish lilac (No. F26) (9)	£200
SF11	6d. pale reddish lilac (No. F27) (9)	£200

(iii) Embossed Inland Revenue Stamps

1860–71. *Underprint* F **15**, *bluish paper, no wmk.* Imperf.

No.	Description	Price
SF12	2d. pink (No. F28) (2, 9)	£125
SF13	9d. pink (No. F33) (2, 9)	£125
SF14	1s. pink (No. F35) (2, 9)	£125
SF15	2s.6d. pink (No. F38) (2, 9)	£125

1861–71. As last but perf 12½.

No.	Description	Price
SF16	2d. pink (No. 39) (9)	75·00
SF17	9d. pink (No. 42) (9)	£125
SF18	1s. pink (No. 44) (9)	£125
SF19	2s.6d. pink (No. 45) (9)	£125

1875. *Underprint* F **16**, *white or bluish paper.* W **47**. P 12½.

No.	Description	Price
SF20	2d. vermilion (No. 50) (9)	£125
SF21	9d. vermilion (No. 51) (9, 10)	£125
SF22	1s. vermilion (No. 52) (9, 10)	£125
SF23	2s.6d. vermilion (No. 54) (9)	£125

1882. As last but *W* **48**.

No.	Description	Price
SF24	2d. vermilion (No. 55) (9)	£150
SF25	9d. vermilion (No. 56) (9)	£150
SF26	1s. vermilion (No. 57) (9)	£150
SF27	2s.6d. vermilion (No. 58) (9)	£150

POST OFFICE STAMP BOOKLETS

The following listing covers all booklets sold by post offices from 1904.

All major variations of contents and cover are included, but minor changes to the covers and differences on the interleaves have been ignored.

From 1913 each booklet carried an edition number, linked to an internal Post Office system of identification which divided the various booklets into series. In 1943 these edition numbers were replaced by edition dates. No attempt has been made to list separate edition numbers for booklets prior to 1943, although notes giving their extent are provided for each booklet. Edition dates from August 1943 are listed separately and exist for all £.s.d. and most Decimal Stitched booklets (except for the 1s. booklets, the 2s. booklets (N1/3), the 5s. "Philympia" booklets (No. HP34), the £1 "Stamps for Cooks" booklet (No. ZP1) and the Decimal Sponsored booklets). They are those found printed upon the booklets, either on the outer back cover or on the white leaves.

ERRORS OF MAKE-UP of booklets exist but we do not list them here. More detailed listings can be found in the 2nd, 3rd and 4th volumes of the *Great Britain Specialised Catalogue*.

ILLUSTRATIONS. The illustrations of the covers are ¾ size except where otherwise stated. Those in Queen Elizabeth II Decimal Sections C to Hare ⅔ size, except where otherwise stated.

PRICES quoted are for complete booklets containing stamps with "average" perforations (i.e. full perforations on two edges of the pane only). Booklets containing panes with complete perforations are worth more.

KING EDWARD VII

2s. Booklets

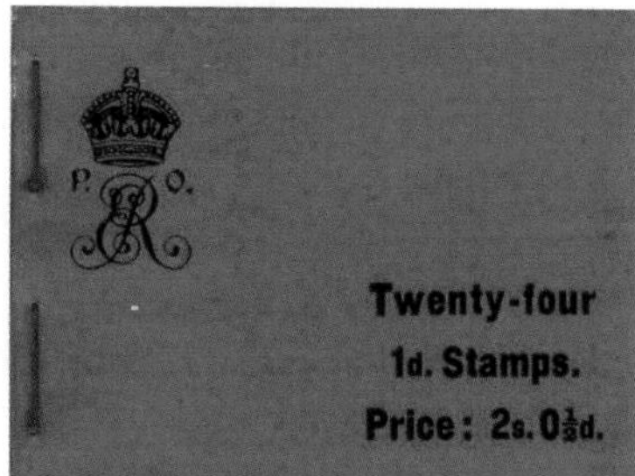

BA 1

1904 (Mar). *Red cover printed in black as Type* BA **1**. *Pages of six stamps:* 24 × 1*d. Wmk Imperial Crown* (*No.* 219).

BA1 .... £325

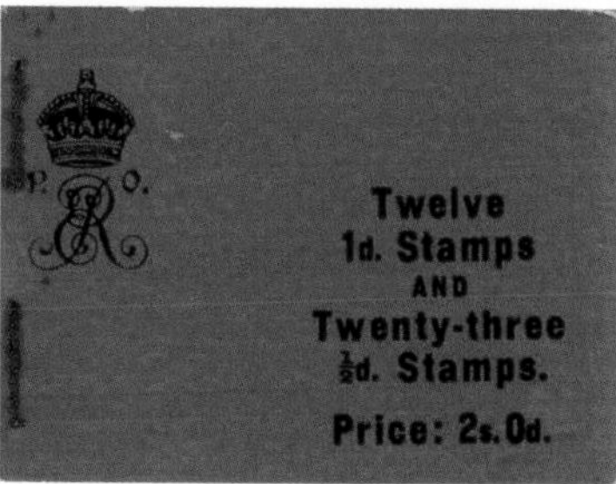

BA 2

1906 (June). *Red cover printed in black as Type* BA **2**. *As before but make-up changed to include* 12 × 1*d. and* 23 × ½*d. and label showing one green cross* (*Nos.* 217 *and* 219).

BA2 .... £1000

1907 (Aug). *Red cover printed in black as Type* BA **2**. *Make-up changed to include* 18 × 1*d. and* 11 × ½*d. and label showing one green cross* (*Nos.* 217 *and* 219).

BA3 .... £1150

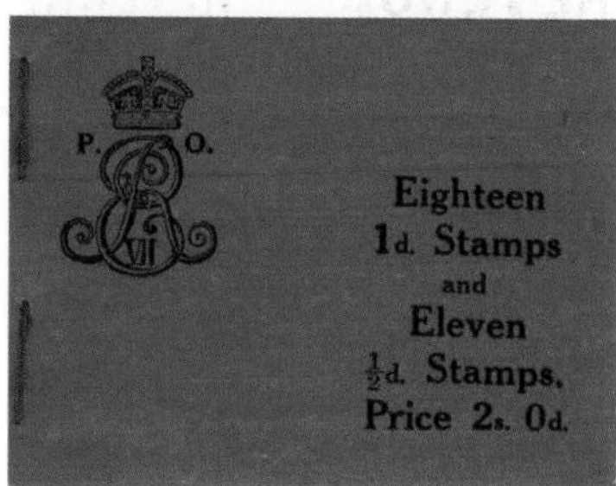

BA 6

1911 (June). *Red cover printed in black as Type* BA **2** *but showing a larger Post Office cypher on cover. As before, but containing stamps by Harrison & Sons* (*Nos.* 267 *and* 272).

BA6 .... £1150

KING GEORGE V

2s. Booklets

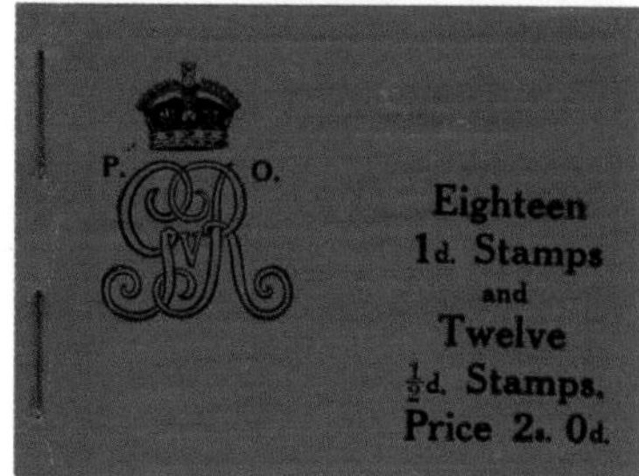

BB 1

1911 (Aug). *Red cover printed in black as Type* BA **2** *showing King George V cypher. Pages of six stamps:* 18 × 1*d. and* 12 × ½*d. Wmk Crown* (*Nos.* 325, 329) *Die* 1B.

BB1 .... £750

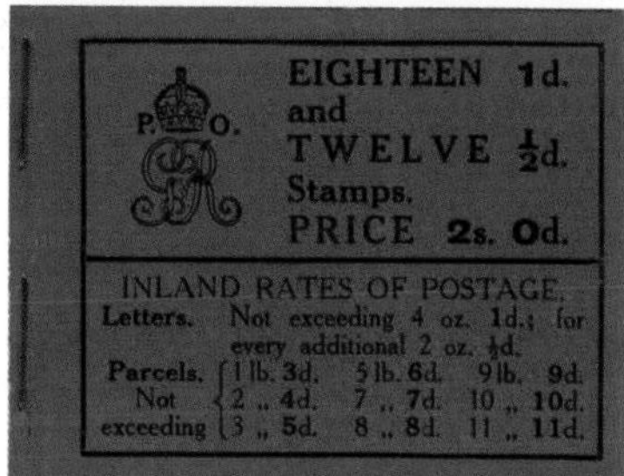

BB 2

1912 (April). *As before, but red cover printed in black as Type* BB **2**.

BB2 .... £1000

1912 (Sept). *As before, but wmk Simple Cypher* (*Nos.* 334, 336) *Die* 1B.

BB3 .... £775

BB 5

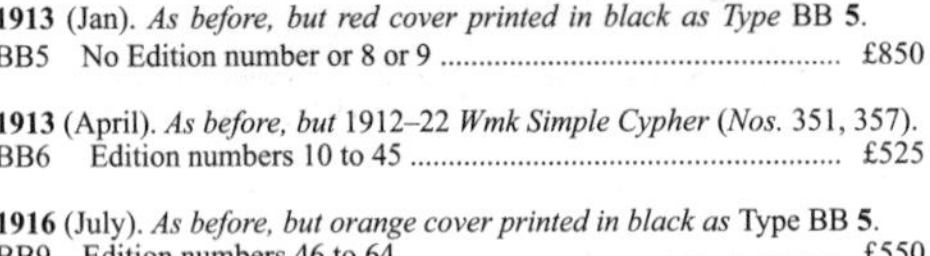

1913 (Jan). *As before, but red cover printed in black as Type* BB **5**.
BB5 No Edition number or 8 or 9 .... £850

1913 (April). *As before, but* 1912–22 *Wmk Simple Cypher* (*Nos.* 351, 357).
BB6 Edition numbers 10 to 45 .... £525

1916 (July). *As before, but orange cover printed in black as* Type BB **5**.
BB9 Edition numbers 46 to 64 .... £550

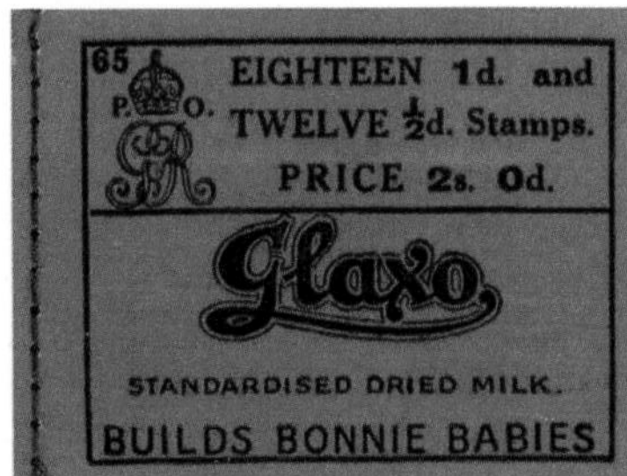

BB 10

1917 (Sept). *As before, but orange cover printed in black as Type* BB **10**.
BB10 Edition numbers 65 to 81 .... £550

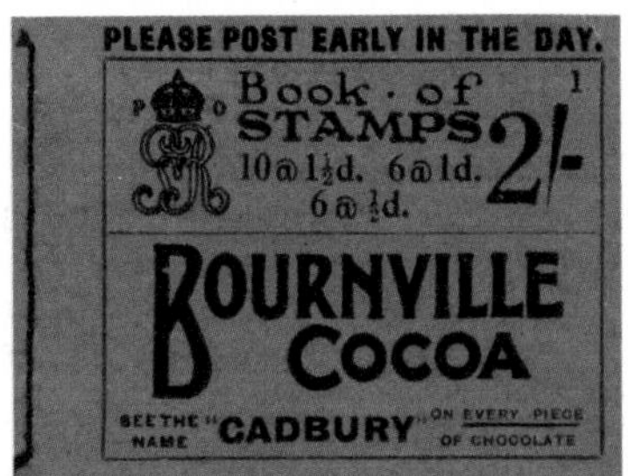

BB 11

1924 (Feb). *Blue cover printed in black as Type* BB **11**. *Pages of six stamps:* 10 × 1½*d.* (*first completed by two perforated labels*), 6 × 1*d. and* 6 × ½*d.* 1912–22 *Wmk Simple Cypher* (*Nos.* 351, 357, 362).
BB11 Edition numbers 1 or 2 .... £1350

1933 (Oct). *As before, but* 1924–26 *Wmk Block Cypher* (*Nos.* 418/20).
BB12 Edition numbers 3 to 102 & 108 to 254 .... £500

BB 13

1929 (May). *Postal Union Congress issue. Cover of special design as Type* BB **13** *printed in blue on buff as before but containing stamps of the P.U.C. issue* (*Nos.* 434/6).
BB13 Edition numbers 103 to 107 .... £500

1934 (Feb). *Blue cover printed in black as Type* BB **11**, *but containing stamps with Block Cypher wmk printed by Harrison & Sons* (*Nos.* 418/20).
BB14 Edition numbers 255 to 287 .... £525

1935 (Jan). *As before, but containing stamps of the photogravure issue with the se-tenant advertisements printed in brown* (*Nos.* 439/41).
BB15 Edition numbers 288 to 297 .... £1300

BB 16

1935 (May). *Silver Jubilee issue. Larger size cover printed in blue on buff as Type* BB **16** *and containing pages of four stamps with no se-tenant advertisements:* 12 × 1½*d.*, 4 × 1*d. and* 4 × ½*d.* (*Nos.* 453/5).
BB16 Edition numbers 298 to 304 .... 90·00

1935 (July). *As No.* BB **15**, *but containing stamps of the photogravure issue with se-tenant advertisements printed in black* (*Nos.* 439/41).
BB17 Edition numbers 305 to 353 .... £375

3s. Booklets

1918 (Oct). *Orange cover printed in black as Type* BB **18**. *Pages of six stamps:* 12 × 1½*d.*, 12 × 1*d. and* 12 × ½*d.* 1912–22 *Wmk Simple Cypher* (*Nos.* 351, 357, 362).
BB18 Edition numbers 1 to 11 .... £675

HAVE YOU READ THE NOTES AT THE BEGINNING OF THIS CATALOGUE?
These often provide answers to the enquiries we receive

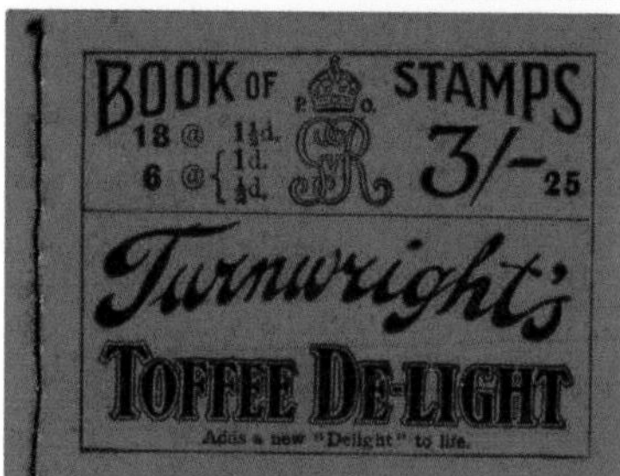

BB **19**

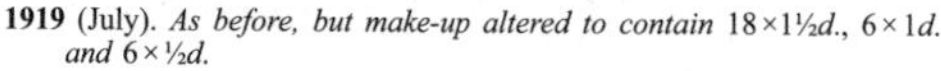

1919 (July). *As before, but make-up altered to contain* 18×1½*d.*, 6×1*d.* *and* 6×½*d.*

BB19 Edition numbers 12 to 26 .... £675

BB **20**

1921 (April). *Experimental booklet bound in blue covers as Type* BB **20**, *containing pages of six stamps:* 18×2*d.* (Die I) (*No.* 368).

BB20 Edition numbers 35 and part 37 .... £850

1921 (Dec). *As before, but containing* 2*d.* (Die II) (*No.* 370).

BB21 Edition numbers 12, 13 and part 37 .... £900

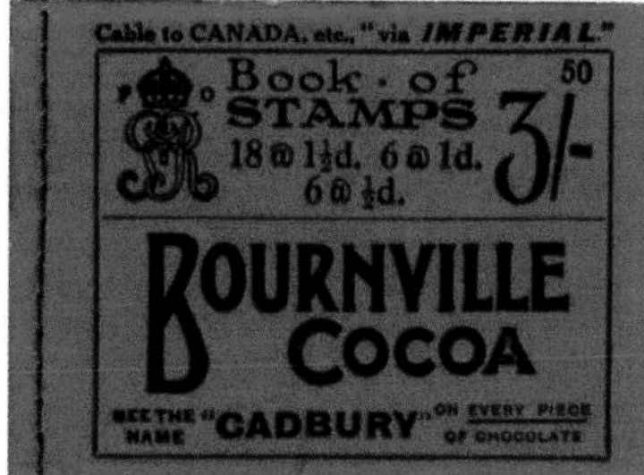

BB **22**

1922 (May). *Scarlet cover printed in black as Type* BB **22**. *Pages of six stamps:* 18×1½*d.*, 6×1*d. and* 6×½*d.* (Nos. 351,357, 362).

BB22 Edition numbers 19, 20, 22, 23 and 25 to 54 .... £850

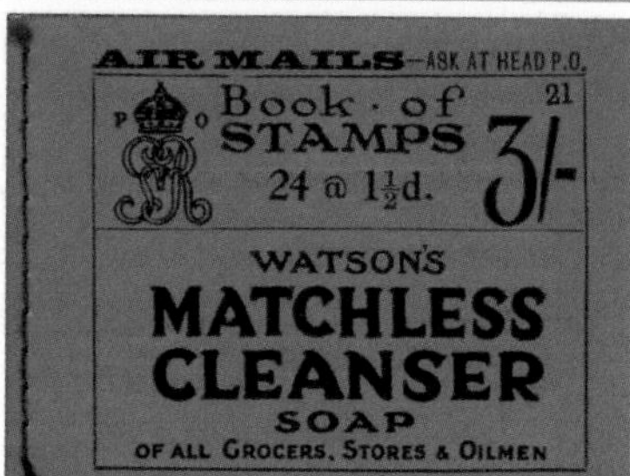

BB **23**

1922 (June). *Experimental booklet as Edition numbers* 12 *and* 13 *bound in blue covers as Type* BB **22**, *containing pages of six stamps:* 24×1½*d.* . (*No.* 362).

BB23 Edition numbers 21 or 24 .... £900

1924 (Feb). *Scarlet cover printed in black as Type* BB **22**, *but containing stamps with Block Cypher wmk, printed by Waterlow & Sons* (*Nos.* 418/20).

BB24 Edition numbers 55 to 167 & 173 to 273 .... £325

1929 (May). *Postal Union Congress issue. Cover of special design as Type* BB **13** *printed in red on buff as before but containing stamps of the P.U.C. issue* (*Nos.* 434/6).

BB25 Edition numbers 168 to 172 .... £380

1934 (Mar). *Scarlet cover printed in black as Type* BB **22**, *but containing stamps with the Block Cypher wmk printed by Harrison & Sons* (*Nos.* 418/20).

BB26 Edition numbers 274 to 288 .... £400

1935 (May). *Silver Jubilee issue. Larger size cover printed in red on buff as Type* BB **16** *and containing pages of four stamps:* 20×1½d.., 4×1*d. and* 4×½d. (*Nos.* 453/5).

BB28 Edition numbers 294 to 297 .... 90·00

1935 (July). *As No.* BB **26**, *but containing stamps of the photogravure issue* (*Nos.* 439/41).

BB29 Edition numbers 289 to 293 & 298 to 319 .... £360

3s.6d. Booklets

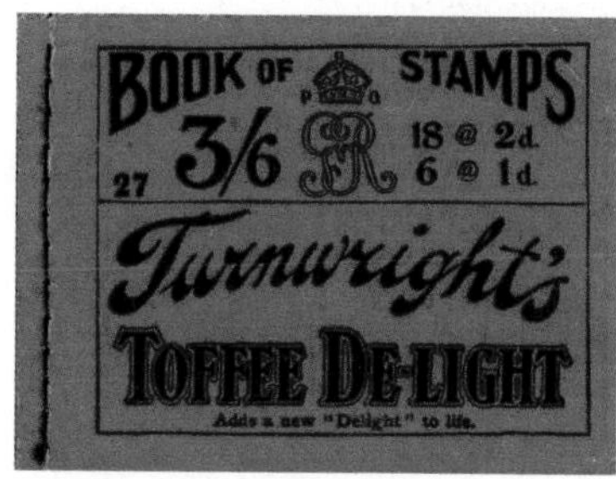

BB **30**

1920 (July). *Orange cover printed in black as Type* BB **30**, *containing pages of six stamps:* 18×2*d. and* 6×1*d.* (*Nos.* 357, 368).

BB30 Edition numbers 27 to 32 .... £900

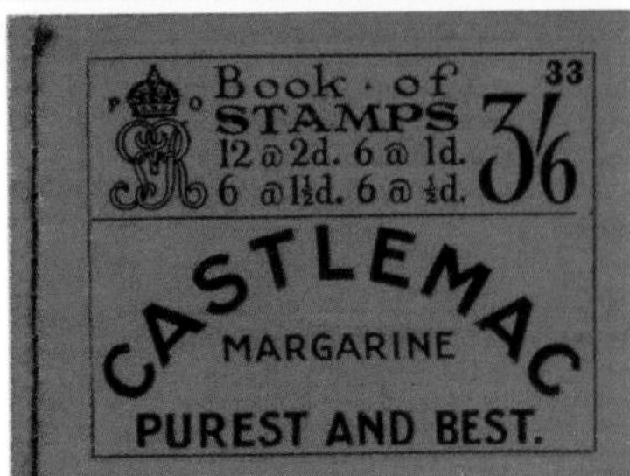

BB 31

1921 (Jan). *Orange-red cover printed in black as Type* BB **31**, *as before but make-up changed to include stamps of* 1912–22 *issue with the Simple Cypher wmk:* 12×2*d.,* 6×1½*d.,* 6×1*d. and* 6×½d. (*Nos.* 351, 357, 362, 368 or 370).

BB31 Edition numbers 1 to 11, 14 to 18, 33, 34, 36 & 38 .... £900

5s. Booklets

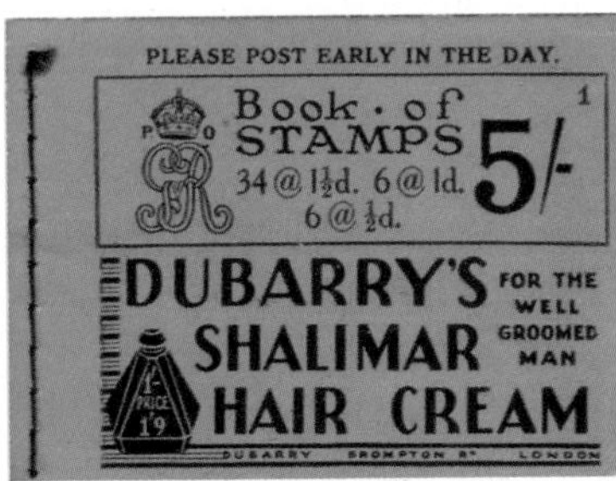

BB 33

1931 (Aug). *Green cover printed in black as Type* BB **33**. *Pages of six stamps:* 34×1½*d.,* 6×1*d. and* 6×½*d.The first* 1½*d. pane completed by two se-tenant advertisements. Printed by Waterlow & Sons on paper with Block Cypher wmk* (*Nos.* 418/20).

BB33 Edition number 1 .... £3250

1932 (June). *As before, but buff cover printed in black.*

BB34 Edition numbers 2 to 6 .... £2200

1934 (July). *As before, but containing stamps with Block Cypher wmk printed by Harrison & Sons* (*Nos.* 418/20).

BB35 Edition numbers 7 or 8 .... £975

1935 (Feb). *As before, but containing stamps of the photogravure issue with se-tenant advertisements printed in brown* (*Nos.* 439/41).

BB36 Edition number 9 .... £2700

1935 (July). *As before, but containing stamps of the photogravure issue with se-tenant advertisements printed in black* (*Nos.* 439/41).

BB37 Edition numbers 10 to 15 .... £380

KING EDWARD VIII

6d. Booklet

1936. *Buff unglazed cover without inscription containing* 4×1½*d.stamps, in panes of two* (*No.* 459).

BC1 .... 65·00

2s. Booklet

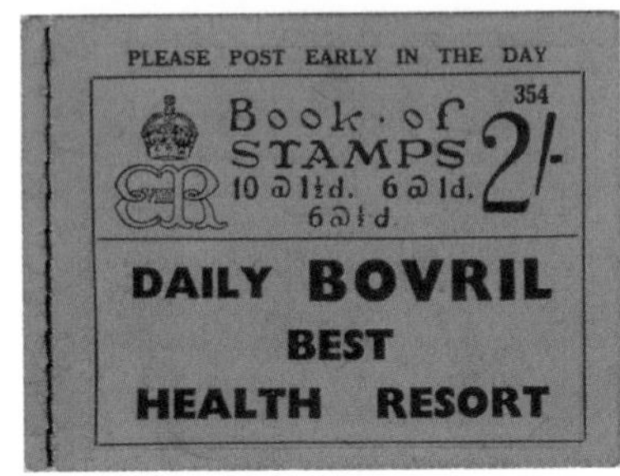

BC 2

1936 (Oct). *As No.* BB **17**. *except for the K.E.VIII cypher on the cover and containing Nos.* 457/9.

BC2 Edition numbers 354 to 385 .... £110

3s. Booklet

1936 (Nov). *As No.* BB **29**, *except for the K.E.VIII cypher on the cover but without* "P" *and* "O" *on either side of the crown, and containing Nos.* 457/9.

BC3 Edition numbers 320 to 332 .... 95·00

5s. Booklet

1937 (Mar). *As No.* BB **37**, *but with the K.E.VIII cypher on the cover and containing Nos.* 457/9.

BC4 Edition numbers 16 or 17 .... £220

KING GEORGE VI

6d. Booklets

1938 (Jan). *As No.* BC **1**, *but containing stamps in the original dark colours. Buff cover without inscription* (*No.* 464).

BD1 .... 65·00

1938 (Feb). *As before, but pink unprinted cover and make-up changed to contain* 2×1½*d.,* 2×1*d. and* 2×½*d. in the original dark colours* (*Nos.* 462/4).

BD2 .... £290

1940 (June). *Pale green unprinted cover and make-up changed to include two panes of four stamps with wmk sideways. Stamps in original dark colours with binding margin either at the top or bottom of the pane:* 4×1*d.,* 4×½*d.* (*Nos.* 462a/3a).

BD3 .... £140

1s. Booklets with Panes of 2

1947 (Dec). *Cream cover, unglazed and without inscription containing panes of two stamps in pale shades, all with wmk normal. Panes of two stamps:* 4×½*d.,* 4×1*d. and* 4×1½*d.* (*Nos.* 485/7).

BD4 .... 25·00

1951 (May). *As before, but containing stamps in changed colours (Nos. 503/5).*

BD5 .... 25·00

1s. Booklets with Panes of 4

1948. *Cream cover as before, but make-up changed to contain 4 × 1½d., 4 × 1d. and 4 × ½d. in panes of four of the pale shades with wmk normal (Nos. 485/7).*

BD6 .... £5250

1951 (May). *As before, but stamps in new colours all wmk normal, margins at either top or at the bottom. (Nos. 503/5).*

BD7 .... 30·00

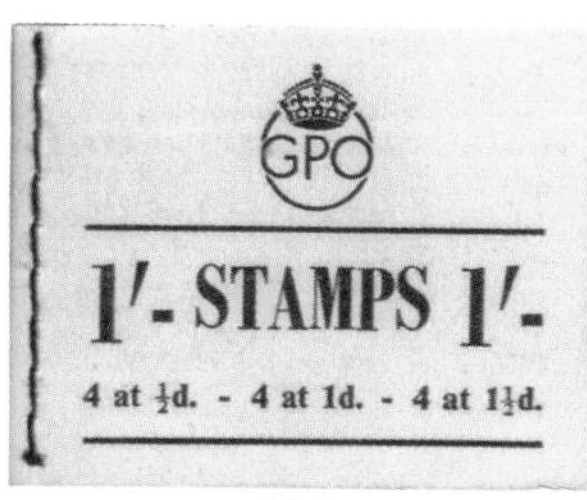

BD 8

1952 (Dec). *Cream cover printed in black as Type* BD **8**. *Make-up as before but with wmk either upright or inverted and margins only at the top (Nos. 503/5).*

BD8 .... 20·00

BD 10

1954. *As before but cover showing GPO emblem with St. Edward's crown and oval frame as Type* BD **10** *(Nos. 503/5).*

BD10 .... 28·00

2s. Booklets

BD 11

1937 (Aug). *Blue cover printed in black as Type* BB **11**, *but with K.G.VI cypher on the cover and containing stamps in the original dark colours. Panes of six stamps: 10 × 1½d.., 6 × 1d. and 6 × ½d. The first 1½d. pane completed by two se-tenant advertisements. (Nos. 462/4).*

BD11 Edition numbers 386 to 412 .... £425

BD 12

1938 (Mar). *Blue cover printed in black as Type* BD **12** *(Nos. 462/4).*

BD12 Edition numbers 413 to 508 .... £425

2s.6d. Booklets

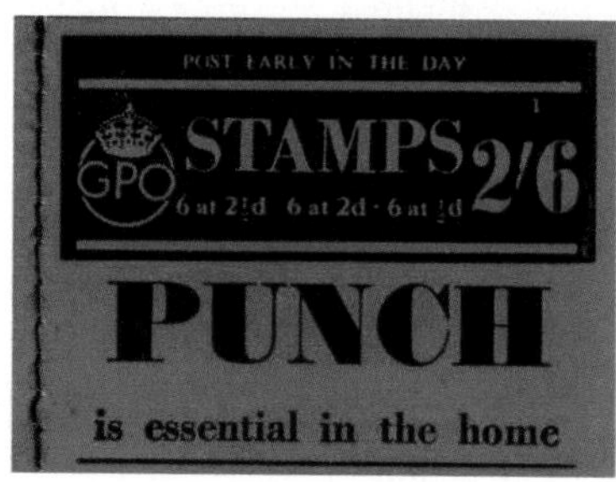

BD 13

1940 (June). *Scarlet cover printed in black as Type* BD **13**, *containing panes of six stamps in original dark colours: 6 × 2½d., 6 × 2d. and 6 × ½d. (Nos. 462, 465/6).*

BD13 Edition numbers 1 to 8 (part) £950

1940 (Sept). *As before, but blue cover printed in black as Type* BD **13**.

BD14 Edition numbers 8 (part) to 13 .... £950

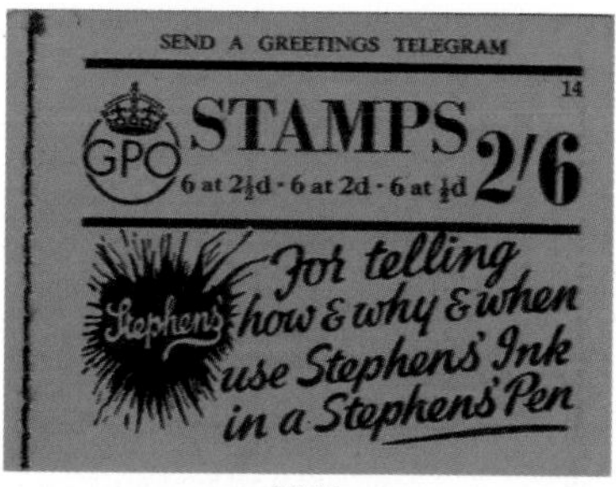

BD 15

1940 (Oct). *As before, but with green cover printed in black as Type* BD **15** (*Nos.* 462, 465/6).

BD15 Edition numbers 14 to 94 .... £485

1942 (Mar). *As before, but containing stamps in pale shades* (*Nos.* 485, 488/9).

BD16 Edition numbers 95 to 214 .... £500

Type **A** Circular GPO Cypher

1943 (Aug). *As before, but green cover printed in black as Type* **A**, *with different contents details* (*Nos.* 485, 488/9).

BD18 Edition dates August 1943 to February 1951 .... 45·00

(1) AUG 1943	70·00
(2) SEPT 1943	90·00
(3) OCT 1943	90·00
(4) NOV 1943	90·00
(5) DEC 1943	90·00
(6) JAN 1944	90·00
(7) FEB 1944	90·00
(8) MAR 1944	90·00
(9) APR 1944	90·00
(10) MAY 1944	90·00
(11) JUNE 1944	90·00
(12) JULY 1944	90·00
(13) AUG 1944	90·00
(14) SEPT 1944	90·00
(15) OCT 1944	90·00
(16) NOV 1944	90·00
(17) DEC 1944	90·00
(18) JAN 1945	90·00
(19) FEB 1945	90·00
(21) APR 1945	90·00
(22) MAY 1945	90·00
(23) JUNE 1945	90·00
(24) JULY 1945	90·00
(25) AUG 1945	90·00
(26) SEPT 1945	90·00
(27) OCT 1945	90·00
(28) NOV 1945	90·00
(29) DEC 1945	90·00
(30) JAN 1946	90·00
(31) FEB 1946	90·00
(32) MAR 1946	90·00
(33) APR 1946	90·00
(34) MAY 1946	90·00
(35) JUNE 1946	90·00
(36) JULY 1946	90·00
(37) AUG 1946	90·00
(38) SEPT 1946	90·00
(39) OCT 1946	90·00
(40) NOV 1946	90·00
(41) DEC 1946	90·00
(42) JAN 1947	90·00
(43) FEB 1947	90·00
(44) MAR 1947	90·00
(45) APR 1947	90·00
(46) MAY 1947	90·00
(47) JUNE 1947	90·00
(48) JULY 1947	90·00
(49) AUG 1947	90·00
(50) SEPT 1947	90·00
(51) OCT 1947	90·00
(52) NOV 1947	90·00
(53) DEC 1947	90·00
(54) JAN 1948	90·00
(55) FEB 1948	90·00
(56) MAR 1948	90·00
(57) APR 1948	90·00
(58) MAY 1948	90·00
(59) JUNE 1948	90·00
(65) JULY 1948	90·00
(61) AUG 1948	90·00
(62) SEPT 1948	90·00
(63) OCT 1948	90·00
(65) DEC 1948	90·00
(66) JAN 1949	90·00
(67) FEB 1949	90·00
(68) MAR 1949	90·00
(69) APR 1949	90·00
(70) MAY 1949	90·00
(71) JUNE 1949	90·00
(72) JULY 1949	90·00
(73) AUG 1949	90·00
(74) OCT 1949	90·00
(75) NOV 1949	90·00
(76) DEC 1949	90·00
(77) JAN 1950	65·00
(78) FEB 1950	65·00
(79) MAR 1950	65·00
(80) APR 1950	65·00
(81) MAY 1950	65·00
(82) JUNE 1950	65·00
(83) JULY 1950	65·00
(84) AUG 1950	65·00
(85) SEPT 1950	65·00
(86) OCT 1950	65·00
(87) NOV 1950	65·00
(88) DEC 1950	60·00
(89) JAN 1951	65·00
(90) FEB 1951	65·00

1951 (May). *As before, but containing stamps in the new colours* (*Nos.* 503, 506/7).

BD19 Edition dates May 1951 to February 1952 .... 40·00

(1) MAY 1951	40·00
(2) JUNE 1951	40·00
(3) JULY 1951	40·00
(4) AUG 1951	40·00
(5) SEPT 1951	50·00
(6) OCT 1951	40·00
(7) NOV 1951	40·00
(8) DEC 1951	40·00
(9) JAN 1952	40·00
(10) FEB 1952	40·00

1952 (March). *As before, but make-up changed to contain:* 6×2½*d.*, 6×1½*d.*, 3×1*d. and* 6×½*d. The* 1*d. pane was completed by three perforated labels in the lower row inscribed* "MINIMUM INLAND PRINTED PAPER RATE 1½*d.*" (*Nos.* 503/5, 507).

BD20 Edition dates March 1952 to May 1953 .... 34·00

(1) MAR 1952	35·00
(2) APR 1952	42·00
(3) MAY 1952	34·00
(4) JUNE 1952	45·00
(5) JULY 1952	42·00
(6) AUG 1952	35·00
(7) SEPT 1952	35·00
(8) OCT 1952	34·00
(9) NOV 1952	35·00
(10) DEC 1952	35·00
(11) JAN 1953	35·00
(12) FEB 1953	35·00
(13) MAR 1953	35·00
(14) APR 1953	35·00
(15) MAY 1953	42·00

3s. Booklets

BD **21**

1937 (Aug). *Scarlet cover printed in black as Type* BB **22** (*without* "P" *and* "O") *except for K.G.VI cypher on the cover and containing stamps in the original dark colours* (*Nos.* 462/4).

BD21 Edition numbers 333 to 343 .... £780

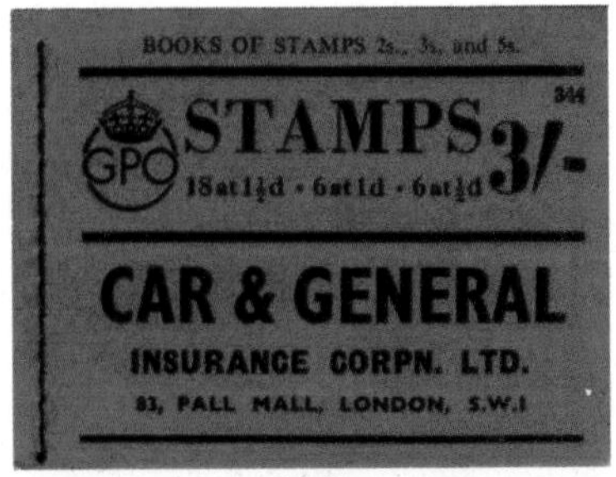

BD **22**

1938 (April). *As before, but scarlet cover printed in black as Type* BD **12** (*Nos.* 462/4).

BD22 Edition numbers 344 to 377 .... £780

5s. Booklets

1937 (Aug). *Buff cover printed in black as Type* BB **33**, *containing stamps of the new reign in the original dark colours. Pages of six stamps:* 34×1½*d.,* 6×1*d. and* 6×½*d. The first* 1½*d. pane completed by two se-tenant advertisements.* (*Nos.* 462/4).

BD23 Edition numbers 18 to 20 .... £900

BD **24**

1938 (May). *As before, but with redesigned front cover showing GPO emblem as Type* BD **24** *instead of royal cypher.*

BD24 Edition numbers 21 to 29 .... £875

1940 (July). *As before, but make-up changed to contain:* 18×2½*d.,* 6×2*d. and* 6×½*d. in the original dark colours* (*Nos.* 462, 465/6).

BD25 Edition numbers 1 to 16 (part) £925

1942 (Mar). *As before, but containing stamps in pale shades* (*Nos.* 485, 488/9).

BD26 Edition numbers 16 (part) to 36 .... £925

1943 (Sept). *As before, but buff cover printed in black as Type* A (*see No.* BD **18**, 2*s.*6*d.*) (*Nos.* 485, 488/9).

BD28 Edition dates September 1943 to December 1950 . ... 95·00

(1) SEPT 1943	£110	(26) JUNE 1947	£110
(2) OCT 1943	£110	(27) AUG 1947	£110
(3) NOV 1943	£110	(28) OCT 1947	£110
(4) DEC 1943	£110	(29) DEC 1947	£110
(5) FEB 1944	£120	(30) FEB 1948	£110
(6) MAR 1944	£120	(31) APR 1948	£110
(7) AUG 1944	£120	(32) JUNE 1948	£110
(8) OCT 1944	£120	(33) JULY 1948	£110
(9) NOV 1944	£120	(34) AUG 1948	£110
(10) JAN 1945	£120	(35) OCT 1948	£110
(11) FEB 1945	£120	(36) DEC 1948	£110
(12) APR 1945	£120	(37) FEB 1949	£110
(13) JUNE 1945	£120	(38) APR 1949	£110
(14) AUG 1945	£120	(39) JUNE 1949	£110
(15) OCT 1945	£120	(40) AUG 1949	£110
(16) DEC 1945	£120	(41) SEPT 1949	£110
(17) JAN 1946	£110	(42) OCT 1949	£110
(18) MAR 1946	£110	(43) DEC 1949	£110
(19) MAY 1946	£110	(44) FEB 1950	95·00
(20) JUNE 1946	£110	(45) APR 1950	95·00
(21) AUG 1946	£110	(46) JUNE 1950	95·00
(22) OCT 1946	£110	(47) AUG 1950	95·00
(23) DEC 1946	£110	(48) OCT 1950	95·00
(24) FEB 1947	£110	(49) DEC 1950	95·00
(25) APR 1947	£110		

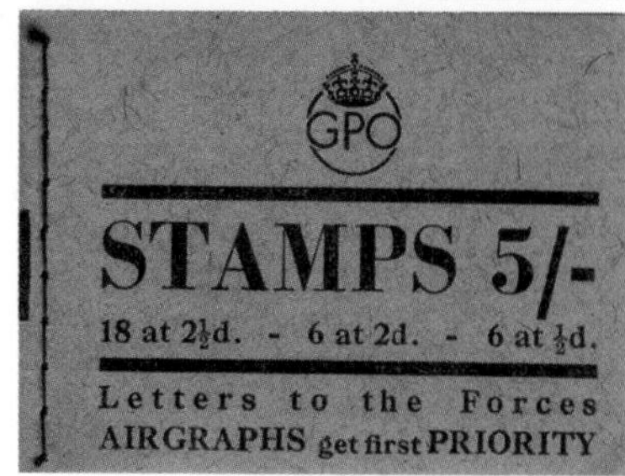

BD **29**

1944 (Apr). *As before, but buff cover printed in black as Type* BD **29** (*Nos.* 485, 488/9).

BD29 Edition dates April or June 1944 .... £1400

(1) APR 1944	£1400	(2) JUNE 1944	£1400

1951 (May). *As before, but buff cover changed back to Type* A (*see No.* BD **18**, 2*s.*6*d.*) *and containing stamps in the new colours* (*Nos.* 503, 506/7).

BD30 Edition dates May 1951 to January 1952 .... 55·00

(1) MAY 1951	55·00	(4) NOV 1951	55·00
(2) JULY 1951	55·00	(5) JAN 1952	55·00
(3) SEPT 1951	55·00		

1952 (Mar). *As before, make-up changed to contain:* 18×2½*d.,* 6×1½*d.,* 3×1*d. and* 6×½*d.. The* 1*d. pane was completed by three perforated labels in the lower row inscribed* "MINIMUM INLAND PRINTED PAPER RATE 1½*d.*" (*Nos.* 503/5, 507).

BD31 Edition dates March to November 1952 .... 45·00

(1) MAR 1952	45·00	(4) SEPT 1952	45·00
(2) MAY 1952	45·00	(5) NOV 1952	45·00
(3) JULY 1952	45·00		

1953 (Jan). *As before, but make-up changed again to include the* 2*d. value and containing:* 12×2½*d.,* 6×2*d.,* 6×1½*d.,* 6×1*d. and* 6×½*d.* (*Nos.* 503/7).

BD32 Edition dates January or March 1953 .... 55·00

(1) JAN 1953	55·00	(2) MAR 1953	55·00

QUEEN ELIZABETH II

I. £.s.d. Booklets, 1953–70.

TYPES OF BOOKLET COVER WITH GPO CYPHER
Type **A** Circular GPO Cypher
(See illustration above No. BD18)

Type **B** Oval Type GPO Cypher

Type **C** New GPO Cypher (small)

Type **D** New GPO Cypher (large)

1s. Booklets

1953 (2 Sept)–**59.** *I. White unprinted cover. Pages of two stamps: 4 × 1½d., 4 × 1d., 4 × ½d.. For use in experimental "D" machines.*

A. *Wmk Tudor Crown* (*Nos.* 515/17) EE

E1	No date	7·00

B. *Wmk St. Edward's Crown* (*Nos.* 540/2)

E2	No date (11.57)	18·00

II. White printed cover as Type **B**. *Pages of four stamps:* 4 × 1½d. 4 × 1*d.*, 4 × ½d.. *For use in* "E" *machines.*

A. *Wmk Tudor Crown* (*Nos.* 515/17)

K1	No date (22.7.54)	6·00

B. *Wmk St. Edward's Crown* (*Nos.* 540/2)

K2	No date (5.7.56)	6·00

C. *Wmk Crowns* (*Nos.* 570/2)

K3	No date (13.8.59)	6·00

2s. Booklets

1959 (22 Apr)–**65.** *Pages of four stamps:* 4 × 3*d.*, 4 × 1½*d.*, 4 × 1*d.*, 4 × ½d..

I. Salmon cover as Type **B**. *Wmk. St. Edward's Crown* (*Nos.*540/2 *and* 545).

N1	No date	5·00

II. Salmon cover as Type **C**. *Wmk Crowns* (*Nos.* 570/2 *and* 575).

N2	No date (2.11.60)	7·00

III. Lemon cover as Type **C**. *Wmk Crowns* (*Nos.* 570/2 *and* 575).

N3	No date (2.61)	7·00

IV. Lemon cover as Type **C**. *Wmk Crowns* (*sideways*) (*Nos.* 570a, 571a, 572b, 575a) *or phosphor* (*Nos.* 610a, 611a, 612a, 615b).

N4	APR 1961	25.00
	p. With phosphor bands	60.00
N5	SEPT 1961	38·00
N6	JAN 1962	40·00
N7	APR 1962	42·00
N8	JULY 1962	40·00
	p. With phosphor bands	80·00
N9	NOV 1962	50·00
	p. With phosphor bands	85·00
N10	JAN 1963	40·00
	p. With phosphor bands	£120
N11	MAR 1963	40·00
N12	JUNE 1963	40·00
	p. With phosphor bands	75·00
N13	AUG 1963	40·00
	p. With phosphor bands	75·00
N14	OCT 1963	40·00
	p. With phosphor bands	£120
N15	FEB 1964	40·00
	p. With phosphor bands	75·00
N16	JUNE 1964	40·00
	p. With phosphor bands	£100
N17	AUG 1964	50·00
	p. With phosphor bands	£100
N18	OCT 1964	40·00
	p. With phosphor bands	65·00
N19	DEC 1964	45·00
	p. With phosphor bands	65·00
N20	APR 1965	38·00
	p. With phosphor bands	60·00

1965 (16 Aug)–**67.** *New Composition. Pages of four stamps:* 4 × 4*d. and pane of* 2 × 1*d. and* 2 × 3*d. arranged se-tenant horiz. Orange-yellow cover as Type* **C** *printed in black. Wmk Crowns* (*sideways*) (*Nos.* 571a, 575a *and* 576ab) *or phosphor* (*Nos.* 611a, 615d *or* 615dEa (*one side phosphor band*) and 616ab).

N21	JULY 1965	3·00
	p. With phosphor bands	15·00
N22	OCT 1965	3·50
	p. With phosphor bands	14·00
N23	JAN 1966	5·00
	p. With phosphor bands	20·00
N24	APR 1966	5·00
	p. With phosphor bands	9·00
N25	JULY 1966	4·00
	p. With phosphor bands	55·00
N26	OCT 1966	5·00
	p. With phosphor bands	12·00
N27	JAN 1967	6·00
	p. With phosphor bands	6·50
N28p	APR 1967. With phosphor bands	7·50
N29p	JULY 1967. With phosphor bands	5·00
N30p	OCT 1967. With phosphor bands	5·00

In the *se-tenant* pane the 3d. appears at left or right to facilitate the application of phosphor bands.

The following illustration shows how the *se-tenant* stamps with one phosphor band on 3d. were printed and the arrows indicate where the guillotine fell. The result gives 1d. stamps with two bands and the 3d. stamps with one band either at left or right.

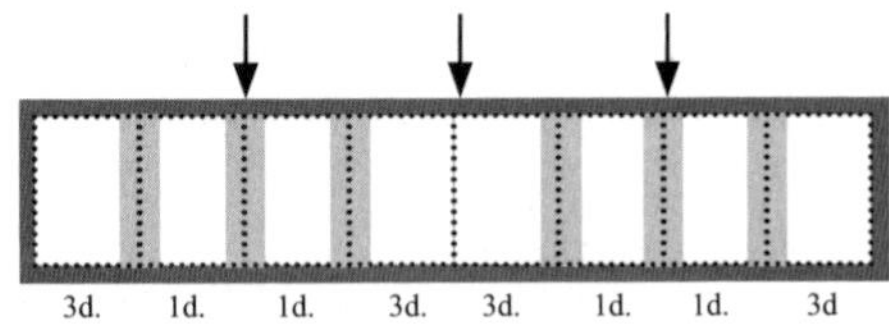

1967 (Nov)–**68.** *Composition and cover as Nos.* N21/30. *Wmk Crowns* (*sideways*) (*Nos.* 611a, 615b (*two phosphor bands*) *and* 616ab).

N31p	JAN 1968	3·00
N32p	MAR 1968	3·50

2s. Booklets with Machin type stamps

1968 (6 Apr–Aug). *Orange-yellow cover as Type* **C**. *Pages of four stamps:* 4 × 4*d. and pane of* 2 × 1*d. and* 2 × 3*d. arranged se-tenant horiz. PVA gum* (*Nos.* 724, 730, 731Ev).

NP27	MAY 1968	1·25
NP28	JULY 1968	1·00
NP29	AUG 1968	4·00

1968 (16 Sept)–**70.** *Grey cover as Type* **C**. *New Composition. 4d. stamps only comprising page of 4 × 4d. with two phosphor bands (No.* 731Ev) *and page of 2 × 4d. with one centre phosphor band (No.* 732) *se-tenant with two printed labels.*

NP30 SEPT 1968 90
NP31 JAN 1969 .... £200

Same composition but all six 4d. stamps have one centre phosphor band (No. 732).

NP31a SEPT 1968 .... £500
NP32 NOV 1968 90
NP33 JAN 1969 90

Same composition but change to 4d. bright vermilion with one centre phosphor band (No. 733).

NP34 MAR 1969 .... 1·25
NP35 MAY 1969 .... 1·50
NP36 JULY 1969 .... 2·00
NP37 SEPT 1969 .... 1·50
NP38 NOV 1969 .... 1·50
NP39 JAN 1970 .... 2·00
NP40 MAR 1970 .... 2·00
NP41 MAY 1970 .... 2·00
NP42 JULY 1970 .... 2·25
NP43 AUG 1970 .... 2·00
NP44 OCT 1970........ 2·00
NP45 DEC 1970 .... 2·00

2s. Booklets for Holiday Resorts

1963 (15 July)–**64.** *I. Lemon cover as Type* **C** *printed in red. New composition. Pages of four stamps: two of 4 × 2½d. and one of 3 × ½d. and 1 × 2½d. arranged se-tenant. Chalky paper. Wmk Crowns (Nos.* 570k *and* 574k).

NR1 No date, black stitching .... 3·50
a. White stitching (3.9.63)........ 4·00

II. Lemon cover as Type **C** *printed in red. Composition changed again. Pages of four stamps 2 × ½d. and 2 × 2½d. arranged sideways, vertically se-tenant. Wmk Crowns (sideways) (No.* 570n × 4).

NR2 1964 (1.7.64)........ 1·60

2s. Booklet for Christmas Cards

1965 (6 Dec). *Orange-yellow cover as Type* **C** *printed in red. Two panes of 4 × 3d. arranged sideways. Wmk Crowns (sideways) (No.* 575a).

NX1 1965........ 80

2s.6d. Booklets

Green cover. Pages of six stamps: 6 × 2½d., 6 × 1½d., 3 × 1d. (page completed by three perforated labels), 6 × ½d..

LABELS. The wording printed on the labels differs as follows:

"PPR" = "MINIMUM INLAND PRINTED PAPER RATE 1½d.."
Two types exist:

A. Printed in photogravure, 17 mm high.
B. Typographed, 15 mm high.

"Shorthand" = "SHORTHAND IN 1 WEEK" (covering all three labels).
"Post Early" = "PLEASE POST EARLY IN THE DAY".
"PAP" = "PACK YOUR PARCELS SECURELY" (1st label)
"ADDRESS YOUR LETTERS CORRECTLY" (2nd label),
"AND POST EARLY IN THE DAY" (3rd label).

1953–54. *Composite booklets containing stamps of King George VI and Queen Elizabeth II.*

A. *K.G.VI ½d.. and* 1*d.* (*Nos.* 503/4) *and Q.E.II* 1½d. *and* 2½d. (*Nos.* 517 *and* 519b). *Cover as Type* **A**. *No interleaving pages.*

F1 MAY 1953 (PPR 17 mm) .... 25·00
F2 JUNE 1953 (PPR 17 mm) .... 28·00
F3 JULY 1953 (PPR 17 mm) .... 32·00
F4 AUG 1953 (PPR 17 mm) .... 28·00

B. *Same composition but with addition of two interleaving pages, one at each end. Cover as Type* **A**.

F5 SEPT 1953 (PPR 17 mm) £160
F6 SEPT 1953 (PPR 15 mm) £100

C. *Same composition and with interleaving pages but with cover as Type* **B**.

F7 OCT 1953 (PPR 17 mm) .... 40·00
F8 OCT 1953 (PPR 15 mm) .... 90·00
F9 NOV 1953 (PPR 17 mm) .... 40·00
F10 NOV 1953 (PPR 15 mm) £140
F11 DEC 1953 (PPR 17 mm) .... 45·00
F12 JAN 1954 (Shorthand) .... 70·00
F13 FEB 1954 (Shorthand) .... 70·00

D. *New composition: K.G.VI* 1*d.* (*No.* 504) *and Q.E.II ½d.,* 1½*d. and* 2½*d.* (*Nos.* 515, 517 *and* 519b).

F14 MAR 1954 (PPR 17 mm) £425
F14a MAR 1954 (Shorthand) ....

1954–57. *Booklets containing only Queen Elizabeth II stamps. All covers as Type* **B**.

A. *Wmk Tudor Crown* (*Nos.* 515/17 *and* 519b).

F15 MAR 1954 (PPR 15 mm) £250
F16 APR 1954 (Post Early) .... 40·00
F17 MAY 1954 (Post Early) .... 40·00
F18 JUNE 1954 (Post Early) .... 40·00
F19 JULY 1954 (Post Early) .... 40·00
F20 AUG 1954 (Post Early) .... 40·00
F21 SEPT 1954 (Post Early) .... 40·00
F22 OCT 1954 (Post Early) .... 40·00
F23 NOV 1954 (Post Early) .... 40·00
F24 DEC 1954 (Post Early) .... 40·00

B. *Same composition but with interleaving pages between each pane of stamps.*

F25 JAN 1955 (Post Early) .... 45·00
F26 JAN 1955 (PAP) £100
F27 FEB 1955 (PAP) .... 40·00
F28 MAR 1955 (PAP) .... 40·00
F29 APR 1955 (PAP) .... 40·00
F30 MAY 1955 (PAP) .... 40·00
F31 JUNE 1955 (PAP) .... 40·00
F32 JULY 1955 (PAP) .... 40·00
F33 AUG 1955 (PAP) .... 40·00

C. *Mixed watermarks. Wmk Tudor Crown* (*Nos.* 515/17 *and* 519b) *and wmk St. Edward's Crown* (*Nos.* 540/2 *and* 544b) *in various combinations.*

F34 SEPT 1955 (PAP)........ *From* 45·00

2s.6d. booklets dated AUGUST, OCTOBER, NOVEMBER and DECEMBER 1955, JANUARY, MAY and JUNE 1956 exist both as listed and with the two watermarks mixed. There are so many different combinations that we do not list them separately, but when in stock selections can be submitted. The SEPTEMBER 1955 booklet (No. F34) only exists in composite form.

D. *Wmk St. Edward's Crown* (*Nos.* 540/2 *and* 544b).

F35 OCT 1955 (PAP) .... 30·00
F36 NOV 1955 (PAP) .... 30·00
F37 DEC 1955 (PAP) .... 30·00
F38 JAN 1956 (PAP) .... 30·00
F39 FEB 1956 (PAP) .... 30·00
F40 MAR 1956 (PAP) .... 30·00
F41 APR 1956 (PAP) .... 35·00
F42 MAY 1956 (PAP) .... 30·00
F43 JUNE 1956 (PAP) .... 30·00
F44 JULY 1956 (PAP) .... 30·00
F45 AUG 1956 (PAP) .... 20·00
F46 SEPT 1956 (PAP) .... 35·00
F47 OCT 1956 (PAP) .... 30·00
F48 NOV 1956 (PAP) .... 30·00
F49 DEC 1956 (PAP) .... 30·00
F50 JAN 1957 (PAP) .... 30·00
F51 FEB 1957 (PAP) .... 30·00
F52 MAR 1957 (PAP) .... 22·00

E. *Same wmk but new composition. Pages of six stamps:* 6 × 2½*d.* (*No.* 544b), 6 × 2*d.* (*No.* 543*b*) *and* 6 × ½*d.* (*No.* 540).

F53 APR 1957 .... 30·00
F54 MAY 1957 .... 30·00
F55 JUNE 1957 .... 25·00
F56 JULY 1957 .... 25·00
F57 AUG 1957 .... 25·00
F58 SEPT 1957 .... 25·00
F59 OCT 1957 .... 25·00
F60 NOV 1957 .... 20·00
F61 DEC 1957 .... 35·00

3s. Booklets

1958–65. *Pages of six stamps:* 6×3*d*., 6×1½*d*., 6×1*d*., 6×½*d*. *I. Red cover as Type* **B**.

A. *Wmk St. Edward's Crown* (*Nos.* 540/2 *and* 545).

M1	JAN 1958	18·00
M2	FEB 1958	18·00
M3	MAR 1958	18·00
M4	APR 1958	18·00
M5	MAY 1958	18·00
M6	JUNE 1958	18·00
M7	JULY 1958	18·00
M8	AUG 1958	20·00
M9	NOV 1958	20·00

The 3s. booklets dated NOVEMBER 1958, DECEMBER 1958 and JANUARY 1959 exist both as listed and with mixed St. Edward's Crown and Crowns wmks.

B. *Wmk Crowns* (*Nos.* 570/2 *and* 575) *or graphite lines* (*Nos.* 587/9 *and* 592).

M10	DEC 1958	25·00
M11	JAN 1959	20·00
M12	FEB 1959	22·00
M13	AUG 1959	25·00
	g. With graphite lines	£200
M14	SEPT 1959	25·00
	g. With graphite lines	£260

II. Brick-red cover as Type **C**. Wmk Crowns (Nos. 570/2 and 575), graphite lines (Nos. 587/9 and 592) or phosphor (Nos. 610/12 *and* 615).

M15	OCT 1959	25·00
	g. With graphite lines	£250
M16	NOV 1959	25·00
M17	DEC 1959	25·00
M18	JAN 1960	25·00
M19	FEB 1960	25·00
	g. With graphite lines	£250
M20	MAR 1960	25·00
	g. With graphite lines	£300
M21	APR 1960	25·00
	g. With graphite lines	£260
M22	MAY 1960	25·00
M23	JUNE 1960	25·00
M24	JULY 1960	25·00
M25	AUG 1960	25·00
	p. With phosphor bands	50·00
M26	SEPT 1960	25·00
M27	OCT 1960	25·00
M28	NOV 1960	25·00
	p. With phosphor bands	55·00

III. Brick-red cover as Type **D**. *Wmk Crowns* (*Nos.* 570/2 *and* 575) *or phosphor* (*Nos.* 610/12 *and* 615).

M29	DEC 1960	25·00
	p. With phosphor bands	60·00
M30	JAN 1961	25·00
M31	FEB 1961	25·00
M32	MAR 1961	22·00
M33	APR 1961	25·00
	p. With phosphor bands	50·00
M34	MAY 1961	25·00
M35	JUNE 1961	25·00
M36	JULY 1961	25·00
	p. With phosphor bands	50·00
M37	AUG 1961	25·00
	p. With phosphor bands	50·00
M38	SEPT 1961	25·00
	p. With phosphor bands	55·00
M39	OCT 1961	25·00
	p. With phosphor bands	50·00
M40	NOV 1961	25·00
M41	DEC 1961	25·00
M42	JAN 1962	25·00
M43	FEB 1962	25·00
	p. With phosphor bands	50·00
M44	MAR 1962	25·00
	p. With phosphor bands	50·00
M45	APR 1962	25·00
	p. With phosphor bands	50·00
M46	MAY 1962	25·00
	p. With phosphor bands	48·00
M47	JUNE 1962	25·00
	p. With phosphor bands	48·00
M48	JULY 1962	22·00
M49	AUG 1962	22·00
	p. With phosphor bands	50·00
M50	SEPT 1962	25·00
	p. With phosphor bands	50·00
M51	OCT 1962	26·00
	p. With phosphor bands	48·00
M52	NOV 1962	25·00
	p. With phosphor bands	50·00
M53	DEC 1962	25·00
	p. With phosphor bands	50·00
M54	JAN 1963	25·00
M55	FEB 1963	22·00
	p. With phosphor bands	48·00
M56	MAR 1963	22·00
	p. With phosphor bands	48·00
M57	APR 1963	22·00
	p. With phosphor bands	48·00
M58	MAY 1963	22·00
	p. With phosphor bands	£200
M59	JUNE 1963	22·00
	p. With phosphor bands	36·00
M60	JULY 1963	22·00
	p. With phosphor bands	50·00
M61	AUG 1963	22·00
	p. With phosphor bands	50·00
M62	SEPT 1963	22·00
M63	OCT 1963	22·00
M64	NOV 1963	22·00
	p. With phosphor bands	48·00
M65	DEC 1963	30·00
	p. With phosphor bands	85·00
M66	JAN 1964	30·00
	p. With phosphor bands	40·00
M67	MAR 1964	25·00
	p. With phosphor bands	50·00
M68	MAY 1964	25·00
	p. With phosphor bands	65·00
M69	JULY 1964	25·00
	p. With phosphor bands	50·00
M70	SEPT 1964	30·00
	p. With phosphor bands	50·00
M71	NOV 1964	30·00
	p. With phosphor bands	40·00
M72	JAN 1965	30·00
	p. With phosphor bands	40·00
M73	MAR 1965	20·00
	p. With phosphor bands	40·00
M74	MAY 1965	20·00
	p. With phosphor bands	40·00

3s.9d. Booklets

1953–57. *Red cover as Type* **B**. *Pages of six stamps:* 18×2½*d*.

A. *Wmk Tudor Crown* (*No.* 519b)

G1	NOV 1953	28·00
G2	JAN 1954	30·00
G3	MAR 1954	30·00
G4	DEC 1954	30·00
G5	FEB 1955	30·00
G6	APR 1955	30·00
G7	JUNE 1955	30·00
G8	AUG 1955	30·00
G9	OCT 1955	28·00
G10	DEC 1955	30·00

3s.9d. booklets dated OCTOBER and DECEMBER 1955 exist both as listed and with the two wkms mixed.

B. Wmk St. Edward's Crown (*No.* 544b). *Same composition but with interleaving pages between each pane of stamps.*

G12	FEB 1956	20·00
G13	APR 1956	20·00
G14	JUNE 1956	20·00
G15	AUG 1956	20·00
G16	OCT 1956	20·00
G17	DEC 1956	20·00
G18	FEB 1957	20·00
G19	APR 1957	20·00
G20	JUNE 1957	12·00
G21	AUG 1957	28·00

4s.6d. Booklets

1957–65. *Pages of six stamps:* 18×3*d*. *I. Purple cover as Type* **B**.

A. *Wmk St. Edward's Crown* (*No.* 545).

L1	OCT 1957	20·00

L2	DEC 1957	20·00
L3	FEB 1958	24·00
L4	APR 1958	20·00
L5	OCT 1958	22·00
L7	DEC 1958	22·00

B. Wmk Crowns (*No.* 575).

L8	DEC 1958	70·00

II. Purple cover as Type **C**. Wmk Crowns (*No.* 575) *or graphite lines* (*No.* 592).

L9	FEB 1959	22·00
L10	JUNE 1959	22·00
L11	AUG 1959	22·00
	g. With graphite lines	28·00
L12	OCT 1959	30·00
L13	DEC 1959	24·00

III. Violet cover as Type **C**. *Wmk Crowns* (*No.* 575), *graphite* lines (*No.* 592) *or phosphor* (*No.* 615).

L14	FEB 1959	30·00
L15	APR 1959	24·00
	g. With graphite lines	20·00
L16	JUNE 1959	24·00
	g. With graphite lines	20·00
L17	DEC 1959	24·00
L18	FEB 1960	24·00
	g. With graphite lines	24·00
L19	APR 1960	24·00
	g. With graphite lines	24·00
L20	JUNE 1960	24·00
L21	AUG 1960	24·00
	p. With phosphor bands	40·00
L22	OCT 1960	24·00

IV. Violet cover as Type **D**. *Wmk Crowns* (*No.* 575) *or phosphor* (*No.* 615).

L23	DEC 1960	40·00
L24	FEB 1961	40·00
	p. With phosphor bands	30·00
L25	APR 1961	28·00
	p. With phosphor bands	30·00
L26	JUNE 1961	28·00
L27	AUG 1961	28·00
	p. With phosphor bands	36·00
L28	OCT 1961	25·00
	p. With phosphor bands	36·00
L29	DEC 1961	25·00
L30	FEB 1962	36·00
	p. With phosphor bands	26·00
L31	APR 1962	36·00
	p. With phosphor bands	36·00
L32	JUNE 1962	36·00
	p. With phosphor bands	45·00
L33	AUG 1962	25·00
	p. With phosphor bands	50·00
L34	OCT 1962	25·00
	p. With phosphor bands	£140
L35	DEC 1962	25·00
	p. With phosphor bands	36·00
L36	FEB 1963	25·00
	p. With phosphor bands	36·00
L37	APR 1963	25·00
	p. With phosphor bands	36·00
L38	JUNE 1963	25·00
	p. With phosphor bands	36·00
L39	AUG 1963	25·00
	p. With phosphor bands	36·00
L40	OCT 1963	25·00
	p. With phosphor bands	36·00
L41	NOV 1963	25·00
	p. With phosphor bands	36·00
L42	DEC 1963	25·00
	p. With phosphor bands	£130
L43	JAN 1964	55·00
L44	FEB 1964	25·00
	p. With phosphor bands	36·00
L45	MAR 1964	55·00
	p. With phosphor bands	70·00
L46	APR 1964	55·00
	p. With phosphor bands	36·00
L47	MAY 1964	25·00
	p. With phosphor bands	36·00
L48	JUNE 1964	25·00
	p. With phosphor bands	36·00
L49	JULY 1964	25·00
	p. With phosphor bands	36·00
L50	AUG 1964	30·00
	p. With phosphor bands	24·00
L51	SEPT 1964	36·00
	p. With phosphor bands	24·00
L52	OCT 1964	25·00
	p. With phosphor bands	36·00
L53	NOV 1964	25·00
	p. With phosphor bands	36·00
L54	DEC 1964	25·00
	p. With phosphor bands	36·00
L55	JAN 1965	20·00
	p. With phosphor bands	36·00
L56	FEB 1965	20·00
	p. With phosphor bands	35·00
L57	MAR 1965	22·00
	p. With phosphor bands	£275
L58	APR 1965	18·00

1965 (26 July)–**67**. *New composition. Pages of six stamps*: 12 × 4*d*., 6 × 1*d*. *Slate-blue cover as Type* **D**. *Wmk Crowns* (*Nos.* 571 *and* 576*a*) *or phosphor* (*Nos.* 611 *and* 616*a*).

L59	JULY 1965	18·00
	p. With phosphor bands	24·00
L60	SEPT 1965	18·00
	p. With phosphor bands	24·00
L61	NOV 1965	18·00
	p. With phosphor bands	24·00
L62	JAN 1966	18·00
	p. With phosphor bands	24·00
L63	MAR 1966	18·00
	p. With phosphor bands	20·00
L64	JAN 1967	15·00
	p. With phosphor bands	15·00
L65	MAR 1967	24·00
	p. With phosphor bands	15·00
L66p	MAY 1967. With phosphor bands	9·00
L67p	JULY 1967. With phosphor bands	10·00
L68p	SEPT 1967. With phosphor bands	10·00
L69p	NOV 1967. With phosphor bands	9·00
L70p	JAN 1968. With phosphor bands	9·00
L71p	MAR 1968. With phosphor bands	8·00

4s.6d. Booklets with Machin type stamps

1968–70. *Slate-blue cover as Type* **D**. *Pages of six stamps*: 12 × 4*d*., 6 × 1*d*. *PVA gum* (*Nos.* 724, 731Ev).

LP45	MAY 1968	6·00

LP **46** Ships Series with GPO Cypher

(Des S. Rose)

Blue cover as Type LP **46**. *Ships Series. Composition as last.*

LP46	JULY 1968 (*Cutty Sark*)	1·50

Same composition but changed to 4*d. with one centre phosphor band* (*No.* 732).

LP47	SEPT 1968 (*Golden Hind*)	2·00
LP48	NOV 1968 (*Discovery*)	2·00

Same composition but changed to 4d. bright vermilion with one centre phosphor band (No. 733).

LP49	JAN 1969 (*Queen Elizabeth 2*)	3·25
LP50	MAR 1969 (*Sirius*)	3·00
LP51	MAY 1969 (*Sirius*)	2·50
LP52	JULY 1969 (*Dreadnought*)	3·00
LP53	SEPT 1969 (*Dreadnought*)	5·00
LP54	NOV 1969 (*Mauretania*)	3·50
LP55	JAN 1970 (*Mauretania*)	5·00
LP56	MAR 1970 (*Victory*)	4·00
LP57	MAY 1970 (*Victory*)	10·00

LP **58** Ships Series with Post Office Corporation Crown Symbol

(Des S. Rose)

As last but cover changed to Type LP **58**.

LP58	AUG 1970 (*Sovereign of the Seas*)	3·75
LP59	OCT 1970 (*Sovereign of the Seas*)	10·00

5s. Booklets

1953–57. *Buff cover. Pages of six stamps.* 12×2½*d.*, 6×2*d.*, 6×1½*d.*, 6×1*d.*, 6×½*d.*

I. Composite booklets containing stamps of King George VI and Queen Elizabeth II.

A. *K.G.VI ½d.*, 1*d. and* 2*d.* (*Nos.* 503/4 *and* 506) *and Q.E.II* 1½*d. and* 2½*d.* (*Nos.* 517 *and* 519b). *Cover as Type* A. *No interleaving pages.*

H1	MAY 1953	35·00
H2	JULY 1953	38·00

B. *Same composition but with addition of two interleaving pages, one at each end. Cover as Type* **A**.

H3	SEPT 1953	38·00

C. *Same composition and with interleaving pages but cover as Type* **B**.

H4	NOV 1953	36·00
H5	JAN 1954	36·00

D. *New composition: K.G.VI* 1*d. and* 2*d.* (*Nos.* 504 *and* 506) *and Q.E.II ½d.*, 1½*d.and* 2½*d.* (*Nos.* 515, 517 *and* 519b).

H6	MAR 1954	£250

E. New composition: K.G.VI 2*d.* (*No.* 506) *and Q.E.II ½d.* 1*d.*, 1½*d.* and 2½*d.*. (*Nos.* 515/17 *and* 519b).

H7	MAR 1954	£140

II. Booklets containing only Queen Elizabeth II stamps. Buff cover as Type **B**. *Two interleaving pages as before.*

A. *Wmk Tudor Crown* (*Nos.* 515/18 *and* 519b).

H8	MAR 1954	£120
H9	MAY 1954	60·00
H10	JULY 1954	70·00
H11	SEPT 1954	35·00
H12	NOV 1954	60·00

B. *Same composition but with interleaving pages between each pane of stamps.*

H13	JAN 1955	60·00
H14	MAR 1955	50·00
H15	MAY 1955	50·00
H16	JULY 1955	50·00

C. *Wmk St. Edward's Crown* (*Nos.* 540/3 *and* 544b).

H17	SEPT 1955	28·00
H18	NOV 1955	30·00
H19	JAN 1956	35·00
H20	MAR 1956	40·00
H21	MAY 1956	36·00
H22	JULY 1956	36·00
H23	SEPT 1956	35·00
H24	NOV 1956	36·00
H25	JAN 1957	40·00

5s. booklets dated SEPTEMBER and NOVEMBER 1955 and JANUARY 1956 exist both as listed and with the two watermarks mixed. There are so many different combinations that we do not list them separately, but when in stock selections can be submitted.

D. *Same watermark. Introduction of* 2*d. light red-brown* (*No.* 543*b*) *in place of No.* 543.

H26	JAN 1957	36·00
H27	MAR 1957	36·00
H28	MAY 1957	35·00
H29	JULY 1957	30·00
H30	SEPT 1957	30·00
H31	NOV 1957	30·00

1958–65. E. *New composition. Pages of six stamps:* 12×3*d.* (*No.* 545), 6×2½*d.* (*No.* 544b), 6×1*d.* (*No.* 541), 6×½*d.* (*No.*540). *Wmk St. Edward's Crown.*

H32	JAN 1958	30·00
H33	MAR 1958	30·00
H34	MAY 1958	30·00
H35	JULY 1958 (11.58)	22·00
H36	NOV 1958	22·00

5s. booklets dated JULY 1958, NOVEMBER 1958 and JANUARY 1959 exist with mixed watermarks.

F. Blue cover as Type **C**. Wmk Crowns (Nos. 570/1, 574/5), graphite lines (Nos. 587/8 *and* 591/2) *or phosphor* (*Nos.*610/11, 614 *and* 615).

H37	JAN 1959	25·00
H38	MAR 1959	30·00
H39	JULY 1959	30·00
	g. With graphite lines	£120
H40	SEPT 1959	30·00
H41	NOV 1959	30·00
H42	JAN 1960	30·00
H43	MAR 1960	30·00
	g. With graphite lines	£130
H44	MAY 1960	35·00
H45	JULY 1960	35·00
H46	SEPT 1960	40·00
	g. With graphite lines	£130
	p. With phosphor bands	95·00
H47	NOV 1960	40·00

G. As last but blue cover as Type **D**. *Same composition.*

I. *Phosphor has two bands on* 2½*d.* (No. 614).

H48	JAN 1961	40·00
H49	MAR 1961	40·00
	p. With phosphor bands	£120
H50	MAY 1961	42·00
H51	JULY 1961	42·00
	p. With phosphor bands	£130
H52	SEPT 1961	42·00
	p. With phosphor bands	£130
H53	NOV 1961	42·00
H54	JAN 1962	42·00
	p. With phosphor bands	£130

II. *As last but phosphor has one band on* 2½*d.* (*No.* 614*a*).

H55	MAR 1962	42·00
	p. With phosphor bands	£135
H56	MAY 1962	42·00
	p. With phosphor bands	£120
H57	JULY 1962	42·00
	p. With phosphor bands	£120
H58	SEPT 1962	42·00
	p. With phosphor bands	£130
H59	NOV 1962	42·00
	p. With phosphor bands	£130
H60	JAN 1963	42·00
	p. With phosphor bands	£400
H61	MAR 1963	42·00
	p. With phosphor bands	£135
H62	MAY 1963	42·00
	p. With phosphor bands	£130
H63	JULY 1963	42·00
	p. With phosphor bands	£130
H64	SEPT 1963	42·00

	p. With phosphor bands	£150
H65	NOV 1963	42·00
	p. With phosphor bands	£130
H66	JAN 1964	42·00
	p. With phosphor bands	90·00
H67	MAR 1964	42·00
	p. With phosphor bands	90·00
H68	MAY 1964	42·00
	p. With phosphor bands	£130
H69	JULY 1964	42·00
	p. With phosphor bands	£120
H70	SEPT 1964	42·00
	p. With phosphor bands	£120
H71	NOV 1964	42·00
	p. With phosphor bands	90·00
H72	JAN 1965	42·00
	p. With phosphor bands	90·00
H73	MAR 1965	36·00
	p. With phosphor bands	£120
H74	MAY 1965	36·00
	p. With phosphor bands	95·00

5s. Booklets with Machin type stamps

HP **26** English Homes Series with GPO Cypher

(Des S. Rose)

1968 (27 Nov)–**70**. *Cinnamon cover as Type* HP **26** (*English Homes Series*). *Pages of six stamps:* 12 × 5*d*. (*No.* 735).

HP26	DEC 1968 (Ightham Mote)	2·40
HP27	FEB 1969 (Little Moreton Hall)	2·40
HP28	APR 1969 (Long Melford Hall)	2·50
HP29	JUNE 1969 (Long Melford Hall)	2·50
HP30	AUG 1969 (Long Melford Hall)	4·00

HP **31** English Homes Series with Post Office Corporation Crown Symbol

(Des S. Rose)

As last but cover changed to Type HP **31**.

HP31	OCT 1969 (Mompesson House)	2·50
HP32	DEC 1969 (Mompesson House)	3·00
HP33	FEB 1970 (Cumberland Terrace)	2·50

HP **34**

(Des P. Gauld)

As last but cover changed to Type HP **34** (*special edition to advertise "Philympia" International Philatelic Exhibition, London, September* 1970).

HP34	(no date) (3.3.70)	2·50

As last but cover changed to Type HP **31**.

HP35	JUNE 1970 (The Vineyard, Saffron Walden)	3·00
HP36	AUG 1970 (The Vineyard, Saffron Walden)	4·00
HP37	OCT 1970 (Mereworth Castle)	3·75
HP38	DEC 1970 (Mereworth Castle)	4·00

6s. Booklets

1965 (21 June)–**67**. *Claret cover as Type* **D**. *Wmk Crowns* (*No.* 576*a*) *or phosphor* (*No.* 616*a*). *Pages of six stamps*: 18 × 4d.

Q1	JUNE 1965	24·00
	p. With phosphor bands	24·00
Q2	JULY 1965	24·00
	p. With phosphor bands	24·00
Q3	AUG 1965	28·00
	p. With phosphor bands	32·00
Q4	SEPT 1965	24·00
	p. With phosphor bands	30·00
Q5	OCT 1965	24·00
	p. With phosphor bands	30·00
Q6	NOV 1965	24·00
	p. With phosphor bands	30·00
Q7	DEC 1965	24·00
	p. With phosphor bands	30·00
Q8	JAN 1966	24·00
	p. With phosphor bands	30·00
Q9	FEB 1966	24·00
	p. With phosphor bands	30·00
Q10	MAR 1966	24·00
	p. With phosphor bands	30·00
Q11	APR 1966	24·00
	p. With phosphor bands	50·00
Q12	MAY 1966	24·00
	p. With phosphor bands	34·00
Q13	JUNE 1966	24·00
	p. With phosphor bands	30·00
Q14	JULY 1966	28·00
	p. With phosphor bands	42·00
Q15	AUG 1966	28·00
	p. With phosphor bands	£100
Q16	SEPT 1966	24·00
	p. With phosphor bands	24·00
Q17	OCT 1966	28·00
	p. With phosphor bands	60·00
Q18	NOV 1966	28·00
	p. With phosphor bands	24·00
Q19	DEC 1966	24·00
	p. With phosphor bands	28·00
Q20	JAN 1967	35·00
	p. With phosphor bands	35·00
Q21	FEB 1967	35·00
	p. With phosphor bands	24·00
Q22	MAR 1967	28·00
	p. With phosphor bands	24·00
Q23	APR 1967	24·00
	p. With phosphor bands	25·00
Q24p	MAY 1967. With phosphor bands	24·00
Q25p	JUNE 1967. With phosphor bands	24·00
Q26p	JULY 1967. With phosphor bands	30·00
Q27p	AUG 1967. With phosphor bands	36·00

6s. Booklets with Machin type stamps

1967–70. *Claret cover as Type* **D**. *Pages of six stamps:* 18 × 4*d. Two phosphor bands. Gum arabic* (*No.* 731).

QP28	SEPT 1967	38·00
QP29	OCT 1967	38·00
QP30	NOV 1967	38·00
QP31	DEC 1967	38·00
QP32	JAN 1968	36·00
QP33	FEB 1968 (No. 731*Ea*)	34·00
QP34	MAR 1968 (No. 731*Ea*)	34·00
QP35	APR 1968 (No. 731*Ea*)	30·00
QP36	MAY 1968 (No. 731*Ea*)	15·00

Change to PVA gum (*No.* 731Ev).

QP37	MAY 1968	£400

QP **38** Birds Series with GPO Cypher

(Des S. Rose)

Orange-red cover as Type QP **38** (*Birds Series*). *Same composition. Two phosphor bands. PVA gum* (*No.* 731Ev).

QP38	JUNE 1968 (Kingfisher) (4.6.68)	1·80
QP39	JULY 1968 (Kingfisher)	11·00
QP40	AUG 1968 (Peregrine Falcon)	1·50

Change to one centre phosphor band (*No.* 732).

QP41	SEPT 1968 (Peregrine Falcon) (16.9.68)	1·80
QP42	OCT 1968 (Pied Woodpecker)	1·80
QP43	NOV 1968 (Pied Woodpecker)	1·90
QP44	DEC 1968 (Great Crested Grebe)	1·90
QP45	JAN 1969 (Barn Owl)	3·00

Change to 4*d. bright vermilion with one centre phosphor band* (*No.* 733).

QP46	FEB 1969 (Barn Owl) (20.2.69)	3·50
QP47	MAR 1969 (Jay)	3·00
QP48	MAY 1969 (Jay)	3·50
QP49	JULY 1969 (Puffin)	3·00
QP50	SEPT 1969 (Puffin)	5·00

QP **51** Birds Series with Post Office Corporation Crown Symbol

(Des S. Rose)

As last but cover changed to Type QP **51**.

QP51	NOV 1969 (Cormorant)	3·50
QP52	JAN 1970 (Cormorant)	4·00
QP53	APR 1970 (Wren)	3·50
QP54	AUG 1970 (Golden Eagle)	3·50
QP55	OCT 1970 (Golden Eagle)	3·50

10s. Booklets

1961 (10 Apr–Oct). *Green cover as Type* **D**. *Pages of six stamps:* 30 × 3*d.*, 6 × 2*d.*, 6 × 1½*d.*, 6 × 1*d.*, 6 × ½*d.*. *Wmk Crowns* (*Nos.* 570/3 *and* 575).

X1	No date	£110
X2	OCT 1961	£125

1962–64. *New Composition. Pages of six stamps:* 30 × 3*d.*, 6 × 2½*d.*, 6 × 1½*d.*, 6 × 2*d.*, 6 × 1*d.* (*Nos.* 571/2 *and* 574/5).

X3	APR 1962	90·00
X4	AUG 1962	£120
X5	MAR 1963	£115
X6	JULY 1963	£115
X7	DEC 1963	£115
X8	JULY 1964	90·00
X9	DEC 1964	£225

1965 (23 Aug)–**66**. *Ochre cover as Type* **D**. *Pages of six stamps:* 24 × 4*d.*, 6 × 3*d.*, 6 × 1*d. Wmk Crowns* (*Nos.* 571, 575, 576*a*).

X10	AUG 1965	24·00
X11	DEC 1965	35·00
X12	FEB 1966	35·00
X13	AUG 1966	24·00
X14	NOV 1966	24·00

1967–68. *Ochre cover as Type* **D**. *Pages of six phosphor stamps:* 24 × 4*d.*, 6 × 3*d.*, 6 × 1*d. Wmk Crowns* (*Nos.* 611, 615*c* (*one side phosphor band*), 616*a*).

X15p	FEB 1967	8·00

Composition as No. X15p. *Wmk Crowns* (*Nos.* 611, 615*e* (*one centre phosphor band*), 616*a*).

X16p	AUG 1967	6·00
X17p	FEB 1968	6·75

10s. Booklets with Machin type stamps

XP **4** Explorers Series with GPO Cypher

(Des S. Rose)

1968 (25 Mar–Aug). *Bright purple cover as Type* XP **4** (*Explorers Series*). *Pages of six stamps:* 24 × 4*d.*, 6 × 3*d.*, 6 × 1*d. PVA gum* (*Nos.* 724, 729Ev, 731Ev).

XP4	MAY 1968 (Livingstone)	5·00
XP5	AUG 1968 (Livingstone)	5·00

1968 (16 Sept)–**70**. *Yellow-green covers as Type* XP **4** (*Explorers Series*) *New composition. Pages of six stamps:* 12 × 5*d.* (*with two phosphor bands*), 12 × 4*d.* (*with one centre phosphor band*) *and pane comprising* 4 × 1*d. se-tenant with vert pair of* 4*d.* (*each with one centre phosphor band*). *PVA gum* (*Nos.* 725, 732 *and* 735).

XP6	SEPT 1968 (Scott)	4·00

Change to 4*d. bright vermilion* (*one centre band*) *but se-tenant pane comprises* 1*d. with two phosphor bands and* 4*d. with one left side phosphor band* (*Nos.* 724 *and* 733/4).

XP7	FEB 1969 (Mary Kingsley) (6.1.69)	3·00
XP8	MAY 1969 (Mary Kingsley)	4·00
XP9	AUG 1969 (Shackleton)	4·00
XP10	NOV 1969 (Shackleton)	6·00

XP **11** Explorers Series with Post Office Corporation Crown Symbol

(Des S. Rose)

As last but cover changed to Type XP **11**.

XP11	FEB 1970 (Frobisher)	6·00
XP12	NOV 1970 (Captain Cook)	6·50

£1 Booklet with Machin type stamps

ZP **1**

1969 (1 Dec). *"Stamps for Cooks". Type* ZP **1** *(150×72 mm) with full colour pictorial cover showing "Baked, Stuffed Haddock". Contains 12 recipes on interleaving pages and on se-tenant labels attached to booklet panes. PVA gum. Stapled.*

ZP1	£1 containing panes of fifteen stamps (5×3): 15×5d. (No. 735), 30×4d. (No. 733) and pane comprising 6×4d. (three each of Nos. 734 and 734Eb) *se-tenant* with 6×1d. (No. 724) and 3×5d. (No. 735)	£250
ZP1a	As last but booklet is sewn with thread instead of being stapled	9·00

II. Decimal Booklets, 1971 onwards.

A. Stitched Booklets.

The 25p., 30p., 35p., 45p. and 50p. booklets have pictorial covers (except for the 35p. and 45p.) without the design inscription. This was no longer necessary as the designs and background information were given on the inside of the front cover. Each series was numbered.

10p. Booklets

DN **46** British Pillar Box Series

(Des R. Maddox)

1971 (15 Feb–1 June). *British Pillar Box Series. Orange yellow cover as Type* DN **46**. *Pages of four stamps:* 2×2p. *se-tenant vertically with* 2×½p. *and* 2×1p. *se-tenant vertically with* 2×1½p. *(Nos.* X8411 *and* X8441).

DN46	FEB 1971 (No. 1 1855 type)	2·50
DN47	APR 1971 (No. 1 1855 type) (19.3.71)	2·00
DN48	JUNE 1971 (No. 2 1856 type) (1.6.71)	2·50

In No. DN47 the pillar box is slightly reduced in size.

1971 (14 July)–**74.** *British Pillar Box Series continued. Orange-yellow cover as Type* DN **46**. *Contents unchanged but panes are se-tenant horizontally (Nos.* X841l/a *and* X844m).

DN49	AUG 1971 (No. 2 1856 type) (14.7.71)	3·00
DN50	OCT 1971 (No. 3 1857–9 type) (27/8/71)	3·00
DN51	DEC 1971 (No. 3 1857–9 type) (6.10.71)	4·00
DN52	FEB 1972 (No. 4 1866–79 type) (8.12.71)	4·00
DN53	APR 1972 (No. 4 1866–79 type) (24.2.72)	2·75
DN54	JUNE 1972 (No. 5 1899 type) (12.4.72)	2·50
DN55	AUG 1972 (No. 5 1899 type) (8.6.72)	2·75
DN56	OCT 1972 (No. 6 1968 type) (2.8.72)	2·75
DN57	DEC 1972 (No. 6 1968 type) (30.10.72)	2·75
DN58	FEB 1973 (No. 7 1936 type) (5.1.73)	2·75
DN59	APR 1973 (No. 7 1936 type) (2.4.73)	4·00
DN60	JUNE 1973 (No. 8 1952 type) (18.4.73)	2·75
DN61	AUG 1973 (No. 8 1952 type) (4.7.73)	15·00
DN62	OCT 1973 (No. 9 1973 type) (16.8.73)	3·50
DN63	DEC 1973 (No. 9 1973 type) (12.11.73)	2·50
DN64	FEB 1974 (No. 9 1973 type) (17.12.73)	3·25
DN65	APR 1974 (No. 10 1974 type) (22.2.74)	2·50
DN66	JUNE 1974 (No. 10 1974 type) (23.4.74)	2·25

DN **67** Postal Uniforms Series

(Des C. Abbott)

1974 (23 July)–**76.** *Postal Uniforms Series. Orange-yellow cover as Type* DN **67**. *Contents unchanged.*

DN67	AUG 1974 (No. 1 1793 type)	1·80
DN68	OCT 1974 (No. 1 1793 type) (27.8.74)	1·80
DN69	DEC 1974 (No. 2 1837 type) (25.10.74)	1·80
DN70	FEB 1975 (No. 2 1837 type) (12.12.74)	1·60
DN71	APR 1975 (No. 3 1855 type) (26.3.75)	1·60
DN72	JUNE 1975 (No. 3 1855 type) (21.5.75)	1·75
DN73	AUG 1975 (No. 3 1855 type) (27.6.75)	1·75
DN74	OCT 1975 (No. 3 1855 type) (3.10.75)	90
DN75	JAN 1976 (No. 3 1855 type) (16.3.76)	90

25p. Booklets

DH **39** Veteran Transport Series

(Des D. Gentleman)

1971 (15 Feb). *Veteran Transport Series. Dull purple cover as Type* DH **39**. *Pages of six stamps:* 5×2½p. *with one printed label,* 4×2½p. *with two printed labels,* 5×½p. *with one printed label* (*Nos.* X841m *and* X851l/m).

DH39 FEB 1971 (No. 1 Knife-board omnibus) .... 3·50

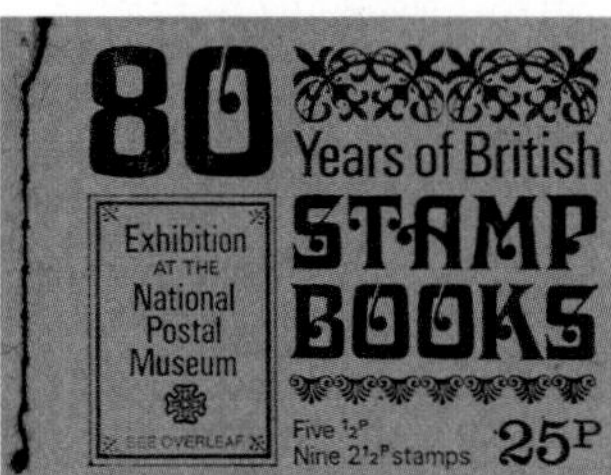

DH **40**

1971 (19 Mar). *Issued to publicise the National Postal Museum Exhibition of* 80 *Years of British Stamp Booklets. Dull purple cover as Type* DH **40**.

DH40 APR 1971 .... 4·25

1971 (11 June)–**73.** *Dull purple cover as Type* DH **39**. *Veteran Transport Series continued.*

DH41 JUNE 1971 (No. 2 B-type omnibus) .... 4·25
DH42 AUG 1971 (No. 2 B-type omnibus) (17.9.71) .... 11·00
DH43 OCT 1971 (No. 3 Showman's Engine) (22.11.71) .... 11·00
DH44 FEB 1972 (No. 4 Mail Van) (23.12.71) .... 7·25
DH45 APR 1972 (No. 4 Mail Van) (13.3.72) .... 8·75
DH46 JUNE 1972 (No. 5 Motor Wagonette) (24.4.72) .... 6·00
DH47 AUG 1972 (No. 5 Motor Wagonette) (14.6.72) .... 11·00
DH48 DEC 1972 (No. 6 Taxi Cab) (19.10.72) .... 11·00
DH50 DEC 1972 "Issues S" (No. 6 Taxi Cab) (6.11.72) . ... 7·25
DH51 FEB 1973 (No. 7 Electric Tramcar) (26.2.73) .... 9·00

Nos. DH42/51 contain panes showing the perforations omitted between the label and the binding margin.

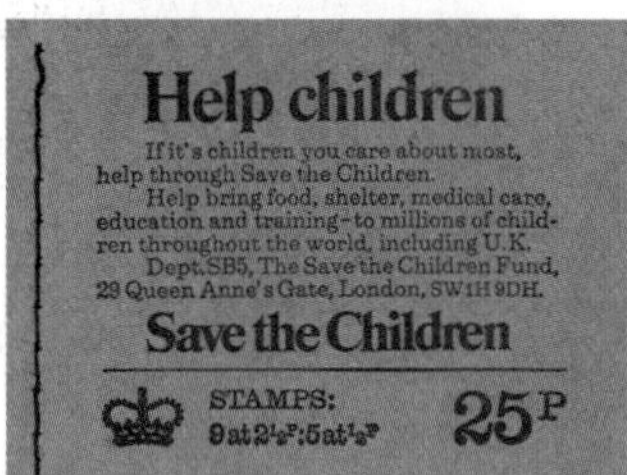

DH **52**

1973 (7 June). *Dull mauve cover as Type* DH **52**.

DH52 JUNE 1973 .... 9·00

No. DH52 contains panes showing the perforations omitted between the label and the binding margin.

30p. Booklets

DQ **56** British Birds Series

(Des H. Titcombe)

1971 (15 Feb). *British Birds Series. Bright purple cover as Type* DQ **56**. *Pages of six stamps:* 2 panes of 5×3p. *with one printed label* (*No.* X855l).

DQ56 FEB 1971 (No. 1 Curlew) .... 4·50

1971 (19 Mar). *Bright purple cover as Type* DH **40**.

DQ57 APR 1971 .... 6·00

1971 (26 May)–**73.** *Bright purple cover as Type* DQ **56**. *British Birds Series continued.*

DQ58 JUNE 1971 (No. 2 Lapwing) .... 6·00
DQ59 AUG 1971 (No. 2 Lapwing) (23.7.71) .... 6·00
DQ60 OCT 1971 (No. 3 Robin) (1.10.71) .... 6·00
DQ61 DEC 1971 (No. 3 Robin) (10.11.71) .... 7·25
DQ62 FEB 1972 (No. 4 Pied Wagtail) (21.12.71) .... 6·00
DQ63 APR 1972 (No. 4 Pied Wagtail) (9.2.72) .... 6·00
DQ64 JUNE 1972 (No. 5 Kestrel) (12.4.72) .... 6·00
DQ65 AUG 1972 (No. 5 Kestrel) (8.6.72) .... 6·25
DQ66 OCT 1972 (No. 6 Black Grouse) (31.7.72) .... 6·75
DQ67 DEC 1972 (No. 6 Black Grouse) (30.10.72) .... 6·75
DQ68 DEC 1972 "Issue S" (No. 6 Black Grouse) (6.12.72) ...... 6·75
DQ69 FEB 1973 (No. 7 Skylark) (29.1.73) .... 6·25
DQ70 APR 1973 (No. 7 Skylark) (2.4.73) .... 5·75
DQ71 JUNE 1973 (No. 8 Oyster-catcher) (8.5.73) .... 6·25
DQ72 AUG 1973 (No. 8 Oyster-catcher) (7.6.73) .... 9·50
DQ72*a* As DQ72 but buff cover (10.8.73)* .... 6·75

Nos. DQ59/72*a* contain panes showing the perforations omitted between the label and the binding margin.*No. DQ 72*a* was printed with a buff cover because of a shortage of the original purple-coloured card.

1974 (30 Jan). *Red cover similar to Type* DH **52**. *Make-up as before but containing panes of* 5×3*p.* (1 *centre band*) (*No.* X856) *with blank label.*

DQ73 SPRING 1974 .... 5·00

1974 (2 June). *Red cover similar to Type* DT **9**. *Make-up as before.*

DQ74 JUNE 1974 .... 5·00

35p. Booklets

DP **1** British Coins Series

(Des P Gauld)

1973 (12 Dec)–**74.** *British Coins Series. Blue cover as Type* DP **1**. *Pages of six stamps:* 2 *pages of* 5×3½p. *with one blank label* (*No.* X858*Eb*).

DP1 AUTUMN 1973 (No. 1 Cuthred's Penny) .... 3·25
DP2 APR 1974 (No. 1 Cuthred's Penny) (10.4.74) .... 6·50
DP3 JUNE 1974 (No. 2 Silver Groat) (4.7.74) .... 3·75

1974 (23 Oct). *Blue cover as Type* DT **9**. *Make-up as before but with No.* X859.

DP4 SEPT 1974 .... 3·50

45p. Booklets

1974 (9 Oct–26 Nov). *British Coins Series continued. Yellow-brown cover as Type* DP **1**. *Pages of six stamps:* 2 *pages of* 5×4½p. (*No.* X 865) *with one blank label.*

DS1 SEPT 1974 (No. 3 Elizabeth Gold Crown) .... 6·00
DS2 DEC 1974 (No. 3 Elizabeth Gold Crown) (1.11.74) .... 6·00
DS2a As DS2 but orange-brown cover (26.11.74)* .... 14·50

*No. DS2*a* was printed with an orange-brown cover because of a shortage of the original yellow-brown card.

50p. Booklets

DT 1

(Des Rosalie Southall)

1971 (15 Feb)–**72.** *British Flowers Series. Turquoise-green cover as Type* DT **1**. *Pages of six stamps:* 6×3*p.*, 4×3*p. setenant horizontally with* 2×2½p. (*side band*), 5×2½p. (*centre band*) *with one printed label and* 5×½p. *with one printed label* (*Nos.* X841m, X851l, X852l *and* X855×6).

DT1	FEB 1971 (No. 1 Large Bindweed)	9·00
DT2	MAY 1971 (No. 2 Primrose) (24.3.71)	10·00
DT3	AUG 1971 (No. 3 Honeysuckle) (28.6.71)	10·00
DT4	NOV 1971 (No. 4 Hop) (17.9.71)	11·00
DT5	FEB 1972 (No. 5 Common Violet) (23.12.71)*	11·00
DT6	MAY 1972 (No. 6 Lords-and-Ladies) (13.3.72)	11·00
DT7	AUG 1972 (No. 7 Wood Anemone) (31.5.72)	11·00
DT8	NOV 1972 (No. 8 Deadly Nightshade) (15.9.72)	9·00

Nos. DT4/8 contain panes showing the perforations omitted between the label and the binding margin.

*Although generally released on 24 December, this booklet was put on sale at the London E.C.1 Philatelic Counter and also at one other Philatelic Counter on 23 December.

DT 9

1973 (19 Jan–June). *Turquoise-green cover as Type* DT **9**.

DT9	FEB 1973	9·00
DT10	APR 1973 (26.2.73)	11·00
DT11	MAY 1973 (2.4.73)	11·00
DT12	AUG 1973 (14.6.73)	17·00

1973 (14 Nov)–74. *Moss-green cover similar to Type* DT **9**. *Pages of six stamps: 2 pages of* 5×3½*p. with one blank label (No.* X858*Eb) and 1 page of* 5×3*p. (centre band) and one blank label (No. X*856*).*

DT13	AUTUMN 1973	8·00
DT14	MAR 1974 (18.2.74)	6·00

85p. Booklet

1974 (13 Nov). *Purple cover similar to Type* DT **9**.

DW 1 Containing 3 pages of 5×4½p. (No. X865) with one blank label and 1 page of 5×3½p.
(No. X859) with one blank label .... 9·00

Sponsored Booklets

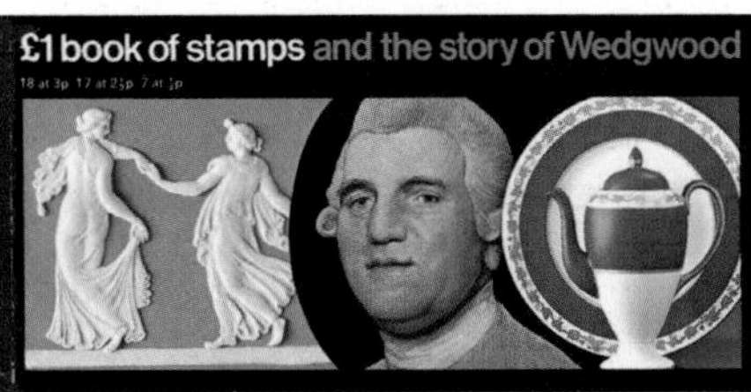

DX 1

(Des J. Wallis)

1972 (24 May). *"The Story of Wedgwood". Full colour pictorial cover, Type* DX **1** (150×72 *mm*). *Containing information and illustrations on interleaving panes and on se-tenant label attached to booklet panes.*

DX1 £1 containing Nos. X841o/p, X851n and X855n booklet panes .... 75·00

Price quoted for No. DX1 is for examples showing the ½p. 1 side band, No. X842, (in pane No. X841p) with full perforations. Examples of the booklet with this ½p. value showing trimmed perforations are priced at £25.

ILLUSTRATIONS. Sponsored booklet covers from No. DX2 are illustrated at one-third linear size *unless otherwise stated.*

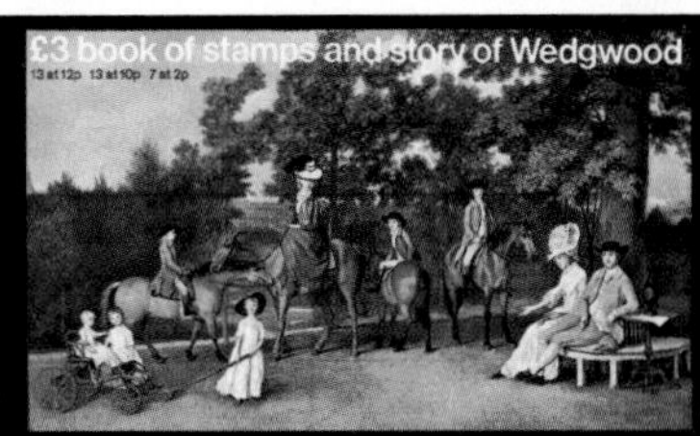

DX 2

(Des J. Wallis)

1980 (16 Apr). *"The Story of Wedgwood". Multicoloured cover, Type* DX **2** (163×97 *mm*) *showing painting "Josiah Wedgwood and his Family" by George Stubbs. Booklet contains text and illustrations on the labels attached to panes and on interleaving pages.*

DX2 £3 containing booklet panes Nos. X849n, X849o, X888l and X895l .... 8·00

No. DX2 is inscribed "January 1980".

DX 3

(Des B. Dedman)

1982 (19 May). *"Story of Stanley Gibbons". Multicoloured cover, Type* DX **3** (163×97 *mm) showing early envelope design on front and stamp album with text on back. Booklet contains text and illustrations on labels attached to panes and on interleaving pages.*

DX3 £4 containing booklet panes Nos. X849p, X899m and X907l/m .... 11·00

No. DX 3 is inscribed "February 1982".

DX **4**

(Des B. West)

1983 (14 Sept). *"Story of the Royal Mint". Multicoloured cover, Type* DX **4** (163×97 *mm) showing current coins, die and tools. Booklet contains text and illustrations on labels attached to panes and on interleaving pages.*

DX4 £4 containing booklet panes Nos. X899m×2, X930b and X949l .... 11·00

DX **5**

(Des P. Miles)

1984 (4 Sept). *"The Story of our Christian Heritage". Multicoloured cover, Type* DX **5** (163×97 *mm) showing mosaic of Christ from Hinton St. Mary Roman villa. Booklet contains text and illustrations on labels attached to panes and on interleaving pages.*

DX5 £4 containing booklet panes Nos. X886bl, X901m×2 and X952l .... 32·00

DX **6**

(Des D. Driver)

1985 (8 Jan). *"Story of The Times" (newspaper). Multicoloured cover, Type* DX **6** (163×95 *mm) showing "Waiting for The Times" (painting by Haydon). Booklet contains text and illustrations on labels attached to panes and on interleaving pages.*

DX6 £5 containing booklet panes Nos. X864l, X900l, X952l and X952m .... 22·00

DX **7**

(Des Trickett and Webb Ltd)

1986 (18 Mar). *"The Story of British Rail". Multicoloured cover, Type* DX **7** (162×95 *mm) showing diesel locomotive. Booklet contains text and illustrations on labels attached to panes and on interleaving pages.*

DX7 £5 containing booklet panes Nos. X896l, X897m, X952l and X952m .... 34·00

DX **8**

(Des Aitken Blakeley Designers)

1987 (3 Mar). *"The Story of P & O". Multicoloured cover, Type* DX **8** (162×95 *mm) showing the "William Fawcett". Booklet contains text and illustrations on labels attached to panes and on interleaving pages.*

DX8 £5 containing booklet panes Nos. X847m, X900l, X900m and X955l .... 28·00

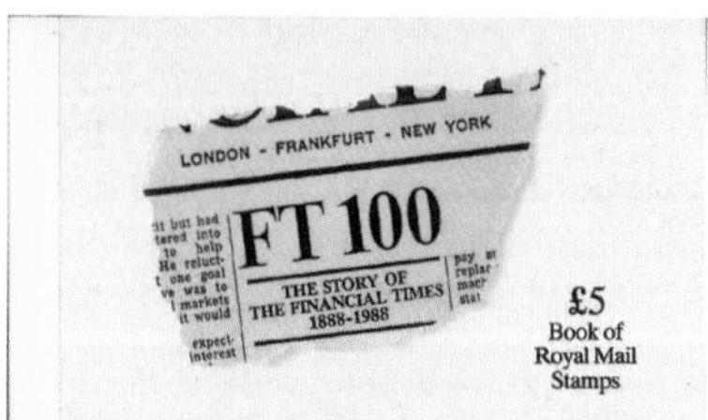

DX **9**

(Des The Partners)

1988 (9 Feb). *"The Story of the Financial Times" (newspaper). Multicoloured cover, Type* DX **9** (162 × 97 *mm*). *Booklet contains text and illustrations on labels attached to the panes and on interleaving pages.*

DX9 £5 containing booklet panes Nos. X1005l, X1006l, X1009l and X1009m .... 43·00

(Des Trickett and Webb Ltd)

1991 (19 Mar). *"Alias Agatha Christie". Multicoloured cover, Type* DX **12** (162 × 97 *mm*). *Booklet contains text and illustrations on labels attached to the panes and on interleaving pages.*

DX12 £6 containing booklet panes Nos. X1008l × 2, X1016l and X1016m .... 25·00

DX **10**

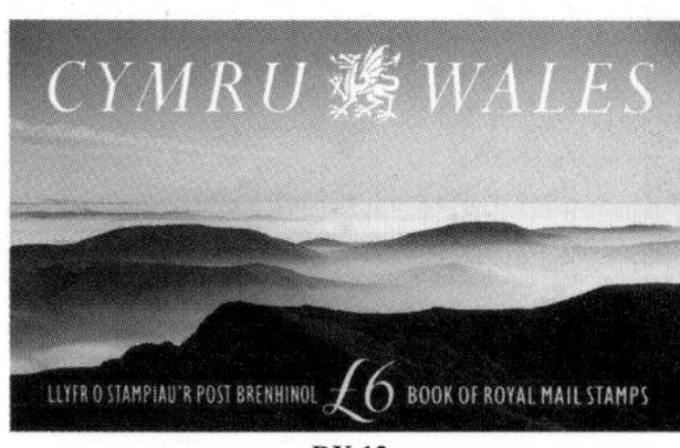

DX **13**

(Des Tayburn)

1989 (21 Mar). *"The Scots Connection". Multicoloured cover, Type* DX **10** (162 × 97 *mm*). *Booklet contains text and illustrations on labels attached to the panes and on interleaving pages.*

DX10 £5 containing booklet panes Nos. S54l, S55l, S62l and S62m .... 24·00

(Des G. Evernden and J. Gibbs)

1992 (25 Feb). *"Cymru–Wales". Multicoloured cover, Type* DX **13** (162 × 97 *mm*). *Booklet contains text and illustrations on labels attached to the panes and on interleaving pages.*

DX13 £6 Containing booklet panes Nos. 1591a, W48a, W49a and W59a .... 20·00

DX **11**

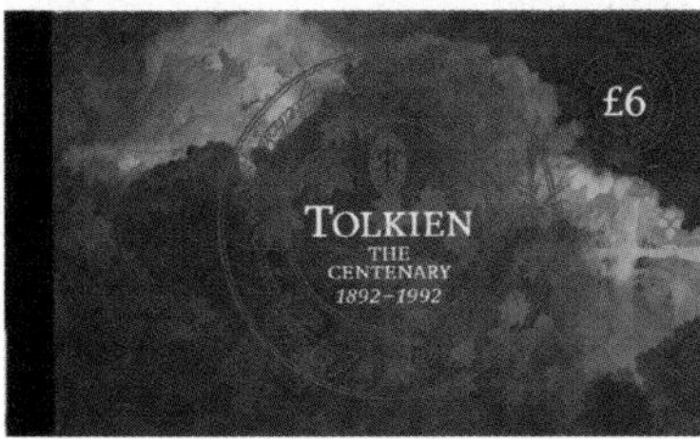

DX **14**

(Des D. Driver)

1990 (20 Mar). *"London Life". Multicoloured cover, Type* DX **11** (162 × 97 *mm*). *Booklet contains text and illustrations on labels attached to the panes and on interleaving pages.*

DX11 £5 containing booklet panes Nos. X906m, 1469n × 2 and 1493a .... 30·00

(Des The Partners)

1992 (27 Oct). *Birth Centenary of J. R. R. Tolkien (author). Multicoloured cover, Type* DX **14** (162 × 97 *mm*). *Booklet contains text and illustrations on labels attached to the panes and on interleaving pages.*

DX14 £6 containing booklet panes Nos. X1011l, X1012l and X1017l × 2 .... 25·00

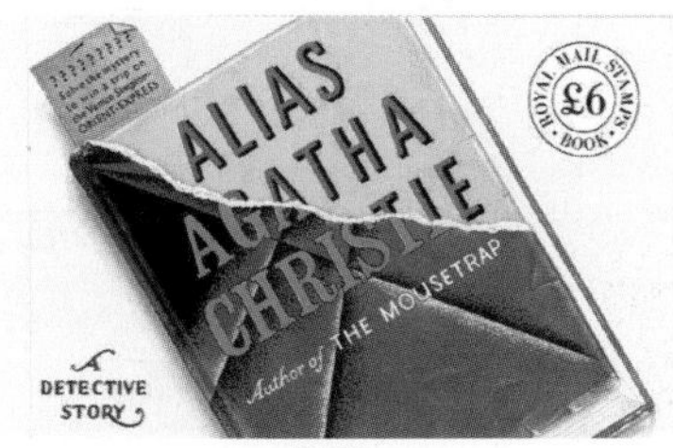

DX **12**

DX **15**

(Des The Partners)

1993 (10 Aug). *"The Story of Beatrix Potter". Multicoloured cover, Type* DX **15** (162×97 *mm*). *Booklet contains text and illustrations on labels attached to the panes and on interleaving pages.*

DX15 £5.64, containing booklet panes Nos. X1012m, 1451al, 1649a and NI48l .... 24·00

Although inscribed "£6.00" No. DX 15 was sold at the face value of its contents, £5.64.

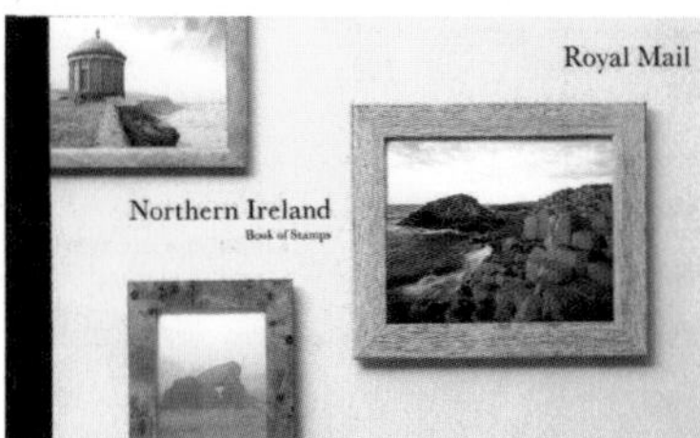

DX **16**

(Des Carroll, Dempsey and Thirkell Ltd)

1994 (26 July). *"Northern Ireland". Multicoloured cover, Type* DX **16** (162×97 *mm*). *Booklet contains text and illustrations on labels attached to the panes and on interleaving pages.*

DX16 £6.04, containing booklet panes Nos. Y1748l, 1812a and NI70a/b, together with a 35p. postal stationery air card .... 28·00

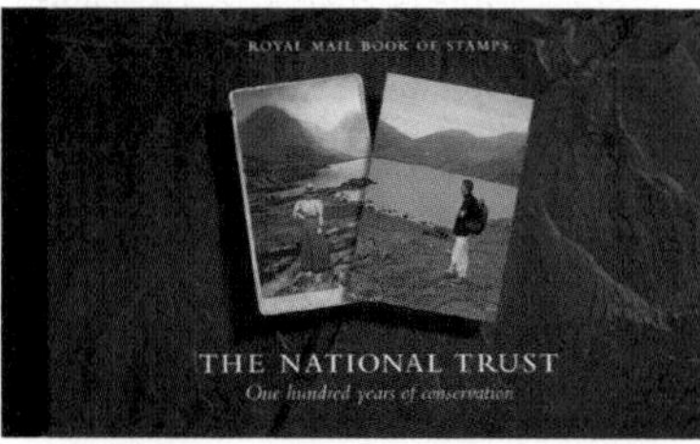

DX **17**

(Des The Partners)

1995 (25 Apr). *Centenary of the National Trust. Multicoloured cover, Type* DX **17** (162×97 *mm*). *Booklet contains text and illustrations on labels attached to the panes and on interleaving pages.*

DX17 £6 containing booklet panes Nos. Y1749l, Y1750l, 1869a and NI70d .... 28·00

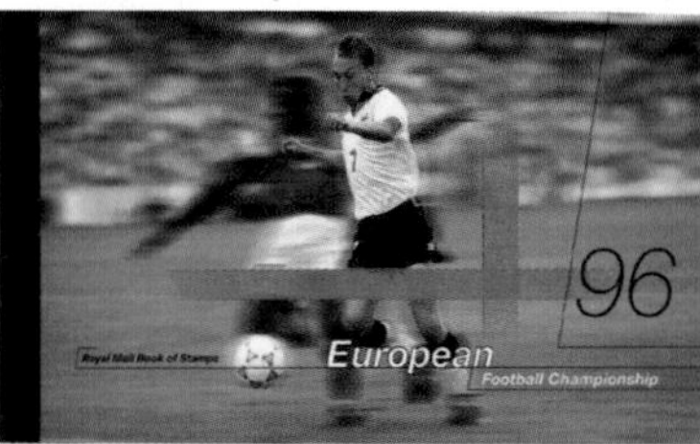

DX **18**

(Des Why Not Associates)

1996 (14 May). *European Football Championship. Multicoloured cover, Type* DX **18** (162×97 *mm*). *Booklet contains text and illustrations on labels attached to the panes and on interleaving pages.*

DX18 £6.48, containing booklet panes Nos. Y1752l, 1925a, 1926a and 1927a .... 18·00

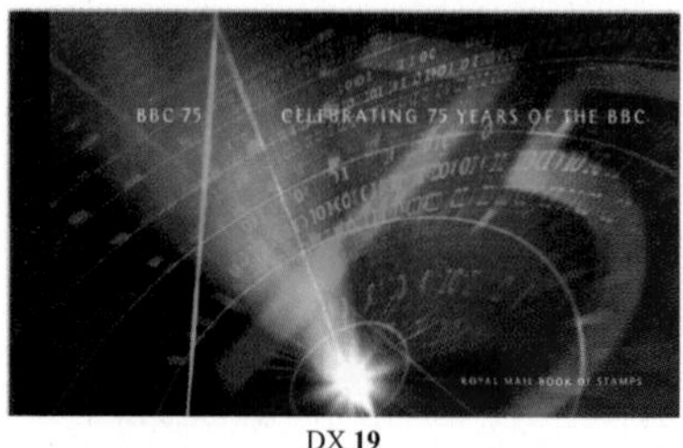

DX **19**

(Des H. Brown)

1997 (23 Sept). *75th Anniv of the B.B.C. Multicoloured cover, Type* DX **19** (162×97 *mm*). *Booklet contains text and illustrations on labels attached to the panes and on interleaving pages.*

DX19 £6.15, containing booklet panes Nos. Y1681l, 1940ab, 1668l and NI81al .... 25·00

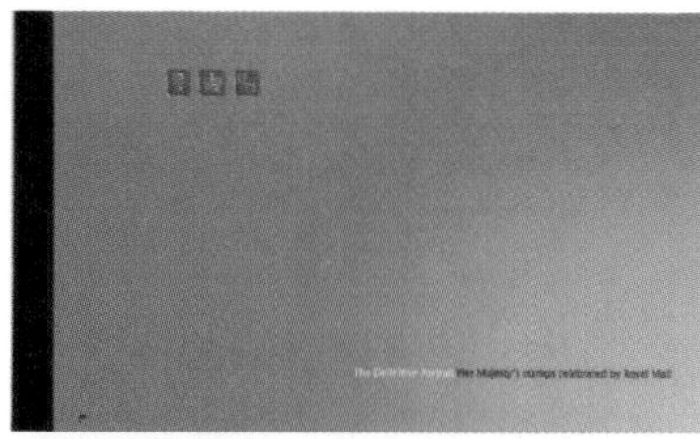

DX **20**

(Des Dew Gibbons Design Group)

1998 (10 Mar). *The Wildings Definitives. Black and gold cover, Type* DX **20** (162×96 *mm*). *Booklet contains text and illustrations on labels attached to the panes and on interleaving pages.*

DX20 £7.49, containing booklet panes Nos. 2031b/c and 2032a/b. .... 26·00

Folder containing DX20, DX22, DX24 *and* **MS**2147 *cancelled on presentation card* £150

DX **21**

(Des Roundel Design Group)

1998 (13 Oct). *"Breaking Barriers". British Speed Record Holders. Multicoloured cover, Type* DX **21** (161 × 96 *mm). Booklet contains text and illustrations on labels attached to the panes and on interleaving pages.*

DX21 £6.16, containing booklet panes Nos.1665l, Y1676l, 2059ac and NI80al .... 30·00

(Des Dew Gibbons Design Group)

1999 (16 Feb). *"Profile on Print". Multicoloured cover as Type* DX **20** (162 × 96 *mm). Booklet contains text and illustrations on labels attached to the panes and on interleaving pages.*

DX22 £7.54, containing booklet panes Nos. 1667l, 1671n and 2077l/9l .... 40·00

DX **23**

(Des Silk Pearce)

1999 (21 Sept). *"World Changers". Multicoloured cover as Type* DX **23** (163 × 96 *mm). Booklet contains text and illustrations on labels attached to the panes and on interleaving pages.*

DX23 £6.99, containing booklet panes Nos. Y1667n, 2072ab, 2080a, 2103BAand 2104ab .... 32·00

(Des Dew Gibbons Design Group)

2000 (15 Feb). *"Special by Design". Multicoloured cover as Type* DX **20** (162 × 96 *mm). Booklet contains text and illustrations on labels attached to the panes and on interleaving pages.*

DX24 £7.50, containing booklet panes Nos. Y1678l, 2124dl, 2133l and NI88al .... 45·00

DX **25**

(Des J. Gibbs)

2000 (4 Aug). *Queen Elizabeth the Queen Mother's 100th Birthday. Brownish grey and grey cover as Type* DX **25** (162 × 96 *mm). Booklet contains text and illustrations on labels attached to the panes and on interleaving pages.*

DX25 £7.03, containing booklet panes Nos. 2124bm, 2160a, **MS**2161a and S94a .... 31·00

DX **26**

(Des Roundel)

2000 (18 Sept). *A Treasury of Trees. Slate-green and bright green cover as Type* DX **26** (162 × 95 *mm). Booklet contains text and illustrations on panes and interleaving pages.*

DX26 £7 containing booklet panes Nos. 2155a, 2156a, 2158a, 2159a and W83al .... 31·00

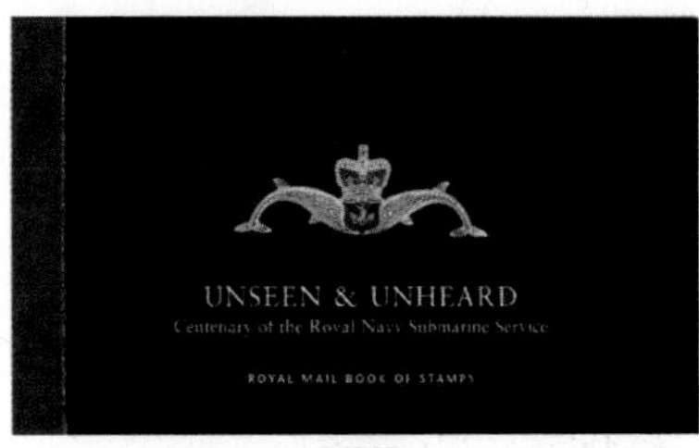

DX **27**

(Des D. Davis)

2001 (22 Oct). *"Unseen and Unheard". Centenary of Royal Navy Submarine Service. Black, greenish yellow, new blue and red cover as Type* DX **27** (162 × 97 *mm). Booklet contains text and illustrations on labels attached to the panes and on interleaving pages.*

DX27 £6.76, containing booklet panes Nos. 2202ab, 2203ab, **MS**2206a and S95a .... 35·00

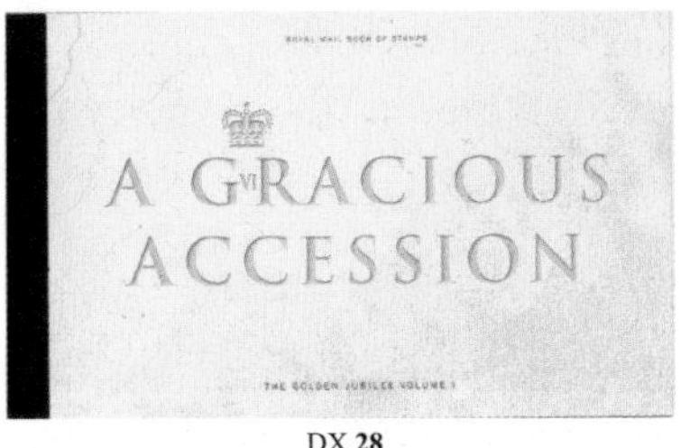

DX **28**

(Des GBH)

2002 (6 Feb). *"A Gracious Accession". Golden Jubilee of Queen Elizabeth II. Multicoloured cover as Type* DX **28** (161 × 96 *mm). Booklet contains text and illustrations on labels attached to the panes and interleaving pages.*

DX28 £7.29, containing booklet panes Nos. 1664n, 2253b/4b and 2258b .... 35·00

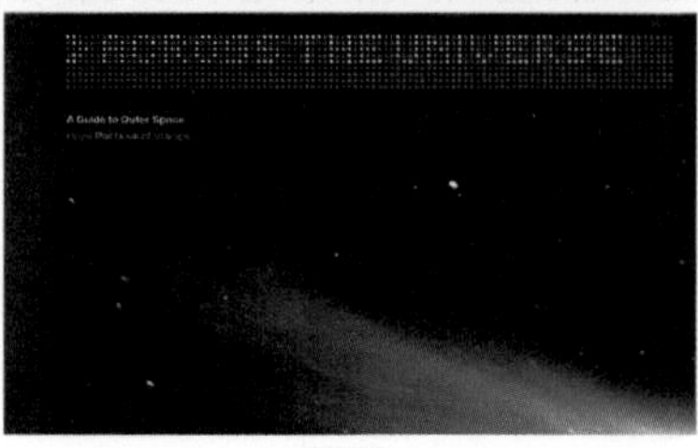

DX **29**

(Des CDT Design)

2002 (24 Sept). *"Across the Universe". Multicoloured cover as Type* DX **29** (164×95 *mm*). *Booklet contains text and illustrations on labels attached to the panes and interleaving pages. Stitched.*

DX29 £6.83, containing booklet panes Nos. 1668m, 2126ac, **MS**2315a and EN1b .... 28·00

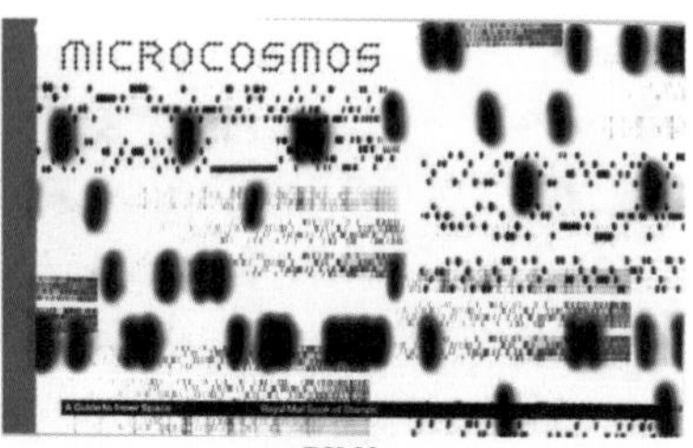

DX **30**

(Des CDT Design)

2003 (25 Feb). *"Microcosmos". 50th Anniv of Discovery of DNA. Multicoloured cover as Type* **DX 30** (164×95 *mm*). *Booklet contains text and illustrations on labels attached to the panes and interleaving pages. Stitched.*

DX30 £6.99, containing booklet panes Nos. 1668n, 2343a, 2345a and NI89a .... 20·00

DX **31**

(Des GBH)

2003 (2 June). *"A Perfect Coronation". 50th Anniv of Coronation. Multicoloured cover as Type* DX **31** (161×96 *mm*). *Booklet contains text and illustrations on labels attached to the panes and on interleaving pages.*

DX31 £7.46, containing booklet panes Nos. 1664o, 2368b/9b and 2378a .... 65·00

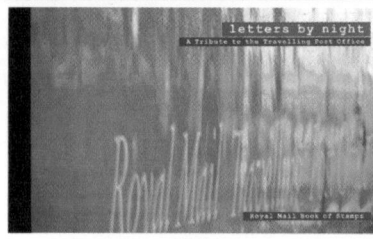

DX **32**

2004 (16 Mar). *"Letters by Night A Tribute to the Travelling Post Office". Multicoloured cover as Type* DX **32** (164×95 *mm*). *Booklet contains text and illustrations on labels attached to the panes and interleaving pages. Stitched.*

DX32 £7.44, containing booklet panes Nos. 1668o, 2392a, 2418a and S109a .... 24·00

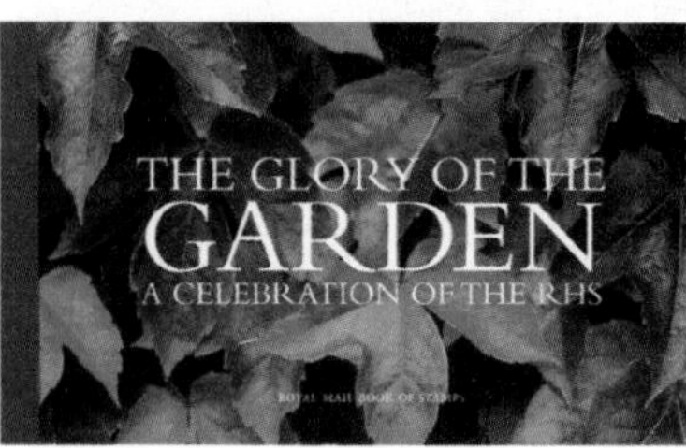

DX **33**

2004 (25 May). *"The Glory of the Garden". Bicentenary of the Royal Horticultural Society. Multicoloured cover as Type* DX **33** (162×96 *mm*). *Booklet contains text and illustrations on labels attached to the panes and interleaving pages. Stitched.*

DX33 £7.23, containing booklet panes Nos. 1668p, 2456a, 2457a and 2463a .... 23·00

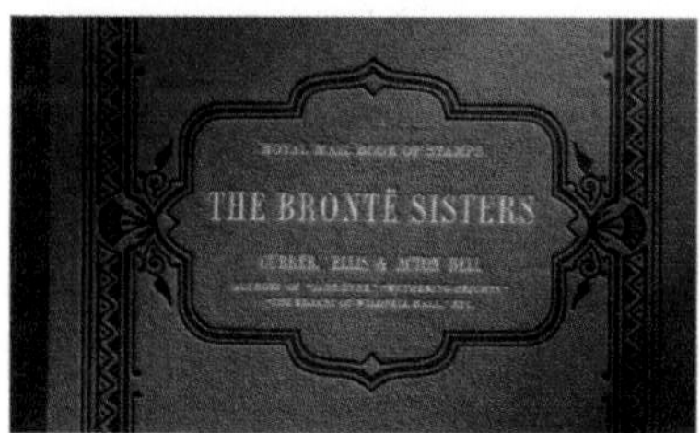

DX **34**

2005 (24 Feb). *The Brontë Sisters. 150th Death Anniv of Charlotte Brontë. Multicoloured cover as Type* DX **34** (162×96 *mm*). *Booklet contains text and illustrations on panes and interleaving pages. Stitched.*

DX34 £7.43, containing booklet panes Nos. 1664p, EN6a, 2518a and 2520a .... 11·00

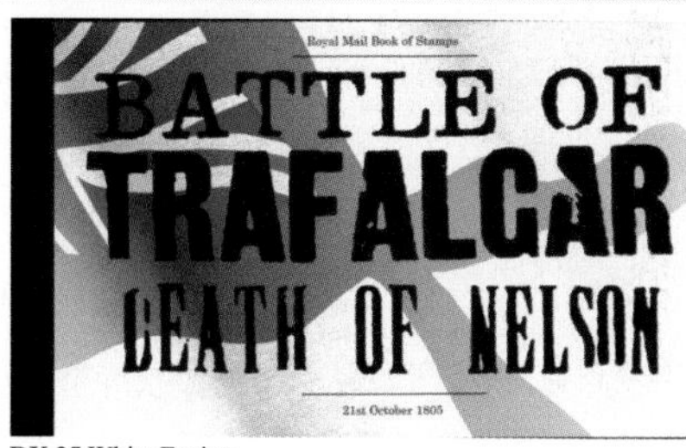

DX **35** White Ensign

2005 (18 Oct). *Bicentenary of the Battle of Trafalgar. Black, scarlet and ultramarine cover as Type* DX **35**. *Booklet contains text and illustrations on labels attached to the panes and interleaving pages. Stitched.*

DX35 £7.26 containing booklet panes Nos. 1668q, 2574b/5b and 2581a .... 17·00

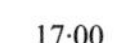

DX **36** Plaque showing Clifton Suspension Bridge

2006 (23 Feb). *Birth Bicentenary of Isambard Kingdom Brunel. Grey and grey-black cover as Type* DX **36**. *Booklet contains text and illustrations on panes and interleaving pages. Stitched.*

DX36 £7.40 containing booklet panes Nos. 1668r, 2607a/8a and 2610a .... 11·00

B. Folded Booklets.

NOTE: All panes are attached to the covers by the selvedge. Inscribed dates are those shown with the printer's imprint.

Illustrations for 10p., 50p., £1 and £2 booklets are 3/4 size; others are 2/3 size.

10p. Booklets

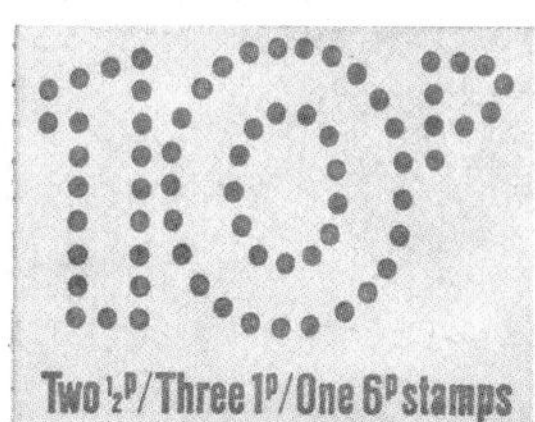

FA 1

1976 (10 Mar)–**77.** *Cover as Type* FA **1** *printed in dull rose on very pale lavender. Containing booklet pane No.* X841r.

FA1	NOV 1975	1·10
FA2	MAR 1976 (9.6.76)	1·20
FA3	JUNE 1977 (13.6.77)	80

FA **4**

(Des N. Battershill)

1978 (8 Feb)–**79.** *Farm Buildings Series. Bistre-brown and turquoise-blue covers as Type* FA **4**, *containing booklet pane No.* X843m.

FA4	Design No. 1, Oast Houses	70
FA5	Design No. 2, Buildings in Ulster (3.5.78)	80
FA6	Design No. 3, Buildings in Yorkshire (9.8.78)	70
FA7	Design No. 4, Buildings in Wales (25.10.78)	70
FA8	Design No. 5, Buildings in Scotland (10.1.79)	70
FA9	Design No. 6, Buildings in Sussex (4.4.79)	70

Nos. FA4/5 are inscribed "January 1978", FA6 "July 1978", FA7 "October 1978", FA8 "December 1978" and FA9 "March 1979".

FA **10**

(Des Hamper and Purssell)

1979 (17 Oct)–**80.** *"London 1980" International Stamp Exhibition. Red and blue cover as Type* FA **10** *showing Post Office exhibition stand and containing No.* X845l.

FA10	Inscr "August 1979"	60
FA11	Inscr "January 1980" (12.1.80)	70

50p. Booklets

All booklets were sold at the cover price of 50p. although some contain stamps to a greater value.

FB **1**

1977 (26 Jan). *Cover as Type* FB **1** *printed in maroon and paleblue.*

FB1A	Containing booklet pane X841s	2·40
FB1B	Containing booklet pane X841sa	2·40

1977 (13 June). *Cover as Type* FB **1**. *Printed in chestnut and stone.*

FB2A	Containing booklet pane X844n	5·00
FB2B	Containing booklet pane X844na	3·00

FB **3**

(Des J. Ireland)

1978 (8 Feb)–**79.** *Commercial Vehicles Series. Olive-yellow and grey covers as Type* FB **3.** A. *Containing booklet pane No.* X844n. B. *Containing booklet pane No.* X844na.

		A	B
FB3	Design No. 1, Clement Talbot van	5·00	3·25
FB4	Design No. 2, Austin taxi (3.5.78)	5·00	3·00
FB5	Design No. 3, Morris Royal Mail van(9.8.78)	5·00	3·00
FB6	Design No. 4, Guy Electric dustcart (25.10.78)	6·50	3·25
FB7	Design No. 5, Albion van (10.1.79)	6·50	6·25
FB8	Design No. 6, Leyland fire engine (4.4.79)	5·25	3·50

Nos. FB3/4 are inscribed "January 1978", FB5 "July 1978", FB6 "October 1978", FB7 "December 1978" and FB8 "March 1979".

1979 (28 Aug). *Contents changed.* A. *Containing booklet pane No.* X849l. B. *Containing booklet pane No.* X849la.

		A	B
FB9	Design No. 6, Leyland fire engine	2·75	2·75

FB **10**

(Des B. Smith)

1979 (3 Oct)–**81.** *Veteran Cars Series. Orange-red and reddish lilac covers as Type* FB **10.** A. *Containing booklet pane No.* X849l. B. *Containing booklet pane No.* X849la.

		A	B
FB10	Design No. 1, 1907 Rolls-Royce Silver Ghost	2·50	2·50

No. FB10 is inscribed "August 1979".

Contents changed. A. *Containing booklet pane No.* X849m. B. *Containing booklet pane No.* X849ma.

		A	B
FB11	Design No. 2, 1908 Grand Prix Austin(4.2.80)	2·75	2·75
FB12	Design No. 3, 1903–5 Vauxhall (25.6.80)	2·75	2·75
FB13	Design No. 4, 1897–1900 Daimler (24.9.80)	2·50	2·50

No. FB11 is inscribed "January 1980", No. FB 12 "May 1980" and No. FB 13 "July 1980".

Contents changed. A. *Containing No.* X841t. B. *Containing No.*X841ta.

		A	B
FB14	Design No. 5, 1896 Lanchester (26.1.81)	2·50	2·50
FB15	Design No. 6, 1913 Bull-nose Morris (18.3.81)	3·00	3·00

Nos. FB14/15 are inscribed "January 1981".

FB **16**

(Des R. Downer)

1981 (6 May)–**82.** *Follies Series. Brown and orange-brown covers as Type* FB **16.** A. *Containing No.* X841t. B. *Containing No.* X841ta.

		A	B
FB16	Design No. 1, Mugdock Castle, Stirlingshire	2·50	2·50

No. FB16 is inscribed "January 1981".

Contents changed. A. Containing No. X854l. B. Containing No. X854la.

		A	B
FB17	Design No. 1, Mugdock Castle, Stirlingshire (26.8.81)	7·25	12·00
FB18	Design No. 2, Mow Cop Castle, Cheshire–Staffs border (30.9.81)	7·00	9·00

Nos. FB17/18 are inscribed "January 1981".

Contents changed. A. Containing No. X841u. B. Containing No. X841ua.

		A	B
FB19	Design No. 3, Paxton's Tower, Llanarthney, Dyfed (1.2.82)	3·00	3·00
FB20	Design No. 4, Temple of the Winds, Mount Stewart, Northern Ireland (6.5.82)	3·00	3·00
FB21	Design No. 5, Temple of the Sun, Stourhead, Wilts (11.8.82)	3·00	3·00
FB22	Design No. 6, Water Garden, Cliveden, Bucks (6.10.82)	3·00	3·00

Nos. FB19/22 are inscribed "February 1982".

FB **23**

(Des H. Titcombe)

1983 (16 Feb–26 Oct). *Rare Farm Animals Series. Bright green and black covers as Type* FB **23.** A. *Containing booklet pane No.* X841u. B. *Containing booklet pane No.* X841ua.

		A	B
FB23	Design No. 1, Bagot Goat	3·25	3·25

Contents changed. Containing No. X845n.

FB24	Design No. 2, Gloucester Old Spot Pig (5.4.83)	6·50
	b. Corrected rate	15·00
FB25	Design No. 3, Toulouse Goose (27.7.83)	6·50
FB26	Design No. 4, Orkney Sheep (26.10.83)	6·50

No. FB23 is inscribed "February 1982" and Nos. FB24/6 "April 1983". The corrected rate reads, "36p. for 200g" instead of "37p. for 200g".

FB **27**

(Des P. Morter)

1984 (3 Sept)–**85.** *Orchids Series. Yellow-green and lilac covers as Type* FB **27.** *Containing booklet pane No.* X845p.

FB27	Design No. 1, *Dendrobium nobile* and *Miltonia* hybrid	4·00
FB28	Design No. 2, *Cypripedium calceolus* and *Ophrys apifera* (15.1.85)	4·00
FB29	Design No. 3, *Bifrenaria* and Vanda tricolor (23.4.85)	4·00
FB30	Design No. 4, *Cymbidium* and *Arpophyllum* (23.7.85)	4·00

Nos. FB27/30 are inscribed "September 1984".

Type FB **31**

(Des M. Thierens Design)

1985 (4 Nov). *Cover as Type* FB **31** *printed in black and bright scarlet. Containing booklet pane No.* X909l.

FB31 Pillar box design .... 4·75

No. FB 31 is inscribed "November 1985".

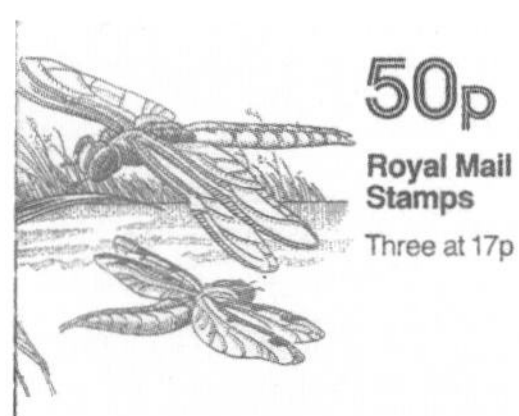

FB **32**

(Des P. Morter)

1986 (20 May–12 Aug). *Pond Life Series. Dull blue and emerald covers as Type* FB **32**. *Containing booklet pane No.* X909l.

FB32 Design No. 1, Emperor Dragonfly, Fourspotted Libellula and Yellow Flag .... 3·00

FB33 Design No. 2. Common Frog, Fennel-leaved Pondweed and Long-stalked Pondweed (29.7.86) .... 4·00

a. Containing booklet pane No. X909Ela(12.8.86)........ 3·75

Nos. FB32/33a are inscribed "November 1985".

FB **34**

(Des N. Battershill)

1986 (29 July). *Roman Britain Series. Brown-ochre and Indian red cover as Type* FB **34**. *Containing booklet pane No.* X845q.

FB34 Design No. 1, Hadrian's Wall .... 11·00

No. FB34 is inscribed "November 1985".

1986 (20 Oct)–**87.** *Pond Life Series continued. Dull blue and emerald covers as Type* FB **32**. *Containing booklet pane No.* X845s.

FB35 Design No. 3, Moorhen and Little Grebe .... 6·00

FB36 Design No. 4, Giant Pond and Great Ramshorn Snails (27.1.87) .... 6·00

No. FB36 is inscribed "October 1986".

1986 (20 Oct)–**87.** *Roman Britain Series continued. Brown ochre and Indian red covers as Type* FB **34**. *Containing booklet pane No.* X847l.

FB37 Design No. 2, Roman Theatre of Verulamium, St. Albans 3·00

FB38 Design No. 3, Portchester Castle, Hampshire (27.1.87) .... 3·00

No. FB38 is inscribed "October 1986".

FB **39**

(Des Patricia Howes)

1987 (14 Apr)–**88.** *Bicentenary of Marylebone Cricket Club Series. Brown and dull ultramarine covers as Type* FB **39**. *Containing booklet pane No.* X847l.

FB 39 Design No. 1, Father Time weather vane .... 3·00

FB 40 Design No. 2, Ashes urn and embroidered velvet bag (14.7.87) .... 3·00

FB 41 Design No. 3, Lord's Pavilion and wrought iron decoration on roof (29.9.87) .... 3·00

FB 42 Design No. 4, England team badge and new stand at Lord's (26.1.88) .... 3·00

Nos. FB39/42 are inscribed "October 1986".

FB **43**

(Des G. Evernden)

1987 (14 Apr)–**88.** *Botanical Gardens Series. Covers as Type* FB **43**. *Containing booklet panes No.* X845s (FB43/4) *or* X845sa (FB45/6).

FB43 Design No. 1 (cover in ultramarine and rosered), Rhododendron "Elizabeth", Bodnant .... 6·00

FB44 Design No. 2 (cover in deep ultramarine and cobalt), Gentiana sino-ornata, Edinburgh (14.7.87) .... 6·00

FB45 Design No. 3 (cover in dull ultramarine and orange-yellow), Lilium auratum and "Mount Stuart" (incorrect inscr) (29.9.87) .... 3·50

a. With corrected spelling "Mount Stewart" (30.10.87) .... 3·50

FB46 Design No. 4 (cover in dull ultramarine and yellow-orange), Strelitzia reginae, Kew (26.1.88)........ 3·50

Nos. FB43/6 are inscribed "October 1986".

The panes from Nos. FB45/6 have imperforate vertical sides.

FB **47**

1988 (12 Apr–5 July). *London Zoo. Children's Drawings Series. Covers as Type* FB **47**.

FB47 Pigs design (cover in black and rose) containing booklet pane No. X847l .... 3·50

FB48 Birds design (cover in black and yellow) containing booklet pane No. X845sa .... 3·50

FB49 Elephants design (cover in black and grey) containing booklet pane No. X847l (5.7.88) .... 3·50

Nos. FB47/9 are inscribed "October 1986". The pane from No. FB48 has imperforate vertical sides.

FB **50**

(Des P. Morter)

1988 (5 July). *Marine Life Series. Blue and orange-brown cover as Type* FB **50**. *Containing booklet pane No.* X845sa.

FB50 Design No. 1, Parasitic Anemone on Common Whelk Shell and Umbrella Jellyfish .... 3·50

No. FB50 is inscribed "October 1986" and has the vertical sides of the pane imperforate.

FB **51**

(Des Lynda Gray)

1988 (5 Sept)–**89.** *Gilbert and Sullivan Operas Series. Black and red covers as Type* FB **51**. *Containing booklet pane No.* X904l.

FB51 Design No. 1, The *Yeomen of the Guard* .... 8·00
FB52 Design No. 2, *The Pirates of Penzance* (24.1.89) .... 8·00
FB53 Design No. 3, *The Mikado* (25.4.89) .... 8·00

1989 (18 July). *Marine Life Series continued. Blue and orange brown cover as Type* FB **50**. *Containing booklet paneNo.* X904l.

FB54 Design No. 2, Common Hermit Crab, Bladder Wrack and Laver Spire Shell .... 8·00

For Design No. 3, see £1 Booklet No. FH17.

FB **55**

(Des P. Hutton)

1989 (2 Oct)–**90.** *Aircraft Series. Turquoise-green and light brown covers as Type* FB **55**. *Containing booklet pane No.* X906l.

FB55 Design No. 1, HP42, Armstrong Whitworth Atalanta and De Havilland Dragon Rapide .... 12·00

No. FB55 was incorrectly inscribed "Atlanta".

As before, but containing Penny Black Anniversary booklet pane No. 1468l.

FB56 Design No. 2, Vickers Viscount 806 and De Havilland Comet 4 (30.1.90) .... 9·00

1990 (4 Sept)–**91.** *Aircraft Series continued. Turquoise-green and light brown covers as Type* FB **55**. *Containing booklet pane No.* X911l.

FB57 Design No. 3, BAC 1-11 and VC10 .... 5·50
FB58 Design No. 4, BAe ATP, BAe 146 and Aérospatiale–BAC Concorde (25.6.91) .... 5·50

FB **59**

(Des A. Drummond)

1991 (10 Sept)–**92.** *Archaeology Series. Covers as Type* FB **59**. *Containing booklet pane No.* X925m.

FB59 Design No. 1 (cover in bright blue and lakebrown), Sir Arthur Evans at Knossos, Crete .... 3·00
a. Corrected rate (10.91) .... 3·25
FB60 Design No. 2 (cover in bright blue and yellow), Howard Carter in the Tomb of Tutankhamun (21.1.92) .... 3·00
FB61 Design No. 3 (cover in bright blue and yellow), Sir Austen Layard at Assyrian site (28.4.92) .... 2·40
FB62 Design No. 4 (cover in new blue and yellow), Sir Flinders Petrie surveying the Pyramids and temples of Giza (28.7.92) .... 3·00

On the inside front cover of No. FB59 the inland letter rates are shown as 1st class 24, 35, 43, 51p. and 2nd class 18, 28, 33, 39p. These were corrected on No. FB59a to read: 1st class 24, 36, 45, 54p. and 2nd class 18, 28, 34, 41p.

FB **63**

(Des J. Matthews)

1992 (22 Sept). 1000*th Anniv of Appointment of Sheriffs. Dull blue and scarlet cover as Type* FB **63**. *Containing booklet pane No.* X925m.

FB63 Design showing Crest, with Helm and Mantling, and Badge of The Shrievalty Association .... 2·00

FB **64**

(Des M. Newton)

1993 (9 Feb–6 July). *Postal History Series. Covers as Type* FB **64**. *Containing booklet pane No.* X925m.

FB64 Design No. 1 (cover in grey-green and greyblack), Airmail postmarks .... 2·50

FB65 Design No. 2 (cover in dull orange and black), Ship mail postmarks (6.4.93) .... 2·50
FB66 Design No. 3 (cover in blue and grey-black), Registered mail postmarks (6.7.93) .... 2·50

1993 (1 Nov). *Postal History Series continued. Rose-red and grey-black cover as Type* FB **64** *containing booklet pane No.* Y1683l.
FB67 Design No. 4, "Paid" postmarks .... 2·50

FB **68**

(Des A. Davidson)

1994 (25 Jan–6 Sept). *Coaching Inns Series. Covers as Type* FB **68.** *Containing booklet pane No.* Y1683l.
FB68 Design No. 1 (cover in myrtle-green and pale myrtle-green), "Swan with Two Necks" .... 2·50
FB69 Design No. 2 (cover in sepia and buff), "Bull and Mouth" (26.4.94) .... 2·50
FB70 Design No. 3 (cover in reddish brown and cinnamon), "Golden Cross" (6.6.94) .... 2·50
FB71 Design No. 4 (cover in black and slate-blue), "Pheasant Inn", Wiltshire (6.9.94) .... 2·50

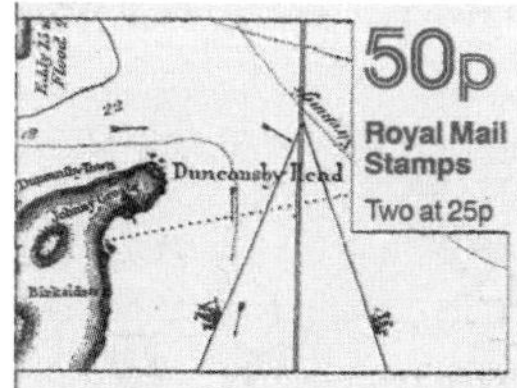

FB **72**

(Des D. Davis)

1995 (7 Feb–4 Apr). *Sea Charts Series. Rosine and black covers as Type* FB **72**, *containing booklet pane No.* Y1683l.
FB72 Design No. 1, John o' Groats, 1800 .... 2·50
FB73 Design No. 2, Land's End, 1808 (4.4.95) .... 2·50

1995 (6 June–4 Sept). *Sea Charts Series continued. Rosine and black covers as Type* FB **72**, *containing booklet pane No.* Y1684l.
FB74 Design No. 3, St. David's Head, 1812 .... 3·25
FB75 Design No. 4, Giant's Causeway, 1828 (4.9.95) .... 3·25

65p. Booklet

1976 (14 July). *Cover as Type* FB **1**, *but larger* (90×49 *mm*). *Printed in turquoise-blue and pale buff.* A. *Selvedge at left.* B. *Selvedge at right.*

		A	B
FC1	Containing ten 6½p. (No. X872)	16·00	9·00

70p. Booklets

1977 (13 June). *Cover as Type* FB **1**, *but larger* (90×49 *mm*). *Printed in purple-brown and dull rose.* A. *Selvedge at left.* B. *Selvedge at right.*

		A	B
FD1	Containing ten 7p. (No. X875)	6·00	6·00

FD **2**

(Des E. Stemp)

1978 (8 Feb)–**79.** *Country Crafts Series. Grey-green and red brown covers as Type* FD **2** (90×49 *mm*). *Containing ten* 7p. (*No.* X875). A. *Selvedge at left.* B. *Selvedge at right.*

		A	B
FD2	Design No. 1, Horse-shoeing	36·00	5·00
FD3	Design No. 2, Thatching (3.5.78)	£200	5·00
FD4	Design No. 3, Dry-stone-walling (9.8.78)	£250	5·00
FD5	Design No. 4, Wheel-making (25.10.78)	9·50	6·75
FD6	Design No. 5, Wattle fence-making (10.1.79)	20·00	7·00

Nos. FD2/3 are inscribed "January 1978", FD4 "July 1978", FD5 "October 1978" and FD6 "December 1978".

FD **7**

(Des F. Wegner)

1979 (5 Feb). *Official opening of Derby Mechanised Letter Office. Pale yellow-green and lilac cover as Type* FD **7** (90×49 *mm*). *Containing ten* 7p. (*No.* X875). A. *Selvedge at left.* B.*Selvedge at right.*

		A	B
FD7	Kedleston Hall	9·00	9·00

No. FD 7 is inscribed "December 1978".

On sale only in the Derby Head Post Office area to promote postcode publicity and also at the Philatelic Bureau and philatelic sales counters.

1979 (4 Apr). *Country Crafts Series continued. Grey-green and red-brown covers as Type* FD **2** (90×49 *mm*). A. *Selvedge at left.* B. *Selvedge at right.*

		A	B
FD8	Design No. 6, Basket-making	8·75	5·00

No. FD8 is inscribed "March 1979".

80p. Booklet

FE **1**

(Des P. Hutton)

1979 (3 Oct). *Military Aircraft Series. Blue and grey cover as Type* FE **1** (90×49 *mm*). *Containing ten* 8p. (*No.* X879) *attached by the selvedge.* A. *Selvedge at left.* B. *Selvedge at right.*

		A	B
FE1	Design No. 1, BE2B, 1914, & Vickers Gun Bus, 1915	4·00	4·00

No. FE1 is inscribed "August 1979".

85p. Booklet

1976 (14 July). *Cover as Type* FB **1** *but larger* (90×49 *mm*). *Printed in light yellow-olive and brownish grey.* A. *Selvedge at left.* B. *Selvedge at right.*

		A	B
FF1	Containing ten 8½p. (No. X881)	9·00	10·00

90p. Booklets

1977 (13 June). *Cover as Type* FB **1**, *but larger* (90×49 *mm*). *Printed in deep grey-blue and cobalt.* A. *Selvedge at left.* B. *Selvedge at right.*

		A	B
FG1	Containing ten 9p. (No. X883)	6·00	8·75

FG **2**

(Des R. Maddox)

1978 (8 Feb)—**79.** *British Canals Series. Yellow-olive and new blue covers as Type* FG **2** (90×49 *mm*). *Containing ten 9p.* (*No.* X883). A. *Selvedge at left.* B. *Selvedge at right.*

		A	B
FG2	Design No. 1, Grand Union	25·00	7·00
FG3	Design No. 2, Llangollen (3.5.78)	5·00	£425
FG4	Design No. 3, Kennet & Avon (9.8.78)	15·00	11·00
FG5	Design No. 4, Caledonian (25.10.78)	7·50	6·00
FG6	Design No. 5, Regents (10.1.79)	17·50	10·00

Nos. FG2/3 are inscribed "January 1978", FG4 "July 1978", FG5 October 1978" and FG6 "December 1978".

(Des F. Wegner)

1979 (5 Feb). *Official Opening of Derby Mechanised Letter Office. Violet-blue and rose cover as Type* FD **7** (90×49 *mm*). *Containing ten 9p.* (*No.* X883). A. *Selvedge at left.* B. *Selvedge at right.*

		A	B
FG7	Tramway Museum, Crich	11·00	11·00

No. FG7 is inscribed "December 1978".

On sale only in the Derby Head Post Office area to promote postcode publicity and also at the Philatelic Bureau and philatelic sales counters.

1979 (4 Apr). *British Canals Series continued. Yellow-olive and new blue cover as Type* FG **2**. A. *Selvedge at left.* B. *Selvedge at right.*

		A	B
FG8	Design No. 6, Leeds & Liverpool	5·00	5·00

No. FG8 is inscribed "March 1979".

£1 Booklets

All booklets were sold at the cover price of £1 although some contain stamps to a greater value.

FH **1**

(Des N. Battershill)

1979 (3 Oct). *Industrial Archaeology Series. Red and green cover as Type* FH **1** (90×49 *mm*). *Containing ten* 10p. (*No.* X887). A. *Selvedge at left.* B. *Selvedge at right.*

		A	B
FH1	Design No. 1, Ironbridge, Telford, Salop	4·50	4·50

No. FH1 is inscribed "August 1979".

1980 (4 Feb—24 Sept). *Military Aircraft Series continued. Blue and grey covers as Type* FE **1** (90×49 *mm*). *Containing ten 10p.* (*No.* X888). A. *Selvedge at left.* B. *Selvedge at right.*

		A	B
FH2	Design No. 2, Sopwith Camel & Vickers Vimy	4·50	4·50
FH3	Design No. 3, Hawker Hart* & Handley Page Heyford (25.6.80)	6·00	6·00
FH4	Design No. 4, Hurricane & Wellington (24.9.80)	4·50	4·50

No FH2 is inscribed "January 1980", No. FH3 "May 1980" and No. FH4 "July 1980".

*On the booklet cover the aircraft is wrongly identified as a Hawker Fury.

FH **5**

(Des M. Newton and S. Paine)

1986 (29 July)–**87.** *Musical Instruments Series. Scarlet and black covers as Type* FH **5**. *Containing six 17p.* (X952).

FH5	Design No 1, Violin	5·00

No. FH5 is inscribed "November 1985".

Contents changed. Containing No. X901n.

FH6	Design No. 2, French horn (20.10.86)	5·00
FH7	Design No. 3, Bass clarinet (27.1.87)	5·00

No. FH7 is inscribed "October 1986".

FH **8**

(Des A. Davidson)

1987 (14 Apr)–**88.** *Sherlock Holmes Series. Bright scarlet and grey-black covers as Type* FH **8**. *Containing booklet pane No.* X901n (FH8/9) *or* X901na (FH10/11).

FH8 Design No. 1, *A Study in Scarlet* .... 5·00
FH9 Design No. 2, *The Hound of the Baskervilles* (14.7.87) .... 5·00
FH10 Design No. 3, *The Adventure of the Speckled Band* (29.9.87) .... 5·00
FH11 Design No. 4, *The Final Problem* (26.1.88) .... 5·00

Nos. FH8/11 are inscribed "October 1986".

The panes from Nos. FH10/11 have imperforate vertical sides.

1988 (12 Apr). *London Zoo. Children's Drawings Series. Cover as Type* FB **47** *in black and brown. Containing booklet pane No.* X901na.

FH12 Bears design .... 5·00

No. FH12 is inscribed "October 1986" and has the vertical sides of the pane imperforate.

FH **13**

(Des Liz Moyes)

1988 (5 July)–**89.** *Charles Dickens Series. Orange-red and maroon covers as Type* FH **13**.

FH13 Designs No. 1, *Oliver Twist,* containing booklet pane No. X901na .... 6·50
FH14 Design No. 2, *Nicholas Nickleby*, containing booklet pane No. X904m (5.9.88) .... 6·50
FH15 Design No. 3, *David Copperfield*, containing booklet pane No. X904m (24.1.89) .... 6·50
FH16 Design No. 4, *Great Expectations*, containing booklet pane No. X1051l (25.4.89) .... 9·50

No. FH13 is inscribed "October 1986" and No. FH16 "September 1988", Nos. FH13/16 have the vertical sides of the pane imperforate.

1989 (18 July). *Marine Life Series continued. Cover as Type* FB **50** *in turquoise-green and scarlet. Containing booklet pane No.* X904m.

FH17 Design No. 3, Edible Sea Urchin, Common Starfish and Common Shore Crab .... 6·00

No. FH17 has the vertical edges of the pane imperforate.

FH **18**

(Des J. Sancha)

1989 (2 Oct)–**90.** *Mills Series. Grey-black and grey-green matt card cover as Type* FH **18**.

FH18 Design No. 1, Wicken Fen, Ely containing booklet pane No. X960l .... 7·00

As Type FH18 *but glossy card cover containing Penny Black Anniversary booklet pane No.* 1476l *printed in litho by Walsall.*

FH19 Design No. 1 (cover in bottle-green and pale green), Wicken Fen, Ely (30.1.90) .... 9·50

No. FH19 was an experimental printing to test a new cover material. This appears glossy when compared with Nos. FH18 and FH20.

As Type FH18 *but changed to matt card cover containing Penny Black Anniversary booklet pane No.* 1469l *printed in photo by Harrison.*

FH20 Design No. 2 (cover in grey-black and bright green), Click Mill, Dounby, Orkney (30.1.90) .... 7·50

1990 (4 Sept)–**91.** *Mills Series continued. Covers as Type* FH **18**. *Containing booklet pane No.* X911m.

FH21 Design No. 3 (cover printed in light blue and buff) Jack and Jill Mills, Clayton, Sussex .... 5·00
FH22 Design No. 4 (cover printed in dull blue and bright yellow-green). Howell Mill, Llanddeusant, Anglesey (25.6.91) .... 5·00

Nos. FH18/22 have the vertical edges of the pane imperforate.Type FH **23**

FH **23**

(Des J. Gibbs)

1991 (10 Sept)–**92.** 150*th Anniv of Punch Magazine. Magenta and grey-black covers as Type* FH **23** *containing booklet pane No.* X927l.

FH23 Design No. 1, Illustrations by Richard Doyle and Hoffnung .... 3·50
a. Corrected rate (10.91) .... 3·50
FH24 Design No. 2, Illustrations by Sir John Tenniel and Eric Burgin (21.1.92) .... 3·50
FH25 Design No. 3, Illustrations by Sir John Tenniel and Anton (28.4.92) .... 3·50
FH26 Design No. 4, Illustrations by Sir John Tenniel and Hewison (28.7.92) .... 3·50

Nos. FH23/6 have the vertical edges of the pane imperforate.

No. FH23a has corrected letter rates as No. FB59a.

(Des J. Matthews)

1992 (22 Sept). 1000*th Anniv of Appointment of Sheriffs. Scarlet and dull blue cover as Type* FB **63** *containing booklet pane No.* X927l.

FH27 Design as Type FB63 but elements in reverse order .... 3·50

No. FH27 has the vertical edges of the pane imperforate.

FH **28**

(Des J. Lawrence)

1993 (9 Feb–6 July). *Educational Institutions Series. Covers as Type* FH **28** *containing booklet pane No.* X1050l *printed in litho by Walsall.*

FH28 Design No. 1 (cover in lake-brown and light blue), University of Wales .... 7·25
FH29 Design No. 2 (cover in deep dull green and lemon), St. Hilda's College, Oxford (6.4.93) .... 7·25
FH30 Design No. 3 (cover in purple-brown and flesh), Marlborough College, Wiltshire (6.7.93) .... 7·25

1993 (1 Nov). *Educational Institutions Series continued. Deep bluish green and lilac cover as Type* FH **28** *containing four 25p. (No.* Y1752) *printed in litho by Walsall.*

FH31 Design No. 4, Free Church of Scotland College, Edinburgh .... 7·00

FH **32**

(Des H. Brockway)

1994 (25 Jan). *20th-century Prime Ministers Series. Brown and pale brown cover as Type* FH **32** *containing four* 25*p.* (*No.* Y1752) *printed in litho by Walsall.*

FH32	Design No. 1, Herbert Asquith	3·00

(Des H. Brockway)

1994 (26 Apr–6 Sept). *20th-century Prime Ministers Series continued. Covers as Type* FH **32**. *Containing four* 25*p.* (*No.* Y1683) *printed in photo by Harrison.*

FH33	Design No. 2 (cover in sepia and buff) David Lloyd-George	3·00
FH34	Design No. 3 (cover in greenish blue and pale blue), Winston Churchill (6.6.94)	3·00
FH35	Design No. 4 (cover in black and yellow-olive), Clement Attlee (6.9.94)	3·00

FH **36**

(Des L. Thomas)

1995 (7 Feb–4 Apr). *50th Anniv of End of Second World War. Covers as Type* FH **36** *containing four* 25*p.* (*No.* Y1683) *printed in photo by Harrison.*

FH36	Design No. 1 (cover in brown-olive and brownish black), Violette Szabo (S.O.E. agent)	3·00
FH37	Design No. 2 (cover in red-brown and black), Dame Vera Lynn (entertainer) (4.4.95)	3·00

1995 (16 May–4 Sept). *50th Anniv of End of Second World War Series continued. Covers as Type* FH **36** *containing four* 25*p.* (*No.* Y1684) *printed in photo by Harrison.*

FH38	Design No. 3 (cover in black and steel-blue), R. J. Mitchell (designer of Spitfire)	3·00
FH39	Design No. 4 (cover in grey-green and black), Archibald Mcindoe (plastic surgeon) (4.9.95)	3·50

FH **40**

1996 (16 Jan). *Multicoloured laminated cover as Type* FH **40**. *Stamps printed in litho by Questa.*

FH40	Containing four 25p. stamps (No. Y1752)	7·00

For an initial test period No. FH40 was only available from machines at twelve post offices, five in London and seven in Scotland, in addition to philatelic outlets. Stocks were distributed nationally from May 1996.

1996 (8 July)–**97**. *Multicoloured laminated cover as Type* FH **40**. *Stamps printed in litho by Questa.*

FH41	Containing booklet pane of 1p. × 2, 20p., 26p. × 3 and 2 labels (No. Y1743l)	6·00
	a. Corrected rate (4.2.97)	5·25

No. FH41 was reissued on 4 February 1997 showing the 200g second class rate on the inside cover altered from 47p. to 45p. A further printing issued 5 May 1998 was without the overseas postage rate table.

1998 (1 Dec). *Multicoloured laminated cover as Type* FH **40**. *Stamps printed in photo by Questa.*

FH42	Containing booklet pane of 1p. × 2, 20p., 26p. × 3 and 2 labels (No. Y1667l)	12·00

1999 (26 Apr). *Multicoloured laminated cover as Type* FH **40**. *Stamps printed in photo by Questa.*

FH43	Containing booklet pane of 1p., 2p., 19p., 26p. × 3 and 2 labels (No. Y1667m)	6·50

2000 (27 Apr)–**01**. *Multicoloured laminated cover as Type* FH **40**. *Stamps printed in photo by Questa.*

FH44	Containing booklet pane of 2nd, 1st × 3 and 4 labels (No. 1664l)	5·00
	a. Containing booklet pane No. 1664la (17.4.01)	5·00

£1.15 Booklets

1981 (26 Jan–18 Mar). *Military Aircraft Series continued. Blue and grey covers as Type* FE **1** (90 × 49 *mm*). *Containing ten* 11½p. (*No.* X893). A. *Selvedge at left.* B. *Selvedge at right.*

		A	B
FI1	Design No. 5, Spitfire & Lancaster	5·00	5·00
FI2	Design No. 6, Lightning & Vulcan (18.3.81)	5·00	5·00

Nos. FI1/2 are inscribed "January 1981".

FI **3**

(Des R. Maddox)

1981 (6 May–30 Sept). *Museums Series. Blue and turquoise green covers as Type* FI **3** (90 × 49 *mm*). *Containing ten* 11½p. (*No.* X893). A. *Selvedge at left.* B. *Selvedge at right.*

		A	B
FI3	Design No. 1, Natural History Museum (British Museum), London	5·00	5·00
FI4	Design No. 2, National Museum of Antiquities of Scotland (30.9.81)	5·00	5·00

Nos. FI3/4 are inscribed "January 1981".

£1.20 Booklets

1980 (4 Feb–24 Sept). *Industrial Archaeology Series continued. Red and green covers as Type* FH **1** *(90×49 mm). Containing ten 12p. (No.* X943). A. *Selvedge at left.* B. *Selvedge at right.*

		A	B
FJ1	Design No. 2, Beetle Mill, Ireland	5·00	5·00
FJ2	Design No. 3, Tin Mines, Cornwall (25.6.80)	5·00	6·50
FJ3	Design No. 4, Bottle Kilns, Gladstone, Stoke-on-Trent (24.9.80)	5·00	5·50

No. FJ1 is inscribed "January 1980", No. FJ2 "May 1980" and No. FJ3 "July 1980".

1986 (14 Jan). *Pillar box "Write Now" cover as Type* FB **31** *(90×49 mm), printed in yellow-green and pale red. Containing ten 12p. (No.* X896). A. *Selvedge at left.* B. *Selvedge at right.*

		A	B
FJ4	"Write Now" (Pillar box design) (no imprint date)	7·00	7·00

FJ 5

(Des R. Maddox)

1986 (29 Apr). *National Gallery cover as Type* FJ **5** *(90×49mm), printed in magenta and blue-green. Containing ten 12p. (No.* X896). A. *Selvedge at left.* B. *Selvedge at right.*

		A	B
FJ5	National Gallery design	6·50	6·50

No. FJ5 is inscribed "November 1985".

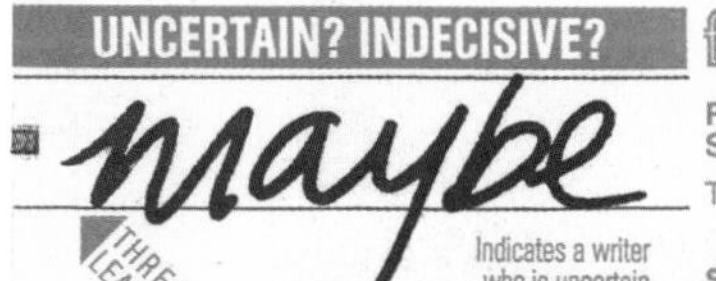

FJ 6

(Des Trickett and Webb Ltd)

1986 (29 July). *Handwriting cover as Type* FJ **6** *(90×49 mm), printed in bright orange and bright blue. Containing ten 12p. (No.* X896). A. *Selvedge at left.* B. *Selvedge at right.*

		A	B
FJ6	"Maybe"	6·50	6·50

No. FJ6 is inscribed "November 1985".

£1.25 Booklets

1982 (1 Feb–6 Oct). *Museums Series continued. Blue and turquoise-green covers as Type* FJ **3** *(90×49 mm). Containing ten 12½p. (No.* X898). A. *Selvedge at left.* B. *Selvedge at right.*

		A	B
FK1	Design No. 3, Ashmolean Museum, Oxford	5·50	5·50
FK2	Design No. 4, National Museum of Wales, Cardiff (6.5.82)	5·50	5·50
FK3	Design No. 5, Ulster Museum, Belfast (11.8.82)	5·50	5·50
FK4	Design No. 6, Castle Museum, York (6.10.82)	5·50	5·50

Nos. FK1/4 are inscribed "February 1982".

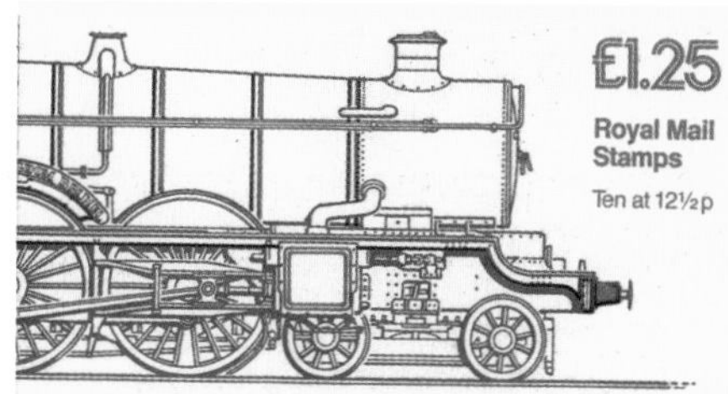

FK 5

(Des S. Paine)

1983 (16 Feb–26 Oct). *Railway Engines Series. Red and blue-green covers as Type* FK **5** *(90×49 mm). Containing ten 12½p. (No.* X898). A. *Selvedge at left.* B. *Selvedge at right.*

		A	B
FK5	Design No. 1, GWR *Isambard Kingdom Brunel*	7·00	7·00
FK6	Design No. 2, LMS Class 4P Passenger Tank Engine (5.4.83)	8·50	8·50
	a. Corrected rate	75·00	£120
FK7	Design No. 3, LNER *Mallard* (27.7.83)	7·00	7·00
FK8	Design No. 4, SR/BR *Clan Line* (26.10.83)	7·00	7·00

No. FK5 is inscribed "February 1982" and Nos. FK6/8 "April 1983". The corrected rate reads "36p. for 200g" instead of "37p. for 200g".

£1.30 Booklets

FL 1

(Des J. Gibbs)

1981 (6 May–30 Sept). *Postal History Series. Covers as Type* FL **1** *(90×49 mm). Containing No.* X894l. A. *Selvedge at left.* B. *Selvedge at right.*

		A	B
FL1	Design No. 1, Penny Black (red & black cover)	7·00	5·50
FL2	Design No. 2, The Downey Head, 1911 (red and green cover) (20.9.81)	9·50	30·00

No. FL1 is inscribed "April 1981" and No. FL2 "September 1981".

FL 3

(Des J. Thirsk)

1984 (3 Sept)–**85**. *Trams Series. Yellow-orange and purple covers as Type* FL **3** (90×49 *mm*). *Containing ten* 13*p*. (No. X900). A. *Selvedge at left*. B. *Selvedge at right*.

		A	B
FL3	Design No. 1, Swansea/Mumbles Railway Car No. 3	5·50	5·50
FL4	Design No. 2, Glasgow Car No. 927 and Car No. 1194 (15.1.85)	6·25	6·25
FL5	Design No. 3, Car No. 717, Blackpool (23.4.85)	6·25	6·25
FL6	Design No. 4, Car No. 120 and "D" Class Car, London (23.7.85)	5·50	5·50

Nos. FL3/6 are inscribed "September 1984".

FL 7

(Des Anne Morrow)

1986 (20 Oct). *Books for Children. Cover as Type* FL **7** (90×49 *mm*) *printed in rose-red and lemon. Containing ten* 13*p*. (*No.* X900). A. *Selvedge at left*. B. *Selvedge at right*.

		A	B
FL7	Teddy bears design	5·50	5·50

FL 8

(Des Trickett and Webb Ltd)

1987 (27 Jan). *"Keep in Touch" cover as Type* FL **8** (90×49 *mm*), *printed in light green and bright blue. Containing ten* 13*p*. (*No.* X900). A. *Selvedge at left*. B. *Selvedge at right*.

		A	B
FL8	Handclasp and envelope design	5·50	5·50

No. FL8 is inscribed "October 1986".

FL 9

(Des Hannah Firmin)

1987 (14 Apr). *"Ideas for your Garden". Cover as Type* FL **9** (90×49 *mm*) *printed in bistre and orange-brown. Containing ten* 13*p*. *stamps* (*No.* X900). A. *Selvedge at left*. B. *Selvedge at right*.

		A	B
FL9	Conservatory design	5·50	5·50

No. FL9 is inscribed "October 1986".

FL 10

(Des Trickett and Webb Ltd)

1987 (4 July). *"Brighter Writer". Cover as Type* FL **10** (90×49 *mm*) *printed in orange and bright reddish violet. Containing ten* 13*p*. *stamps* (*No.* X900). A. *Selvedge at left*. B. *Selvedge at right*.

		A	B
FL10	Flower design	5·50	5·50

No. FL10 is inscribed "October 1986".

FL 11

(Des E. Stemp)

1987 (29 Sept). *"Jolly Postman". Cover as Type* FL **11** (90×49 *mm*) *printed in pale blue and deep blue. Containing ten* 13*p*. *stamps* (*No.* X900). A. *Selvedge at left*. B. *Selvedge at right*.

		A	B
FL11	Boy drawing design	5·75	5·75

No. FL11 is inscribed "October 1986".

FL **12**

(Des E. Hughes)

1988 (26 Jan). *Bicentenary of Linnean Society. Cover as Type* FL **12** (90×49 *mm*) *printed in blue and claret. Containing ten* 13*p. stamps* (*No.* X900). A. *Selvedge at left.* B. *Selvedge at right.*

		A	B
FL12	Mermaid, fish and insect (from "Hortus Sanibatis", 1497)	6·75	6·75

No. FL12 is inscribed "October 1986".

FL **13**

(Des Hannah Firmin)

1988 (12 Apr). *Recipe Cards. Cover as Type* FL **13** (90×49 *mm*) *printed in brown and green. Containing ten* 13*p. stamps* (*No.* X900). A. *Selvedge at left.* B. *Selvedge at right.*

		A	B
FL13	Vegetables design	5·50	5·50

No. FL13 is inscribed "October 1986".

FL **14**

(Des Trickett and Webb Ltd)

1988 (5 July). *"Children's Parties". Cover as Type* FL **14** (90×49 *mm*) *printed in blue-green and bright purple. Containing ten* 13*p. stamps* (*No.* X900). A. *Selvedge at left.* B. *Selvedge at right.*

		A	B
FL14	Balloons and streamers design	5·50	5·50

No. FL14 is inscribed "October 1986".

£1.40 Booklets

1981 (26 Jan–18 Mar). *Industrial Archaeology Series continued. Red and green covers as Type* FH **1** (90×49 *mm*). *Containing ten* 14*p.* (*No.* X946). A. *Selvedge at left.* B. *Selvedge at right.*

		A	B
FM1	Design No. 5, Preston Mill, Scotland	5·50	5·50
FM2	Design No. 6, Talyllyn Railway, Tywyn (18.3.81)	5·50	5·50

Nos. FM1/2 are inscribed "January 1981".

FM **3**

(Des E. Stemp)

1981 (6 May–30 Sept). *19th-century Women's Costume Series. Claret and blue covers as Type* FM **3** (90×49 *mm*). *Containing ten* 14*p.* (*No.* X946). A. *Selvedge at left.* B. *Selvedge at right.*

		A	B
FM3	Design No. 1, Costume, 1800–15	5·50	5·50
FM4	Design No. 2, Costume, 1815–30 (30.9.81)	5·50	5·50

Nos. FM3/4 are inscribed "January 1981".

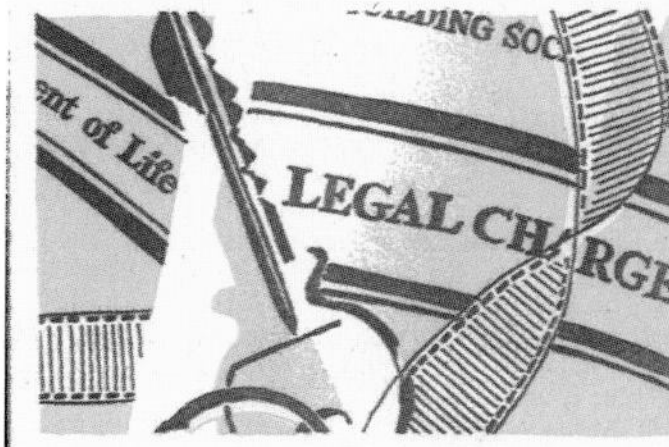

FM **5**

(Des A. Drummond)

1988 (5 Sept). *"Pocket Planner". Cover as Type* FM **5** (90×49 *mm*) *printed in grey-black and yellow. Containing ten* 14*p. stamps* (No. X903). A. *Selvedge at left.* B. *Selvedge at right.*

		A	B
FM5	"Legal Charge" design	5·50	5·50

FM **6**

(Des Debbie Cook)

1989 (24 Jan). *150th Anniv of Fox Talbot's Report on the Photographic Process to Royal Society. Cover as Type* FM **6** *(90×49 mm) printed in reddish orange and black. Containing ten* 14*p. stamps (No.* X903). A. *Selvedge at left.* B. *Selvedge at right.*

		A	B
FM6	Photographs and darkroom equipment	5·75	5·75

No. FM6 is inscribed "September 1988".

£1.43 Booklets

1982 (1 Feb–6 May). *Postal History Series continued. Covers as Type* FL **1** *(90×49 mm). Containing No.* X899l. A. *Selvedge at left.* B. *Selvedge at right.*

		A	B
FN1	Design No. 3, James Chalmers (postal reformer) (orange and turquoise-blue cover)	6·00	6·00
FN2	Design No. 4, Edmund Dulac (stamp designer) (brown and red cover) (6.5.82)	6·00	6·00

FN **3**

(Des J. Gardner)

1982 (12 July). *"Holiday Postcard Stamp Book". Purple and turquoise-blue cover as Type* FN **3** *(90×49 mm). Containing No.* X899l. A. *Selvedge at left.* B. Selvedge at right.

		A	B
FN3	Golden Hinde on front, postcard voucher on back	6·00	6·00

1982 (21 July)–**83**. *Postal History Series continued. Covers as Type* FL **1** *(90×49 mm). Containing No.* X899l. A. *Selvedge at left.* B. *Selvedge at right.*

		A	B
FN4	Design No. 5, "Forces Postal Service" (grey and violet cover)	6·00	6·00
FN5	Design No. 6, The £5 Orange (orange and black cover) (6.10.82)	6·00	6·00
FN6	Design No. 7, Postmark History (bright scarlet and deep dull blue cover) (16.2.83)	6·00	6·00

No. FN1 is inscribed "February 1982". FN2/3 "May 1982", FN4 "July 1982", FN5 "October 1982", FN6 "November 1982".

For booklet No. FS2 with cover price of £1.45, see £1.60 booklets.

£1.46 Booklets

1983 (5 Apr–26 Oct). *Postal History Series continued. Covers as Type* FL **1** *(90×49 mm).* A. *Containing No.* X899n. B. *Containing No.* X899na.

		A	B
FO1	Design No. 8, Seahorse High Values (blue and green cover)	11·00	11·00
	a. Corrected rate	48·00	24·00
FO2	Design No. 9, Parcel Post Centenary (turquoise-blue and carmine cover) (27.7.83)	9·50	9·50
FO3	Design No. 10, Silver Jubilee of Regional Stamps (dull green & reddish violet cover) (26.10.83)	9·50	9·50

No. FO1 is inscribed "March 1983", No. FO2 "May 1983" and No. FO 3 "June 1983".

The corrected rate reads "36p. for 200g" instead of "37p. for 200g".

£1.50 Booklets

1986 (14 Jan). *Pillar box "Write Now" cover as Type* FB **31** *(90×49 mm), printed in ultramarine and red.* A. *Containing No.* X897l. B. *Containing No.* X897la.

		A	B
FP1	"Write Now" (Pillar box design)	7·00	7·00

No. FP1 shows no imprint date.

1986 (29 Apr). *National Gallery cover as Type* FJ **5** *(90×49 mm), printed in violet and vermilion.* A. *Containing No.* X897l. B. *Containing No.* X897la.

		A	B
FP2	National Gallery design	7·00	7·00

No. FP2 is inscribed "November 1985".

1986 (29 July). *Handwriting cover as Type* FJ **6** *(90×49 mm), printed in blue-green and bright blue.* A. *Containing No.* X897l. B. *Containing No.* X897la.

		A	B
FP3	"No"	7·00	7·00

No. FP3 is inscribed "November 1985".

£1.54 Booklets

1984 (3 Sept)–**85**. *Postal History Series continued. Covers as Type* FL **1** *(90×49 mm).* A. *Containing No.* X901l. B. *Containing No.* X901la.

		A	B
FQ1	Design No. 11, Old and new Postage Dues (reddish purple and pale blue cover)	6·00	6·00
FQ2	Design No. 12, Queen Victoria embossed stamps (yellow-green and blue-cover) (15.1.85)	6·00	6·00
FQ3	Design No. 13, Queen Victoria surface printed stamps (blue-green and carmine cover) (23.4.85)	6·00	6·00
FQ4	Design No. 14, 17th-century mounted and foot messengers (deep brown & orange-red cover) (23.7.85)	6·00	6·00

No. FQ1 is inscribed "July 1984" and Nos. FQ2/4 are inscribed "September 1984".

£1.55 Booklets

1982 (1 Feb–6 Oct). *19th-century Women's Costume Series continued. Claret and blue covers as Type* FM **3** *(90×49 mm). Containing ten* 15½p. *(No.* X948). A. *Selvedge at left.* B. *Selvedge at right.*

		A	B
FR1	Design No. 3, Costume, 1830–50	5·75	5·75
FR2	Design No. 4, Costume, 1850–60 (6.5.82)	5·75	5·75
FR3	Design No. 5, Costume, 1860–80 (11.8.82)	5·75	5·75
FR4	Design No. 6, Costume, 1880–1900 (6.10.82)	5·75	5·75

Nos. FR1/4 are inscribed "February 1982".

£1.60 Booklets

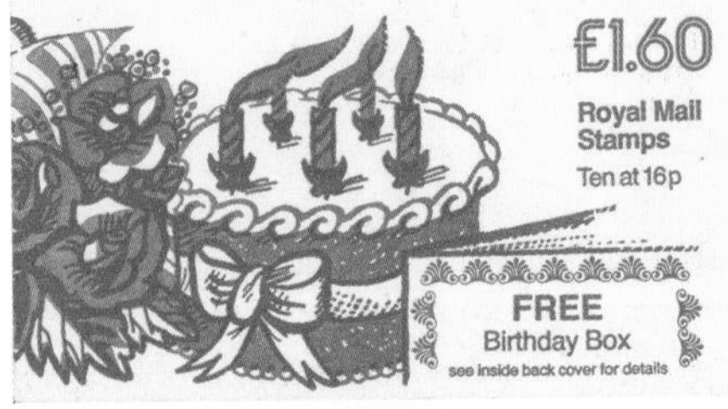

FS **1**

(Des Carol Walklin)

1983 (5 Apr). *"Birthday Box" Design. Magenta and red-orange cover as Type* FS **1** *(90×49 mm). Depicting birthday cake and associated items.* A. *Selvedge at left.* B. *Selvedge at right.*

		A	B
FS1	Containing ten 16p. stamps (No. X949) (no imprint date)	7·00	7·00
	a. Rates altered and "February 1983" imprint date	70·00	£120

FS **2**

(Des R. Maddox)

1983 (10 Aug). *British Countryside Series. Special Discount Booklet (sold at £1.45). Greenish blue and ultramarine cover as Type* FS **2** (90×49 *mm*). *Containing ten* 16*p. stamps* (*No.* X949Eu). A. *Selvedge at left.* B. *Selvedge at right.*

		A	B
FS2	Design No. 1, Lyme Regis, Dorset	9·00	9·00

Stamps from No. FS2 show a double-lined "D" printed in blue on the reverse over the gum.

No. FS2 is inscribed "April 1983".

1983 (21 Sept). *British Countryside Series continued. Dull green on violet cover as Type* FS **2** (90×49 *mm*). *Containing ten* 16*p. stamps* (*No.* X949). A. *Selvedge at left.* B. *Selvedge at right.*

		A	B
FS3	Design No. 2, Arlington Row, Bibury, Gloucestershire	6·00	6·00

No. FS3 is inscribed "April 1983".

FS **4**

(Des M. Newton)

1984 (14 Feb). *"Write it" Design. Vermilion and ultramarine cover as Type* FS **4** (90×49 *mm*). *Containing ten* 16*p. stamps* (*No.* X949). A. *Selvedge at left.* B. *Selvedge at right.*

		A	B
FS4	Fountain pen	7·00	7·00

No. FS4 is inscribed "April 1983".

£1.70 Booklets

FT **1**

(Des G. Hardie)

1984 (3 Sept). *Social Letter Writing Series. Rose and deep claret cover as Type* FT **1** (90×49 *mm*). *Containing ten* 17*p.* (*No.* X952). A. *Selvedge at left.* B. *Selvedge at right.*

		A	B
FT1	Design No. 1, "Love Letters"	7·00	7·00

No. FT1 is inscribed "September 1984".

1985 (5 Mar). *Social Letter Writing Series continued. Special Discount Booklet (sold at* £1.55). *Turquoise-blue and deep claret cover as Type* FT **1** (90×49 *mm*). *Containing ten* 17*p.* (*No.* X952Eu). A. *Selvedge at left.* B. *Selvedge at right.*

		A	B
FT2	Design No. 2, "Letters abroad"	7·00	7·00

Stamps from No. FT2 show a double-lined "D" printed in blue on the reverse over the gum.

No. FT2 is inscribed "September 1984".

1985 (9 Apr). *Social Letter Writing Series continued. Bright blue and deep claret cover as Type* FT **1** (90×49 *mm*). *Containing ten* 17*p.* (*No.* X952). A. *Selvedge at left.* B. *Selvedge at right.*

		A	B
FT3	Design No. 3, "Fan letters"	6·50	6·50

No. FT3 is inscribed "September 1984".

FT4

(Des B. Smith)

1985 (30 July). 350 *Years of Royal Mail Public Postal Service. Special Discount Booklet (sold at* £1.53). *Cover Type* FS **4** (90×60 *mm*), *printed in rosine and bright blue. Containing ten* 17*p.* (*No.* 1290Eu) *with selvedge at top.*

FT4	Datapost Service design	7·00

The stamps from this booklet show double-lined letters "D" printed on the reverse over the gum.

No. FT4 is inscribed "September 1984".

1985 (8 Oct)–**86**. *Social Letter Writing Series continued. Black and bright scarlet cover as Type* FT **1** (90×49 *mm*). *Containing ten* 17*p.* (*No.* X952). A. *Selvedge at left.* B. *Selvedge at right.*

		A	B
FT5	Design No. 4, "Write Now" (Pillar box)	6·50	6·50
	a. Revised rates (2nd class (60g) 12p.) (1.86)	25·00	15·00

1986 (29 Apr). *National Gallery cover as Type* FJ **5** (90×49 *mm*), *printed in blue-green and blue. Containing ten* 17*p.* (*No.* X952). A. *Selvedge at left.* B. *Selvedge at right.*

		A	B
FT6	National Gallery design	7·00	7·00

No. FT6 is inscribed "November 1985".

1986 (29 July). *Handwriting cover as Type* FJ **6** (90×49 *mm*) *printed in red and bright blue. Containing ten* 17*p.* (*No.* X952). A. *Selvedge at left.* B. *Selvedge at right.*

		A	B
FT7	"Yes"	7·00	7·00

No. FT7 is inscribed "November 1985".

£1.80 Booklets

1986 (20 Oct). *Books for Children. New blue and orange-brown cover as Type* FL **7**. *Containing ten* 18*p.* (*No.* X955). A. *Selvedge at left.* B. *Selvedge at right.*

		A	B
FU1	Rabbits design	7·00	7·00

1987 (27 Jan). *"Keep in Touch" cover as Type* FL **8** *printed in magenta and bright blue. Containing ten* 18*p.* (*No.* X955). A. *Selvedge at left.* B. *Selvedge at right.*

		A	B
FU2	Handclasp and envelope design	7·00	7·00

No. FU2 is inscribed "October 1986".

1987 (14 Apr). *"Ideas for your Garden". Claret and brown-olive cover as Type* FL **9** (90×49 *mm*). *Containing ten* 18*p. stamps* (*No.* X955). A. *Selvedge at left.* B. *Selvedge at right.*

		A	B
FU3	Garden path design	7·00	7·00

No. FU3 is inscribed "October 1986".

1987 (14 July). *"Brighter Writer". Turquoise-green and reddish orange cover as Type* FL **10** (90×49 *mm*). *Containing ten* 18*p. stamps* (*No.* X955). A. *Selvedge at left.* B. *Selvedge at right.*

		A	B
FU4	Berries and leaves design	7·00	7·00

No. FU4 is inscribed "October 1986".

1987 (29 Sept). *"Jolly Postman". Cover as Type* FL **11** (90×49 *mm*) *printed in deep blue and claret. Containing ten* 18*p. stamps* (*No.* X955). A. *Selvedge at left.* B. *Selvedge at right.*

		A	B
FU5	Girl drawing design	7·00	7·00

No. FU5 is inscribed "October 1986".

1988 (26 Jan). *Bicentenary of Linnean Society. Cover as Type* FL **12** (90×49 *mm*) *printed in dull yellow-green and dull claret. Containing ten* 18*p. stamps* (*No.* X955). A. *Selvedge at left.* B. *Selvedge at right.*

		A	B
FU6	Wolf and birds (from "Hortus Sanitatis", 1497)	7·00	7·00

1988 (12 Apr). *Recipe Cards. Cover as Type* FL **13** (90×49 *mm*) *printed in claret and Indian red. Containing ten* 18*p. stamps* (*No.* X955). A. *Selvedge at left.* B. *Selvedge at right.*

		A	B
FU7	Fruits, pudding and jam design	7·00	7·00

No. FU7 is inscribed "October 1986".

1988 (5 July). *"Children's Parties". Cover as Type* FL **14** (90×49 *mm*) *printed in violet and rosine. Containing ten* 18*p. stamps* (*No.* X955). A. *Selvedge at left.* B. *Selvedge at right.*

		A	B
FU8	Balloons and party hats design	7·00	7·00

No. FU8 is inscribed "October 1986".

£1.90 Booklets

1988 (5 Sept). *"Pocket Planner". Cover as Type* FM **5** (90×49 *mm*) *printed in yellow-green and magenta. Containing ten* 19*p. stamps* (*No.* X956). A. *Selvedge at left.* B. *Selvedge at right.*

		A	B
FV1	"Marriage Act" design	8·75	8·75

1989 (24 Jan). 150*th Anniv of Fox Talbot's Report on the Photographic Process to Royal Society. Cover as Type* FM **6** (90×49 *mm*) *printed in emerald and black. Containing ten* 19*p. stamps* (*No.* X956). A. *Selvedge at left.* B. *Selvedge at right.*

		A	B
FV2	Fox Talbot with camera and Lacock Abbey	8·75	8·75

No. FV2 is inscribed "September 1988".

£2 Booklets

FW1

(Des Debbie Cook)

1993 (1 Nov)–**94**. *Postal Vehicles Series. Covers as Type* FW **1**. *Containing eight* 25*p.* (*No.* Y1683).

FW1	Design No. 1 (cover in dull vermilion and deep blue), Motorised cycle-carrier	6·50
FW2	Design No. 2 (cover in green and deep violet-blue), Experimental motor-mail van (26.4.94)	6·50
FW3	Design No. 3 (cover in red and black), Experimental electric mail van, 1932 (6.9.94)	6·50

FW **3**

(Des The Four Hundred)

1995 (7 Feb–4 Apr). *Birth Bicentenary of Sir Rowland Hill. Covers as Type* FW **3**. *Containing eight* 25*p.* (*No.* Y1683).

FW4	Design No. 1 (cover in purple and new blue), Rowland Hill as director of London and Brighton Railway Company	6·50
FW5	Design No. 2 (cover in deep mauve and greenish blue), Rowland Hill and Hazlewood School (4.4.95)	6·50

1995 (6 June–4 Sept). *Birth Bicentenary of Sir Rowland Hill Series continued. Covers as* Type FW **3**. *Containing eight* 25*p.* (*No.* Y1684).

FW6	Design No. 3 (cover in deep blue-green and dull orange), Rowland Hill as Secretary to the Post Office	7·00
FW7	Design No. 4 (cover in red-brown and orange), Uniform Penny Postage petition and Mulready envelope (4.9.95)	7·00

1996 (16 Jan). *Multicoloured laminated cover as Type* FH **40**. *Stamps printed in litho by Questa.*

FW8	Containing eight 25p. stamps (No. Y1752)	7·00

For an initial test period No. FW 8 was only available from machines at twelve post offices, five in London and seven in Scotland, in addition to philatelic outlets. Stocks were distributed nationally from May 1996.

1996 (8 July)–**97**. *Multicoloured laminated cover as Type* FH **40**. *Stamps printed in litho by Questa.*

FW9	Containing booklet pane of 20p. and 26p. × 7 (No. Y1751l)	8·00
	a. Corrected rate (4.2.97)	8·00

No. FW9 was reissued on 4 February 1997 showing the 200g second class rate on the inside cover altered from 47p. to 45p. A further printing issued 5 May 1998 was without the overseas postage rate table.

1998 (1 Dec). *Multicoloured laminated cover as Type* FH **40**. *Stamps printed in photo by Questa.*

FW10	Containing booklet pane of 20p. and 26p. × 7 (No. Y1680l)	18·00

1999 (26 Apr). *Multicoloured laminated cover as Type* FH **40**. *Stamps printed in photo by Questa.*

FW11	Containing booklet pane of 19p. and 26p. × 7 (No. Y1677l)	13·00

2000 (27 Apr). *Multicoloured laminated cover as Type* FH **40**. *Stamps printed in photo by Questa.*

FW12	Containing booklet pane of 2nd × 2 and 1st × 6 (No. 1664m)	7·00

Christmas Booklets

FX **1**

(Des J. Matthews)

1978 (15 Nov). *"Christmas Greetings". Cover Type* FX **1** (90×49 *mm*). *Printed in rose-red and sage-green.*

FX1 £1.60, containing booklet pane No. X875l .... 5·00

No. FX1 is inscribed "August 1978".

FX **2**

(Des P. Sharland)

1979 (14 Nov). *"Christmas Greetings". Red and green cover as Type* FX **2** (90×49 *mm*), *showing Christmas cracker.*

FX2 £1.80, containing booklet pane No. X879l .... 6·00

No. FX2 is inscribed "October 1979".

FX **3**

(Des E. Fraser)

1980 (12 Nov). *Christmas. Red and blue cover as Type* FX **3** (90×49 *mm*), *showing Nativity scene.*

FX3 £2.20, containing booklet pane No. X888m .... 6·50

No. FX3 is inscribed "September 1980".

FX **4**

(Des W. Sanderson)

1981 (11 Nov). *Christmas. Red and blue cover as Type* FX **4**, (90×49 *mm*), *showing skating scene.*

FX4 £2.55, containing booklet pane No. X893l .... 8·50

No. FX4 is inscribed "January 1981".

FX **5**

(Des A. Davidson)

1982 (10 Nov). *Christmas. Red and green cover as Type* FX 5 (90×49 *mm*), *showing Christmas Mummers.*

FX5 £2.50, containing booklet pane No. X898l .... 9·50

No. FX5 is inscribed "February 1982" and was sold at a discount of 30p. off the face value of the stamps.

Each stamp in the pane has a blue star printed on the reverse over the gum.

FX **6**

(Des Barbara Brown)

1983 (9 Nov). *Christmas. Brown-lilac and yellow cover as Type* FX **6** (90×49 *mm*), *showing pantomime scenes.*

FX6 £2.20, containing twenty 12½p. (No. X898Ev) .... 8·50

No. FX6 is inscribed "April 1983" and was sold at a discount of 30p. off the face value of the stamps.

Each stamp in the pane has a double-lined blue star printed on the reverse over the gum.

FX 7

(Des Yvonne Gilbert)

1984 (20 Nov). *Christmas. Light brown and red-orange cover as Type* FX **7** (90 × 60 *mm*), *showing Nativity scene.*

FX7 £2.30, containing twenty 13p. (No. 1267Eu) .... 9·50

No. FX7 is inscribed "September 1984" and was sold at a discount of 30p. off the face value of the stamps.

The stamps from this booklet show double-lined blue stars printed on the reverse over the gum.

FX **8**

(Des A. George)

1985 (19 Nov). *Christmas. Bright blue and rose cover as Type* FX **8** (90 × 60 *mm*), *showing The Pantomime.*

FX8 £2.40, containing twenty 12p. (No. 1303Eu)...................... 9·00

The stamps from this booklet show double-lined blue stars printed on the reverse over the gum.

FX **9**

(Des Lynda Gray)

1986 (2 Dec). *Christmas. Red and dull blue-green cover as Type* FX **9** (90 × 49 *mm*), *showing Shetland Yule cakes.* A. *Selvedge at left.* B. *Selvedge at right.*

		A	B
FX9	£1.20, containing ten 13p. (No. X900Eu)	8·50	9·00

No. FX9 is inscribed "October 1986" and was sold at a discount of 10p. off the face value of the stamps.

Each stamp in the pane has a blue star printed on the reverse over the gum.

For 1990 and later Christmas stamps, see Barcode Booklets Section G.

£1.90 Greetings Booklet

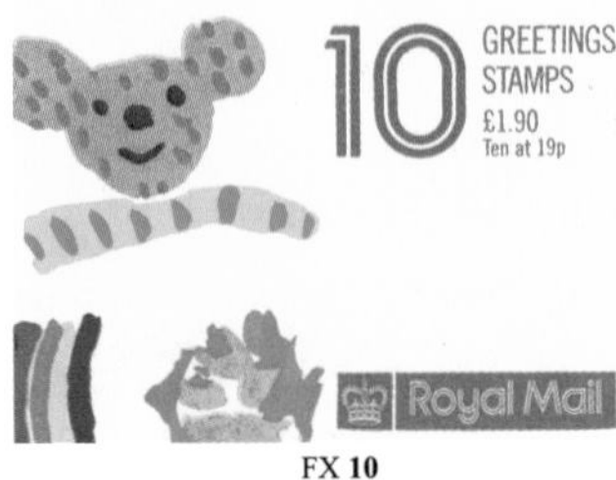

FX **10**

(Des L. Moberly)

1989 (31 Jan). *Greetings Stamps. Multicoloured cover as Type* FX **10** (89 × 60 *mm*). *Containing booklet pane No.* 1423a, *including twelve special greetings labels in a block* (3 × 4) *at right, attached by the selvedge.*

FY1 Greetings design .... 50·00

No. FY1 is inscribed "September 1988".

The cover of No. FX10 shows an overall pattern of elements taken from the stamp designs. Due to the method of production the position of these elements varies from cover to cover.

For Greetings stamps in Barcode booklets, see Barcode Booklets Section F.

BARCODE BOOKLETS

These booklets are listed in eight sections.

SECTION C.	G numbers containing Machin stamps with face values
SECTION D.	Hnumbers containing Machin NVI stamps
SECTION E.	J numbers containing Machin Penny Black Anniversary stamps
SECTION F.	KX numbers containing Greetings stamps
SECTION G.	LX numbers containing Christmas stamps
SECTION H.	M numbers containing self-adhesive NVI definitive stamps
SECTION I.	N numbers containing self-adhesive definitive stamps with face values
SECTION J.	PM numbers containing both special and definitive self-adhesive NVI stamps

These are produced for sale in both post offices and commercial outlets.

NOTE: All panes are attached to the covers by the selvedge. Barcode booklet covers are illustrated at two-thirds linear size *unless otherwise stated.*

C. Barcode Booklets containing Machin stamps with values shown as Type 367.

COVERS. These are all printed in scarlet, lemon and black with the barcode on the reverse. Type GA1 has a clear "window" to view the contents. Type GB3 is shorter and has a stamp illustration printed on the cover to replace the "window". These illustrations show an oblique white line across the bottom right-hand corner of the "stamp". Unless otherwise stated all covers were printed by Harrison.

From early 1997 the printer of each booklet is identified by a small capital letter below the barcode on the outside back cover.

52p. Booklet

GA 1

1987 (4 Aug). *Laminated cover Type* GA **1** (75 × 60 *mm*).
GA1 Containing booklet pane No. X900n .... 4·00
No. GA1 is inscribed "20 October 1986".

56p. Booklets

1988 (23 Aug). *Laminated cover as Type* GA **1** (75 × 56 *mm*).
GB1 Containing booklet pane No. X903l .... 6·00

1988 (11 Oct). *Laminated cover as Type* GA **1** (75 × 56 *mm*) *printed by Walsall.*
GB2 Containing booklet pane No. X903l .... 9·50

GB **3** Large Crown

1988 (11 Oct). *Laminated cover as Type* GB **3** (75 × 48 *mm*) *with stamp printed on the cover in deep blue.*
GB3 Containing booklet pane No. X903n .... 7·75
No. GB3 is inscribed "5 September 1988" and has the horizontal edges of the pane imperforate.

1989 (24 Jan). *Laminated cover as Type* GB **3** (75 × 48 *mm*) *with stamp printed on the cover in deep blue by Walsall.*
GB4 Containing booklet pane No. X903q .... 40·00
No. GB4 is inscribed "5 September 1988" and has the three edges of the pane imperforate.

72p. Booklet

1987 (4 Aug). *Laminated cover as Type* GA **1** (75 × 60 *mm*).
GC1 Containing booklet pane No. X955m .... 4·00
No. GC1 is inscribed "20 October 1986".

76p. Booklets

1988 (23 Aug). *Laminated cover as Type* GA **1** (75 × 56 *mm*).
GD1 Containing booklet pane No. X956l .... 7·75

1988 (11 Oct). *Laminated cover as Type* GA **1** (75 × 56 *mm*) *printed by Walsall.*
GD2 Containing booklet pane No. X956l .... 8·00

1988 (11 Oct). *Laminated cover as Type* GB **3** (75 × 48 *mm*) *with stamp printed on the cover in bright orange-red.*
GD3 Containing booklet pane No. X956n .... 9·50
No. GD3 is inscribed "5 September 1988" and has the horizontal edges of the pane imperforate.

1989 (24 Jan). *Laminated cover as Type* GB **3** (75 × 48 *mm*) *with stamp printed on the cover in bright orange-red by Walsall.*
GD4 Containing booklet pane No. X956q .... 40·00
No. GD4 is inscribed "5 September 1988" and has the three edges of the pane imperforate.

78p. Booklet

GD **4a** (As Type GL **1** but without "4")

1992 (28 July). *Multicoloured laminated cover as Type* GD **4a** (75 × 49 *mm*) *with stamp printed on the cover in bright mauve by Walsall.*
GD4*a* Containing two 39p. stamps (No. X1058) (pane No. X1058l with right-hand vert pair removed) and pane of 4 air mail labels .... 3·50
Stamps in No. GD4*a* have top or bottom edge imperforate. Booklet No. GD4*a* was produced in connection with a Kellogg's Bran Flakes promotion.

£1.04 Booklet

1987 (4 Aug). *Laminated cover as Type* GA **1** (75 × 60 *mm*).
GE1 Containing booklet pane No. X971bl .... 20·00
No. GE1 is inscribed "20 October 1986".

£1.08 Booklets

1988 (23 Aug). *Laminated cover as Type* GA **1** (75 × 56 *mm*).
GF1 Containing booklet pane No. X973l .... 14·00

1988 (11 Oct). *Laminated cover as Type* GB **3** (75 × 48 *mm*) *with stamp printed on the cover in chestnut.*
GF2 Containing booklet pane No. X973m .... 35·00
No. GF2 is inscribed "5 September 1988" and has the horizontal edges of the pane imperforate.

£1.16 Booklets

GG **1** Redrawn Crown

1989 (2 Oct). *Laminated cover as Type* GG **1** (75 × 48 *mm*) *with stamp printed on the cover in deep mauve by Walsall.*

GG1 Containing booklet pane No. X1054l .... 17·00

No. GG1 has three edges of the pane imperforate.

1990 (17 Apr). *Laminated cover as Type* GG **1** (75 × 48 *mm*) *with stamp printed on the cover in deep mauve by Walsall.*

GG2 Containing booklet pane No. X1055l .... 20·00

No. GG2 has three edges of the pane imperforate.

£1.20 Booklets

GGA1 ("BY AIR MAIL *par avion*" at bottom left)

1998 (5 May). *Multicoloured laminated cover as Type* GGA **1** (75 × 50 *mm*) *with stamps printed on cover in olive-grey by Walsall. Inscr* "For items up to 20g" *on yellow tab at right.*

GGA1 Containing four 30p. (photo) (No. Y1688) and a pane of 4 air mail labels .... 4·25

GGA2 "Create a card Design"

1998 (3 Aug). *Multicoloured laminated cover as Type* GGA **2** (75 × 50 *mm*) *printed by Walsall. Inscr* "See inside for offer details" *on yellow tab at right.*

GGA2 Containing four 30p. (photo) (No. Y1688) and a pane of 4 air mail labels .... 4·25

This booklet was not placed on philatelic sale until 7 September 1998.

£1.24 Booklet

GH1 Crown on White

1990 (17 Sept). *Multicoloured laminated cover as Type* GH1 (75 × 49 *mm*) *with stamp printed on the cover in ultramarine by Walsall.*

GH1 Containing booklet pane No. X1056l .... 7·00

No. GH1 has the horizontal edges of the pane imperforate.

£1.30 Booklet

1987 (4 Aug). *Laminated cover as Type* GA **1** (98 × 60 *mm*).

GI1 Containing booklet pane No. X900o .... 6·00

No. GI1 is inscribed "20 October 1986".

£1.32 Booklet

GJ **1**

1991 (16 Sept)–**92.** *Multicoloured laminated cover as Type* GJ **1** (75 × 49 *mm*) *with stamp printed on the cover in light emerald by Walsall. Inscr* "For letters up to 10g" *on yellow strip at right.*

GJ1 Containing booklet pane No. X1057l and a pane of 4 air mail labels .... 6·50

a. Inscr "For Worldwide Postcards" on yellow strip (8.9.92) .... 12·00

Nos. GJ1/a have the horizontal edges of the pane imperforate.

£1.40 Booklets

1988 (23 Aug). *Laminated cover as Type* GA **1** (97 × 56 *mm*).

GK1 Containing booklet pane No. X903m .... 18·00

1988 (11 Oct). *Laminated cover as Type* GA **1** (97 × 56 *mm*) *printed by Questa.*

GK2 Containing ten 14p. (No. X1007) .... 18·00

1988 (11 Oct). *Laminated cover as Type* GB **3** (75 × 48 *mm*) *with stamp printed on the cover in deep blue.*

GK3 Containing booklet pane No. X903p .... 10·00

No. GK3 is inscribed "5 September 1988" and has horizontal edges of the pane imperforate.

1988 (11 Oct). *Laminated cover as Type* GB **3** (75 × 48 *mm*) *with stamp printed on the cover in deep blue by Questa.*

GK4 Containing ten 14p. (No. X1007) .... 18·00

1993 (1 Nov). *Laminated cover as Type* GJ1 (76 × 50 *mm*) *with stamp printed on the cover in yellow by Walsall.*

GK5 Containing four 35p. (No. Y1755) and a pane of 4 air mail labels .... 6·25

Type GK6 (without diagonal white line across corners of stamps)

1995 (16 May). *Multicoloured laminated cover as Type* GK **6** (75 × 48 *mm*) *with stamps printed on the cover in yellow by Walsall.*

GK6 Containing four 35p. (No. Y1755) and a pane of 4 air mail labels .... 6·25

1996 (19 Mar). *Multicoloured laminated cover as Type* GK **6** (75 × 48 *mm*) *without "International" and showing Olympic symbols on the back. Stamps printed on the cover in yellow by Walsall.*

GK7 Containing four 35p. (No. Y1755) and a pane of 4 air mail labels .... 6·50

£1.48 Booklets

GL **1** ("Worldwide Postcard Stamps" ranged left without diagonal white lines across corner of stamps)

1996 (8 July). *Multicoloured laminated cover as Type* GL **1** (75×48 *mm) showing Olympic symbols on the back. Stamps printed on the cover in bright mauve by Walsall. Inscribed* "For Worldwide Postcards" *on yellow tab at right.*
GL1 Containing four 37p. (No. Y1756) and a pane of 4 air mail labels .... 10·00

1997 (4 Feb). *Multicoloured laminated cover as Type* GL **1** (75×48 *mm) without Olympic symbols on the back. Stamps printed on the cover in bright mauve by Walsall. Inscribed* "For Worldwide Postcards" *on yellow tab at right.*
GL2 Containing four 37p. (No. Y1756) and a pane of 4 air mail labels .... 10·00

GL **3**

1997 (26 Aug)–**98.** *Multicoloured laminated cover as Type* GL **3** (75×48 *mm) printed by Walsall. Inscribed* "For Worldwide Postcards" *on yellow tab at right.*
GL3 Containing four 37p. (photo) (No. Y1697) and a pane of 4 new design air mail labels .... 5·50
a. Showing validity notice on inside backcover (5.5.98).... 4·50

No. GL3 has the postage rate table on the inside back cover.

1998 (3 Aug). *Multicoloured laminated cover as Typ*e GGA **2** (*"Create a card" design*) (75×50 *mm) printed by Walsall.*
GL4 Containing four 37p. (photo) (No. Y1697) and a pane of 4 air mail labels .... 4·50

This booklet was not placed on philatelic sale until 7 September 1998.

£1.52 Booklets

1999 (26 Apr). *Multicoloured laminated cover as Type* GGA **1** (76×50 *mm) with stamps printed on cover in ultramarine by Walsall. Inscr* "For Worldwide Postcards" *on yellow tab at right.*
GLA1 Containing four 38p. (photo) (No. Y1701) and a pane of 4 air mail labels .... 5·00

£1.56 Booklet

GM **1**

1991 (16 Sept). *Multicoloured laminated cover as Type* GM **1** (75×49 *mm) with stamp printed on the cover in bright mauve by Walsall.*
GM1 Containing booklet pane No. X1058l and a pane of 4 air mail labels .... 11·00

No. GM1 has the horizontal edges of the pane imperforate.

£1.60 Booklet

2000 (27 Apr). *Multicoloured laminated cover as Type* GGA **1** (76×50 *mm) with stamps printed on cover in deep azure by Walsall. Inscr* "For Worldwide Postcards" *on yellow tab at right.*
GMA1 Containing four 40p. (photo) (No. Y1704) and a pane of 4 air mail labels .... 7·50

£1.64 Booklets

1993 (1 Nov). *Laminated cover as Type* GM **1** (76×50 *mm) with stamp printed on the cover in drab by Walsall.*
GN1 Containing four 41p. (No. Y1757) and a pane of 4 air mail labels .... 7·00

1995 (16 May). *Multicoloured laminated cover as Type* GK **6** (75×48 *mm) with stamps printed on the cover in drab by Walsall.*
GN2 Containing four 41p. (No. Y1757) and a pane of 4 air mail labels .... 7·00

1996 (19 Mar). *Multicoloured laminated cover as Type* GK **6** (75×48 *mm) without* "International" *and showing Olympic symbols on the back. Stamps printed on the cover in drab by Walsall.*
GN3 Containing four 41p. (No. Y1757) and a pane of 4 air mail labels .... 7·00

£1.80 Booklet

1987 (4 Aug). *Laminated cover as Type* GA**1** (98×60 *mm*).
GO1 Containing booklet pane No. X955n .... 9·00

No. GO1 is inscribed "20 October 1986".

£1.90 Booklets

1988 (23 Aug). *Laminated cover as Type* GA **1** (97×56 *mm*).
GP1 Containing booklet pane No. X956m .... 12·00

1988 (11 Oct). *Laminated cover as Type* GA **1** (97×56 *mm) printed by Questa.*
GP2 Containing ten 19p. (No. X1013) .... 24·00

1988 (11 Oct). *Laminated cover as Type* GB **3** (75×48 *mm) with stamp printed on the cover in bright orange-red.*
GP3 Containing booklet pane No. X956o .... 12·00

No. GP 3 is inscribed "5 September 1988" and has the horizontal edges of the pane imperforate.

1988 (11 Oct). *Laminated cover as Type* GB **3** (75×48 *mm) with stamp printed on the cover in bright orange-red by Questa.*
GP4 Containing ten 19p. (No. X1013) .... 24·00

£2.40 Booklets

1994 (9 Aug). *Laminated cover as Type* GM **1** (75×49 *mm) with stamp printed on the cover in dull blue-grey by Walsall.*
GQ1 Containing four 60p. (No. Y1758) and a pane of 4 air mail labels .... 8·00

GQ **2**

1994 (4 Oct). *Laminated cover as Type* GQ **2** (75×49 *mm*) *with stamp printed on the cover in dull blue-grey by Walsall.*
GQ2 Containing four 60p. (No. Y1758) and a pane of 4 air mail plus 4 "Seasons Greetings" labels .... 8·00

1995 (16 May). *Laminated cover as Type* GK **6** (75×48 *mm*) *with stamps printed on the cover in dull blue-grey by Walsall.*
GQ3 Containing four 60p. (No. Y1758) and a pane of 4 air mail labels .... 8·00

1996 (19 Mar). *Multicoloured laminated cover as Type* GK **6** (75×48 *mm*) *without* "International" *and showing Olympic symbols on the back. Stamps printed on the cover in dull grey blue by Walsall.*
GQ4 Containing four 60p. (No. Y1758) and a pane of 4 air mail labels .... 8·00

£2.52 Booklets

1996 (8 July). *Multicoloured laminated cover as Type* GL **1** (75×48 *mm*) *showing Olympic symbols on the back. Stamps printed on the cover in light emerald by Walsall. Inscribed* "For items up to 20g" *on yellow tab at right.*
GR1 Containing four 63p. (No. Y1759) and a pane of 4 air mail labels .... 12·00

1997 (4 Feb). *Multicoloured laminated cover as Type* GL **1** (75×48 *mm*) *without Olympic symbols on the back. Stamps printed on the cover in light emerald by Walsall. Inscribed* "For items up to 20g" *on yellow tab at right.*
GR2 Containing four 63p. (No. Y1759) and a pane of 4 air mail labels .... 12·00

1997 (26 Aug). *Multicoloured laminated cover as Type* GL **1** (75×48 *mm*), *but inscr* "Worldwide Airmail Stamps". *Stamps printed on the cover in light emerald by Walsall. Inscribed* "For items up to 20g" *on yellow tab at right.*
GR3 Containing four 63p. (photo) (No. Y1720) and a pane of 4 air mail labels .... 7·25

No. GR3 shows a "W" on the outside back cover below the barcode.

1998 (5 May). *Multicoloured laminated cover as Type* GGA **1** (75×50 *mm*). *Stamps printed on the cover in light emerald by Walsall. Inscr* "For items up to 20g" *on yellow tab at right.*
GR4 Containing four 63p. (photo) (No. Y1720) and a pane of 4 new design air mail labels .... 7·25

£2.56 Booklets

1999 (26 Apr). *Multicoloured laminated cover as Type* GGA **1** (75×50 *mm*). *Stamps printed on cover in turquoise-green by Walsall. Inscr* "For items up to 20g" *on yellow tab at right.*
GS1 Containing four 64p. (photo) (No. Y1721) and a pane of 4 air mail labels .... 8·00

£2.60 Booklet

2000 (27 Apr). *Multicoloured laminated cover as Type* GGA **1** (76×50 *mm*) *with stamps printed on cover in greenish blue by Walsall. Inscr* "For items up to 20g" *on yellow tab at right.*
GT1 Containing four 65p. (photo) (No. Y1722) and a pane of 4 air mail labels .... 9·50

D. Barcode Booklets containing No Value Indicated stamps with barcodes on the back cover.

HA **1** Redrawn Crown (small)

1989 (22 Aug). *Laminated cover as Type* HA **1** (75×48 *mm*) *with stamp printed on the cover in bright blue by Walsall.*
HA1 Containing booklet pane No. 1449b .... 7·00

No. HA1 has three edges of the pane imperforate.

No. HA1 was initially sold at 56p., which was increased to 60p. from 2.10.89.

1989 (28 Nov). *Laminated cover as Type* HA **1** (75×48 *mm*) *with stamp printed on the cover in bright blue by Walsall containing stamps printed in photo by Harrison.*
HA2 Containing booklet pane No. 1445b .... 22·00

No. HA2 has three edges of the pane imperforate and was sold at 60p.

HA **3** Crown on white

1990 (7 Aug). *Multicoloured laminated cover as Type* HA **3** (75×48 *mm*) *with stamp printed on the cover in deep blue by Walsall.*
HA3 Containing booklet pane No. 1515a .... 3·75

No. HA3 has the horizontal edges of the pane imperforate.

No. HA3 was initially sold at 60p., which was increased to 68p. from 17.9.90 and to 72p. from 16.9.91.

1991 (6 Aug). *Multicoloured laminated cover as Type* HA **3** (75×48 *mm*) *with stamp printed on the cover in bright blue by Walsall.*
HA4 Containing booklet pane No. 1449c .... 3·50

No. HA4 has the horizontal edges of the pane imperforate.

No. HA4 was initially sold at 68p., which was increased to 72p. from 16.9.91.

HA **5** Olympic Symbols

1992 (21 Jan). *Multicoloured laminated cover as Type* HA **5** (75×48 *mm*) *with stamp printed on the cover in bright blue by Walsall.*
HA5 Containing booklet pane No. 1449BC .... 7·00

No. HA5 has the horizontal edges of the pane imperforate and was sold at 72p.

PERFORATIONS. Booklets from No. HA6 show perforations on all edges of the pane.

1993 (6 Apr). *Multicoloured laminated cover as Type* HA **3** (75×48 *mm*) *with stamp printed on the cover in bright blue by Walsall.*
HA6 Containing four 2nd Class stamps (No. 1670) .... 4·00

No. HA6 was initially sold at 72p., which was increased to 76p. from 1.11.93.

No. HA6 was re-issued on 6 December 1994 showing the inscriptions on the inside of the cover re-arranged.

1993 (7 Sept). *Multicoloured laminated cover as Type* HA **3** (75×48 *mm*) *with stamp printed on the cover in bright blue by Harrison.*
HA7 Containing four 2nd Class stamps (No. 1664) .... 4·00

No. HA7 was initially sold at 72p., which was increased to 76p. from 1.11.93.

Type HA **8** ("Second Class Stamps" centred) (with diagonal white line across corners of stamps)

1995 (10 Jan). *Multicoloured laminated cover as Type* HA **8** (75×48 *mm*) *with stamps printed on the cover in bright blue by Harrison.*
HA8 Containing four 2nd Class stamps (No. 1664) .... 4·00

No. HA8 was initially sold at 76p, which was increased to 80p. from 8.7.96.

1995 (12 Dec). *Multicoloured laminated cover as Type* HA **8** (75×48 *mm*) *with stamps printed on the cover in bright blue by Walsall.*
HA9 Containing four 2nd Class stamps (No. 1670) .... 4·00

No. HA9 was initially sold at 76p, which was increased to 80p. from 8.7.96.

1996 (6 Feb). *Multicoloured laminated cover as Type* HA **8** (75×48 *mm*) *showing Olympic symbols on the back. Stamps printed on the cover in bright blue by Walsall.*
HA10 Containing four 2nd Class stamps (No. 1670).................. 4·00

No. HA10 was initially sold at 76p, which was increased to 80p. from 8.7.96.

NOTE: From No. HA11 onwards, the printer of each booklet is identified by a small capital letter below the barcode on the outside back cover.

HA **11** ("Second Class Stamps" ranged left) (without diagonal white line across corners of stamps)

1997 (4 Feb). *Multicoloured laminated cover as Type* HA **11** (75×48 *mm*). *Stamps printed on the cover in bright blue by Walsall.*
HA11 Containing four 2nd Class stamps (No. 1670) .... 4·00

No. HA11 was sold at 80p.

1997 (26 Aug). *Multicoloured laminated cover as Type* HA **11** (75×48 *mm*). *Stamps printed on the cover in bright blue by Walsall.*
HA12 Containing four 2nd Class stamps (photo) (No. 1664)....... 3·75

No. HA12 was initially sold at 80p. It was re-issued on 5 May 1998 showing the positions of the imprint and the post code notice transposed, and again on 14 March 2000 with changed telephone number and added website address. The booklet was sold at 76p. from 26.4.99.

Panes of 4 1st Class stamps

1989 (22 Aug). *Laminated cover as Type* HA **1** (75×48 *mm*) *with stamp printed on the cover in brownish black by Walsall.*
HB1 Containing booklet pane No. 1450a .... 8·50

No. HB1 has three edges of the pane imperforate.

No. HB1 was initially sold at 76p., which was increased to 80p. from 2.10.89.

1989 (5 Dec). *Laminated cover as Type* HA **1** (75×48 *mm*) *with stamp printed on the cover in brownish black by Walsall containing stamps printed in photo by Harrison.*
HB2 Containing booklet pane No. 1447b .... 40·00

No. HB2 has three edges of the pane imperforate and was sold at 80p.

1990 (7 Aug). *Multicoloured laminated cover as Type* HA **3** (75×48 *mm*) *with stamp printed on the cover in bright orange-red by Walsall.*
HB3 Containing booklet pane No. 1516a .... 4·00
a. Containing pane No. 1516ca .... 12·00

No. HB3 has the horizontal edges of the pane imperforate.

No. HB3 was initially sold at 80p., which was increased to 88p. from 17.9.90 and to 96p. from 16.9.91.

1992 (21 Jan). *Multicoloured laminated cover as Type* HA **5** (75×48 *mm*) *with stamp printed on the cover in bright orange-red by Walsall.*
HB4 Containing booklet pane No. 1516a .... 4·00

No. HB4 has the horizontal edges of the pane imperforate and was initially sold at 96p., which was increased to £1 from 1.11.93.

PERFORATIONS. Booklets from No. HB5 show perforations on all edges of the pane.

1993 (6 Apr). *Multicoloured laminated cover as Type* HA **3** (75×48 *mm*) *with stamp printed on the cover in bright orange-red by Harrison.*
HB5 Containing four 1st Class stamps (No. 1666) .... 5·50

No. HB5 was initially sold at 96p., which was increased to £1 from 1.11.93.

1993 (17 Aug). *Multicoloured laminated cover as Type* HA **3** (76×50 *mm*) *with stamp printed on the cover in bright orange-red by Walsall.*
HB6 Containing four 1st Class stamps (No. 1671)..................... 4·00

No. HB6 was initially sold at 96p., which was increased to £1 from 1.11.93.

1994 (27 July). *Multicoloured laminated cover as Type* HA **3** (76×50 *mm*) *with stamp printed on the cover in bright orange-red by Questa.*
HB7 Containing booklet pane No. 1671l which includes a label commemorating the 300th anniv of the Bank of England . 9·50

No. HB7 was sold at £1.

1995 (10 Jan). *Multicoloured laminated cover as Type* HA **8** (75×48 *mm*) *with stamps printed on the cover in bright orange-red by Walsall.*
HB8 Containing four 1st Class stamps (No. 1671) .... 4·00

No. HB8 was initially sold at £1, which was increased to £1.04 from 8.7.96.

1995 (16 May). *Multicoloured laminated cover as Type* HA **8** (75×48 *mm*) *with stamps printed on the cover in bright orange-red by Walsall.*
HB9 Containing booklet pane No. 1671la which includes a label commemorating the birth centenary of R. J. Mitchell (designer of Spitfire) .... 6·00

No. HB9 was sold at £1.

1996 (6 Feb–Aug). *Multicoloured laminated cover as Type* HA **8** (75×48 *mm*) *showing Olympic symbols on the back. Stamps printed on the cover in bright orange-red by Walsall.*
HB10 Containing four 1st Class stamps (No. 1671) .... 6·00
a. Without diagonal white line across corners of stamps (Aug) .... 75·00

No. HB10 was initially sold at £1, which was increased to £1.04 from 8.7.96.

1996 (16 Apr). *Multicoloured laminated cover as Type* HA **11** (75×48 *mm*) *with stamps printed on the cover in bright orange-red by Walsall. Inscribed* "Commemorative Label Inside" *on yellow tab at right.*
HB11 Containing booklet pane No. 1671la (includes label commemorating the 70th birthday of Queen Elizabeth II) .. 6·00

No. HB11 was initially sold at £1, which was increased to £1.04 from 8.7.96.

NOTE: From No. HB12 onwards, the printer of each booklet (with the exception of No. HB19) is identified by a small capital letter below the barcode on the outside back cover.

1997 (4 Feb). *Multicoloured laminated cover as Type* HA **11** *(75×48 mm). Stamps printed on the cover in bright orange-red by Walsall.*
HB12 Containing four 1st Class stamps (No. 1671) .... 3·50
No. HB12 was sold at £1.04.

1997 (12 Feb). *Multicoloured laminated cover as Type* HA **11** *(75×48 mm). Stamps printed on the cover in bright orange-red by Walsall. Inscribed* "Special Label Inside" *on yellow tab at right.*
HB13 Containing booklet pane No. 1671la (includes label commemorating "Hong Kong '97" international stamp exhibition) .... 6·00
No. HB13 was sold at £1.04.

1997 (26 Aug). *Multicoloured laminated cover as Type* HA **11** *(75×48 mm). Stamps printed on the cover in bright orange-red by Walsall.*
HB14 Containing four 1st Class stamps (photo) (No. 1667) .... 4·00
No. HB14 was sold at £1.04. It was re-issued on 5 May 1998 showing the positions of the imprint and the post code notice transposed, on 16 March 1999 with "Please note that the First Class rate is no longer valid to Europe" added to inside back cover and again on 14 March 2000 with changed telephone number and added website address.

1997 (21 Oct). *Multicoloured laminated cover as Type* HA **11** *(75×48 mm). Stamps printed on the cover in bright orange-red by Walsall. Inscribed* "Commemorative Label Inside" *on yellow tab at right.*
HB15 Containing booklet pane No. 1671la (litho) (includes label commemorating Commonwealth Heads of Government Meeting, Edinburgh) .... 9·50
No. HB15 was sold at £1.04.

1998 (14 Nov). *Multicoloured laminated cover as Type* HA **11** *(75×48 mm). Stamps printed on the cover in bright orange-red by Walsall. Inscribed* "Commemorative Label Inside" *on yellow tab at right.*
HB16 Containing booklet pane No. 1671la (litho) (includes label commemorating 50th birthday of the Prince of Wales) .... 7·00
No. HB16 was sold at £1.04.

1999 (12 May). *Multicoloured laminated cover as Type* HA **11** *(75×48 mm). Stamps printed on the cover in bright orange-red by Walsall. Inscribed* "Commemorative Label Inside" *on yellow tab at right.*
HB17 Containing booklet pane No. 1667m (photo) (includes label commemorating 50th anniv of Berlin Airlift) .... 8·00
No. HB17 was sold for £1.04.

1999 (1 Oct). *Multicoloured laminated cover as Type* HA **11** *(76×50 mm). Stamps printed on the cover in bright orange-red by Walsall. Inscribed* "Commemorative Label Inside" *on yellow tab at right.*
HB18 Containing booklet pane No. 1667m (photo) (includes label commemorating Rugby World Cup) .... 4·50
No. HB18 was sold at £1.04.

2000 (21 Mar). *Multicoloured laminated cover as Type* HA **11** *(75×48 mm). Stamps printed on the cover in olive-brown by Walsall with Postman Pat. Inscribed* "Postman Pat Label Inside" *on yellow tab at right.*
HB19 Containing booklet pane No. 2124bl (photo) (includes label commemorating "Stamp Show 2000", Earls Court) 6·00
No. HB19 was initially sold at £1.04, which was increased to £1.08 from 27.4.2000.

2000 (4 Apr). *Opening of National Botanic Garden of Wales. Multicoloured laminated cover as Type* HA **11** *(75×48 mm). Stamps printed on the cover in olive-brown by Walsall. Inscribed* "Botanic Garden Label Inside" *on yellow tab at right.*
HB20 Containing booklet pane No. 2124bl .... 6·00
No. HB20 was initially sold at £1.04, which was increased to £1.08 from 27.4.2000.

Panes of 8 1st Class Stamps plus pane of 2 Millennium commemoratives

HBA1

1999 (12 May). *Multicoloured laminated cover as Type* HBA**1** *(76×50 mm) showing Millennium and Machin stamps printed by Walsall.*
HBA1 Containing booklet pane No. 2085a and eight 1st Class stamps (photo) (No. 1667) .... 8·00
No. HBA1 was sold at £2.60.

1999 (21 Sept). *Multicoloured laminated cover as Type* HBA**1** *(76×50 mm) showing Millennium and Machin stamps printed by Walsall.*
HBA2 Containing booklet pane No. 2108a and eight 1st Class stamps (photo) (No. 1667) .... 8·00
No. HBA2 was sold at £2.60.

2000 (26 May). *Multicoloured laminated cover as Type* HBA**1** *(76×50 mm) showing Millennium and Machin stamps printed by Walsall.*
HBA3 Containing booklet pane No. 2126ab and eight 1st Class stamps (photo) (No. 2124) .... 10·00
No. HBA3 was sold at £2.70.

2000 (5 Sept). *Multicoloured laminated cover as Type* HBA**1** *(76×50 mm) showing Millennium and Machin stamps printed by Walsall.*
HBA4 Containing booklet pane No. 2153a and eight 1st Class stamps (photo) (No. 2124) .... 11·00
No. HBA4 was sold at £2.70.

Panes of 10 2nd Class stamps

1989 (22 Aug–2 Oct). *Laminated cover as Type* HA **1** *(75×48 mm) with stamp printed on the cover in bright blue by Harrison.*
HC1 Containing booklet pane No. 1445a .... 11·00
a. Inside cover with new rates (2 Oct) .... 12·00
Nos. HC1/a have the horizontal edges of the pane imperforate.
No. HC1 was initially sold at £1.40, which was increased to £1.50 from 2.10.89. No. HC1a was sold at £1.50.

1989 (19 Sept). *Laminated cover as Type* HA **1** *(75×48 mm) with stamp printed on the cover in bright blue by Questa.*
HC2 Containing ten 2nd Class stamps (No. 1451) .... 9·50
No. HC2 has perforations on all edges of the pane and was initially sold at £1.40, which was increased to £1.50 from 2.10.89.

1990 (7 Aug). *Multicoloured laminated cover as Type* HA3 *(75×48 mm) with stamp printed on the cover in deep blue by Harrison.*
HC3 Containing booklet pane No. 1511a .... 12·00
No. HC3 has the horizontal edges of the pane imperforate.
No. HC3 was initially sold at £1.50, which was increased to £1.70 from 17.9.90.

1990 (7 Aug). *Multicoloured laminated cover as Type* HA **3** *(75×48 mm) with stamp printed on the cover in deep blue by Questa.*
HC4 Containing ten 2nd Class stamps (No. 1513) .... 15·00
No. HC4 has perforations on all edges of the pane and was initially sold at £1.50, which was increased to £1.70 from 17.9.90.

1990 (7 Aug). *Multicoloured laminated cover as Type* HA **3** *(75×48 mm) with stamp printed on the cover in deep blue by Walsall.*
HC5 Containing booklet pane No. 1515b .... 8·50
No. HC5 has the horizontal edges of the pane imperforate.
No. HC5 was initially sold at £1.50, which was increased to £1.70 from 17.9.90, and to £1.80 from 16.9.91.

1991 (6 Aug). *Multicoloured laminated cover as Type* HA **3** *(75×48 mm) with stamp printed on the cover in bright blue by Questa.*
HC6 Containing ten 2nd Class stamps (No. 1451) .... 8·00
No. HC6 has perforations on all edges of the pane and was initially sold at £1.70, which was increased to £1.80 from 16.9.91.

1991 (6 Aug). *Multicoloured laminated cover as Type* HA **3** (75×48 *mm) with stamp printed on the cover in bright blue by Walsall.*

HC7 Containing booklet pane No. 1449d .... 7·50

No. HC7 has the horizontal edges of the pane imperforate.

No. HC7 was initially sold at £1.70, which was increased to £1.80 from 16.9.91.

1992 (21 Jan). *Multicoloured laminated cover as Type* HA **5** (75×48 *mm) with stamp printed on the cover in bright blue by Walsall.*

HC8 Containing booklet pane No. 1449d .... 6·00

No. HC8 has the horizontal edges of the pane imperforate and was initially sold at £1.80, which was increased to £1.84 from 1.11.93.

1992 (31 Mar). *Multicoloured laminated cover as Type* HA **5** (75×48 *mm) with stamp printed on the cover in bright blue by Questa.*

HC9 Containing ten 2nd Class stamps (No. 1451) .... 8·50

No. HC9 has perforations on all edges of the pane and was sold at £1.80.

1992 (22 Sept). *Multicoloured laminated cover as Type* HA **3** (75×48 *mm) with stamp printed on the cover in bright blue by Harrison.*

HC10 Containing booklet pane No. 1445a .... 8·00

No. HC10 has the horizontal edges of the pane imperforate and was sold at £1.80.

PERFORATIONS. Booklets from No. HC11 show perforations on all edges of the pane.

1993 (6 Apr). *Multicoloured laminated cover as Type* HA **3** (75×48 *mm) with stamp printed on the cover in bright blue by Questa.*

HC11 Containing ten 2nd Class stamps (No. 1670) .... 7·75

No. HC11 was initially sold at £1.80, which was increased to £1.90 from 1.11.93.

No. HC11 was re-issued on 17 August 1993 showing changes to the text on the inside of the cover and again on 6 September 1994 showing further changes.

1993 (1 Nov). *Multicoloured laminated cover as Type* HA **3** (75×48 *mm) with stamp printed on the cover in bright blue by Walsall.*

HC12 Containing ten 2nd Class stamps (No. 1670) .... 7·75

No. HC 12 was sold at £1.90.

1995 (10 Jan). *Multicoloured laminated cover as Type* HA **8** (75×48 *mm) with stamps printed on the cover in bright blue by Questa.*

HC13 Containing ten 2nd Class stamps (No. 1670) .... 7·75

No. HC13 was initially sold at £1.90, which was increased to £2 from 8.7.96.

1995 (12 Dec). *Multicoloured laminated cover as Type* HA **8** (75×48 *mm) with stamps printed on cover in bright blue by Harrison.*

HC14 Containing ten 2nd Class stamps (No. 1664) .... 6·00

No. HC14 was initially sold at £1.90, which was increased to £2 from 8.7.96.

1996 (6 Feb). *Multicoloured laminated cover as Type* HA **8** (75×48 *mm) showing Olympic symbols on the back. Stamps printed on the cover in bright blue by Harrison.*

HC15 Containing ten 2nd Class stamps (No. 1664)..................... 6·50

No. HC15 was initially sold at £1.90, which was increased to £2 from 8.7.96.

1996 (6 Feb). *Multicoloured laminated cover as Type* HA **8** (75×48 *mm) showing Olympic symbols on the back. Stamps printed on the cover in bright blue by Questa.*

HC16 Containing ten 2nd Class stamps (No. 1670) .... 9·00

No. HC16 was initially sold at £1.90, which was increased to £2 from 8.7.96.

NOTE: From No. HC17 onwards, the printer of each booklet is identified by a small capital letter below the barcode on the outside back cover.

1996 (6 Aug). *Multicoloured laminated cover as Type* HA **11** (75×48 *mm) but with diagonal white lines across corners of stamps, showing Olympic symbols on the back. Stamps printed on the cover in bright blue by Harrison.*

HC17 Containing ten 2nd Class stamps (No. 1664) .... 6·50

No. HC17 was sold at £2.

1996 (6 Aug). *Multicoloured laminated cover as Type* HA **11** (75×48 *mm) showing Olympic symbols on the back. Stamps printed on the cover in bright blue by Questa.*

HC18 Containing ten 2nd Class stamps (No. 1670) .... 8·75

No. HC18 was sold at £2.

1997 (4 Feb). *Multicoloured laminated cover as Type* HA **11** (75×48 *mm). Stamps printed on the cover in bright blue by Harrison.*

HC19 Containing ten 2nd Class stamps (No. 1664)..................... 6·50

No. HC19 was sold at £2.

1997 (4 Feb). *Multicoloured laminated cover as Type* HA **11** (75×48 *mm). Stamps printed on the cover in bright blue by Questa.*

HC20 Containing ten 2nd Class stamps (No. 1670) .... 7·00

No. HC20 was initially sold at £2. It was re-issued on 5 May 1998 showing the positions of the imprint and the post code notice transposed. The booklet was sold at £1.90 from 26.4.99.

1998 (5 May). *Multicoloured laminated cover as Type* HA **11** (75×48 *mm). Stamps printed on the cover in bright blue by De La Rue.*

HC21 Containing ten 2nd Class stamps (No. 1664) .... 6·00

No. HC21 was initially sold at £2, which was decreased to £1.90 from 26.4.99.

1998 (1 Dec). *Multicoloured laminated cover as Type* HA **11** (75×48 *mm). Stamps printed on the cover in bright blue by Questa.*

HC22 Containing ten 2nd Class stamps (No. 1664a) (photo)....... 8·75

No. HC22 was initially sold at £2, which was decreased to £1.90 from 26.4.99. It was re-issued on 14 March 2000 with changed telephone number and added website address.

Panes of 10 1st Class stamps

1989 (22 Aug–2 Oct). *Laminated cover as Type* HA **1** (75×48 *mm) with stamp printed on the cover in brownish black by Harrison.*

HD1 Containing booklet pane No. 1447a .... 15·00

a. Inside cover with new rates (2 Oct) .... 13·00

Nos. HD1/a have the horizontal edges of the pane imperforate.

No. HD1 was initially sold at £1.90, which was increased to £2 from 2.10.89. No. HD1a was sold at £2.

1989 (19 Sept). *Laminated cover as Type* HA **1** (75×48 *mm) with stamp printed on the cover in brownish black by Questa.*

HD2 Containing ten 1st Class stamps (No. 1452) .... 20·00

No. HD2 has perforations on all edges of the pane and was initially sold at £1.90, which was increased to £2 from 2.10.89.

1990 (7 Aug). *Multicoloured laminated cover as Type* HA **3** (75×48 *mm) with stamp printed on the cover in bright orange-red by Harrison.*

HD3 Containing booklet pane No. 1512a .... 10·00

No. HD3 has the horizontal edges of the pane imperforate. No. HD3 was initially sold at £2, which was increased to £2.20 from 17.9.90 and to £2.40 from 16.9.91.

1990 (7 Aug). *Multicoloured laminated cover as Type* HA **3** (75×48 *mm) with stamp printed on the cover in bright orange-red by Questa.*

HD4 Containing ten 1st Class stamps (No. 1514) .... 8·50

No. HD4 has perforations on all edges of the pane and was initially sold at £2, which was increased to £2.20 from 17.9.90 and to £2.40 from 16.9.91.

1990 (7 Aug). *Multicoloured laminated cover as Type* HA **3** (75×48 *mm) with stamp printed on the cover in bright orange-red by Walsall.*

HD5 Containing booklet pane No. 1516b .... 8·75

No. HD5 has the horizontal edges of the pane imperforate and was intially sold at £2, which was increased to £2.20 from 17.9.90 and to £2.40 from 16.9.91.

1992 (21 Jan). *Multicoloured laminated cover as Type* HA **5** (75×48 *mm) with stamp printed on the cover in bright orange-red by Harrison.*

HD6 Containing booklet pane No. 1512a.................................. 10·00

No. HD6 has the horizontal edges of the pane imperforate and was sold at £2.40.

1992 (21 Jan). *Multicoloured laminated cover as Type* HA **5** (75×48 *mm) with stamp printed on the cover in bright orange-red by Walsall.*

HD7 Containing booklet pane No. 1516b .... 7·75

No. HD7 has the horizontal edges of the pane imperforate and was sold at £2.40.

1993 (9 Feb). *Multicoloured laminated cover as Type* HA **3** (77×44 *mm) with advertisement for Greetings Booklet on reverse showing Rupert Bear as in Type* KX5. *Stamp printed on the cover in bright orange-red by Walsall.*

HD8 Containing booklet pane No. 1516b .... 7·75

No. HD8 has the horiziontal edges of the pane imperforate and was sold at £2.40.

PERFORATIONS. Booklets from No. HD9 show perforations on all edges of the pane.

1993 (6 Apr). *Multicoloured laminated cover as Type* HA **3** (75×48 *mm) with stamp printed on the cover in bright orange-red by Harrison.*

HD9 Containing ten 1st Class stamps (No. 1666) .... 12·00

No. HD9 was initially sold at £2.40, which was increased to £2.50 from 1.11.93.

No. HD9 was re-issued on 17 August 1993 showing changes to the text on the inside of the covers.

1993 (6 Apr). *Multicoloured laminated cover as Type* HA **3** (75×48 *mm) with stamp printed on the cover in bright orange-red by Walsall.*

HD10 Containing ten 1st Class stamps (No. 1671) .... 7·75

No. HD10 was initially sold at £2.40, which was increased to £2.50 from 1.11.93.

No. HD10 was re-issued on 17 August 1993 showing changes to the text on the inside of the covers.

1993 (1 Nov). *Laminated cover as Type* HA **3** (75×50 *mm) with stamp printed on the cover in bright orange-red by Questa.*

HD11 Containing ten 1st Class stamps (No. 1671) .... 7·75

No. HD11 was sold at £2.50.

No. HD11 was re-issued on 4 October 1994 showing changes to the text on the inside of the cover.

1993 (1 Nov). *Laminated cover as Type* HA **3** (75×50 *mm) with advertisement for Greetings Booklet on reverse showing Rupert Bear as in Type* KX5. *Stamp printed on the cover in bright orange-red by Walsall.*

HD12 Containing ten 1st Class stamps (No. 1671) .... 8·75

1994 (22 Feb). *Multicoloured laminated cover as Type* HA **3** (75×48 *mm) with stamp printed on the cover in bright orange-red by Walsall. Inscribed* "FREE POSTCARDS" *on yellow tab at right.*

HD13 Containing ten 1st Class stamps (No. 1671) and additional page giving details of Greetings Stamps postcard offer .... 7·75

No. HD13 was sold at £2.50.

1994 (1 July). *Multicoloured laminated covers as Type* HA **3** (76×50 *mm) with advertisement for Greetings Booklet on reverse showing Rupert Bear as in Type* KX5. *Stamp printed on the cover in bright orange-red by Walsall. Inscribed* "OPEN NOW Chance to win a kite" *on yellow tab at right.*

HD14 Containing ten 1st Class stamps (No. 1671) with "Better luck next time." etc on inside back cover .... 8·00

HD15 Containing ten 1st Class stamps (No. 1671) with "You've Won!" etc on inside back cover .... 8·00

Nos. HD14/15 sold at £2.50 each and were initially only available from branches of W.H. Smith and Son. They were issued in connection with a competition in which the prizes were Paddington Bear kites. The booklets were not available from Royal Mail philatelic outlets until 4 October 1994.

Prices

Prices are for stamps in fine condition. Please see the notes at the front of the catalogue for details

HD **16**

1994 (20 Sept). *Multicoloured laminated covers as Type* HD **16** (76×50 *mm) printed by Walsall. Inscribed* "ORDER YOURS INSIDE" *on yellow tab at right.*

HD16 Containing ten 1st Class stamps (No. 1671) with "DO NOT OPEN UNTIL....."on front cover .... 8·00

HD17 Containing ten 1st Class stamps (No. 1671) with "KEEP IN TOUCH" on front cover .... 8·00

HD18 Containing ten 1st Class stamps (No. 1671) with "HAPPY BIRTHDAY" on front cover .... 8·00

HD19 Containing ten 1st Class stamps (No. 1671) with "What's Happenin'?" on front cover .... 8·00

Nos. HD16/19 were sold at £2.50 each.

1995 (10 Jan). *Multicoloured laminated cover as Type* HA **8** (75×48 *mm) with stamps printed on the cover in bright orange-red by Harrison.*

HD20 Containing ten 1st Class stamps (No. 1666) .... 12·00

1995 (10 Jan). *Multicoloured laminated cover as Type* HA **8** (75×48 *mm) with stamps printed on the cover in bright orange-red by Questa.*

HD21 Containing ten 1st Class stamps (No. 1671) .... 7·75

1995 (10 Jan). *Multicoloured laminated cover as Type* HA **8** (75×48 *mm) with stamps printed on the cover in bright orange-red by Walsall.*

HD22 Containing ten 1st Class stamps (No. 1671) .... 7·75

Nos. HD20/2 were initially sold at £2.50 each, which was increased to £2.60 from 8.7.96.

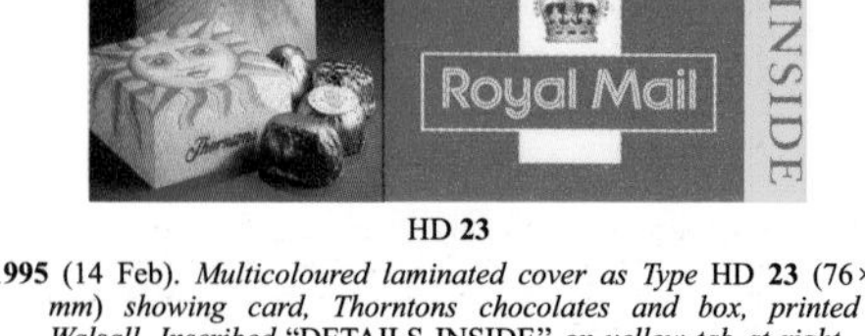

HD **23**

1995 (14 Feb). *Multicoloured laminated cover as Type* HD **23** (76×50 *mm) showing card, Thorntons chocolates and box, printed by Walsall. Inscribed* "DETAILS INSIDE" *on yellow tab at right.*

HD23 Containing ten 1st Class stamps (No. 1671) .... 7·75

No. HD23 was sold at £2.50.

1995 (4 Apr). *Multicoloured laminated cover as Type* HA **8** (76×48 *mm) with stamps printed on cover in bright orange-red by Harrison.*

HD24 Containing ten 1st Class stamps (No. 1667)....................... 7·75

No. HD24 was sold at £2.50.

1995 (24 Apr). *Multicoloured laminated cover as Type* HA **8** (75×48 *mm*) *with stamps printed on cover in bright orange-red by Walsall. Inscribed* "W H Smith Special Offer" *on yellow tab at right.*

HD25 Containing ten 1st Class stamps (No. 1671) .... 7·75

No. HD25 was sold at £2.50 and was initially only available from W. H. Smith branches and offered 50p. off the purchase of own brand stationery. The booklet was not placed on philatelic sale until 3 October 1995. Its price was increased to £2.60 on 8.7.96.

1995 (26 June). *Multicoloured laminated cover as Type* HA **8** (76×48 *mm*) *with stamps printed on cover in bright orange red by Questa. Inscribed* "Sainsbury's Promotion" *on yellow tab at right.*

HD26 Containing ten 1st Class stamps (No. 1671) .... 7·75

No. HD26 was sold at £2.50 and was initially only available from Sainsbury's branches and offered the chance to win a year's free shopping. The booklet was not placed on philatelic sale until 5 September 1995. Its price was increased to £2.60 on 8.7.96

1995 (4 Sept). *Multicoloured laminated cover as Type* HD **23** (76×48 *mm*) *showing ceramic figures of Benjy Bear and Harry Hedgehog, printed by Harrison.*

HD27 Containing ten 1st Class stamps (No. 1667) .... 7·75

No. HD27 was initially sold at £2.50, which was increased to £2.60 from 8.7.96.

1996 (6 Feb). *Multicoloured laminated cover as Type* HA **8** (76×48 *mm*) *showing Olympic symbols on the back. Stamps printed on the cover in bright orange-red by Walsall.*

HD28 Containing ten 1st Class stamps (No. 1671)..................... 7·75

No. HD28 was initially sold at £2.50, which was increased to £2.60 from 8.7.96.

1996 (19 Feb). *Multicoloured laminated cover as Type* HD **23** (76×48 *mm*) *showing Walt Disney World, printed by Harrison.*

HD29 Containing ten 1st Class stamps (No. 1667) .... 7·75

No. HD 29 was initially sold at £2.50, which was increased to £2.60 from 8.7.96.

1996 (19 Mar). *Multicoloured laminated cover as Type* HA **8** (76×48 *mm*) *showing Olympic symbols on the back, printed by Harrison.*

HD30 Containing ten 1st Class stamps (No. 1667) .... 8·75

No. HD30 was initially sold at £2.50, which was increased to £2.60 from 8.7.96.

HD 31

1996 (13 May). *Multicoloured laminated covers as Type* HD **31** (76×48 *mm*) *showing woman lighting Olympic torch, printed by Harrison, with each booklet showing a scratchcard on the reverse based on different Olympic events.*

HD31 Containing ten 1st Class stamps (No. 1667) (Shot Put)...... 7·75
HD32 Containing ten 1st Class stamps (No. 1667) (Hurdles)....... 7·75
HD33 Containing ten 1st Class stamps (No. 1667) (Archery)...... 7·75

Nos. HD31/3 were initially each sold at £2.50, which was increased to £2.60 from 8.7.96.

NOTE: From No. HD34 onwards, the printer of each booklet is identified by a small capital letter below the barcode on the outside back cover.

1996 (15 July). *Multicoloured laminated cover as Type* HA **11** (76×48 *mm*) *showing Olympic symbols on the back. Stamps printed on the cover in bright orange-red by Walsall. Inscribed* "WHSmith Offer Inside" *on yellow tab at right.*

HD34 Containing ten 1st Class stamps (No. 1671) .... 7·75

No. HD34 was sold at £2.60 and was initially only available from branches of W. H. Smith and Sons. It was issued in connection with a special offer of AA/OS Leisure Guides. The booklets were not available from Royal Mail philatelic outlets until 17 September 1996.

1996 (16 Aug). *Multicoloured laminated cover as Type* HA **11** (76×48 *mm*), *but with diagonal white line across corners of stamps and showing Olympic symbols on the back. Stamps printed on the cover in bright orange-red by Harrison.*

HD35 Containing ten 1st Class stamps (No. 1667) .... 8·75

No. HD35 was sold at £2.60.

1996 (16 Aug). *Multicoloured laminated cover as Type* HA **11** (76×48 *mm*) *showing Olympic symbols on the back. Stamps printed on the cover in bright orange-red by Walsall.*

HD36 Containing ten 1st Class stamps (No. 1671) .... 7·75

No. HD36 was sold at £2.60.

1996 (9 Sept). *Multicoloured laminated cover as Type* HD **31** (76×48 *mm*) *showing iced cakes on front and back, printed by Walsall. Inscribed* "OPEN FOR DETAILS" *on yellow tab at right.*

HD37 Containing ten 1st Class stamps (No. 1671) .... 7·75

No. HD37 was sold at £2.60.

1996 (7 Oct). *Multicoloured laminated cover as Type* HA **11** (76×48 *mm*) *showing Olympic symbols on the back. Stamps printed on cover in bright orange-red by Walsall. Inscribed* "Offer Inside" *on yellow tab at right.*

HD38 Containing ten 1st Class stamps (No. 1671) .... 7·75

No. HD38 was sold at £2.60 and was initially only available from ASDA stores and offered £1 off greetings cards. The booklet was not placed on philatelic sale until 13 January 1997.

1997 (4 Feb). *Multicoloured laminated cover as Type* HA **11** (76×48 *mm*). *Stamps printed on the cover in bright orange-red by Harrison.*

HD 39 Containing ten 1st Class stamps (No. 1667) .... 7·75

No. HD39 was sold at £2.60.

1997 (4 Feb). *Multicoloured laminated cover as Type* HA **11** (76×48 *mm*). *Stamps printed on the cover in bright orange-red by Walsall.*

HD40 Containing ten 1st Class stamps (No. 1671) .... 7·00

No. HD40 was sold at £2.60.

1997 (21 Apr). *Royal Golden Wedding. Multicoloured laminated cover as Type* HA **11** (76×48 *mm*). *Stamps printed on the cover in gold by Harrison.*

HD41 Containing ten 1st Class stamps (No. 1668) .... 8·50

No. HD41 was sold at £2.60.

1997 (21 Apr). *Royal Golden Wedding. Multicoloured laminated cover as Type* HA **11** (76×48 *mm*). *Stamps printed on the cover in gold by Walsall.*

HD42 Containing ten 1st Class stamps (No. 1668) .... 8·50

No. HD42 was sold at £2.60.

1997 (15 Sept). *Multicoloured laminated cover as Type* HD **31** (76×48 *mm*) *showing a tropical beach scene printed by Harrison. Inscr* "FIRST CLASS TRAVEL" *on front, and* "OPEN FOR DETAILS" *on yellow tab at right.*

HD43 Containing ten 1st Class stamps (No. 1668) .... 8·00

No. HD43 was sold at £2.60.

1997 (8 Nov). *Multicoloured laminated cover as Type* HA **11** (76×48 *mm*). *Stamps printed on the cover in bright orange-red by Walsall.*

HD44 Containing ten 1st Class stamps (photo) (No. 1667) .... 7·75

No. HD44 was sold at £2.60. It was re-issued on 5 May 1998 showing the positions of the imprint, which was now vertical, and the post code notice transposed and again on 16 March 1999 with "Please note that the First Class rate is no longer valid to Europe" added to inside back cover.

HD **45**

1998 (2 Feb). *Multicoloured laminated cover as Type* HD **45** (76×48 *mm*) *showing Disney illustration printed by De la Rue, with a scratch card on the reverse. Inscr* "See reverse for Scratch and Win" *on yellow tab at right.*

HD45 Containing ten 1st Class stamps (photo) (No. 1667) .... 7·75

No. HD45 was sold at £2.60.

HD **46**

1998 (27 Apr). *Multicoloured laminated cover as Type* HD **46** (76×48 *mm*) *showing Peugeot* 106 *printed by De La Rue. Inscr* "WIN A PEUGEOT 106" *on yellow tab at right.*

HD46 Containing ten 1st Class stamps (photo) (No. 1667) .... 7·75

No. HD46 was sold at £2.60. This booklet was not placed on philatelic sale until 23 June 1998.

1998 (5 May). *Multicoloured laminated cover as Type* HA **11** (76×48 *mm*). *Stamps printed on the cover in bright orange-red by De La Rue.*

HD47 Containing ten 1st Class stamps (photo) (No. 1667) .... 7·75

No. HD47 was initially sold at £2.60, which was increased to £2.70 from 27.4.2000.

1998 (1 July). *Multicoloured laminated cover as Type* HD **46** (76×48 *mm*) *showing JVC Camcorder printed by De La Rue. Inscr* "WIN A JVC CAMCORDER" *on yellow tab at right.*

HD48 Containing ten 1st Class stamps (photo) (No. 1667) .... 7·75

No. HD48 was sold at £2.60. This booklet was not placed on philatelic sale until 27 August 1998.

1998 (3 Aug). *Multicoloured laminated cover as Type* GGA **2** (76×48 *mm*) *inscr* ("Create a card design"), *printed by De La Rue.*

HD49 Containing ten 1st Class stamps (No. 1667) .... 7·75

No. HD49 was sold at £2.60. This booklet was not placed on philatelic sale until 7 September 1998.

1998 (7 Sept). *Multicoloured laminated cover as Type* HA **11** (75×49 *mm*), *with stamps printed on the cover in bright orange-red by Questa.*

HD50 Containing ten 1st Class stamps (litho) (No. 1671)........... 7·75

No. HD50 was sold at £2·60.

1998 (1 Dec). *Multicoloured laminated cover as Type* HA **11** (75×48 *mm*). *Stamps printed on the cover in bright orange-red by Questa.*

HD51 Containing ten 1st Class stamps (photo) (No. 1667a) .... 14·00

No. HD51 was sold at £2.60. It was re-issued on 16 March 1999 with "Please note that the First Class rate is no longer valid to Europe" added to inside back cover.

2000 (6 Jan). *Multicoloured laminated cover as Type* HA **11** (75×48 *mm*). *Millennium definitives printed on the cover in olive-brown by Questa.*

HD52 Containing ten 1st Class stamps (photo) (No. 2124d)........ 7·75

No. HD52 was initially sold at £2.60, which was increased to £2.70 from 27 April 2000. It was re-issued on 14 March 2000 with a changed telephone number on the inside back cover.

2000 (6 Jan). *Multicoloured laminated cover as Type* HA **11** (75×48 *mm*). *Millennium definitives printed on the cover in olive-brown by Walsall.*

HD53 Containing ten 1st Class stamps (photo) (No. 2124).......... 7·75

No. HD53 was initially sold at £2.60, which was increased to £2.70 from 27 April 2000. It was re-issued on 14 March 2000 with a changed telephone number on the inside back cover.

Panes of 4 European Air Mail Stamps

HF **1**

1999 (19 Jan). *Multicoloured laminated cover as Type* HF **1** (75×50 *mm*). *Stamps printed on the cover in deep blue by Walsall. Inscr* "For items up to 20g" *on yellow tab at right.*

HF1 Containing four European Air Mail stamps (No. 1669) and pane of four air mail labels.. 4·50

No. HF1 was initially sold at £1.20 which was increased to £1.36 from 25.10.99 and £1.44 from 27.4.2000.

It was re-issued on 27 April 2000 showing an amended Customer Services telephone number on the inside back cover.

E. Barcode Booklets containing Penny Black Anniversary stamps with barcodes on back cover.

60p. Booklet

JA **1**

1990 (30 Jan). *Laminated cover as Type* JA **1** (75×48 *mm*) *showing Penny Black Anniversary stamp in bright blue. Containing booklet pane No.* 1475l, *printed in litho by Walsall.*

JA1 Containing booklet pane No. 1475l .... 7·00

No. JA1 has three edges of the pane imperforate.

80p. Booklets

1990 (30 Jan). *Laminated cover as Type* JA **1** (75×48 *mm*) *showing Penny Black Anniversary stamp in brownish black and cream. Containing booklet pane No.* 1476m, *printed in litho by Walsall.*

JB1 Containing booklet pane No. 1476m .... 10·00

No. JB1 has three edges of the pane imperforate.

1990 (17 Apr). *Laminated cover as Type* JA **1** (75×48 *mm*) *showing Penny Black Anniversary stamp printed on the cover in brownish black by Walsall. Containing stamps printed in photo by Harrison.*
JB2 Containing booklet pane No. 1469r .... 8·00
No. JB2 has three edges of the pane imperforate.

£1.50 Booklets

1990 (30 Jan). *Laminated cover as Type* JA **1** (75×48 *mm*) *showing Penny Black Anniversary stamp in bright blue. Containing booklet pane No.* 1467l *printed in photo by Harrison.*
JC1 Containing booklet pane No. 1467l .... 10·00
No. JC1 has the horizontal edges of the pane imperforate.

1990 (17 Apr). *Laminated cover as Type* JA **1** (75×48 *mm*) *showing Penny Black Anniversary stamp printed on the cover in bright blue, printed in litho by Questa.*
JC2 Containing ten 15p. (No. 1477) .... 20·00

1990 (12 June). *Laminated cover as Type* JA **1** (75×48 *mm*) *showing Penny Black Anniversary stamp in bright blue. Containing booklet pane No.* 1475m, *printed in litho by Walsall.*
JC3 Containing booklet pane No. 1475m .... 12·00
No. JC3 has three edges of the pane imperforate.

1990 (30 Jan). *Laminated cover as Type* JA **1** (75×48 *mm*) *showing Penny Black Anniversary stamp in brownish black and cream. Containing booklet pane. No.* 1469m, *printed in photo by Harrison.*
JD1 Containing booklet pane No. 1469m .... 11·00
No. JD1 has the horizontal edges of the pane imperforate.

1990 (17 Apr). *Laminated cover as Type* JA **1** (75×48 *mm*) *showing Penny Black Anniversary stamp printed on the cover in brownish black, printed in litho by Questa.*
JD2 Containing ten 20p. (No. 1478) .... 22·00

1990 (12 June). *Laminated cover as Type* JA **1** (75×48 *mm*) *showing Penny Black Anniversary stamp in brownish black and cream. Containing booklet pane No.* 1476n, *printed in litho by Walsall.*
JD3 Containing booklet pane No. 1476n .... 16·00
No. JD3 has three edges of the pane imperforate.

F. Barcode Booklets containing Greetings stamps with barcodes on the back cover.

£2 Greetings Booklet

KX **1** (*Illustration reduced. Actual size* 135×85 *mm*)

(Des Michael Peters and Partners)

1990 (6 Feb). *Greetings Stamps. Cover printed in scarlet, lemon and black as Type* KX **1** (135×85 *mm*). *Containing booklet pane No.* 1483a, *and a separate sheet of* 12 *greetings labels.*
KX1 "Smile" design cut-out showing stamps inside .... 30·00

Greetings Booklets containing No Value Indicated stamps

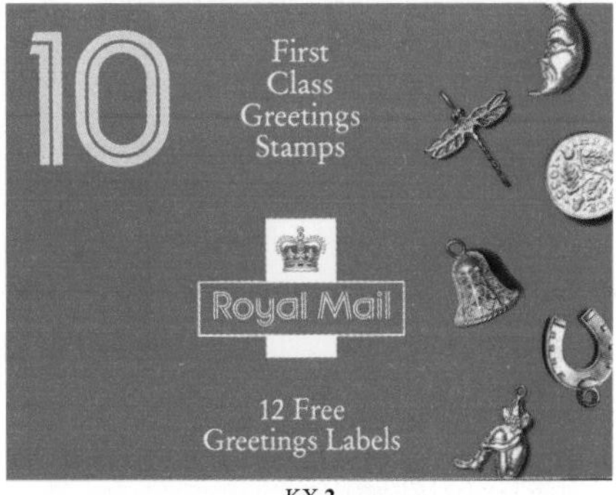

KX **2**

(Des T. Meeuwissen)

1991 (5 Feb). *Greetings Stamps. Multicoloured laminated cover as Type* KX **2** (95×69 *mm*). *Containing booklet pane No.* 1536a, *including twelve special greetings labels in a block* (3×4) *at right, attached by the selvedge.*
KX2 "Good Luck" charms design .... 15·00
No. KX2 was initially sold at £2.20, which was increased to £2.40 from 16.9.91.

KX **3**

(Des Michael Peters and Partners)

1991 (26 Mar). *Greetings Stamps. Multicoloured laminated cover as Type* KX **3** (95×69 *mm*). *Containing booklet pane No.* 1550a, *including twelve special greetings labels in a block* (3×4) *at right, attached by the selvedge.*
KX3 Laughing pillar box design .... 12·00
No. KX3 was initially sold at £2.20, which was increased to £2.40 from 16.9.91 and to £2.50 from 1.11.93.

KX 4

(Des Trickett and Webb)

1992 (28 Jan). *Greetings Stamps. Multicoloured laminated cover as Type* KX **4** (95×69 *mm*). *Containing booklet pane No.* 1592a, *including twelve special greetings labels in a block* (3×4) *at right, attached by selvedge.*

KX4 Pressed Flowers design .... 13·00

No. KX4 was initially sold at £2.40, which was increased to £2.50 from 1.11.93 and to £2.60 from 8.7.96.

KX 5

(Des Newell and Sorrell)

1993 (2 Feb). *Greetings Stamps. Multicoloured laminated cover as Type* KX **5** (96×60 *mm*). *Containing booklet pane No.* 1644a *and pane of twenty special greetings labels in a block* (5×4), *both panes attached by a common gutter margin.*

KX5 Children's Characters design .... 11·00

No. KX5 was initially sold at £2.40, which was increased to £2.50 from 1.11.93.

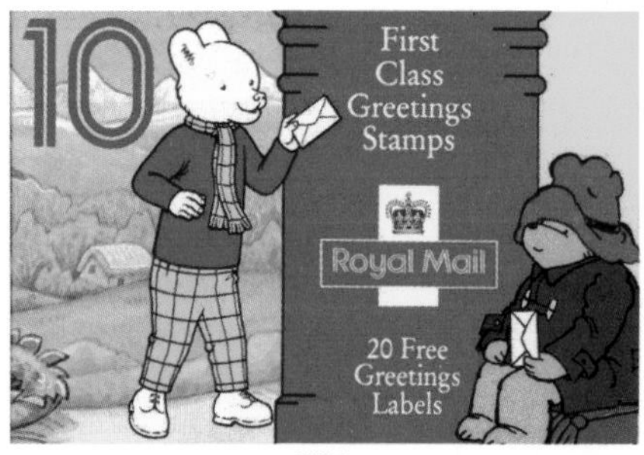

KX 6

(Des Newell and Sorrell)

1994 (1 Feb). *Greetings Stamps. Multicoloured cover as Type* KX **6** (96×60 *mm*). *Containing booklet pane No.* 1800a *and pane of twenty special greetings labels in a block* (5×4), *both panes attached by a common gutter margin.*

KX6 Children's Characters design .... 13·00

No. KX6 was initially sold at £2.50, which was increased to £2.60 from 8.7.96.

KX 7

(Des Newell and Sorrell)

1995 (21 Mar)–**96.** *Greetings Stamps. Multicoloured cover as Type* KX **7** (96×60 *mm*). *Containing booklet pane No.* 1858a *and pane of twenty special greetings labels in a block* (5×4), *both panes attached by a common gutter margin. Inscr* "Pull Open" *on yellow strip at right.*

KX7 Clown design .... 11·50
a. No inscr on yellow strip (5.2.96) .... 12·00

Nos. KX7/a were initially sold at £2.50, which was increased to £2.60 from 8.7.96.

KX 8

(Des M. Wolf)

1996 (26 Feb–11 Nov). *Greetings Stamps. Multicoloured cover as Type* KX **8** (96×60 *mm*). *Containing booklet pane No.* 1905a *and pane of twenty special greetings labels in a block* (5×4), *both panes attached by a common gutter margin.*

KX8 "MORE! LOVE" design .... 10·00
a. Containing pane No. 1905pa (11 Nov) .... 28·00

No. KX8 was initially sold at £2.50, which was increased to £2.60 from 8.7.96.

No. KX8a shows a redesigned inside front cover which omits references to 1996 dates.

KX **9**

(Des Tutssels)

1997 (6 Jan). *Greetings Stamps. 19th-century Flower Paintings. Multicoloured cover as Type* KX **9** (96×61 *mm*). *Containing booklet pane No.* 1955a *and pane of twenty special greetings labels in a block* (5×4), *both panes attached by a common gutter margin.*

KX9 *Gentiana acaulis* design .... 11·25

No. KX9 was sold at £2.60. It was re-issued on 16 March 1999 with "Please note that the First Class rate is no longer valid to Europe" added to inside front cover.

1997 (3 Feb). *Greetings Stamps. 19th-century Flower Paintings. Multicoloured cover as Type* KX **9** (96×61 *mm*) *but with box inscribed* "WIN A BEAUTIFUL BOUQUET INSTANTLY?" *printed in yellow on red over the flower on the front and with a scratch card on the inside back cover. Inscribed* "Open now – See if you've won" *on yellow tab at right. Containing booklet pane No.* 1955a *and pane of twenty special greetings labels in a block* (5×4), *both panes attached by a common gutter margin.*

KX10 *Gentiana acaulis* design .... 12·00

No. KX10 was sold at £2.60.

KX **11**

1998 (5 Jan). *Greetings Stamps. 19th-century Flower Paintings. Multicoloured cover as Type* KX **11** (96×61 *mm*). *Inscribed* "See reverse for special offer" *on yellow tab at right. Containing booklet pane No.* 1955a *and pane of twenty special greetings labels in a block* (5×4), *both attached by a common gutter margin.*

KX11 Chocolate design .... 12·00

No. KX11 was sold at £2.60.

1998 (3 Aug). *Greetings Stamps. 19th-century Flower Paintings. Multicoloured cover as Type* GGA **2** (88×61 *mm*) *printed by Walsall. Containing booklet pane No.* 1955a *and pane of twenty special greetings labels in a block* (5×4), *both attached by a common gutter margin.*

KX12 "Create a card" design .... 12·00

No. KX12 was sold at £2.60. This booklet was not placed on philatelic sale until 7 September 1998.

G. Barcode Booklets containing Christmas stamps with barcode on the back.

LX **1**

(Des A. Davidson)

1990 (13 Nov). *Christmas. Multicoloured laminated cover as Type* LX **1** (96×60 *mm*). *Containing booklet pane No.* 1526a, *attached by the selvedge.*

LX1 £3.40, Snowman design .... 11·00

1991 (12 Nov). *Multicoloured laminated cover as Type* LX **1**, *but* 95×70 *mm. Containing booklet pane No.* 1582b *attached by the selvedge.*

LX2 £3.60, Holly design .... 11·00

LX **3**

(Des Karen Murray)

1992 (10 Nov). *Multicoloured laminated cover as Type* LX **3** (95×70 *mm*). *Containing booklet pane No.* 1634a *attached by the selvedge.*

LX3 £3.60, Santa Claus and Reindeer design .... 11·00

1993 (9 Nov). *Multicoloured laminated covers as Type* LX **3**, *but* 95×60 *mm, each showing Santa Claus and Reindeer. Panes attached by selvedge.*

LX4 £2.50, containing ten 25p. stamps (No. 1791) .... 10·00

LX5 £3.80, containing twenty 19p. stamps (No. 1790) .... 12·00

No. LX4 was only available from Post Offices in the Central T.V. area and from philatelic outlets.

LX **6**

(Des Yvonne Gilbert)

1994 (1 Nov). *Multicoloured laminated covers as Type* LX **6** (95 × 60 *mm*), *showing different Nativity Play props. Panes attached by selvedge.*

LX6 £2.50, containing ten 25p. stamps (No. 1844) .... 7·75
LX7 £3.80, containing twenty 19p. stamps (No. 1843) .... 11·00

LX **8**

(Des K. Lilly)

1995 (30 Oct). *Multicoloured laminated covers as Type* LX **8** (95 × 60 *mm*), *showing Robins as depicted on the contents. Panes attached by selvedge.*

LX8 £2.40, containing four 60p. stamps (No. 1900) plus 4 air mail labels .... 7·50
LX9 £2.50, containing ten 25p. stamps (No. 1897) .... 7·50
LX10 £3.80, containing twenty 19p. stamps (No. 1896) .... 12·00

LX **11**

1996 (28 Oct). *Multicoloured laminated covers as Type* LX **11** (95 × 60 *mm*), *showing scenes from the Nativity as depicted on the contents. Panes attached by selvedge.*

LX11 Containing ten 1st Class stamps (No. 1951) .... 8·50
LX12 Containing twenty 2nd Class stamps (No. 1950) .... 11·00

No. LX11 was sold at £2.60 and No. LX12 at £4.

LX **13**

1997 (27 Oct). *Multicoloured laminated covers as Type* LX **13** (95 × 60 *mm*), *showing Father Christmas and crackers as depicted on the contents. Panes attached by selvedge.*

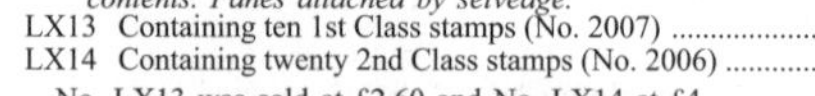

LX13 Containing ten 1st Class stamps (No. 2007) .... 8·75
LX14 Containing twenty 2nd Class stamps (No. 2006) .... 12·00

No. LX13 was sold at £2.60 and No. LX14 at £4.

LX **15**

1998 (2 Nov). *Multicoloured laminated covers as Type* LX **15** (95 × 60 *mm*), *showing angels as depicted on the contents. Panes attached by selvedge.*

LX15 £2.60 booklet containing ten 26p. stamps (No. 2065) .... 7·75
LX16 £4 booklet containing twenty 20p. stamps (No. 2064) ...... 12·00

LX **17**

1999 (2 Nov). *Multicoloured laminated covers as Type* LX **17** (95 × 70 *mm*), *showing designs as depicted on the contents. Panes attached by selvedge.*

LX17 £2.60 booklet containing ten 26p. stamps (No. 2116) .... 8·50
LX18 £3.90 booklet containing twenty 19p. stamps (No. 2115) 12·00

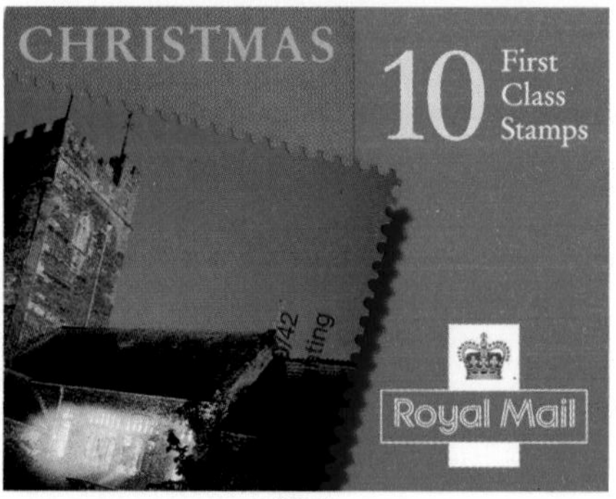

LX **19**

2000 (7 Nov). *Multicoloured laminated covers as Type* LX **19** (96×70 *mm*), *showing designs as depicted on the contents. Inscribed* "Season's Greetings" *on yellow tab at right. Panes attached by selvedge.*

LX19 £2.70, containing ten 1st Class stamps (No. 2171) .... 8·50
LX20 £3.80, containing twenty 2nd Class stamps (No. 2170) .... 11·50

2001 (6 Nov). *Self-adhesive booklet panes Nos.* 2238a *and* 2239a, *each with a multicoloured header label showing barcode and Royal Mail emblem and further label at foot with telephone numbers, folded to form booklets* 119×81 *mm.*

LX21 £3.24, booklet containing pane of twelve 1st Class stamps (No. 2239a) .... 9·00
LX22 £4.56, booklet containing pane of twenty-four 2nd Class stamps (No. 2238a) .... 13·50

Nos. LX21/2 show the surplus self-adhesive paper around each stamp retained.

2002 (5 Nov). *Self-adhesive booklet panes Nos.* 2321a *and* 2322a, *each with a multicoloured header label showing barcode and Royal Mail emblem and further label at foot with telephone numbers, folded to form booklets* 105×72 *mm.*

LX23 £3.24, booklet containing twelve 1st Class stamps (No. 2322a) .... 8·00
LX24 £4.56, booklet containing twenty-four 2nd Class stamps (No. 2321a) .... 10·00

No. LX23 was sealed into a cellophane packet which also contained a Lord of the Rings game card.

Nos. LX23/4 show the surplus self-adhesive paper around each stamp retained.

2003 (4 Nov). *Self-adhesive booklet panes Nos.* 2410a *and* 2411a, *each with a multicoloured header label showing barcode and Royal Mail emblem and further label at foot with telephone numbers, folded to form booklets* 106×71 *mm.*

LX25 £3.36, booklet containing twelve 1st Class stamps (No. 2411a) .... 5·00
LX26 £4.80, booklet containing twenty-four 2nd Class stamps (No. 2410a) .... 7·25

Nos. LX25/6 have the surplus self-adhesive paper around each stamp removed.

2004 (2 Nov). *Self-adhesive booklet panes Nos.* 2495a *and* 2496a, *each with a multicoloured header label showing barcode and Royal Mail emblem and further label at foot with contact information, folded to form booklets* 105×71 *mm.*

LX27 £3.36 booklet containing twelve 1st Class stamps (No. 2496a) .... 11·00
LX28 £5.04 booklet containing twenty-four 2nd Class stamps (No. 2495a) .... 16·00

Nos. LX27/8 have the surplus self-adhesive paper around each stamp removed.

2005 (1 Nov). *Self-adhesive booklet panes Nos.* 2582a *and* 2583a, *each with a multicoloured header label showing barcode and Royal Mail emblem and further label at foot with contact information, folded to form booklets* 106×71 *mm.*

LX29 £3.60 booklet containing twelve 1st Class stamps (No. 2583a) .... 5·25
LX30 £5.04 booklet containing twenty-four 2nd Class stamps (No. 2582a) .... 7·00

Nos. LX29/30 have the surplus self-adhesive paper around each stamp removed.

H. Self-adhesive Barcode Booklets containing No Value Indicated stamps.

NOTE. All booklets in this section show the surplus self adhesive paper around each stamp retained, unless otherwise stated.

Panes of six 2nd class stamps.

MA **1**

2001 (29 Jan). *Multicoloured laminated cover as Type* MA **1** (74×56 *mm*). *Stamps printed on the cover in bright blue by Walsall.*

MA 1 Containing six 2nd Class self-adhesive stamps (No. 2039) .... 4·00

No. MA 1 was sold at £1.14. It was re-issued on 1 August 2001 showing "Cod Post" added to the "Ffôn Testun" inscription on the back cover.

Panes of six 1st Class stamps

2001 (29 Jan). *Multicoloured laminated cover as Type* MA **1** (74×56 *mm*). *Stamps printed on the cover in bright orange-red by Walsall.*

MB1 Containing six 1st Class self-adhesive stamps (No. 2040) 5·50

No. MB1 was sold at £1.62. It was re-issued on 1 August 2001 showing "Cod Post" added to the "Ffôn Testun" inscription on the back cover.

MB **2**

2001 (29 Jan). *Multicoloured laminated cover as Type* MB **2** (74×56 *mm*). *Stamps printed on the cover in bright orange-red with portrait of Queen Victoria by Walsall.*

MB2 Containing booklet pane No. 2040l (includes label commemorating death centenary of Queen Victoria) .... 9·50

No. MB2 was sold at £1.62.

MB 3

2002 (5 June). *Gold laminated cover as Type* MB **3** *(74×56 mm) by Questa.*

MB3 Containing six 1st Class self-adhesive stamps (No. 2295) 5·00

No. MB3 was sold at £1.62. It shows the surplus self-adhesive paper around each stamp removed and a single notch at the top right hand edge to facilitate identification by the blind.

2002 (5 June). *Gold laminated cover as Type* MB **3** *(74×56 mm) by Walsall.*

MB4 Containing six 1st Class self-adhesive stamps (No. 2295) 5·00
a. Inside cover with Smilers advertisement (23.3.05) 1·80

No. MB4 was sold at £1.62. It shows the surplus self-adhesive paper around each stamp removed and a single notch at the top right hand edge to facilitate identification by the blind.

No. MB4 was re-issued on 22 March 2005 with a Smilers advertisement (showing no 2262 and photograph of baby) on the inside front cover. It was re-issued again on 26 July 2005 with a different Smilers advertisement (showing No. 2261 and photograph of bride).

2002 (4 July). *Multicoloured laminated cover as Type* MA **1** *(74×56 mm) with stamps printed on the cover in bright orange-red by Questa.*

MB5 Containing six 1st Class self-adhesive stamps (No. 2040) 5·00

No. MB5 was sold at £1.62.

MB **6** ("The Real Network" added below logo)

2003 (27 Mar). *Gold cover with multicoloured emblem as Type* MB **6** *(74×56 mm) by Walsall.*

MB6 Containing six 1st Class self-adhesive stamps (No. 2295) 2·40

No. MB6 was initially sold at £1.62. It shows the surplus self-adhesive paper around each stamp removed and has a single notch at top right.

MB **7**

(Supporting London 2012)

2004 (15 June). *London's Bid to host Olympic Games,* 2012. *Gold cover with multicoloured emblem as Type* MB **7** *(74×56 mm) by Walsall.*

MB7 Containing six 1st Class self-adhesive stamps (No. 2295) 5·50

No. MB7 was sold at £1.62. It has the surplus self-adhesive paper around each stamp removed and a single notch at top right for identification by the blind.

Panes of 10 2nd Class stamps
(Supporting London 2012)

2001 (29 Jan). *Multicoloured laminated cover as Type* MA **1** (74×56 *mm). Stamps printed on the cover in bright blue by Questa.*

MC1 Containing ten 2nd Class self-adhesive stamps (No. 2039) 6·00

No. MC1 was sold at £1.90 and was intended for use in stamp machines.

Panes of 10 1st Class stamps
(Supporting London 2012)

2001 (29 Jan). *Multicoloured laminated cover as Type* MA **1** (74×56 *mm). Stamps printed on the cover in bright orange-red by Questa.*

MD1 Containing ten 1st Class self-adhesive stamps (No. 2040) 8·50

No. MD1 was sold at £2.70 and was intended for use in stamp machines.

Panes of 12 2nd Class stamps
(Supporting London 2012)

2001 (29 Jan). *Multicoloured laminated cover as Type* MA **1** (74×56 *mm). Stamps printed on the cover in bright blue by Questa.*

ME1 Containing twelve 2nd Class self-adhesive stamps (No. 2039) .... 7·00

No. ME1 was sold at £2.28. It was re-issued on 1 August 2001 showing "Cod Post" added to the "Ffôn Testun" inscription on the back cover.

ME **2**

(Supporting London 2012)

2002 (4 July). *Multicoloured laminated cover as Type* ME **2** (74×57 *mm) printed by Questa with the surplus self-adhesive paper around each stamp removed.*

ME2 Containing twelve 2nd Class self-adhesive stamps (No. 2039) .... 7·00

No. ME2 was sold at £2.28. It shows the surplus self-adhesive paper around each stamp removed and two notches at the top right hand edge to facilitate identification by the blind.

ME **3** ("The Real Network" added below logo)

2003 (27 Mar). *Blue cover with multicoloured emblem as Type* ME **3** (74×57 *mm) by Walsall.*

ME3 Containing twelve 2nd Class self-adhesive stamps (No. 2039) .... 3·50

No. ME3 was initially sold for £2.28. It shows the surplus self-adhesive paper around each stamp removed and has two notches at top right.

2004 (15 June). *Blue cover with multicoloured emblem as Type* ME **2** (74×56 *mm) by Walsall.*

ME4 Containing twelve 2nd Class self-adhesive stamps (No. 2039) .... 8·25

No. ME4 was sold for £2.52. It has the surplus self-adhesive paper around each stamp removed and has two notches at top right.

Panes of 12 1st Class stamps

2001 (29 Jan). *Multicoloured laminated covers as Type* MA **1** *(*74×56 *mm). Stamps printed on the covers in bright orange-red by Questa (No.* MF1*) or Walsall (No.* MF2*).*

MF1 Containing twelve 1st Class self-adhesive stamps (No. 2040) (Questa) .... 10·00

MF2 Containing twelve 1st Class self-adhesive stamps (No. 2040) (Walsall) .... 10·00

Nos. MF1/2 were each sold at £3.24. They were re-issued on 1 August 2001 showing "Cod Post" added to the "Ffôn Testun" inscription on the back covers.

2002 (5 June). *Gold laminated cover as Type* MB **3** (74×56 *mm) by Walsall.*

MF3 Containing twelve 1st Class self-adhesive stamps (No. 2295) .... 10·00

No. MF3 was sold at £3.24. It shows the surplus self-adhesive paper around each stamp removed and a single notch at the top right hand edge to facilitate identification by the blind.

2003 (27 Mar). *Gold cover with multicoloured emblem as Type* ME **3** (74×57 *mm) by Walsall.*

MF4 Containing twelve 1st Class self-adhesive stamps (No. 2295) .... 4·75

No. MF4 was initially sold for £3.24. It shows the surplus self adhesive paper around each stamp removed and has a single notch at top right.

Panes of 20 1st Class stamps

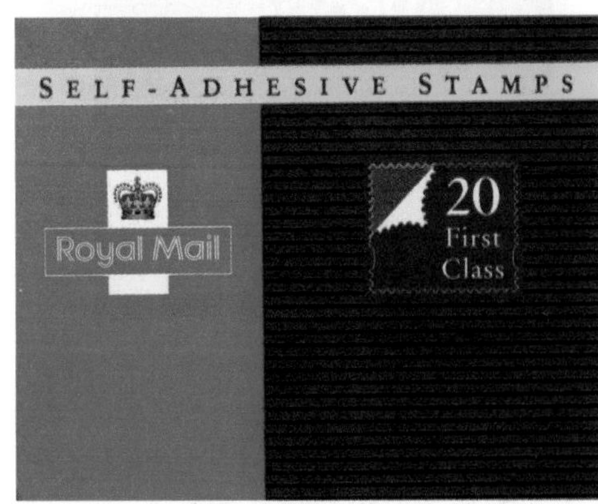

MG **1**

1993 (19 Oct). *Multicoloured cover as Type* MG **1** (91×77 *mm).*

MG1 Containing booklet pane No. 1789a........ 20·00

No. MG1 was initially sold at £4.80 which was increased to £5 from 1.11.93.

Panes of 6 E stamps

2002 (4 July). *Multicoloured laminated cover as Type* ME **2** *(*74×57 *mm) printed by Walsall with the surplus self-adhesive paper around each stamp removed.*

MH1 Containing six E stamps (No. 2296) and six Air Mail labels .... 6·50

No. MH1 was sold at £2.22. It shows the surplus self-adhesive paper around each stamp removed.

2003 (28 May). *Multicoloured cover as Type* MB **6** (74×57 *mm with* "The Real Network" *added below logo) printed by Walsall with the surplus self-adhesive paper around each stamp removed.*

MH2 Containing six E stamps (No. 2296) and six Air Mail labels .... 3·50

No. MH2 was sold at £2.28.

Panes of 4 Europe stamps

All booklets in this section show the surplus self-adhesive paper around each stamp removed.

MI **1**

2003 (27 Mar). *Ultramarine cover with multicoloured emblem as Type* MI **1** *(*74×57 *mm) by Walsall.*

MI1 Containing four Europe self-adhesive stamps (No. 2358) and four Air Mail labels .... 3·00

MI 2

2004 (15 June). *Ultramarine cover with multicoloured emblem as Type* MI **2** (74×57 *mm) by Walsall.*

MI2 Containing four Europe self-adhesive stamps (No. 2358) and four Air Mail labels ... 7·25

No. MI2 was sold at £2.28.

Panes of 4 Worldwide stamps

All booklets in this section show the surplus self-adhesive paper around each stamp removed.

2003 (27 Mar). *Red cover with multicoloured emblem as Type* MI **1** *(74×57 mm) by Walsall.*

MJ1 Containing four Worldwide self-adhesive stamps (No. 2359) and four Air Mail labels ... 6·75

2003 (27 Mar). *Red cover with multicoloured emblem as Type* MI **1** *(74×57 mm) by Walsall.*

MJ1 Containing four Worldwide self-adhesive stamps (No. 2359) and four Air Mail labels ... 6·75

2004 (15 June). *Red cover with multicoloured emblem as Type* MI **2** *(74×57 mm) by Walsall.*

MJ2 Containing four Worldwide self-adhesive stamps (No. 2359) and four Air Mail labels ... 14·50

No. MJ2 was sold at £4.48.

Pane of 4 Worldwide postcard stamps

All booklets in this section have the surplus self-adhesive paper around each stamp removed.

2004 (1 Apr). *Grey-black cover with multicoloured emblem as Type* MI **1** *(74×57 mm) but without* "The Real Network" *by Walsall.*

MJA1 Containing four Worldwide postcard self-adhesive stamps (No. 2357a) and four Air Mail labels ... 2·50

No. MJA1 was sold for £1.72.

I. Self-adhesive. Barcode Booklets containing stamps with face values.

NOTE. All booklets in this section show the surplus self-adhesive paper around each stamp removed.

£2.52 Booklet

2002 (4 July). *Multicoloured laminated cover as Type* ME **2** *(74×57 mm) printed by Walsall with the surplus self-adhesive paper around each stamp removed.*

NA1 Containing six 42p. stamps (No. 2297) and six Air Mail labels ... 7·25

2003 (28 May). *Multicoloured cover as Type* MB **6** *(74×57 mm with* "The Real Network" *added below logo) printed by Walsall.*

NA2 Containing six 42p. stamps (No. 2297) and six Air Mail labels ... 3·75

£4.08 Booklet

2002 (4 July). *Multicoloured laminated cover as Type* ME **2** (74×57 *mm) printed by Walsall with the surplus self-adhesive paper around each stamp removed.*

NB1 Containing six 68p. stamps (No. 2298) and six Air Mail labels ... 11·00

2003 (28 May). *Multicoloured cover as Type* MB **6** (74×57 *mm with* "The Real Network" *added below logo) printed by Walsall.*

NB2 Containing six 68p. stamps (No. 2298) and six Air Mail labels ... 6·00

J. Self-adhesive Barcode Booklets containing No Value Indicated Special or Occasions issues, with Definitive stamps.

NOTE. All booklets in this section show the surplus self-adhesive paper around each stamp retained, unless otherwise stated.

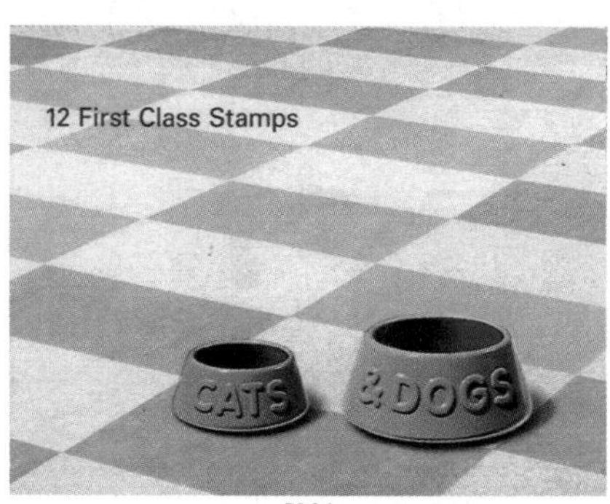

PM 1

2001 (13 Feb). *Cats and Dogs. Multicoloured cover as Type* PM **1** *(84×64 mm). Printed by Walsall.*

PM1 (£3.24) booklet containing pane of twelve 1st stamps (No. 2187b) ... 15·00

PM 2

2001 (17 Apr). *Centenary of Royal Navy Submarine Service. Multicoloured cover as Type* PM **2** *(75×57 mm). Printed by Questa.*

PM2 (£1.62) booklet containing pane No. 2207a ... 80·00

2001 (4 Sept). *Punch and Judy Show Puppets. Multicoloured cover as Type* PM **2** *(74×57 mm). Printed by Questa.*

PM3 (£1.62) booklet containing pane No. 2230a ... 20·00

2001 (22 Oct). *Flags and Ensigns. Multicoloured cover as Type* PM **2** *(74×57 mm). Printed by Questa.*
PM4 (£1.62) booklet containing pane No. 2208a .... 24·00

2002 (2 May). *50th Anniv of Passenger Jet Aviation. Airliners. Multicoloured cover as Type* PM **2** *(74×57 mm). Printed by Questa.*
PM5 (£1.62) booklet containing pane No. 2290a .... 12·00

2002 (21 May). *World Cup Football Championship, Japan and Korea. Multicoloured cover as Type* PM **2** *(74×57 mm). Printed by Walsall.*
PM6 (£1.62) booklet containing pane No. 2293a .... 10·00

PM **7**

2002 (10 Sept). *Bridges of London. Gold cover with multicoloured emblem and stamp illustration as Type* PM **7** *(74×57 mm). Printed by Questa.*
PM7 (£1.62) booklet containing pane No. 2314a .... 14·00

No. PM7 shows the surplus self-adhesive paper around each stamp removed and a single notch at the top right hand edge to facilitate identification by the blind.

2003 (4 Mar). *"Occasions" Greetings Stamps. Gold cover with multicoloured emblem and stamp illustration as Type* PM **7** *(74×57 mm). Printed by Questa.*
PM8 (£1.62) booklet containing pane No. 2264ab .... 10·00

No. PM8 shows the surplus self-adhesive paper around each stamp removed and a single notch at the top right hand edge to facilitate identification by the blind.

PM **9** ("The Real Network" added below logo)

2003 (29 Apr). *Extreme Endeavours. Gold cover with multicoloured emblem and stamp illustration as Type* PM **9** *(74×57 mm). Printed by De La Rue.*
PM9 (£1.62) booklet containing pane No. 2366a .... 10·00

No. PM9 shows the surplus self-adhesive paper around each stamp removed and has a single notch at top right.

2003 (15 July). *A British Journey: Scotland. Gold cover with multicoloured emblem and stamp illustration as Type* PM **9** *(74×57 mm). Printed by De La Rue.*
PM10 (£1.68) booklet containing pane No. 2391a .... 10·00

No. PM10 shows the surplus self-adhesive paper around each stamp removed and has a single notch at top right.

2003 (18 Sept). *Classic Transport Toys. Gold cover with multicoloured emblem and stamp illustration as Type* PM **7** *(74×57 mm). Printed by De La Rue.*
PM11 (£1.68) booklet containing pane No. 2403a .... 12·00

No. PM11 shows the surplus self-adhesive paper around each stamp removed and has a single notch at top right.

2004 (16 Mar). *A British Journey: Northern Ireland. Gold cover with multicoloured emblem and stamp illustration as Type* PM **7** *(74×57 mm). Printed by De La Rue.*
PM12 (£1.68) booklet containing pane No. 2445a .... 10·00

No. PM12 shows the surplus self-adhesive paper around each stamp removed and has a single notch at top right.

2004 (13 Apr). *Ocean Liners. Gold cover with multicoloured emblem and stamp illustration as Type* PM **7** *(74×57 mm). Printed by De La Rue.*
PM13 (£1.68) booklet containing pane No. 2455a .... 10·00

No. PM13 has the self-adhesive paper around each stamp removed and has a single notch at top right.

2004 (15 June). *A British Journey: Wales. Gold cover with multicoloured emblem and stamp illustration as Type* PM **7** *(74×57 mm). Printed by De La Rue.*
PM14 (£1.68) booklet containing pane No. 2472a .... 12·00

K. Self-adhesive Barcode Booklets containing No Value Indicated "Smilers" stamps in definitive size.

QA **1**

2005 (4 Oct). *Gold cover with multicoloured emblem as Type* QA **1** *(74×56 mm) by Walsall.*
QA1 (£1.80) booklet containing booklet pane No. 2567a .... 2·50

HAVE YOU READ THE NOTES AT THE BEGINNING OF THIS CATALOGUE?

These often provide answers to the enquiries we receive

POST OFFICE LABEL SHEETS

At the Stamp Show 2000 International Stamp Exhibition visitors could purchase sheets of 10 × 1st class stamps in the "Smiles" designs (as Nos. 1550/9), each stamp having a *se-tenant* label on which the exhibition visitor's picture was printed, the photographs being taken in a booth at the exhibition.

For those unable to visit the exhibition, the same sheet could be purchased from the Philatelic Bureau and from Post Office philatelic outlets with a "Stamp Show 2000" label in place of the photograph.

For Christmas 2000, sheets of 20 × 19p stamps in the "Robin in Pillar Box" design (as No. 1896) or 10 × 1st class "Father Christmas with Cracker" design (as No. 2007) were available through the Philatelic Bureau, with *se-tenant* labels as part of a "customised" service, purchasers supplying their own photographs for reproduction on the *se-tenant* label.

This service has continued under the name "Smilers", after the initial set of stamp designs employed, and was also made available at photo-booths at selected post offices. Corporate label panes, allowing commercial and charitable organisations to have their logo or message reproduced on the *se-tenant* labels were made available through the Bureau from 2000.

Label sheets have continued to be offered with a standard greeting or message. These "Generic Smilers" have been available from the Philatelic Bureau or from philatelic outlets.

As "personalised", "corporate" and "generic" label sheets could only be purchased at a premium over the face value of the stamps within them, they are not given full listing in this catalogue; neither are individual stamps (with or without their *se-tenant* label), some of which are identifiable as having come from Label Sheets, due to perforation, phosphor or printing differences.

The list which follows comprises the "generic" sheets only. Differences between the stamp in the Label Sheets and those of the standard issues are given under the respective listings in this catalogue.

LS 1

2000 (22 May). *The Stamp Show 2000. Type* LS **1**. *Photo Questa. Original selling price* £2.95.

LS1 10×(1st) "Smiles" stamps, as Nos. 1550/9 and attached labels .... 55·00

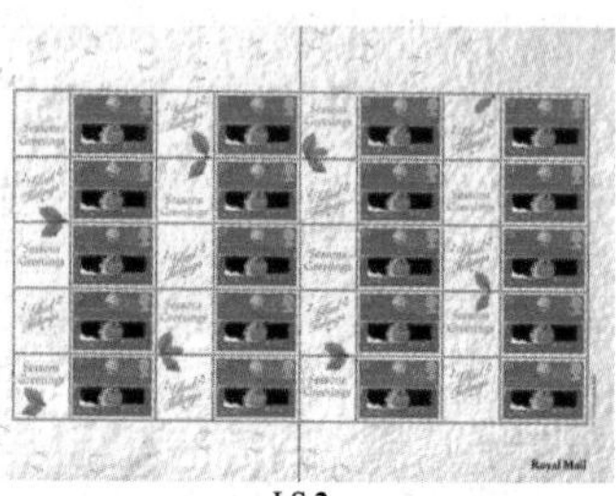

LS 2

LS 3

2000 (3 Oct)–**01**. *Christmas. Types* LS **2** *and* LS **3**. *Photo Questa. Original selling price* £3.99 *(*LS **2/2a***) and* £2.95 *(*LS **3/a***)*.

LS2 20×19p. "Robin in Pillar Box" stamps, as No. 1896 and attached labels (Imprint "Post Office 2000") £200

a. Imprint "Consignia 2001" (9.10.01) ....

LS3 10×(1st) "Father Christmas with Cracker" stamps, as No. 2007 and attached labels (Imprint "Post Office 2000") £200

a. Imprint "Consignia 2001" (9.10.01) ....

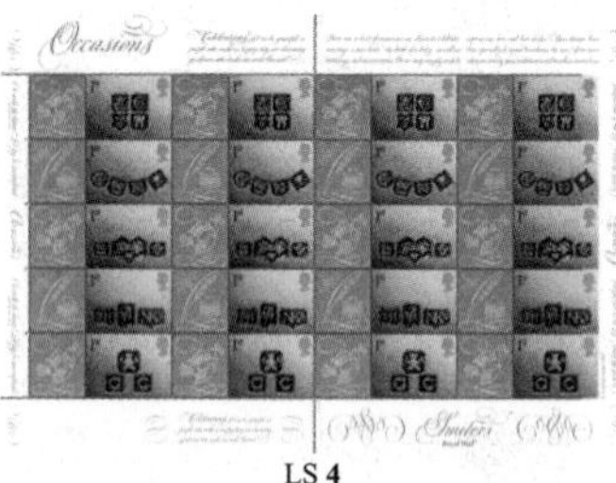

LS 4

2001 (5 June)–**01**. *"Occasions". Type* LS **4**. *Litho Questa. Original selling price* £5.95.

LS4 20×(1st) "Occasions" stamps as Nos. 2182/6 in four vertical columns of five with attached labels £200

2001 (3 July)–**01**. *"Smiles". As Type* LS **1** *but with greetings shown in attached labels. Litho Questa. Original selling price* £2.95.

LS5 10×(1st) "Smilesî" stamps, as Nos. 1550/9 and attached labels £200

LS 6

2001 (18 Dec)–**01**. *"Greetings Cartoons". Type* LS **6**. *Litho Questa. Original selling price* £2.95.

LS6 10×(1st) Greetings Cartoons, as Nos. 1905p/14p and attached labels .... 70·00

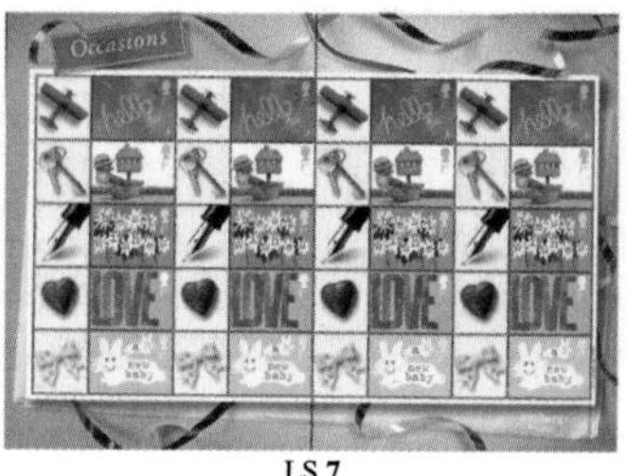

LS 7

2002 (23 Apr)–**01**. *"Occasions" Stamps. Type* LS **7**. *Litho Questa. Original selling price* £5.95.

LS7 20×(1st) "Occasions" stamps as Nos. 2260/4 in four vertical columns of five with attached labels .... 70·00

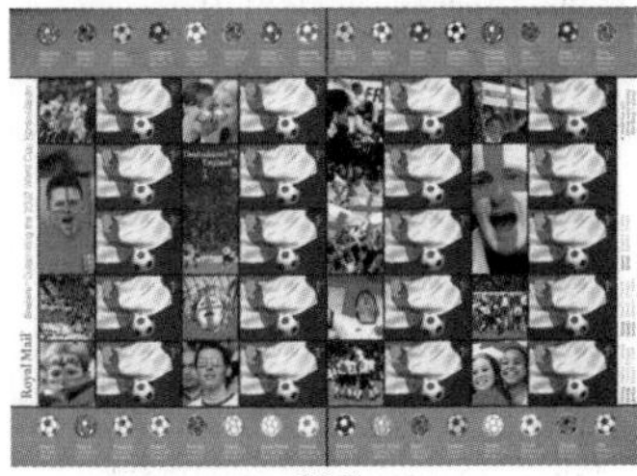

LS **8**

2002 (21 May). *Football World Cup. Type* LS **8**. *Litho Questa. Original selling price* £5.95.

LS8 20×(1st) as bottom right quarter of flag stamp in MS**2292** and attached labels .... 35·00

LS **9**

2002 (1 Oct). *"Smiles". Type* LS **9**. *Litho Questa. Original selling price* £5.95.

LS9 10×(1st) "Teddy Bear" and 10 × (1st) Dennis the Menace, as Nos. 1550/1, each with attached labels .... 35·00

LS **10**

2002 (1 Oct). *Christmas. Type* LS **10**. *Litho Questa. Original selling price* £5.95.

LS10 20×(1st) "Father Christmas with Cracker", as No. 2007, with attached greetings labels .... 35·00

LS **11**

2003 (21 Jan). *Flower Paintings. Type* LS **11**. *Litho Questa. Original selling price* £5.95.

LS11 20×(1st) Flowers Greetings Stamps, as Nos. 1955/64 (two of each design) with floral labels attached .... 30·00

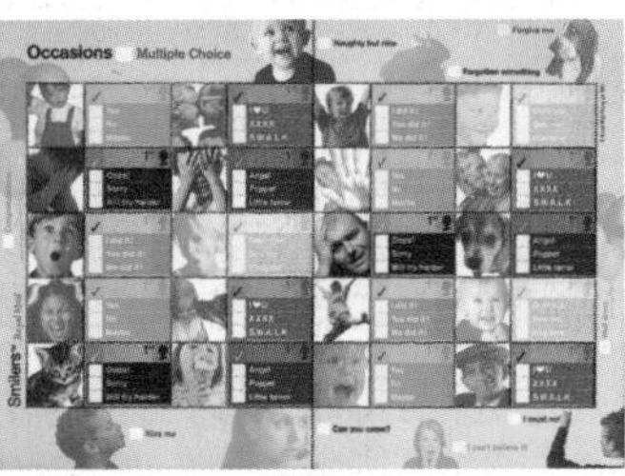

LS **12**

2003 (4 Feb). *"Occasions". Type* LS **12**. *Litho Questa. Original selling price* £5.95.

LS12 20×(1st) "Tick box" Occasions stamps, as Nos. 2337/42 (four of Nos. 2338 and 2340 and 3 each of the others) with attached labels .... 30·00
a. "Multiple Choice" in green ....

"Multiple Choice" at top left of sheet is generally in red. LS12a is believed to have come from trial sheets which were put on sale in error.

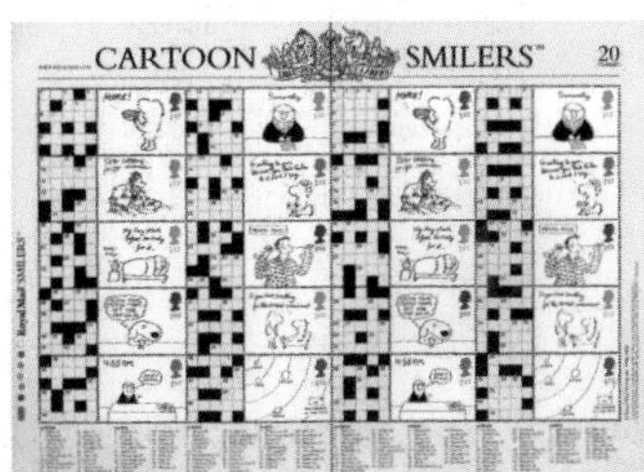

LS **13**

2003 (29 July). *Crossword Cartoons. Type* LS **13**. *Litho Questa. Original selling price* £6.15.

LS13 20×(1st) Cartoons as Nos. 1905/14 with "Crossword" labels attached .... 30·00

LS **14**

2003 (30 Sept). *Christmas. "Winter Robins". Type* LS **14**. *Litho De La Rue. Original selling price* £6.15.

LS14 20×(1st) Winter Robins, self-adhesive, as No. 2239 with labels alongside .... 30·00

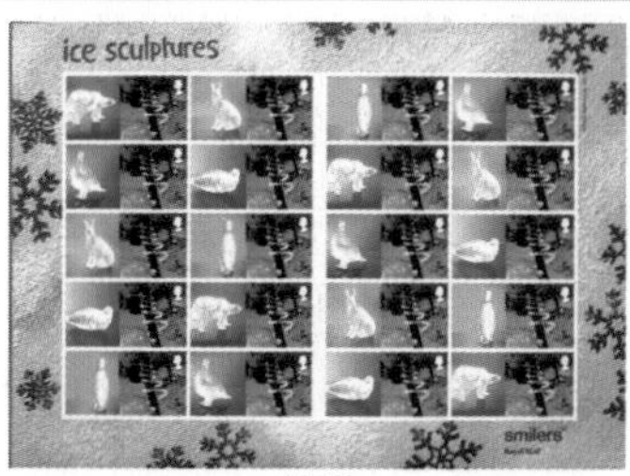

LS **15**

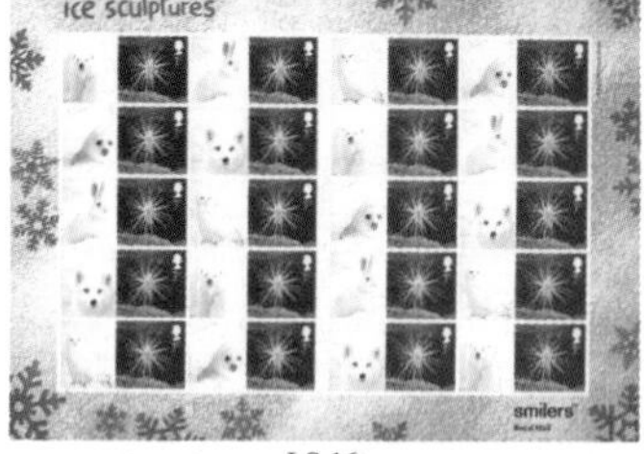

LS **16**

2003 (4 Nov). *Christmas. Types* LS **15** *and* LS **16**. *Litho De La Rue. Original selling prices* £4.20 (2nd) *and* £6.15 (1st).

LS15 20×(2nd) Ice Sculptures, self-adhesive, as No. 2410 with labels showing ice sculptures of polar fauna alongside ..... 18·00

LS16 20×(1st) Ice Sculptures, self-adhesive, as No. 2411 with labels showing photographs of polar fauna alongside .... 30·00

2004 (30 Jan). *Hong Kong Stamp Expo. Litho Walsall. Original selling price* £6.15.

LS17 20×(1st) "Hello" greetings stamps, as No. 2262 with labels alongside .... 20·00

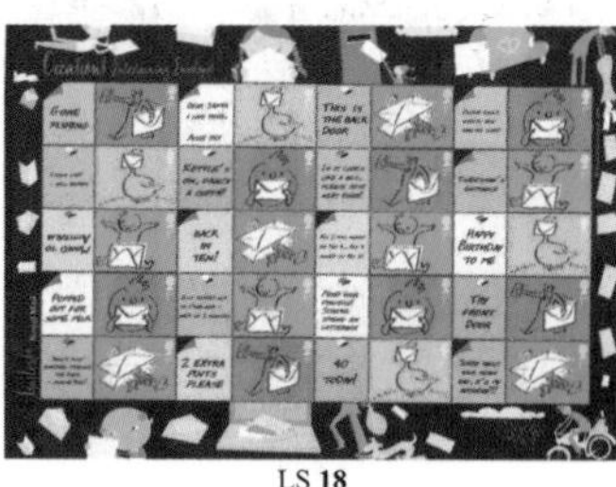

LS **18**

2004 (3 Feb). *Occasions "Entertaining Envelopes". Type* LS **18**. *Litho De La Rue. Original selling price* £6.15.

LS18 20×(1st) "Entertaining Envelopes" greetings stamps, as Nos. 2424/8 (four of each design) with attached labels..... 20·00

LS **19**

2004 (25 May). *Royal Horticultural Society. Type* LS **19**. *Litho Walsall. Original selling price* £6.15.

LS19 20×(1st) Dahlia, as No. 2457 with attached labels .... 30·00

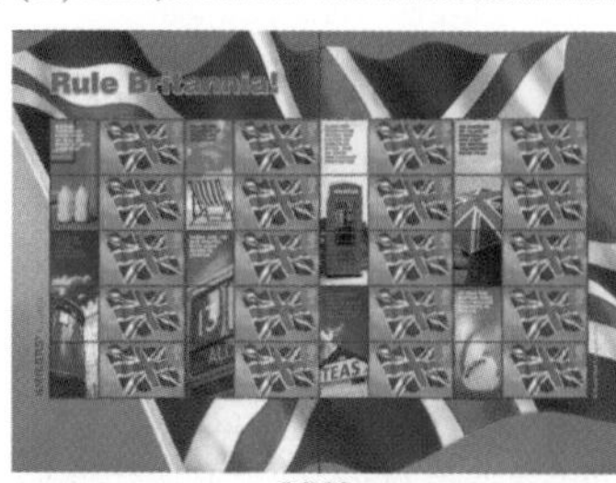

LS **20**

2004 (27 July). *"Rule Britannia". Type* LS **20**. *Litho Walsall. Original selling price* £6.15.

LS20 20×(1st) Union Flag, as Type **1517** with attached labels... 20·00

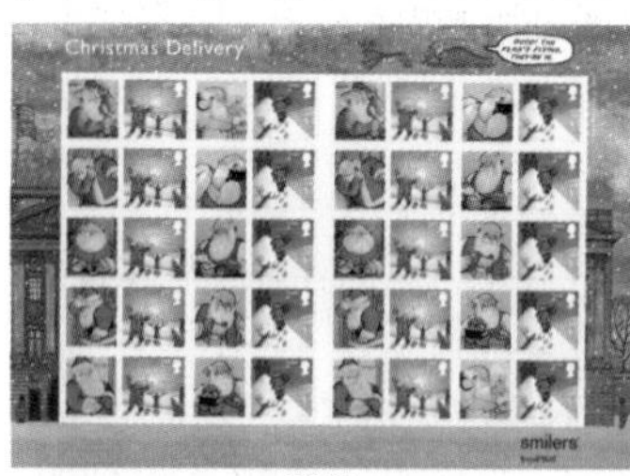

LS **21**

2004 (2 Nov). *Christmas. Type* LS **21**. *Litho De La Rue. Original selling price* £5.40.

LS21 10×(2nd) and 10×(1st) "Father Christmas", as Nos. 2495/6 with attached labels........ 20·00

LS **22**

2005 (11 Jan). *Farm Animals. Type* LS **22**. *Litho Walsall. Original selling price* £6.15.

LS22 20×(1st) Farm Animals, as Nos. 2502/11 with attached labels .... 19·00

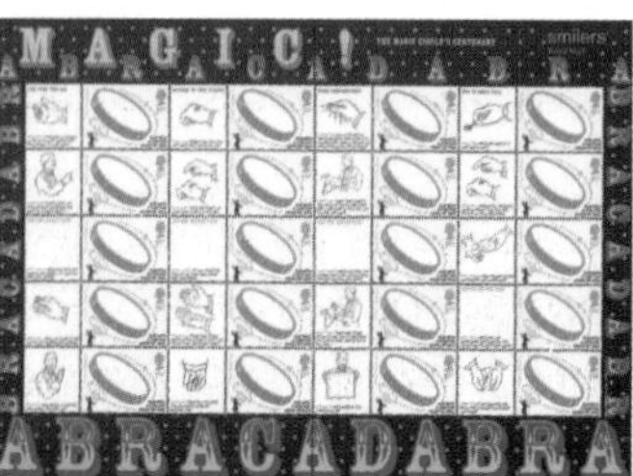

LS **23**

2005 (15 Mar). *Centenary of the Magic Circle. Type* LS **23**. *Litho Walsall. Original selling price* £6.15.
LS23 20×(1st) Spinning Coin, as No. 2525 with attached labels 9·25

LS **24**

2005 (21 Apr). *Pacific Explorer 2005 World Stamp Expo. Type* LS **24**. *Litho Walsall. Original selling price* £6.55.
LS24 20×(1st) "Hello" greetings stamps, as No. 2262 with attached labels .... 9·75

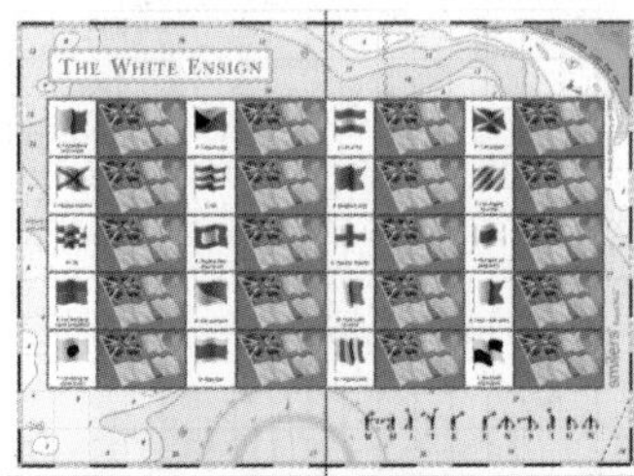

LS **25**

2005 (21 June). *The White Ensign. Type* LS **25**. *Litho Cartor. Original selling price* £6.55.
LS25 20×(1st) White Ensign stamps, as Type 1516 with attached labels .... 9·75

LS **26**

2005 (15 Sept). *Classic ITV. Type* LS **26**. *Litho Walsall. Original selling price* £6.55.
LS26 20×(1st) Emmerdale stamps, as No. 2562 with attached labels .... 9·75

HAVE YOU READ THE NOTES AT THE BEGINNING OF THIS CATALOGUE?
These often provide answers to the enquiries we receive

LS **27**

2005 (1 Nov). *Christmas. "Christmas Robins". Type* LS **27**. *Litho Cartor. Original selling price* £5.60.
LS27 10×(2nd) and 10×(1st) Robins, self-adhesive, as Nos. 2238/9 with attached labels .... 8·50

LS **28**

2006 (10 Jan). *A Bear called Paddington. Type* LS **28**. *Litho De La Rue. Original selling price* £6.55.
LS28 20×(1st) Paddington Bear, self-adhesive, as No. 2592 with attached labels .... 9·75

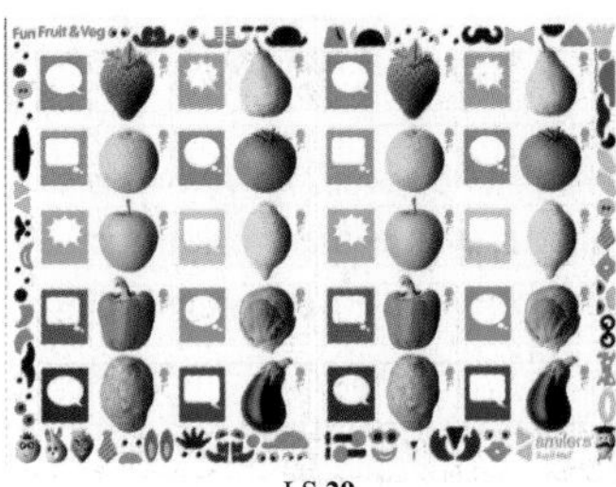

LS **29**

2006 (7 Mar). *Fun Fruit and Veg. Type* LS **29**. *Litho Cartor. Original selling price* £6.55.
LS29 20×(1st) Fruit and Vegetables stamps, self adhesive as Nos. 2348/557 with attached labels .... 9·75

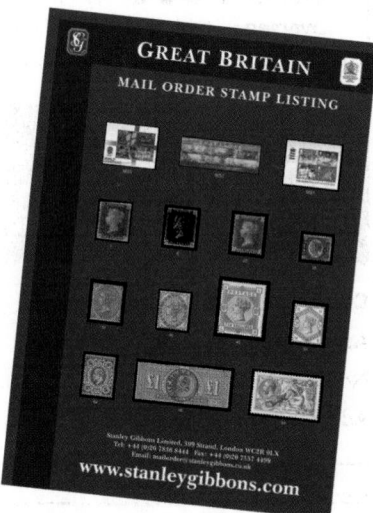

COLLECT
BRITISH STAMPS

Condition (mint/UM/used)	Country	SG No.	Description	Price	Office use only
			POSTAGE & PACKAGING	£3.60	
			GRAND TOTAL	£	

m price. The minimum catalogue price quoted is 10p. For individual stamps, prices between 10p and 95p are provided for catalogue users. The lowest price charged for individual stamps or sets purchased from Stanley Gibbons Ltd is £1

e complete payment, name and address details overleaf